ISRAEL'S MEDITERRANEAN GAS

This book examines the internal and external implications of Israel's natural gas discoveries in the Eastern Mediterranean. The nation's changed status from being an importer of coal and oil to that of an exporter of natural gas has consequences not only for the energy sector but also for the fragile geopolitics of the region.

The book:

- Explores the challenges and issues of energy economics and governance;
- Analyses Israel's gas diplomacy with its neighbours in the Middle East and North Africa and its potential positive impact on the amelioration of the Arab-Israeli conflict;
- Studies how Israel can avoid the deleterious impact of the Dutch disease once the government's share of the export revenues start flowing.

The author traces a consummate picture of history, politics, and conflicts that shape the economics of energy in Israel and its future trajectories. A major intervention in Middle East studies, this volume will be of great interest to scholars and researchers of energy studies, development studies, strategic studies, politics, diplomacy, and international relations. It will also be of interest to government agencies, think-tanks, and risk management firms.

Sujata Ashwarya is an Associate Professor in the Centre for West Asian Studies in Jamia Millia Islamia, New Delhi, India. She has published more than 30 research articles in the field of Middle Eastern studies and has written, edited, and co-edited: *India-Iran Relations: Progress, Problems and Prospects* (2017); *Contemporary West Asia: Perspectives on Change and Continuity* (co-edited; 2017); *Essays on Iran and Israel: An Indian Perspective* (2014); and *Civil Society, Democracy and State in West Asia* (edited; 2010).

"Through an empirically rich and analytically sophisticated book about the emerging natural gas sector in Israel, Sujata Ashwarya makes an important contribution to the study of the challenges faced by Israel in formulating a comprehensive policy on its newly found natural gas resource, and the trials and tribulations of establishing partnerships for export of gas in the Mediterranean region."

−Özden Oktav, Mediniyat University, Istanbul

"Initially lacking natural resources of its own, Israel has recently become a major gas producer, with ensuing dilemmas for its leaders and citizens. In this insightful and timely book, Sujata Ashwarya vividly presents Israel's gas discoveries and the domestic and external challenges arising from them."

−Oren Barak, The Hebrew University of Jerusalem, Israel

"This is a must-read book. Sujata Ashwarya, a well-established scholar, examines the economic, political and environmental issues of energy between Israel and its neighbours. The volume makes a significant a contribution to both the academic literature and the political debate."

−Gawdat Bahgat, National Defense University, Washington, DC

ISRAEL'S MEDITERRANEAN GAS

Domestic Governance, Economic Impact, and Strategic Implications

Sujata Ashwarya

Routledge
Taylor & Francis Group

LONDON AND NEW YORK

First published 2019
by Routledge
2 Park Square, Milton Park, Abingdon, Oxon OX14 4RN

and by Routledge
52 Vanderbilt Avenue, New York, NY 10017

Routledge is an imprint of the Taylor & Francis Group, an informa business

© 2019 Sujata Ashwarya

Maps not to scale. The international boundaries, coastlines,
denominations, and other information shown in any map in this work
do not necessarily imply any judgement concerning the legal status of
any territory or the endorsement or acceptance of such information. For
current boundaries, readers may refer to the Survey of India maps.

Trademark notice: Product or corporate names may be trademarks
or registered trademarks, and are used only for identification and
explanation without intent to infringe.

British Library Cataloguing-in-Publication Data
A catalogue record for this book is available from the British Library

Library of Congress Cataloging-in-Publication Data
Names: Ashwarya, Sujata, author.
Title: Israel's Mediterranean gas : domestic governance, economic
    impact and strategic implications / Sujata Ashwarya.
Description: Milton Park, Abingdon, Oxon ; New York, NY :
    Routledge, 2019. | Includes bibliographical references and index.
Identifiers: LCCN 2018061439 | ISBN 9781138099074 (hardback :
    alk. paper) | ISBN 9780429260636 (pbk. : alk. paper)
Subjects: LCSH: Gas industry—Israel. | Natural gas—Economic
    aspects—Israel. | Natural gas—Government policy—Israel. |
    Energy policy—Israel. | Energy security—Israel. | Israel—Foreign
    economic relations—Middle East. | Middle East—Foreign economic
    relations—Israel. | Israel—Foreign relations—Middle East. |
    Middle East—Foreign relations—Israel.
Classification: LCC HD9581.I772 A84 2019 | DDC
    333.8/233095694—dc23
LC record available at https://lccn.loc.gov/2018061439

ISBN: 978-1-138-09907-4 (hbk)
ISBN: 978-0-367-20275-0 (pbk)
ISBN: 978-0-429-26063-6 (ebk)

Typeset in Bembo
by Apex CoVantage, LLC

Printed and bound in Great Britain by
TJ International Ltd, Padstow, Cornwall

CONTENTS

FIGURES

TABLES

ACKNOWLEDGEMENTS

This book is an outcome of the two-year research project on Israel's natural gas resources in the Eastern Mediterranean that was sponsored by the Indian Council of Social Science Research (ICSSR) in 2014. In researching and writing this book, I received immense help from a number of people in academia, journalism, and public service in Israel, Turkey, Egypt, and India. Thanks to their informed commentaries and clarifications, I have been able to pack a sweeping number of issues relating to Israel's emerging natural gas sector within the ambit of four chapters.

The contents of this volume have been greatly enriched by panels on 'security in the Middle East,' 'Middle East governance,' and 'politics of the Middle East' at conferences held at National Taiwan University, Shanghai International Studies University (SISU), and Sakarya University, Turkey. At all these places, I presented papers on various facets of Israel's gas sector and energy security. A travel grant from the World International Studies Committee (WISC) to participate in the 5th Global International Studies Conference in Taipei and the generous hospitality of the organisers at the Middle East Studies Institute in SISU gave me the opportunity to discuss my views with a wider audience.

This book would not have been written without the munificence of Professor Gideon Shelach of the Hebrew University of Jerusalem, who facilitated my stay on the campus in January 2016, during which I conducted most of the interviews for this book. I am grateful to Professor Rafik Turan for assisting my stay (and that of my family) in Ankara during my visit for research in Turkey. I want to thank my students, who listened to my lectures on the 'geopolitics of energy' during the course of their learning on energy and international relations and asked useful questions that, in turn, have enhanced the sense and tenor of some of my arguments.

I want to express my deep gratitude to my family, my parents and my sister, for their rock-solid support and reassuring presence in all my difficult times. I am especially grateful to my teenage daughter for holding me in high esteem, which drives me to measure up and become better every day. A huge thank you goes out to my husband for helping me prepare the tables and maps. His flair for numbers and cool artistic bent have greatly enriched this book's content. One could not have asked for more.

I want to thank everyone at Routledge, especially Shloka Chauhan and Matthew Twigg, for their invaluable help during the production stages and the anonymous referee for the useful feedback. I remain indebted to Shoma Choudhury, who accepted the book proposal and saw it expeditiously through the review process. Needless to say, the errors and imperfections are entirely mine.

This book is dedicated to the loving memory my mother, Professor Rita Rani Sinha, an incredible woman who was at once a thorough professional, a devoted wife, an ambitious mother, and a loving grandmother. She would have been elated to see it in print.

ABBREVIATIONS

APC	Arab Potash Company
ATC	Antitrust Commissioner
bbl	billion barrels
bcf	billion cubic feet
bcm	billion cubic metre
BDS	Boycott, Divestment and Sanctions
BG	British Gas Group
BL	Bank Leumi
BNC	Boycott National Committee
BoI	Bank of Israel
BOTAŞ	Petroleum Pipeline Corporation (state-owned company of Turkey)
bpd	barrels per day
BTC	Baku–Tbilisi–Ceyhan pipeline
BTUs	British thermal units
CAGR	Compound Annual Growth Rate
CARB	California Air Resources Board
CBS	Central Bureau of Statistics
CCC	Consolidated Contractors Company
CHP	cogeneration or combined heat and power
CIA	Central Intelligence Agency
CNG	compressed natural gas
CO_2	carbon dioxide
CSP	concentrated solar power
DME	Dimethyl ether
DMO	Domestic market obligations
DSM	domestic supply module

E&P	exploration and production
EAC	Economics Affairs Committee
EAF	Egyptian Armed Forces
EAPC	Eilat-Ashkelon Pipeline Company
EastMed	East Mediterranean
EDF-EN	EDF Energies Nouvelles
EESI	Environment and Energy Study Institute
EEZ	Exclusive Economic Zone
EGAS	Egyptian Natural Gas Holding Company
EGPC	Egyptian General Petroleum Corporation
EIA	Energy Information Administration
ELNG	Egyptian Liquefied Natural Gas Company
EMG	East Mediterranean Gas
EU	European Union
F-T	Fischer–Tropsch (synthesis)
FCA	Fiat Chrysler Automobiles
FCI	Fuel Choices Initiative (of Israel)
FCSMI	Fuel Choices and Smart Mobility Initiative
FDP	field development plan
FFV	flex-fuel vehicle
FGD	flue gas desulfurisation
FID	final investment decision
FPSO	floating production, storage, and offloading
FSRU	floating storage and regasification unit
GASCO	Egyptian Natural Gas Company
GDP	Gross Domestic Product
GEA-IL	Green Energy Association of Israel
GHG	greenhouse gas
GIC	Government Investment Corporation
GPCA	Gulf Petrochemical and Chemicals Association
GSPAs	gas sales and purchase agreements
GTL	gas-to-liquid
GWh	gigawatt hour
HCJ	High Court of Justice
HCL	Haifa Chemicals Ltd.
IAA	Israel Antitrust Authority
ICC	International Chamber of Commerce
ICE	The Israel Chemist and Engineer
ICL	Israel Chemicals Ltd.
ICSID	International Centre for Settlement of International Disputes
IDF	Israel Defence Forces
IEA	International Energy Agency
IEC	Israel Electricity Company
IEF	Israel Energy Forum

INGL	Israel Natural Gas Lines Ltd.
INOC	Israel National Oil Company
IOCs	international oil companies
IPM	IPM Beer Tuvia Ltd.
IPO	initial public offering
IPPs	independent power producers
ISIS	Islamic State of Iraq and Syria
ITLOS	International Tribunal for the Law of the Sea
KRG	Kurdistan Regional Government
KWh	Kilowatt hour
LAFN	Lebanese Armed Forces-Navy
LIBOR	The London Interbank Offered Rate
LNG	liquefied natural gas
LoI	letter of intent
LPA	Lebanese Petroleum Authority
LPG	liquefied petroleum gas
mbl	million barrels
mcm	million cubic metres
MoA	Memorandum of Agreement
MoE	Ministry of Energy
MoF	Ministry of Finance
MoU	Memorandum of Understanding
MPA	maritime patrolling aircraft
mt	million tonne
MTO	methanol to olefins
mtoe	million tonnes of oil equivalent
MW	Megawatt
NEC	National Economic Council
NEDC	New European Driving Cycle
NEPCO	National Electric Power Company
NGA	Natural Gas Authority
NGF	Natural Gas Framework
NGV	natural gas vehicle
NICs	newly industrialised countries
NIS	New Israeli Shekel
NOx	oxides of nitrogen
NPPs	Nuclear Power Plants
OEC	The Observatory of Economic Complexity
OECD	Organisation for Economic Cooperation and Development
OIC	Organisation of Islamic Countries
OPEC	Organisation of Petroleum Exporting Countries
PA	Palestinian Authority
PE	primary energy
PIF	Palestine Investment Fund

PRMS	pressure reducing and metering station
PNA	Palestinian National Authority
PUA	Public Utilities Authority-Electricity
PV	photovoltaic
R-factor	recovery factor
R&D	research and development
REM	regional export module
RFI	request for information
RFS	renewable fuel standard
RoC	Republic of Cyprus
SCAF	Supreme Council of the Armed Forces
SCP	South Caucasus Pipeline
SCPI	State Company for Petrochemical Industries (of Iraq)
SEGAS	Spanish Egyptian Gas Company
SGC	southern gas corridor
SPP	small power producers
SPV	special purpose vehicle
STL	submerged turret-loading
SWF	sovereign wealth fund
TANAP	Trans-Anatolian Gas Pipeline
TAP	Trans Adriatic Pipeline
tcf	trillion cubic feet
tcm	trillion cubic metre
TCO	Total cost of ownership
tCO_2	tonnes of carbon dioxide (1,000 kg of carbon dioxide)
TJ	terajoule
ToP	Take-or-pay
TPES	total primary energy supply
TRNC	Turkish Republic of Northern Cyprus
UCS	Union of Concerned Scientists
UFG	Union Fenosa Gas
ULEV	ultra low emission vehicle
UN	United Nations
UNCLOS	United Nations Convention on the Law of the Sea
UNFCC	United Nations Framework Convention on Climate Change
UNIFIL-MTF	United Nations Interim Forces in Lebanon-Maritime Task Force
USGS	US Geological Survey
USV	unmanned surface vessel
VOCs	volatile organic compounds
WND	West Nile Delta

INTRODUCTION

"Where need takes us" – the tagline of Israel Chemicals – aptly sums up the Israeli gas story. From being a historically energy-deficient economy, importing 99 percent of its fossil fuel requirement, Israel's gas discoveries in the Eastern Mediterranean at the turn of the 20th century radically changed its supply side vulnerability. Although small commercial production of oil and gas from onshore wells did take place in the 1950s and 1960s as a result of years of drilling activity,[1] these discoveries were woefully inadequate to sustain the demands of a growing economy. Israel was dependent on imported oil and coal to fulfil almost all of its energy requirements. Significantly, natural gas was never a part of Israel's energy mix until the Mediterranean discoveries, given the difficulties involved in importing the fuel (transportation cost, non-competitive pricing, and restrictive contracts)[2] and Israel's typical geopolitical situation, which prevented cooperation with gas-rich regional countries.

The desire for enhanced energy security and the prospect of importing gas from Egypt presented an opportunity that could secure Israel's energy supply and ensure carbon reductions advantages, having signed the United Nations Framework Convention on Climate Change (UNFCCC) in 1996.[3] In 2000, the Israel Electricity Corporation (IEC) began the process of converting its diesel and fuel oil power plants to natural gas operations and invited bids for a long-term natural gas purchase contract. In the immediate purlieu, the British Gas Group, majority leaseholder and operator of the Gaza Marine field discovered in 1999, offered to supply gas to the IEC. However, the utility refused the offer, claiming that East Mediterranean Gas (EMG) – the Israeli–Egyptian consortium of state-owned Egyptian General Petroleum Corporation and the private Israeli company, Merhav – having the concession to import gas from Egypt was less expensive. Ariel Sharon, the then Prime Minister of Israel, vetoed any purchase of Palestinian gas, believing that anti-Israeli fighters could benefit from the sale of gas from the Gaza reservoirs.

The IEC then took the decision to acquire half of the requisite gas from EMG and the other half from the Yam Tethys fields, Noa and Mari-B, discovered by an Israeli–American consortium in Israel's economic waters during 1999–2000. It is pertinent to remember here that when the Palestinian Authority (PA) awarded the concession of the Gaza Marine to BG in 1999, a precondition was that Israel would also receive a share of the gas supply. Nonetheless, Israel bargained on a price below the market rate, and as political expediencies thwarted the development contracts and guarantees of uninterrupted gas supplies from Gaza and continuous flow of funds to the PA, the BG group pulled out of negotiations and the development of Gaza Marine was prevented in time.

After a series of complex negotiations, held secretly, against the background of the Second Intifada and severe criticism facing the Egyptian regime for its Israeli policy (President Hosni Mubarak of Egypt refused to break off diplomatic relations with Israel as was the popular demand), the contract between the IEC and EMG was finally signed in July 2005. A vague memorandum of understanding (MoU) between the governments of the two countries affirmed the deal, though there seems to have been a great amount of unease on the Egyptian side now that the tryst with Israel was public.[4] To deliver the gas, EMG built and operated a 60 km undersea pipeline starting from Al-Arish in North Sinai to the Israeli coastal town of Ashkelon,[5] which started to deliver natural gas from Egyptian fields to Israeli shores in 2008.

Between 2008 and 2012, the gas through the Arish-Ashkelon pipeline fulfilled over 40 percent of Israel's electricity needs; in April 2012, the arrangement fell through, owing to Arab Spring disturbances and the decline in gas production in Egypt leading to its diversion for local use. For about a year, until Israel's giant Tamar field began to supply gas in March 2013 four years after its discovery, the IEC had to switch to expensive fuel oil to offset the shortfall of electricity in the domestic market. Alongside the renewed availability of natural gas from its Mediterranean field, Israel began importing liquefied natural gas (LNG) in January 2013 via the deep water LNG receiving terminal and mooring system – anchored to receive gas from the floating storage and regasification unit (FSRU) – located approximately 10 km west of Hadera's coastline in north-western Israel. The LNG imports enters the onshore transmission system through a maritime flowline maintained and operated by the state-owned Israel Natural Gas Lines Ltd. (INGL) or 'Natgaz,' its Hebrew acronym. The Hadera terminal can receive some 2.5 bcm per year of natural gas,[6] representing a fifth of the country's current gas needs. The LNG imports, though marginal, add the critical amount required to augment security of supply to the Israeli market.

The Yam Tethys fields inaugurated an era of gas substitution in the mix of fossil fuel supply in Israel. Further discoveries – the 318 billion cubic metres (bcm) Tamar, as well as the 606 bcm Leviathan, which will go on stream in early 2019 – have consolidated Israel's energy supply in unprecedented ways. Growing availability of natural gas in the market and its adoption as the fuel of choice for electricity production in Israel has seen consumption rise by leaps and bounds.

By 2030, Israel aims to produce 80 percent of power from natural gas and 17 percent from zero polluting renewable energy sources.[7] More and more industrial enterprises and factories are being encouraged through governmental support and subsidies to incorporate natural gas into their operations.

Gas from Israel's offshore fields moves through the pipelines owned and operated by the field developers to the receiving station in Ashdod. After processing, the gas enters into the transmission network constructed and maintained by the state-owned INGL, whose about 700 km long transmission pipelines service some of the largest consumers of natural gas – major power stations and industry. Since the high pressure in the network (at a high rate of pressure equal to 80 bars) does not allow most factories to connect to it, the Ministry of Energy (MoE) permits the transmission of natural gas to small customers (factories and manufacturing units) in various regions of the country through a grid of smaller diameter, low-pressure pipelines. Six private companies, each responsible for different regions in Israel, have received regional operating licenses to create a distribution network at a rate of pressure of up to 16 bar.

Natgaz is in the process of expanding the gas distribution network to cover Jerusalem and surrounding areas and to serve small and medium-sized industrial customers. Until 2016, the INGL had invested $1,200 million in the construction of its pipeline grid, receiving terminals, pressure reducing and metering stations (PRMS), and other facilities of the high pressure network and is about to invest another $500 million by 2020. Expanding the low pressure distribution network and the conversion of about 400 manufacturing enterprises (recommended for optimal utilisation of gas in the industrial/manufacturing sector in the near future) to natural gas operation would expectedly cost another $0.5–$0.8 billion by 2020.[8] INGL's plan is to enlarge the scope of the transmission network to send out between 10 and 15 bcm of natural gas (from the receiving terminals to the customers) per year, and approximately 1.8 million cubic metres (mcm) per hour, a majority of the 18 bcm projected consumption until 2030.[9]

The extant rules, procedures, and infrastructure vis-à-vis the gas resources inadvertently bury the fact that when large quantities of gas were discovered following Tamar, Israel was ill-prepared on several regulatory fronts. Since Israel took the political decision to allow private players to build the petroleum sector, the field developers had to draw up the entire natural gas sector from scratch. That required the establishment of a close working relationship between the foreign and Israeli investors and government to create methods and procedures with respect to drilling, extracting, and marketing gas in a secure and reliable manner.

One of the most important aspects of Israel's successful gas story – rules and regulations regarding gas governance – came into existence following protracted and often contentious public discussions and debates. As the developers were assured adequate compensation and profit for undertaking an inherently risky endeavour of gas exploration and extraction, the people of Israel received the guarantee of a share in the gas profits through increased public spending and creation of a sovereign wealth fund (SWF). The impact of the natural gas industry on Israeli society has been wide-ranging – from a decline in the price of electrical power and low-cost manufacture of goods for export to increased savings in the economy and a stable Gross Domestic Product (GDP) growth rate.

Natural gas discoveries have reshaped Israel's broader geopolitical realities. Strategically and politically speaking, Israel is now less dependent on overseas energy imports and has even become an exporter. Regional states are beginning to work together with Israel, signing contracts for the import of natural gas from Israel, or attempting to create a regime whereby they can export natural gas to far off customers. In effect, Israel is no longer an isolated energy island, cut off from its regional and proximate neighbours.

Companies in Jordan and Egypt have signed contracts with the Tamar and Leviathan developers to import Israeli gas for ten years, backed by the political support from their respective governments. Although deteriorating relations with Turkey and Palestine significantly limit Israel's export options, and while the Arab world remains fundamentally opposed to trading relations with Israel, Cyprus and Greece, which did not consider Israel as a friendly country until recently, are showing great interest in cooperating with the Jewish state on economic and security matters.[10] Turkey's power struggles with Greece and Cyprus[11] over energy reserves in the Eastern Mediterranean have provided impetus to the burgeoning relations between Greece and Israel – despite the well-known anti-Zionist stance of Greece's incumbent Syriza Party – and Cyprus and Israel.

Disputes over the demarcation of the Exclusive Economic Zone (EEZ) with Greece in the Aegean Sea and Cyprus in the Mediterranean Sea have resurfaced on Turkey's strategic agenda. Ankara is ready to use warships to block offshore exploration of gas by the Republic of Cyprus, arguing, first, that the latter has sovereignty only over the southern part of the island with an EEZ of 12 nautical miles – same as its territorial waters. Moreover, Turkey says, the benefits of gas discoveries should take into account the interests of the Turkish Cypriots in the northern part.[12] Added to this is the dimension of an Israeli-Turkish bitter clash over the blockade of the Gaza Strip and Ankara's support for Hamas.

The leaders of Israel, Greece, and Cyprus are holding regular trilateral summits to develop the oil and gas resources in the Eastern Mediterranean region. Together with Egypt's vast resources and Cyprus' potential for more discoveries (besides the medium-sized Aphrodite field), Israel is the prime mover behind the idea of a trans-Mediterranean pipeline that would transport the gas of the Eastern Mediterranean region to European shorelines. If that happens, the region will become an integral part of the global gas trade network, as more and more countries shift from the more polluting coal and oil to cleaner and environmental-friendly natural gas.

Gas discoveries and regulatory changes

In 1999, the 'Yam Tethys' partnership forged between Israel's Delek Group and Texas' Noble Energy (the company name, assumed in 2002, derives from Noble

Affiliates, created as a holding company for Samedan in the 1970s) made its first small, non-commercially viable natural gas discovery in Israeli territorial waters. The field named Noa foretold of larger discoveries in the Eastern Mediterranean. One year later, Mari-B, or Yam Tethys field as it is known locally, was discovered. Its approximately 25 bcm of natural gas heralded the founding of the gas market in Israel. Almost a decade following, the Noble-Delek consortium's dramatic discovery of the Tamar field altered Israel's status from an energy importing to an energy exporting economy.

Tamar's reserves at 320 bcm represented at the time the largest-ever natural gas find in the Levant basin of the Eastern Mediterranean. In December 2010, less than two years following Tamar's discovery, Leviathan, containing double the gas in Tamar, increased the prospect of Israel's natural gas supplies in a significant way. Scheduled to come on stream towards the end of 2019, Leviathan not only has the potential to strengthen Israel's energy security and augment state revenues but also consolidate the country's export credentials.

While Tamar's development was fairly quick, the flow of gas from the Leviathan field was delayed due to regulatory and taxation issues. One of the primary reasons was the rancorous disagreement between the government, citizens, and the Noble-Delek consortium over taxation, the export quota, and monopoly questions. The Israeli public was concerned that the Petroleum Law of 1952 (henceforth, Petroleum Law) was not adequate to deal with the enormous amount of wealth that would accrue to the fortune of the field developers. Under the Petroleum Law, royalty for the petroleum resource was capped at 12.5 percent and it allowed for a massive tax write-off in the form of 'depletion allowance.' In other words, the developers would pay a negligible tax and claim deductions on depletion of the resource every year as a result of production and other 'losses' from the gas fields.

In response to the public outcry and criticism against the enrichment of the gas field developers, the government of Israel instituted a commission to investigate the shortcomings in the Petroleum Law and suggest new methods of taxation for the country's oil and gas resources. The Sheshinski Committee (the popular name for the commission headed by Eytan Sheshinski, an Economics professor) recommended changes in taxation that sought to square the interests of the public to whom the resource belonged and those of the gas companies who were taking the risk to develop the resource. During the existence of the commission, the gas companies, in cahoots with some parliamentarians, carried out a sustained attack on the task of the committee and its various members, fearing a reduced profit from the committee's impending proposals. Eventually, they acquiesced to the committee recommendations once it became clear that the government was inclined to accept them wholly.

The Sheshinski Committee in its proposals to the government struck down the concession-based taxation regime for hydrocarbon production. While cancelling the depletion (or exhaustion) allowance, the new tax provisions, while retaining the 12.5 percent royalty set in 1952, introduced the provision of 'progressive taxation' (in addition to regular corporate tax) on 'excess profits' (not revenues) of the gas companies. Called the 'levy,' this tax would begin after the developers have recovered investment expenses plus a return allowance. The tax will start at 20 percent of taxable income after a return of 150 percent on the investment and will rise incrementally to reach 50 percent once the return on the investment reaches 230 percent. Increase in the total take (including the 12.5 percent royalty) of the state thus cannot exceed 62.5 percent. The maximum profits levy is reduced to 45.5 percent, due to a change in the regular corporate tax rules in 2012, and any future change will initiate a corresponding change in the profits' levy.

Although the Sheshinski tax regime would apply to all future oil and gas development projects, some existing gas projects and Tamar (which was due to start within a year of the committee's proposals) were placed under transitional provisions to soften the tax burden and give a boost to their development. All in all, the new fiscal regime raised the applicable tax on oil and gas significantly to bring it on par with the level in other gas-rich countries. Subsequently, a Supreme Court ruling upheld the state's right to increase its share of the revenues from the profits of oil and gas companies.

The other regulatory issue that seized Israel' gas sector was that of export. There were no obvious restrictions under the Petroleum Law on the amount of natural gas that the developers could export to foreign buyers. They could export the gas from the fields they had developed based exclusively on commercial considerations, raising the question of energy security for a country that has historically lacked domestic sources of energy. Following hectic lobbying by NGOs, highlighting the threat to Israel's energy security if the gas developers retained the right to sell as much Israeli gas as possible to external markets, the government appointed yet another committee.

A public debate on how much gas to preserve for domestic consumption and how much to export ensued alongside the appointment of the Tzemach Committee in October 2011, headed by Shaul Tzemach, the then Director General of the MoE. The Tzemach Committee received a mandate to consider a range of domestic supply-demand scenarios and propose comprehensive government policy for the development of the emerging natural gas sector in Israel. Ultimately, the focus of the committee's conclusions rested on its core objective, of outlining a policy to safeguard the country's natural gas reserves for domestic consumption on one hand and determining a quota for export on the other. The committee was expected to take into account the geopolitical uniqueness of Israel and that it must sustain its newly found energy independence, even though there has not been a single instance when Israel has experienced an energy crisis.

After examining several consumption scenarios, the Tzemach Committee in its recommendations in September 2012, determined a period of 25 years as reasonable to recommend a quota of 450 bcm for the domestic consumption up to 2037 (on the basis of the demand scenario of approximately 500 bcm by 2040) and limited the exports to 500 bcm. These distributions were based on a recoverable volume of 950 bcm at that time. Among its several recommendations for the advancement of the natural gas industry in Israel, the committee emphasised the importance of exports as an incentive for private companies to continue investing in exploration and to obtain the necessary financing for development of the gas fields and attendant infrastructures. Given the fact that domestic consumption was low, the committee was of the opinion that a total ban on gas export would be counter-productive to the growth of the natural gas sector in the country. A further consideration in favour of export as mentioned by the committee related to the potentially large revenues likely to reach the state coffers from the profits incurred from tax on gas exports.

In face of the strong opposition to the Tzemach Committee proposals from the NGOs, a section of the Knesset members, and several experts – that had vigorously campaigned to keep all the gas within Israel – the government decided to shore up the export restriction, beyond the committee's allocation. While adopting the committee's recommendations, the government modified the quantity apportioned for the domestic market to 540 bcm (about 57 percent of the estimated gas deposits), which would guarantee consumption for 27 years from the date of the government's decision. The gas companies were left with an export quota of 43 percent irrespective of the price of gas in the international market or the demand for gas for domestic use. In response to the modification of the recommendation of the Tzemach Committee, the group, which believed no export should be allowed, challenged the government's decision in the Supreme Court. In its decision, the court approved the volume revised for local use, stating that the government's decision to allow export of gas did not immediately exhaust the resource, and that a future government could always reconsider the decision in case of contingencies.

A further regulatory change in the gas story pertained to the antitrust issue raised against the dominant position of Noble Energy and Delek Group in the Israeli gas market. In 2012, the Israel Antitrust Authority (IAA) noted that the Noble-Delek consortium had majority holdings in all the discovered fields. However, it must be said here that it was not by design but because the partnership was lucky enough to have discovered these fields, even as in the past both domestic and foreign companies had unsuccessfully trawled Israel's economic waters for petroleum resources. Still, the control of the two companies in concert with the country's entire gas supply, raised serious monopoly concerns with the antitrust commissioner. Once this aspect received attention, significant structural changes ensued in the emergent Israeli gas market.

Within the purview of the Natural Gas Framework (NGF) agreed between the government and the gas companies, Noble and Delek undertook to sell off their entire holdings in Karish and Tanin reservoirs. Delek would sell all its stakes in Tamar and, while Noble Energy could remain the field's operator, it needed to reduce its holdings in the field. In the Leviathan field, Noble and Delek, along with Ratio Oil Explorations Ltd., would be able to remain without any change in ownership, provided they would commit to production from the field by the end of 2019. In return for the fulfilment of these obligations, designed to ensure competition in the natural gas market, the companies received the required exemptions from the antitrust prohibitions. The framework, among others, includes an outline of price control mechanisms for the sale price of natural gas in the local market, the proviso ensuring internal prices of gas will always be lower than export prices, directions on how to execute the export quotas, the imperatives of local content requirements, and the assurance of the government of a stable regulatory environment.

Uses of natural gas in the Israeli economy

The highest demand for natural gas in Israeli economy comes from the power generation sector. In 2016, the electricity sector absorbed 83 percent of the total natural gas consumption, of which the IEC consumed approximately half of the total natural gas consumption in the economy and about 63 percent of the consumption of natural gas for the production of electricity. The private power producers consumed the rest.[13]

The integration of natural gas in the industry has been slow owing to a combination of factors, including lack of a widespread gas delivery network and high cost of integration to gas operations in the context of low oil prices. A growing adoption of the fuel for onsite electricity production in industrial parks is a welcome trend for the natural gas market in the country.

One of the downstream consumptions that the Israeli government is encouraging, is the use of natural gas as a transportation fuel, beginning with large and heavy vehicles. The companies interested in setting up compressed natural gas (CNG) stations across the country are being supported with quick clearance of proposals and subsidies. Israel's natural gas also has a huge potential in the chemical and petrochemical industry. By using domestic natural gas instead of imported crude oil in petrochemical production, industries could save a considerable amount on their production costs. Production of methanol and olefins – utilising domestic natural gas as feeder – could become the starting point for a host of enterprises, manufacturing industrial and household products. Similarly, the fertiliser industry would get a definite fillip if an ammonia plant using local gas supply is established.

Integration of natural gas in the downstream sector, however, requires a concerted policy effort on the part of the government. As Cohen and Korner observe,[14] the whole sector is standing still. What is needed is a complete revision of the sector to comprehend the kind of "investment guarantees or other means of support needed to help develop the infrastructure,"[15] either on the supply side with the development of pipeline or on the demand side to incentivise the consumers through grants and concessions to move over their processes to natural gas.

No conversation about the importance of natural gas can be complete without a discussion of the establishment of the SWF in Israel. The Israeli SWF will be constituted of the 'windfall profit' tax or excess profit tax from the sales of gas and mineral resources, particularly potash from the Dead Sea. It will become operational once the deposits reach a billion dollars. Meanwhile, the Bank of Israel (BoI), since 2013,[16] has repeatedly intervened in the local foreign exchange market to purchase foreign exchange to offset the impact of natural gas production (foreign exchange payments by the gas companies) on the balance of payments and its effect on the exchange rate. This plan of action will receive a thorough review when the SWF becomes operational, presumably in 2020.

Natural gas as an instrument of diplomacy

Apart from providing long-term energy security and lowering domestic energy prices, Israel hopes that its offshore gas deposits can serve as a vital diplomatic tool to improve relations with its neighbours. Constructive economic exchange through gas trade will meaningfully contribute to regional integration, and shared economic benefits could mitigate conflicts that have long informed the political landscape of the region. The beginning of gas supplies from Leviathan in 2019 can fulfil growing domestic demand as well as provide cost-efficient volumes for export to neighbours such as Jordan and Egypt with whom Israel has concluded gas supply agreements.

However, a significant question facing the Israeli gas developers is: can the volumes agreed in any of these deals (46.8 bcm to Jordan and 64 bcm to Egypt for 10–15 years) anchor the development of the second phase of the Leviathan field meant, exclusively for export? A related and equally crucial question is: will investment in Israel remain attractive to investors if the export option appears so difficult? However, if a larger deal with Egypt or Turkey were to happen, it would allow Noble and Delek to continue to invest in the export phase of the Leviathan project.

While two companies on the Jordanian side of the Dead Sea have started receiving gas from Tamar through a short-distance pipeline since January 2017, a longer overland pipeline under construction in the northern part of Israel will transport gas from the Leviathan field to Jordan's National Electric Power Company (NEPCO) for 15 years. An agreement between Noble-Delek and Egyptian entities concluded in September 2018, will allow the Israeli field developers to use the Al-Arish-Ashkelon pipeline for the delivery of gas from Tamar and Leviathan to Dolphinus Holding, once the requisite engineering to reverse the flow of the pipeline is accomplished.

Besides, with some level-headed diplomacy, Israel's could export to Turkey through a technically feasible maritime pipeline connecting Leviathan production wells to the southern Turkish ports on the Mediterranean. Although at this stage, Israel's deteriorating relations with Turkey and the Turkish-Cypriot conflict make it far-fetched option, in view of the geopolitical and economic gains, the Israeli-Turkish pipeline option may be worth pursuing. The more distant exports of Western Europe could be realised by laying an underwater pipeline in cohort with Cyprus and Greece or by utilising the liquefaction facilities in Egypt. The opportunities to export gas in the region and trans-regionally are immense, even as security, political, and commercial issues hinder or, at least, delay the materialisation of the ideas.

Israel's gas deals with Jordan and Egypt are not without its share of challenges. A combination of strong political and commercial considerations within Jordan threatens Israeli gas supplies. Gas import from Israel is a highly political issue in Jordan, even though the Jordanian King has been able to circumvent the opposition to the deal. NEPCO's decision in 2016 to import gas from Israeli fields is facing incessant opposition from civil society. In July 2018, Jordan's Professional Associations Council went on strike to protest against the construction of the gas pipeline, which will transport Israeli gas to Jordan, declaring "we are against normalization with the Zionist enemy in all aspects."[17]

While NEPCO will start receiving gas from Leviathan in early 2020, the Jordanian gas import from Egypt resumed in September 2018. The gas supplies from Israel and Egypt will satisfy the Jordanian demand for power generation and industrial production for a few years. However, when Jordan starts to build the planned desalination plant in Aqaba and distribution grid for delivery of gas to local households, domestic sensitivity to the issue of import from Israel dictates that any additional Jordanian requirements would be obtained from Egypt.

Israel's gas export to Egypt is also not without its share of challenges. The security situation in the Sinai Peninsula remains grave with numerous militant groups holed up in the vast expanse of the desert. In this context, it is important to remember that the Egyptian gas pipeline carrying gas to Israel through the Sinai Peninsula was bombed numerous times in the wake of the Arab Spring uprising in 2011. Another challenge, and not the least, is the question of the need for gas from Israel, when Egypt has revamped its own production from Zohr and Nooros fields (in the Nile delta) – both contributing the lion's share of the country's natural gas output. With other finds in the West Nile Delta (WND) and expectations of more discoveries onshore in the Nile delta and Western Desert, along with a reform of the gas market in tow, Egypt is expected to have a gas surplus as early as 2019. So, the question now is whether the Egyptian consumers would pay for Israeli gas, given the fact that it is not only politically problematic, but also costlier than the domestic supply because of the added cost of import.

Even the export of gas from the Israeli fields to European buyers, through the Egyptian LNG facility appears problematic for two reasons: First, with increasing production surplus, Egypt would be using the capacity of its two liquefaction plants at Idku and Damietta for exports from its fields; and, second, the fee paid for liquefaction would push up the price and damage the competitiveness of Israeli gas in the global market. Nonetheless, the government of Israel has supported Noble-Delek's export contract with Dophinus to preserve the Egyptian export outlet and make the deal a springboard for future contracts. However, Egypt's discovery of a supergiant Noor gas field in the Mediterranean and continuing exploration activities of international oil companies (IOCs) in the Red Sea may well tip the economies of scale and spell an end to the Israeli endeavour to sell gas in a cost-efficient manner and leverage it as a diplomatic tool.

As the export to Turkey appears shaky, the government is forcefully pursuing the East Mediterranean (EastMed) underwater pipeline running from Israeli gas fields through Cyprus to Greece and Italy. Again, the economies of scale do not justify the cost and logistical challenges involved in its construction. Israel and Cyprus do not have the extractable volume of gas required to make a pipeline of such scale and magnitude viable. Egypt, which might have the volumes to do so (given the strong prospects of discoveries in the Red Sea and Greater Nile Delta), would instead export gas as LNG, utilising its terminals than pay for piped transit.[18] That leaves Israel with Egypt as the only route to sell gas and the only customer to sell gas, whether it is for its domestic consumption or export.

Turkey is the sole Eastern Mediterranean country, which has the capacity to fully absorb gas exports from Israel, given its rapidly growing demand and import dependency of oil and gas. Further, since Turkey wants to build geopolitical and geo-economic leverage in its international relations, it is also willing to host energy infrastructure projects on its territory, including providing a transit hub for pipelines.[19] Turkey is, therefore, strategically located to receive gas at its southern port of Ceyhan from Israel's offshore fields, which is a distance of 450 km, and can provide an onward entry to Europe through the southern gas corridor (SGC).

However, Israel relations with Turkey have soured since the killing by Israeli commandos of ten Turkish activists on board the Mavi Marmara, the flagship of an aid flotilla led by an alliance of pro-Palestinian activists, attempting to breach the Gaza blockade on 31 May 2010.[20] Relations were restored in 2016 after a six-year rift with the exchange of ambassadors, following the Israeli Prime Minister's apology to Turkish President Erdoğan in March 2013 for the killing of Turks aboard the ship. Israel also agreed to disburse $20 million as compensation for the families of the victims, as well as allow Turkish humanitarian aid to Gaza through the port of Ashdod in southern Israel. Backed by the US, which pushed the parties to resolve their differences, hoping to enlist two long-time allies to advance mutual interests and stability[21] and lubricated by an "energy deal that could transform Israel into a gas exporter and bolster Turkey as a key gas portal for Europe,"[22] the fragile reconciliation predictably did not hold for long as tensions mostly focused on the Palestinian–Israeli conflict were not resolved.

The Israel–Turkey relations went from bad to worse in April-May 2018 over the killing of dozens of Palestinians by Israeli forces in the weekly 'great march of return' protests. Turkey expelled Israeli ambassador in Ankara with Israel retaliating by doing the same to a senior Turkish diplomat. In each instance of Israeli military escalation in Gaza since Operation Cast Lead in 2008–2009, Erdoğan has vociferously condemned Israel, accusing Israel of "ethnic cleansing" and labelling Israel a "terrorist state".[23] Ankara also voiced sharp criticism of the opening of the US embassy in Jerusalem and, in an address to the Turkish parliament, Erdoğan called Israel "the most fascist and most racist country of the world," referring to the Nation States Law.[24]

Israel and Turkey have a bilateral trade of over $4 billion, and businesses in the two countries have been mature enough to steer clear of political developments. In March 2014, Israeli media[25] announced that more than ten companies, including two Turkish energy firms, have submitted offers for the tender to build a maritime pipeline that would transport natural gas from Israel's offshore Leviathan gas field to Turkey. Bidders included Turkey's Zorlu Group, which already holds an indirect stake in an Israeli power plant, and a joint bid by Turcas Petrol and German electricity utility RW. What is interesting is that the pipeline would have run from Leviathan's floating production, storage and offloading (FPSO) ship to the Ceyhan port had it not been abandoned in favour of a production platform close to the Israeli shore. As the idea of an FPSO for the Leviathan field fell into disfavour owing to security considerations, the tender was allowed to lapse.

After the 2016 reconciliation, energy talks on the export of gas from Israel through a pipeline resumed, but did not go too far. The march of return protests saw both Erdoğan and Israeli Prime Minister Benjamin Netanyahu engage in a very public verbal duel, inflaming the public on both sides. These public condemnations of each other and tit-for-tat ripostes have already delayed and perhaps killed what could have been a lucrative energy bargain for Israeli gas.

It is pertinent, however, to note that Turkey has neither downgraded not severed relations with Israel so that a diplomatic space may still be open for negotiations. Many in Israel believe that relations with Turkey should be restored through "quiet, efficient and professional diplomacy"[26] as it is a significant ally in the Middle Eastern region, and energy relations, if institutionalised, will open up many economic and diplomatic gates. That being so, a critical issue standing in the way is the conflict between Cyprus and Turkey.

The ideal route for an Israeli–Turkish pipeline would be along the Levantine coastline of Lebanon and Syria because of the shallow seabed. However, political and security risks, in addition to open hostility of the two countries towards Israel, prevents its realisation. On the other hand, the alternative route through Cypriot waters requires the approval of the Republic of Cyprus (the southern part which makes up two-thirds of the island, RoC), necessitating a Turkish–Cypriot rapprochement. The RoC has refused to allow a pipeline to Turkey unless Ankara agrees to end the island's 40-year-old division. Hence, without resolution of the Cypriot–Turkish problem, a subsea gas pipeline operative in the Eastern Mediterranean is still a difficult proposition.

The question here is, has Israel's dream of selling cost-efficient gas to its neighbours and link them in long-term interdependent relations soured? Israel has been contemplating a multiplicity of export options, contingent on the understanding that energy ties could be a game changer in its fractured relations with several regional and trans-regional actors. Israel's new gas agreements with the Arab governments of Jordan and Egypt are not only significant for the monetary dividend, but also for the potential positive impact on Arab-Israeli relations. Nonetheless, Israel's latent or overt conflict with its neighbours, because of the persistence of the Palestinian–Israeli conflict in all its complexity of "conflicts over demography and land,"[27] is far-removed from any resolution.

All the same, the deals with Jordanian and Egyptian entities reveal that cardinal rule of the game: Energy deals take place and pipelines get built when political relations between states are normal rather than the reverse.[28] Any change or perversion of political relations can jeopardise energy trade. Egyptian–Israeli gas trade fell off the radar in 2011 in large part due to political factors manifested in the bombings of the supply pipeline and wide-ranging local opposition to the deal. Therefore, an Israeli–Turkish gas pipeline will have an improved chance for success if the political relations between the former allies get on track.

In the Middle East, a host of changes have occurred since the formation of the states in the wake of the Great War. Alliances have formed and transformed, economic development has had great successes and massive failures, and societies are constantly negotiating between tradition and modernity. What has endured, however, amid the shifting sands of time is the fact that politics always trumps over economics. If it were not so, Jordan, Egypt, and Turkey would have readily signed energy deals with Israel much earlier to generate interdependent relationships and escalate the cost of conflict. Contrary to liberal belief,[29] trade-related incentives have not driven economic interdependence in the region or led to the diminution of international conflicts. As it appears, Israel's gas reserves have a vast utilisation potential in the internal market. However, it is very small as compared to the large external markets, and if gas companies focus solely on the domestic market, their remuneration could potentially be far less than what they would accumulate from exports. Israel may be facing a 'resource curse' of a different kind.

The organisation of the volume

Chapter 1 delineates and reviews the key features of Israel's energy sector, in particular, the supply side vulnerability, which still exists today. Imported coal and oil even after the gas discoveries now constitute two-thirds of the country's primary energy consumption, despite the increasing adoption of natural gas, highlighting the need for a broad-based use of the indigenous resource across the economy. The principal demand for natural gas in the Israeli economy comes from the electricity sector. Here, gas has steadily substituted coal and oil, such that oil has fallen off the power generation sector. Oil is used overwhelmingly in the transportation sector, along with its utilisation in a small amount in the industrial sector, both manufacturing and petrochemicals. Israel imports 99.5 percent of its oil needs, creating a profound dependence on foreign sources and intense pressure on the state's exchequer. To alleviate Israel's oil dependency in transportation, the Prime Minister's office in Israel has launched the Fuel Choice and Smart Mobility Initiative with an ambitious goal of dramatically decreasing the reliance on oil in transportation through development of alternatives fuels and mobility solutions.

Besides, the chapter also throws light on the energy intensity of Israel's growth. The presence of a small energy-intensive manufacturing sector as a result of the expansion of the service sector in the economy over a 20-year growth period, has brought down the intensity of electricity use. Lack of gas flaring and low-level losses in transmission have contributed to lowering of the energy intensity of growth, unlike the regional countries of the Gulf. The chapter also looks into the high carbon dioxide emission in Israel as a consequence of the high percentage of the coal and gas usages. It goes on to delineate Israel's multipronged energy supply strategy, which has five essential components, including: a) diversification of import; b) pursuit of the proximate source of supply; c) search for an indigenous supply source; d) physical security of energy installations; and e) use of renewables and alternative sources. The chapter studies each of these components to assess the ongoing transformation of Israel's status from import-dependency to energy self-sufficiency.

The second chapter delineates the essential characteristics of Israel's gas regulatory regime and highlights its distinctive features in comparison with other gas-producing countries. It goes on to provide a historical overview of Israel's natural gas discoveries, including the year of discovery, size of the fields, and their developmental position at the time of writing. Legal and institutional mechanisms to manage petroleum resources in Israel have also been investigated in the chapter to understand the existing environment for the development of the gas sector. An analysis of the evolution of gas regulations relating to three key issues of taxation, export, and competition, constitutes a significant portion of the chapter. The political context and the public debates surrounding each of these issues have been treated in-depth to understand the unique aspects of the resultant governmental policies, as have the Supreme Court orders, which served to illuminate them.

The third chapter involves a discussion of the structure of Israel's natural gas market along with the potential for expansion of the use of gas in newer sectors of the economy. One of the most important implications of the natural gas framework has been to impel the rapid development of the Leviathan field, Israel's largest natural gas field to date, and the concomitant signing of several gas sales and purchase agreements (GSPAs), buttressing its economic viability. Karish and Tanin gas fields, meant to provide exclusively for the domestic market and create competition locally, will receive governmental support in the form of subsidies because of the higher relative cost of developing small fields.

While examining the utilisation of natural gas use in power generation (by the IEC, private power producers, and as part of the self-generation power supply system in industrial complexes), this chapter also analyses both demand and supply constrains that hinder the integration of natural gas in the industrial sector. The use of gas in the downstream segment of the petroleum industry, such as, in ammonia plant, methanol production, or gas-to-liquid fabrication, has immense scope, as the chapter uncovers, but is at a standstill for lack of coherent and sustained governmental initiatives. The use of natural gas in transportation, however, is receiving a thrust with governmental support for the setting up of CNG filling stations, and the chapter examines this development in some detail. Chapter 3 also explores the creation and usefulness of Israel's SWF for the stability of the currency and its intergenerational use.

Chapter 4 seeks to analyse Israel's natural gas export potential to neighbouring countries in the East Mediterranean region as well as to Europe. Together with a study of the political dynamics between Israel and its neighbours, as well as geopolitics of emerging gas trade in the Eastern Mediterranean, this chapter attempts to examine the feasibility of exporting gas to Jordan, Egypt, Turkey, Palestinian Territories, Cyprus, and Greece. There are both opportunities and challenges. While opportunities include political as well as monetary dividends for Israel, challenges include territorial disputes and contesting claims over resources among regional countries. The gas supply contracts to two Jordanian companies and an Egyptian entity are the only favourable trade deals yet for Israeli field developers. In the absence of demarcation of the EEZ among the players in the Eastern Mediterranean region and given the long-standing Turkey–Cyprus, Israel–Lebanon, Israel–Palestinian, and Israel–Turkey political disputes, Israeli gas export plans predicated on the idea that trade can bring stability and security is erroneous. Notably, Israel has been able to conclude trade deals only where political and diplomatic ties already exist.

Even in the Jordanian and Egyptian deals, challenges abound. Internal opposition in Jordan to trade deals with Israel in the broader context of the Israel-Palestinian conflict persists, as does the security side of transporting piped gas through the Sinai Peninsula – where an affiliate of the Islamic State group has taken root. Hence, while Israel's gas discoveries might have a wide export potential, many believe their best utilisation would be within the sphere of domestic consumption.

Notes

1 Israel discovered its first onshore gas deposits in Zohar, Kidod and Hakanaim near Arad (a city located on the north-eastern part of the Negev desert). Small commercial production of oil also took place from Zuk-Tamrur deposits near the SW coastline of the Dead Sea and Heletz oil field southeast of Ashkelon. See Michael Gardosh et al., "Hydrocarbon Exploration in the Southern Dead Sea," in Zvi Ben-Avraham, Tina M. Niemi, and Joel R. Gat (eds.), *The Dead Sea: The Lake and Its Setting* (New York and Oxford: Oxford University Press, 1997), p. 58; Lev Eppelbaum, Youri Katz, and Zvi Ben-Avraham, "Israel – Petroleum Geology and Prospective Provinces," *Search and Discovery*, No. 10533 (2013), www.searchanddiscovery.com/pdfz/documents/2013/10533eppelbaum/ndx_eppelbaum.pdf.html (accessed on May 3, 2018); *Oil & Gas in Israel – Exploration History*, Ministry of Energy, State of Israel, undated, www.energy-sea.gov.il/English-Site/Pages/Oil%20And%20Gas%20in%20Israel/History-of-Oil-Gas-Exploration-and-Production-in-Israel.aspx (accessed on May 3, 2018).
2 Andre Barbe and David Riker, *Obstacles to International Trade in Natural Gas*, Office of Industries, US International Trade Commission, Washington, DC, No. ID-15-043, December 2015, pp. 12–15, www.usitc.gov/publications/332/obstacles_natural_gas_final_pdf_accessible.pdf (accessed on May 3, 2018).
3 *United Nations Framework Convention on Climate Change*, Israel Ministry of Environmental Protection, State of Israel, September 24, 2017, www.sviva.gov.il/English/env_topics/InternationalCooperation/IntlConventions/Pages/UNFCCC.aspx (accessed on May 5, 2018).
4 Galia Press-Barnathan, *The Political Economy of Transitions to Peace* (Pittsburgh: University of Pittsburgh Press, 2009), pp. 46–47.
5 "At the Weekly Cabinet Meeting," *Prime Minister's Office*, July 31, 2005, www.pmo.gov.il/english/mediacenter/secretaryannouncements/pages/govmes310705.aspx (accessed on May 5, 2018).

6   *The Deep Water LNG Terminal*, Israel Natural Gas Lines, Ministry of Energy, State of Israel, 2013, www.ingl.co.il/the-deep-water-lng-terminal/?lang=en (accessed on May 5, 2018).

7   Matthew Kalman, "Israel Minister Seeks End to Coal, Diesel and Gasoline by 2030," *Bloomberg*, April 17, 2018, www.bna.com/israel-minister-seeks-n57982091179/ (accessed on May 5, 2018).

8   Gina Cohen and Miki Korner, *Israeli Oil & Gas Sector, Economic and Geopolitical Aspects: Distinguish Between the Impossible, the Potential and the Doable*, Samuel Neaman Institute, Haifa, Israel, April 2016, pp. 14–15, www.neaman.org.il/Files/6-459.pdf (accessed on May 9, 2018).

9   *Consumption and Demand*, Israel Natural Gas Lines, Ministry of Energy, State of Israel, 2013, www.ingl.co.il/facts-and-information/national-transmission-network/?lang=en (accessed on May 9, 2018).

10 Vassilios Damiras, "Greece, Cyprus and Israel in an Era of Geostrategic Friendship and Geoeconomic Cooperation," *Mediterranean Affairs*, January 9, 2015, http://mediterra neanaffairs.com/greece-cyprus-and-israel-in-an-era-of-geostrategic-friendship-and-geoeconomic-cooperation/ (accessed on May 10, 2018).

11 "East Med Natural Gas Reserves Could Meet Turkey's Energy Needs for 572 Years," *Yeni Safak*, July 24, 2018, www.yenisafak.com/en/news/east-med-natural-gas-reserves-could-meet-turkeys-energy-needs-for-572-years-3437159 (accessed on September 5, 2018).

12 A. Necdet Pamir, "Cyprus and Its Natural Resources Are a Vital Part of Our 'Blue Homeland'," *Insight Turkey*, February 23, 2018, https://sigmaturkey.com/2018/02/23/cyprus-natural-resources-vital-part-blue-homeland/ (accessed on May 13, 2018).

13 *Review of Developments in the Natural Gas Economy 2017* [Hebrew], Ministry of Energy and Natural Gas Authority, State of Israel, April 26, 2018, p. 9, www.gov.il/BlobFolder/guide/natural_gas_basics/he/ng_2017.pdf (accessed on May 13, 2018).

14 Cohen and Korner, *Israeli Oil & Gas Sector*, April 2016, p. 27.

15 Ibid.

16 *Bank of Israel to Offset Effect of Natural Gas*, Israeli Missions Around the World, undated, http://embassies.gov.il/MFA/InnovativeIsrael/economy/Pages/Bank-of-Israel-to-offset-effect-of-natural-gas.aspx (accessed on September 6, 2018); "Israel: Monetary Policy Status Quo," *BNP Paribas*, January 30, 2018, http://economic-research.bnpparibas.com/html/en-US/Monetary-policy-status-1/30/2018,30610 (accessed on May 13, 2018); *Will the Bank of Israel Succeed Once Again to Stop the Shekel From Strengthening?* Bank Leumi, Tel Aviv, Israel, April 2013, p. 1, https://english.leumi.co.il/static-files/10/LeumiEnglish/June2013shekelstrengthening.pdf (accessed on May 13, 2018).

17 "Jordan Unions Protest Against Israel Gas Deal," *Middle East Monitor*, July 25, 2018, www.middleeastmonitor.com/20180725-jordan-unions-protest-against-israel-gas-deal/ (accessed on September 8, 2018).

18 See *Memorandum of Understanding on a Strategic Partnership on Energy Between the European Union and the Arab Republic of Egypt 2018–2022*, European Commission, April 23, 2018, p. 6, https://ec.europa.eu/energy/sites/ener/files/documents/eu-egypt_mou.pdf (accessed on May 13, 2018).

19 Sinan Ülgen and Mitat Çelikpala, "*TurkStream: Impact on Turkey's Economy and Energy Security*," Centre for Economics and Foreign Policy Studies (EDAM), Istanbul, Turkey, November 11, 2017, p. 9, http://edam.org.tr/wp-content/uploads/2017/11/turkstream_report_eng.pdf (accessed on May 17, 2018).

20 For an analysis of the developments in Israeli-Turkish relations, see Dan Arbell, *The US-Turkey-Israel Triangle*, Centre for Middle East Policy at Brookings, Washington, DC, Analysis Paper No. 34, October 2014, pp. 1–54, www.brookings.edu/wp-content/uploads/2016/07/USTurkeyIsrael-Triangle.pdf (accessed on May 17, 2018).

21 Shira Efron, *The Future of Israeli-Turkish Relations*, RAND Corporation, 2018, pp. viii–ix, www.rand.org/content/dam/rand/pubs/research_reports/RR2400/RR2445/RAND_RR2445.pdf (accessed on September 10, 2018).

22 Keith Johnson, "Israel's Reconciliation With Turkey Could Lead to New Energy Deals," *Foreign Policy*, June 27, 2016, https://foreignpolicy.com/2016/06/27/israels-reconciliation-with-turkey-could-lead-to-new-energy-deals/ (accessed on May 17, 2018).

23 *Israel-Turkey Reconciliation: A Progress Report*, Britain Israel Communications and Research Centre (BICOM) Briefing, 2017, www.bicom.org.uk/wp-content/uploads/2017/04/Turkey-paper-2017-Final-pdf.pdf (accessed on May 19, 2018).

24 "Erdoğan Says Israel Is the World's 'Most Fascist, Racist' State," *TRT World*, July 24, 2018, www.trtworld.com/turkey/erdogan-says-israel-is-the-world-s-most-fascist-racist-state-19119 (accessed on September 10, 2018).

25 "At Least 10 Firms Bid for Israel-Turkey Gas Pipeline: Report," *Hurriyet Daily News*, March 25, 2014, www.hurriyetdailynews.com/at-least-10-firms-bid-for-israel-turkey-gas-pipeline-report-64066 (accessed on May 19, 2018).

26 Keren Setton, "Rocky Israel-Turkey Ties Hit New Low, But Full-blown Crisis Could be Prevented," *Xinhua* (Beijing, China), May 17, 2018, www.xinhuanet.com/english/2018-01/12/c_136889167.htm (accessed on May 19, 2018).

27 Omro Boehm, "Did Israel Just Stop Trying to Be a Democracy?" *The New York Times*, July 26, 2018, www.nytimes.com/2018/07/26/opinion/israel-law-jewish-democracy-apartheid-palestinian.html (accessed on September 11, 2018).

28 Gulshan Dietl, *India and the Global Game of Gas Pipelines* (New Delhi: Routledge, 2017), p. 42.

29 According to the Liberal view, states have no reason to forsake the benefits from trade, especially if defection from the trading agreement will only lead to losses. Given this presupposition, liberals can argue that interdependence – as reflected in high trade at any particular point in time – will foster peace, given the advantages of trade over conflict and war. For an understanding of the debate on interdependence and conflict, see Edward D. Mansfield and Brian M. Pollins (eds.), *Economic Interdependence and International Conflict: New Perspectives on an Enduring Debate* (Ann Arbor: University of Michigan Press, 2003), pp. 1–30.

1

ISRAEL'S ENERGY SECTOR

Features, policies, and challenges

From energy scarcity to energy sufficiency

> The starting point for energy security today as it has always been is diversification
> of supplies and sources.
>
> *—Daniel Yergin*[1]

The above quote captures the essence of Israel's energy policies since its establishment in 1948. Diversification has been the underpinning feature of Israel's quest for energy supply security. Ensuring non-dependence on a single source or a particular type of energy has led to the development of a dynamic gas industry and the emergence of a burgeoning renewable energy sector.

Until 2004, when indigenously produced gas from its offshore fields in the Eastern Mediterranean came on stream, Israel imported 98 percent of its domestic energy requirements. Therefore, securing energy supply had been a major concern of Israeli policymakers for most of their country's history. Energy consumption in Israel primarily comes from hydrocarbon fuels – coal, oil, and gas. Renewable energy still has to find a larger share in the total energy mix – and it is a miniscule fraction of fossil fuels – even as Israel's started using solar energy in the 1970s. A transformative consequence of the 1973 oil crisis for Israel was the promulgation of a special national guideline requiring the installation of solar-thermal panels for water heating on all residential buildings.

Although located in the oil-and-gas-rich Middle East, political enmity with the producers (Arabs as well as Iran after 1979) effectively rendered the Jewish state an 'energy island,' isolated from regional energy trade networks and electricity grid connections. An exception was Egypt, which supplied gas through a maritime pipeline for less than four years during 2008–2012. That arrangement collapsed with the beginning of the Arab Spring rebellion in 2011. Since the discovery of natural gas in its EEZ, Israel has been able to reduce its almost complete reliance on imported coal and oil in significant ways. Estimated reserve of natural gas has been revised upwards from the time of the initial discovery in 1999–2000, and production has increased substantially with the on streaming of the Tamar field in 2013. Both these factors have improved Israel's energy security as never before.

Israel plans to reduce its dependence on oil imports through an expansion of its newly emerging natural gas sector. The beginning of gas production from Yam Tethys' Mari-B field in 2004, together with the gas imported from Egypt, initiated a 'gas revolution' in Israel's energy market. Electricity generation saw an increasing use of natural gas, such that it completely replaced diesel and fuel oil in 2016. Natural gas has also substituted coal in a sizeable way in the power sector. An noticeable exception to the trend of natural gas substitution in the power sector was in 2012. That year, the IEC purchased diesel and fuel oil in substantial quantities to compensate for the shortfall in natural gas, stemming from depletion of the Mari B reservoirs, as wells as disruption and eventual termination of supplies from Egypt.[2]

The proportion of natural gas in Israel's primary energy (PE) consumption has steadily increased over the last decade to become the second largest source of fuel in 2017. On the contrary, the share of renewables has been marginal and remained so in the same year, despite the fact that the country is a leader in renewable energy technologies.[3] Israel barely uses renewable power[4] and many observers believe that the discovery of large quantities of natural gas since 2009 has lowered government's interest in renewables. Officially, however, Israel upholds the goal of generating 10 percent of its energy needs from renewable sources by 2020.[5]

Israel's desire for energy security and independence is defined by a ceaseless quest for indigenous sources of supply. Since Israel's founding in 1948, companies searching for oil across the territory have drilled 530 onshore exploratory wells, and not even one long-term commercially viable oil well that could alleviate Israel's import dependency, has come to light. More recently, companies are carrying out exploratory drillings for oil in the disputed Golan Heights area in the north[6] and in the Dead Sea region of the country. The World Energy Council reported in November 2010 that Israel's underground oil-shale (marinate) deposits, which underlay some 15 percent of the country, could yield four billion barrels (bbl) of oil.[7] Buoying the country's optimism further is the Beicip-Franlab's estimate of the presence of up to 6.6 bbl of oil and 2135 bcm of gas in the offshore portion of Israel's Levant basin.[8]

Exploratory drillings for oil in the Golan Heights have yielded some results.[9] Afek reported in October 2015 that it had discovered a stratum of the shale deposit that could contain significant quantities of oil. The exact quantity is still not known, and it is yet to be determined whether the crude can be extracted profitably from under once volcanically active areas, given also the relatively high cost of shale extraction through hydraulic fracturing or 'fracking.'[10] Another obstacle is the opposition from environmental groups and Golan residents who are up in arms at the prospect of the development of shale wells in the area. As a result, further drilling is likely to be delayed. Afek also operates an oil shale project near Beit Shemesh (a city between Jerusalem and Tel Aviv), which is also facing fierce opposition from environmental groups concerned about damage to groundwater.[11]

An exploratory drilling by the Israel Opportunity-Energy Resources Ltd.–led consortium at the Hatrurim oil and gas exploration license near the Dead Sea on the Israeli side has found a reservoir containing an estimated 7 to 11 million barrels (mbl) of oil.[12] The appraisal by an independent Australia-based Dunmore Consulting sorted the discovery as 'contingent resource,' a classification that indicates 100 percent geological certainty about oil recovery from that accumulation, once the project is commercialised.[13] Israeli companies Delek Group and Avner Oil have already produced oil in 1995 from the license's reservoirs in the Halamish section, before they moved on offshore and found gas in the Eastern Mediterranean. Delek decided not to proceed with oil production due to low oil prices at that time. Israel Opportunity and its partners want to re-enter the Halamish drilling using advanced technologies and, according to public information, the spud date was in October 2018.[14]

Israel's energy sector: key features

Israel's PE consumption in 2017 was 25.8 million tonnes of oil equivalent (mtoe) – of which imported coal and oil constituted 65.5 percent of the supply – 45 percent or 11.7 mtoe was oil and other liquids, and 20 percent or 5.2 mtoe was coal. The remaining 33.4 percent or 8.9 mtoe of primary energy consumption consisted mostly of indigenously supplied natural gas, of which a meagre 0.4 mtoe was from the renewable sector (Figure 1.1). During the ten-year period from 2007 to 2017, PE consumption from natural gas grew by a whopping 240 percent. The increase in gas consumption from 1.1 mtoe in 2004 to 8.5 mtoe in 2017 (Table 1.1 and Figure 1.1) – nearly all being met by domestic production – can be attributed to the supplies from Yam Tethys and Tamar offshore gas fields. A miniscule percentage of gas came from imported LNG.[15] Despite the increasing use of natural gas, demand for imported oil and coal still constitutes about 65 percent of the total PE consumption.[16]

Use of coal and natural gas substitution

Israel does not produce coal in any amount: It imports its entire coal requirement. While coal has long been Israel's chief source of electricity, its use is declining as the use of natural gas in the power generation sector expands rapidly and gas-fired generation supplants coal-fired capacity. Coal's share in electricity production out of its total usage is 100 percent, i.e., the fuel is not used in any other transformation in Israel.[17] A fuel of choice in electricity generation, natural gas

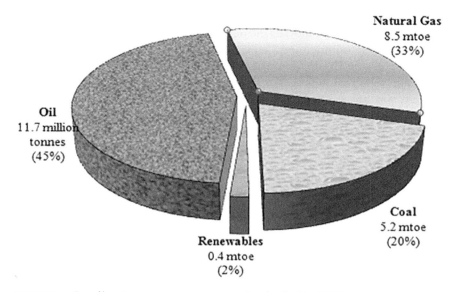

FIGURE 1.1 Israel's primary energy consumption by fuel in 2017

Source: BP Statistical Review of World Energy (henceforth, BP Statistical Review), June 2018

TABLE 1.1 Israel's total primary energy consumption by fuel, 2004–2016

(Oil consumption is measured in million tonnes; other fuels in mtoe)

Year	Oil	Natural gas	Coal	Nuclear energy	Hydro electricity	Renewables*	Total
2016	10.8	8.0	5.7	–	+	0.4	24.9
2015	11.4	7.6	6.7	–	+	0.3	26.0
2014	10.6	6.8	6.9	–	+	0.2	24.5
2013	11.5	6.2	7.4	–	+	0.1	25.2
2012	13.9	2.3	8.8	–	+	0.1	25.2
2011	11.8	4.5	7.9	–	+	0.1	24.3
2010	11.2	4.8	7.7	–	+	+	23.8
2009	10.8	3.8	7.7	–	+	+	22.3
2008	12.0	3.4	7.9	–	+	+	23.3
2007	12.3	2.5	8.0	–	+	+	22.8
2006	11.7	2.1	7.8	–	+	+	21.7
2005	12.1	1.5	7.9	–	+	+	21.6
2004	11.9	1.1	8.0	–	+	+	21.0

+Less than 0.05 MTOE

Source: BP Statistical Review (relevant years)

*Based on gross generation from renewable sources including wind, geothermal, solar, biomass, and waste. Converted by thermal equivalence assuming 38% conversion efficiency in a modern thermal power station steadily replaced coal and oil (diesel oil and fuel oil) to become the dominant fuel in electricity production in Israel during 2013–2017 (Table 1.2a).

Despite gas substitution, coal remains the second most important source for electrical power in Israel, given that in 2017 a critical 32.6 percent of electricity came from power stations operated on steam coal. In contrast, power produced from oil was just 1.2 percent, reflecting the governmental policy of phasing out expensive and polluting electricity fuel and substituting it with natural gas. While there is a relative increase in the use of renewables for electricity production, it is still a tiny fraction of over 2 percent of the total energy supply (Table 1.2a–c). Uri Bialer rightly observes, "There are still imponderables in Israel's supplies, despite the inclusion of natural gas in the energy consumption mix."[18]

The use of natural gas for electricity production witnessed a continuous growth at the expense of coal up until the imports from Egypt became erratic in 2011 and the production from the Mari-B began to decline almost coterminously. Consequently, Israel's power production from natural gas in 2011, witnessed a fall from the 2010 level, and 2012 witnessed a precipitous drop from 2011, as Mari-B reservoirs trickled to an end. A rapid recovery in

TABLE 1.2A Electricity generation by type of fuel (percentages)

Source	Non-renewable energy					Renewable energy					Total
	Total	Natural gas	Coal	Diesel oil	Residual fuel oil	Other	Total	Solar power	Wind power	Hydropower	Others	
2017	97.5	63.2	32.6	1.1	0.1	0.4	2.5	2.2	–	–	–	100
2016	97.5	60.7	35.9	0.3	0.1	0.4	2.5	2.3	–	–	–	100
2015	98.1	51.6	45.4	0.6	0.1	0.4	2.0	1.8	0.01	0.04	0.11	100
2014	98.5	48.9	49.1	0.1	0	0.4	1.5	1.4	0.01	0.02	0.10	100
2013	99.1	43.1	52.3	2.4	0.8	0.5	0.9	0.8	0.01	0.05	0.07	100

Source: Central Bureau of Statistics (CBS), State of Israel, Jerusalem, September 4, 2018

TABLE 1.2B Israel electricity fuel mix, 2013–2017 (in GWh, thousand MWh, or million KWh)

Year/ Source	Natural gas	Coal	Diesel oil	Residual fuel oil	Other	Renewable energy	Total
2017	42797	22029	773	95	289	1691	67674
2016	40825	24162	230	58	278	1703	67256
2015	33149	29161	355	65	283	1261	64275
2014	29945	30105	52	10	263	921	61295
2013	26462	32101	1485	467	283	571	61368

Source: CBS, State of Israel, Jerusalem, September 4, 2018

TABLE 1.2C Electricity production from coal, oil, gas, and renewables: export and domestic supply (in GWh or million KWh)

Year	Electricity production						Export**	Domestic supply
	Coal	Oil	Gas	Renewables*	Other sources	Total		
2016	24206	288	40824	1658	0	66976	−5553	61423
2015	29444	419	33149	1214	0	64226	−5197	59029
2014	30136	299	29457	921	0	60813	−4844	55969
2013	32138	2245	26378	571	0	61322	−4675	56647
2012	38760	13193	10566	484	0	63003	−4434	58569
2011	35191	4359	19748	294	80	59679	−4222	55457
2010	34289	2145	21955	170	32	58591	−3966	54625
2009	34398	2227	18016	99	268	55008	−3783	51225
2008	35378	5990	15382	32	220	57002	−3666	53336
2007	37402	5797	10569	24	0	53792	−2081	51711
2006	35835	5613	9085	25	0	50558	−1844	48714
2005	36282	6654	5657	39	0	48602	−1667	46935
2004	36611	6288	4341	39	0	47279	−1459	45820

*Includes biofuels (primary solid biofuels and biogases), hydro (includes production from pumped storage plants), solar PV, wind, and other sources
**Export to West Bank and Gaza Strip

Source: Israel: Electricity and Heat, International Energy Agency (IEA) Electricity Information, 2017 and 2018

2013 with the linking of Tamar field to the distribution pipelines onshore saw the consumption of coal plummet by 17 percent (Table 1.2c).[19]

Between 2013 and 2017, the use of natural gas showed a substantial increase. In 2017, the share of natural gas for the generation of electricity in Israel stood over 63 percent, compared to 43 percent in 2013. In contrast, the share of coal tumbled from over 52 percent to about 33 percent during the same period. The use of coal and gas was equivalent in 2014, but the latter took the lead in 2015 (Tables 1.2a and b) aided by several governmental measures (discussed in Chapter 3) to promote the use of natural gas over coal in the power sector. According to the MoE with the closure of four coal-fired units at the Hadera power station in July 2018, only 28 percent of all electricity production in Israel remained coal-based in that year.[20]

Oil usage and the impact of natural gas

Given the negligible local supply, Israel imports almost all of its oil needs. While crude oil is the most significant component of oil imports, Israel also imports a small amount of refinery feedstock, naphtha, Liquefied Petroleum Gas (LPG), motor gasoline, kerosene, diesel, and fuel oil. It also exports a few oil products, mainly to the Palestinian territories (Table 1.3). Oil retains its most significant share in Israel's primary energy consumption given its overwhelming use in

TABLE 1.3 Israel's oil import, export, and domestic supply (in 1000 tonnes)

Year	Production	Import*	Export**	Stock changes	Total domestic supply	Statistical differences	Transformation
2016	115	15053	−5682	386	21525	−156	13946
2015	76	15995	−6142	399	22061	−57	14503
2014	82	15646	−6886	0	11175	−424	13970
2013	64	14955	−6017	232	21267	−424	13897
2012	12	16574	−3143	0	21498	−288	14963
2011	20	14379	−4238	577	20959	338	13376
2010	4	14620	−3202	−6	21690	473	13393
2009	6	13957	−2893	0	21275	−221	12671
2008	6	14890	−3374	584	23259	−367	13736
2007	4	14261	−3350	−121	19818	1159	12913
2006	7	13919	−3173	149	20555	632	13298
2005	2	13651	−4089	223	19960	1382	13761
2004	2	13994	−3628	−192	19403	1050	12595

*Including crude oil, refinery feedstock, LPG, motor gasoline, other kerosene, gas/diesel, and fuel oil
**Including naphtha, LPG, motor gasoline, other kerosene and gas/diesel (export mainly to the Palestinian areas of West bank and Gaza)

Source: IEA, 2017 and 2018

the transportation sector. In 2016, the land transport sector consumed around 2.9 million tonnes (mt) of gasoline and 2.6mt of diesel out of the total domestic supply of 3.1mt and 2.8mt respectively (both production in refinery plus import). From the country's import of 10.3mt of crude oil, the total consumption in the form of gasoline and diesel from refining was as high as 44.4 percent.[21] A small amount of crude oil goes into industry, residential, and commercial uses in the form of LPG and chemical/petrochemical industry in the form of LPG and naphtha (Table 1.4). Israel also exports some amount of gasoline and diesel to the Palestinians. The West Bank and Gaza receive 558 thousand tonnes of gasoline and 1.9mt of diesel in 2016.[22]

Given the high cost of importing crude oil, together with the international commitment of the state to curb emissions from the use of fossil fuels, the Israeli government's stated policy is to bring down the use of oil in transportation (both public and private) through an increasing use of natural gas and alternative fuels.[23] The use of natural gas in public transportation is becoming more commonplace worldwide due to its lower price as compared to gasoline and diesel fuel and relatively cleaner combustion. At present, there is no gas-powered vehicle (or gas-filling station) in the country, the prime obstacle being the lack of a coherent policy on the taxes to be levied on such vehicles.[24]

There is a strong sentiment in Israel in favour of the adoption of natural gas as transportation fuel, especially as "it is cheaper than diesel, it is a 'clean' fuel that meets the requirements to reduce air emissions and reduce noise, does not

TABLE 1.4 Israel's oil consumption (in 1000 tonnes)

Year	Electricity plants (diesel and fuel oil)	Oil refineries (crude oil, refinery feedstock)	Energy industry's own use (fuel oil)	Industry (LPG, other kerosene, gas/diesel, fuel oil)	Transport (motor gasoline, gas/diesel, jet kerosene, and LPG)	Residential, commercial space (LPG), and agriculture	Other (non-specified, other kerosene, fuel oil)	Non-energy use (petrochemicals) naphtha etc.
2016	74	13872	0	437	5570	266	247	898
2015	114	14389	0	451	5362	230	223	690
2014	30	13940	0	560	5356	237	34	686
2013	477	13420	616	537	5018	235	35	625
2012	3098	11865	141	196	5433	576	501	362
2011	968	12408	479	184	4969	907	501	881
2010	579	12814	919	276	5208	868	730	769
2009	570	12075	639	344	4969	916	750	803
2008	1350	12386	654	340	5060	718	368	1068
2007	1562	11351	647	308	4594	821	634	1066
2006	1560	11738	889	282	4361	833	661	845
2005	1822	11939	657	260	4262	727	598	677
2004	1802	10793	649	170	4475	858	813	818

Source: IEA, 2017 and 2018

contaminate the soil and water, is lighter than the air and therefore very volatile and safe to use, in contrast to LPG."[25] In addition, the shift from oil to gas use has tremendous financial benefit for the economy: It can generate consumer savings and taxable income, save precious foreign exchange, and help meet the global requirement of reducing greenhouse gas emission. Nonetheless, a 2014 Bank Leumi study reports that any meaningful adoption of CNG in the transportation sector would take place only after 2025 and that during the 15-year period between 2025 and 2040, the largest investment in the CNG-fuelled vehicles would occur in the segment of truck fleets. Further, investments in CNG buses and taxi fleets would be relatively marginal and CNG will probably represent a meagre 10 percent of all private vehicles by 2040.[26]

The use of natural gas as CNG to power vehicles is a well-established technology, and there are expected benefits in terms of fuel and cost saving. In sharp contrast to Israel, where only three experimental vehicles run on natural gas, global gas market includes 26 million vehicles and more than 31,000 gas stations.[27] A comprehensive study by Haifa-based Neaman Institute's Energy Forum,[28] notes that the development of the natural gas-driven transport economy in Israel is thwarted by regulatory obstacles, including the lack of infrastructure for fuelling, high erection costs of refuelling stations coupled with the problems associated with the need to connect to the gas distribution/transmission system, and the costs associated with conversion of diesel engines to run on gas. Besides, the report highlights how the ambiguity about the cost of the transportation gas due to uncertainty regarding the Excise Tax that will be imposed looms large over any meaningful adoption of CNG vehicles in the country.

The industrial sector is another oil consuming segment of the Israeli market. In 2016, consumption of LPG and fuel oil was 168 and 251 thousand tonnes, respectively; 898 thousand tonnes of naphtha were also used to produce chemical and petrochemical products (Table 1.4).[29] However, several important industries have been integrating natural gas in their operations, in addition to onsite electricity production. Natural gas is an input chemical in the refining process as well as in heating systems (Table 1.5). While in the long term, the natural gas discoveries have created the potential for the growth of new industries based on methanol, studies reveal that the investment in a methanol plant will not occur before 2020 and production will commence closer to 2030.[30] Israel's MoE forecasts a 15 percent increase in the use of natural gas in domestic industrial applications during 2017–2026 and a 39 percent jump by 2040.[31]

Promotion of natural gas in transportation

In his 'Vision 2030,' Israel's Energy Minister Yuval Steinitz sets out 2030 as the cut-off year through which the polluting sectors of the economy – electricity production, transportation, and industry – will completely shift to natural gas and renewable energy usage, thereby eliminating the need for coal, gasoline, and diesel fuel.[32] In keeping with this vision, the MoE initiated a series of reforms in March 2018 to augment the use of natural gas in the diesel and gasoline segment.

TABLE 1.5 Israel's natural gas usage on a gross calorific value basis (in terajoule (TJ))

Year	Domestic supply			Total (domestic supply/ consumption)	Consumption			
	Production	Import	Statistical differences		Electricity plants	Energy industry own use*	Industry	Other non-specified
2016	352712	13653	16841	383206	317669	7693	53748	4096
2015	314234	6130	12184	332548	262263	44068	23105	3112
2014	288144	4606	4161	296911	263695	44552	23359	1305
2013	244788	22262	43971	311021	258879	33981	17816	345
2012	95536	2303	0	97839	76692	13877	7270	0
2011	163448	26484	−2337	187595	171628	10478	5489	0
2010	124306	80583	−3044	201845	193347	5573	2925	0
2009	100849	58150	8612	167611	155310	4520	7781	0
2008	130310	12323	−5496	137137	134699	2438	0	0
2007	103493	0	4386	107879	105016	2863	0	0
2006	86496	0	3366	89862	87092	2770	0	0
2005	61044	0	1563	62607	62607	0	0	0
2004	44294	0	1191	45485	45485	0	0	0

Source: IEA, 2017 and 2018

*Energy industry own use contains the primary and secondary energy consumed by transformation industries for heating, pumping, traction, and lighting purposes. These quantities are shown as negative figures. Included here are own use of energy consumed in power plants (which includes net electricity consumed for pumped storage) and energy used for gas extraction. See "Energy Industry Own Use," Balances Definitions, IEA, www.iea.org/statistics/resources/balancedefinitions/#eiou

The *Globes* summarises the major aspects of the reforms, including changes in taxes on fossil fuels to create a favourable milieu for the adoption of natural gas.[33] First, reimbursement for the excise tax on diesel fuel, which enables transporters of taxicabs, buses, and commercial vehicles to obtain tax refunds on the use of diesel, will be eliminated so as to create natural gas preference for the owners of heavy vehicles. Second, the tax on natural gas, which will take effect gradually starting in 2024, will apply if there are at least 25 CNG filling stations to supply natural gas for transportation. While taxes on CNG will amount to New Israeli Shekel (NIS) 0.02 per kg in the initial years, a raise gradually after six years will see excise tax reaching NIS 1.40 per kg in 2028. According to the plan, starting in March 2019, the excise tax on coal will be raised from NIS 46 to NIS 142 per tonne.[34] The government has also announced a $28.5 million (NIS 100 million) grants programme for companies willing to integrate CNG fuelling infrastructure within the public gas stations as well as stations that fuel large vehicles fleets.[35]

Significantly, a consultancy study on Israel's natural gas sector mentions the need for the concurrent promotion of electric vehicles along with those powered by CNG, in order to completely eliminate or reduce to the highest extent possible the use of fossil fuels: "Israel Railways, the state owned national railway system, has begun a process of conversion of its entire network from diesel to electric trains. A new electric light rail system in Tel Aviv is also under construction, with the first line (the red line) planned to begin operation in 2021."[36] Adopting an electricity-based train system will necessitate an increased use of natural gas for generating additional electrical power.

In conjunction with the CNG initiative, the Prime Minister's office launched a special programme to give impetus to the development of energy substitutes for oil in the transportation sector. The Fuel Choices Initiative (FCI), 2010, is a 10-year, NIS 1.5 billion ($430 million) international programme for research and development (R&D) concentrating on the evolution of technologies that reduce oil-dependent transportation not only in the domestic market but also globally. Indeed, the Israeli government considers FCI a "programme dedicated to reducing the world's dependency on oil for transport."[37] The focus of the programme is to make Israel a breeding ground and a test bed for alternative technologies and innovations in transportation, including the development and promotion of electric vehicles, along with hybrid, hydrogen, fuel cells, and CNG vehicles.[38] The programme also includes forging partnerships with international alternative fuel developers and creating joint pilot projects.

By establishing Israel as a centre of knowledge and industry in the field of alternative transportation fuels, the FCI is intended to serve as a support for start-up companies to secure funding, conduct research, and commercialise their projects.[39] It includes an annual $1 million prize to international innovators in the field. The Eric and Sheila Samson Prize, awarded for the first time in 2013, is the world's largest monetary prize awarded in the field of alternative fuels.[40]

Building on the FCI, the Israeli government in January 2017 launched a National Plan for Smart Mobility, allocating a budget of NIS 250 million for the plan that will be spread over five years. The project, now known as Fuel Choices and Smart Mobility Initiative (FCSMI), will assist start-ups to come up with innovative alternatives for transportation and commercialise their projects, boosting the position of Israel as the leader in transportation technologies.[41]

Energy intensity of growth

Israel has undergone rapid economic development in the past 15–20 years and attained a high standard of living comparable to some Organisation for Economic Cooperation and Development (OECD) countries such as France and Germany, but compares on a lesser scale to US, Canada, Australia, or Sweden. In 2017, Israel's overall GDP was approximately $350.85 billion and its GDP per capita was approximately $40270.25, comparable to France, $36,870.22, Germany, $44469.91, and, in the same year, the European Union, $33715.13 as a whole.[42]

However, Israel's energy intensity per capita and energy intensity relative to GDP ranks lower on an international scale as compared to several high performing newly industrialised and other OECD countries (Table 1.6) – a feature that can be attributed to the structural changes in the composition of the GDP. A BoI report (2016)[43] argues that in recent decades (over the last 20 years or so), the share of service sector in the Israeli economy has swelled (Table 1.7 and

TABLE 1.6 Energy intensity (TPES/GDP) for Israel, select newly industrialised countries (NICs), and select OECD countries: 1996, 2006, 2016 (toe/thousand 2005 USD)

Country	Energy intensity		
	2016	*2006*	*1996*
Israel	0.08	0.1	0.11
Select NICs			
Brazil	0.13	0.12	0.12
China	0.31	0.48	0.48
Indonesia	0.22	0.3	0.3
Malaysia	0.26	0.31	0.31
South Africa	0.33	0.38	0.38
Thailand	0.34	0.34	0.34
Select OECD countries			
Chile	0.14	0.15	0.17
France	0.09	0.1	0.12
Germany	0.08	0.1	0.12
New Zealand	0.12	0.12	0.15
Norway	0.06	0.06	0.07
Spain	0.08	0.1	0.1
United States	0.13	0.16	0.2

Source: IEA Atlas of Energy, 2018

TABLE 1.7 Israel's value added manufacturing, industries, and services in the 20-year period (% of GDP)

Year	Services, etc.	Manufacturing	Industries	Agriculture
2016	77.858	13.036	20.839	1.304
2015	77.696	13.148	20.995	1.309
2014	76.749	13.566	21.968	1.283
2013	76.501	13.787	22.162	1.336
2012	76.364	15.033	22.275	1.361
2011	76.376	14.779	21.914	1.71
2010	75.418	15.495	22.895	1.687
2009	75.481	15.437	22.571	1.948
2008	75.221	16.129	23.109	1.67
2007	74.648	16.938	23.734	1.617
2006	74.443	16.737	23.873	1.683
2005	75.199	16.219	23.05	1.751
2004	75.707	15.822	22.805	1.488
2003	75.405	15.774	23.018	1.577
2002	75.625	15.612	22.687	1.688
2001	75.457	16.172	22.903	1.641
2000	73.87	17.915	24.716	1.414
1999	73.428	17.739	24.96	1.612
1998	72.604	17.559	25.522	1.874
1997	71.976	17.556	26.35	1.674
1996	71.939	17.194	26.271	1.79
1995	71.883	17.014	26.161	1.956

Source: The World Bank, 2018

Figure 1.2) and since the intensity of energy use (electricity) in services is less than that in manufacturing, which has gradually shrunk, the result has been an overall drop in the intensity of electricity use in the Israeli economy.

Further, the share of industries with relatively low electricity usage has multiplied within both services and manufacturing, according to the above-mentioned BoI report. In manufacturing, energy-intensive enterprises (petrochemical, steel, and aluminium) are small and the share of high-technology industries (pharmaceuticals and electronic components) that use less electricity have proliferated, as have the share of financial and business services within the service sector. The report concludes that if the decline in electricity consumption continues in the manufacturing and services sectors, it will lead to an added diminution in the intensity of electricity use and a reduction in the rate of increase in demand for electricity relative to GDP.[44]

With natural gas becoming ever more available to the energy-intensive factories and to household for heating, the BoI report advances the view that it will substitute for electricity and moderate the demand growth for electricity in Israel, similar to how fuel products had substituted electricity in industrial production

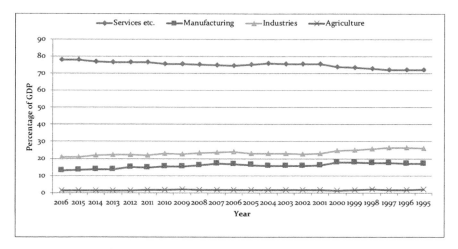

FIGURE 1.2 Israel's value added manufacturing, industries, and services in the 20-year period (% of GDP)

Source: The World Bank, 2018

TABLE 1.8 Electric power transmission and distribution losses, 2010–2014 (% of output)

Year	Israel	Iran	Kuwait	Qatar	Saudi Arabia	UAE
2014	2.858	12.603	1.661	6.05	6.781	7.177
2013	4.186	14.499	12.131	6.228	7.048	7.176
2012	2.755	14.47	14.194	6.232	8.753	7.176
2011	2.748	14.541	12.326	6.232	9.4	7.176
2010	2.758	14.192	12.087	6.278	8.909	7.176

Source: The World Bank, 2018

processes in the early 1990s. Demand for electricity will also be moderated as the proportion of households owning an air conditioner is expected to reach close to 100 percent by the beginning of the next decade.[45] Israel's past decline in the intensity of electricity use, reflected in the decline in energy intensity of growth, will continue in coming decades and are consistent with the significant downward trend in OECD countries. In the last two decades, the highest energy intensity of growth in Israel was recorded as 0.11 total primary energy supply (TPES)/GDP in 1996 (Table 1.6).

A reasonably favourable climate, high population density, and average ranking GDP per capita have also contributed to the low energy intensity of growth.[46] Israel does not have two other technical factors that contribute to high level of energy intensity characteristics of Persian Gulf states, namely, gas flaring in oil and gas production, and transmission and distribution losses in the power system (Table 1.8), which adds to their energy intensity.[47] For instance, Israel's electric power transmission and

TABLE 1.9 CO_2 emissions/population (tCO_2/capita)

Year	Israel	Germany	France	New Zealand
2016	7.46	8.88	4.38	6.45
2015	7.44	8.93	4.37	6.74
2014	7.46	8.93	4.32	6.89
2013	8.18	9.47	4.81	6.94
2012	9.33	9.26	4.75	7.07
2011	8.7	9.11	4.75	6.75
2010	8.98	9.45	5.23	6.96
2009	8.53	8.95	5.16	7.03
2008	8.77	9.60	5.54	7.83
2007	8.9	9.47	5.44	7.70

Source: IEA, 2018

distribution losses is low, a 2.86 percent of total output in 2014, as compared to 12.6 percent in Iran, 7.2 percent in UAE, and 6.8 percent in Saudi Arabia.[48]

Carbon dioxide emissions

Israel, discernibly, ranks less favourably on carbon dioxide (CO_2) emission per capita. In comparative terms, larger OECD economies such as Germany[49] and France, which have about eight and six times the population of Israel respectively,[50] have comparable or less CO_2 emission per capita. However, Israel's performance is better than New Zealand, which has GDP per capita of $39412.5, comparable to $37180.5 of Israel,[51] and has about half the population of Israel.[52] Due persistently to the high share of coal and oil in the primary energy mix, Israel's CO_2 emission per capital remains high in the ten-year period (Table 1.9), thus limiting the advantages of low energy intensity.[53]

The projected reduction on the use of coal and oil in the future, as natural gas becomes the primary fuel in electricity generation, and transportation sector adopts gas-based and other high-technology locomotives will have a salutary impact of the lowering the levels of CO_2 emission. However, it is unlikely to be eliminated mainly because a share of coal-fired plants will be retained or converted to combined-cycle power plants with coal backup for considerations of energy security and price uncertainty. Quite naturally, then, CO_2 intensity for Israel is the highest at the 2014 level among the OECD countries considered: Israel (2.9), New Zealand (1.7), France (1.3), and Germany (2.35).[54]

Israel's energy supply strategy

The geopolitics surrounding Israel dictates that energy security is a prominent issue and it is often equated with national security. An energy island, political animosity due to the Arab-Israeli conflict has prevented Israel from procuring energy produced in the Middle East, as well as establishing electricity grid interconnections with any neighbouring Arab country. Like any other country, Israel must devise strategies to minimise the risk arising from vagaries of energy supply. In Israel's case, energy security is not only connected to the easy availability of energy at a reasonable price, but also the management of risks arising from attack on its energy infrastructure by an enemy state or non-state actor in the region.

Import of coal

Without an internal supply option, Israel imports coal from countries as varied as Australia, South Africa, Columbia, and Russia.[55] In the aftermath of the oil crisis of 1973, Israel replaced oil with coal as the primary fuel for electricity generation so as to distance itself from the vagaries of the oil market. Coal continues to be a significant source for electricity generation despite the increasing use of natural gas.

Geopolitics also plays a role in the persistence of coal in Israel's primary energy supply. Most of the most significant coal exporters – South Africa, Poland, Australia, and Colombia[56] – are on good political terms with Israel and are located outside of areas of major political instability, unlike oil and natural gas. Coal can be readily obtained from different sources, making it difficult to embargo. It is easy to transport and store and thus enhances energy security of a country.[57] Many believe that the continued salience of coal in Israel's power generation reflects a bias at the highest level of policymaking, which does not consider natural gas or renewables as secure sources of energy.[58]

Crude oil supply from Iran: 1958–1979

In view of the country's high oil consumption and virtually no crude oil and condensate production, Israeli oil supply comes from a wide variety of sources. For reasons of national security, the Israeli government does not identify the sources of oil supply. Until the late 1970s, it is widely known that Iran was the primary source of Israel's oil supply. Crude oil from Iran was shipped to Eilat, Israel's southern port on the Gulf of Aqaba, directly accessible from the Iranian ports through the Red Sea. In order to ensure the supply of Iranian crude to the Haifa refinery, Israel built a pipeline, which began pumping oil from Eilat to Haifa via Ashkelon in 1958.[59]

Following the 1967 War, Israel agreed to partner with Iran for the construction of a bigger crude oil pipeline from Eilat to Ashkelon aimed at serving the interests of both countries equally. It provided Iran with an alternative route for the portage of its oil to European customers via the Ashkelon's port[60] in the wake of the closure of the Suez Canal. Israel gained another opening here to move crude oil to Haifa refineries, using the section of the old line north of Ashkelon (Figure 1.3).[61] The Eilat-Ashkelon Pipeline Company (EAPC) was set up in 1968 as an equal partnership joint venture between Israel and Iran to design and operate the pipeline.[62]

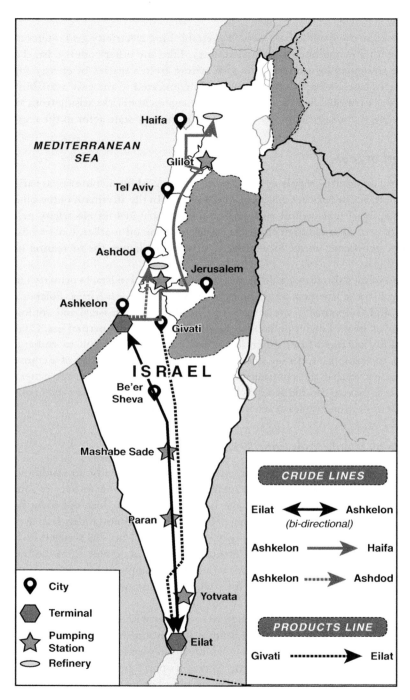

FIGURE 1.3 Eilat–Ashkelon–Haifa pipeline system

Source: Author's figure; referenced from EAPC, 2018

Disclaimer: Map not to scale

Once the new pipeline was inaugurated in February 1970, it was able to rapidly control a transit trade of about one MT of oil per month from Iran, of which half went to the Haifa refinery.[63] Until the establishment of the Islamic regime following the disposal of Shah of Iran Mohammad Reza Shah Pahlavi in 1979, Israel continuously bought oil from Iran – one of the reasons for its firm relations with the Shah's regime – despite Iran's official participation in the Arab oil embargo on Israel.

In addition, the EAPC pipeline also accommodated tonnes of crude oil from Sinai oil fields under Israel's control since the 1967 June Arab-Israeli War.[64] EAPC also built another line from Ashkelon to a new refinery in Ashdod, which commenced operations in 1973. However, when the Islamic regime in Iran decided to sever all ties with the Jewish state, the Israeli government took control of EAPC's assets and sold off its international interests and operations. The company, however, continued to operate the pipeline in Israel and further develop its operations.[65]

Sinai oil fields and American guarantee

The capture of Sinai during the 1967 War had major implications for Israel's energy position as the peninsula was rich in oil along the Gulf of Suez. However, when Israel took control of the oilfields from Egypt, they were found to be in very poor condition due to damages caused by war and neglect. A substantial investment was made by the Israeli government to bring them back into full production. Among others (Ras Sudr, Asl, Sidi, and Belayim), Abu Rudeis was the most prolific field (Figure 1.4) and it was brought back on stream at the rate of 50,000 barrels per day (bpd) by October 1967 and, following the restoration of its onshore portion, output reached some 90,000 bpd a month later.

By 1971, the total supply from Sinai peaked at 120,000 bpd, so much so that the peninsular fields produced a total of 43.2 million barrels of oil, approximating Israel's annual domestic consumption and delivering the country self-sufficiency for the first time. Under the 4 September 1975 Sinai Interim Agreement (also known as Sinai II Agreement), Israel retuned the rich Abu Rudeis oilfield to Egyptian control.[66]

In April 1982, Israel handed over the Alma oilfield (now called the Shuab Ali field) (Figure 1.4), which it had discovered in the Suez Gulf in November 1977 and developed with great rapidity within two years.[67] By November 1979, Alma's seven wells were producing some 40,000 bpd, about 22 percent of Israel's demand.[68] When Israel ceded the Alma field to Egypt, it had become the Jewish state's largest single source of oil, supplying about half of the country's energy needs.[69] Israel had considered the Alma field as integral to its energy security and expected it to deliver energy self-sufficiency by 1990.[70]

According to an Egyptian Petroleum Authority report, Israel managed to produce a total of 165 million barrels of crude oil (and 70 billion cubic feet of natural gas) – worth roughly $15 billion at 1975 values – during its occupation of

FIGURE 1.4 Oil and gas fields in Sinai

Source: Author

Disclaimer: Map not to scale

the Sinai peninsula.[71] The historic Israeli–Egyptian peace treaty of 1979, which included Egypt's commitment to sell oil to Israel in light of the loss of Sinai fields,[72] substituted for the cessation of oil export from Iran in the wake of the revolution. An average of about 1.5mt of oil from Egyptian wells arrived annually in tankers at Eilat, from where it was transported via the EAPC's pipeline to Ashkelon and then carried forward to the Haifa and Ashdod refineries.[73] However, due to deterioration in Egypt-Israel relations following the outbreak of the Intifada in 1987, these exports were terminated.[74] The EAPC also upgraded the pipeline and enhanced its capacity to handle bi-directional traffic, allowing Russia to sell oil to Asia.[75]

In order to shield Israel against the vagaries of dependence on imported oil, both the Sinai withdrawal and the Egyptian-Israeli peace agreements were accompanied by the US-Israel deal on oil. In light of the fact that Iran had joined the Arab oil producers in the oil embargo of 1973, the United States and Israel signed a five-year Memorandum of Agreement (MoA) on oil, parallel to the Sinai II Agreement, which came into force on 27 February 1976.[76]

The American-Israeli oil agreement included a promise to assist Israel in securing oil supply should it fail to procure the fuel to "meet all its normal requirements for domestic consumption"[77] on the international market. US would also secure the necessary means to transport such oil to Israel. Further, if the United States were to be prevented from purchasing oil, such as quantitative restrictions under an embargo, it would "make oil available for purchase by Israel"[78] in accordance with the International Energy Agency (IEA) guidelines. It was an extraordinary commitment, binding US to part with its share of oil in case of emergency, as Washington would also give "special attention"[79] to Israel's oil needs when providing foreign assistance.

Another MoA between the United States and Israel, which accompanied the Egypt-Israel Treaty of Peace signed in Washington on 26 March 1979, upheld the oil supply agreement of September 1975 and gave it an extension of 15 years.[80] It too required the United States to make "every effort"[81] to help transport oil to Israel if it was unable to secure tankers in the open market. By pledging Israel continued access to oil, the US-Israel agreement alleviated Israeli anxieties about rise in oil prices and disruption of supply in the wake of the Iranian revolution. The MoA was extended in 1994 and 2004 but it was not renewed by the Obama Administration when the extension last expired in November 2014. Israel has, however, never needed to invoke this 'emergency oil' supply agreement.

Oil from Russia, Central Asia, and Kurdistan regional governments

In recent decades, Israel has imported crude oil from Russia, Caspian Sea and Africa.[82] At least since 2005, Israel has turned to Russia and Caspian Sea littoral, Azerbaijan and Kazakhstan, for most of its oil requirements.[83] Crude oil bound for Israel is transported via the Baku–Tbilisi–Ceyhan pipeline (BTC) that runs from the Azeri capital of Baku, through the Georgian capital of Tbilisi, and to the Mediterranean port of Ceyhan in Turkey's south. From Ceyhan port, oil tankers move the crude to Israel's eastern Mediterranean ports of Haifa and Ashdod.[84] The exclusive tanker deliveries meant for the Israeli shores come via the Black Sea and Turkish-controlled Bosporus and Dardanelles.[85]

Iraqi Kurdistan started supplying oil to Israel from June 2014, shortly after Kurdish Peshmarga forces – the Kurdistan Regional Government's (KRG's) independent army – seized the oil-rich town of Kirkuk in northern Iraq from the radical Islamic State of Iraq and Syria (ISIS). In 2015–2016, most of Israel's oil supply came from KRG via Turkey's Ceyhan port. More specifically, Israeli refineries located in Haifa and Ashdod imported more than 19 million barrels of Kurdish oil between the beginning of May and August 2015, worth $1 billion and an equivalent of about 77 percent of average Israeli demand.[86] "Kurdish oil flows easily through Turkey to Israel," claims Necdet Pamir, "riding on the

AKP's emphasis on commercial aspect as opposed to the political facet of energy transactions."[87]

The relationship between Israel and Kurds dates to the mid-1960s. Kurds were an integral part of the Israel's 'periphery doctrine' or 'alliance of periphery' advanced by Israeli Prime Minister David Ben-Gurion. This doctrine/alliance was premised on the rule that Israel should cultivate ties with non-Arab states and minorities with which it had no direct conflict and who had long-standing problems with Arab states.[88] In this way, Israel sought to offset the political and economic boycott of the Arab world that made it a regional pariah.

Although the alliance of periphery became redundant with the collapse of the Pahlavi regime in Iran, and as Israel's regional position improved with the signing of peace treaties with Egypt and Jordan, the Kurds still have salience in Israel's regional policy. Since the 1960s, Israel has provided military training, armaments, intelligence, and funding to the Kurds,[89] viewing the minority ethnic group – whose indigenous population is split between Iraq, Turkey, Syria, and Iran – as a buffer against Arab adversaries in the north and as an anchor of stability since the emergence of ISIS and initiation of the civil war in Syria. While Iraqi Kurdistan's quest for independence does not have much international support, Prime Minister Benjamin Netanyahu made Israeli support for an independent Kurdish state in northern Iraq official in September 2017, stating that Israel "supports the legitimate efforts of the Kurdish people to achieve their own state,"[90] days ahead of the Kurdish independence referendum that Baghdad opposed.

Israeli officials have openly stated a number of times that Israel has never had a problem obtaining oil, even during the most difficult times, including from countries with which it has no diplomatic relations.[91] Israel has also built a highly fortified 'underground facility' to store its strategic reserves of oil in case supply lanes are disrupted due to war or embargo, situations not unknown to Israel. One of the recommendations of the Arganat Commission – headed by chief justice Shimon Arganat and appointed to investigate the circumstances leading the outbreak of the Yom Kippur War in October 1973 – was to build a fuel reserve facility for emergency situations. The October War revealed some glaring shortcomings, one of which was the lack of fuel reserve to fly the fighter jets. A fuel reserve facility was inaugurated in 1996 and used once during the 2006 second Lebanon War, when oil tankers could not approach Israel's shores.[92]

Natural gas supply and MoU with Qatar

In view of the difficulties involved in import of natural gas, Israel began to see natural gas as an energy option only in the early 1990s. Natural gas is relatively hard to transport, requiring the construction of expensive infrastructure. The cost of investment implies that suppliers want long-term commitments that preclude other potential supply source from trade, making it relatively easy to embargo. Israel's enmity with gas-rich countries of the region ensured that there were no regional pipelines from Egypt or Iran in the first four decades of the nation's existence.

With the warming of regional relations once the 1993 Oslo Accord was signed, Israel pursued the idea of natural gas import from Qatar, signing a MoU for natural gas supplies. Israel also participated in a mutual feasibility study as part of Qatar's goal to become the leading gas provider in the region.[93] The Qatari government commissioned Houston-based energy company Enron to conduct feasibility studies relating to LNG supplies to Israel and India. France's Sofregaz concluded a survey on behalf of the Israeli government that found it was viable to offload LNG at both the Eilat and Ashdod ports.[94]

Although the discussions progressed to an advanced stage, the ambitious plan to import natural gas from Qatar soon encountered political difficulties, as the project had been considered contingent on the progress of the Arab-Israeli peace process, which had begun to unravel in the late 1990s. As the Oslo rapprochement dissolved with the onset of the second Palestinian *Intifada*, provoked as it was by the visit of Israeli opposition leader Ariel Sharon's visit to the Al-Aqsa mosque in September 2000, Qatar came under increasing pressure from the Arab countries to abandon economic relations with Israel. Officially, Qatar surrendered to Arab pressure, closing down the trade office established in Doha in October 1995.

In practice, however, Qatar's business ties with Israel continued in a discreet manner so much so that in May 2003, Doha declared that it would broaden relations with Israel if there were to be a progress in peace process with the Palestinians.[95] Further, Israel's then-Foreign Minister Tzipi Livni stated after her trip to Qatar in April 2008 that the Arab country was willing to go "all the way"[96] towards normalisation of relations with Israel. In the same vein, several newspapers in the Arab world reported that Qatar was not averse to selling gas to Israel for an "unlimited period of time."[97]

Parallel to talks with Qatar, Israel also explored the possibility of importing gas from Egypt. Former Egyptian oil minister Hamdi Ali al-Bandi, visited Israel in August 1994 to discuss gas trade between the two countries. The possibility of constructing a 180-km pipeline to transport gas from the Baltim and Timsa offshore fields near Port Said was also discussed,[98] although there was no progress on a potential gas deal until 1999, the year Israel entered the 'gas game.'

British Gas and Gaza fields

For several years Israel negotiated with the British Gas (BG)-led consortium, including the Consolidated Contractors Company (CCC)[99] and the Palestine Investment Fund (PIF),[100] licensed to commercially develop the Gaza gas fields. Within Gaza's territorial waters, the two primary gas fields, Gaza Marine, the main field and the second smaller field, the 'Border Field' that straddles the maritime boundary separating Gaza's territorial waters from Israel's territorial waters, contains an estimated 28 bcm of gas. When the fields were discovered in 1999, it was commonly believed Israel would contract to buy gas from Gaza Marine and this was "widely believed to be an Israeli precondition for allowing the development of the fields to go ahead."[101]

Israel viewed the Gaza fields as essential to its energy security, believing that its own gas resources discovered around the same time as the Gaza Marine would soon run out. However, with the beginning of the Al-Aqsa Intifada in September 2000, Israel started to block the development of Gaza fields, citing security reasons. Israeli officials argue that they do not want the revenue from the gas sales to end up in the hands of Hamas, which took over the control of the Gaza Strip in 2006.[102]

A US diplomatic cable revealed by Wikileaks[103] discloses that the PA, along with the BG-led consortium, made serious efforts to create "a transparent and auditable mechanism" for gas taxes and royalties that will "not run afoul with US and European regulatory restrictions"[104] to assuage Israel's security concerns. The same cable goes on to say that several rounds of negotiations between BG and successive Israeli governments did not produce a deal, even as the consortium partners agreed that the primary onshore delivery terminal should be in Ashdod, the Israeli coastal city. Negotiations took a beating on the issue of how to deliver a portion of the gas to the Gaza Power Plant.

A melange of reasons (discussed in Chapter 4) have held up the development of Gaza Marine since 1999, not least Israel's intent to prevent Palestinians from earning a profit from gas sales and becoming energy independent.[105] Israel went on to discover Tamar and Leviathan fields, so the argument in favour of importing gas from Gaza Marine to allay Israel's energy supply crunch became superfluous. Now owing large quantities of gas, Israel maintains that the Gaza's offshore fields should be developed when their legal status is clarified in an EEZ delineation agreement with the future Palestinian state.[106]

Indigenous discoveries and import from Egypt

Israel's gas story begins in 1999–2000 with the discovery of Noa and Mari B reserves off the country's Eastern Mediterranean coast. In June 1999, the American-Israeli Yam Tethys consortium, comprising Noble Energy, Avner Exploration, and Delek Drilling, found commercially viable gas reserves in the Noa lease area, followed in February 2000 by more discoveries in the Mari lease area. Larger fields such as Tamar and Leviathan in what Israel calls its EEZ[107] have given Israel energy self-sufficiency in a significant way. Along with a few smaller ones discovered during 2012–2013,[108] Israel has consolidated its position as a regional gas power. Around 40 percent of total reserve would be headed for export under a new law approved by the government in June 2013 (discussed in Chapter 2).

Galvanised by the discoveries in Yam Tethys reserves, the IEC decided to convert a series of its diesel and fuel oil power stations to natural gas operations. The government, bearing in mind Israel's ratification of Climate Change Convention in 1996 (although it did not have any binding limitation on Israel's greenhouse gas emissions),[109] allowed IEC to negotiate a long-term natural gas purchase contract with local and foreign suppliers. After several rounds of negotiations, IEC signed a $3 billion deal with EMG, an Egyptian-Israeli company,[110] in August 2005. The contract stipulated a supply of 1.7 bcm of natural gas per year (1.2 bcm to be purchased in the first year) for 15 years to Israel from the Egyptian gas fields, with an option of a 5-year extension. The EMG also contracted to supply natural gas to several large Israeli industries, but its most important customer was the IEC.

Gas started flowing through the Al-Arish-Ashkelon pipeline (Figure 1.5) in July 2008 and reached full capacity to the extent that Egypt was supplying Israel with 43 percent of its natural gas needs by 2010. However, in the wake of the Arab Spring disturbances in Egypt starting in February 2011, the Sinai section of the Egyptian gas pipeline supplying to the Al-Arish-Ashkelon pipeline became the target of the widespread anger against President Mubarak's regime.[111] It suffered bombings at

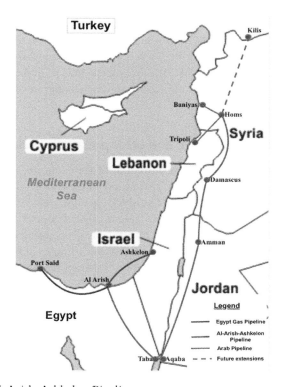

FIGURE 1.5   Al-Arish-Ashkelon Pipeline

Source: Author

Disclaimer: Map not to scale

least a dozen times, severely impairing supplies to Israel for extended periods. Gas deliveries to Israel dried up for a total of 225 days in 2011 and 66 days during the first three months of 2012, and ceased after an explosion on 5 March of that year.[112]

During 2011, the Egyptian gas supply was reduced to 30 percent of the contractual quantity, such that EMG's supply to the IEC was only about 16 percent of the natural gas used for electricity generation.[113] The suppliers to the EMG, state-owned Egyptian General Petroleum Corporation (EGPC), and Egyptian Natural Gas Holding Company (EGAS) eventually announced in April 2012 that they could no longer supply gas for export to Israel.[114] Meanwhile, the Yam Tethys' Mari-B reserve, in full production since February 2004 and the sole indigenous supplier to the IEC, made up for the shortfall. From October 2011, however, the extraction rate from Mari B reserve decreased gradually due to the depletion of the field and the collapse of its wells resulting from over extraction, as Israel's power generation had relied heavily on it when the gas supply from Egypt became unreliable.[115] Production from Mari-B continued to plummet throughout 2012, and the field trickled to an end in December 2013. Some gas began to flow from Yam Tethys's Noa North and Pinnacles I reserves in June–July 2012 to allow for additional supplies to the market, but it was not enough. The daily aggregate quantity of natural gas supplied by the Yam Tethys fields to the IEC, including Mari B reserve, at this stage was about 50 percent of the daily contractual quantity.[116] As a result of these events, Israel faced severe energy shortage in the summer of 2012 forcing the IEC to make a costly immediate transition to expensive liquid fuels for power generation to counter for the shortfall in the supply of gas.[117]

FSRU, production from Tamar, and other prospective fields

Israel's electric utility, faced with termination of Egyptian gas and depletion of Mari-B, turned to LNG imports as a stopgap until gas from the Tamar reservoir was integrated into the market. The INGL inaugurated a deep-water LNG receiving terminal off the coast of Hadera in 2012. Cargoes of the liquefied fuel are offloaded ship-to-ship on sea into the floating storage and regasification unit (FSRU) moored to a submerged turret-loading (STL) buoy. Once the FSRU turns back LNG into gas on-board, it is injected into the STL system and pumped onshore through the attached pipelines.[118] The IEC being the sole LNG importer and the main gas consumer in the country, most of the gas imports are for its own use. The IEC leased the US-based Excelerate Energy's FSRU *Excellence* in 2013 for five years; the lease was extended by a further two years to September 2019.[119]

Most cargoes to Hadera have come from BP's LNG operations in Trinidad and Tobago. Israel also received a cargo of US LNG – from the nation's two operating LNG export terminals – Sabine Pass and Dominion Energy's Cove Point facility in Maryland – for the first time in May 2018, since exports from America's shores began in 2016.[120]

The Israeli Natural Gas Authority, a department in the Ministry of Energy, supports more LNG imports and is in favour of building a second terminal and leasing another FSRU. Promoters of this idea argue that a new terminal is required as a backup to the gas system when more than half of Israel's power generation is gas-dependent. It would increase energy security in view of the fact that Israel has no gas storage facilities[121] and a disruption in the supply chain would impede the availability of gas to the consumers and cause power outages. They also argue that small industrial units can avail gas supply, which they do not because of shortages.

Equally, there are those who say that building another LNG terminal is unnecessary while the existing LNG terminal is operating below par at 0.06–0.36 bcm per year. Instead, they favour the expeditious development of Karish and Tanin, Israel's smaller gas fields, and building another pipeline from Tamar to generate redundancy of supply in the domestic market.[122]

At present, Israel's natural gas supply is almost wholly dependent on a single source – the Tamar gas field. The Tamar field project consists of a system of underwater pipes that transport gas from the production wells to the production platform located at a distance of 150 km, which is about 45 km from the shore. A single flowline carries gas from the production platform to the Ashdod gas-receiving terminal (Figure 1.6). In case of attack or technical failure, Tamar, connected to the electricity transmission structure through a single carriage line, could pose a significant risk to Israel's electricity generation.[123]

While the floating LNG import terminal was hailed as capable of relieving Israel's gas shortage until the start of production from Tamar reservoir, it remains a component of the country's energy security as a crucial backup measure. The development of the Leviathan field by the end of 2019, as well as Tanin and Karish, which are expected to come on stream in the early 2020s, will dramatically improve the security of gas supply to the Israeli economy.

Regional unrest and the resultant domestic energy crisis in 2012 deepened Israel's resolve to develop its natural gas resources. If all the discovered fields go through favourable development in the coming years, Israel would be able to fortify its energy security for several decades and even acquire greater strategic edge through gas export that can transform energy supply and economic relations in the Eastern Mediterranean region.

Diversification of electricity production

As nations become conscious of environmental degradation and climate change caused by the burning of fossil fuels, they are making efforts to replace them by cleaner sources of energy. Israel signed and ratified the 2015 Paris Agreement that determined a global temperature rise must be kept well below 2°C by means of varying national greenhouse gas (GHG) reduction targets. The target approved for the country by Government Decision Number 542 of 20 September 2015 aims at a 26 percent per capita reduction in CHG emissions by 2030 from its

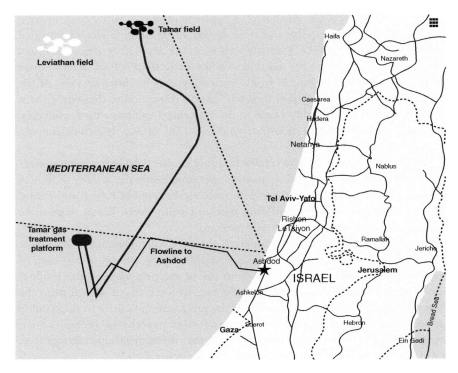

FIGURE 1.6 Single flowline from production platform to Ashdod receiving terminal

Source: Author

Disclaimer: Map not to scale

2005 base year per capita emissions level. In order to meet the national goal for GHG emissions, the government took the decision[124] to draw up a national plan, targeting electricity-based energy efficiency programme and increased share of renewable energy in electricity production to the tune of 10 percent by 2020, 13 percent by 2025, and 17 percent by 2030.[125]

Reduction in coal usage

Israel's energy and environment ministries in 2015 issued a directive requiring the IEC to reduce its use of coal at the coal-fired power stations (Table 1.10) in Orot Rabin (Hadera) and Rotenberg (Ashkelon)[126] by 15 percent in 2016 and to use more natural gas. The ministries also mandated a further 5 percent reduction in coal use for power generation in 2017.[127] As a result, the consumption of coal in electricity generation dropped by 20 percent in 2016.[128]

Coal demand fell further in 2017 due to the closure of a 575-Megawatt (MW) unit at the Orot Robin power complex in order to instal filters/scrubbers as part

TABLE 1.10 Israel's coal power generation units

Location	Orot Rabin (Hadera)		Rotenberg (Ashkelon)	
	Stage A	Stage B	Stage A	Stage B
Turbines (total 10)	4 × 360	2 × 575	2 × 575	2 × 550
MW	1,440	1,150	1,150	1,100
Year(s) of commissioning	1981–84	1995–96	1990–91	2000–01

Source: IEC

of its programme to meet environment ministry's guidelines for reducing emissions at coal plants.[129] In the first six months of 2017, the IEC's electricity generation from coal dropped to 43.93 percent as compared to 51.72 percent in the first six months of 2016. During the same period, power production from natural gas (including LNG) appreciated from 47.68 in June 2016 to 55.35 in June 2016.[130]

As of December 2017, approximately 57 percent of the total installed generation capacity of the IEC was powered by natural gas.[131] In compliance with the 'emission permit' under the Clean Air Law, 2008, the IEC is obliged to continue installing emission reduction devices in all the units at the Rotenberg site and in units 5 and 6 at the Orot Rabin site.[132]

In keeping with the international commitment on climate change and domestic concerns about loss of lives due to pollution, Israel's Ministry of Energy has instructed the IEC to reduce the share of coal generation in its installed capacity to 20 percent in 2022 and to zero by 2025 (Table 1.10).[133] While the four oldest coal-based electricity generation units at Orot Rabin (coal units 1–4) will be closed by 2022 and replaced with private cogeneration power stations that run on natural gas and coal-backed for emergency,[134] the IEC will construct and operate two new combined-cycle gas turbines at Orot Rabin, the very last of its development of new generation sites.[135]

The other decisions by the government to reduce the consumption of coal, include "establishing a loading priority," i.e., giving priority to natural gas over coal in power stations.[136] A January 2018 decision taken by Energy Minister Steinitz and Environmental Protection Minister Zeev Elkin called for a 30 percent reduction in coal use for electricity generation in 2018 compared to 2015 – the base year. As part of the decision, one of the four coal-fired units in the Orot Rabin power plant was shut down in September.[137] According to the environment ministry's bulletin, by the end of 2018, 70 percent of electricity generation in Israel will be based on natural gas and renewable energy.[138]

However, coal capability will be maintained at the IEC power stations in Ashkelon and units 5–6 in Hadera.[139] Overall, most of the coal power units of the IEC will be decommissioned in the middle of the next decade and the remaining units will be in reserve. The government's mid-term target is for natural gas to account for 80 percent of electricity production, with 10 percent or more from renewables – solar radiation, wind, biogas, and biomass – and the remainder from coal by 2020.[140]

Integration of renewable energy

Development of renewable energy has lagged behind in Israel as compared to OECD countries, although it has always been a part of the strategy to reduce reliance on imported fossil fuels. It is worth remembering that one of the first acts of Prime Minister Ben-Gurion was to set up the Research Council of Israel to promote research and development that would harness scientific knowledge towards the development of a new nation having virtually no natural resources.

In the wake of the Organisation of Petroleum Exporting Countries' (OPEC's) oil embargo of Israel in 1973 and the Iranian Revolution of 1979 that resulted in the decade's second oil crisis, the country passed its first solar energy legislation in 1980 aimed at reducing dependence on foreign oil. The law made it mandatory for all new residential building up to 20 metres high to instal solar-thermal water heaters. Over the years, this reduced electric power consumption by 3 percent and made Israel a world leader in solar water heating system, with 85 percent of households today using solar thermal energy.[141] Hence, some electricity consumption or other type of heating fuel consumption has been replaced by a renewable source.

Given the combination of import dependency and growth in energy demand, the logical trajectory for Israel's energy security is to diversify sources of supply and, to begin with, develop the renewable energy sector. Despite attempts at energy diversification, the share of renewable energy as a percentage of the total primary energy consumption or electricity production has been minor. In 2009, the Israeli government established a target for renewables to reach 5 percent power generation from renewable sources by 2014, 10 percent by 2020, and 17 percent by 2030.[142] These figures are far below the OECD mid-term targets of 20 percent share of renewables by 2020, and 27 percent by 2030.[143] Many countries are well beyond that: In 2016, 32 percent of the country's electricity consumption, an exceptionally large proportion by global standards, came from renewable energy.[144]

Despite ample sunshine and suitable climatic conditions for renewable energy, Israel fell far behind the initial 5 percent target, today producing only 2.5 percent of its electricity from renewables.[145] Bureaucratic bottlenecks, cumbersome regulations, a lack of land, and anticipation of more gas coming online that can produce electricity at a lower cost than solar are often cited as factors explaining the lower than expected use of solar energy.[146] Although Israeli inventors are leading the technological developments in the field of renewables, particularly solar energy, many of them have taken their expertise abroad and focused on markets outside of Israel because they found it difficult to implement their ideas at home.[147]

According to a 2018 OECD survey, an investment of about NIS 38 billion (3.1 percent of GDP) is required to increase the share of electricity generated by renewable sources from 2.6 percent in 2016 to 17 percent in 2030.[148] To achieve these targets, the authorities are promoting the construction of gas-fired and solar power stations by independent power producers (IPPs), because the IEC has not been building power stations since 2009 so as to enhance competition in the power sector. The share of IPPs in total power production has gone up more than fourfold during 2013–2016, from 6.9 percent to 27.5 percent.[149] As electricity production from renewables would come from private entities, the IEC needs to upgrade the network surrounding the new renewable energy installations.

The IEC also needs to prepare for absorbing excess electricity produced from private houses' rooftop solar installations (once more and more people adopt these) and draw up a plan on how to charge people who would be both consumers and producers of electricity. At present, the grid can only absorb between 5 and 20 percent of its energy from renewable sources, and investment will be required to meet renewable energy generation targets.[150] As the share of renewable energy in the grid increases, the need to find energy storage solutions will also become prominent. The Samuel Neaman Institute's report on leveraging Israel's energy potential rightly notes:

> Israel's relative advantages in the renewable energy sector are a potential which must be leveraged, especially given that the industry is both labour- and knowledge-intensive, and that its growth expected to provide significant direct benefits for the Israeli such as employment and exports, as well as external benefits such as emissions reduction and energy savings.[151]

With an annual budget of about US $300 million, the Ministry of Industry, Trade and Labor is giving a push to technological companies to conduct research and develop solutions in field of renewable energy. To date there are 200 renewable energy companies involved in the programme, about 30 percent of which are start-ups.[152] In recent years, solar and wind power generation have made some progress.

With more than 300 days of sunshine per year and some of the highest levels of solar radiation in the world, Israel is particularly suited to the development of solar energy sector. Ketura Sun, Israel's first commercial solar project using photovoltaic panels, was built in the Arava Valley, a sparsely populated tract in southern Israel between the Dead Sea and Eilat. Inaugurated in 2011, the solar field built as a joint venture between Israel's Arava Power and Germany's Siemens AG, has a power capacity of 5 MW. Since then, Arava Power has built more than 100 MW of Photo Voltaic (PV) projects, all situated in the country's southern Negev desert and the Arava valley.[153]

Another large solar power station, named after the nearby town of Ashalim, is under construction on the vast swathe of the Negev. The Ashalim complex is made up of three solar power generation projects, each using a different technology.[154] The first is Negev Energy's 121 MW power plant that employs the concentrated solar power (CSP)-thermal method. Thousands of parabolic troughs, fitted with half a million rotatable mirrors, concentrate the sun's radiation on special tubes that are positioned at the centre of the trough. The radiation heats up the thermal oil flowing through the tubes to 390OC and by using heat exchangers, the thermal energy is then transferred to water in a boiler, producing steam to drive the turbine and generate electricity. The second, a 110 MW power project built by Megalim Solar Power, uses the thermo-solar method. Around 50,000 computer-controlled heliostat mirrors focus the sun's rays onto a special type of boiler atop a 250-metre-high tower. Once the boiler heats up, it produces steam that turns the turbine to generate electricity. The third project, a 30 MW solar plant owned by French group EDF Energies Nouvelles (EDF EN), is a photovoltaic (PV) park that uses solar cells to generate electrical power. Together, these projects will generate some 310 MW of power, contributing around 2.5 percent towards the country's goal of generating 10 percent of its energy from renewable sources by 2020.

In addition to solar PV resources, Israel has a small amount of hydroelectric power in its pool of renewables. In 2015, Israel produced 24 GWh of hydroelectric power. While Israel has been producing hydroelectric power since 1990, the recent data on hydroelectric generation is not available for the years 2016 and 2017.

Plans to utilize geothermal energy are either in the planning process or under consideration. Power generated from wind is miniscule, and the earliest data available for wind generation is 2001 when it was 10 GWh of the gross electricity production. Since then wind power generation rose to 12 GWh in 2003 and then declined to 11 GWh in 2011 and 7 GWh in 2015. No data is available for 2016 and 2017. Although, the potential of wind energy in Israel is as high as an estimated 1,000 MW, wind turbines have aroused vigorous opposition within Israel, ironically from environmental organizations, which are concerned about injury to rare birds nesting on the Golan Heights, where the wind assessment is the best for setting up a wind farm. As of now, only two wind farms, which were built in the 1990s, are active in Israel. Around 15 wind power projects are in the construction stages and the government is considering granting approval to several others. In June 2018, a consortium led by Enlight Renewable Energy (an Israeli company) received permission from the Ministry of Energy in June 2018 to build a 96–99 MW wind power plant in the Bekaa Valley in northern Golan Heights. The Emek Habacha wind farm, as the project is also known, will be the largest of its kind in Israel when complete in 2020–21, and will supply power to the IEC under a 20-year purchase agreement, significantly augmenting the renewable energy production in Israel.[155] The proposals to utilise geothermal energy are either in the planning process or under consideration. Finally, Israel has no nuclear power plant but the nation from time to time has considered possibility of building a nuclear power plant to diversify its energy sector.

The master plan for energy sector in Israel (2013) commissioned by the Ministry of National Infrastructures and prepared by energy consultancy group Tahal recommends construction of Nuclear Power Plants (NPPs) as a part of the electrical production system in Israel, starting from 2030. It calls for nuclear power to contribute 5 percent of Israel's energy by 2030 and 15 percent of production by 2050.[156]

Supply from indigenous sources

Natural gas began to flow into the Israeli economy in 2004. During 2004–2012 the economy relied on natural gas from the Yam Tethys reservoirs, primarily for electricity generation. Since April 2013 Tamar reserve, which has been the primary source of natural gas, provided 96 percent of the total supply of 9.66 bcm in 2016, jump of about 76 percent as compared to 2013 when it was 5.49 bcm.[157] Tamar's expansion project, which is currently underway, will allow an increase in the production capacity of the reservoir to about 20.4 bcm annually to fully meet the total demand of domestic requirement and export commitments to Jordan under contract with Tamar developers.[158]

The development of the Leviathan field, which would supply additional gas to the Israeli market, has been postponed a number of times over recent years for want of administrative approval pertaining to regulatory issues. In June 2016, the government accepted a framework for the development of Leviathan, as well as Karish and Tanin. According to the reservoir development plan, Leviathan is expected to reach a maximum production capacity of 21 bcm per year: The first stage includes the development of 12 bcm output per year intended to be divided between the Israeli economy and the Jordanian electric company and the second phase would have the output of 9 bcm per year entirely for export. It is important to note that within the plan there is a clause permitting a lower magnitude of development of the reservoir (only in the initial stage – 12 bcm) if an export agreement is not signed.

The Leviathan reservoir will not only boost supply to the domestic market and ensure Israel's energy security, but will also serve as an export outlet for Israel's immediate neighbours and the wider Mediterranean region. Karish and Tanin reservoirs (which include 60 bcm of proven gas reserves and another 25 bcm with a high level of probability) would provide exclusively for the local market. If these fields go through favourable development in the coming years, Israel would be able to fortify its energy security for several decades and even acquire greater strategic edge through gas export, transforming energy supply and economic relations in the Eastern Mediterranean region.

Physical security of energy installations

In the situation of geopolitical instability in Lebanon, missile and terror attacks aiming to inflict long lasting damages to Israel's natural gas facilities in the Eastern Mediterranean are an issue of critical importance for Israel. The offshore gas infrastructure is crucial to Israel energy security and, therefore, attacking them might present the enemy with a significant achievement. The oil rigs are particularly vulnerable because of their substantial size and distance from the shore.

Israel vulnerabilities vis-à-vis its north are two-pronged: First, tussle with Lebanon, an enemy state, with regard to delimitation of its EEZ and, secondly, defending its infrastructure from attacks by the virulently anti-Israeli Hizbullah operating from southern Lebanon.[159] Israel and Lebanon have never agreed on a delimitation of their maritime boundaries. According to international law, splitting maritime territory between neighbouring states is done through a mutual agreement. However, given the lack of any diplomatic relations between the two countries, efforts by the United States and United Nations to mediate a peaceful resolution to the maritime dispute have been unproductive.

Tensions have escalated with both nations claiming the rights to the potential petroleum reserves in their disputed maritime border zone. Hizbullah has threatened to attack Israel if the Jewish state attempts to extract oil or natural gas in that area.[160] It is worth remembering here that in 2006, the Hizbullah fought the Israeli army to a draw in a border war and has since maintained a tense standoff, while making clear that even the slightest of Israeli 'provocation' could lead to a new conflict. It is not wholly unimaginable that in the next regional war, the Israeli and Lebanese military could target each other's natural gas drills. Some commentators have referred to these rigs as 'sitting ducks'[161] for terrorist attacks.

Indeed, a report published in Israel's national newspaper *Haaretz*[162] brings to light the fact that the Israeli army had advised the MoE a couple of years ago to sanction offshore gas production rigs in the Mediterranean Sea close to the shoreline so as to protect them better through the air defence Iron Dome system. The army has been of the opinion that the rig up to 15 nautical miles (28 km) from the shore was ideal to thwart any plot by terrorists, particularly Hizbullah, from harming the facility. The army, according to the report, has once again advised the Ministry of Energy to decide on building the production platform for Karish–Tanin in close proximity to the shore. The ministry officials feel Karish–Tanin are not so strategically important to Israel and have gone ahead to approve the main field development plan of Karish, which envisages drilling three wells using a FPSO unit that will be located approximately 90 km offshore near the wells of the fields.

As mentioned in the Introduction to this book, Noble Energy originally planned to locate processing gas from the Leviathan field using an FPSO installation anchored about 120 km (75 miles) into the sea closer to the drilling site, instead of a production rig on fixed platform near the shore. While the gas would be brought from the FPSO to the shore through a pipeline, the condensate would be loaded onto tankers for export or transport to internal market.[163] The National Planning and Building Council charged with proposing what has come to be known as National Outline Plan 37 H (for natural gas treatment facilities) for all of Israel's gas fields, favoured a land-based processing facility in its June 2013 survey,[164] which was what the MoE approved when it gave the green light to the Leviathan's development plan involving fixed production platform in June

2016.[165] But in response to a petition of the environmentalist, the Supreme Court subsequently supported the Environmental Protection Ministry's view of processing gas away from the population centres and as much as possible out at sea.

Both the army and navy had serious reservations about the FPSO on grounds that, due to its massive size, Leviathan is a valuable field and in order to defend its production platform adequately from attacks, it needed to be located inside Israel's territorial waters. It would be dangerous to leave the facility exposed far away from the shore. Taking into consideration the questions of safety and security of the production facilities, the government decided to permit the construction of the platform less than 10 km from Dor beach.[166]

Risks and Israel's maritime strategy

Israel has been adjusting its maritime strategy to protect offshore assets from possible attack by both state and non-state actors. The Israeli navy charged with the defence of drilling platforms and rigs out at sea[167] identifies three main kinds of risks to Israel's gas installations in the Mediterranean – maritime terror attacks, below-surface activity, and aerial threats. But the first step starts with intelligence gathering and assessments. Terror attacks could involve armed militants physically entering the rigs to take control, and airborne threats could include a scenario where missiles are fired into the northern gas fields, while another situation could be of miniature submarines striking from below.

Israel's navy has traditionally been the smallest part of the Israel Defence Forces (IDF), but the navy is getting a boost. To secure its Mediterranean gas rigs, the Israeli Ministry of Defence announced in 2014 that Israel has ordered the procurement of four German-made corvette warships to defend the Mediterranean gas rigs. These corvettes, likely to be delivered by the end of 2019, would be classed as Saar-6 missile boats – suggesting a major improvement in capabilities.[168]

In a letter dated July 6 2016, to the US Senate, the Defence Security Cooperation Agency said the new helicopters would be used to defend Israel's natural gas infrastructure: "Israel has purchased four new frigates [German] to secure the Leviathan Natural Gas Field. The SH-60F helicopters will be used on board these new frigates to patrol and protect these gas fields as well as other areas under threat."[169]

Israel has pressed its corvettes and other ships to secure its offshore natural gas fields. The three corvettes of the Saar 5-class, manufactured by the US company Northrop Grumman – INS Eilat, INS Lahav, and INS Hanit – are the most prominent warships of the Israeli navy. Outfitted with Harpoon and Gabriel sea-to-sea missiles, Barak-8 sea-to-air missiles, and a helicopter hangar, these three vessels are capable of covering a range of maritime missions, including surface strikes, naval interdiction, sea patrol, and search and rescue.[170] In July 2006, while taking part in the Israeli Navy blockade of Lebanese ports, INS Hanit was hit by a surface to sea anti-ship Iranian-made version of the Chinese

C-802 missile fired by the Hizbullah, causing serious damage.[171] In response, Israel announced that it would acclimatise its Saar 5-class to accommodate the eight Sikorsky Seahawk helicopters, SH-60F, approved for sale by the Pentagon in July 2016, to add more firepower to the navy.[172]

INS Lahav corvette, fitted with a battery of Iron Dome anti-missile system in November 2017, makes the much-vaunted rocket interceptor operational at sea for the first time and adds "another operational layer to defend and protect Israel's energy assets in the Mediterranean Sea."[173] A new generation of Saar class vessels, the Saar S-72 – that can be configured to cover a range of maritime missions, including surface attack, maritime surveillance and interdiction, EEZ patrol, and search and rescue – incorporated into the naval arsenal will fulfil Israel's growing demand for security of its gas fields.[174]

In December 2013, the Israeli navy signed contracts to acquire two hi-tech German-built MEKO class F221 frigates for patrol of the Mediterranean gas fields and build up its maritime firepower. The two frigates with Barak 8 medium-range air defence systems produced by the Israel Aerospace Industries will have the capability to intercept subsonic and supersonic missiles, fighter aircraft, maritime patrolling aircraft (MPA), helicopter and sea-skimming missiles.[175]

The Israeli navy has also deployed unmanned surface vessel (USV), Shomer Hayam, or Protector developed by state-owned Rafael to patrol around the deep-sea platforms. Three more USVs were procured from the US via the US Navy's International Program Office at the end of 2016.[176] Rig owners have also deployed private security guards on each platform, armed with radars to monitor sea traffic in the area and designed to link up with those operated by the IDF.[177]

Lebanon's military preparedness

As the Lebanese government moves towards commercial extraction of the country's natural gas and petroleum resources in its maritime EEZ, the Lebanese navy is expanding its capability to secure the gas resources. At present, the United Nations Interim Forces in Lebanon-Maritime Task Force (UNIFIL-MTF) is working with Lebanon's naval forces to monitor the territorial waters, with an emphasis upon search-and-rescue and smuggling interdiction operations, under the expanded UNIFIL mandate by United Nations Security Council resolution 1701 following the 2006 war with Israel.

Lebanese Navy chief Admiral Nazih Baroudi in a piece for the US Naval Institute's *Proceedings* magazine acknowledged that the high probability of finding gas and oil reserves in the seabed of Lebanon's EEZ placed immense responsibility on the Lebanese Armed Forces-Navy (LAFN) to develop the ability to patrol the EEZ of the country and protect future oil and gas platforms from attack.[178] In 2013, Baroudi outlined a five-year plan to give LAFN the capability of operating independently of the UNIFIL-MTF through the acquisition of new vessels and equipment as well as multipronged training of the force. The

Lebanese naval commander put the cost of the plan at $450 million, which he hoped to come from the government, donations, and allies of the country.[179]

However, there is a lingering concern in Israel that as the LAFN dispenses with the presence of the maritime task force operating under UNIFIL in Lebanon, a confrontation between Israeli naval forces and LAFN could occur. A minor cross-border incident or an inadvertent discharge of fire could spark a broader conflict between the two countries. Lebanon has issued exploration licenses for two blocks that Israel claims overlap with its maritime area. If these contentions lead to a confrontation between Israeli and Lebanese naval forces, it is not unlikely that the Hizbullah might launch its attack on Israel's offshore installations.

Israel's natural gas in perspective

Almost 60 percent of the world's total proven conventional gas reserves are in five countries, Russia, Qatar, Turkmenistan, Saudi Arabia, and Iran, of which the first three are dominant suppliers to Europe and Asia. Although Iran has the second largest gas reserves in the world, its development was hit by the slew of sanctions emanating from the controversy over the country's nuclear programme, depriving the nation of the technology and the economic means of bringing the resource to market.

Saudi Arabia gas development has been slow as compared to oil, but the gas produced is all utilised in the domestic market. If both conventional and shale gas resources are accounted for, United States is the fourth largest gas producer in the world. However, gas as a resource has wide geographical distribution with all significant regions holding recoverable resources. Compared to 1973, the year of the first energy crisis, many countries have now developed a gas infrastructure to feed power plants, industry, and household requirements.

The world consumption is still vastly dominated by a few countries: the United States, the Russian Federation, the People's Republic of China, the Islamic Republic of Iran, Japan, and Canada account for half of the world consumption. Given the high cost of development of infrastructure involved in extraction, processing, storage, transportation, and distribution to customers, adoption of gas in the global energy mix has been slow. However, with growing environmental concerns about pollution from the burning of oil and coal, and given the fact that natural gas is low in carbon content when compared with conventional fossil fuels, more and more countries all over the world have developed a natural gas sector.

In 2011, the International Energy Agency (IEA) predicted that the world would rapidly enter into "a golden age of gas," during which gas demand would reach 5.1 trillion cubic metres (tcm) by 2035. The share of natural gas in the global energy mix would increase from 21 percent to 25 percent in 2035, forcing the share of coal into decline and eventually overtaking it by 2030.[180] Natural gas production has risen every year since the economic crisis of 2009. In 2016, global production of natural gas was as high as 3,613 bcm, 0.8 percent higher than 2015, indicative of the fact that natural gas has progressively become a crucial component of the world's energy supply, producing geopolitical contestations for availability of the resource in several parts of the world.[181]

Israel natural gas reserves rank 44th on the ranking of proven reserve of gas.[182] Israel's natural gas comes in the market at a time when advancements in technology and international dynamics of fuel use have made it an alternative fuel for both coal and crude oil. Israel's offshore gas reserve, as of now located in 'gas-only' wells, makes it easier to exploit than gas found associated with oil. Many countries like Iraq and Nigeria still vent or flare a lot of associated gas because of the technical difficulties and economic costs involved in its exploitation.

Given Israel energy vulnerabilities and its location in one of the unstable regions of the world, natural gas discoveries have given the country the flexibility to manage its own needs. The Tamar field has made Israeli access to energy more secure and stable than at any other point in the country's modern history. Considering that the Tamar field meets its consumption needs for the next 25 years, Israel sees itself positioned as a new natural gas source for the neighbouring countries as well as Europe with the development of the Leviathan gas field.

Israel's electricity generation is one of the most carbon-intensive in the OECD. The tax rates on fuels used for electricity generation are low compared to many other countries. Coal, which accounts for the majority of electricity generation and CO_2 emissions in Israel, is taxed well below most estimates of social costs. Natural gas is not taxed at all when used for electricity generation.

However, as a fuel, natural gas produces on average half the carbon dioxide emissions when compared to lignite, and owing to the energy conversion efficiency of combined-cycle power plants that Israel has introduced in the past decade, electricity production has become less polluting and more efficient. Israel has a long way to go in adding renewables into energy production, but gas power plants with shortest start-up time when compared to both coal and nuclear power plants in conjunction are particularly suited to electricity consumption patterns to satiate high demand for electricity.

With the discovery of Yam Tethys fields, Israel got an opportunity to become independent from external energy suppliers and become a natural gas-based economy, meaning a reduction of energy prices, reduction of air pollution and greenhouse gas emission, and an important source of income for the state both now and in the future.

Notes

1 Daniel Yergin is an American author, energy expert and economic historian known for his work, *The Quest: Energy, Security, and the Remaking of the Modern World* (2011).
2 The reservoir had depleted much faster than expected and with the change in the Egyptian regime in 2011 as a consequence of the 'Arab Spring.' Egyptian gas supply was reduced to only 30 percent of the contractual quantity to the IEC. Yiftach Ron-Tal and

Eli Glikman, *Israel Electric Corporation Ltd.*, 2012, p. 302, www.iec.co.il/Community/Documents/Hevrat%20Hashmal_eng_2012.pdf (accessed on April 4, 2017).

3 *BP Statistical Review of World Energy* (henceforth, *BP Statistical Review*), 2016 & 2017.

4 International Energy Agency (IEA) Statistics, 2017.

5 In January 2009, Government Decision No. 4450 declared 10 percent of Israel's electricity will come from renewable sources by 2020 and a 2011 decision reaffirmed that target and set quotas for the electricity generation from certain types of renewables. *Policy on the Integration of Renewable Energy Sources Into the Israeli Electricity Sector*, Ministry of Energy, State of Israel, February 14, 2010, p. 2, http://archive.energy.gov.il/English/PublicationsLibraryE/REPolicy.pdf (accessed on April 4, 2017); *Renewable Energy*, Israel Ministry of Environmental Protection, February 2, 2017, www.sviva.gov.il/English/env_topics/climatechange/renewable-energy/Pages/RE-default.aspx (accessed on July 2, 2018); *Market Overview: Renewables*, Green Energy Association of Israel (GEA-IL), 2018, www.greenrg.org.il/he-il/english.htm (accessed on July 2, 2018).

6 Golan Heights is a part of Syria, which Israel has occupied since 1967 and annexed in 1981 in violation of international law. However, In May 2012, Minstry of Energy under Uzi Landau approved exploratory drilling for petroleum in the Golan Heights, nearly 20 years after Israel decided in 1994, at the height of Oslo Peace Process, not to explore the area for diplomatic reasons. The Ministry argued that under the Golan Heights Law, 1981, which applies Israel's government and laws to the Golan Heights – determined null and void by United Nations Security Council 497) – the Petroleum Law (5711–1951) also applied to the Golan Heights and that oil exploration could be carried out. The ministerial approval was followed by the Israel's Petroleum Council decision in February 2013 to permit Afek Oil and Gas through exclusive licensing to drill at ten possible locations throughout the disputed territory. Afek is a subsidiary of Genie Energy Ltd., a New Jersey-based company with some high profile investors and advisors across banking, media, and political sectors. In the six months that followed the approval for drilling of the Northern District Committee for Planning and Building in July 2014, a High Court petition filed by environmental group, Adam Teva V'Din (Israel Union for Environmental Defense), temporary froze Afek's work – until the petition was dismissed in December. "Energy Minister Uzi Landau Has Decided to Renew Exploration Licenses on the Golan, Despite Syrian Objections," *Globes*, May 13, 2013, www.globes.co.il/en/article-1000748091 (accessed on April 5, 2017); Ilan Ben-Zion, "Government Secretly Approves Golan Heights Drilling," *The Times of Israel*, May 13, 2012, www.timesofisrael.com/government-secretly-approves-golan-heights-drilling/ (accessed on April 5, 2017); "Israel Council Approves First License to Drill for Oil in Golan Heights," *Platts*, February 21, 2013, www.platts.com/latest-news/oil/jerusalem/israel-council-approves-first-license-to-drill-8167166 (accessed on April 5, 2017); Paul Fallon, "Israel Uses Syrian Chaos to Drill for Oil in the Golan Heights," *The Citizen*, July 27, 2015, www.thecitizen.in/index.php/en/newsdetail/index/1/4524/israel-uses-syrian-chaos-to-drill-for-oil-in-the-golan-heights; Michelle Malka Grossman, "Oil Drilling to Go on in Golan Heights," *Jerusalem Post*, February 1, 2016, www.jpost.com/business-and-innovation/environment/drilling-to-go-on-in-the-golan-443533 (accessed on April 5, 2017).

7 *Israel*, Fossil Fuel Support Country Note, Organization for Economic Cooperation and Development (OECD), September 2016, p. 1.

8 *Offshore Levant Basin Petroleum System and HC Resource Assessment*, Petroleum Unit, Natural Resources Administration, Ministry of National Infrastructures, Energy and Water Resources, Government of Israel, p. 3.

9 "Allowing U.S. Oil Drilling in Golan Breaches UN Resolutions," *Syrian Times*, February 25, 2013, http://syriatimes.sy/index.php/golan/3229-allowing-u-s-oil-drilling-in-golan-breaches-un-resolutions (accessed on April 6, 2017); "Syria to UN: Israel's Licensing US Company to Drill for Oil in Occupied Syrian Golan Violates

SC Resolution," *Tishreen* (Damascus) [Arabic], March 2, 2013, http://archive.tishreen. news.sy/tishreen/public/read/281451 (accessed on April 6, 2017).

10 Andy Tully, "Major Shale Find Could Guarantee Israel's Oil Supply For Years," *Nasdaq*, October 9, 2015, www.nasdaq.com/article/major-shale-find-could-guarantee-israels-oil-supply-for-years-cm528693 (accessed on April 6, 2017); "Black Gold Under the Golan," *The Economist*, November 7, 2015, www.economist.com/news/middle-east-and-africa/21677597-geologists-israel-think-they-have-found-oilin-very-tricky-territory-black-gold (accessed on April 6, 2017).

11 Eran Azran, "Geologist Reports Major Oil Find in Israel; Firm Stays Mum," *Haaretz*, October   8,   2015,   www.haaretz.com/israel-news/business/.premium-geologist-reports-golan-oil-find-firm-stays-mum-1.5406510 (accessed on April 9, 2017).

12 "Energy Firm says Old Dead Sea Well Could Hold $322 mln of Oil," *energy-pedia News*, May 1, 2016, www.energy-pedia.com/news/israel/new-167342 (accessed on April 9, 2017); *Israel Science & Technology: Oil & Natural Gas*, Jewish Virtual Library, 2018, www.jewishvirtuallibrary.org/oil-and-natural-gas-in-israel (accessed on July 4, 2018).

13 Amir Rosenbaum, "Hatrurim Land License Drilling Finds Oil Near Dead Sea; Israeli Oil Reserve Worth $319 Million," *Jewish Business News*, May 1, 2016, http:// jewishbusinessnews.com/2016/05/01/hatrurim-land-license-drilling-finds-oil-near-dead-sea-israeli-oil-reserve-worth-319-million/ (accessed on April 9, 2017).

14 *Hatrurim License*, Israel Opportunity Energy Resources, undated, www.oilandgas.co.il/ englishsite/assetsmap/hatrurim-license.aspx (accessed on July 4, 2018).

15 During 2008–2011, about 40 percent of gas consumption, primarily for electricity generation, was met by pipeline import from Egypt. Since January 2013, a small amount of gas is imported by ship as Liquefied Natural Gas (LNG) to an offshore buoy where it is re-gasified and pumped into the gas distribution pipeline. In 2014, 0.06 bcm out of the total natural gas supply of 7.60 bcm, was imported; in 2015, it was 0.13 bcm out of 8.40 bcm; and in 2016, it was 0.36 bcm out of 9.66 bcm. See *Review of Developments in the Natural Gas Market During 2016* [Hebrew], Ministry of Energy, State of Israel, 2016, p. 12.

16 *BP Statistical Review*, 2017.

17 *International Energy Agency (IEA) Coal Information*, 2018.

18 Author's interview with Prof Uri Bialer, emeritus professor of International Relations at the Hebrew University of Jerusalem and Maurice B. Hexter Chair in International Relations – Middle Eastern Studies, Jerusalem, Israel, January 19, 2016.

19 During 2013, approximately 5.55 bcm of natural gas was supplied from Tamar. Together with LNG import through a marine buoy, which became operational in January of that year, 0.51 bcm of natural gas was supplied to the economy, constituting approximately 7.3 percent of the total natural gas supply. *Review of Developments in the Natural Gas Economy 2016* [Hebrew], Ministry of Energy and Natural Gas Authority, State of Israel, 2017, http://archive.energy.gov.il/Subjects/NG/Documents/Publication/ NGPublication2016.pdf (accessed on July 4, 2018).

20 *The Ministry of Energy's Plan to Rescue Israel From Energy Pollution*, Ministry of Energy, Government of Israel, October 22, 2018, www.gov.il/en/Departments/news/plan_2030 (accessed on July 4, 2018).

21 *IEA Oil Information*, 2018.

22 Ibid.

23 "Government decision no. 5327 calls for advancing the switch to oil substitutes in transportation in the years 2013 to 2025 and for reducing the share of oil in Israel's transportation by 30 percent by 2020 and 60 percent in 2025, in relation to the forecasted consumption for those years. The resolution calls, among other things, for pilots and demonstrations of new technologies, including natural gas technologies such as Compressed Natural Gas (CNG) and Gas-To-Liquid (GTL)." "Addressing Oil Shale Extraction in Israel," *Environment Bulletin*, Volume 41 (January 2015), Israel Ministry of Environmental Protection, p. 28; *Reducing Israeli Dependence on Petroleum-Based Fuels in Transportation*, Government Resolution No. 5327, Prime Minister's Office.

24 Hedy Cohen, "US Instructing Israel on Gas-Powered Vehicles," *Globes*, September 9, 2015, www.globes.co.il/en/article-us-instructing-israel-on-gas-powered-public-trans port-1001068073 (accessed on April 12, 2017).

25 See Gershon Grossman and Naama Shapira, *Natural Gas for Transportation in Israel: Summary and Recommendations of the Discussion* [Hebrew], The Samuel Neaman Institute of Energy, The Samuel Neaman Institute of National Policy Research, July 2017, p. 1, www.neaman.org.il/EN/Energy-Forum-40-Natural-gas-for-transportation-in-Israel (accessed on July 4, 2018).

26 *The Potential of Natural Gas in the Israeli Economy*, Finance and Economics Division, Bank Leumi, State of Israel, April 2014, p. 10, www.chamber.org.il/media/150344/ the-potential-of-natural-gas-in-the-israeli-economy-april-2014.pdf (accessed on April 12, 2017).

27 "Natural Gas Vehicle Statistics," *NGV Global*, July 6, 2018, www.iangv.org/current-ngv-stats/ (accessed on September 2, 2018).

28 See Gershon Grossman and Naama Shapira, *Natural Gas for Transportation in Israel (Summary)*, July 2017, pp. 1–2, www.neaman.org.il/EN/Energy-Forum-40-Natural-gas-for-transportation-in-Israel (accessed on July 4, 2018).

29 *IEA Oil Information*, 2018.

30 *The Potential of Natural Gas*, Bank Leumi, April 2014, p. 11.

31 *The Natural Gas Sector in Israel*, Ministry of Energy, State of Israel, undated, http:// archive.energy.gov.il/English/Subjects/Natural%20Gas/Pages/GxmsMniNG Economy.aspx (accessed on April 13, 2017).

32 While it is possible to imagine a situation of 100 percent electricity from natural gas and renewables in the scenario of current power production, complete elimination of gasoline and diesel from the transport sector appears far-fetched. There are neither installed refuelling stations nor CNG vehicles on the nations' road as of 2018. Many contest that the Ministry of Energy's push towards the elimination of gasoline and diesel vehicle imports by 2030, would severely affect the country's haulage industry, which have incorporated low-emission vehicles conforming to stringent European emission standards. Shoshanna Solomon, "Israel Aims to Eliminate Use of Coal, Gasoline and Diesel by 2030," *The Times of Israel*, February 27, 2018, www.timesofisrael.com/israel-aims-to-eliminate-use-of-coal-gasoline-and-diesel-by-2030/ (accessed on July 5, 2018); Kalman, "Israel Minister Seeks End to Coal, Diesel and Gasoline by 2030," April 17, 2018.

33 Sonia Gorodeisky, "Knesset C'tee Approves 'Green Tax' to Boost Gas Use," *Globes*, March 15, 2018, www.globes.co.il/en/article-knesset-ctee-approves-green-taxation-to-boost-natgas-usage-1001227926 (accessed on July 5, 2018).

34 Ibid.

35 Lior Gutman, "Israel Announces $28.5 Million Grants Program for CNG Fueling Infrastructure," *Calcalist-Tech*, March 29, 2018, www.calcalistech.com/ctech/ articles/0,7340,L-3735247,00.html (accessed on July 5, 2018).

36 Chen Herzog, Norden Shalabna, and Guy Maor, *Israel Natural Gas Demand Forecast 2017–2040*, BDO Consulting Group, July 2, 2017, p. 7.

37 "Fuel Choices Initiative," Israel Energy Week, *Ministry of Economy and Industry* (Foreign Trade Administration), http://itrade.gov.il/india/events/israel-energy-week-december-3-9-2014-tel-aviv-israel/ (accessed on April 17, 2017).

38 Prachi Patel, "Israel Makes an Ambitious Move on Alternative Fuels," *Energy Quarterly*, Volume 39 (March 2014), p. 2; *Fuel Choice and Smart Mobility Initiative*, Prime Minister's Office, State of Israel, www.fuelchoicesinitiative.com/our-mission/ (accessed on April 17, 2017); See Kfir Noy and Moshe Givoni, "Is 'Smart Mobility' Sustainable? Examining the Views and Beliefs of Transport's Technological Entrepreneurs," *Sustainability*, Volume 10, Issue 2 (February 2018), p. 3.

39 Eyal Rosner, *Israel's Fuel Choices Initiative*, Fuel Choices Initiative, Prime Minister's Office, State of Israel; Ari Rabinovitch, "Israel's New Motor Fuels Strategy Leans on Gas," *Reuters*, December 17, 2013, www.reuters.com/article/us-israel-cars-fuels/

israels-new-motor-fuels-strategy-leans-on-gas-idUSBRE9BN0BC20131224 (accessed on April 18, 2017).

40 *The Winners of the Eric And Sheila Samson Prime Minister's Prize For Innovation In Alternative Fuels For Transportation*, Fuel Choices and Smart Mobility Initiatives, Prime Ministers' Office, State of Israel, 2017, www.fuelchoicessummit.com/Award.aspx (accessed on July 5, 2018).

41 *Cabinet Approves National NIS 250 Million Plan to Advance Smart Transportation*, Prime Minister's Office, State of Israel, January 22, 2017, www.pmo.gov.il/English/Media Center/Spokesman/Pages/spokeTransportation220117.aspx (accessed on July 5, 2018).

42 *GDP at Current US$*, The World Bank, 2018.

43 "The Economy and Economic Policy," *Bank of Israel Annual Report – 2015*, April 2016, p. 29, www.boi.org.il/en/NewsAndPublications/RegularPublications/Pages/Doch-BankIsrael2015.aspx (accessed on April 18, 2017).

44 Ibid.

45 "The Economy and Economic Policy," *BoI Annual Report – 2015*, April 2016, p. 30.

46 See Philip Hemmings, *Assessing Challenges to the Energy Sector in Israel*, OECD Economics Department Working Paper No. 914, December 6, 2011, p. 7.

47 See Gawdat Bahgat, *Alternative Energy in the Middle East* (Basingstoke, Hampshire: Palgrave Macmillan, 2013), p. 136.

48 The World Bank data, 2018.

49 Germany, long a frontline player for more ambitious international climate targets, has pledged to cut its carbon emissions 40 percent below 1990 levels by 2020, one of the most aggressive global targets. Yet Germany's greenhouse gas emissions remain high, at 37 percent in 2016, because, at the same time that subsidies have produced more wind and solar power, domestic compulsions as well as the vagaries of the global energy market have induced the country's power producers to burn more lignite, a particularly cheap and the dirtiest kind of coal. The electricity lignite exerts downward pressure on prices as much as it also generates employment. High prices for Russian gas and low prices for coal, given a glut due to US exports, work in favour of lignite. Hard coal and lignite have a share of 40 percent in German power production (compared to 29 percent from renewables, 13 percent from nuclear and 12 percent from natural gas in 2016). If Germany lignite-fired power plants offline, it would have little difficulty reaching its 40 percent emissions-reduction target. See "Coal in Germany," *Clean Energy Wire*, December 5, 2017, www.cleanenergywire.org/factsheets/coal-germany (accessed on July 6, 2018); Editors, "Germany Is Burning Too Much Coal," *Bloomberg*, November 14, 2017, www.bloomberg.com/view/articles/2017-11-14/germany-is-burning-too-much-coal (accessed on July 6, 2018); "The End of Lignite Coal for Power in Germany," *Deutsche Welle*, October 27, 2015, www.dw.com/en/the-end-of-lignite-coal-for-power-in-germany/a-18806081 (accessed on April 18, 2017).

50 *Population, Total*, The World Bank, 2018.

51 Ibid.

52 Population of Israel as of 2017 was approximately 8 million and 71 thousand, while the population of New Zealand was approximately 4 million and 79 thousand. *The World Bank*, 2018.

53 New Zealand's energy intensity level of primary energy (MJ/$2011 PPP GDP) is 5.4, whereas that of Israel is 3.6. *Energy Intensity Level of Primary Energy* (MJ/$2011 PPP GDP), The World Bank data, 2018.

54 CO_2 *Intensity (kg per kg of Oil Equivalent Energy Use)*, The World Bank, 2018.

55 *About National Coal Supply Corporation*, The National Coal Supply Corporation Ltd., undated, http://ncsc.co.il/?page_id=101&lang=en (accessed on April 18, 2017).

56 Gawdat Bahgat, "Energy and the Arab-Israeli Conflict," *Middle Eastern Studies*, Volume 44, Issue 6 (November, 2008), p. 938; See Pao-Yu Oei and Roman Mendelevitch, *Perspectives and Colombian Coal Exports on the International Steam Coal Market Until 2030*, Rosa Luxemburg Stiftung, November 2016, p. 14, www.rosalux.de/en/publication/id/9251/perspectives-on-colombian-coal/ (accessed on April 18, 2017).

57 Luca Franza, Dick de Jong, and Coby van der Linde write that since subsequent to the Arab Spring (2011) and the Euromaidan street protests in Kiev (2013), a 'new arc of instability' has emerged that stretches from the Arabian peninsula, the Sahel, and the Levant to Russia and the Former Soviet republics – roughly corresponding to the MENA [Middle East and North Africa] and FSU [Former Soviet Union] regions. These two regions happen to host three-quarters of the world's total proven conventional gas reserves. This region also roughly holds 60 percent of the proven oil reserves. "The Future of Gas: The Transition Fuel?" in Silvia Colombo, Mohamed El Harrak, and Nicolò Sartori (eds.), *The Future of Natural Gas Markets and Geopolitics* (Diepenheim: The Netherlands: Istituto Affari Internazionali, OCP Policy Centre and Lenthe Publishers/European Energy Review, 2016), pp. 33–34.

58 Noam Segal, *Israel: The 'Energy Island's' Transition to Energy Independence*, Heinrich Boll Stiftung (Israel), July 7, 2016, https://il.boell.org/en/2016/07/07/israel-energy-islands-transition-energy-independence (accessed on April 20, 2017).

59 *Oil Development in Israel*, Intelligence Memorandum (Secret), Central Intelligence Agency (CIA), June 1970, Date of Release, October 30, 2011, p. 9.

60 Two independent refineries, one in Sardinia and the other in Portugal were known to have received crude oil from the pipeline. Some oil was also transhipped to Romania from Ashkelon. *Oil Development in Israel*, Intelligence Memorandum (Secret), CIA, June 1970, pp. 12, 13; Mordechai Abir, *Oil, Power and Politics: Conflict of Arabia, the Red Sea and the Gulf* (London: Frank Cass and Co. Ltd., 1974. Republished by Taylor & Francis e-Library, 2005), p. 77.

61 *Oil Development in Israel*, CIA, June 1970, p. 12.

62 John Reed, "Israel: Oil Secrets to Spill," *Financial Times*, January 27, 2016, www.ft.com/content/6260b762-c067-11e5-846f-79b0e3d20eaf?mhq5j=e5 (accessed on April 22, 2017).

63 *Oil Development*, CIA, June 1970, p. 12.

64 The flow of oil from Iran to Eilat rose from about 400,000 tonnes per month in January and February 1970 to nearly 650,000 in March and to almost 850,000 tonnes in April. In addition the system probably accommodated approximately 170,000 tonnes of Sinai crude oil a month. Of the total shipments to Eilat in April of about 1mt, almost 500,000 tonnes probably were destined for the Haifa refinery and about 140,000 tonnes were transhipped to Romania. Two independent refineries, one in Sardinia and the other in Portugal, are also known to have received crude oil from the pipeline. A substantial part of the remainder probably was required to fill the pipeline and to build up inventory at Eilat and Ashkelon. *Oil Development in Israel*, Intelligence Memorandum (Secret), CIA, June 1970, p. 12.

65 Iran's national oil company, the partner in the EAPC, has been seeking financial redress worth billions of dollars from Israel in international arbitration since 1989. Margit Cohn, *Energy Law in Israel* (Alphen an den Rijn, The Netherlands: Kluwer Law International BV, 2010), p. 59. *Israel's Fuel Economy*, Ministry of Energy, State of Israel, http://energy.gov.il/English/Subjects/Subject/Pages/GxmsMniIsraelsFuelEconomy.aspx (accessed on April 25, 2017); *About the Company*, Eilat Ashkelon Pipeline Co. Ltd. (EAPC), 2018, www.eapc.com (accessed on July 7, 2018).

66 Edward R. Rosen, "The Effect of Relinquished Sinai Resources on Israel's Energy Situation and Policies," *Middle East Review*, Volume 14, Issue 3–4 (1982), p. 7.

67 Europa Publication, *The Middle East and North Africa 2004* (London and New York: Taylor and Francis Group, 2004), p. 578; Louise Lief, "Egypt Puts Stamp on Sinai," *Christian Science Monitor*, April 22, 1982, www.csmonitor.com/1982/0422/042255.html (accessed on April 25, 2017).

68 Rosen, "The Effect of Relinquished Sinai Resources," 1982, p. 7.

69 Mitchell Bard and Moshe Schwartz, *1001 Facts Everyone Should Know About Israel* (Oxford: Rowman and Littlefield Publishers, 2005), p. 145.

70 Mitchell Bard and Moshe Schwartz, *1001 Facts*, 2005, p. 145; Rosen, "The Effect of Relinquished Sinai Resources," 1982, p. 8.

71 "Egypt to Develop Sinai Oil Fields 'Over-Exploited' by Israel," *World Bulletin News* (Istanbul), November 25, 2013, www.worldbulletin.net/news/123659/egypt-to-develop-sinai-oil-fields-over-exploited-by-israel (accessed on April 27, 2017).

72 More specifically, the establishment of regular economic relations between the parties would include, "normal commercial sales of oil by Egypt to Israel, and that Israel shall be fully entitled to make bids for Egyptian-origin oil not needed for Egyptian domestic oil consumption, and Egypt and its oil concessionaires will entertain bids made by Israel, on the same basis and terms as apply to other bidders for such oil." *Egypt-Israel Peace Treaty*, Israel Ministry of Foreign Affairs, State of Israel, March 26, 1979, www.mfa.gov.il/mfa/foreignpolicy/peace/guide/pages/israel-egypt%20peace%20treaty.aspx (accessed on April 27, 2017).

73 Yossi Melman, "How Israel Lost to the Iranians," *Haaretz*, November 1, 2017, www.haaretz.com/print-edition/features/how-israel-lost-to-the-iranians-1.209838 (accessed on July 7, 2018).

74 "A Shortcut for Russian Oil to Asia," *Energy Security*, Institute for the Analysis of Global Security, March 31, 2004, www.iags.org/n0331044.htm (accessed on April 28, 2017); Maureen S. Crandall, *Energy, Economics, and Politics in the Caspian Region: Dreams and Realities* (Westport: Praeger Security International, 2006), p. 36; Anthony H. Cordesman, *Energy Developments in the Middle East* (Westport: Praeger Publishers, 2004), p. 230.

75 *Reverse Flow Project*, EAPC, 2018, http://eapc.com/reverse-flow-project/ (accessed on July 8, 2018).

76 Sinai II Agreement was a diplomatic agreement signed by Egypt and Israel on September 4, 1975 in Geneva, Switzerland, subsequent to the Disengagement Agreement of 18 January, 1974, which resulted in the redeployment of Egyptian forces west of the Suez Canal and Israeli forces east of it, with a buffer zone on both sides of the canal monitored by the United Nations Emergency Force (UNEF). A similar agreement was signed between Israel and Syria on 31 May, 1974. Sinai II Agreement, in addition to the further redeployment of their armed forces, the two countries resolved, "not to resort to the threat or use of force or military blockade against each other," to observe the ceasefire ending the 1973 War, and to pursue a peace settlement based on UN Security Council Resolution 338. Most significantly, it placed American observers in the Sinai Peninsula to monitor the demilitarised zones established between the two countries. Quiet in Sinai resulted in the reopening of the Suez Canal in June 1975. *Israel-Egypt Disengagement Agreement (1974)*, Economic Cooperation Foundation (ECF), January 1, 1974, https://ecf.org.il/issues/issue/179 (accessed on April 28, 2017); *Israeli-Egyptian Interim Agreement (Sinai II, 1975)*, ECF, September 4, 1975, https://ecf.org.il/issues/issue/180 (accessed on April 28, 2017); *Sinai II Accords, Egyptian-Israeli Disengagement Agreement*, Centre for Israel Education (Atlanta, Georgia), September 4, 1975, https://israeled.org/resources/documents/sinai-ii-accords-egyptian-israeli-disengagement-agreement/ (accessed on April 28, 2017).

77 *Memorandum of Agreement Between the Governments of Israel and the United States*, September 1, 1975, Volume 1252, No. 20410, p. 68, https://treaties.un.org/doc/Publication/UNTS/Volume%201252/volume-1252-I-20410-English.pdf (accessed on April 30, 2017).

78 Ibid.

79 Ibid.

80 *US-Israel Memorandum of Agreement,* Ministry of Foreign Affairs, State of Israel, March 26, 1979; *Memorandum of Agreement Between the Governments of the United States of America and Israel-Oil*, Ministry of Foreign Affairs, State of Israel, March 26, 1979; Jeremy M. Sharp, *1979 Memorandum of Agreement Between the United States and Israel on Oil*, Congressional Research Service, May 8, 2014, p. 1; David Aviel, "Economic Implications of the Peace Treaty Between Egypt and Israel," *Case Western Reserve Journal of International Law*, Volume 12, Issue 1 (Winter 1980), pp. 60–61.

81 *Memorandum of Agreement*, September 1, 1975.

82 See Bahgat, "Energy and the Arab-Israeli Conflict," November 2008, p. 938.
83 More than 70 percent of our oil is imported from Azerbaijan and Russia, says Amit Mor, CEO of Eco Energy, an Israel-based energy consultancy firm. Sandy Rashty, "Roll Out Israel's Oil Barrels," *The Jewish Chronicle*, August 4, 2013, www.thejc.com/business/features/roll-out-israel-s-oil-barrels-1.47310 (accessed on April 30, 2017); Nick Childs, "Russia Seeks Mid-East Role," *BBC News*, April 27, 2005, http://news.bbc.co.uk/2/hi/middle_east/4490447.stm (accessed on April 30, 2017); *Israel Science and Technology: Oil and Natural Gas, Jewish Virtual Library*, 2018, www.jewishvirtuallibrary.org/oil-and-natural-gas-in-israel (accessed on July 8, 2018).
84 Author's interview with Ambassador Ron Adams, Envoy on Energy Policy, Ministry of Foreign Affairs, Government of Israel, Jerusalem, January 11, 2016.
85 Shamkhal Abilov, "The Azerbaijan-Israel Relations: A Non-Diplomatic, But Strategic Partnership," *The Journal of Central Asian and Caucasian Studies* (OAKA) (USAK, Ankara International Strategic Research Organization), Volume 4, Issue 8 (2009), pp. 155, 159 (147–167); Gawdat Bahgat, "Israel's Energy Security: The Caspian Sea and the Middle East," *Israel Affairs*, Volume 16, Issue 3 (2010), pp. 406–415.
86 David Sheppard, John Reed, and Anjli Raval, "Israel Turns to Kurds for Three-Quarters of Its Oil Supplies," *Financial Times*, August 23, 2015, www.ft.com/content/150f00cc-472c-11e5-af2f-4d6e0e5eda22 (accessed on May 1, 2017); Sharon Udasin, "Report: Majority of Israeli Oil Imported From Kurdistan," *The Jerusalem Post*, August 24, 2015, www.jpost.com/Business-and-Innovation/Israel-importing-77-percent-of-itsoil-from-Iraqi-Kurdistan-report-says-413056 (accessed on May 1, 2017).
87 Author's interview with Necdet Pamir, instructor of world energy politics at Bilkent University, chairman of the Committee on Energy Policies, Chamber of Petroleum Engineers, Ankara, June 7, 2017.
88 See Trita Parsi, "Israeli Iranian Relations Assessed," in Homa Katouzian and Hossein Shahidi (eds.), *Iran in the 21st Century: Politics, Economics & Conflict* (London: Routledge, 2008), pp. 136–138; Joseph Alper, "Israel and the Iran-Iraq War," in Efraim Karsh (ed.), *The Iran-Iraq War: Impact and Implications* (New York: Palgrave Macmillan, 1989), pp. 156–157; Leon Hadar, "The Collapse of Israel's 'Periphery Doctrine'," *Foreign Policy*, June 26, 2010, http://foreignpolicy.com/2010/06/26/the-collapse-of-israels-periphery-doctrine/ (accessed on May 3, 2017).
89 Sergey Minasian, "The Israeli-Kurdish Relations," *21st Century*, No. 1 (2007), pp. 15–32; Ofra Bengio, "Surprising Ties Between Israel and the Kurds," *Middle East Quarterly*, Volume 21, Issue 3 (Summer 2014), p. 5.
90 Rhys Dubin, "Netanyahu Finally Supports a Two-State Solution – In Iraq," *Foreign Policy*, September 13, 2017, http://foreignpolicy.com/2017/09/13/netanyahu-finally-supports-a-two-state-solution-in-iraq/ (accessed on July 10, 2018).
91 See Daniel Engber, "Where Does Israel Get Oil," *Slate*, July 14, 2006, www.slate.com/articles/news_and_politics/explainer/2006/07/where_does_israel_get_oil.html (accessed on May 3, 2017).
92 Barakat, "Turkey Cannot Block," September 22, 2011.
93 Tal Samuel-Azran, *Al Jazeera and US War Coverage* (New York: Peter Lang, 2010), p. 134.
94 Dov Hoch, "Israel Discusses Import of Gas From Egypt, Qatar," *JOC.com*, August 25, 1994, www.joc.com/israel-discusses-import-gas-egypt-qatar_19940825.html (accessed on May 3, 2017).
95 In an interview with Al-Jazeera, Qatari Foreign Minister Sheikh Hamad bin Jassem al-Thani, who had met his Israeli counterpart Silvan Shalom a day earlier, stated that, "We are committed for a certain time to long talks with the Israelis because we must adopt practical steps to put an end to the killing between Israelis and Palestinians." Faisal Baatout, "Qatar Ready to Boost Ties With Israel," *Middle East Online*, May 15, 2003, www.middle-east-online.com/english/?id=5562 (accessed on May 3, 2017).
96 Samuel-Azran, *Al Jazeera and US War Coverage*, 2016, p. 135.
97 Doron Peskin, "Report: Qatar Offering Israel Gas," *Ynet News*, May 5, 2011, www.ynetnews.com/articles/0,7340,L-4064547,00.html (accessed on May 4, 2017).

98 Hoch, "Israel Discusses Import of Gas From Egypt, Qatar," August 25, 1994.

99 CCC is one of the largest construction companies in operation in the Middle East and is headquartered in Athens.

100 PIF PLC is a Sovereign Wealth Fund of the State of Palestine founded in 2000. It specialises in investments in start-ups, early stage, growth capital, spin-off, and capital raising or business development investments. "Company Overview of Palestine Investment Fund PLC," *Bloomberg*, 2018, www.bloomberg.com/research/stocks/private/snapshot.asp?privcapId=62147909 (accessed on July 10, 2018).

101 Victor Kattan, "The Gas Fields off Gaza: A Gift or a Curse?" *Al-Shabaka*, April 24, 2012, https://al-shabaka.org/briefs/gas-fields-gaza-gift-or-curse/#fnref-390-2 (accessed on May 4, 2017).

102 Moshe Yaalon, *Does the Prospective Purchase of British Gas From Gaza Threaten Israel's National Security?* Jerusalem Issue Briefs, Jerusalem Centre for Public Affairs, Volume 7, No. 17, October 19, 2007, http://jcpa.org/article/does-the-prospective-purchase-of-british-gas-from-gaza-threaten-israel%E2%80%99s-national-security/ (accessed on May 6, 2017).

103 Consul General Jake Walles, *Update on Commercial Development of Offshore Gaza Natural Gas Field*, Confidential, Wikileaks, February 27, 2007, https://wikileaks.org/plusd/cables/07JERUSALEM401_a.html (accessed on May 6, 2017).

104 *Update on Commercial Development of Offshore Gaza Natural Gas Field*, Wikileaks, February 27, 2007.

105 See Dania Akkad, "Why Hasn't Gaza Marine Produced Gas," *Mid East Eye*, April 26, 2015, www.middleeasteye.net/news/why-hasnt-gaza-marine-produced-gas-257418634 (accessed on May 6, 2017).

106 Many believe that the strategy is to deliberately prevent the Palestinian from exploiting their own natural resources because the resulting economic transformation could improve their bargaining position vis-à-vis Israel. Antreasyan, writing in the *Journal of Palestine Studies* says that Israel's stranglehold over Gaza has been designed to make "Palestinian access to the Marine-1 and Marine-2 gas wells impossible." Israel's long-term goal "besides preventing the Palestinians from exploiting their own resources, is to integrate the gas fields off Gaza into the adjacent Israeli offshore installations." This is part of a wider strategy of "blocking Palestinian economic development." Anais Antreasyan, "Gas Finds in the Eastern Mediterranean: Gaza, Israel and other Conflicts," *Journal of Palestine Studies*, Volume XLII, Issue 3 (Spring 2013), pp. 29–47.

107 Israel has an EEZ agreement with Cyprus only in the Eastern Mediterranean region. Lebanon, Egypt, and the PA have refused to delineate EEZ with Israel for reasons related to the Arab-Israeli conflict.

108 These smaller fields are discussed in detail in Chapter 2.

109 "From Kyoto to Copenhagen," in *Coping With Climate Change in Israel*, Special Bulletin, State of Israel, Ministry of Environmental Protection, December 2009, p. 3.

110 A joint venture owned by two prominent Egyptian businessman Hussein Salem (65%) and Israeli businessman Yossi Meiman's Merhav Group (25%), two prominent Egyptian and Israeli businessmen with close ties to the governments in Jerusalem and Cairo, respectively, and state-owned Egyptian Natural Gas Holding Company (10%). The Egyptian Natural Gas Holding Company (EGAS), a subsidiary of the state-owned Egyptian General Petroleum Corporation (EGPC), was formed in the same year as the EMG, to manage the state stakes in gas projects. According to a cable from the US Embassy in Cairo on June 30, 2005, leaked by the Wikileaks, the GOE encouraged the formation of the EMG to negotiate the deal with the IEC because "having a private company negotiate with the Israel Electric Corporation made the arrangement more palatable for the GOE." Egypt had significant gas reserves and wanted to find buyers. However the only promising market in the region was that of Israel. The decision to sell gas to Israel was made by President Mubarak, who "appreciated the lucrative economic dividend that would result from such a deal." *ECPO Counsellor John Desrocher, Egypt and Israel Signed Gas Deal*, Confidential, Wikileaks, June 30, 2005, https://wikileaks.org/plusd/cables/05CAIRO4972_a.html (accessed on May 9, 2017); Galia

Press-Barnathan, *The Political of Transitions to Peace: A Comparative Perspective* (Pittsburgh and Pasadena: University of Pittsburgh Press, 2009), p. 47.

111 The agreement to supply gas to Israel was an extremely unpopular project of the Mubarak regime. There were allegations that Egyptian gas was being sold to Israel cheaply with the collusion of authorities at the highest level. Daniel Fink writes: "The basic accusation has been that the Egyptian government was selling gas to EMG at below market rates (which allowed the company to mark up its prices for the IEC and pocket the profits). Members of the regime, including Mubarak himself, his sons, and members of the intelligence service were thought to be personally benefiting from the deal. . . .The price is generally believed to have been around US$1.50 per million British thermal units (BTUs), though the exact amount was not revealed. Though there is no global benchmark for gas prices, industry experts maintained that gas was underpriced and was costing the country US$13 million a day in lost revenues. Nikos Tsafos, an analyst at PFC Energy said that at the time, Turkey, Greece and Italy were paying $7 to $10 per million BTUs in comparable deals." Daniel Fink, "Turning Off the Egyptian Gas Spigot: Implications for Israel," *Journal of Energy Security*, May 31, 2011, http://ensec.org/index.php?option=com_content&view=article&id=313:turn ing-off-the-egyptian-gas-spigot-implications-for-israel&catid=116:content0411&Ite mid=375 (accessed on May 11, 2017).

112 "Egypt Scraps Gas Supply Deal," *BBC News*, April 23, 2012, www.bbc.com/news/ world-middle-east-17808954 (accessed on May 11, 2017).

113 *Financial Reports For The Year Ended December 31, 2011*, The Israel Electric Corporation Limited (IEC), p. 79, www.iec.co.il/EN/IR/SiteAssets/Pages/FinancialStatements/ Financial%20Statements%20-%20December%202011.pdf (accessed on May 11, 2017); Ron-Tal and Glikman, *Israel Electric Corporation Ltd.*, 2012, p. 302.

114 IEC Board of Directors decided in September 2011, in an arbitration process versus the Egyptian national gas supply companies and EMG, to receive compensation for the damages incurred by non-delivery gas supply. The International Arbitration Tribunal in Paris ordered the two Egyptian gas companies, EGAS and EGPC, to pay $1.76 billion in compensation to the IEC. EMG, which oversaw Israeli-Egyptian gas deals from 2008 to 2012, was awarded $288 million in compensation. The Egyptian government has since appealed the arbitration outcome and ordered its gas companies to freeze any negotiations with Israeli gas companies over future deals. See, *IEC Financial Reports*, December 31, 2012, pp. 68–69; Ya'acov Zalel, "Day of High Drama Sees Egypt Freeze Gas Negotiations With Israel," *Natural Gas Europe*, October 2, 2012, www.naturalgaseurope.com/egypt-freezes-gas-negotiations-israel-after-ordered-to-pay-1.76-billion-compensation-26965 (accessed on May 14, 2017).

115 *Financial Reports for Three Months*, IEC, March 31, 2012, p. 6, www.iec.co.il/EN/IR/ Documents/Financial_Reports_March_2012.pdf (accessed on May 14, 2017).

116 *Financial Reports for Three Months*, IEC, March 31, 2013, p. 78, www.iec.co.il/en/ir/ pages/financialstatements.aspx (accessed on May 14, 2017); "Noble Brings Noa North Gas Field on Stream," *OffshoreEnergyToday.com*, June 25, 2012, www.offshoreenergytoday. com/noble-brings-noa-north-gas-field-on-stream-israel/ (accessed on May 15, 2017).

117 *IEC Financial Reports for Three Months*, March 31, 2013, p. 78, www.iec.co.il/en/ir/ pages/financialstatements.aspx (accessed on May 15, 2017).

118 *Marine Buoy to Absorb Natural Gas From LNG Ships* [Hebrew], Israel Natural Gas Lines, 2013, www.ingl.co.il/%D7%A0%D7%AA%D7%95%D7%A0%D7%99-%D7%94%D7 %9E%D7%A2%D7%A8%D7%9B%D7%AA/%D7%A4%D7%A8%D7%95%D7%99% D7%A7%D7%98%D7%99%D7%9D/%D7%94%D7%9E%D7%A6%D7%95%D7%A3- %D7%94%D7%99%D7%9E%D7%99-%D7%9C%D7%A7%D7%9C%D7%99%D7%9 8%D7%AA-%D7%92%D7%96-%D7%98%D7%91%D7%A2%D7%99-%D7%9E%D7 %90%D7%A0%D7%99%D7%95%D7%AA-lng-%D7%9E%D7%92%D7%96%D7%96/ (accessed on May 17, 2017); *Transmission and Distribution System* (Hebrew), Ministry of Energy, State of Israel, www.gov.il/he/Departments/Guides/distribution_area (accessed on July 10, 2018); Melanie Lidman, "10 Things to Know About Israel's Natural Gas," *The*

Times of Israel, November 29, 2015, www.timesofisrael.com/top-10-things-to-know-about-israels-natural-gas/ (accessed on May 17, 2017); *"Hadera Deepwater LNG Terminal: Israel's First LNG Import Terminal,"* Excelerate Energy, undated, http://excelerateenergy.com/project/hadera-deepwater-lng-terminal/ (accessed on May 17, 2017).

119 "Eastern Mediterranean Gas Discoveries Redefine LNG Playing Field," *LNG World Shipping,* March 28, 2018, www.lngworldshipping.com/news/view,eastern-mediter ranean-gas-discoveries-redefine-lng-playing-field_51240.htm (accessed on July 10, 2018).

120 Ryan Collins and Kevin Varley, "A U.S. Shale Gas Cargo Is Heading to Israel for the First Time," *Bloomberg,* May 11, 2018, www.bloomberg.com/news/articles/2018-05-10/a-u-s-shale-gas-cargo-is-heading-to-israel-for-the-first-time (accessed on May 18, 2017); "Israel to Import Natural Gas for Less than Its Own Field's Rates," *JewishPress.com,* April 6, 2016, www.jewishpress.com/news/breaking-news/israel-to-import-natural-gas-for-less-than-its-own-fields-rates/2016/04/06/ (accessed on May 18, 2017); Yaccov Zalel, "Israel Electric Company Signed an Agreement to Import LNG," *Natural Gas World,* April 6, 2016, www.naturalgasworld.com/report-israel-to-import-lng-cheaper-than-local-natural-gas-28946 (accessed on May 18, 2017); *What We Do,* British Petroleum, 2018, www.bp.com/en_tt/trinidad-and-tobago/about-bp-in-trinidad-and-tobago/BPinTT.html (accessed on July 13, 2018).

121 Israel's only natural gas storage comes from the FSRU storage tanks on the FSRU in Hadera.

122 See *Review of Developments in the Natural Gas Market,* Ministry of Energy, State of Israel, 2016, p. 12; Gina Cohen, "Israel: More Gas Customers, Please," *Petroleum Economist,* September 12, 2017, www.petroleum-economist.com/articles/midstream-downstream/lng/2017/israel-more-gas-customers-please (accessed on July 13, 2018); "Israel Eyes Second Import Terminal," *Hellenic Shipping News,* August 11, 2016, www.hellenicshippingnews.com/israel-eyes-second-import-terminal/ (accessed on May 18, 2017).

123 These fears came true when a pipeline crack was detected during scheduled field maintenance in September 2017. It took about a week before regular supplies were restored after a total cut off. The consumers had about 5 percent added to their electricity bill to cover the additional cost of alternate expensive fuels – diesel, coal, and fuel oil. The days-long shutdown also presented a picture of the national security, environmental, and economic challenges that the current reliance on one source and a single supply pipe pose to the nation. See Max Schindler, "Pipeline Failure for Tamar Gas Field to Cause Hiccup in Electricity Rates," *Jerusalem Post,* September 24, 2017, www.jpost.com/Business-and-Innovation/Environment/Israelis-electric-bills-to-increase-following-gas-pipeline-failure-505827 (accessed on July 13, 2018); Ya'acov Zalel, "Tamar Gas Supply to Israel Halted," *Natural Gas World,* September 22, 2017, www.naturalgasworld.com/gas-supply-from-tamar-to-israel-completely-stopped-55492 (accessed on July 13, 2018).

124 *National Plan for Implementation of the Greenhouse Gas Emissions Reduction Targets and for Energy Efficiency,* Government Decision No. 1403, Ministry of Environmental Protection, State of Israel, April 10, 2016, pp. 1–8, http://www.sviva.gov.il/English/env_topics/climatechange/NatlEmissionsReductionPlan/Documents/Govt-Decision-1403-National-GHG-Reduction-Plan-April-2016.pdf (accessed on July 13, 2018).

125 *Israel National Plan for Implementation of the Paris Agreement,* Israel Ministry of Environmental Protection, State of Israel, September 2016, pp. 4, 14, http://www.sviva.gov.il/InfoServices/ReservoirInfo/DocLib2/Publications/P0801-P0900/P0836eng.pdf (accessed on July 13, 2018); Honi Kabalo, *The Israeli Net Metering Scheme – Lessons Learned,* Public Utilities Authority-Electricity, State of Israel, September 29, 2014, https://pua.gov.il/English/Documents/The%20Israeli%20Net%20Metering%20Scheme%20%20lessons%20learned.pdf (accessed on May 18, 2017).

126 Rutenberg power station is the newest thermal power station in Israel and the second largest in terms of generation capacity.

127 This directive comes after the IEC was remiss in its obligation to instal scrubbers or filters at the power stations, which it was obligated to do by 2016 under a personal order of the then-environmental protection minister, Gilad Erdan. The orders have been crafted to bring Israel in line with global trends. Filters or scrubber system is the informal name for flue gas desulfurisation (FGD) technology, which removes, or 'scrubs,' sulphur dioxide SO2 emissions from the exhaust of coal-fired power plants. A reduction in sulphur emissions reduces air pollution and the harm caused to public health, and reduces the cost of healthcare, saving the economy direct economic costs. Installing the filters requires shutting down the coal-fired power plants, so the work has been spaced out over five years to prevent power outages. Ehud Zion Waldoks, "All Coal-Fired Power Stations to Get Filters," *Jerusalem Post*, December 27, 2010, www. jpost.com/enviro-tech/all-coal-fired-power-stations-to-get-filters (accessed on May 21, 2017); *Ministry Is Ordering Israel Electric Corp. to Reduce Coal Use*, Ministry of Environmental Protection, State of Israel, December 13, 2015, www.sviva.gov.il/English/ResourcesandServices/NewsAndEvents/NewsAndMessageDover/Pages/2015/12-Dec/Ministry-is-Ordering-Israel-Electric-Corp-to-Reduce-Coal-Use.aspx (accessed on May 21, 2017); Hedy Cohen, "Israel Electric Corp to Reduce Coal Use Friday," *Globes*, December 29, 2015, www.globes.co.il/en/article-iec-to-reduce-coal-use-from-friday-1001091820 (accessed on May 21, 2017); "Sulphur Dioxide Scrubbers," *Duke Energy*, undated, www.duke-energy.com/our-company/environment/air-quality/sulfur-dioxide-scrubbers (accessed on May 21, 2017).

128 "Israel Targets Coal-for-Power Use at Less than 10% of Fuel Mix by 2025," *Platts*, April 5, 2017, www.platts.com/latest-news/electric-power/telaviv/israel-targets-coal-for-power-use-at-less-than-26704398 (accessed on July 13, 2018).

129 "Israel Electric Coal Consumption to Drop Further in 2017," *Platts*, March 15, 2017, www.platts.com/latest-news/coal/telaviv/israel-electric-coal-consumption-to-drop-further-26685600 (accessed on July 13, 2018).

130 *Financial Reports for Six and Three Months*, IEC, June 6, 2017, p. 4, www.iec.co.il/en/ir/pages/financialstatements.aspx (accessed on July 13, 2018).

131 *Financial Reports*, IEC, December 31, 2017, p. 20, www.iec.co.il/en/ir/pages/financial statements.aspx (accessed on July 13, 2018).

132 Ibid., p. 50.

133 "Israel Plans to Close Coal Power Plants Until 2025," *Front News International*, September 27, 2017, https://frontnews.eu/news/en/14344 (accessed on July 13, 2018).

134 As part of the reformation of the IEC's structure and in a bid to increase competition in electricity supply, a notice published by the Ministry of Energy on 28 May 2017 states that the private sector will construct the natural gas operated power stations at Orot Rabin. These four coal units at Orot Rabin power station, according to the ministry, are responsible for 25 percent of all air pollution in Israel. Each kilowatt produced by coal is between 10 and 1000 times more than pollution from natural gas. *IEC Financial Reports for Six and Three Months*, June 6, 2017, p. 3; *IEC Financial Reports*, December 31, 2017, p. 50; *Government OKs Decision to Shut Coal-Fired Power Plants in Hadera by 2022*, Ministry of Environmental Protection, State of Israel, August 9, 2018, www.sviva.gov.il/English/ResourcesandServices/NewsAndEvents/NewsAndMessage Dover/Pages/2018/08-Aug/Government-OKs-Decision-to-Shut-Coal-Fired-Power-Plants-in-Hadera-by-2022.aspx (accessed on July 14, 2018).

135 "Notes to the Consolidated Financial Statements," *IEC Financial Reports*, December 31, 2017, pp. 9, 22.

136 "Israel's Energy Minister: No Coal, Gasoline by 2030," *Globes*, December 4, 2017, www. globes.co.il/en/article-israels-energy-minister-no-coal-gasoline-by-2030-1001214304 (accessed on July 14, 2018).

137 *Ministers Elkin and Steinitz: "Electric Company Must Reduce Use of Coal by 30% Compared to 2015,"* Ministry of Environmental Protection, State of Israel, January 3, 2018, www.sviva.gov.il/English/ResourcesandServices/NewsAndEvents/NewsAndMessage-Dover/Pages/2018/01-Jan/Ministers-Elkin-and-Steinitz-Electric-Company-Must-Reduce-Use-of-Coal-by-30-Compared-to-2015.aspx (accessed on July 14, 2018).

138 "Launching a Clean Car Revolution in Israel," *Israel Environmental Bulletin*, Ministry of Environmental Protection, Volume 44, March 2018, p. 4, www.sviva.gov.il/English/SearchResults/Pages/GeneralSearchResults.aspx (accessed on July 14, 2018).

139 "Israel's Energy Minister: No Coal, Gasoline by 2030," *Globes*, December 4, 2017.

140 *Policy on the Integration of Renewable Energy Sources Into the Israeli Electricity Sector*, Ministry of National Infrastructures, Energy and Water Resources, February 14, 2010; Sharon Udasin, "Hadera Coal Chimneys to be Shut Down, Replaced by Gas Within Six Years," *Jerusalem Post*, August 25, 2016, www.jpost.com/Israel-News/Hadera-coal-chimneys-to-be-shut-down-replaced-by-gas-within-six-years-465968 (accessed on May 24, 2017).

141 *Renewable Energy Planning and Policy: An Overview: Lawmakers Pass First Solar Energy Legislation*, February 19, 2017, Ministry of Environmental Protection, State of Israel, www.sviva.gov.il/English/env_topics/climatechange/renewable-energy/Pages/Renewable-Energy-Planning-And-Policy.aspx (accessed on July 14, 2018); "Israel's Ketura Solar Farm Connected to Grid," *Energy Matters*, July 30, 2015, www.energymatters.com.au/renewable-news/ketura-solar-farm-em4960/ (accessed on May 24, 2017).

142 *Israel Commits to Reducing GHG Emissions 26% by 2030*, Ministry of Environmental Protection, State of Israel, October 7, 2015, www.sviva.gov.il/English/ResourcesandServices/NewsAndEvents/NewsAndMessageDover/Pages/2015/Oct-10/Israel-Commits-to-Reducing-GHG-Emissions-26-percent-by-2030.aspx (accessed on May 24, 2017); *Market Overview: Renewables*, Green Energy Association of Israel (GEA-IL), 2018; Itay Zetelny, Ernst and Young, "Renewable Energy Recap: Israel," *Renewable Energy World*, January 2, 2012, www.renewableenergyworld.com/articles/2012/01/renewable-energy-recap-israel.html (accessed on May 24, 2017); "Israel – Energy," *Export.gov*, June 9, 2017, www.export.gov/apex/article2?id=Israel-Energy (accessed on July 14, 2018).

143 *Renewable Energy: Catalyst for a Clean Energy Transition*, OECD, 2016, www.oecd.org/environment/renewable-energy-catalyst-clean-energy-transition.htm(accessedonMay24, 2017).

144 Jeffrey Ball, "Germany's High-Priced Energy Revolution," *Fortune*, March 14, 2017, http://fortune.com/2017/03/14/germany-renewable-clean-energy-solar/ (accessed on May 24, 2017).

145 Central Bureau of Statistics, Government of Israel, Jerusalem, Israel, September 2017.

146 *Israel – Energy*, Export.gov, June 9, 2017.

147 See, "Israeli co Enlight to Buy PV, Wind in Central Europe," *Renewables Now*, January 22, 2018, https://renewablesnow.com/news/israeli-co-enlight-to-buy-pv-wind-in-central-europe-598988/ (accessed on July 14, 2018); Melanie Lidman, "With $1b Africa Deal, Israel's Solar Power Exports Eclipse Local Usage," *The Times of Israel*, June 5, 2017, www.timesofisrael.com/with-1b-africa-deal-israels-solar-power-exports-eclipse-local-usage/ (accessed on July 14, 2018); Viva Sarah Press, "Enlight, Migdal to Invest $147 Million in Renewable Energy," *Israel21c*, January 3, 2016; Melanie Lidman, "Israelis to Dedicate Largest Solar Field in East Africa," *The Times of Israel*, February 4, 2015, www.timesofisrael.com/israelis-to-dedicate-largest-solar-field-in-east-africa/ (accessed on May 24, 2017).

148 *OECD Economic Surveys: Israel 2018*, Organisation for Economic Co-operation and Development (OECD), Paris, France, March 2018, p. 140, www.oecd-ilibrary.org/economics/oecd-economic-surveys-israel-2018_eco_surveys-isr-2018-en (accessed on September 18, 2018).

149 Central Bureau of Statistics, State of Israel, 2017.

150 Zetelny, Ernst and Young, "Renewable Energy Recap: Israel," January 2, 2012.

151 *The Israeli Renewable Energy and Energy Efficiency Industry: Executive Summary*, Samuel Neaman Institute, Israel Institute of Technology, October 2015, p. 1, www.neaman.org.il/Files/6-449.pdf (accessed on May 25, 2017).

152 *Israel's Renewable Energy Sector*, National Sustainable Energy and Water Program, Ministry of Economy and Industry, Government of Israel, undated, http://israelnewtech.gov.il/English/Energy/Pages/aboutus.aspx (accessed on July 14, 2018).

153 "Historic Inauguration of Ketura Sun – Israel's First Solar Field," *Arava Power Company*, June 5, 2011, www.aravapower.com/Ketura%20Sun (accessed on May 25, 2017); "Israel's Ketura Solar Farm Connected to Grid," *Energy Matters*, July 30, 2015.

154 "Belectric Cuts Ribbon on 30-MW Solar Park in Israel," *Renewables Now*, January 31, 2018, https://renewablesnow.com/news/belectric-cuts-ribbon-on-30-mw-solar-park-in-israel-600026/ (accessed on July 14, 2018); "Ashalim's Solar Tower Is World's Tallest," *Renewable Energy Magazine*, December 27, 2017, www.renewableenergymagazine.com/solar_thermal_electric/ashalima-s-solar-tower-is-worlda-s-20171227 (accessed on July 14, 2018); Karen Graham, "Israel Will Soon Have World's Tallest Solar Power Tower," *Digital Journal*, January 8, 2017, www.digitaljournal.com/tech-and-science/technology/israel-will-soon-have-world-s-tallest-solar-power-tower/article/483220 (accessed on July 14, 2018); "Israel to Build World's Tallest Solar Tower in Symbol of Renewable Energy Ambition," *Independent*, January 5, 2017, www.independent.co.uk/news/world/middle-east/israel-solar-tower-power-energy-renewable-tech-ambitions-a7510901.html (accessed on July 14, 2018); *Ashalim Power Station, Israel*, GE Renewable Energy, 2016, www.ge.com/content/dam/gepower-renewables/global/en_US/downloads/brochures/solar-csp-ashalim-gea32278.pdf (accessed on May 27, 2017); *Ashalim*, BrightSource, 2015, www.brightsourceenergy.com/ashalim-solar-project#.WP9ScCN962w (accessed on May 27, 2017); *Thermo Solar Power*, Negev Energy, undated, http://www.negevenergy.co.il/en/ (accessed on February 6, 2019).

155 Yoram Gabizon, "Largest Wind Energy Project in Israel Commences – Will Bring in NIS 105 Million Per Year," The Marker [in Hebrew], June 10, 2018, https://www.themarker.com/markets/1.6159248 (accessed on August 27, 2018); "Israeli project secures funding," Wind Power Monthly, July 18, 2018, https://www.windpowermonthly.com/article/1487419/israeli-project-secures-funding (accessed on August 27, 2018); Press Release, Central Bureau of Statistics, State of Israel, Jerusalem, January 6, 2019, https://www.cbs.gov.il/he/mediarelease/DocLib/2019/001/03_19_001b.pdf (accessed on February 8, 2019); IEA Electricity Information, 2018; "Israel's Ketura Solar Farm," *Energy Matters*, July 30, 2015; "Analysis: Israel's Plans to Tap Into Wind Power Take Shape," *Wind Power Monthly*, January 30, 2015, www.windpowermonthly.com/article/1331651/analysis-israels-plans-tap-wind-power-shape (accessed on May 27, 2017); "Israel: Production Capacities," *The Wind Power*, December 27, 2016, www.thewindpower.net/country_en_60_israel.php (accessed on July 15, 2018).

156 Zafrir Rinat, "Energy Plan Sees Need for Nuclear Power Plants in Israel," *Haaretz*, January 26, 2016, www.haaretz.com/israel-news/.premium-1.699485 (accessed on May 27, 2017); Shlomo Wald and Ilan Yaar, "The Need for Nuclear Power Stations in Israel," *IAEA Panel*, February 11, 2014, www.iaea.org/inis/collection/NCLCollectionStore/_Public/45/114/45114735.pdf (accessed on May 27, 2017).

157 Natural Gas Authority, Ministry of Energy, 2016.

158 *Tamar Gas Field*, Delek Drilling, 2018, www.delekdrilling.co.il/en/project/tamar-gas-field (accessed on July 15, 2018).

159 The details of the Israel's two-pronged conflict with the Lebanese state and the Hezbollah group are discussed in Chapter 4.

160 "Lebanese Army Chief Urges Military to Remain Alert to 'Defy Israeli Enemy'," *Almasdarnews* (Lebanon), July 31, 2018, www.almasdarnews.com/article/lebanese-army-chief-urges-military-to-remain-alert-to-defy-israeli-enemy/ (accessed on July 15, 2018).

161 Sara Parker Musarra, "Israel Attempts to Balance Regulations, Infrastructure With LNG Growth," *Offshore Engineer*, October 22, 2013, www.oedigital.com/geoscience/item/4277-israel-attempts-to-balance-regulations-infrastructure-with-lng-growth (accessed on May 27, 2017).

162 Amos Harel, "Fearing Hezbollah Attacks, Israeli Military Insists Gas Rigs Be Close to Shore," *Haaretz*, July 31, 2018, www.haaretz.com/israel-news/.premium-fearing-hezbollah-attacks-israeli-military-insists-gas-rigs-be-close-to-shore-1.6334588 (accessed on July 15, 2018).

163 See "Leviathan Gas Field Group Submits \$6.5 b Development Plan," *Ynetnews.com*, October 1, 2014, www.ynetnews.com/articles/0,7340,L-4576570,00.html (accessed on May 28, 2017); "Leviathan Partners Submit FPSO Field Development Plan," *Gas Strategies*, October 1, 2016, www.gasstrategies.com/information-services/gas-matters-today/leviathan-partners-submit-fpso-field-development-plan (accessed on May 28, 2017); Noble Energy, *Eastern Mediterranean*, Energy Analysts Conference presentation, December 6, 2012, http://files.shareholder.com/downloads/ABEA-2D0WMQ/247 3688728x0x620347/477d484f-655f-4c8e-8c6f-390ad9a75988/NBL_Analyst_Day_ Presentation.pdf (accessed on May 28, 2017).

164 "Description of Actions Resulting From Implementation of the Proposed Plan," *National Outline Plan NOP 37/H – Marine Environment Impact Survey*, June 2013, Chapters 3, https://www3.opic.gov/Environment/EIA/nobleenergy/ESIA/Translated TAMA37HEIAOffshoresections/Offshore_EIA_Chapters_3_4_5.pdf (accessed on May 28, 2017).

165 "Israel Approves Noble's Leviathan Development Plan," OffshoreEnergyToday.com, June 2, 2016, www.offshoreenergytoday.com/israel-approves-nobles-leviathan-development-plan/ (accessed on May 28, 2017); *Approval of the Development Plan for the Leviathan Field of 21 bcm Per Year by the Petroleum Commissioner*, Delek Group, June 7, 2016, https://ir.delek-group.com/news-releases/news-release-details/approval-development-plan-leviathan-field-21-bcm-year-petroleum (accessed on May 28, 2017).

166 Since the government's decision, the Citizens' groups, several local authorities, environmental NGOs, and academic experts have come under the umbrella of Citizens Coalition to oppose the government's decision arguing that an operational gas platform near the shore increases pose a threat to public health and the marine environment, in case of a malfunction or a hostile attack on the facility. Besides the offshore facilities, there is concern about an onshore processing station for the highly toxic and carcinogenic condensate, a natural gas by-product, at the Hagit power station. *The Times of Israel* reported in August 2018 that the State Comptroller would investigate into the extent to which the security concerns influenced the government's decision to allow the location of the gas platform close to the shore. Yisrael Price, "Natural-Gas Facilities Too Close for Safety, Say Northern Residents," *Hamodia*, August 20, 2017, https://hamodia.com/2017/08/20/natural-gas-facilities-close-safety-say-northern-residents/ (accessed on July 15, 2018); Sue Surkes, "State Comptroller Probing Why Gas Platform Being Built Close to Israeli Coast," *The Times of Israel*, August 10, 2018, www.timesofisrael.com/state-comptroller-probing-why-gas-platform-being-built-close-to-israeli-coast/ (accessed on July 15, 2018); Zafrir Rinat, "Building New Natural Gas Rig Off Israel's Shores Poses High Ecological Risks, Expert Warns," *Haaretz*, July 30, 2018, www.haaretz.com/israel-news/.premium-expert-warns-of-ecological-risk-posed-by-offshore-natural-gas-rig-1.6334688 (accessed on July 30, 2018).

167 Dov Benovadia, "Israel Navy Completes Gas Platforms Defensive Drill," *Hamodia*, June 6, 2018, https://hamodia.com/2018/06/06/israel-navy-completes-gas-platforms-defensive-drill/ (accessed on July 15, 2018).

168 "Germany Subsidizes Sale of Four Warships to Israel," *Reuters*, May 11, 2015, http://in.reuters.com/article/germany-israel-warships/germany-subsidizes-sale-of-four-warships-to-israel-idINL5N0Y21IL20150511 (accessed on May 29, 2017).

169 *Israel – Excess SH-60F Sea-Hawk Helicopter Equipment and Support*, Defence Security Cooperation Agency, News Release, July 6, 2016, www.dsca.mil/major-arms-sales/

israel-excess-sh-60f-sea-hawk-helicopter-equipment-and-support (accessed on May 29, 2017).

170 "Eilat Class Multi-Mission Naval Corvettes," *Naval Technology*, undated, www.naval-technology.com/projects/saar5/ (accessed on July 16, 2018).

171 *Summary of Attack on IDF Ship*, Ministry of Foreign Affairs, State of Israel, July 15, 2006, www.mfa.gov.il/mfa/foreignpolicy/terrorism/hizbullah/pages/summary%20 of%20attack%20on%20idf%20missile%20ship%2015-jul-2006.aspx (accessed on May 29, 2017); "Hizbullah Hits Israel's INS Hanit With Anti-ship Missile," *Jane's Defence Weekly*, July 18, 2006, www.janes.com/defence/news/jdw/jdw060718_1_n.shtml (accessed on May 29, 2017); "Eilat Class Multi-Mission," *Naval Technology*.

172 "US: Israel to Get 8 Seahawk Helicopters, Related Equipment," *Israel Hayom*, July 11, 2016, www.israelhayom.com/2017/07/20/us-israel-to-get-8-seahawk-helicopters-related-equipment/ (accessed on May 29, 2017).

173 "'Iron Dome of Seas': Israel's Navy Version of Missile Defence System Declared Operational," *RT*, November 28, 2017, www.rt.com/news/411189-israel-iron-dome-warship/ (accessed on July 16, 2018).

174 Tamir Eshel, "Israel Shipyards Introduces the SAAR 72 Mini-Corvette Design," *Defense Update*, May 16, 2013, http://defense-update.com/20130516_saar-72.html (accessed on May 29, 2017).

175 "Israeli Navy to Get 2 German Frigates to Shield Natural Gas Fields," *United Press International*, December 17, 2013, www.upi.com/Business_News/Security-Industry/2013/12/17/Israeli-navy-to-get-2-German-frigates-to-shield-natural-gas-fields/UPI-40851387306062/ (accessed on May 29, 2017); "Long-Range Surface-to-Air Missile (LRSAM) / Barak 8," *GlobalSecurity.org*, undated, www.globalsecurity.org/military/world/india/lr-sam.htm (accessed on May 29, 2017).

176 Barbara Opall-Rome, "Israel Navy Readies for Third-Generation USV," *Defense News*, July 27, 2016, www.defensenews.com/naval/2016/07/27/israel-navy-readies-for-third-generation-usv/ (accessed on May 29, 2017).

177 Paul Alster and David Andrew Weinberg, "The Daunting Challenge of Defending Israel's Multi-Billion Dollar Gas Fields," *Forbes*, January 1, 2014, www.forbes.com/sites/realspin/2014/01/08/the-daunting-challenge-of-defending-israels-multi-billion-dollar-gas-fields/#ce039c03b929 (accessed on May 29, 2017).

178 Admiral Nazih Baroudi, "The Commanders Respond: Lebanese Navy," *Proceedings*, Volume 138/3/1,309 (March 2012), www.usni.org/magazines/proceedings/2012-03/commanders-respond-lebanese-navy (accessed on May 31, 2017).

179 Admiral Nazih Baroudi, "The Commanders Respond: Lebanese Navy," *Proceedings*, Volume 139/3/1,321 (March 2013), www.usni.org/magazines/proceedings/2013-03/commanders-respond-lebanese-navy (accessed on May 31, 2017).

180 *Are We Entering the Golden Age of Gas?* Special Report, World Energy Outlook, International Energy Agency, 2011, p. 7; "Introduction," in Silvia Colombo, Mohamed El Harrak, and Nicolò Sartori (eds.), *The Future of Natural Gas Markets and Geopolitics Editors* (The Netherlands: Lenthe Publishers/European Energy Review, 2016), p. 19.

181 *IEA Gas Information*, IEA statistics, 2018.

182 *Country Comparison: Natural Gas – Proved Reserves*, The World Factbook, Central Intelligence Agency, undated, www.cia.gov/library/publications/the-world-factbook/rankorder/2253rank.html (accessed on May 31, 2017).

2

ISRAEL'S NATURAL GAS DISCOVERIES

Evolution of the regulatory framework for resource governance

Development of energy sector with private investment and governmental regulations

> A comprehensive national energy policy is critical to our nation's economy and our national security . . .
>
> *−Heather Wilson*[1]

The above, spoken in the context of the United States, may well be applied to Israel's formulation of the energy regulations relating to oil and gas resources through a comprehensive process of public consultations, Knesset debates, and judicial interpretations. These regulations incorporated into laws have alleviated industry uncertainty and created opportunities for investment in this critical sector of the economy. Energy regulations have ensured that Israel's resource is first and foremost available for utilisation in the domestic economy, thus contributing to energy security and by implication to national security, as securing energy has always been one of the most important tasks of the state.

In the last three decades, several large offshore gas fields have been discovered in the Eastern Mediterranean region comprising of countries like Cyprus, Egypt, Israel, Jordan, Lebanon, Syria, and the Palestinian territories. A 2010 report of the US Geological Survey (USGS) estimated the mean probable undiscovered reserves of oil at 1.7 billion barrels and 122 trillion cubic feet (tcf or 3500 bcm) of natural gas in the Levantine basin of the Eastern Mediterranean region.[2] The Levantine Sea is the easternmost part of the Mediterranean that includes the territorial waters of Israel, Gaza Strip, Lebanon, and Syria. The discovery of large quantities of natural gas in the EEZ of Israel, Cyprus, and Egypt significantly alters the supply–side forecasts for the Mediterranean region, hitherto poor in petroleum resources as compared to its Persian Gulf counterparts.

Israel is leading the Eastern Mediterranean region in the development of gas resources. The Tamar gas reservoir producing for the domestic market since 2013 started supplying small amounts of gas to two Jordanian companies in early 2017. Leviathan, the largest discovered field in Israel's economic waters, is in the process of development and would provide the gas volumes for both the domestic market and export. Smaller fields – Karish–Tanin and Dalit – expected to come online in the early to late 2020s would further keep the internal market well supplied and enhance Israel's energy security.

The new energy industry has revolutionised Israel's economy, as well as provided the country with greater strategic leverage. But the new discoveries have also opened up a Pandora's box of thorny social, financial, security, and foreign policy concerns. Israel did not have a set of regulations suitable for the level of the discoveries in 2009–2010. The enormous size of the discoveries in Tamar and Leviathan mandated changes in rules on taxation and profits, as much as they brought forth the need to address monopoly concerns in the Israeli gas market.

Accordingly, the government took several measures to introduce changes in Israel's regulatory environment. Unlike other gas-rich countries, where states have played an effective role in exploration and production (E&P) through national oil and gas companies, Israel sought to build a semi-independent regulatory structure of directives and regulations embedded in the state's policy measures. Israel's gas regulatory regime is thus characterised by five fundamental features:

a) Gas development led by private players: Israel took the ideological decision to develop its gas resource through private sector participation. While it is common to have state-owned enterprises in critical sectors of the economy that manage government's stakes, Israeli policymakers did not consider the establishment of a national energy company as essential to their nation's gas management strategy.[3] Israel deregulated its petroleum sector in the 1990s – a marker of the neoliberal reforms of the day – to encourage private domestic and foreign investments. All the state holdings in oil exploration companies were privatised, including that of the Israel National Oil Company (the government-owned holding company, INOC), which threw the petroleum sector open to competition. The Petroleum Law of 1952, amended in 1957, 1965, and 1989, to encourage foreign interest in exploration activities, has remained the primary set of guidelines rules governing E&P activities in Israel's upstream sector.

The Israeli government enacted the Natural Gas Sector Law, 2002 (henceforth, 'Gas Law'), to institute a competitive private sector in the midstream and downstream phases too. Amendment Number 4, 2007, to the Gas Law elucidated that transmission, storage, marketing, sale, and the setting up and operation of a LNG installation would be part of the licensing obligation. The Natural Gas Authority (NGA), established in the MoE, would supervise these processes.

Iran and Qatar, Israel's near-neighbours and holders of the second and third largest gas reserves in the world, have state-owned companies that control the majority stakes in consortiums often constituted of IOCs to operate in the upstream, midstream, and downstream sectors of the petroleum industry. In a political domain similar to that of Israel, the world's third-largest natural gas exporter, Norway, has a state-owned company that manages the commercial aspects of government's financial interests in petroleum operations. The Norwegian government is also the largest shareholder of Statoil ASA, one of the most important energy companies operating in the international market, holding 67 percent of the stakes. In the gas-rich Mediterranean region, state's control of oil and gas industry is the norm.

Algeria's Sonatrach, the state oil and gas company, dominates the gas industry and state-owned Sonelgaz currently controls the retail gas industry. Algeria has increasingly allowed foreign participation in the upstream gas sector, although Sonatrach has a controlling 51 percent interest in all joint ventures. In Egypt, the state-owned EGAS always participates with a private investor in exploration, development, and production of natural gas through conventional production sharing agreements and is closely involved in the management of gas projects.

A fully owned subsidiary of the Egyptian Natural Gas Company (GASCO), is responsible for planning and operation of the transportation system, distribution and marketing, and operating LNG projects in conjunction with private owners. The system of having private players to develop the entire value chain of the gas industry in a competitive manner is unique to Israel. State ownership is confined the INGL, established in 2003 for the construction and operation of the national natural gas transmission infrastructure.

b) Public policy formation process: Several critical aspects of the gas regulatory regime related to taxation of 'profit oil,' export, and competition in the gas industry emerged through public hearings before the expert committees, constituted to recommend policy measures to the government. The committees heard across-the-board opinions on issues within the purview of their mandate. Interest groups ranging from field developers, environmentalist, health activists, opposition lawmakers in the Knesset, to those concerned with the commercial aspects of the gas industry appeared before the committees to present their views or sent them in writing.

Public hearings introduced transparency in the functioning of the expert committees just as the divergent positions and perspectives helped the committees to delineate policy proposals that reconciled the interest of the Israeli people who owned the resource and the interests of gas companies who developed it for public use. The complicated issues of tax on profit from gas sales, export quota for the gas developers, and monopoly holdings of the dominant consortium in the gas market were publicly discussed. One salutary impact of the public policy formation process has been the deepening of public understanding of the gas economy and its bearings on the policies of the state, such as those related to public spending and use of gas earnings for developmental needs.

c) State ownership of resource and taxation rate: Through changes in taxation rules, the government reiterated that the mineral resource belonged to the state. One of the most important changes was the revocation of the claim of gas developers to 'field degradation' subsidy in the calculation of profits, leading to an increase in government's share of revenues from gas development. Unlike the US and Canada, which have a privatised ownership of petroleum resources, the rights-holders to the Israeli gas fields are not the owners of those fields. The developers did not buy the gas fields from the state (or the field is not found on their private estate) and, therefore, the mineral in the fields did not belong to them but to the state and, by that token, to the people. Nonetheless, to incentivise the developers, the government sought to ensure through regulations that they were entitled to recover at least 150 percent of the invested cost before a system of progressive taxation in the form of levy or tax on excess profit[4] would take effect.

d) Result of democratic decision-making: The state took into account the public opinion while drawing up policies on the gas sector. Without public scrutiny and debate, the prioritisation of internal usage over export option, considered a critical incentivise for the gas developers, would not have seen the light of the day. A central aspect of the public debate that ensued consequent to the Tzemach Committee hearings was the emphasis on the continued availability of gas, first and foremost for domestic consumption. In effect, gas as a transgenerational resource required careful utilisation strategies so that it did not run out earlier than the development of alternatives and put Israel once again in a precarious position of complete energy dependency.

e) Foreign policy and gas: The Israeli government believes that natural gas export can serve as a strategic foreign policy tool for Israel to transform antagonistic regional ties into interdependent ones. Gas contracts are typically long-term, tethered to transmission structures that are difficult to replace. Gas demand and supply relationships function with an understanding of the strategic context and, therefore, even modest exports or imports carry leverage related to availability for the consumers and revenue for the suppliers. According to the National Security Council position submitted to the MoE in July 2015:

> There are substantial political-security benefits to be derived from the possibility of anchoring elements of Israel's relations with neighboring states and partners to peace agreements through the export of natural gas, thereby making a significant contribution to the national security of the State of Israel in a regional environment that is turbulent and dangerous. Intelligent use of the gas reserves could expand the sphere of influence of the State of Israel in the international arena, both in nearby and more distant areas.[5]

Israel's gas discoveries: a historical overview

Economic requirements and political environment bound Israel's energy and national security consideration in a tight embrace, motivating the country to engage in on-and-off exploration activities since the 1970s with the strategic aim of reducing dependence on energy imports. Israel from its founding had no choice but to import all of its energy – oil, gas, and coal. Israeli Prime Minister Golda Meir often joked that God had guided the Jewish people through the desert to the only land in the Middle East with no oil.[6] Despite assiduous search that continues to this date, Israel has not found any commercially viable onshore or offshore oil field.

Israel discovered its first oil field in the Heletz area, southeast of the port city of Ashkelon as early as 1955 that yielded as little as 17.2 million barrels of oil and is now dry. In the 1960s, Kokhav, Brur, Ashdod, and Zuk Tamrur also turned in small, insignificant quantities of oil. The search for natural gas began in 1950, and by the end of that decade, small but commercial quantities of reserves were found in the Zohar field in 1958, followed by Kidod in 1960 and Kanaim in 1961; some shallow gas surfaced in Ashdod, Shiqma, Notera, and Mazal.[7] The oil crisis in 1973 drove the Israeli government to make further efforts to find oil and gas close to its territory.

Israel discovered and developed the Sadot/Raad onshore gas field and Alma oil fields in the Gulf of Suez in 1975 and 1977, respectively, during its 12-year occupation of the Sinai Peninsula from 1967–1979.[8] However, under the Sinai disengagement agreement, Israel relinquished the petroleum fields, with an estimated total investment worth $5 billion worth of investment, to the Egyptian government.[9] The real breakthrough in the discovery of indigenous petroleum resource came in the years 1999–2000, when Israel discovered two commercially viable natural gas reserves in the Eastern Mediterranean economic waters. Over the past two decades, significant amounts of natural gas have been found in Israel's EEZ, a real breakthrough for a country, which has had negligible energy resources of its own.

In the early 1990s, the Israeli government introduced structural changes to expedite of oil and gas E&P, including deregulation of the market and privatisation of the state-owned energy companies. Intending to attract foreign investment and technology into E&P, the government eased the terms of the exploration licenses and promised extensive tax benefits.[10] Yet, few internationally known oil and gas companies evinced interest owing to concerns that business with Israel would damage their prospects in the Arab world. Texas-based Samedan, now Noble Energy, was a notable exception. With no exposure to the Arab markets, it entered Israeli E&P in 1998, in partnership with private Israeli companies.[11]

Commercially viable discoveries: Yam Tethys gas fields

In June 1999, Yam Tethys – a partnership comprised of Noble Energy and Delek Group[12] – discovered the Noa field, Israel's first commercially extractable natural gas reserve containing about 1.2 bcm of gas. A few months later in February 2000, the Noble-Delek consortium found an estimated 25 bcm of gas in the Mari-B lease; its satellite reservoir Pinnacles was discovered in 2012. Located 25km off the coastal towns of Ashdod and Ashkelon, the Yam Tethys fields – Noa and Mari-B – marked the beginning of a new era in the Israel's energy supply. Natural gas increasingly became the preferred source of energy for electricity generation and for use in the large industries.

Gaza marine field

Simultaneously, the Palestinian National Authority (PNA) awarded the BG-led consortium that included CCC[13] and the PIF[14] a 25-year exploration license for the entire maritime area off the Gaza Strip. Awarded in 1999, the license provided BG the right to explore the area for gas, develop those gas reserves, and build the necessary infrastructure to bring gas onshore.[15] In the following year, the consortium discovered the Gaza Marine gas field 30km offshore Gaza.

BG drilled two wells named Gaza Marine-1 and Gaza Marine-2, leading to the discovery of the field. Based on these drilling results, BG conducted a developmental survey for the field in 2001, which established its technical and economic feasibility.[16] Estimated to contain 28 bcm of gas, Gaza Marine is mired in the Palestinian – Israeli conflict and still awaits development.

Tamar, Leviathan, and other discoveries

The Yam Tethys breakthrough and the local natural gas market that ensued from it, injected dynamism in the exploration activities, paving the way for small and large deep-water discoveries that followed a decade later. Beginning in 2009, a series of additional discoveries in the Eastern Mediterranean, this time off the northern coast, sharply increased Israel's natural gas reserves.

Noble Energy-led consortium comprising Isramco Negev 2, Delek Drilling, Avner Oil Exploration, and Dor Gas Exploration ('Tamar Partnership')[17] discovered the Tamar field in January 2009, some 90 km west of the port of Haifa. With a recoverable reserve of about 281 bcm of gas and about 13 million barrels of condensate, Tamar was the biggest gas find in the Levant Basin at the time of its discovery. In 2013, another 26 bcm of gas and 2 million barrels of condensate were discovered at Tamar South West, bringing the combined total proved and probable reserves in the reservoir (2P)[18] reserves available from Tamar and Tamar SW to approximately 307 bcm.[19]

According to the updated report of the Tamar partners as of July 2017, the volume of 2P, including Tamar SW, is about 318 bcm of natural gas and about 14.6 million barrels of condensate, up 13 percent of what was initially estimated.[20] Tamar is a world-class reservoir containing high quality dry gas. Production from Tamar has seen consistent increase, from 7.5 bcm in 2014, to 8.3 bcm in 2015, to 9.3 bcm in 2016, and to 9.7 bcm in 2017.[21]

Noble-Delek consortium's discovery of a natural gas reservoir at the Dalit drill site off the coast of Hadera in March 2009 added an estimated 14.2 bcm contingent and prospective resources to the total gas reserve.[22] The partnership's string of success continued as it announced the discovery of Leviathan in June 2010, 50 km to the west of Tamar and located at comparable depth of 5 km below sea level. With 2P and 2C[23] contingent resources totalling 606 bcm of natural gas and almost 40 million barrels of condensate, Leviathan contains about two-thirds of all the gas resources discovered off the coast of Israel.[24] An appropriate name for a humongous reservoir, Leviathan is one of the world's largest deep-water natural gas reserves.

In February 2012, Noble-Delek announced its sixth offshore discovery at the deep-water Tanin field located about 20 km north of Tamar, which holds about 22.3 bcm of gas and 4.1 million barrels of liquids of 2C contingent resources. The Karish discovery in May 2013, north of Tanin and approximately 30 km northeast of the Tamar, with 2C contingent resource size over 46.2 bcm and 28.7 million barrels of condensate, was also the seventh consecutive field discovery for Noble Energy and its partners.[25] The Karish and Tanin fields are approximately 40 km apart and located in the north of Israel's EEZ at depths exceeding 1.7 km. Noble and Delek have since sold off their entire stakes in Tanin and Karish pursuant to their agreement with the government to reduce their cross-holdings in Israel's natural gas fields, which gave them a monopolistic status in the gas market.

Israel's offshore gas potential continued to grow as a group of Norwegian and Israeli drillers[26] made a discovery within the Aphrodite-2 exploration well in December 2012 in the Ishai license block, 160 km northwest of Haifa. Drilling at Aphrodite-2, which is adjacent to Aphrodite (discovered towards the end of 2011 by Noble energy in block 12 license, at the edge of the Cypriot's EEZ with Israel) and Leviathan, yielded an estimated reserve of 7–10 bcm of 2C resources.[27] Gas in the Aphrodite-2 well is believed to be part of one continuous geological stratum with Cyprus' Aphrodite field.[28] The discovery of Shimson deposit in 2012,[29] with further appraisal work carried out in 2015, revealed 5 bcm of 2C contingent resources at the best estimate.[30]

Data from Israel's MoE show that Israel's natural gas supply, including reserves, contingent, and prospective,[31] could be as high as 1,480 bcm (for discovered gas fields and their size, see Table 2.1 and Figure 2.1).[32]

Institutional and legal mechanisms

To develop its natural gas resources, Israel has established a sound institutional and legal structure for the development of its gas sector. Oil and natural gas exploration, development, and production in Israel are subject to a multi-layered and wide-ranging regulations. Midstream sector, such as the establishment of the infrastructure to transport and distribute gas, is also under the purview of well-formulated rules and regulations. The allied areas, namely, royalties, taxation, environmental regulation, and antitrust issues are also part of the comprehensive institutional and regulatory framework.

Petroleum Law and Natural Gas Law

Petroleum sector in Israel is regulated by way of two primary laws: the Petroleum Law, including the Petroleum Regulations, 1953, and the Gas Law. The

TABLE 2.1 Israel's natural gas fields

Field	Year of discovery	Resources (bcm)	Remaining reserves (bcm)	Water depth (metre)	Category	First gas/ status	Operator
Noa	1999	1.3	Produced	790	2P	2004/Depleted	Noble Energy
Mari-B	2000	25	<3	235	2P	2004/Depleted	Noble
Tamar and Tamar Southwest	2009	318	275	1700	2P	2013/Producing	Noble Energy
Dalit	2009	14.2	14.2	1,380	2C	Not developed	Noble Energy
Leviathan	2010	606	606	1,650	2P and 2C	Under Development	Noble Energy
Tanin	2011	22.3	22.3	1,750	2C	Not developed	Energean
Karish	2013	46.2	46.2	1,750	2C	Under Development	Energean
Shimshon	2012	5	5	1,100	2C	Under Development	AGR/Isramco
Ishai	2012	7–10	7–10	1700 m	2C	Not developed	Petroleum Services Holdings (PSH) AS

Source: Author's table; figures from Delek Drilling, Energean, Israel Opportunity Energy Resources, and BDO Analysis

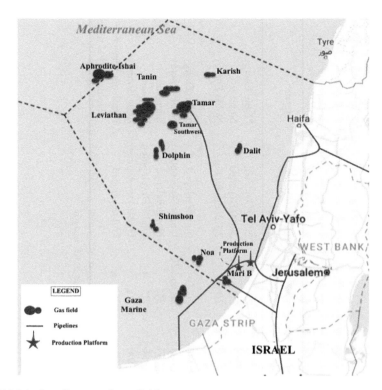

FIGURE 2.1 Israel's natural gas fields

Source: Author's figure; referenced from Ministry of Energy, State of Israel, 2018.

Disclaimer: Map not to scale

Petroleum Law and the Petroleum Regulations provide a broad regulatory framework for licensing, exploration, and production of oil and gas, both onshore and offshore.

Under the Petroleum Law, oil and gas resources are the property of the State, whether or not located on state lands. All petroleum resources in Israel and its continental shelf belong to the state. No person is allowed to explore for or produce petroleum without receiving a right under the Petroleum Law. Through a competitive bidding process, executed by the Ministry of National Infrastructures, a private company can acquire the right to explore and produce oil and gas. As per the Petroleum Law, a Petroleum Commissioner appointed by the MoE presides over upstream oil and gas activities in conjunction with the Petroleum Council, comprising 15 members with at least seven representing the public. According to the Article 82 of the Petroleum Law, the Ministry of Energy is authorised to formulate rules and regulations on matters relating to its implementation, including safety and environmental aspects.

The regulatory supervision on petroleum E&P begins with an application under the licensing system specified in the Petroleum Law and includes the following stages: a) the permit stage, which provides rights for preliminary exploration for up to 18 months; b) the license stage, which provided exclusive right to conduct petroleum surveys and test or development drilling for up to three years (with a possible annual extension of up to a further three years); and c) the lease stage, which provides the exclusive right to explore and produce. The lease is initially granted for 30 years with the possibility of renewal for an additional term of 20 years. Notably, the leaseholder is obliged to begin commercial production within three years of the grant of the lease.

The Gas Law, as the companion regulation governing the midstream and downstream activities in the petroleum sector, includes a licensing system aimed at encouraging competition in natural gas infrastructure, including distribution, transmission, storage, and LNG facilities. It establishes a regulatory body, the NGA. In particular, it is involved in "licensing and supervision of natural gas licensees, establishing tariffs and criteria for the provision of services, arbitrating disputes and defining arrangements between the players in the market, and investigating consumer complaints against licensees."[33] Although endowed with a separate budget, the Director of the NGA retains his position at the pleasure of the Minister of National Infrastructure, which, many believe, compromises the autonomy of the Authority vis-à-vis regulation and supervision.

For the purpose of distribution of natural gas from the receiving stations located in Ashdod and Ashkelon (two port cities on Israel's coast in the southwest), the INGL or Natgaz has received a license from the Ministry of Energy in 2004 for a period of 30 years to build and operate the natural gas transmission system. INGL is subject to the decisions of the NGA. Through a network of 600 km of pipelines that wind around the country, the Natgaz supplies high-pressure gas to major consumers, such as electric power consumers, large industrial plants, and to six private companies that have been granted the regional distribution license each.[34] Thus, while the gas distribution network for the biggest users has been developed as a state-run project, the government has let the market forces decide if and when to develop a network for small users.

Natural gas produced at the Tamar field (from the five subsea wells) flows through the longest subsea tieback[35] in the world for about 150 km to a platform installed 1.5 km north the Mari-B platform. The Tamar platform is tied into the existing pipeline, the one that delivered gas from Mari-B to the onshore reception station in Ashdod. From the reception station, the gas is pumped at high pressure through wide pipes, built and maintained by IGNL, that make up the national transmission system. The offshore pipeline that runs from Ashdod to Dor serves as a main artery for the flow of gas to IEC's Reading and Orot Rabin power stations. An 8.5 km INGL-built marine pipeline connection from the buoy-based LNG receiving terminal links up with the with the Ashdod-Dor pipeline in Hadera.

Antitrust institution and legislations

Another regulatory institution affecting the country's natural gas sector is the Israel Antitrust Authority (IAA) that operates according to two sets of laws: These are the Restrictive Trade Practices Law, 5748–1988 (the Antitrust Law), and Promotion of Competition and Reduction of Concentration Law, 5774–2013 (the Anti-Concentration Law).

The Antitrust Law provides the legal grounds upon which the Antitrust Commissioner (ATC/Director General) of the IAA regulates restrictive arrangements, merger transactions, monopolies, and concentration groups.[36] In particular, "the law prohibits a monopolist from using its position to reduce competition or harm the public, inter alia, through setting exorbitant prices, engaging in predatory pricing, engaging in price discrimination, or stipulating unreasonable terms."[37] The Authority also responds to monopolist behaviour that block, drive out, or harm competing suppliers from the market.[38] It has the power to make policy recommendations and can advise the Attorney General to pursue criminal proceedings in cases of antitrust violations. All these recommendations and directions can be dismissed by an Israeli court of law.

The Anti-Concentration Law is perhaps the most significant economic policy measures taken by the Israeli government to effect changes in its corporate law with the purpose of reducing economy-wide concentration and promoting competition in various sectors of the economy. The law "requires investors deemed to be overly concentrated in the Israeli market to sell or take other actions regarding prime assets. By the same token, these investors may also be restricted from acquiring further Israeli assets."[39]

Following the persistent reporting by *TheMarker*[40] on the concentration of economic power in few hands and its effect on competitiveness, production, pricing, and income inequality, Prime Minister Benjamin Netanyahu instituted a committee to suggest ways to increase competition in the economy.[41] The Concentration Committee,[42] headed jointly by the director general of the Finance Ministry, Haim Shani, and the director general of the Prime Minister's Office, Eyal Gabai, set up on 24 October 2011, handed over the final recommendations to the government in February 2012.

The committee's work took a dramatic turn and accelerated considerably following the wave of social justice protests that swept Israel during the summer of 2011 directed towards the high cost of living attributed to limited competition and weak antitrust regulation. In its interim report,[43] released on 11 October 2011, the committee arrived at the conclusion that the Israeli economy is highly concentrated, both in the real and financial sectors; that a few holding groups control a number of public companies mainly through the use of a pyramidal holding structure; and that this structure creates an outcome where they are competitors, suppliers, and customers of each other. As an outcome of this ownership structure, a large share of economic activity in Israel is controlled by a relatively small number of capitalists.[44]

The committee's recommendations were adopted by the Israeli government and included in the Anti-Concentration Law more than a year later in December 2013, which dealt with three areas: that considerations relating to market centralisation and sectorial competitiveness be taken into account in the allocation of public assets (e.g., concessions and licenses granted by the government in the areas of telecommunications, natural gas exploration, etc.) and in transferring significant amounts of governmental holdings to non-state entities (e.g., by privatisation); a prohibition on multi-layered corporate holding structures; and the separation between financial and non-financial assets.[45] The law is especially important in public tenders for exploration of oil and gas resources.

Evolution of gas regulations: the Sheshinski Committee

As Israel exulted at the discovery of natural gas in its economic waters and high project value of the reserves, it simultaneously came to light that the nation's tax system pertaining to oil and gas industry was extremely lenient by international standards, and the government take[46] in natural resources was much smaller than many developed countries. Israel did not have a set of rules suitable for the level of discoveries in its economic waters since 2000, a fact highlighted regularly by the media in the wake of the Tamar and Leviathan discoveries, fields large enough to fulfil Israel's dream of energy self-sufficiency and even turn the country into a gas exporter.

In this scenario, the gas field developers – who had acquired licenses for E&P in the early 1990s when Israel's petroleum resources were few and far between – wanted to keep operating under the generous terms of their permits, which included numerous tax benefits and unrestricted export opportunity. However, in view of the scale of the natural gas finds in Tamar and Leviathan, the Israeli public demanded that the state exercising its sovereign rights over natural gas resource and claim a larger share in the massive profits that would accrue to the investors from the development of these two gas fields. They also demanded that the government should gurantee them long-term security of energy supply before the allocation of an export quota to the developers.

With public interest sufficiently aroused, social activists who founded an NGO, Forum for Civil Action, supported by the opposition lawmakers in the Labour Party, advocated that the government should raise the taxes to an appropriate level so that the people of Israel as a whole could benefit from the discovery of the gas deposits. After all, gas being a public resource, enjoined the state to collect more proceeds from its profitable development on behalf of the citizens, just like any other petroleum-rich country. The gas developers, however, supported by some right-wing Knesset members, opposed these demands on two counts – 'risk' and 'retroactivity.'

First, the gas companies argued that they had invested millions of dollars in exploratory drilling, an inherently high-risk venture, believing that the taxes would remain low. Indeed, the gas developers argued that, among other things, low taxation (and the possibility of higher profit) served as an incentive for undertaking the risk of oil and gas exploration.[47] Second, they contended that the government should not be allowed to make retroactive changes to the laws that existed at the time when they decided to take the plunge to drill for gas in Israel's economic waters. The developers' argument rested on the reasoning that they made a certain cost-benefit evaluation on the basis of the existing tax rate and invested accordingly while there was no guarantee of finding oil or gas.

As the public debate on taxation of gas companies descended into accusations and counter-accusations by rival camps, Finance Minister Yuval Steinitz weighed the public mood and seized upon the opportunity to reform the oil and gas fiscal and taxation regime to reflect the new reality of gas discoveries and to bring it up-to-date with prevailing international practices. On 12 April 2010, the Committee to Examine the Policy on Oil and Gas Resources in Israel was convened by the Ministry of Finance (MoF). Popularly known as the 'Sheshinski Committee,' it was headed by Eytan Sheshinski, a well-known economist at the Hebrew University of Jerusalem.

In the letter of appointment, the Minister of Finance tasked the committee members with the responsibility to examine the fiscal system in practice relating to oil and gas resources (taxation, royalties, and fees) in order. The committee was asked to determine whether the existent system framed in 1952 could still be relevant and appropriate in view of the significant discoveries of gas in Israel's maritime zone over the past one decade.[48]

More specifically, it set out the committee's assignments as:

a)   To examine Israel's extant fiscal system with regard to petroleum reserves in its entirety and to compare it to countries with similar macroeconomic and democratic characteristics, keeping in mind the economic and geopolitical conditions unique to Israel.
b)   To propose an informed fiscal policy that addresses the current status of Israel as a gas producer, as well as address the various licensing and discovery phases of the reserve areas in progress at the time of the establishment of this Committee.
c)   To examine the implications of current and future discoveries for the Israeli economy.[49]

The committee comprised of another seven members that included five senior government officials and two observers from the legal and banking sectors.[50] Its working mode involved an 'open door' policy, receiving positions of the public in writing as well as economic and legal opinions from groups and organisations that requested to present their views in committee hearings, including the oil and gas developers.[51] The committee's hearings were a unique way of channelling public opinion on the subject.

Not content with simply the domestic views on a matter as critical as fiscal policy for the burgeoning petroleum sector in Israel, the Sheshinski Committee sought professional opinions from two prominent experts, Daniel Johnson and Robert S. Pindyck, Professor of Economics and Finance at the Sloan School of Management, Massachusetts Institute of Technology, US. Once the interim recommendations were published in November 2010 on the website of the MoF, the committee invited the interested parties to present their opinions on the draft proposal. After receiving the public's positions in writing as well as oral comments, the committee re-examined its draft and submitted its final recommendations to the finance minister on 3 January 2011.

During the 11-month duration of its existence, the committee weathered enormous pressures from various quarters. The companies that stood to profit from gas extraction lobbied the committee and intensified their argument against any increase of the gas royalties – even US officials reportedly complained to their Israeli counterparts about hurting Noble Energy's income.[52] On the other hand, social and environmental groups demanded that the wealth generated from Israel's only major natural resource should be used to help the poor and strengthen social programmes. Therefore, the government should collect more taxes from the gas developers on behalf of the people.

The Sheshinski Committee was subject to a sustained pressure campaign to prevent changes in the extant taxes paid by the gas companies to the state. Attempts were made to delegitimise the committee, particularly its chairman, citing his conflict of interest based on his wife's volunteer role at the New Israel Fund, an organisation often accused by its detractors of promoting a socialistic agenda. A vilification campaign accused Sheshinski of supporting 'Arab gas,' meaning a raised tax regime would drive away investors, thus reinforcing Israel's dependence on gas imported from Egypt.[53] Sheshinski even received anonymous threats threatening him of dire consequences if the committee did not amend its recommendations.[54]

The Sheshinski Committee grappled with two fundamental questions: First, what should be the mechanism for distribution of profits from gas sales? Second, how can the gas industry, run by private companies, have enough incentive to develop the known reserves and invest in further exploration and drilling? To resolve these questions, the committee remained true to its letter of appointment. It studied the best practices in oil and gas E&P markets in countries with similar macroeconomic and democratic characteristics to that of Israel and then thoroughly examined the fiscal system in Israel for the gas industry, along with corresponding financial tools and systems around the world.

In its review of the existing fiscal regime for petroleum industry in Israel, the committee underlined its inherent incompatibility with emerging circumstances. An estimate of the economic value of the tax benefits involved in fiscal system – which is essentially composed of royalties under the Petroleum Law and taxation under the Income Tax Regulations (Deductions from Income of Oil Rights Holders) 1961 – led the committee to believe that the extant system did not reflect the public's ownership of the natural resources in an accurate manner and was actually regressive, implying that as the project got more profitable, the state's share of profit became smaller. In saying this, the committee was referring to the 'depletion allowance' or 'depletion deduction' in the Income Tax Regulations, which allowed the developers to reduce their taxable income significantly.

The depletion allowance was meant to reflect the exhaustion of the resource and thus a decrease in the value of the asset. Since there has been no payment for the resource in the deposit in the first place and the state owned the depleting asset, it was a subsidy given to the industry through tax benefit. Therefore, the Sheshinski Committee pointed out that the depletion allowance had no economic justification and was inconsistent with international practice, where the oil and gas resources are public properties.

While the resource tax regime imposed a 12.5 percent royalty on petroleum revenues, for income tax purposes, the system allowed the taxpayer to deduct a depletion allowance from profits – amounting to 27.5 percent of revenues but no more than 50 percent of profits. In other words, the state and the public received almost no benefit in the form of remuneration for the ownership of the oil and gas resources, as royalty and depletion allowance largely balanced each other out. The Sheshinski Committee, therefore, pointed out that the depletion allowance had no economic justification. Its abolition, the committee deemed, was the first and essential component towards creating a reasonable fiscal system in the E&P industry in Israel. Where oil and gas resources are public properties, such a reform, in the committee's opinion, was consistent with international practice.

Other key aspects of the reforms proposed by the Sheshinski Committee included the following:[55]

a) Tax royalty rates left unchanged: The committee decided to leave the 12.5 percent rate of the royalty established in the Petroleum law unchanged because it was similar to that of other countries around the world. Royalties, the members of the committee noted, are not the primary fiscal tools used to obtain remuneration for the exploitation of their oil and gas deposits in those countries and are accompanied by complementary collection through dedicated financial tools that are unique to the industry. The committee examined the issue of raising the royalty rates but decided that it was better to implement alternative fiscal tools to increase the state's share of income. It opined that increasing the royalties would have an adverse impact on the development of less profitable fields, as well as the impact on the profitability of the deposits under variable market conditions.

b) Progressive taxation: One of the most important recommendations of the committee was the scheme for the imposition of a special tax or 'levy' ranging from 20 to 50 percent. The levy or tax on excess profit would enlarge the government take (taxes and royalties) from about one-third to two-thirds (52–62 percent) during the life of a profitable project. However, this levy would be imposed only after the developers have recovered 150 percent of the amount invested in exploration and development of the project, representing the recovery factor (R-factor) of 1.5.

The rate of the levy would start at 20 percent if the R-factor were 1.5 (recovery of 150 percent of the amount invested) and range progressively up to 50 percent when the R-factor reached 2.3 (recovery of 230 percent of the amount invested).[56] In other words, the government can collect the levy only when the developers accumulate profits in the range of 1.5 to 2.3 times their investment in E&P.[57]

The R-factor is calculated as: R-factor = Cumulative net revenues ÷ Exploration and development expenses

In the calculation of the R-factor, the following considerations would apply:

i   A greater weight is to be given to the exploration expenses in the totalling of expenses in the R-factor denominator.
ii During the development and setup period, until the commercial production of gas/oil, an annual financing cost will be added to the investment expenses in the R-factor denominator, set at the average annual LIBOR rate,[58] plus a fixed 3 percent premium. This mechanism will lead to a significant reduction in the entrepreneurs' risk if an unanticipated delay occurs during the setup period.
iii The levy would be imposed on each field separately, a practice known as ring fencing, and redirecting revenues or expenses among the deposits will not be allowed. In other words, there were will be no consolidation of taxable income.

c) Accelerated depreciation: The committee introduced an accelerated depreciation mechanism to costs accumulated during the lease stage in the development of petroleum assets at a rate of 10 percent. Separate arrangements apply to the exploration (permit and license) and production (lease) phases.[59]

d) Application of transition provisions: The committee established a gradual track for transition from the existing to proposed fiscal system. For example, the minimum R-factor for the imposition of the levy is higher for production commencing before January 2014.[60]

The following transition provisions were included:

i   Higher rate of accelerated depreciation for investments made by the end of 2013: Such investments will receive a maximum accelerated depreciation rate of 15 percent.
ii Deposits in which commercial production began before the establishment of the committee will enter the bottom of the levy track, so that the rate of the initial levy applicable to them will be the lowest rate in the first year of payment. The levy payments that will be required from such deposits will be reduced by 50 percent for any given levy, i.e., multiplied by a factor of 0.5, until the end of production of the gas that is currently in the deposit.[61]
iii In deposits where production will begin after the establishment of the committee, but no later than 1 January 2014, the levy at its minimum rate will apply only after their revenues reach double the value of the investment

(R-factor ratio of 2). The maximum rate of the levy on these deposits will apply after they come to an R-factor ratio of 2.8.[62]

The Sheshinski Committee through its recommendations concluded that the objective for reform of the fiscal system was to strike a balance between allocating appropriate remuneration to the public for the utilisation of the state's natural resources and providing sufficient incentive to those engaged in natural gas exploration. A survey conducted in January 2011 showed that a large proportion of the public (48.3 percent) supported the Sheshinski conclusions, 14.3 percent believed that the committee sided with the gas companies, and only 10.9 percent believed that the committee recommendations hurt the gas companies.[63]

The petitions, lectures, and citizen meetings organised by NGOs on the issue of taxation of gas profits, generated unprecedented public interest in the workings of the economy and tremendous outrage against the concentration of wealth in a few hands. A widespread perception that the gas companies were making huge profits at the expense of the people, permeated the subsequent disagreements in the formulation of regulations for the natural gas sector. In the backdrop of the Knesset's reading of the Sheshinski bill, a wave of strikes and demonstrations hit throughout the country. People from across the social spectrum protested the mounting cost of living and the pervasive inequality in Israeli society.[64]

Broadly supported by both the coalition and opposition members, the Knesset accepted the Sheshinski Committte recommendations on 30 March 2011, giving them a solid anchor in law. Energy Minister Uzi Landau and the other ministers from Yisrael Beiteinu, a right wing party of Netanyahu's coalition, voted against the 'Sheshinski bill.' Landau had consistently opposed the committee's findings and fought against increase of taxes on energy companies, telling that if the tax reforms were implemented, Israel's petroleum reserves will remain underground. In a letter to PM Netanyahu, he demanded an exemption for the Tamar gas discovery from the draft recommendations, warning any delay in its development on account of change in taxation rules would drive the power companies to purchase gas from alternative suppliers. While Netanyahu remained non-committal, Sheshinski did not heed to such an argument. As a consequence, two committee members of the Ministry of National Infrastructures opposed the recommendations and issued a minority report.[65]

The Oil Profits Tax Law, 2011 (later renamed the Natural Resources Profits Taxation Law),[66] largely based on the Sheshinski Committee's report, filled the legal vacuum that existed in the regulations on oil and gas. Accordingly, the owners of the gas fields became liable to a significant increase in tax on the profits than what existed when they acquired the concessions for offshore exploration.

Risk, retroactivity, and incentive

In defence of the petroleum tax reforms in Israel, many experts are of the opinion that it is inaccurate to presume oil and gas exploration is enormously risky and, therefore, that companies need high returns to remain sufficiently invested in the industry. Deep-water drilling involves sufficient risks, but most of them can be hedged or moderated "throughout project execution by selecting appropriate field development plans, risk management, and modifying project implementation methods."[67] While the odds against a single well yielding proven reserve are quite high, most of the companies down wells at multiple sites, to reduce the risk of complete failure. Noam Segal, policy director of Israel Energy Forum (IEF), believes that drilling is much less risky now than what the drilling companies construe it to be because of the innovative technology, which precisely tells the best places to drill and, hence, reduces the probability of drilling into dry wells.[68]

A related argument advanced by the companies that Israel's specific risks – terrorism and military conflict – justify higher rate of return to continue investing in the industry, is again fallacious. According to Robert Pindyck, "country-specific risks are largely diversifiable by investors through holding the stocks of companies operating in different areas of the world."[69] Managing risks is not unique to gas companies, and they face similar conditions as any other company in the world. Moreover, the government of Israel gives sovereign guarantees to gas installations against the threat of terrorism and war.

The retroactive argument of the gas companies was also misleading. Israel's laws governing royalty and taxation were created in the 1950s, as 'point of departure' regulations subject to change when petroleum reserves were discovered. Carol Nakhle, a research fellow at the Surrey Energy Economics Centre, University of Surrey, writes on the need for dynamism in the tax system in response to exogenous conditions,[70] which in the case of Israel, was not the rise in energy prices – responsible for the so-called 'retroactive tax increases' in response to externalities in many developed countries – but the discovery of two large gas reservoirs[71] (the larger, Leviathan, discovered during the committee's work).

In view of the discovery of Tamar and Leviathan, the Sheshinski Committee's consideration on the change in the tax structure to reflect "greater prospectivity revealed by recent exploration successes" is not uncommon and "is regularly tested in the oil and gas industry as host governments reappraise, with the benefit of hindsight, the risks that were taken by the investor,"[72] stresses IHS CERA[73] in a special report submitted to the committee for opinion. Similarly, David Johnston,[74] in his opinion to the Sheshinski Committee, quotes a Wood Mackenzie write-up to emphasise the logic of the increase in government take as risk decreases following the successful prospecting:

> One of the key parameters in determining the attractiveness of a country for exploration is the level of Government Take – the lower the take, the more attractive the opportunity. *A low tax rate, however, can be associated with a high risk that this will be changed in the future if windfall profits are realized.*[75]

As Friedman argues in the BoI study,[76] because of the rise in the probability of finding natural gas in Israel's economic waters accompanied by the discovery of

Tamar and Leviathan reservoirs, the high-risk – low-tax linkage was reduced and warranted a change in tax regime in view of the prospect for future windfall profits, without any real damage to oil and gas exploration. He draws attention to the fact that the issue of tax raises was considered at the beginning of the 2000s after the discovery of the Yam Tethys reservoirs, but it was finally decided in 2007 that there was no justification for increase in royalties (or taxes), as numerous drills at sea had not led to new discoveries. With the success of Tamar and Leviathan, however, there was an acceptable reason for raising the tax rate in Israel's E&P industry, as the tax rate in Israel was fairly low in international comparison. The 'retroactive' argument of the gas companies also did not hold water in view of the evolution and changes in the Israeli fiscal structure and corporate tax system during the last 60 years since the legislation of the Petroleum Law.

The complaint of the gas companies that they will not have the incentive to invest in E&P if the profits are not high enough does not measure up to the provisions of the 2011 Oil Profits Taxation Law. Behind the smokescreen of this objection is the clear fact that Sheshinski Committee tax proposals made matters better rather than worse for the gas companies. While on the one hand, the state increased its share of the profit, on the other, it became the main 'stockholder,' willing to wait for years for its share of the money and preferring that the developers recover their cost and collect revenues before giving away the dividend as taxes. Since the Sheshinski fiscal provisions taxed only 'excess profits' – a tax levied on a project only after the entrepreneurs were promised a high rate of profit from those projects – not revenues, they improved the position of the gas companies, since it apportioned a part of the risk to the government too. If the companies turned substantial profits, the government would get its tax; if they didn't, the government would bear the brunt equally.[77]

The legal challenge

Some oil and gas exploration companies and their shareholders challenged the so-called Sheshinski law.[78] Isramco, a partner in the Tamar and Shimshon fields, and Givot Olam, owner and operator of the Meged oil-field license, led the petitions, arguing that their rights in the concessions were formulated and completed prior to the establishment of the committee and hence the law would harm them retroactively. The companies added that they relied on the extant legal situation – which preceded the adoption of the new fiscal law – on which they had official assurances and, therefore, they had a legitimate expectation of stability of fiscal arrangements that preceded the changes of 2011. Another claim of the exploration companies was that the law was unconstitutional because it infringed their property rights in the holdings and appealed for the restoration of the depletion allowance.

The Supreme Court justices, headed by Vice President Miriam Naor, dismissed the petition in August 2012, stating that the new law did not apply to income generated in the past and therefore rejected the claims that it was a retroactive imposition of a tax. The judges also rejected the companies' claim on government promises that the tax regime would not change and determined that there were several opinions amongst the decision-makers, and that the mechanism adopted, which guarantees 150 percent profit, is satisfactory.

Naor ruled that taxation of future profits of the companies did not harm the assets of the companies as it did not involve changing the terms of the licenses and holdings under the Petroleum Law. The Court held that oil and gas being a public and limited resource, the government had the right to update an archaic legislation to increase its stake in oil and gas discoveries for worthy expenditures in the future. The Supreme Court judgement stated that the companies' claim of damage to property pertained to reduction in the expected value of future profits derivable from their petroleum rights and upheld the legality of the new taxation law on oil profits.

Evolution of gas regulations: the Tzemach Committee

In the background of the incredible Leviathan discovery, there arose a need to formulate a comprehensive policy for the country's gas sector. On 2 October 2011, PM Netanyahu and energy minister Uzi Landau appointed an inter-ministerial committee to formulate a comprehensive governmental policy on the natural gas industry in Israel.

Since a multi-member committee appeared more befitting than a single member committee for the purpose of formulating a policy that would affect a number of regulatory issues, the government appointed members of the Tzemach Committee – which got its name from its chairman, Shaul Tzemach, the Director General of the MoE and Water Resources – from a wide range of ministries, authorities, and offices. These included the National Economic Council (NEC)[79] in the Prime Minister's Office, MoF, Antitrust Authority, Ministry of Environmental Protection, National Security Council, Ministry of Foreign Affairs, and Attorney General's office.

The Committee aimed to achieve the following three goals as per its appointment letter:

a) To examine various models of government policies for natural gas in countries which possess similar characteristics to Israel, while taking into consideration Israel's unique geopolitical situation.
b) To examine projected supply and demand according to different scenarios and assumptions. On the supply side, to estimate both present discoveries and potential future discoveries.
c) To propose a policy for development of the natural gas sector in Israel, balancing the following goals: secure domestic supply, facilitate competition in the local gas market, leverage the environmental benefits of natural gas, and maximise economic and political gains. The committee was particularly requested to examine the mechanisms that would achieve a balance between domestic consumption and exports.[80]

As specified in its letter of appointment, the committee examined the various models of governmental policies in the natural gas sector around the globe, which displayed similar characteristics to Israel. Out of the 30 largest natural gas-producing countries in the world, 12 countries with characteristics similar to Israel were chosen with natural gas resources of a similar scale and location in order to carry out a comprehensive comparative survey. The goal was to learn from international experience and best practices in the industry around the world and, accordingly, recommend the most favourable policy in the light of Israel's need and requirement as well as its unique geopolitical situation.[81]

The Tzemach Committee followed the mode of working of Sheshinski Committee: It met over a period of several months and held a number of public hearings of interested parties and incorporated their views in the protocols of more of than 2,000 pages. The committee also sought opinions from international consulting firms. On April 5 2012, the committee published a draft of the main recommendations for public review.

In the committee's hearings, several interested parties participated, including environmental organisations, oil and gas companies, consulting companies, and major government companies, IEC and INGL. In addition to the hearings, and in light of the matter's importance, the energy ministry organised a conference on the subject to ensure that each party that desired to express its opinion had more than one opportunity to do so. After 11 months of deliberations, it submitted its final report to the government in September 2012.

The issue of gas export

Charged with the task of exploring ways to ensure long-term energy needs of the Israeli economy, one of the more extensive discussions of the committee revolved around the question whether gas field developers should be allowed to export gas and how much. Until the appointment of the committee, there were no restrictions on the amount of gas that developers could export to foreign buyers. They were free to decide how much they wanted to export and to whom depending on the commercial agreements. Following heightened public awareness over gas issues and persistent campaign by several NGOs calling for a total ban on gas exports – in order to ensure long-term availability of the environment-friendly fuel for the Israeli market – the government decided to entrust the committee to suggest a mechanism to reconcile the domestic requirements with export option.

The Tzemach Committee decided to let the gas producers ship from Israel's existing and prospective gas resources, based on the understanding that if the producers did not invest the millions of dollars required for developing the gas fields, the resource buried under the sea was worth nothing. Accordingly, the committee found the developers' demand for export – to raise the capital necessary for further exploration and development of Israel's gas resources for the benefit state and its citizens – within reasonable limit: "In the economy in which the volume of domestic demand is limited, without granting owners the rights in the gas fields for the monetization of part of the gas, there will be no research and development activities in the coming years as required."[82] The committee noted that:

> The possibility of exporting gas does not mean that all gas supplied will be exported immediately. It should be emphasized that the committee recommends that exports be permitted only from fields that received possession. That is, exports will be possible only if gas is found in the appropriate quantities, or, in other words, permitting export depends on the supply of gas (and not the potential) in the economy and at a limited rate for each field.[83]

If the government were to prohibit export of gas, the committee was of the opinion that it would hinder advancements required in Israel's gas sector. In other words, the need for export arose from the fact that local market was not big enough to absorb all the gas, and, since private companies were solely developing the upstream industry, there was the important element of profit considerations, says Ron Adam.[84] At the same time, the committee also acknowledged the importance of ensuring supply to the domestic market as a top priority and set out four basic elements:

a) Fields will be required to supply a certain percentage of natural gas for the benefit of the local economy.
b) Each producing field will be required to connect to the local economy at the specified time and volume.
c) Consumers in the Israeli economy will have priority to purchase natural gas from fields under Israeli control.
d) Specific conditions will be set for common fields for Israel and its neighbours under individual arrangements.[85]

The Tzemach Committee, while accepting the figures of the NEC that the total gas discoveries (including contingent and prospective) could reach as high as 1,480 bcm, decided to base its policy recommendations on a smaller volume of 950 bcm (Table 2.2). It was of the opinion that given the volume of domestic demand, it would be reasonable to guarantee supply security for the next 25 years.[86] Taking into consideration the existing demand of the economy and gas utilization scenarios in the future, the committee decided to allocate 450 bcm for domestic consumption and 500 bcm for export from all natural gas fields until 2040. Export of gas, the committee suggested, should be through licensing and determination of an export quota for each field.[87]

TABLE 2.2 The Tzemach Committee: natural gas reserves/resources and projected demand

Natural gas supply	bcm
Prospective resources are known today	Approx. 680
Of these, prospective resources with over 90 percent probability	Approx. 150
Reserves and contingent resources	Approx. 800
Total natural gas supply (reserves, contingent resources and prospective resources)	Approx. 1,480
Total natural gas supply to set policy	Approx. 950
Cumulative demand for natural gas for 25 years	Approx. 450
Maximum quantity allowed for export	500

Source: Full Report of the Tzemach Committee, p. 93

TABLE 2.3 Supply to the domestic market of the total volume in the field

Volume of natural gas in the field*	Minimum domestic market obligation (DMO)
More than 200 bcm (inclusive)	50 percent of this quantity
100–200 bcm	40 percent of this quantity
25–100 bcm	25 percent of this quantity
Less than 25 bcm	To be fixed by the Petroleum Commissioner

Source: Full report of the Tzemach Committee, pp. 9 and 95

*Determination of field scope is based on 2P reserves

In general, all fields would have to abide by the minimum supply requirement for the local economy, i.e., their domestic market obligations (DMO) (Table 2.3):

a) If the volume of the field is greater than or equal to 200 bcm, DMO will be 50 percent of the volume.
b) If the volume of the field is greater than or equal to 100 bcm, but lower than 200 bcm, DMO will be 40 percent of the volume.
c) If the volume of the field is greater than or equal to 25 bcm, but lower than 100 bcm, DMO will be 25 percent of the volume.
d) Fields whose volume is less than 25 bcm will have a DMO, but not a specified volume.[88]

While maintaining a priority supply to the domestic economy for an optimal period of time, the Tzemach Committee recommended a policy that provided the gas field developers "freedom to choose whether to sell any surplus natural gas (above and beyond local demand) for other industrial or commercial uses, or to export it,"[89] and to enlarge "the benefits of Israel's natural gas potential for the society as a whole, particularly because natural gas is a public resource."[90] It being so, it was argued in the hearings of the committee that selling gas abroad would enhance Israel political weight and strategic leverage, especially with Arab neighbours, who could enter into long-term gas trading relationship with Israel. According to the committee, the natural gas policy must join the needs of the local energy industry with political objectives of the state.

Those who argued in support of gas export also emphasised the fact that there has not been a single episode in Israel's history when there had been a shortage of energy supply to the economy. "Even if the gas ran out in a few decades, Israel as an innovative nation would develop alternative sources to fuel the economy's needs. To let gas buried in the ground served no purpose."[91]

Tzemach committee recommendations and its critics

The changes proposed by the Tzemach Committee were met with strong disagreement and criticism from opposition lawmakers in the Knesset. Joined by environmental groups and professional organisations, such as the IEF, Adam Teva V'Din (Israel Union for Environmental Defence), and the Movement for Quality Government, they argued for the need to reserve gas for the Israel's growing needs and for the benefit of future generations. They claimed that the Tzemach Committee appeared to be overwhelmed by the companies' warning that a ban on export would deter the development of Leviathan and other reservoirs and hence unduly favoured the developers at the expense of people's interest. The oppositionists asserted that gas being a public resource should primarily benefit the domestic economy by lowering prices, reducing pollution, and strengthening country's growing energy independence.

The recommendations of the Tzemach Committee were also subject to scrutiny on two other counts: First, the purely speculative assumption of the gas reserves and, secondly, the conservative estimate of consumption or gas usage in the 25-year optimal period. The committee's assumption of 950 bcm in the total natural gas supply for setting policy included contingent and prospective resources. If the contingent and prospective reserves do not materialise, then the reserve base is much narrower and the gas available for domestic use shrinks. In that light, critics pointed out the error of using unavailable resources for allocating the domestic and export quota.[92]

When the committee published its interim report, environmental protection ministry's director general Alona Sheafer-Caro, a member of the committee, sent the minority opinion to committee chairman. Strongly opposing the conclusions of the draft report, Sheafer-Caro argued that the conclusions of the Tzemach Committee were based on overestimating the country's gas production potential and underestimating Israel's future demand for gas.[93] The minority opinion noted, "allowing such a large amount of gas to be exported, based not on facts, but on unreliable forecasts of future discoveries of resources, exhibits a lack of national responsibility."[94] Shaffer-Caro emphasised that the committee's draft ignored the findings of an internal report of the Ministry of Energy, which drew the attention of the committee members to the potentially much higher demand for gas in Israel and the need to ensure the energy security of the nation.

In a report authored by Sinai Netanyahu and Shlomo Wald, the chief scientists at the MoE, and submitted to the Tzemach Committee in March 2012 stated there was a gap of 100 to 150 bcm between the demand projection presented to the committee by NGA and assessments carried out in the calculation of up to 2040 in their report. In the opinion of Netanyahu and Wald, "the State of Israel must improve and develop the capabilities of the Israeli economy to switch to large-scale use of natural gas by 2020 and should not export gas."[95] The source of the gap, they asserted, was their recognition of the future demand for natural in transportation and establishment of industries using use natural gas (ammonia production, natural gas for gas-to-liquid plants, or plants using methanol as fuel substitute).[96]

The report stated that by 2040, Israel would require around of gas 600 bcm and consumption beyond that year would be in the order of about 40 bcm per year.[97] At this rate, Israel would exhaust all known and prospective reserves by the mid-2055, even if there were no export. Notwithstanding the improvement in energy efficiency, demand will not go down in absolute terms; indeed, the gas reserves were expected to last even less than 40 years.[98] That was true even when mitigating factors such as the existence of 'trapped gas,' the impossibility of extracting gas from the reservoirs due to the exhaustion of the flow, and the inevitable operational damage to the reservoirs, were not included.[99]

Netanyahu and Wald were also not persuaded by the committee's postulation that export would be necessary to give gas companies the necessary financial reinforcement for their operations. "If proven that financing the development of the gas sources by the entrepreneurs constitutes an economic risk for them," the two scientists recommended that the "state should consider the possibility of purchasing gas from entrepreneurs to avoid losing this strategic resource – an informed risk premium that Israel should consider paying."[100] Moreover,

> even if all the potential gas reserves within Israel's exclusive waters are discovered, Israel will never be a global player in the gas arena. A minimal level of modesty is required to understand that there are 44,000 bcm of proven reserves in Russia, while Iran, Algeria, Qatar, and Egypt have tens of thousands of bcm of proven gas reserves and the United States has massive quantities of shale gas. Israel is thus a marginal player.[101]

They also rejected the contention that exporting gas would give Israel a diplomatic advantage or secure Israel's geopolitical stature:

Gas exports require billions of shekels of investment in the construction of an export facility that will require providing export approval on a large scale. Such exports would bring Israel back in 30 years to total dependence on the import of energy sources. Promotion of political interests by managing the gas sector can only be in the local area of Cyprus, Jordan, and the Palestinian Authority. This area deserves consideration from the fact that Israel is a minor gas player.[102]

Neither would export of gas bring down gas prices in the domestic market, say Netanyahu and Wald as "gas exports will cause an increase in gas prices in Israel since producers will have another channel to market that will set the threshold."[103]

Sinaia Netanyahu, at a meeting of the Economic Affairs Committee of the Knesset, reiterated her argument that the Tzemach Committee's interim report lacked clarity on the speed of development of the demand for industry and transportation. She believed that the government did not have a serious report that examined the requirements of industries that use gas as a raw material.[104] Then-environmental protection minister Amir Peretz, opposed the of the Tzemach Committee recommendations, stating rather accurately that Israel was not a gas empire to allow such a large export of gas. He argued if the committee had looked into the use of gas in transportation, not only for public vehicles but also private cars – one of the most polluting sectors in Israel – more rigorously, the gas allocation for domestic use would have turned out much higher.[105]

Ehud Keinan, a professor at the Technion, Haifa, and president of the Israel Chemical Society, reaffirmed the conclusions of scientists Netanyahu and Wald in an affidavit to the Supreme Court. He believed that "the added value gained from building and enlarging Israel's chemical industry based on natural gas would be far more extensive and significantly outweigh taxes proceeds received from exporting the gas."[106] In addition, Sinaia Netanyahu told the Economics Affairs Committee (EAC) of the Knesset in a hearing that the government did not have a serious report that examined the requirements of industries that use gas as raw material or feeder.[107]

Adoption of the recommendations and the court challenge

Given the opposition to the notion of gas export, the government through Decision No. 442 of 23 June 2013, adopted a plan (on the subject of "Adopting the main recommendations of the Committee for the Examination of the Government Policy in the Area of the Natural Gas Economy in Israel, the Tzemach Committee Report") that increased gas allocation for domestic use to 540 bcm 20 percent more than the recommendations of the Tzemach Committee, based on 29 years of projected needs of the economy from the date of the decision (the committee referred to a period of 25 years) (Table 2.4).[108] Despite a formal appeal by half the Knesset members to bring the decision to a vote, the government refused fearing a defeat on the floor of the House.

In the wake of the government decision, several Knesset members, were joined by environmental groups, petitioned the Supreme Court, arguing that no export of natural gas should be allowed and that it should all be reserved for domestic consumption and for the use of the future generation of Israelis. The main legal argument of the petitioners was that the Cabinet lacked the authority to decide on a matter as critical and with wide-ranging implications for the economy and environment.

That being so, the petitioners, inter alia, requested the court to revoke the government's decision and called for an absolute anchoring of the recommendations of the committee on natural gas policy through the Knesset's primary legislation. Their argument was based on the "non-delegation doctrine" whereby the designation of the volume of natural gas exports constituted a "preliminary/primary arrangement" that cannot be delegated to the executive and should be determined by the legislator.

On 21 October 2013, a panel of seven judges in the Supreme Court, sitting as the High Court of Justice, decided by a 5–2 majority opinion to reject the petition on the basis that non-delegation of primary arrangement could not be ascertained in the present case. It is pertinent to note here that in Israel's constitutional law there are different and contradictory positions on the rule prohibiting Knesset from delegating the power to establish primary arrangements to the executive branch.

Judge Asher Grunis, the President of the Supreme Court, who wrote the majority opinion, expressed the prevailing position that the non-delegation doctrine is an "interpretative presumption" which can be contradicted. The presumption here is, legislature cannot delegate the authority to determine primary legislation to the executive branch, but can only authorise its implementation, according to the basic criteria defined by the legislator. It implies, "the issue of all the primary arrangements is the extent of the discretion that Knesset has left

TABLE 2.4 Gas export proposed by the Tzemach Committee and Government's decision

	Tzemach Committee's recommendations, August 2012		Government's decision, No. 442, June 2013	
	Bcm	% of gas	bcm	% of gas
Domestic use	450	47.4	540	56.8
Balance for export	500	52.6	410	43.2
Total potential reserve for setting policy	950	100	950	100

Source: Author

in the hands of the executive."[109] However, where it is found that arrangements established by the executive branch violated Basic Laws on human rights or "hard core issues," the non-delegation rule and requirement of authorisation by Knesset would be more strictly applied, than in the event of absence of such violation. In the latter case, then, "the terms of the authorization can be examined in a more lenient manner."[110]

In the case, the petitioners argued there was indeed a violation of human rights because the government's decision harms the rights of future generations of Israelis, who may not be able to enjoy a cheap and clean source of energy due to export-induced deprivation of natural gas and, therefore, government's decision is a primary arrangement. Their argument was dismissed by the majority opinion on the ground that it was not clear how the government's decision may lead to a certain and concrete violation basic human rights.[111] Further, since the gas is being extracted slowly and gradually spread over many years, there is ample scope for a future government or Knesset to change the decision to the benefit of future generations. Therefore, the matter did not qualify as a preliminary arrangement requiring explicit authorisation from the legislator.[112]

Further, the court drew attention to the fact that Knesset authorizes the Minister of Energy to determine the volume of petroleum[113] (here natural gas) a leaseholder would have to supply for the needs of the Israeli economy in the first instance, in accordance with Article 33 (a) of the Petroleum Law, 5712–1952:

> The Minister may, after consultation with the Authority, require lessees to supply first, at the market price, out of the petroleum produced by them in Israel and the petroleum products produced therefrom, such quantity of petroleum and petroleum products as, in his opinion, is required for Israeli consumption, and to refine it in Israel as far as they have refining facilities and to sell it in Israel.[114]

Judge Grunis interpreted Article 33 (a) within the context of various other regulatory provisions in the Petroleum Law, to arrive at the conclusion that it conferred broad authority on the officials in charge of its implementation: Gas being a limited resource required regulation for the purpose of the Law, which is the aggregate welfare of the economy as a whole. Further, Judge Grunis explained, even as Article 33 (a) does not contain an express authorisation for determination of an "overall policy regarding the export of natural gas, it certainly exists in the provision's implicit authority to determine such policies."[115]

In addition, the court observed that a key facet of Petroleum Law is to create an appropriate balance between public interest and developers' incentive, so as to maximise the overall welfare of the populace. In this context, the court opined it would be very difficult to legislate concrete and specific provisions in a series of primary legislations of the Knesset, and therefore it is reasonable to assume the legislative branch would delegate the authority to establish an overall policy for Israel's gas sector to the executive branch.[116]

Court's Vice-President Judge Miriam Naor stressed that in her reading, Article 34 of Petroleum Law[117] grants unrestricted right to export petroleum by contractual provisions or regulations, unless the minister under Article 33 limits this right in order to preserve the needs of the economy. In the absence of a provision on limitation on export in Article 33 and since Article 34 does not limit it, the right to export is virtually unlimited. Both the articles are intertwined and mirror images of each other – and, by that token, Article 33 limits the scope of permissibility of Article 34.[118] In order that basic principles underlying the Petroleum Law are fulfilled, such as the desire of the State of Israel to become energy independent, Article 33 constitutes a general authorisation for the formulation of a policy.

The two dissenting judges, Judge Salim Joubran and Justice Elyakim Rubinstein, were of the opinion that determining a policy on exports quota and the amount of natural gas required for the Israeli economy is a primary arrangement, requiring a primary legislation of the Knesset. According to Justice Joubran, the adoption of the Tzemach Committee's proposals by government's decision "violates the principle of public participation and transparency in the democratic process," especially as there is "fear of excessive depletion of natural gas resources belonging to the Israeli public."[119]

In the opinion of Judge Rubinstein, regulating the issue of exporting natural gas "is a first-rate primary arrangement" in view of the high public interest and ramifications for generations. Therefore, the issue "needs to be regulated by the Knesset, in an orderly legislative process."[120] In the opinion of Judges, Joubran and Rubinstein, Article 33 of the Petroleum Law does not grant express authorisation to the Minister to set rules. In order words, the provision does not delegate the authority of the Knesset to the executive. Rather, it requires the minister to implement policy determined by a legislative process in Knesset.[121]

In its decision, the court approved the volume determined for local use in Decision 442, thus:

> The government continued to decide to leave for the purposes of the economy 540 bcm of natural gas, 20 percent above the recommended quantity of the Tzemach Committee. The government decision therefore assumes that the natural gas resources, which will be saved for the benefit of the Israeli economy, will be exhausted within decades. This is not an immediate exhaustion of the resource. A future Knesset, and a future government, will be able to reconsider the issue. The government is not, therefore, the end of the story.[122]

The High Court's decision would have paved the way for the development of Leviathan gas reserve, but another controversy regarding governance of the gas industry brewed simultaneously.

The antitrust issue

Five months after assuming the charge of the Director General or ATC of the IAA, Professor David Gilo, announced in a press release on 6 September 2011[123] that Noble Energy, Delek Group, and Ratio Oil had violated antitrust laws when they joined the Ratio-Yam project, encompassing the Leviathan prospect. Ratio, which held 100 percent interest in the Ratio Yam Preliminary Permit Area, farmed-out a share of its working interests to Delek Drilling, Avner, and Noble Energy in 2007–2008. The inclusion of the Noble-Delek partnership in Ratio-Yam preliminary permit, while they held Israel's other natural gas assets, constituted a restrictive arrangement that had not received the antitrust approval. In other words, IAA saw the Noble-Delek partnership as a de facto cartel or monopoly in the upstream gas sector.

In the same press release,[124] the ATC also announced that he would soon declare Noble Energy and Delek Group as having a monopoly on natural gas supply to the Israeli market in light of their holdings in Yam Tethys. In November 2012, more than a year later and after examining the holdings in Israel's gas market, the IAA declared the Tamar partners – Delek Drilling, Avner, Noble, Isramco Negev 2 Partnership Ltd. (Isramco), and Dor Gas Exploration Ltd. Partnership (Dor) – jointly and severally, as having a monopoly in Israel's natural gas supply as of mid–April 2013 (after the onset of Tamar scheduled for March),[125] placing sale and purchase contracts of Tamar under the provisions and prohibitions of the Restrictive Trade Practices Law, 5748–1988.[126] The ATC's decision came in the backdrop of depleting Mari-B reservoir and Tamar's expected supply. Before the announcement, an investigation conducted by the antitrust authority revealed that Tamar would remain a dominant force in the Israeli gas market for at least 15 years: Until 2020, the Tamar reserve would provide for more than half of the domestic demand, and – according to the forecasts by the NGA regarding the supply of natural gas up to 2040 – Tamar was expected to provide most of Israel's domestic demand until at least till 2027.[127]

In the hearings conducted prior to the decision, the Noble-Delek partnership claimed until mid-2013 there could be no certainty that the Tamar reservoir would supply more than half of Israel's natural gas. ATC rejected this argument and held that the Tamar partnership is expected, with high probability, to provide far more than half of Israel's natural gas supply from July 2013, being the only reservoir to begin operation. Given that Tamar would remain the only supplier for the next several years, the IAA, in addition, decided to address the agreements signed between Tamar partners and IEC, IPPs, and other large industrial consumers.

The Tamar developers had already signed GSPAs that covered a high percentage of the domestic demand and were the only gas suppliers in the market, a situation that limited the ability of consumers to negotiate prices, according to IAA. That potentially put Noble-Delek partnership in a position where they could substantially influence prices. The sale of gas at a price to the consumers above the level that would result from competition could raise electricity prices, causing public harm.

Since Israel was a relatively nascent and small market for gas in 2012, with more than 85 percent consumed only by the IEC and supply restricted to Tamar alone, there was little scope for demand elasticity or supply flexibility. It is hard to see how competition could emerge in such a situation. Further, few international companies evinced interest in Israel's upstream gas sector during the almost ten year interregnum between the Yam Tethys finds and discoveries of Tamar and Leviathan, which gave the Noble-Delek partnership a default dominance. Significantly, the difficulty in raising funds and recruiting top-tier operators for deep-sea exploration in Israel still trails Israel's E&P sector.[128]

Before taking the decision to declare Tamar partners a monopoly, the anti-trust commissioner intervened in a number of gas contracts.[129] He shortened them significantly to enable natural gas consumers to enjoy the benefits of competition between Tamar and competing gas reservoirs whenever they entered the market. The Tamar partners were prohibited from worsening the commercial terms for the gas purchasers as a response to the conditions he stipulated. As the activities of Tamar partners were placed under the anti-trust provisions, the goings-on in Leviathan reservoir too were brought under the purview of the prohibitions and provisions relating to monopolies.

A series of protracted negotiations commenced between the IAA and the developers in an attempt to reach a deal that would open up the gas market to competition and save the Noble Energy and Delek Group from legal proceedings. These culminated in March 2014 in the form of the 'Antitrust Agreement,' whereby David Gilo sought to break the Noble-Delek monopoly through a sale of their cross-holdings in Israel's natural gas fields.

Under the terms of the agreement with IAA, Noble Energy and Delek Group could continue to own the rights in Tamar and Leviathan fields, provided they divested completely from two smaller gas reserves, Karish and Tanin, to a third party that should agree to sell gas from these fields only to the domestic consumers. This buyer will have the right to purchase 15.2 bcm of gas from Leviathan if the aggregate proven reserves at Karish and Tanin are less than 70 bcm. Further, Noble-Delek can market the gas from Tamar and Leviathan till early January 2020, when the ATC will reassess the competitive situation in the gas market.[130] In light of the agreement, the Australian energy company Woodside pulled out of a preliminary agreement in May 2014 to buy a quarter of Leviathan, reasoning that the sale of Israel's largest reservoir may take years, and therefore the IAA had decided to force Noble-Delek to sell some of the smaller gas fields to expeditiously resolve their monopolistic status.[131]

The Antitrust Agreement was incorporated into a draft consent decree and presented to the public for comment before its submission for approval to the

Antitrust Tribunal. After releasing the details, Gilo embarked on a lengthy process of hearings on the agreement and it seemed that the monopoly issue was on its way to a resolution. However, on 24 December 2014, the ATC rescinded on the decree and decided not to defend it in a dramatic turn of events. The likely reasoning was that the shared stakes of Noble Energy and Delek Group in Tamar (67 percent) and Leviathan (85 percent), which together constitute more than 90 percent of Israel's proven gas reserves, would not "produce a competitive environment that would solve the problem of the existence of a monopoly."[132] Gilo declared that the "entry of Delek and Noble into the Leviathan project constitutes a restraint of trade that did not receive prior approval as required by Israeli antitrust law."[133] In other words, the ATC declared Noble Energy and Delek's holdings a de facto monopoly in the gas market and recommended breaking up of their control in Israel's two largest fields.

David Gilo's ostensibly 'fickle' decision-making raised a lot of concern from various quarters. In response, Noble Energy decided to declare a freeze on its investments in upstream gas in Israel. The developers, who had already begun negotiating gas exports from Tamar and Leviathan in deals with Egyptian and Jordanian clients, argued that the IAA's position would not only lead to delay in the development of the Leviathan for many years, but the resulting 'regulatory uncertainty' will also cast a shadow over the future investments in Israel's oil and gas industry. The government perceived the situation as a threat to Israel's energy national security. Tamar reserves as the sole indigenous source of gas – providing for about 50 percent of the country's electricity generation – would remain so until the Leviathan is developed.

Following the IAA's turnaround, and with elections scheduled three months later, public debate on natural gas swelled. What had begun as an isolated antitrust issue over the Leviathan license, soon spiralled into an all-out public debate on the Noble-Delek partnership's monopoly status in E&P and monetisation of the gas resource. Besides the considerable resentment over enormous profits accruing to the owners of the gas companies, the price IEC paid for gas became the issue of a class action suit against the Tamar developers.

In order not to undermine the position of the IAA and cognisant of the fact that a cartel can only be broken with the court's approval, entailing extensive delays as the matter worked its way up to the Supreme Court, PM Netanyahu appointed an inter-ministerial panel chaired by head of NEC Professor Eugene Kandel to negotiate a new agreement with the gas companies. The team comprising ministers from various government ministries, as well as ATC, was meant to be representative since it was charged with the responsibility of evolving a comprehensive arrangement that would reduce cross-ownership in reservoirs, foster competition, and encourage new investment in the oil and gas sector. Hence, the chief task of the Kandel Committee was to suggest a strategy that would strike a balance between the imperatives of gas development and monopoly concerns raised by the IAA. The deliberations of the committee took the entire year of 2015, once again involving the parliament and public, as well as heated debates in the media.[134]

Natural gas framework

After nearly six months of meetings and discussions, Israel's Energy Minister Yuval Steinitz on 30 June 2015 released the terms of the agreement, the so-called Natural Gas Framework (NGF), between the government and field developers for public commentary.[135] While giving approval to the development of Leviathan and expansion of Tamar, the NGF dealt with multiple issues under different sets of laws, including the outstanding regulatory issues rankling the Israel Antitrust Authority. These included the monopolistic status of Noble Energy and Delek Group in Israel's main gas fields, future pricing of gas in the local market because of the Noble-Delek's monopoly over gas sales, regulatory stability demanded by the gas companies, and the allocation of quota for export from different gas fields, which has the potential to significantly affect investment in E&P. It was understood by the parties that the adoption of the framework would grant Noble-Delek partnership exemptions from the antitrust restrictions and create an environment of competition in Israel's natural gas market. The key aspects of NGF were:

a) Transfer and reduction of rights in gas fields: With a view to create multiple and separate ownership of the natural gas reservoirs offshore Israel, NGF required Delek subsidiaries, Delek Drilling and Avner Oil Corporation, to completely sell their rights in Tamar within six years of the adoption of NGF. Noble Energy could remain Tamar's operator but needed to reduce its holding from 36 percent to 25 percent over the same period. Noble Energy and Delek Group would sell off their entire holdings in Karish and Tanin within 14 months after the framework is approved. Because the buyer would be required to sell gas only to Israel, export allocations intended for these reservoirs would be transferred to Leviathan. While Noble, Delek, and Ratio Oil could remain invested in Leviathan without any change in their holdings, the commencement date for commercial production and gas supply to the local market was set at 48 months after the approval date of the gas framework, i.e., December 2019 (Table 2.5).

b) Provisions related to domestic pricing: Although the government will not impose price supervision on annual contracts for gas already signed, it set a price ceiling for the next six years, pertaining to the period of transition during which Karish and Tanin would be completely sold off to a third party and Delek would have divested from Tamar. The developers of Tamar and Leviathan would offer a base price to their prospective consumers, derived by dividing the total revenues from natural gas sales by the total amount of natural gas supplied to consumers by the applicable leaseholder, both during the previous quarter.

Nevertheless, the parties to a particular agreement may choose any reasonable and accepted method for linkage of the base price (Israeli Hub or average domestic market price, Brent, Public Utilities Authority-Electricity (PUA)/IEC indexation, or export price agreement),[136] which will be updated quarterly by the NGA, with the renewed pricing applicable to agreements already in effect. The long-term customers of the Tamar fields would get a two-year "window of opportunity" (anticipated during 2020–2022 but subject

TABLE 2.5 Holdings in Israel's major gas fields as of 2014 (in %)

Fields developers	Tamar#	Leviathan*	Karish*	Tanin*	Dalit*
Noble	36	39.66	47	47	32.5
Delek Group	31.25	45.34	53	53	22
Isramco	28.75	–	–	–	28.75
Dor Gas	4	–	–	–	4
Ratio oil LP	–	15	–	–	–
Everest	–	–	–	–	3.4
Total stakes	100	100	100	100	100

Source: Author's table; figures from Delek Drilling

#Israel's only producing field
*Fields yet to be developed

to change) to reduce the quantities committed for purchase by up to 50 percent. In addition, all customers will be permitted to resell 15 percent of their contractually purchased quantity in secondary sales without pricing restrictions. The framework also warranted that the domestic prices of gas would always be lower than the export price, in accordance with the notion that the natural resource belongs to the Israeli people and they have the first right to enjoy its benefits.

c) Modification of export provisions: The NGF relaxed some of the export limitations set out in Government Decision 442 of 2013 and added new procedures on how to calculate and administer the export quota. It provided for the calculation of the amount of natural gas for export as a pro rata percentage of the total natural gas resources and amended the estimation of the volume of gas in the field for the purpose of calculating the domestic market obligations on the basis of both 2P and 2C categories cumulatively. It granted the right to sign an export contract from the Tamar reservoir before Leviathan started production in a significant relief to the developers. The provision was meant to encourage local competition between the gas from the Tamar and Karish-Tanin, which are meant solely for the local market.

d) Stability of regulatory provisions: A crucial provision stipulated in the NGF at the demand of the gas companies was the controversial 'stability clause.'[137] According to Chapter Ten of the framework titled, 'A Stable Regulatory Environment,' the government took an undertaking to maintain stable regulatory environment in natural gas E&P on three issues – taxation, export, and antitrust – for a period of ten years from the date of the approval of the NGF. The government also undertook to oppose any private member bill aimed at changing the main parameters of the framework and present regulations. These undertakings were contingent upon the compliance of the developers with their commitment to develop the gas fields under the terms to the framework.

Chapter Ten of NGF included two targets: First, by the end of two years (2017), Leviathan leaseholders must enter into binding agreements for the purchase of equipment and services amounting to at least $1.5 billion, in addition to the sums previously invested. Second, the government would be entitled to evaluate its policy regarding the encouragement of foreign investment five years from the NGF approval date (2020). However, if by that date either the Leviathan field produces gas for the local market or Leviathan partners have invested an accumulated sum of US$ 4 billion and they are in an advanced stage of development of the Leviathan, the policy will not be changed for ten years from the NGF approval date.

The NGF was accepted by the gas companies and recommended by all the committee members. In their first addresses following its release, officials from the Delek Group and Noble Energy pledged their commitment to developing the Leviathan field, while criticising the harsh terms of the framework itself. The government countered that the provisions delineated in the framework would foster an environment of competition in Israel's upstream petroleum sector with the entry of a new operators, reduce the existence of cross-ownership between gas reservoirs in the current scenario, and encourage new investment by providing long-term regulatory stability.

Critics, however, contended the framework only slightly reduced each ownership stakes in the Israel's gas fields and did not actually break the partners' control of Israel's largest fields, Tamar and Leviathan, and as a single company or joint venture selling gas to the Israeli market from both reservoirs would raise prices. ATC Gilo underscored these lacunae in a speech at the annual conference of the Israeli Institute of Energy on 26 May 2015, shortly after announcing his resignation from the IAA, to protest the gas framework:

> The main problem with the arrangement taking shape is that Noble will continue to be the owner of 25 percent of Tamar. This means that Noble will take part in commercial negotiations and in the setting of the price and commercial conditions for all of Tamar's customers. Since Noble also holds about 40 percent of Leviathan, this will create a situation in which Tamar will not want to compete with Leviathan. In addition, since Nobel holds 25 percent of Tamar, the incentive for Leviathan to compete with Tamar is also small. Accordingly, competition cannot be expected between the large fields.[138]

Political manoeuvrings and the NGF

To circumvent objections of the IAA, the economy minister, following consultation with the Knesset's Economics Affairs Committee (EAC), can invoke Article 52 of the 1988 Restrictive Trade Practices Law (The Antitrust Law) to "exempt a restrictive trade practice from all or some of the provisions of this Law, if he believes that such action is necessary for reasons of foreign policy or national security."[139]

After the public hearing, however, Minister of Economy Aryeh Deri in June 2015 declined to activate his authority to invoke the Article 52, reckoning that the clause was untested and he could not take the sole responsibility for authorising such an agreement where there were monopoly concerns, and the IAA awaited the appointment of a new head.[140] Instead, in a Security Cabinet meeting that deemed the development of natural gas an issue of national security, Deri agreed to transfer his authority to invoke the article to the Cabinet – a move that required the authorisation of both the Cabinet and Knesset.[141]

While the transfer quickly received Cabinet approval,[142] Netanyahu delayed a Knesset vote after at least three Cabinet members cited conflicts of interest – personal or business-related – in withholding support for the agreement. A unanimous Cabinet approved the NGF on 16 August 2015 (Government Decision 476 regarding the "Framework for the expansion of natural gas production from Tamar and the speedy development of Leviathan, Karish, Tanin, and other natural gas fields"),[143] but fully activating the deal required that economy minister invoke Article 52 to circumvent the IAA's objections.

On 7 September 2015, the government, aiming to advance the legitimacy of the gas framework, presented it for approval by the Knesset – although it was not a bill but a political resolution and as such a Knesset vote was not obligatory. The deal did pass a vote in the Knesset by a 59 to 51 majority[144] but still faced the antitrust challenge because the government coalition could not cobble up a majority on the crucial vote to transfer the economy minister's authority on the matter to the Cabinet.[145] Deri's refusal to invoke Article 52, and his preference for letting a new antitrust commissioner endorse the NGF, spelled more uncertainty and long delays. Netanyahu then convinced Deri to resign from his post for another portfolio in the government, and the Ministry of Economy passed into the Prime Minister's hands.

As per the Antitrust Law, the gas framework came up for hearing before the EAC. Chaired by Eitan Cabel, a member of the opposition Zionist Union party, the EAC heard officials and companies involved in delineating the framework, as well as representatives of activists and organisations opposing it, and, finally, Netanyahu himself – and took the decision to advise Prime Minister not to invoke Article 52.[146] However, the recommendation of the EAC, which amounted to the disapproval of the NGF, was non-binding and Netanyahu chose to ignore it.

On 17 December 2015, Netanyahu – exercising his right as economy minister under Section 52 of the Antitrust Law – granted the antitrust exception and brought the much-debated framework into force (the date became the NGF 'approval date').[147] Netanyahu's political cartwheel to seek approval for the NGF in the name of national security received criticism from several quarters, ranging from academic experts to civil society leaders, who were battling cartelisation of Israeli economy. The use of Article 52 in order to circumvent the objections of the ATA, "amounted to 'securitization' of the gas issue,"[148] implying that it was moved out of normal politics – of deference to public opinion and of the primacy of legislative process – to the security sphere, where expeditious action and prevention of public discussions become the rules of the game.[149] PM Netanyahu's use of Article 52 in the manner it was "amounted to a violation of the spirit of the antitrust law," says Amnon Portugali, because "a cartel without a permit [Noble-Delek were in Leviathan] amounted to a civil and criminal offence which should have drawn prosecution."[150]

The judicial challenge

Within a matter of two weeks, several NGOs, public advocacy groups and left and centrist opposition parties in the Knesset (Zionist Union and Meretz) challenged the framework in the Supreme Court, where the State of Israel and the gas companies defended the NGF. Prime Minister Netanyahu himself testified before the panel of judges to introduce the government's arguments on the importance of the framework, making the case one of the most prominent of all cases of 2016.

The Supreme Court, sitting as the High court of Justice (HCJ) as a five-member bench, emphasised that the Court was not examining the economic wisdom of the framework but the legal–constitutional question of the limits of the government's authority to act when the Knesset did not explicitly authorise it, and the unwillingness of Cabinet to enact the framework in the form of a bill, when the economic consequences of the deal are so extraordinarily immense:

> The gas deal that was presented in the outline [framework] included many legal and regulatory aspects, all of which were concentrated by the government into a single contract with the gas companies. For that reason, the HCJ was confronted with the need to determine the limits of executive authority, and to rule on questions of delegation and granting an exemption from antitrust law in the energy sector through a government contract, which in effect reorganized the entire energy sector.[151]

Thus, the judges addressed three central issues brought up in the challenge:

a) Whether the reasons of foreign policy and national security proffered by the government genuinely justify the exemption in the exercise of authority under Article 52 of the Antitrust Act.
b) Whether the stabilisation clause that prevented the current and future government to legislate and regulate the gas sector is reasonable.
c) Whether the gas framework in all its complexity and importance to the economy of Israel requires primary legislation (Acts of the Knesset) instead of a government decision.

In its judgement on 27 March 2016, the HCJ delivered a blow to the government and gas companies, striking down the entire framework. In a 4–1 judgement, the court found that the stability clause – a key part of the framework that requires the government not to execute any regulatory changes on the gas industry for at least ten years – was markedly restrictive and constituted an encroachment upon the authority of the present and future government to regulate key components of the gas market if a situation were to arise. Therefore, the HCJ barred the government from giving such a guarantee to the companies.

In its judgement, the majority of the bench held the clause null and void on the basis of the administrative rule that power and authority also create an obligation – the obligation of exercising discretion. In other words, "the government does not have the power and authority to decide not to decide or not to take action," especially when the matter at hand "is a real political dispute, and when the its decision restricts the discretion of its successors." By deciding in the framework that the government shall avoid regulatory changes for a decade, it has "unlawfully relieved itself from its discretion."[152]

Judge Joubran added that the gas framework was prescribed without authority, since the Government was not entitled to "restrict either its own discretion or the discretion of the Knesset."[153] In his opinion, the sweeping wording of the stability provisions, "could compromise Israel's international standing, if the circumstances so emerged that required the State to renege on undertakings it had previously given."[154]

Judge Uzi Vogelman joined the opinions of Judge Rubinstein and Judge Joubran, in support of the argument that the regulatory stability clause in its current format could not hold the test of legality. In this regard, Justice Vogelman "emphasized that the scope and duration of the stability clause, as well as the 'price tag' that accompanies its anticipated breach, create a de facto prohibited restriction of administrative discretion."[155] Therefore, a commitment in the framework that binds the government not to initiate any changes in legislation and to oppose legislative initiatives for ten years cannot stand. The government's undertaking to thwart a private bill, according to Judge Esther Hayut, "crosses all permissible boundaries in a parliamentary democracy and renders the restrictive provisions as clearly and blatantly illegal."

Judge Hayut was further of the opinion that "the restrictive provisions create a legislative and regulatory freeze due to the exposure to a significant damages claim on the part of the gas companies of an unknown scope," curbing the flexibility of the government, "as the one that de facto controls the legislative process in the Knesset in initiating legislation."[156]

Judge Noam Sohlberg who dissented on the stability clause believed that the proviso did not restrict the Knesset's sovereign power to legislate. What the stability clause did was to limit the government's discretion, and "is a necessary consequence of the mere existence of administrative contracts and promises." However, since the stability clause is anchored in Government Decision, it gives the government more flexibility than if it were anchored in legislation. Moreover, "the regulatory stability clause is part of an entire 'package deal,' which is the result of long and complex professional negotiations. . . . In investments of this kind, an undertaking for 10 years is acceptable, and is required in order to prescribe policy and execute long-term important projects."[157]

In many ways, the stability clause has symbolic value, stated Justice Sohlberg, given the "huge economic investment on the part of the entrepreneurs at a significant risk on their part." Furthermore, if the government is entitled to sell all or part of the gas reservoirs according to the State Assets Law (a greater act, of selling), then, *a fortiori* it is permitted to perform a lesser one (the Gas Outline, including its regulatory stability clause). Based on these grounds, Judge Sohlberg reached the conclusion that the regulatory stability clause is not illegal.[158]

In its declaration before the court, the government has claimed that the stability clause was a *conditio sine qua non* (an indispensable condition), the proposition emphasised by Netanyahu when he filed a personal affidavit before the Supreme Court[159] – an unprecedented move in Israel's history when a sitting PM appeared in the court and addressed the bench in person, urging it to approve the regulation. Since, the court in its majority opinion decided that the clause was illegal, it reached the conclusion that the whole Framework had to be struck down.

The two other challenges that the petitioners had raised against the Framework were dismissed. A majority of three judges – Hayut, Vogelman, and Sohlberg – ruled that the validity of the framework was not contingent upon being anchored by primary legislation, i.e., it need not be legislated in its entirety by the Knesset. In addition, a majority of four judges – with the exception of Judge Joubran – did not object to the national security and foreign policy imperatives argument in the government's exercise of Section 52 of the Antitrust Law, to override antitrust objections in approving the framework. The Court suspended the effect of its ruling for a year, however, in order to allow the government time to revise the gas agreement.[160]

In effect, the court had not touched any other point of the framework, most importantly the use of Article 52 of the Antitrust Law, which meant that if the stability clause mechanism was altered, the rest of the plan could stand. The government moved swiftly in view of the Supreme Court's ruling. A government-backed committee renegotiated the outline with the gas companies and reached a compromise deal.

Modification of the gas framework

On 22 May 2016, Energy Minister Yuval Steinitz announced the Cabinet's approval (Government Decision Number 1465)[161] of the compromise deal between the government and developers that addressed the concerns of the court. The government re-adopted Government Decision 476, with the exception of Chapter 10, which was revised to make it more flexible and reflect a new version of the stability clause. While the new clause still talks of a ten-year-long regulatory climate in the gas sector (with the intention to attract investment), it does not guarantee nor does it direct the government to desist from and oppose the enactment of changes in taxation, ownership of the reservoirs, and exports. In contrast to the previous stability clause, the government will not oppose private members' bills seeking to alter regulations; "it proposes to let officials decide about any financial compensation due to the gas companies for regulatory changes that could have a material adverse effect on the leaseholders."[162] According to the MoE, the new term "obviates the government's obligation to oppose private legislation seeking to change policy relating to Israel's offshore gas fields, and provides greater leeway for future government administrations to revise natural gas policy, should the need arise."[163]

The first licensing round and lack of investment

In November 2016, the Ministry of Energy issued its first tender ever for rights to drill in 24 offshore blocks in Israel's EEZ (Figure 2.2), each of about 400 square kilometres. The original deadline for the submission of tenders was March 2017, but lack of a sufficient number of applications led the authorities to advance the deadline to July. The deadline was extended again to November 2017, after only one company, Energean, submitted a bid, that too because it was interested in taking control of licensing blocks between the Karish and Tanin fields it operates. The blocks offered under the bidding round were located adjacent to other blocks leased or licensed to other operators, which have shown significant reserves (Figure 2.2).

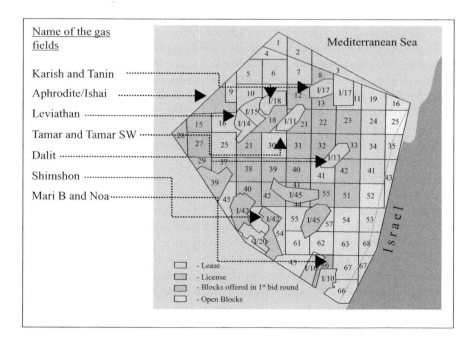

FIGURE 2.2   Israel's offshore exploration blocks

Source: Author's figure; referenced from Ministry of Energy, State of Israel, 2017

Disclaimer: Map not to scale

However, no Israeli companies submitted offers, indicating that they were unable to partner with European or American companies required as operators for their bids. Despite two deadline extensions, Israel's offshore licensing round that closed on 15 November 2017 saw only two submissions: One was from Energean Israel and the other from a consortium of four Indian oil corporations, namely, ONGC Videsh, Bharat PetroResources, Indian Oil, and Oil India.

Out of 24 tendered, five blocks were awarded to Energean and one to the Indian consortium led by ONGC. Energean received five offshore exploration licenses comprising blocks 12, 21, 22, 23, and 31, which are located near the Karish and Tanin; only one block near the Dalit field was awarded to Indian oil companies. Each of the six had received only a single bid, and India had bid for right to explore in all the tendered blocks. The winners would get an exploration license for three years, which could be extended by an additional three years, if the licensee has implemented the work plan and commits to carry out drilling during the extension period.

The question one might ask at this stage is, has the regulatory turmoil experienced by Noble Energy had a negative impact on the investment climate in Israel for foreign investors? It is a known fact, however, that major oil companies have exercised historical caution about doing business with the Jewish state, wanting not to antagonise their Arab oil clients. Top firms like Eni, Total, and JSC Novatek placed bids in Lebanon's license round, which took place almost concurrently with that of Israel, despite the country's political crises, and Novatek even bid on the disputed block 9, a part which Israel claims to be within its EEZ.[164]

That said, while economic decisions are complicated, with a variety of factors influencing investors' decision on whether and where to invest and how much and when, one cannot say with certainty what factors may have deterred foreign investment in the Israeli gas sector. Nevertheless, it is still possible to identify some of these factors, which can be tackled to create a favourable investment climate in Israel's E&P sector.

The rapid pace of regulatory changes related to the gas sector, which benefit the consumers to the detriment of the developers, occurred over a short duration of time creating uncertainty about what to expect next, says Friedman, the author of a BoI report referred to previously in this chapter, and may have caused a decline in their investments in Israel. The study also addresses the issue of restrictions on the export of gas on the investment in Israeli E&P, underlining the fact the developers interested in maximising their profits "will have difficulty in financing expensive development of the natural gas reserves which will create a surplus of supply in the domestic market, in particular when they are not permitted or are unable to export the gas [beyond the quota]."[165]

When Italian company Edison International Spa – one of the oldest foreign investors in the Israeli gas exploration market[166] – closed down its activity in Israel in July 2018, market insiders interpreted the decision as a testimony to the waning enthusiasm of the companies in gas exploration in Israel due to restrictions on gas exports imposed by the Tzemach Committee's decision. Notably, Edison, which had competed for the Karish–Tanin licenses and lost the rights to the reservoirs to Energean, did not participate in the licensing round conducted by the MoE in the latter half of 2017.[167]

Moreover, the 'anti-tycoon' atmosphere that has evolved over the last few years, along with a very strong anti-establishment civil society fighting for what it believes are the 'people's rights' has also chilled the enthusiasm of gas companies to invest in Israel.[168] "This fighting on the streets, in the media and in the courts, have been at least partly successful, often at the expense of the investors" may also have scared some of them off the Israeli market.[169] Given the miniscule amount of gas in Israel's possession – 0.09 percent of the world's total proven natural gas reserves and the expected combined annual production from Tamar and Leviathan fields amounting to only 0.2 percent of global annual production (2015)[170] – Israel needs to maintain a competitive investment climate comparable with other gas-producing countries to attract foreign players. For this, the government needs to provide foreign investors with "international, legally binding, guarantees that will minimize the political risks that jeopardize their investments."[171]

Adiri Committee: incentives for investment?

Since the Tzemach Committee asserted that its recommendations – export quotas from each gas field and domestic market obligations (DMO) of the field leaseholder – would boost the upstream gas sector, there has been extreme lethargy in exploratory drilling in the past five years. More so, the industry has come to view the idea of an export quota for each field as a hindrance to investment in exploration. A stipulation of Tzemach Committee that the government should review its recommendations five years after the date of their approval, led the government to appoint a committee, headed by Director General of the Ministry of Energy, Udi Adiri, on 4 January 2018. The Adiri Committee – a common moniker for this newly appointed committee – included representatives from the ministries and authorities that participated in the deliberations of Tzemach Committee.

Much like the committee headed by Shaul Tzemach, the Adiri Committee was guided by principles identical to its predecessor, including ensuring energy security for the domestic market, incentivising the development of new fields, and ensuring competition among the suppliers in the market. It released the interim report[172] of its proposals in July 2018 for public comments, some of which were incorporated in its final report published on 12 December 2018.[173] To begin with, the Adiri Committee recognised that the developers' ability to export gas was a requisite to encourage the entry of investors into E&P, even as, redundancy, energy security, and competition in the local market were, as the previous committee, its prime consideration.

The Adiri Committee acknowledged at the outset in its final proposals that since Government Decision 442, which accepted the Tzemach Committee recommendations in June 2013, there has been a retreat in "continued and significant development of the exploration and production segment offshore Israel."[174] No drilling has been carried out over the years between 2013 and 2018, and the last two exploration drills in offshore Israel were in 2013. Further, while in 2012, when the Tzemach Committee deliberated and submitted its report, there were 36 licenses and 4 leases in Israel's maritime zone in 2012, while as of December 2018, when the Adiri Committee submitted its final report, there are only 8 licenses and 10 leases offshore Israel. As a result, the outlook for prospective resources – assumed by the Tzemach Committee to be 150 bcm – has diminished and of which only 51 bcm have been discovered till date.[175] Many licenses included in the calculation of prospective resources were returned without the exploratory drilling.

For the reason of maximizing the benefit of gas resources to the people, the Adiri Committee, in the first instance, examined eight demand scenarios, predicting natural gas utilisation in the Israeli economy in the next 25 years (2018–2042),[176] and adopted the consumption volume of 452 bcm as best representing the potential penetration of natural gas.[177] It observed this volume allowed for compliance with the governmental targets in the power generation, transportation, industrial and petrochemical sectors, including the target for closure of coal stations by 2030, 17 percent energy efficiency by 2030, and 17 percent of electricity generation from renewables (Table 2.6).[178] However, in view of the uncertainty regarding the parameters that constitute the demand scenario and the vagaries of the market, the review committee suggested no change to the quantity determined in Government Decision 442, i.e., 540 bcm for protection of the local economy minus 43 bcm that have been consumed since 2013, or about 500 bcm in total that will serve the domestic market in contingencies, unless and until additional supplies materialise.[179] In effect, the total volume for export is retained at the existing 460 bcm, although the volume of gas above the 500 bcm quantity could be directed to export with manifold benefits to the economy.[180]

In order to accelerate investment in the upstream gas sector, the Adiri Committee made a distinction between 'obligation to connect' to the domestic market and 'obligation to supply to the local economy' according to the size of the field, in contrast to Tzemach Committee report in which all producing fields were obliged to connect to the local market and supply irrespective of the size

TABLE 2.6 Natural gas demand forecast, 2018–2042

Year/Sectors	2018	2020	2025	2030	2035	2040	2042	2018–2042
Electricity	8.8	8.4	11.0	13.5	14.7	16.0	16.5	321
Heavy industry and distribution	2.0	2.5	2.7	3.0	3.2	3.4	3.5	73.1
Transportation	0.0	0.1	0.3	1.3	3.0	4.7	5.1	47.0
Petrochemical industries	–	–	0.3	0.5	0.7	0.7	0.7	11.2
Total local demand	10.9	11	14	18	22	25	26	452

Source: *Conclusions of the Professional Team* [Hebrew] [Adiri Committee recommendations], December 2018, p. 42.

of the field under minimum domestic market obligation. While the Tzemach Committee saw the obligation to connect to the domestic market as necessary to create supply security and redundancy, and increase the number of suppliers to the domestic market to encourage competition, the Adiri Committee believed the changes in ground realities provided room to think differently. In view of the expected energy redundancy and energy security situation with the connection of Leviathan at the end of 2019 and Karish and Tanin fields by early 2021, Adiri Committee recognised that:

> the economic costs and additional statutory and planning difficulties which the obligation to connect to the domestic market impose on the entrepreneurs, create a precursory cooling effect on the exploration and development of natural gas fields. Consequently, imposing the sweeping obligation to connect to the local economy today is liable to harm competition because it creates a significant entry barrier for additional investments in the sector.[181]

In light of Government Decision 2592 of 2 April 2017, titled, "Encouraging small and medium reservoirs and declaring an emergency in the natural gas sector," which instructed the Petroleum Commissioner to examine the clause in Decision 442 requiring the leaseholder to connect all natural gas fields in the lease area, for the purpose of encouraging small and medium-sized reservoirs, the Adiri Committee proposed the following: a) prospective fields up to 50 bcm do not have the obligation to connect to the local market and b) fields that contain less than 50 bcm are exempt from DMO.[182] By implication, small fields up to 50 bcm can be developed solely for the purpose of export, and investors encouraged by this option would be willing to drill for and develop such fields. Further, fields between 51 and 200 bcm that start commercial production before 1 January 2028 will be required to connect to the domestic market by 31 December 2032.[183] This is to ensure that the market is well supplied during the expected shortage in hourly supply in the years 2033–2035.[184] However, any further postponement of connection obligation for such fields can be granted at the discretion of Petroleum Commissioner, who will take a decision on the basis of the state of market redundancy and the amount of natural gas connected to the Israeli market (Tables 2.7 and 2.8).[185]

Sluggishness in exploration and production is the most worrisome issue in Israel's upstream sector with implications for long-term energy security. It is not yet certain if the alterations in the 'obligation to connect' and DMO would kick start drilling in Israel's upstream sector. While Israel's first gas tender for granting new drilling licenses in November 2017 failed to attract major oil companies, neighbouring Lebanon's licensing round saw IOCs picking up bids for oil and gas blocs in the same year. The Israeli gas industry is hoping that Adiri Committee recommendations, adopted by the government in January 2019[186] will make a significant change in the diminished outlook on E&P in offshore Israel in the second licensing round launched in November 2018, with bids due in June 2019.[187]

TABLE 2.7 Size of the gas field and obligation to connect to the domestic market

Size of the gas field	Obligation to connect
> 200 bcm	Must connect to the domestic market prior to the date of commercial flow
>50 and up to 200 bcm	Fields that begin commercial production before the first day of January 2028 must connect to the domestic market by the last day of 2032; fields that begin commercial production after the first day of January 2028 must connect upon development, and prior to commercial supply
Up to 50 bcm	Not required to connect to the domestic market

Source: *Conclusions of the Professional Team* [Hebrew] [Adiri Committee recommendations], December 2018, p. 8

TABLE 2.8 Size of the field and obligation of minimum supply to the domestic market

Size of the gas field	Obligation to supply
< 50 bcm	Not obliged to supply to the domestic market
For each 1 BCM added from 50 bcm to 200 bcm	Must supply 50% to domestic market and can export 50%
For each 1 BCM added from 200 BCM and above	Must reserve 55% to domestic market and can export 45%

Source: *Conclusions of the Professional Team* [Hebrew] [Adiri Committee recommendations], December 2018, p. 9.

Moving ahead

Since the discovery of gas in its territorial waters at the end of the last century, Israel has formulated a comprehensive fiscal, tax, and export policy for its resources. Being a democratic country, the policy decisions made by the government were vigorously debated in the public domain. Public opinion played a decisive role in moulding the policies in a way that people got their rightful share in the resources and income from resources. The scale of natural gas finds in Tamar and Leviathan brought forth matters of distribution of profits between gas developers and public, energy security and exports of gas, as well as monopoly holdings in the gas fields and pricing of gas to the forefront of public debate.

While the developers wanted to keep generously benefitting from tax breaks and subsidies, keeping almost all the profit and exercising export options, the Israeli public demanded that the government take a larger share from the development of the state's petroleum resources. A popular demand also underlined the need for governmental assurance of energy security to the domestic consumers, before the developers are allowed to export gas. The question of cross-holdings of Noble-Delek in Israel's gas fields raised the issue of how to break the monopoly of the partnership to guarantee equal conditions for existing and prospective players in Israel's offshore gas sector.

In the short-term, the room for building a competitive gas market is limited; an effective competition would evolve with the entry of new companies in E&P and further commercial discoveries. Price regulations, which constitutes an important aspect of the framework, is required in the present circumstances of insufficient competition in the gas market. However, this is not an ideal situation but only a stopgap to a more competitive situation. The post-NGF initiatives by the government to incentivise the development of smaller fields, such as, subsidy for infrastructure (pipeline capacity and storage facilities) advancement and price incentive for those purchasing from such fields, will go a long way in correcting the distortions of monopoly and pricing in the Israeli gas market. In addition, governmental measures to accelerate the expansion of gas distribution network across the country and simultaneous provision of incentives to local firms to access this network and switch to natural gas use,[188] discussed in Chapter 3, will generate a vibrant dynamic between supply and demand, which will have a salutary impact on investments in Israel's E&P.

In a small gas market like Israel, where the total reserve is small, regulatory stability is the key to attracting investors who need clear profitability prospects in return for pledging costly investments over the long period. One such prospect is export of gas for which the policy based on Tzemach Committee recommendations has set out clear regulations. The Israeli government has been acting as a facilitator for export of natural gas by signing MoUs with Cyprus, Greece, and Italy for gas export to Europe. The NEPCO deal with Jordan (2016) and the gas export agreements with Egypt's Dolphinus group (2018), discussed in Chapter 4, are the results of political efforts on the part of the government to find an outlet for the country's gas resources. However, the discoveries of new gas reserves of large commercial value such as Zohr and Calypso in Egyptian and Cypriot economic waters, respectively, could have important implications for Israeli gas development by potentially reducing its export options and increasing regional competition in this sector. Conversely, the discovery of new gas fields in Israel's neighbourhood raises the potential for greater regional cooperation in the gas sector in terms of creating joint infrastructure projects and establishing procedures for the shared use of existing facilities.

Notes

1 Former Republican member of the United States House of Representatives representing New Mexico's 1st congressional district from 1998 to 2009.
2 *Assessment of Undiscovered Oil and Gas Resources of the Levant Basin Province, Eastern Mediterranean*, United States Geological Survey (USGS), Virginia, United States, March 12, 2010, https://pubs.usgs.gov/fs/2010/3014/ (accessed on June 3, 2017).

3 State-owned oil and gas companies largely involved in onshore exploration and funded by the government budget existed in Israel until the 1990s, which caused significant financial losses as a result of their limited success. However, since the late 1990s, discovery of offshore natural gas in large quantities by a consortium of private players have transformed the nature of Israel's energy economy.

4 Excess profit is the profit over and above what is deemed to be a normal (market equilibrium) return on capital investment. Excess profits tax is assessed in addition to any corporate income tax already in place and is primarily imposed on selective businesses to prevent those business owners from reaping inordinate profits. This tax is not popular with free-market enterprise thinkers who feel that it discourages productivity with its removal of the profit motive. See "Excess Profits Tax," *Investopedia*, www.investopedia.com/terms/e/excess-profits-tax.asp (accessed on June 3, 2017).

5 *National Security and Foreign Relations*, Delek Drilling, Herzeliya Pituach, Israel, undated, www.delekdrilling.co.il/en/natural-gas/national-security-and-foreign-relations (accessed on June 3, 2017).

6 Martin Flectcher, "Israel's Big Gusher," *Slate*, February 26, 2014, www.slate.com/articles/news_and_politics/moment/2014/02/israel_s_natural_gas_deposits_tel_aviv_s_offshore_gas_fields_will_make_it.html (accessed on June 4, 2017).

7 "Exploration History," Zion Oil, 2006, www.sec.gov/Archives/edgar/data/1131312/000113131206000077/exploration.htm (accessed on June 4, 2017); Shiri Shaham, Simon Weintraub, Noam Meir and Josh Hersch, "Israel," in Christopher B. Strong, *The Oil and Gas Law Review*, 2nd edition (London: Law Business Research Ltd., 2014), p. 179, www.arnon.co.il/files/e3b84790d602b8d3179de6a92b2be89a/The%20Oil%20and%20Gas%20Review.pdf (accessed on June 4, 2017).

8 Edward Tawadros, *Geology of North Africa* (Boca Raton: BRC Press, 2011), p. 607; "Alma Oilfields Re Turned to Egypt," *Jewish Telegraphic Agency*, November 26, 1979, www.jta.org/1979/11/26/archive/alma-oilfields-re-turned-to-egypt (accessed on June 7, 2017).

9 Edward R. Rosen, "The Effect of Relinquished Sinai Resources on Israel's Energy Situation and Policies," *Middle East Review*, Volume 14, Number 3–4 (1982), p. 8; William J. Levitt, "Israel Told to Keep Sinai Oil," *The New York Times*, November 6, 1978, www.nytimes.com/1978/11/06/archives/israel-told-to-keep-sinai-oil.html (accessed on June 7, 2017).

10 The Petroleum Law of 1952 that regulated exploration and production in the initial years of the establishment of the state, and offered extremely favourable term for E&P, was substantially amended in 1965 to encourage international investment in the oil and gas sector.

11 Since the early 1990s, some small Israeli publicly traded limited partnerships conducted the bulk of exploration activities without significant outside assistance. *Zion Oil and Gas*, Zion Oil & Gas, Inc., 2001–2006, www.sec.gov/Archives/edgar/data/1131312/000113131206000077/exploration.htm (accessed on June 8, 2017).

12 The right holders in the Yam Thetis partnership were Noble Energy (47.059 percent), Delek Drilling (25.5 percent), Avner Oil and Gas Exploration (23 percent), and Delek Investments and Properties (4.441 percent). Delek Drilling, Avner Oil, and Delek Investments constitute the Delek Group. See *The Natural Gas Sector in Israel*, Ministry of Energy, State of Israel, undated, http://archive.energy.gov.il/English/Subjects/Natural%20Gas/Pages/GxmsMniNGEconomy.aspx (accessed on July 16, 2018); *Yam Tethys: The Transition to Natural Gas*, Delek Drilling, undated, www.delekdrilling.co.il/en/project/yam-tethys (accessed on June 8, 2017).

13 Founded by three Palestinian businessmen in 1952, it is the largest construction company in the Middle East and is now headquartered in Greece.

14 The PIF, which was founded in 2003, is a publicly owned company based in Ramallah and similar in structure to a sovereign wealth fund – although instead of investing surplus money in foreign markets, it reinvests this money in Palestinian resources.

15 "Gaza Marine Gas Field," *Offshore Technology*, 2018, www.offshore-technology.com/projects/gaza-marine-gas-field/ (accessed on July 16, 2018).

16 "The Gaza Marine Field: Left Behind," *Natural Gas Europe*, May 11, 2015, www. naturalgaseurope.com/the-gaza-marine-field-left-behind-23564 (accessed on June 8, 2017); "Gaza Marine Gas Field," *Offshore Technology*, 2018.

17 The current stakes in the Tamar project are Delek Drilling (22 percent), Noble Energy (25 percent), Isramco (28.75 percent), Tamar Petroleum (16.75 percent) Dor Gas (4 percent), and Everest (3.5 percent).

18 Oil and gas reserves are frequently classified as proved (1P), probable (2P), or possible (3P) depending on the reasonable certainty of being recovered in the existing technical and economic conditions. Proved reserves are considered to have a 90 percent certainty of being produced, probable to have a 50 percent certainty, and possible to have only a 10 percent certainty. See Jack Bogart Maverik, "What Is the Difference Between Proven and Probable Reserves in the Oil and Gas Sector?" *Investopedia*, September 14, 2018, www.investopedia.com/ask/answers/060115/what-difference-between-proven-and-probable-reserves-oil-and-gas-sector.asp (accessed on July 16, 2018).

19 *Tamar Gas Field*, Delek Drilling, undated, www.delekdrilling.co.il/en/project/tamar-gas-field.

20 Ibid.; "Partners in Israel's Tamar Raise Gas Reserves Estimate by 13 pct," *Reuters*, July 2, 2017, www.reuters.com/article/israel-natgas-idUSL8N1JT09K (accessed on July 16, 2018).

21 *Tamar Petroleum: Investors Presentation*, Tamar Petroleum, Herzeliya Pituach, Israel, February 2018, https://ir.tamarpetroleum.co.il/wp-content/uploads/2018/02/Tamar-P-Investors-Presentation-Feb-2018-Eng.pdf (accessed on July 16, 2018).

22 *Additional Prospect: Dalit*, Delek Group, Netanya, Israel, 2017, www.delek-group.com/our-operations/east-med/ (accessed on June 11, 2017).

23 Contingent Resources are those quantities of petroleum estimated to be potentially recoverable from known accumulations using established technology but which are not currently considered to be commercially recoverable due to one or more contingencies. Contingent resources are divided into three different classes: 1C, 2C, and 3C, which in theory will become 1P, 2P, and 3P, respectively, when contingencies are removed. See *Petroleum Resources Classification System and Definitions*, Society of Petroleum Engineers, Texas, United States, 2003–2018, www.spe.org/industry/petroleum-resources-classification-system-definitions.php (accessed on July 16, 2018); *Calculation of Reserves*, Tethys Oil, Stockholm, Sweden, undated, www.tethysoil.com/en/operations/oil-and-natural-gas/calculation-of-reserves (accessed on July 16, 2018).

24 *Leviathan Gas Field*, Delek Drilling, undated, www.delekdrilling.co.il/en/project/leviathan-gas-field (accessed on June 11, 2017); *Leviathan: The Levant Basin's Game Changing Discovery*, East Med and Our Assets, Delek Group, 2017, www.delek-group.com/our-operations/east-med/ (accessed on June 11, 2017).

25 *Tanin*, Energean Oil and Gas, Tel Aviv and Haifa, Israel, undated, www.energean.com/operations/israel/tanin/ (accessed on June 11, 2017); *Karish*, Energean Oil and Gas, undated, www.energean.com/operations/israel/israel/karish/ (accessed on June 11, 2017).

26 The current stakeholders of the Ishai field are Israel Opportunity Energy Resources, LP (21 percent), MAMMAX Oil & Gas ltd (63 percent), Eden Energy Ltd (11 percent) and Petroleum Services Holdings AS [PSH, former AGR, Norwegian] (5 percent). PSH is the operator of the Ishai lease. See *Ownership in Petroleum Rights*, Oil and Gas Section, Ministry of Energy, State of Israel, January 8, 2018, p. 2, www.gov.il/Blob-Folder/guide/oil_gas_license/he/OwnershipPetroleumRights_1.pdf (accessed on July 16, 2018).

27 *Israeli Gas Opportunities*, Ministry of Energy, State of Israel, 2016, 2016, http://archive. energy.gov.il/English/Subjects/Natural%20Gas/Pages/GxmsMniNGLobby.aspx (accessed on June 12, 2017); "AGR, Partners Make Big Israeli Gas Find," *Platts*, January 3, 2013, www.platts.cn/latest-news/natural-gas/jerusalem/agr-partners-make-big-israeli-gas-find-6978742 (accessed on June 12, 2017); *Ishai Lease*, Israel Opportunity Energy Resources LP., Ramat Gan, Israel, www.oilandgas.co.il/englishsite/assetsmap/pelagic-licenses.aspx (accessed on June 12, 2017).

28 Gas production in the Cyprus' Aphrodite field as well as Ishai field depends on agreements between the two countries. In 2010, Israel and Cyprus signed an EEZ agreement delineating the border between the two countries' economic waters. However, the supposed unitisation agreement on arrangements for developing the cross-border fields was never signed. A year later, toward the end of 2011, Noble Energy announced the discovery of Aphrodite, containing about 110–120 bcm of gas. Exactly how much natural gas spills into the Ishai license is not known for certain. The Cypriots claim it is only a negligible fraction, possibly around 3 percent of the reservoir or less, but in Israeli, professional opinion deems it at least 5 percent of the field. According to MoE figures, Ishai constitutes about 10 percent of the Aphrodite reserve, anywhere between 7 and 10 bcm. Encouraged by this discovery of Aphrodite, when holders of the Ishai license drilled a well in November 2012, it demonstrated that Aphrodite did partly extend into their license, though it only showed negligible quantities of natural gas. To the disbelief of the Cypriot side, in November 2015 the Ministry of Energy declared the findings a discovery, a term implying a commercial value. Following a report that Cyprus was in talks with Egypt to export gas from Aphrodite in March 2018, the owners of the Ishai lease, who have already spent $120 million on exploratory drilling, wrote to the petroleum commissioner and Minister of Energy, claiming that the extraction of gas on the Cypriot side would lead to the depletion of gas from Ishai. While Cyprus rebuffs the claim, Israel is in a strange situation. Israel has stakes on both sides of the EEZ, given that the Aphrodite field is developed by Noble-Delek-British Gas partnership, and Shell is also reportedly considering a plan to buy gas from the Aphrodite and Israel's Leviathan reservoirs for liquefaction at its lNG terminal in Idku. Israel and Cyprus will turn to international arbitration to resolve the dispute or might agree on unitised development of the reservoir. An agreement on this issue is important to speed up the construction of the Eastern Mediterranean pipeline for export of Israeli and Cypriot gas to Europe as well as exports to Egypt. Mona Sukkarieh, "Aphrodite's Blues: Cyprus and Israel Diverge Over Shared Gas Reservoir," *Executive Magazine*, June 6, 2018, www.executive-magazine.com/economics-policy/aphrodites-blues (accessed on July 16, 2018); *Aphrodite Gas Field*, Delek Drilling, undated, www.delekdrilling.co.il/en/project/aphrodite-gas-field; "Owners of Israeli Field Seek to Stop Cyprus Deal With Egypt," *Cyprus Mail Online*, March 14, 2018, https://cyprus-mail.com/2018/03/14/owners-israeli-field-seek-stop-cyprus-deal-egypt/ (accessed on July 16, 2018); "Egypt, Cyprus to Sign Deal to Connect Aphrodite Gas Field With Egypt," *Economic Times*, April 30, 2018, https://energy.economictimes.indiatimes.com/news/oil-and-gas/egypt-cyprus-to-sign-deal-to-connect-aphrodite-gas-field-with-egypt/63966328 (accessed on July 16, 2018); Hana Levi Julian, "Israel, Cyprus Move to International Arbitration on Aphrodite Gas Reservoir," *JewishPress.com*, May 1, 2018, www.jewishpress.com/news/business-economy/israel-cyprus-move-to-international-arbitration-on-gas-reservoir/2018/05/01/ (accessed on July 16, 2018); Ora Cohen, "Israel's 5% Claim on Gas in Cypriot Field Causes Dispute With Nicosia," *Haaretz*, May 11, 2018, www.haaretz.com/israel-news/business/israel-s-5-claim-on-gas-in-cypriot-field-causes-dispute-with-nicosia-1.6075918 (accessed on July 16, 2018).

29 Stakeholders of the field are, Isramco Negev 2 LP (50 percent), Naphta Israeli Oil Company Ltd. (20 percent), Israel Oil Company (10 percent), Modiin Energy Partnership Ltd. (5 percent), ATP Oil & Gas Corporation (5 percent), and Petroleum Services Holdings AS (5 percent). See *Ownership in Petroleum Rights*, January 8, 2018, p. 2.

30 Epstein Rosenblum Maoz, "Israel Launches First International Bid Round for Offshore Oil and Gas Exploration Blocks," *Mondaq*, April 28, 2017, www.mondaq.com/x/589814/Oil+Gas+Electricity/Israel+Launches+First+International+Bid+Round+For+Offshore+Oil+And+Gas+Exploration+Blocks (accessed on June 15, 2017); "The Underbelly of Eastern Mediterranean Gas," *Journal of Energy Security*, August 13, 2013, www.ensec.org/index.php?option=com_content&view=article&id=445:the-under-belly-of-eastern-mediterranean-gas&catid=137:is (accessed on June 15, 2017).

31 All potentially recoverable volumes from undiscovered accumulations on a given date are classified as Prospective Resources. If a discovery is made, the potentially recoverable volumes from that discovery are classified as Contingent Resources. When the development plan has been defined and progressed to the point where commerciality is determined, the resource would be reclassified as Reserves. See, *I Know What Reserves Are, But What Are*, Gaffney, Cline and Associates, July 29, 2016, http://gaffney-cline-focus.com/i-know-what-reserves-are (accessed on June 15, 2017).

32 Executive Summary of *The Recommendations of the Inter-Ministerial Committee to Examine the Government's Policy Regarding Natural Gas in Israel* (Tzemach Committee Report), Natural Resources Administration, Ministry of Energy, State of Israel, September 2012, p. 8, www.gov.il/BlobFolder/reports/tzemach_report/en/pa3161ed-B-REV%20main%20recommendations%20Tzemach%20report.pdf (accessed on June 15, 2017).

33 *The Natural Gas Authority*, The Ministry Energy, State of Israel, July 4, 2018, www.gov.il/en/Departments/Guides/natural_gas_authority_cuncil?chapterIndex=1 (accessed on July 16, 2018).

34 INGL delivers to eight large power stations owned by Israel Electric Corporation and to independent power producers. In addition, INGL also delivers natural gas to industrial customers including ORL, Haifa Chemicals, Makhteshim, Agan, Dead Sea Works, Mashab, Phoenicia Glass Works, and others. The aim of granting distribution licenses is to extend the network to small and medium consumers. See *Infrastructure for Energy Independence*, Israel Natural Gas Lines, Tel Aviv, Israel, 2013, www.ingl.co.il/?page_id=105&lang=en (accessed on June 22, 2017); *The Distribution Network* [Hebrew], Ministry of Energy, State of Israel, undated, http://archive.energy.gov.il/Subjects/NG/Pages/GxmsMniNGDistributionNetwork.aspx (accessed on July 16, 2018).

35 Subsea tieback is a connection between new (or untapped) oil and gas discovery and an existing production centre. See, *What Is the Foremost Consideration for Subsea Tiebacks?* Audubon Companies, Houston, Texas, US, November 5, 2015, www.auduboncompanies.com/what-is-the-foremost-consideration-for-subsea-tiebacks/ (accessed on June 22, 2017).

36 Shai Bakal, "Israel: Competition Regulation in Israel: The Law, Recent Trends and Insights," *Mondaq*, May 2, 2017, www.mondaq.com/x/590348/Trade+Regulation+Practices/Competition+Regulation (accessed on June 22, 2017).

37 See *The General Director of Restrictive Trade Practices Declares the Partners in the Natural Gas Reservoir 'Tamar' to Have a Monopoly on Israel's Natural Gas Supply*, The Antitrust Authority, State of Israel, Press Release, November 13, 2012, www.antitrust.gov.il/eng/subject/182/item/32858.aspx (accessed on June 22, 2017).

38 Ibid.

39 Shirin Herzog, "Israel's Anti-Concentration Law: An Opportunity for New Players," *The Times of Israel*, November 30, 2017, http://blogs.timesofisrael.com/israels-anti-concentration-law-an-opportunity-for-new-players/ (accessed on July 18, 2018).

40 *TheMarker* is the financial supplement of Israel's leading national daily, *Haaretz*.

41 See Eran Azran, "Israel's Capital Market: A Swamp of Concentration," *Haaretz*, August 1, 2011, www.haaretz.com/israel-news/business/1.5038269 (accessed on June 22, 2017).

42 See *Annual Report on Competition Policy Developments in Israel*, Directorate for Financial and Enterprise Affairs, Organisation for Economic Co-operation and Development, June 11, 2013, pp. 1–17, www.oecd.org/officialdocuments/publicdisplaydocumentpdf/?cote=DAF/COMP/AR(2013)15&docLanguage=En (accessed on June 22, 2017).

43 *Draft Recommendations: Committee for Increasing Competition in the Economy* [Hebrew], Israel's Finance Ministry, October 11, 2011, p. 1, http://mof.gov.il/Committees/CompetitivenessCommittee/TyuyatRec_Report.pdf (accessed on June 24, 2017).

44 Ibid., p. 1.

45 *Law for Promotion of Competition and Reduction of Concentration*, The Antitrust Authority, State of Israel, 2013, www.antitrust.gov.il/eng/Law%20of%20Concentration.aspx (accessed on June 24, 2017).

46 'Government take' in upstream projects is a term that describes the combination of direct royalties and corporate income taxes, as well as service fees and profit sharing.

47 Position of Noble Energy and Delek group submitted to the Sheshinski Committee.

48 *The Minister of Finance Appoints a Committee to Examine the Policy on Oil and Gas Resources in Israel*, Press Release [Hebrew], Ministry of Finance, State of Israel, April 13, 2010, https://mof.gov.il/Releases/Documents/2010-667.doc (accessed on June 27, 2017).

49 Ibid.

50 The Committee members were Eugene Kandel, head of the National Economic Council; Shaul Tzemach, director general of the Ministry of National Infrastructures; Yaakov Mimran, petroleum commissioner, Ministry of National Infrastructures; Yehuda Nasradishi, director of the Tax Authority; and Udi Nissan budget director, Ministry of Finance. Avi Licht, assistant attorney general (economic fiscal) and Amit Friedman from the Bank of Israel (BOI) were observers. Ibid.

51 Momi Dahan, "Policy Analysis in the Treasury: How Does the Israeli Ministry of Finance Arrive at a Policy Decision," in Gila Menahem and Amos Zehavi (eds.), *Policy Analysis in Israel* (Bristol: Policy Press, 2016), p. 135.

52 Noam Sheizaf, "Bill Clinton Tried to Dismantle Israeli Natural Gas Revenue Committee," *+972 Magazine*, April 16, 2013, https://972mag.com/bill-clinton-tried-to-dismantle-israeli-natural-gas-revenue-committee/69394/ (accessed on June 29, 2017).

53 Avi Bar-Eli, "Steinitz Blasts 'Pressure Campaign' Against Gas Royalties Committee," *Haaretz*, August 26, 2010, www.haaretz.com/1.5105440 (accessed on June 29, 2017).

54 Moti Bassok, "Chairman of Israel's Gas Panel Receives Death Threats," *Haaretz*, January 24, 2011, www.haaretz.com/israel-news/business/cabinet-approves-sheshinski-committee-recommendations-1.338809 (accessed on July 1, 2017).

"Sheshinski Eases Proposed Tax for Gas Exploration Firms," *Jerusalem Post*, April 1, 2011, www.jpost.com/National-News/Sheshinski-eases-proposed-tax-for-gas-exploration-firms (accessed on July 1, 2017); Avi Bar-Eli, Moti Bassok and Zvi Zrahiya, "Cabinet Approves Sheshinski Committee Recommendations," *Haaretz*, January 24, 2011, www.haaretz.com/israel-news/business/cabinet-approves-sheshinski-committee-recommendations-1.338809 (accessed on July 1, 2017).

55 The key aspects of the reforms are summarised from the Sheshinski Committee Report. *Summary of Main Conclusions of the Committee for the Examination of Fiscal Policy on Oil and Gas Resources in Israel Headed by Prof. Eytan Sheshinski* [Hebrew], Ministry of Finance, State of Israel, January 3, 2011, https://mof.gov.il/Releases/Documents/2011-19.doc (accessed on July 6, 2017); *Conclusions of the Committee for the Examination of the Fiscal Policy on Oil and Gas Resources in Israel, State of Israel* [Sheshinski Committee] [Hebrew & English], Ministry of Finance, State of Israel, January 2011, https://mof.gov.il/Budget Site/reform/Documents/shashinskiFullReport_n.pdf (accessed on July 6, 2017).

56 By that measure, Tamar – the only field in production at present – must earn more than $8 billion before the Sheshinski levy kicks in, a figure that would be reached not before 2021. As of the end of 2015, Tamar Partners have invested more than $4 billion, and are currently carrying out a significant expansion project, whose cost is approximately $1.5 to 2 billion. See *Tamar Gas Field*, Delek Drilling; Meirav Arlosoroff, "Why Hasn't Israel's Windfall-profit Tax Blown in Yet?" *Haaretz*, August 30, 2017, www.haaretz.com/israel-news/business/why-hasnt-israels-windfall-profit-tax-blown-in-yet-1.5446722 (accessed on August 30, 2017).

57 It is estimated that the levy would only kick in after about eight years of production in the case of a medium to a large field or after about 15 years in the case of a small field. The idea of levy is to incentivise companies to explore for oil and gas and those that are successful earn back an adequate return. See Leon Harris, "Your Taxes: What the Sheshinski Committee Report Means?" *Jerusalem Post*, November 16, 2010, www.jpost.com/Business/Commentary/Your-Taxes-What-the-Sheshinski-Committees-report-means (accessed on July 9, 2017).

58 The London Interbank Offered Rate (LIBOR) is the annualised, average interest rate at which banks offer to lend short-term funds (wholesale money) to one another in the

international interbank market. Lenders, including banks and other financial institutions, use LIBOR as the benchmark reference for determining interest rate for various debt instruments. "Definition of Libor," *Financial Times*, http://lexicon.ft.com/Term?term=LIBOR; "What Is Libor," *Investopedia*, www.investopedia.com/terms/l/libor.asp (accessed on July 9, 2017); "Libor," www.fedprimerate.com/libor/index.html (accessed on July 9, 2017).

59 Many experts believe that the committee included this provision perhaps in compensation for abolishing the depletion allowance. Shlomo Swirski with Guy Pade, Yaron Dishon and Adi Sofer, *No Paradigm Change in Sight: The Economic Policies of the Second Netanyahu Government (2009–2012)*, Friedrich Ebert Stiftung and the Adva Centre (Jerusalem, Israel), November 2013, p. 17, http://adva.org/wp-content/uploads/2015/01/miracle21.pdf (accessed on July 12, 2017).

60 This provision was meant to lighten the fiscal burden for the discoveries existing before the establishment of the committee (i.e., the Yam Tethys and Tamar fields). In doing so, the Sheshinski Committee considered the views of those who (some Knesset members such as Energy Minister Uzi Landau and the representatives of the gas companies) raised the issue of 'retroactivity' in the proposed fiscal system.

61 This provision was clearly included to give a boost to the developers of the Yam Tethys project.

62 This provision was directed at the Tamar field, which was being developed at that time and was expected to come online in mid-2013. It was meant to be an incentive for the developers to expedite the completion of the project.

63 Shir Hever, "Flammable Politics: Political-Economic Implications of Israel's Natural Gas Find," *The Economy of the Occupation: A Socioeconomic Bulletin*, No. 27–28, Alternative Information Centre, Jerusalem, December 2011, p. 27, www.shirhever.com/wp-content/uploads/2018/01/Bulletin-27-28-Natural-Gas-Discovery.pdf (accessed on July 17, 2018).

64 A report of the OECD found Israel to have the highest poverty rate in the developed world (2.5 times the average) and the second-highest gap between rich and poor.

65 However, it is worth noting that the 'transitional provisions' in the final recommendations did specify tax benefits for the Mari B and Tamar fields, providing an incentive for the Tamar partners to develop the field and begin production within three years, i.e., by 1 January, 2014. In fact, the main beneficiary of the provision has been Tamar, which came on stream in March 2013. The provision also gave Tamar an increased R-factor of 2–2.8 (as opposed to 1.5–2.3 levy range), which meant that the developers would begin to pay the tax on profit only after they have recovered a 200 percent return on the investment in E&D of the reserves. See Zvi Lavi, "Landau: Energy Firm May Favor Egypt Gas," *Ynetnews.com*, December 13, 2010, www.ynetnews.com/articles/0,7340,L-3997847,00.html (accessed on July 24, 2017); *Economic & Commercial Report for October 2010*, Embassy of India, Tel Aviv, pp. 5, 7, http://pharmexcil.org/uploadfile/ufiles/293698897_Israel_Annual_Eco_and_Com_Rep_2010.pdf (accessed on July 24, 2017); Amiram Barakat, "Sheshinski: Bring Gas Ashore Early, Pay Less Tax," *Globes*, January 31, 2011, www.globes.co.il/en/article-1000613046 (accessed on July 24, 2017).

66 See *The Ministerial Committee on Legislation Approved the Oil Profits Tax Law, Which Regulates the New Taxation System for Gas and Oil Discoveries* [Hebrew], Ministry of Finance, State of Israel, February 23, 2011, https://mof.gov.il/Releases/Pages/News_320.aspx (accessed on July 25, 2017).; *Oil Profits Tax Law, 5771–2011* [Hebrew], April 10, 2011, https://mof.gov.il/Committees/NatureResourcesCommittee/MoreFiles_TaxesLaw.pdf (accessed on July 25, 2017).

67 "Deepwater Risks-1: Challenges, Risks Can Be Managed in Deepwater Oil and Gas Projects," *Oil and Gas Journal*, November 27, 2006, www.ogj.com/articles/print/volume-104/issue-44/exploration-development/deepwater-risks-1-challenges-risks-can-be-managed-in-deepwater-oil-and-gas-projects.html (accessed on July 25, 2017).

68 Author's telephonic interview with Noam Segal, January 26, 2016, Jerusalem, Israel.

69 Robert S. Pindyck and Analysis Group, Inc., *A Framework for the Taxation of Natural Resources in Israel*, Ministry of Finance, State of Israel, September 22, 2014, p. 32, https://mof.gov.il/Committees/NatureResourcesCommittee/Maskanot_Appendix3. pdf (accessed on July 27, 2017).

70 "Much as taxpaying enterprises would like it, governments cannot be expected to cast their tax systems in stone. Flexibility there has to be in any tax system if it is to respond to differing conditions and to evolve as a result of major changes in the external environment." Carole Nakhle, *Petroleum Taxation: Sharing the Oil Wealth: A Study of Petroleum Taxation Yesterday, Today and Tomorrow* (London and New York: Routledge, 2008), p. 15; See also, Carole Nakhle, *Licensing and Upstream Petroleum Fiscal Regimes: Assessing Lebanon's Choices* (Ras Beirut: The Lebanese Center for Policy Studies, 2015), p. 32, www.lcps-lebanon.org/publications/1436792630-edt_lcps_carol_n_policy_paper_2015_high_res.pdf (accessed on July 27, 2017).

71 In the backdrop of the increase in oil prices in the 1970s, which led to a sharp and unexpected increase in the profitability of entrepreneurs, the UK introduced the Petroleum Revenue Tax in 1975 and raised its level in 1980. After the second oil crisis, in response to the same rise in prices, Norway in 1975 introduced the Special Tax, whose level was raised after the 1979 oil crisis. Similarly, Alaska raised the Production Tax, which was 3 percent in the late 1960s, to 15 percent in 1981 (12.5 percent during the first years of production). Yoav Friedmann, *The Government's Policy in the Field of Natural Gas Production, Seven Years After the Discovery of 'Tamar'* [Hebrew], Bank of Israel, Periodical Papers 2016, March 1, 2016, p. 6, www.boi.org.il/he/NewsAnd Publications/PressReleases/Documents/%D7%9E%D7%97%D7%A7%D7%A8-%20 %D7%9E%D7%93%D7%99%D7%A0%D7%99%D7%95%D7%AA%20%D7%94%D7 %9E%D7%9E%D7%A9%D7%9C%D7%94%20%D7%91%D7%A2%D7%A0%D7%A-3%20%D7%94%D7%A4%D7%A7%D7%AA%20%D7%94%D7%92%D7%96%20 %D7%94%D7%98%D7%91%D7%A2%D7%99.pdf (accessed on July 28, 2017).

72 *A Comparison of Fiscal Regimes: Offshore Natural Gas in Israel*, Special Report, IHS CERA, 2010, www.mof.gov.il/Committees/PreviouslyCommittees/PhysicsPolicyCommittee/ ServedOpinion_NovelEnergy_Appendix_d.pdf (accessed on July 29, 2017).

73 IHS Cambridge Energy Research Associates or IHS CERA is US-based consulting company that specialises in advising governments and private companies on energy markets, geopolitics, industry trends, and strategy. "IHS Cambridge Energy Research Associates Inc.," *Bloomberg*, 2018, www.bloomberg.com/profiles/companies/376925Z:US-ihs-cambridge-energy-research-associates-inc (accessed on July 18, 2018).

74 Daniel Johnston & Co. Inc. is one of the world's leading consultancies for upstream oil and gas exploration and licensing. See http://david01010.wixsite.com/daniel-johnston (accessed on August 2, 2017).

75 Graham Kellas, "The Pitfalls of Windfalls," Wood Mackenzie Ltd., 2006 [Emphasis mine]. Quoted in Daniel Johnston, *Israel Hydrocarbon Fiscal Analysis and Commentary*, Daniel Johnston & Co., Inc., November 15, 2010, p. 6, www.eisourcebook.org/cms/ Israel,%20Hydrocarbon%20Fiscal%20Analysis%20and%20Commentary.pdf (accessed on August 2, 2017).

76 Friedmann, *The Government's Policy in the Field of Natural Gas Production*, March 2016, p. 7.

77 Amiram Barkat, reporter and commentator associated with Israeli financial daily, *Globes*, makes this argument. Amiram Barkat, "Gas Developers, Owe Sheshinski Debt of Gratitude," *Globes*, May 20, 2015, www.globes.co.il/en/article-gas-developers-owe-sheshinski-a-debt-of-gratitude-1001038366 (accessed on August 2, 2017).

78 The summary of the judgement is from: Hila Raz, "The Petitions Against the Sheshinski Law Were Rejected: 'There Is No Retroactive Taxation Here'," *The Marker* [Hebrew], August 15, 2012, www.themarker.com/law/1.1801962 (accessed on August 2, 2017).

79 The National Economic Council, established by Government Resolution No. 430 in September 2006, serves as a coordinating body for the Prime Minister on issues

that require macroeconomic perspective and methodological economic thinking. It assists the Prime Minister in decision-making processes and is staffed with a team of economists with advanced degrees and proficiency in the public, private, and academic sectors. *About the National Economic Council*, Prime Minister's Office, http://www.pmo.gov.il/English/PrimeMinistersOffice/DivisionsAndAuthorities/TheNationalEconomicCouncil/Pages/About.aspx (accessed on February 7, 2019).

80 *Letter of Appointment Establishing Inter-Ministerial Committee to Examine the Government's Policy Regarding Natural Gas in Israel*, Ministry of Energy, State of Israel, October 4, 2011, www.gov.il/he/Departments/news/gas_com (accessed on August 5, 2017).
81 See Executive Summary of *The Recommendations of the Inter-Ministerial Committee to Examine the Government's Policy Regarding Natural Gas in Israel*, September 2012, pp. 1–2.
82 *Full Report of the Tzemach Committee* [Hebrew], Ministry of Energy, State of Israel, September 2012, p. 85, http://archive.energy.gov.il/Subjects/NG/Documents/NGReportSep12.pdf (accessed on August 5, 2017).
83 Ibid.
84 Author's interview with Ambassador Ron Adam, Envoy on Energy Policy, Ministry of Foreign Affairs, State of Israel, January 11, 2016.
85 *Full Report of the Tzemach Committee*, September 2012, p. 4.
86 In the 10 scenarios projected by the Tzemach Committee relating to demand forecast for natural gas in the Israeli economy, the range of years is 2013–2040. Ibid., pp. 115–124.
87 Ibid., pp. 4–5.
88 Ibid. pp. 9, 95.
89 *Tzemach Committee Report*, Executive Summary, September 2012, p. 4.
90 Ibid., p. 3.
91 Author's interview with Ambassador Oded Eran, Senior Research Fellow at the Institute for National Security Studies and Israel's ambassador to Jordan (1997–2000), Tel Aviv, January 13, 2016.
92 Drilling at the sites of Sara, Mira, Ishai, and Shimshon licenses has yielded 'dry' or 'almost dry' wells. With quantities of gas discovered in these drillings being 90 percent below forecasts that reportedly cut about 130 bcm from the total reserves. See Ron Steinblatt, "National Capital Markets Recommends Ratio: Improving Prospects for Exports," *Globes*, May 6, 2013, www.globes.co.il/news/article.aspx?did=1000841866 (accessed on August 8, 2017); *Ministry Director General: The Tzemach Committee Should Reconsider Its Gas Export Policy Recommendations*, Israel Ministry of Environmental Protection, State of Israel, October 25, 2012, www.sviva.gov.il/English/Resourcesand-Services/NewsAndEvents/NewsAndMessageDover/Pages/2012/10_October_2012/TzemachCmteRecommendations.aspx (accessed on August 8, 2017).
93 See Alona Sheafer-Caro, *The Position of the Ministry of Environmental Protection – Recommendations of the Committee to Examine Government Policy in the Natural Gas Industry* [Hebrew], September 12, 2012, Ministry of Energy, State of Israel, http://archive.energy.gov.il/Subjects/NG/Documents/NGSviva.pdf (accessed on August 11, 2017).
94 *Adoption of Tzemach Committee Conclusions Could Harm the Public and Could Cause Irreparable Damage to the Economy and the Environment*, Ministry of Environmental Protection, State of Israel, April 4, 2013, www.sviva.gov.il/English/ResourcesandServices/NewsAndEvents/NewsAndMessageDover/Pages/2012/08_August_2012/Tzemach-CommitteeConclusionsHarmful.aspx (accessed on August 11, 2017).
95 Sinaia Netanyahu and Shlomo Wald, *The Policy of Managing Natural Gas Resources in Israel Opinion on the Subject of Natural Gas Export Option From Israel* [Hebrew], March 19, 2012, pp. 5, 6, http://archive.energy.gov.il/Subjects/NG/Documents/%D7%94%D7%AA%D7%99%D7%99%D7%97%D7%A1%D7%95%D7%AA/NGExportMarch2012.pdf (accessed on August 11, 2017).
96 Ibid., pp. 4, 8, 22, 23.
97 Ibid., p. 8.

98 Ibid., p. 9.

99 Ibid.

100 Ibid., pp. 5, 8; Itai Trilnick, "Israel's Gas Reserves Insufficient for Exports," *Haaretz*, July 18, 2012, www.haaretz.com/israel-news/business/israel-s-gas-reserves-insufficient-for-exports-1.451838 (accessed on August 16, 2017).

101 Sinaia Netanyahu and Shlomo Wald, *The Policy of Managing Natural Gas Resources*, p. 20.

102 Ibid.

103 Ibid.

104 See "Minister of Environment at the Economic Affairs Committee: 'We Are Not a Gas Empire, We Should Keep Reserves of the bcm 600 for the Israeli Market'," *Press Release* [English], The Knesset, June 5, 2013, www.knesset.gov.il/spokesman/eng/PR_eng.asp?PRID=10766 (accessed on August 16, 2017).

105 Ibid.; See, "At a Glance: News in Brief About the Environment in Israel," *Israel Environment Bulletin*, Volume 39 (July 2013), Israel Ministry of Environmental Protection, State of Israel, pp. 6–7, www.sviva.gov.il/English/ResourcesandServices/Publications/Bulletin/Documents/Bulletin-Vol39-July2013.pdf (accessed on August 16, 2017).

106 Ariella Berger, "Natural Gas at the Supreme Court: Far-Reaching Consequences," *Jerusalem Post*, August 7, 2013, www.jpost.com/Opinion/Op-Ed-Contributors/When-the-wider-public-sphere-becomes-the-correct-forum-322380 (accessed on August 19, 2017).

107 See "Minister of Environment at the Economic Affairs Committee: 'We Are Not a Gas Empire, We Should Keep Reserves of the bcm 600 for the Israeli Market'," *Press Release* [English], The Knesset, June 5, 2013.

108 *Adoption of the Main Recommendations of the Committee to Examine the Government's Policy Regarding the Natural Gas Market in Israel*, Government Resolution 442, June 23, 2013, Ministry of Energy, State of Israel, https://www.gov.il/he/Departments/policies/2013_des442 (accessed on August 19, 2017); *Cabinet Approves Increase in Quantity of Gas for the Israeli Economy*, Prime Minister's Office, State of Israel, June 23, 2013, www.pmo.gov.il/English/MediaCenter/Spokesman/Pages/spokegas230613.aspx (accessed on August 19, 2017); *PM Netanyahu's Remarks on the Decision to Increase to 60% the Amount of Natural Gas Designated for the Israeli Market*, Prime Minister's Office, State of Israel, June 16, 2013, www.pmo.gov.il/english/mediacenter/events/pages/eventgas190613.aspx (accessed on August 19, 2017); "Israeli government approves 40 pct limit on natural gas exports," *Reuters*, June 23, 2013, www.reuters.com/article/israel-natgas-idUSL5N0EZ0BQ20130623 (accessed on August 19, 2017).

109 In the Supreme Court sitting as the High Court of Justice, HCJ 4491/13 [Hebrew], October 21, 2013, para 26 of the opinion of Justice Grunis.

110 Ibid., para 23, 26 of the opinion of Justice Grunis.

111 Ibid., para 28.

112 Ibid., para 33.

113 The term is often used to refer to the liquid form, commonly called crude oil, but, as a technical term, petroleum also includes natural gas.

114 Petroleum Law, 5712 – 1952, *State of Israel*, http://www.energy-sea.gov.il/English-Site/SiteAssets/PETROLEUM%20%20LAW,%201952.pdf (accessed on August 19, 2017)

115 HCJ 4491/13, para 40 of the opinion of Justice Grunis.

116 Ibid., para 42.

117 Article 34 of the Petroleum Law provides: "A Lessee May, Subject to the Regulations, Import Petroleum and Petroleum Products Into Israel and May Refine Petroleum, Whether Produced in Israel or Imported From Abroad and May Process, Transport, *Export* and Trade in Such Petroleum and Petroleum Products." Emphasis mine.

118 HCJ 4491/13, para 2, opinion of Justice Miriam Naor.

119 HCJ 4491/13, para 3, opinion of Justice Salim Joubran.

120 HCJ 4491/13, para 4, opinion of Justice Elyakim Rubinstein.

121 HCJ 4491/13, para 3, opinion of Justice Joubran and para 15 of Justice Rubinstein.

122 In the Supreme Court sitting as the High Court of Justice, HCJ 4491/13 [Hebrew], p. 24; Edna Adato, Hezi Sternlicht, Ze'ev Klein, and Dan Lavie, "High Court Upholds Government's Gas Export Policy," *Israel Hayom*, October 22, 2013, www.israelhayom. com/site/newsletter_article.php?id=12749 (accessed on August 24, 2017).

123 *The General Director of Restrictive Trade Practices Considers Declaring Delek to Have a Monopoly in the Supply of Natural Gas and to Determine That Delek, Avner, Noble and Ratio Were Sides to a Restrictive Arrangement in Relation to the 'Leviathan' Joint Venture*, The Antitrust Authority, Government of Israel, Press Release, September 6, 2011, www. antitrust.gov.il/eng/subject/182/item/32860.aspx (accessed on August 24, 2017).

124 Ibid.

125 *The General Director of Restrictive Trade Practices Declares the Partners in the Natural Gas Reservoir 'Tamar' to Have a Monopoly*, The Antitrust Authority, November 13, 2012.

126 Under antitrust legislation, monopolists are subject to special restrictions, and in order to prevent anti-competitive behaviour or harm to the public, the General Director may issue instructions to the monopolist regarding the measures it must take. In particular, the law prohibits a monopolist from using its position to reduce competition or harm the public, inter alia, through setting exorbitant prices, engaging in predatory pricing, engaging in price discrimination, or stipulating unreasonable terms. Prohibitions against unreasonable refusal to supply the product also apply. Among other actions, the General Director may respond to monopolist behaviour that may block the entry of competing suppliers into the market, drive them out of the market, or harm competition between the monopolist's customers.

127 *The General Director of Restrictive Trade Practices*, Press Release, The Antitrust Authority, State of Israel, November 13, 2012.

128 Friedmann, *The Government's Policy in the Field of Natural Gas Production*, March 2016, p. 2.

129 *The General Director of Restrictive Trade Practices*, The Antitrust Authority, November 13, 2012.

130 "Regulator Orders Delek, Noble Energy to Sell Gas Fields," *Globes*, March 27, 2014, www.globes.co.il/en/articleregulator-orders-delek-noble-energy-to-sell-gas-fields-1000927892 (accessed on August 27, 2017); Avi Bar-Eli, "Antitrust Chief Warns He May Break Up Natural Gas Monopoly," *Haaretz*, December 23, 2014, www.haaretz.com/israel-news/business/.premium-1.633228 (accessed on August 27, 2017).

131 Michael Hochberg, *Israel's Natural Gas Potential: Securing the Future*, Middle East Institute, Policy Focus Series, August 2016, p. 7, www.mei.edu/sites/default/files/publications/PF20_Hochberg_IsraelGas_web.pdf (accessed on August 30, 2017).

132 *Update on the Natural Gas Issue*, The Antitrust Authority, State of Israel, December 24, 2014, www.antitrust.gov.il/eng/item/33459/search/785c3118847a4ee381ae044651cb82b3.aspx (accessed on August 30, 2017).

133 Ibid.

134 Shiri Shaham and Simon Weintraub, "Israeli Natural Gas Industry – Where Do We Go Now?" *Oilfield Technology*, June 24, 2016, www.energyglobal.com/upstream/drilling-and-production/24062016/israeli-natural-gas-industry-where-do-we-go-now-part-1/ (accessed on September 1, 2017).

135 See, Shiri Shaham and Simon Weintraub, *Update on Israeli Natural Gas Industry*, Yigal Arnon & Co., Tel Aviv and Jerusalem, January 11, 2017, www.engineerlive.com/content/update-israeli-natural-gas-industry (accessed on September 1, 2017); *Israel's Upstream Natural Gas Sector Against the Backdrop of the New Gas Framework*, Meitar Law Firm, June 7, 2016, http://meitar.com/files/Publications/2016/1-israels_upstream_natural_gas_sector_against_the_backdrop_of_the_new_gas_framework.pdf (accessed on September 1, 2017).

136 *Israeli Government's Vision of the Natural Gas Market*, Delek Group, 2017, www.delek-group.com/our-operations/east-med-our-business-environment/ (accessed on September 2, 2017).

137 The stability clause was inserted because the gas companies contended that the $6 billion or more needed to develop Leviathan, Israel's biggest field, would be too risky otherwise. A government in the future could opt to change tax policy and other regulations that would affect the return on their investment.

138 *Speech of Professor David Gilo, Israel Antitrust Authority General, at the Annual Conference of the Israeli Institute of Energy*, The Antitrust Authority, State of Israel, May 26, 2015, www.antitrust.gov.il/eng/subject/182/item/33641.aspx (accessed on September 5, 2017).

139 The narrowly defined circumstances where Article 52 can be used have been incorporated to protect the Antitrust Authority's independence and its overall status of key regulator in the Israeli economy. See *Article 52, Restrictive Trade Practices Law, 5748–1988*, The Antitrust Authority, State of Israel, undated, www.antitrust.gov.il/eng/Antitrust-law.aspx (accessed on July 20, 2018); *Annual Report on Competition Policy Developments in Israel – 2015*, Organisation for Economic Co-operation and Development (OECD), 15–17 June 2016, p. 4, www.oecd.org/officialdocuments/publicdisplaydocumentpdf/?cote=DAF/COMP/AR(2016)5&docLanguage=En (accessed on September 5, 2017).

140 Moran Azulay, "Netanyahu Fighting to Build Majority for Natural Gas Plan," *Reuters*, June 29, 2015, www.reuters.com/article/israel-gas-idUSL8N0ZG0J820150630 (accessed on September 5, 2017).

141 *Security Cabinet Unanimously Approves Moving Quickly to Develop and Expand Israel's Gas Fields*, Prime Minister's Office (PMO), State of Israel, June 25, 2015, www.pmo.gov.il/English/MediaCenter/Spokesman/Pages/spokeGaz250615.aspx (accessed on September 8, 2017).

142 *At the Weekly Cabinet Meeting*, PMO, State of Israel, June 28, 2015, www.pmo.gov.il/english/mediacenter/secretaryannouncements/pages/govmes280615.aspx (accessed on September 8, 2017).

143 *At the Weekly Cabinet Meeting*, PMO, State of Israel, August 16, 2015, www.pmo.gov.il/english/mediacenter/secretaryannouncements/pages/govmes160815.aspx (accessed on September 8, 2017).

144 "Controversial Natural Gas Deal Passes Knesset," *Times of Israel*, September 7, 2015, www.timesofisrael.com/controversial-natural-gas-deal-passes-knesset/ (accessed on September 8, 2017).

145 Lahav Harkov, "Gas Deal Still Stuck Despite Knesset Approval," Jerusalem Post, September 7, 2015, https://www.jpost.com/Israel-News/Politics-And-Diplomacy/Gas-deal-still-stuck-despite-Knesset-approval-415489 (accessed on September 8, 2017).

146 *Economic Affairs Committee Advises PM Netanyahu Not to Activate Article 52 of Antitrust Law in Order to Implement Natural Gas Deal; Chairman Cabel: In Israel It Is Easy to Make Everything a Security Issue*, The Knesset, Press Release, December 14, 2015, www.knesset.gov.il/spokesman/eng/PR_eng.asp?PRID=11815 (accessed on September 9, 2017).

147 The government decision of August 2015 introduced some amendments in the framework. One related to the ten-year regulatory stability clause: In case a private member bill passed the Knesset proceedings, the government would initiate another bill to reinstate the status quo ante. Another important amendment related to the 'domestic content': The Tamar and Leviathan leaseholders were enjoined to invest at least $500 million over eight years in pertinent Israeli goods and services, R&D, personnel and professional training as part of the local content requirement.

148 Author's interview with Oren Barak, professor of Political Science and International Politics, Hebrew university of Jerusalem, Jerusalem, Israel, January 12, 2015.

149 Buzan et al. (1998) opine that, "Securitization is an extreme version of politicization that enables the use of extraordinary means in the name of security." State practitioners who implement policies securitise issues that are not necessarily essential to the survival of the state, but rather they have been successful in constructing these issues into existential problems. Thus, as Silva says, it becomes "convenient to implement policies that,

otherwise, would have to be profoundly debated, contested and justified (2016)." Barry Buzan, Ole Wæver, and Jaap de Wilde, *Security: A New Framework for Analysis* (Boulder: Lynne Rienner Publishers, 1998), p. 25; Marta Silva, "Securitization as a Nation-building Instrument," *Politikon: The IAPSS Academic Journal*, Volume 29 (March 2016), p. 203; See also Barry Buzan, *People, States and Fear: An Agenda for International Security Studies in the Post-Cold War Era*, 2nd edition (Colchester: ECPR Press, 2009).

150 Author's telephonic interview with Amon Portugali, January 26, 2016, Jerusalem, Israel, January 24, 2016. Portugali is a research fellow at the Chazan Center for Social Justice and Democracy at the Van Leer Institute, Jerusalem. He is the founder and leader of the Forum for Civilian Action which led the struggle for Israel's natural gas royalties.

151 Justice Uzi Vogelman, Nadiv Mordechay, Yaniv Roznai, and Tehilla Schwartz, "Developments in Israeli Constitutional Law: The Year 2016 in Review," *I-CONnect: Blog of the International Journal of Constitutional Law*, October 4, 2017, www.iconnectblog. com/2017/10/developments-in-israeli-constitutional-law-the-year-2016-in-review/ (accessed on September 11, 2017).

152 High Court of Justice 4374/15, 7588/15, 8747/15, 262/16, *The Movement for Quality Government v. The Prime Minister, Summary* of Judgment [English translation], p. 2, http://versa.cardozo.yu.edu/sites/default/files/upload/opinions/Movement%20for%20Quality%20Government%20v.%20Prime%20Minister_0.pdf (accessed on July 23, 2018).

153 Ibid., p. 4.

154 Ibid.

155 Ibid., p. 6.

156 Ibid., p. 8.

157 Ibid., p. 5.

158 Ibid., p. 4.

159 This was evident from the fact that a few hours after Netanyahu's affidavit, the judges asked the state attorney to respond within seven days as to the 'stability aspect' of the agreement could be passed in the Knesset instead of being authorised merely in PM's capacity as economy minister. Yonah Jeremy Bob, "Netanyahu to High Court: Gas Deal Helps Chance of Peace With Many Countries," *Jerusalem Post*, February 14, 2016, www.jpost.com/Israel-News/Politics-And-Diplomacy/Netanyahu-confronts-High-Court-to-defend-natural-gas-policy-in-unprecedented-personal-appearance-444846 (accessed on September 16, 2017).

160 Deputy President E. Rubinstein and Justice S. Joubran and U. Vogelman favoured the entire framework be cancelled, whereas Justice E. Hayut was of the opinion that only the restrictive provisions that are in Chapter 10 of the NGF should be ruled void. *Summary of Judgment the Supreme Court*, High Court of Justice 4374/15, 7588/15, 8747/15, 262/, pp. 8–9.

161 *Amendment of the Outline for Increasing the Quantity of Natural Gas Produced From the Tamar Natural Gas Field and the Rapid Development of the Leviathan, Karish and Tannin Natural Gas Fields and Other Natural Gas Fields*, Government Decision 1465, PMO, State of Israel May 22, 2016, www.gov.il/he/Departments/policies/2016_dec1465 (accessed on September 17, 2017).

162 Shaham and Weintraub, "Israeli Natural Gas Industry – Where Do We Go Now?" June 24, 2016.

163 *Solution Found for Framework for Developing Israel's Natural Gas Fields – The Stability Provision Will Be Revised*, Ministry of Energy, State of Israel, May 19, 2016, www.gov.il/en/departments/news/framework_developing_natural_gas_fields (accessed on September 23, 2017).

164 "Lebanon's Oil & Gas Licensing Round Attracts Bids From Total-Eni-Novatek," *Middle East Strategic Perspective*, October 13, 2017, www.mesp.me/2017/10/13/lebanons-oil-gas-licensing-round-attracts-bids-total-eni-novatek/ (accessed on July 25, 2018).

165 Friedmann, *The Government's Policy in the Field of Natural Gas Production*, March 2016, p. 17.

166   Edison still remains a partner in the Royee license on the southern side of Israel's exclusive economic zone, along the maritime border with Egypt. Ratio currently holds 70 percent of the rights in the license along with Edison (20 percent – operator) and Israel Opportunity (10 percent). *Royee*, Ratio Oil, 2017, www.ratioil.com/en/assets/royee/ (accessed on September 24, 2017).

167   "Edison Stops Gas Exploration in Israel," *Trend News Agency*, August 7, 2018, https://en.trend.az/world/europe/2937789.html (accessed on July 27, 2018).

168   Arie Reich, *Israel's Foreign Investment Protection Regime in View of Developments in Its Energy Sector*, European University Institute Department of Law, EUI Working Paper LAW, February 2017, p. 21, https://poseidon01.ssrn.com/delivery.php ?ID=674066 09202008107212100500508101710 10380460070200590341270660891101261 0209 90 72029028056033058006042055014025020105118119091096053082054 0010601 22115073004110103078006061053066087028066090075031125012071024 0650241 2108702902508212707707700181220980770241 04&EXT=pdf (accessed on September 24, 2017).

169   Ibid., See also, Ori Redler, "Crime and Punishment: The Social Protests Chase Away Investors," *Mida* [Hebrew], December 9, 2015, https://mida.org.il/2015/12/09/%D7%94%D7%97%D7%98%D7%90-%D7%95%D7%A2%D7%95%D7%A0%D7%A9%D7%95-%D7%94%D7%9E%D7%97%D7%90%D7%95%D7%AA-%D7%94%D7%97%D7%91%D7%A8%D7%AA%D7%99%D7%95%D7%AA-%D7%9E%D7%91%D7%A8%D7%99%D7%97%D7%95%D7%AA-%D7%90/ (accessed on September 24, 2017).

170   *Country Comparison: Natural Gas – Proved Reserves*, The World Factbook, Central Investigation Agency (CIA), undated, www.cia.gov/library/publications/the-world-factbook/rankorder/2253rank.html (accessed on September 27, 2017).

171   Reich, *Israel's Foreign Investment*, p. 21.

172   *Report of the Professional Team's Conclusions for Periodic Review of the Recommendations of the Government Policy Review Committee on the Issue of the Natural Gas Sector in Israel that Were Adopted in Government Decision 442 of 23 June 2013: Draft for Public Reference* [Adiri Committee Interim Report] [Hebrew], Ministry of Energy, State of Israel, July 2018, www.gov.il/BlobFolder/rfp/ng_160718/he/Israel_Natural_Gas_report_draft.pdf (accessed on August 31, 2018).

173   *Conclusions of the professional committee for the periodic review of the recommendations of the Committee for the Examination of Government Policy on the Natural Gas Sector in Israel, which were adopted in Government Decision 442 of 23 June 2013* [Adiri Committee] [Hebrew], Final Report, Ministry of Energy, State of Israel, December 2018, https://www.gov.il/BlobFolder/reports/periodic_examination/he/ng_dec_18.pdf (accessed on February 5, 2019); *Conclusions of the Professional Team for the Periodic Examination of the Recommendations of the Committee on Examining the Government's Policy in the Natural Gas Market Adopted in Government Decision 442 Dated June 23 2013* [Adiri Committee], Executive Summary, December 2018, Ministry of Energy, State of Israel, December 2018, http://www.energy-sea.gov.il/English-Site/PublishingImages/Pages/Forms/EditForm/Adiri%20Committee%20Final%20Recommendations%2018.12.2018%20Executive%20Summary%20-%20Translation.pdf (accessed on February 11, 2019).

174   *Conclusions of the professional committee*, Final Report, p. 5.

175   Ibid.

176   Ibid., p. 41.

177   Ibid., p. 6.

178   Ibid., p. 6.

179   Ibid., pp. 5, 6, 46

180   See Yaniv Bar, *The Natural Gas Sector in Israel: An Economic Survey*, Bank Leumi, August 2018, p. 1, https://english.leumi.co.il/static-files/10/LeumiEnglish/Israel_Capital_Markets/Natural_Gas_in_Israel_August_2018_global.pdf?reffer=deposit_check_hp_banner (accessed on August 31, 2018).

181   Ibid., p. 7.

182 Ibid., pp. 8, 9.
183 Ibid., p. 8.
184 Ibid., pp. 7, 46, 55.
185 Ibid., p. 8.
186 *Adopting the main recommendations of the professional team for the periodic review of the recommendations of the Committee to Examine the Government's Policy on the Natural Gas Sector in Israel and the Amendment of the Government Decision*, Government Decision 442, Prime Minister's Office, January 6, 2019, https://www.gov.il/he/Departments/policies/dec4442_2019 (accessed on February 11, 2019).
187 *2nd Bid Round*, Ministry of Energy, State of Israel, November 2018, http://www.energy-sea.gov.il/English-Site/Pages/Offshore%20Bid%20Rounds/2nd-Bid-Round.aspx (accessed on February 11, 2019).
188 *Council Decisions*, Council for Natural Gas Affairs, Ministry of Energy, State of Israel, undated, http://archive.energy.gov.il/Subjects/NG/Pages/GxmsMniNGPublicationsAggregator.aspx (accessed on July 28, 2018).

3

ECONOMIC IMPLICATIONS FOR ISRAEL

Prospects for development of new gas-based sectors

Natural gas is a very flexible source of energy that can help us bridge the gap between our current high-carbon economy and our zero-carbon future.

–Katharine Hayhoe[1]

Israel's gas discovery has indeed been a game changer for the country's economy, leading to a change in the nature of fuel used for electricity production and manufacturing. Natural gas has displaced coal in power production and has created the potential for fuelling the transportation fleet and the development of the petrochemical sector. Coal import has gone down and so have the externalities associated with environmental degradation.

With dramatic structural changes in Israel's energy sector stemming from a change in the fuel mix, the impact of natural gas in raising the economy's relative advantage is only beginning to appear. Until 2004, Israel was completely dependent on imported oil and coal for its primary energy supply. The beginning of supply from the Yam Tethys in 2004 and boost from Tamar field since 2013 have substantially nudged out oil and coal in the generation of electricity. While the use of fuel oil in electricity generation has been negligible in recent years, coal still has a strong show, but figures indicate a continuous downward trend with gas substitution.[2] In 2016–2017, Israel took some major decisions to reduce the use of coal in the power sector. A 'load order' was established according to which natural gas will have priority over coal in power stations while operating coal units at a minimal load and the substitution of coal-fired units in power stations with gas-powered units.[3] Such measures will eventually allow Israel to absorb more gas when the Leviathan reservoir comes on stream in 2019.

The obvious monetary benefits to the economy of using indigenous natural gas instead of imported coal and oil – in terms of reduced fuel costs for electricity generation and production costs in energy-intensive industries – cannot be over-emphasised. According to the assessment of the NGA, Israel's savings during the 14-years transition (2004–2017) to natural gas is approximately NIS 54.4 billion. More than 76 percent or NIS 41.5 billion of savings was in the electricity sector; a significant reduction in fuel oil use in the industrial sector saved about NIS 12.8 billion.[4]

Natural gas not only brings down the strategic and economic dependence on imported oil and coal, it also significantly reduces the emission of contaminants to the environment. The improvement in air quality thereby reduces the huge indirect cost associated with the pollution and health damage. There has been a substantial decrease in emission of pollutants following the reduction in the use of diesel oil, fuel oil, and coal in electricity generation and industrial production. In the five years between 2012 and 2016, carbon dioxide (CO_2) emissions in Israel from all sources registered a downward trend from about 74 thousand tonnes to 64 thousand tonnes. In tandem, CO_2 emissions per capita reduced from 9.3 tCO_2 /capita in 2012 to 7.5 tonne tCO_2/capita in 2016.[5] Similarly, Nitrogen dioxide (NO_2) emission went down from 182.7 thousand tonnes to 123.5 thousand tonnes between the years 2012 and 2016.[6] Natural gas, thus, has significant mitigation potential for GHG emissions. It is a much more efficient fuel and can produce almost 20 percent added electricity as compared to coal or oil.

The energy economy objectives of the MoE[7] instruct a reduction in the use of polluting fossil fuels by 2030. More specifically, the goal is to completely terminate the use of coal and nearly end the use of distillate fuels in the three main sectors of the economy, namely, electricity production, transportation, and industrial sector. In power generation, the goal is to generate 80 percent of electricity requirement from natural gas, with the rest generated by a mix of renewable energy. The coal-based power stations of the IEC in Hadera and Ashkelon will be shuttered. Industry, both heavy and light, will be based on natural gas, the goal being the achievement of 95 percent use of natural gas for the production of energy and steam from 2030. In the transportation sector, the plan calls for a gradual switch of public transportation and heavy fleet from gasoline to natural gas-burning engines and electricity. By 2030, import of vehicles powered by diesel and gasoline will be totally banned and all the cars sold in Israel will be electric vehicles. The objective, if achieved, will reduce air pollution by at least 60 percent, and save the state over NIS 78 billion by 2040, according to the ministry's estimate.

However, an increased utilisation of gas in the Israeli economy in the last ten years was limited by both supply and demand constraints, including termination of gas import from Egypt in 2012,[8] rapid depletion of the Yam Tethys reservoirs, delay in the development of Leviathan and other gas fields due to regulatory issues, lack of sufficient onshore natural gas distribution network, and high cost of establishment of facilities for use of gas in transportation and petrochemical industry. Each of these aspects will be discussed in this chapter. Israel's gas sector will require the elimination of these limitations to enable the market to fully utilise the economic and environmental benefits of domestically produced natural gas.

The Tamar reservoir will continue to be the primary source of supply of natural gas for the Israeli economy until Leviathan is connected to the supply system towards the end of 2019, and the beginning of gas production from Karish planned for the first quarter of 2021. These independent sources will be able to provide a total annual supply of 26 bcm per year, starting 2021 (10 bcm from Tamar + 12 bcm from Leviathan, and 4 bcm from Karish).[9] With an accelerated pace of deployment of natural gas distribution network throughout the country and the beginning of the use of natural gas in transportation and petrochemicals, the key economic benefit of gas supply from Leviathan and Karish would be the further reduction in the import of energy and energy products. The drop in import of fuels would lead to a decline in negative trade balance of $5.1 billion in net imports in 2016 and support an increase in the current account of the balance of payments. However, a consequent strengthening of the shekel would be problematic for export of manufacturing goods, requiring the national bank to employ foreign-currency purchase mechanism, as it is doing currently to manage royalties and tax proceeds from the gas sector.

According to the 2018 OECD economic survey of Israel, the beginning of gas production from Leviathan will have just a slight initial positive impact of 0.3 percent on GDP compared to 1.1 percent of GDP (2013–2014) from the commencement of production from Tamar – that is because the domestic demand for natural gas is limited in the current scenario, which will be supplied mostly from Tamar. The longer-term impact of Leviathan on GDP will depend on export opportunities, according to the report.[10] Contracts for export of gas to Jordan and Egypt from the Leviathan field, and ongoing discussions with the European countries to export gas, will encourage the development of the field and draw the interest of IOCs in potential oil and gas resources in Israeli offshore area. In addition, contribution to Israel's GDP will come from the tax on excess profit of the gas companies starting in 2020. It could represent 10 percent of GDP in 2040[11] and will be invested in a SWF in foreign currencies to reduce the risks of 'Dutch disease.'

Post-NGF developments

One of the important implications of NGF is the improved potential for an augmented flow of gas into the economy in a competitive environment. Under the framework, stakeholders of the Leviathan are obliged to develop the reservoir by 2020. In February 2017, the Leviathan developers made the final investment decision (FID) for the development of the first phase (Phase 1A) or the domestic supply module (DSM) of the Leviathan field (Figure 3.1).[12] The first phase includes capacity development of up to 12 bcm per year, primarily intended for the Israeli economy and Jordan's NEPCO. In the second stage (Phase 1b) or the regional export module (REM) of the field,[13] the company targets a capacity

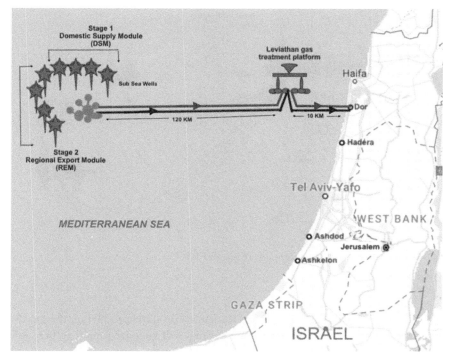

FIGURE 3.1 Leviathan's development modules (Phase 1A and 1B)

Source: Author

Disclaimer: Map not to scale

development of 9 bcm per year, meant for export (Figure 3.1).[14] With the development of both phases, the Leviathan reservoir is expected to reach a maximum production capacity of 21 bcm per year.

The total sale of Karish and Tanin gas fields to an unrelated third party marks another milestone in the fulfilment of the developers' obligation under NGF. With the goal of increasing competition within the upstream sector, the energy ministry approved the sale of Karish and Tanin to Greek energy company Energean Oil in December 2016 and granted the approval to transfer the two leases to Energean Israel, the gas subsidiary. A year later, with the financial backing of its partner Kerogen Capital (50 percent interest), Energean Israel's field development plan (FDP) was approved by the Israeli Petroleum Commissioner in August 2017.

Energean approved the FID to proceed with the development of Karish–Tanin in March 2018, having secured the finances and equity funding for the project. Energean will develop the project through a FPSO vessel (Figure 3.2),[15] which will be built some 90 km offshore. The company believes FPSO will ease gas processing and storage and could also be used for other projects.[16] The company will develop Tanin after Karish, depending upon the number of GSPAs

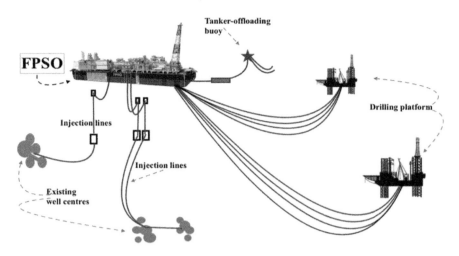

FIGURE 3.2 Oil and gas development through FPSO

Source: Author

secured and growth in gas sales. Once Karish–Tanin starts producing, the Israeli gas market, with 26 bcm of gas in circulation, will become supply secure and achieve redundancy (Figure 3.3).

As far as Tamar field is concerned, Delek Drilling has started selling its stakes to be able to exit the field by 2022, in accord with its commitment under the gas framework. Equally, Noble Energy has started to trim itself in Tamar through the sale of some of its holdings. In July 2016, Noble Energy sold 3.5 percent of its Tamar holdings to Israel's Harel Investments and Financial Services Ltd. and Israel Infrastructure Fund. In July 2017, Delek Drilling, established the Tamar Petroleum, a special purpose vehicle (SPV) to sell its rights in the Tamar field. Following a successful initial public offering (IPO), Tamar Petroleum started trading on the Tel Aviv Stock Exchange.[17]

Delek Drilling sold its 9.25 percent working interest in Tamar and Dalit Leases to Tamar Petroleum and, in exchange, Delek received approximately NIS 3 billion (approximately $850 million) as well as a shareholding in Tamar Petroleum amounting to 40 percent. Once Noble transfers 7.5 percent of Tamar rights, Tamar Petroleum will hold 16.75 percent of the rights in the two leases.[18]

Gas sale agreements: Leviathan

Once the Leviathan reservoir starts producing commercially, it will significantly increase the volume of gas supply to the domestic market (to about 20 bcm per annum), establishing energy security and redundancy, which does not exist at

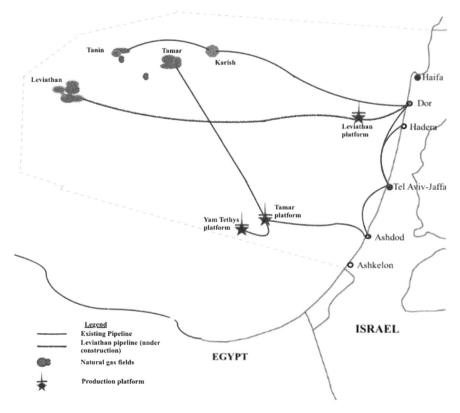

FIGURE 3.3   Israel's domestic market for natural gas by 2021

Source: Author's figure; referenced from Delek Group, 2017

present given the economy's reliance solely on Tamar. The connection of the Leviathan to the onshore pipeline system will more than double the amount of gas available to the domestic market and that will bring about significant changes. In addition to the fact that it will expand the production of electricity based on natural gas with the increase in consumption of existing customers and entry of new producers, big and small businesses in the manufacturing sector will switch over to natural gas for their energy requirements, assured of a local and reliable supply.

Leviathan development is the largest privately financed infrastructure project in Israel's history. The estimated cost of development of the domestic phase is $3.5–4 billion out of the total cost of $5–6 billion.[19] It is important that Leviathan partners sign long-term agreements for the supply of gas that will ensure the flow of revenues for investment in the future development of the field. Some of the Leviathan's GSPAs are:

a) Edeltech and Zorlu: Israel's largest private power producer Edeltech and its Turkish partner Zorlu Enerji have signed two deals to buy 6 bcm of gas worth $1.3 billion over 18 years. Gas would be supplied to Edeltech's two new power plants – the 140 MW Tamar power plant located in the Haifa Chemicals factory and 77 MW Solad power plant at a site next to the CHS factory in Ashdod.

b) IPM Beer Tuvia Ltd. (IPM): The private producer has agreed to buy 13 bcm of natural gas over a period of 18 years at an estimated $3 billion for its 413 MW power plant planned for the Be'er Tuvia industrial zone, 60km west of Jerusalem. Any surplus electricity will be sent via the IEC grid to other consumers.

c) Paz Ashdod Oil Refinery: A subsidiary of Paz Oil Company Ltd. engaged in producing oil refining products, signed an agreement with the Leviathan partners to buy 3.12 bcm of gas over a period of 15 years at the cost of $700 million. Paz will produce electricity for both its own use and sale to external customers.

d) Dalia Power Energies Ltd.: The Leviathan partners signed a $2 billion deal to sell 8.8 bcm of gas to Dalia for over 20 years. Gas will be used to operate the second power plant that Dalia plans to build at its Tzafit power station (the largest in Israel) near Kibbutz Kfar Menahem in south-central Israel, which will produce about 800 MW of electricity.

e) Israel Chemicals Ltd. (ICL): The company has agreed to buy 0.38 bcm a year (with an option of increase to 0.76 bcm a year) from Leviathan on a binding basis. While the deal is a backup in case of Energean failing to supply from Karish and Tanin, it will become effective when gas starts flowing from the Leviathan project, and is valid until September 2020. If gas from the Energean's reservoirs is delayed, the agreement would be extended for six-month-periods until either gas starts flowing from Karish and Tanin or the end of 2025, whichever is earlier.

f) NEPCO: In September 2016, the Leviathan partners signed an agreement with NEPCO for the supply of approximately 45 bcm of natural gas for a period of 15 years worth $10 billion.

g) Dolphinus Holdings: In February 2018, Leviathan partners signed an export agreement with Dolphinus Holdings for the supply of up to 32 bcm annually for 12 years to the Egyptian domestic market.

The Leviathan partners are promoting a number of contacts with Egypt, Turkey, Cyprus, and Europe to find anchor customer(s) to secure funds needed for investment in the REM phase of the project. Leviathan developers are keen to export to Turkey, as most of its local gas demand is met by imports. Several proposals on how to construct a pipeline from the Leviathan production platform to Ceyhan port are on the table. There is a plan to also link Leviathan with Aphrodite, the neighbouring Cypriot gas field, in which Noble and Delek Group also have the majority stakes, to provide gas to Europe through a long-distance pipeline. Leviathan being an enormous reservoir can serve the variable regional demand easily and competitively, and the government is playing an active role, initiating talks at the political level for GSPAs.

Gas sale agreements: Karish and Tanin

The gas from Karish and Tanin reservoirs (which contain around 68 bcm of gas) are exclusively for the local market. Before proposing the FID for the two fields, Energean signed 12 GSPAs for the supply of 42 bcm, enabling competition in the gas sector and lowering the price of gas paid by the consumers, thereby fulfilling the two aims of NGF. These agreements will enable the diversification of natural gas supply for Israeli customers, underpinned by Take-or-pay (ToP) arrangements for a minimum annual offtake and underpinned by a firm floor price:

a) ICL: The company along with Bazan Group Oil Refineries (bay area, Haifa) and OPC Energy (formerly known as IC Power Ltd.) signed agreements to buy 39 bcm of gas from the Karish and Tanin fields over 15 years, or 2.6 bcm annually. ICL will also use the gas for operating a new 250 MW power station in Sodom.

b) Dorad Energy Ltd.: Private power producer Dorad will purchase 6.75 bcm over 14 years from the Karish and Tanin reservoirs for over $500 million. Dorad power plant in Ashkelon has a production capacity of about 860 MW. Dorad is planning to build another power station Dorad B in the existing station, and to produce 650 MW of electricity.

c) Rapac Communications and Infrastructure: Rapac has signed a contract to buy gas 0.8 bcm annually for 17 years from Energean for its two power stations, Alon Tavor and Ramat Gabriel, each with a capacity of 73 MW.

d) Ramat Negev Energy Ltd. and Ashdod Energy Ltd.: These subsidiaries of the Edeltech Group will purchase a total amount of up to 2.65 bcm of gas from Energean Israel over 14 years. The companies operate at the site of Adama Company. Ramat Negev operates in the Adama Machteshim site in Neot Hovav, at a capacity of 125 MW, and Ashdod Energy with a capacity of 65 MW operates at the Adama Agan site in Ashdod industrial area. Both power plants provide electricity to the on-site consumers and steam to the host factories.

e) Dalia Power: Energean Israel has signed two agreements with Dalia Power and its sister company, Or Power Energies, for the supply of 1.3 bcm annually or 23 bcm of natural gas over the lifetime of the contracts. The period of the supply agreements will start from the date natural gas starts flowing

from Karish–Tanin and conclude at the point when the purchasers' generation licenses need extension. Dalia and Or will purchase part of their gas
requirements to operate the Dalia power plant in Tzafit as well as future
power plants planned by Or.

Governmental measures for small fields

In view of the high unit cost of developing small and medium-sized reserves and
to create competition locally between the gas from Tamar and Karish–Tanin fields,
the Israeli government through Government Decision 2592 approved a package
of incentives for small and medium reservoirs.[20] Among others, it included subsidies for laying pipeline from offshore fields and commitments from all producers
to back each other up if supplies are interrupted. More specifically, it involves
the subsidy of NIS 100 million for joint infrastructure projects to facilitate the
connection of Karish–Tanin as well as other reservoirs to the shore. The MoE
intends to secure backup for customers of Karish and Tanin in case of malfunction
through a mechanism of mutual guarantee between the different gas fields.

Decision 2592 also determined that INGL would establish and operate a segment of a transmission system for small reservoirs (Karish and Tanin, currently),
consisting of a 10 km long line and a connection on land of about 2 km at an estimated at NIS 386.3 million.[21] The significance of this move is to encourage the
connection of the two fields to Israel's gas transmission system and thus increase
the number of gas suppliers to the market. Moreover, new connections to the gas
transmission system increase redundancy and reliability of supply. The government
has also allocated NIS 10 million in 2017 for the conversion of car fleets, buses, and
trucks to natural gas operation to utilise the availability of added gas.[22] Finally, the
Electricity Authority would provide financial incentives such as low gas prices to
customers in the electric power market if they choose marginal fields as their suppliers. These measures amount to an implementation of one of the major aims of
NGf, which is the creation of a competitive milieu in Israel's natural gas industry.
With the development of Leviathan on track, it is unlikely that there will be a
disruption in supply as in 2013, when the Mari-B reservoirs dwindled and Tamar
was still in the process of being developed.

The surety of uninterrupted supply will encourage manufacturing units to
make the investment to convert to natural gas. A further expansion of production from Tamar is still possible as two of its wells are still undeveloped and it is
possible that there will be an increase in output from Leviathan over its production years as technology for gas extraction becomes more advanced.

Natural gas consumption trend: power generation

The main drivers an the increase in demand for natural gas comes from the
growth in demand for electricity together with the increasing weight of natural
gas in the industrial sector. The entire increase in the electricity production

capacity (combined cycle, cogeneration, open cycle) in the coming years (except for a relatively small rate of renewables) is in natural gas. In addition, demand is expected from energy-intensive industry, manufacturing of chemical and petrochemical products based on natural gas, and natural gas-based transportation. Due to the limitations of natural gas supply,[23] the market is still far from utilising the full potential of the use of local natural gas.

Israel added gas to its energy mix with the onset of the Mari–B reservoir, paving the way for significant changes in the economy. Natural gas consumption has climbed from 1.19 bcm in 2004 to 10.35 bcm in 2017, with a compound annual growth rate of 18.1 percent from 2004 to 2017 (Figure 3.4). Electricity generation from natural gas constituted the entire gas consumption for the first two years. Except for the short interlude of 2011–2012, during which the Mari–B field had begun to exhaust and supply for Egypt became erratic (and eventually stopped), gas intake of the economy has progressed steadily (Table 3.1).

Since Tamar started production in 2013, the percentage growth in gas consumption in the economy has been more than 50 percent, with a high annual growth of 12.6 percent (2013–2017). About 9.83 bcm or 95 percent of gas supply in 2017 were from the Tamar wells and the balance came from bouy-based LNG imports (Figures 3.4 and 3.5). The Tamar reservoir is the main source of gas supply and has so far provided about 40.5 bcm of gas to the Israeli consumers.[24] As robust reservoir, Tamar clocks an average hourly and daily flow of 1.18 mcm and 28.4 mcm respectively, and is likely to continue as the mainstay supply source of Israel's

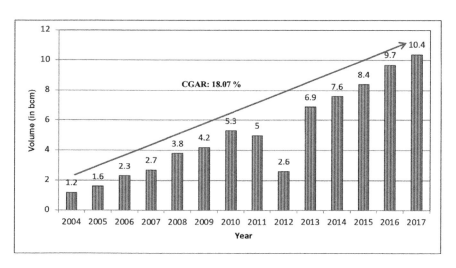

FIGURE 3.4   Total natural gas consumption in Israel, 2004–2017

Source: Author; figures from the Ministry of Energy, Israel, 2018

*Figures have been rounded off at several places for clarity

TABLE 3.1 Total natural gas consumption and natural gas consumption in electricity generation

	Consumption (bcm)	NG consumption in production of electricity	
		(bcm)	(%)
2017	10.35	8.54	83
2016	9.7	8.4	83
2015	8.4	6.6	79
2014	7.6	5.9	78
2013	6.9	5.6	81
2012	2.6	2.0	77
2011	5.0	4.6	91
2010	5.3	5.1	96
2009	4.2	3.9	93
2008	3.8	3.7	98
2007	2.8	2.7	97
2006	2.3	2.2	97
2005	1.7	1.7	100
2004	1.2	1.2	100
Total	71.85	61.04	84.95

Source: Author; Figures from the Ministry of Energy, Israel, April 2018; BP Statistical Review of World Energy, 2018; IEA Atlas of Energy, 2018

*Figures have been rounded off at several places for clarity

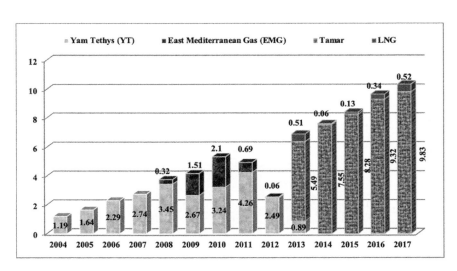

FIGURE 3.5 Distribution of natural gas supply in 2004–2017 by supplier (in bcm)

Source: Author; figures from the Ministry of Energy, Israel, 2018

natural gas market.[25] The successful completion of the drilling of Tamar-8 well (in addition to five producing wells of the first stage of the Tamar's development) in early 2017, as part of the expansion of supply from the Tamar field and its connection to the existing Tamar and Yam Tethys production platforms, has augmented the volume of gas available to the Israeli economy.[26]

The use of natural gas has swelled in recent years, led by an increase in consumption in the electricity sector, whose total consumption amounted to 8 bcm 2016, a sharp increase of about 19 percent as compared with consumption in 2015. Most of the increase was due to energy minister's order to reduce the use of coal for electricity generation.[27] Moreover, since the Tamar reservoir started to produce, electricity generation from natural gas climbed rapidly from 43 percent in 2013 to more than 63 percent in 2017: In 2016 and 2017, consumption of natural gas for the generation of electricity constituted about 83 percent of total natural gas consumption in the economy.[28] As a whole, the use of natural gas in electricity generation from 2004 to 2017 was 61 bcm, which is about 85 percent of the 72 bcm of natural gas consumed in the economy during this period (Table 3.1 and Figure 3.4). According to MoE, the total installed natural gas-fired power generation in 2020 would reach about 69 percent of the total installed power generation capacity in Israel.[29]

In tandem with the rise in the use of natural gas for power production, there is a constant decline in coal-fired electricity production, which will become more pronounced from 2020 onward as Leviathan goes online. Coal consumption in electricity generation saw a decline of more than 9 percent year-to-year – from 9,135 thousand tonnes in 2016 to about 8,306 thousand tonnes in 2017. The percentage reduction in coal usage from 2010 to 2017 – the years during which gas usage in power generation amplified – is a substantial 32.5 percent, i.e., a drop of 3,998 thousand tonnes from 12,304 thousand tonnes.[30] These figures reveal a sustained effort by IEC, backed by the government, to incorporate indigenous fuel into a critical sector of the economy. In 2017, MoE took the decision to reduce the use of coal by closing down coal-operated units in power production by 2023 and in January 2018 the ministry set a further reduction of 30 percent in coal use relative to 2017.

Projections regarding electricity consumption

According to Yaniv Bar in a Bank Leumi (BL) study,[31] the use of natural gas for electricity production during the years 2004–2015 was supported by an average annual increase of 3.3 percent in demand, which will clock a similar rate through 2030, owing to the use of natural gas in new areas, such as, water desalination. Afterwards, the rate of demand is expected to moderate to an average of 2.5 percent annually.

On the other hand, a 2017 the BoI study of 2017 authored by Lior Gallo[32] projects a slightly lower rate of increase in demand for electricity in the 2020s and 2030s, which is expected to be between 2.7 and 3 percent, slightly lower than in the past. BoI's estimate is based on the projected slowdown in GDP, as the weight of the high-tech sector increases – which is less electricity intensive than the industry average – and the likely installation of air-conditioners in every household. However, the study does not consider the demand from desalination plants or electrification of trains "since at the moment there is no forecast of their magnitude."[33]

In addition to expansion of the use of electricity in desalination facilities, the BDO report[34] includes the high population growth rate, expected increase in the standard of living (based on both penetration rate and usage intensity of household electric appliances), electrification of the Israeli railway system, expectation for a reduction in electricity tariffs, decline in coal-based power generation, and increased Palestinian need to the demand scenario. It predicts a demand growth in the electricity sector at the rate of 3.5 percent per annum until 2040.

The above projections explain low growth (BOI: 2.7–3 percent), business as usual (Bank Leumi: 3.3 percent), and high growth (BDO: 3.5 percent) scenarios electricity demand growth (Table 3.2):

a) BOI's estimate corresponds to MoE's medium growth scenario of 2.57 per-cent through the 2020s until 2030,[35] creating a total demand of 172.9 bcm from the 2018 baseline. In 2030, the projected annual requirement of gas would be 16.5 bcm.

b) Bank Leumi's estimate of electricity growth corresponds to the MoE's high growth projection of 3.07 percent growth in electricity demand up until 2030. In that year, the consumption of gas in the economy would reach 17.9 bcm and the total amount of gas required would be 184.5 bcm from the 2018 starting line.

c) BDO's 'super growth' scenario would require a total of 255.8 bcm until 2030 taking 2018 as the starting point. The report predicts the annual gas con-sumption of 25 bcm in 2030.

The above-mentioned reports project a scenario of continuous growth in demand for natural gas, stemming from an increasing use of electricity in transportation, household usage, and desalination. Demand redundancy is mentioned only in the context of installation of air conditioners – a robust electricity-consuming item. All the above-mentioned reports point to an increase in the penetration rate and usage intensity of household electric appliances as contributing to the growth in electricity demand.

In Israel today, natural gas for electricity generation is favoured by govern-ment institutions across board – Ministry of Finance, Public Utilities Author-ity, and MoE itself. The conversion of the IEC's heavy-fuel-oil-based thermal power plants to natural gas at the Eshkol power plant in Ashdod, Reading in Tel Aviv, and Haifa power station is already complete. It should be noted, however,

TABLE 3.2 Gas utilisation in different electricity demand scenarios, 2015–2030

Year	Low (2.57 percent annual growth in electricity demand)	Business as usual (3.07 percent annual growth in electricity demand)	High* (3.8 percent annual growth in electricity demand)
2015	8.4	8.6	8.4
2016	9.6	9.8	9.7
2017	10.0	10.3	10.4
2018	10.3	10.7	11.2
2019	10.4	10.9	11.5
2020	11.6	12.1	14.3
2021	12.0	12.6	15.9
2022	12.4	13.0	18.0
2023	12.7	13.5	18.7
2024	13.3	14.2	19.5
2025	13.7	14.7	20.5
2026	14.1	15.1	21.3
2027	14.8	16.0	22.3
2028	15.3	16.6	23.4
2029	15.8	17.2	24.2
2030	16.5	17.9	25.0
Total	**200.9**	**213.2**	**254.8**
CAGR (2018–2030)	**4%**	**4.38%**	**6.92%**

Source: Figures from Ministry of Energy, State of Israel,http://archive.energy.gov.il/Subjects/NG/Pages/GxmsMniNGEconomy.aspx; Chen Herzog, Israel Natural Gas Demand Forecast 2017–2040, BDO Consulting Group, p. 12, www.delek-group.com/wp-content/uploads/2017/09/BDO-Gas-Market-Forecast-2-07-2017-for-Delek-Group-with-final-letter-1.pdf; and Author

that fuel oil remains a backup fuel in these production units. These have been turned into combined cycle electricity generation, which have a high efficiency of 50–58 percent compared to 38–42 percent for heavy fuel oil and coal-powered stations.[36]

In August 2016, the MoE decided to phase out 4 coal units at the Orot Rabin power plant in Hadera (Rabin A, Units 1 through 4), the oldest and most polluting coal units in Israel – with a total capacity of 1,440 MW and comprising 30 percent of Israel's coal production capacity – no later than June 2022.[37] The government has accepted the decision of the energy ministry as part of electricity sector reforms (Government Decision 3859). The termination of the coal-powered stations is predicated on two conditions.[38] First, a redundancy in natural gas supply to the Israeli market after Leviathan and Karish fields are linked to the overland transmission system by a separate pipelines. Second, the start of operation of the first combined cycle power plant of 600 MW capacity, constructed by the IEC's daughter company, no later than June 1 2022.

TABLE 3.3 Electricity generation by renewable energy sources

Year	Renewable Energy (million KWh)				
	Solar power	Wind power	Hydropower	Others	Total
2017	1,511	(. . .)	(. . .)	(. . .)	**1,691**
2016	1,526	(. . .)	(. . .)	(. . .)	**1,703**
2015	1,159	7	24	70	**1,261**
2014	840	6	13	62	**921**
2013	494	6	28	43	**571**

Source: Author; figures from Central Bureau of Statistics, State of Israel, September 4, 2018

(. . .) = Unknown

With the twin aim of diversification of energy supply and curbing pollution arising from the use of fossil fuels, MoE is also advancing guidelines to increase the production of renewable energy. The target is to use renewable energy sources to produce 10 percent of electricity by 2020, 13 percent in 2025, and 17 percent in 2030. In 2017, Israel generated 1,691 million KWh of renewable energy – more than three times the value in 2013 – in which the major chunk of 1,511 was that from solar energy, which has registered a steady increase in the past five years (Table 3.3).

To create a synergy between natural gas and renewable energy, NGA has approved the flow of natural gas to two solar thermal power stations in Ashalim. Natural gas will support the capacity of these stations (not more than 15 percent) to generate electricity when the sun is mild, during winter, and at night. A 32km pipeline built by the regional contractor for the Negev, connects the solar power stations to the natural gas station in Neot Hovav.[39] It appears a unique method to back up the national electricity grid and keep the power solar plant running, just as it promotes the deployment of natural gas throughout the country. Energy security warrants that Israel must continue to expand natural gas network to the remotest areas and continue to diversify supplies so as to avoid reliance on a single source of energy.

IEC and private electricity producers

The composition of electricity producers using natural gas is changing as private power producers enter the fray, evident in the declining share of IEC in the total consumption of natural gas used for electricity generation. In 2004, 100 percent of the natural gas supply was used for generation of electricity; IEC was the sole buyer of natural gas as well as the electricity producer. IPPs have since increased their share of natural gas intake for electricity generation. With abundance in supply as Tamar started production in 2013, there was a sharp rise of about 170 percent year-by-year between 2013 and 2014 in IPPs' natural gas consumption for power production (Table 3.4). In contrast, the share of IEC registered

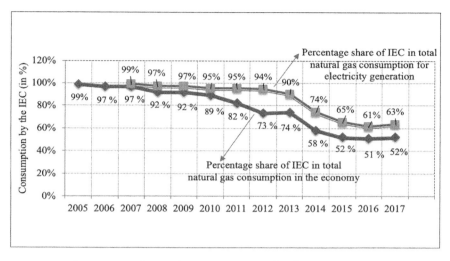

FIGURE 3.6   Percentage of natural gas consumption by the IEC, 2007–2017

Source: Author; figures from Ministry of Energy, State of Israel, 2018

TABLE 3.4 Natural gas consumption for electricity generation by producer

Period	Total gas consumption (thousand TOE)	Gas consumption by IEC (thousand TOE)	Gas consumption by private companies (thousand TOE)
2013	4,780.7	4,150.9	629.9
2014	5,252.9	3,552.9	1,700.1
2015	5,637.7	3,423.1	2,214.6
2016	6,878.2	4,024.9	2,853.3
2017	7,361.5	4,344.4	3,017.1

Source: Author; figures from Databank, Central Bureau of Statistics, State of Israel, November 5, 2018

a drop of about 14.4 percent and 16 percentage points over the same duration (Table 3.4 & Figure 3.6).

In terms of the volume of gas consumption, private electricity producers consumed 3.2 bcm or 31 percent (including absorption in industrial plants for electricity generation) in 2017, whereas IEC consumed 5.34 bcm or 62.5 percent out of a total supply of 8.54 bcm.[40] The growing role of IPPs in the electricity sector is evident from the fact that in 2017, private producers generated 27.9 percent of electricity, compared to five years ago in 2013, when it was a meagre 6.9 percent. Table 3.5 shows a steady growth in share of the private sector in total power production and, with power sector reforms, this trend is likely to continue in the coming years.

TABLE 3.5 Israel: electricity generation by producer (all fuels)

Unit	In percentage					In million KWh or GWh			
Year	2017	2016	2015	2014	2013	2016	2015	2014	2013
TOTAL	100.0	100.0	100.0	100.0	100.0	67,210	64,230	61,295	61,368
Israel Electric Corporation	72.1	72.4	78.8	84.4	93.1	48,713	50,627	51,726	57,119
Private electricity producer	27.9	27.6	21.2	15.6	6.9	18,497	13,603	9,569	4,249

Source: Author; figures from Central Bureau of Statistics, State of Israel, September 4, 2018

Private sector participation and competition throughout the electricity supply became a possibility with the establishment of the Electricity Law in 1996 – concurrent with the expiration of the 70-year-old concession of IEC – which laid the groundwork for structural reform of the electric utility. This Law instituted a framework for licensed private sector participation and paved the way for a multiple-provider system, similar to those adopted in other OECD countries. It established an independent regulatory body, the Public Utilities Authority-Electricity (PUA), charged with three major tasks, including fixing of the electricity tariffs and the means of updating them, setting required standards for the level, nature, and quality of the service provided by the various entities operating in the electricity market, and issuing of licenses to operate in the electricity market, besides supervision of compliance to the conditions stated in the licenses.

The PUA became operational immediately but the reform to initiate private sector partnership in the entire supply chain was sluggish. However, the discovery of natural gas opened up a historic opportunity and provided the much-needed impetus to jump-start privatisation in the electricity production sector. Production licenses were the first to come but detailed regulations on the design of IPP contracts for the sale of electricity were not established until 2004, and the first license was awarded only in 2009.

With the participation of the private sector, two kinds of power generation systems have emerged in the Israeli electricity market (Table 3.6): First, the owners of the private power stations sell electricity to large consumers, both industrial and commercial, through the national distribution grid of IEC. These include major stand-alone IPPs, such as the 450 MW OPC Rotem's combined cycle power station in Mishor Rotem in the Negev desert operational in July 2013, 840 MW Dorad plant near Ashkelon operational since the summer of 2014, and 870 MW Dalia Power Energies IPP at Tzafit near Tel Aviv, which commenced its commercial operation in July 2015. Second, industrial complexes have installed private cogeneration facilities, thereby creating a self-generating energy supply system.[41] Through the establishment of self-generation power plants with cogeneration or combined heat and power

(CHP) facilities, these factories are able to generate electricity and utilise the residual thermal energy (hot water and steam) in their operations.[42] They even sell the surplus electricity to the national electricity grid when the plant is not at the full performance levels.

The MoE published a series of regulations in 2004 (amended in 2009, 2012, and 2014) and 2005 that organised and formalised private electric power generation in general and the building of cogeneration power plants in particular.[43] On 18 July 2018, the Knesset approved a ten-year, NIS 7.1 billion ($1.9 billion) historic reform of electricity sector, titled, "The Reform in the Electricity Sector and Structural Change in the Israel Electric Corporation," (Decision 3859) aimed at increasing competition and streamlining the national utility.[44] The corporation agreed to open up the power production market and transfer system management and planning to another state-owned company.

At the end of the reform process, IEC will manufacture just 30 percent of the country's electricity, compared to 70 percent today. Most of the production will move into the hands of private producers. As part of the reform, IEC agreed to sell off 19 production units in five sites – Eshkol, Reading, Alon Tavor, Ramat Hovav, and the eastern part of the Hagit site – to third parties in a bid to increase competition in electricity supply over five years. The reform allows for IEC to form a subsidiary to build and manage two new natural gas-operated combined-cycle power turbines with a total installed capacity of approximately 1,200 MW at the Orot Rabin site in Hadera. The IEC, however, will remain a monopoly in transmission and distribution of electricity, although electricity supply will be gradually opened to competition.

Natural gas consumption trend: industrial use

Natural gas is being increasingly used to leverage the development of Israel's industrial sector. In addition to cogeneration plant producing electricity and heat for self-use on factory premises, natural gas is used as a combustion substitute for *mazut* (low quality fuel oil; when blended or broken down, the end product being diesel) diesel, crude oil, and LPG to produce and process a variety of products including fuels, paper, minerals, pharmaceuticals, food, rubber, and building materials.

Significant use of natural gas in the Israeli industrial sector began in 2006 at the Paz oil refinery in Ashdod and at the Hadera paper mills in 2007. Both are connected to the national natural gas distribution grid operated by INGL. Several large and small companies have invested in the integration of natural gas in their operations (along with onsite electricity production) (see Table 3.6) by linking up to INGL's large pipeline system and regional distribution systems. The INGL supply grid delivers natural gas to large industrial plants, including in the Haifa Bay area, Ramat Hovav, Mishor Rotem, and Sodom. Its industrial customers include ORL, Haifa Chemicals, Sugat Industries in Kiryat Gat, America-Israel Paper Mills (Hadera Papers Ltd.), Adama Agan crop protection chemicals

TABLE 3.6 Independent power producers (IPP) in Israel: electricity production and self-generation in indus◆

Plant name	Location	Year of commissioning	Holding(s)	Capacity of plant
OPC Rotem	Mishor Rotem, Near Dimona, Negev desert	2013	IC Power, a subsidiary of the Israel Corporation, and Dalkia Israel Ltd., a subsidiary of Veolia Environment	466 MW
Dorad	Ashkelon (EAPC Complex)	2014	Dorad Energy Ltd., Eilat-Ashkelon Infrastructure Services Ltd. (EAIS), a subsidiary of Eilat Ashkelon Pipeline Company (EAPC), Zorlu Enerji, a Turkish company and Edelcom Ltd., an associate company of Edeltech private Israeli company	840
Dalia	Tzafit, 40km south-east of Tel Aviv and Kfar Menahem in south-central Israel	2015	Dalia Power Energies	900 MW
Ramat Gabriel plant	Nilit factory premises, Migdal Ha'emek Industrial zone, Haifa	2018	RD Energy	70 MW
Alon Tavor power plant	Tnuva Dairy premises, Alon Tavor Industrial Zone, Afula city, Northern District	2018	RD energy	70 MW
Ashdod Energy power plant	Adama Agan Chemical Plant premises, Northern Industrial Zone, Ashdod	2015	Edeltech Group and Zorlu Energy Electricity Generation Inc.	55 MW
Ramat Negev Energy Co. Ltd.	Makhteshim Chemical Plant premises in Ramat (Noet) Hovav industrial zone	2015	Edeltech Group and Zorlu Energy Electricity Generation Inc.	120 MW
Sorek power plant	Sorek, south of Tel Aviv	2016	Delek Sorek Ltd. (subsidiary of Delek Group), IDE Technologies (Israel Chemicals), and Hutchison Whampoa	140 MW

Technology used	Type of fuel	Fuel provider	End users	Type of operation
Combined cycle	Gas	Tamar	IEC and others	Other-generation
Combined cycle	Gas	Tamar	Ministry of Defence, Israeli Aerospace Industries, Dan Hotels, Isrotel, Keter Plastics etc. through national grid	Other-generation
Combined cycle	Gas/ Diesel backup	Tamar 200 bcf/17 years	IEC and business customers	Other-generation
Cogeneration	Gas	Tamar/15-year agreement	Nilit factory (Manufacturer of nylon fibres and thermoplastic is the main client)	Self-generation and other-generation
Cogeneration	Gas	Tamar/15-year agreement	Tnuva Dairy (manufacturer of a range of dairy products), is the main client	Self-generation and other-generation
Cogeneration with Combined cycle backup	Gas	Tamar	Adama Agan and others	Self-generation and other-generation
Cogeneration with Combined cycle backup	Gas	Tamar	Machteshim Chemical Plant (manufacturer of herbicides, insecticides, and fungicides), other plants in Noet Hovav; through national grid to IEC and others	Self-generation and other-generation
Cogeneration	Gas	Tamar/3.3 bcm for 15 years	Sorek Desalination Company Ltd.	Self-generation and other-generation

TABLE 3.6 (Continued)

Plant name	Location	Year of commissioning	Holding(s)	Capacity of plant
Delek Eshkelon power plant	Ashkelon's desalination compound	2008	Delek Power Plants Ltd. (Delek Group)	87 MW
Paz Ashdod Refinery power plant (two in operation, one commissioned for 2018)	Ashdod Refineries compound	2008; 2018	Paz Oil Company Ltd.	109 MW + 70 MW (commissioned for 2018)
Nesharim power plant	Ramla	2010–2014 (gradual expansion)	Mashav Energy (Mashav Initiating and Development Ltd.)	122 MW
Etgal Ashdod power station	Ashdod	2005; 2018	Shikun and Binui renewable energy (Etgal Energy Investments Ltd.)	28 MW +64 MW (gas turbine commissione for 2018)
Hadera Paper power plant	Hadera paper facility	2018	IC Power (a subsidiary of Kenon Holdings Ltd.)	120 MW
Oil Refineries Ltd. (ORL, Bazan Group)				135 MW +340 MW
Dead Sea Works (DSW) power station	Sodom	2018	DSW, a subsidiary of ICL Fertilisers	240 MW powe plant

Sources: Author; various

company at the Northern Industrial Zone in Ashdod, Adama Machteshim chemicals company in the Ramat Hovav industrial zone near Beersheva, Dead Sea Works potash plant in Sodom, and several others.[45]

Small energy consumers in the small-and-medium-sized industrial segment, such as, Shaniv Paper Ltd, Phoenicia Glass Works Ltd., Fireproof Industries Ltd., and Asian Chemical Industries Ltd., have converted to natural gas operation. These received a grant of NIS 1 million from the government in 2012 to switch to the gas-based setup. Phoenicia Glass Works, which faced economic difficulties related to high cost of manufacturing from oil-based fuels was saved from closure upon conversion. Others, like Hadassah Medical Centre in Jerusalem, are beginning to convert their facilities to natural gas use.

Further expansion of distribution network to cover factories not connected to natural gas is ongoing, albeit not at a pace visualised by MoE. For example, in February 2016, the energy minister signed a license for the establishment of a natural gas distribution network in the Jerusalem Region. The Rotem Natural

Technology used	Type of fuel	Fuel provider	End users	Type of operation
Combined cycle	Gas	Yam Tethys	Ashkelon's desalination facility	Self-generation and other-generation
Cogeneration	Gas	Yam Tethys/ Tamar	Paz Ashdod Oil Refinery, kibbutzim (collective settlements) in the area, high-tech companies, and industrial customers such as Coca Cola Enterprises	Self-generation and other-generation
Combined cycle	Gas	Yam Tethys/ Tamar	Nesher Cement Enterprises of Cement Industries	Self-generation and other-generation
Combined cycle/ Cogeneration	Fuel oil and Gas (new plant)	Tamar	Exclusively to IEC (power plant acts as "peaker," available to the grid during peak consumption)	Other-generation
Cogeneration	Gas	Tamar	Hadera Papers	Self-generation and other-generation
Cogeneration	Gas	Tanin and Karish	ORL	Self-generation and other-generation
Combined cycle and cogeneration	Gas	Tamar	Dead Sea Works	Self-generation

Gas Company agreed construct a pipeline network to connect industrial zones, enterprises, and major consumers in Jerusalem and surrounding areas to natural gas.[46] Further, under an agreement signed by the Airports Authority with SuperNG Natural Gas Distribution Company,[47] Ben Gurion Airport will be disconnected from the IEC's transmission grid and switch to electricity produced exclusively from natural gas. The Airports Authority's power station, which currently runs on diesel fuel and uses electricity backup from IEC, will be upgraded and converted to natural gas operation by early 2021.[48] Besides, factories isolated from the gas transmission and distribution networks are receiving CNG as a stopgap arrangement.[49]

Despite significant connectivities, only 10 percent of the 627 Israeli factories, hospitals, hotels, and government institutions that were slated to switch to natural gas have actually been connected to the pipeline network by 2017.[50] There were 15 large industrial customers connected to the gas transmission system, 57 relatively small customers (of which 20 linked up in 2017) connected to the distribution network, and eight received CNG (an additional four added in the same year). It is important to note that over 90 percent of the consumers of natural gas in 2017 were in the distribution areas of the Negev and south,[51] a trend boosted by the construction of the PRMS in Eshel HaNasi that enabled distribution company Negev Natural Gas to inject gas at low pressure to the industrial zones.[52] As this finding highlights, the penetration of distribution network in other regions is slow, accounting for low utilisation of gas in the manufacturing sector.

Distribution companies complain that they face many bureaucratic difficulties in laying the pipeline network, including complexities related to pipeline passage jurisdiction, problems defining and applying safety standards, a lack of cooperation among public agencies, as well as lack of interest among small factor owners wanting to connect to the gas network.[53] To remove these impediments, a comprehensive reform was carried out within the framework of the Arrangements Law of 2015–2016,[54] along with a subsidy scheme to encourage manufacturing unit to switch to natural gas operations.

Recognising the huge cost associated with building the gas distribution network for small factories, MoE has created a pool of subsidy worth NIS 40 million.[55] In May 2018, MoE issued a public tender[56] for submission of applications for grants to connect remote consumers to the distribution network in three complementary ways, including deployment of distribution lines, upgrades of existing lines, and construction of pressure reduction and measurement stations. In addition, 46 plants whose consumption exceeded 100,000 cubic metres per year, received a cache of grants in 2017 to convert their operations to natural gas. In order to keep up the momentum, MoE decided to extend the scheme of grants till August 2018.[57]

In addition, the launch of the eastern line in June 2017, a two-way main artery for transmission of natural gas from the Nesher cement factory in Ramla to the Hagit station in Elyakim, will boost natural gas usage. About 90km long, the arterial pipeline will enable customers along the pipeline passage access to gas and absorb the flows from Leviathan into the transmission system.[58] The eastern line is meant to serve as a backup to the sea line – the single artery for gas flow from Ashdod to Dor in the north via Tel Aviv – and increase the storage capacity of the system (Figure 3.6).

The total consumption of natural gas in the industrial sector in 2017 amounted to 1.81 bcm, a 6.5 percent increase compared to 1.7 bcm in 2016 (Table 3.7) Most of the growth came from the addition of new consumers to the distribution network and additional CNG consumers. Yet, industrial uptake did not match MoE's projection of 2.5 bcm in 2016 and 2.6 bcm in 2017 (Figure 3.8). If the Compound Annual Growth Rate (CAGR) of 2.11 percent (2014–17) in industrial consumption is compared to CAGR of 13.4 percent in MoE's projection for the same period, the ministry's future projection appears vastly overestimated. However, the onset of Leviathan, Karish, and Tanin will inject substantial amount of gas into the economy by 2022. In conjunction with the expansion of

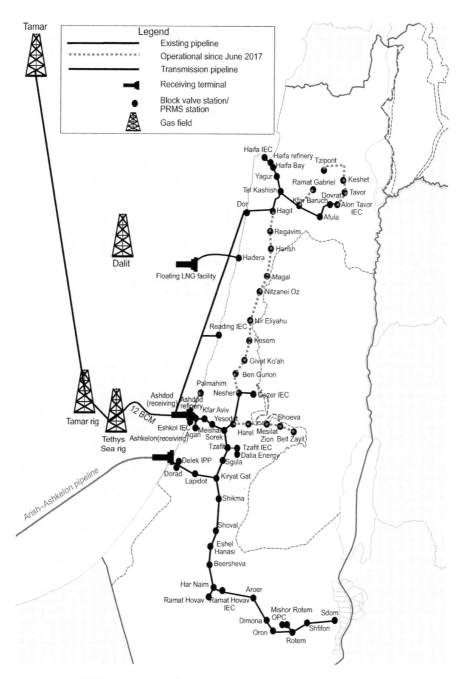

FIGURE 3.7 IGNL pipelines and natural gas reservoirs

Source: Author and based on "Israel Natural Gas Lines Map," https://commons.wikimedia.org/wiki/
File:Israel_Natural_Gas_Lines_Map_EN.svg

Disclaimer: Map not to scale

TABLE 3.7 Natural gas consumption in industry

Year	Consumption (bcm)	NG consumption in production of electricity**		NG consumption in industry	
		(bcm)	(%)	(bcm)	(%)
2017	10.35	8.54	83	1.81	17.5
2016	9.7	8	83	1.7	17
2015	8.4	6.6	79	1.8	21
2014	7.6	5.9	78	1.7	22
2013	6.9	5.6	81	1.3	19
2012	2.6	2.0	77	0.6	23
2011	5.0	4.6	91	0.4	9
2010	5.3	5.1	96	0.2	4
2009	4.2	3.9	93	0.3	7
2008	3.8	3.7	98	0.1	2
2007	2.8	2.7	97	0.1	3
2006	2.3	2.2	97	0.1	3

Source: Author; BP Statistical Review of World Energy, 2018; IEA Atlas of Energy, 2018; Ministry of Energy, Israel, 2017

Figures are rounded off for clarity

gas supply network riding on governmental facilitations, including simplification of procedures and subsidy to the licensees to expand the gas distribution network, a likely increase in the absorption of gas in the economy is presumable. In the long term, use of natural gas can also lead to the development of new industries that use gas as a raw material for the production of petrochemicals. The MoE foresees the beginning of methanol production in 2020, which may be an overestimation, given that until 2018 there is no standing proposal from private enterprises to do so.

Two critical advantages for the local industry integrating natural gas into their processes include savings in energy costs and decline in production costs. It is important to note that the absorption of gas in industrial operations depends upon the nature of industry and technology employed. The likely impact of natural gas varies across the industrial sector, as can be seen in the table that follows.[59] Energy intensity is invariably high in less technologically intensive industries and, therefore, the benefits or profits from the penetration of natural gas into traditional industries are high, including drop in cost of production and increase in competitiveness of the product in the export market. Industries making chemical products, mineral products, and textiles could especially benefit from the use of natural gas, given that the difference between export and import in these three categories is to the tune of $11.1 billion (Table 3.8).

Those in medium–high and medium categories of energy intensity such as paper goods as well as animal and vegetable products (both food and nonfood items) could create a comparative advantage through cost reduction for

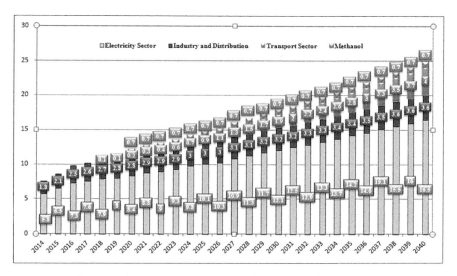

FIGURE 3.8 Forecasted increase in natural gas demand until 2040

Source: Author; figures from Ministry of Energy, State of Israel, 2017

manufacturers. Sectors across the medium–high, medium, medium–low, and high categories of technology have substantial contribution to export – prefabricated buildings, stone and glasses, food stuff, paper good, mineral product, metals, and textiles – and require cheaper energy (natural gas) as a crucial component of manufacturing to bring down cost of production of the industrial sector worth $6.11 billion (Table 3.8). Appreciation of the shekel in view of rent from natural gas and savings in the economy create further imperative to use natural gas to strengthen exports.

Natural gas offers the Israeli economy new opportunities for the development of the chemical/petrochemical industry. It opens up the possibility of reducing the need for the import of crude oil, refined products, and organic chemical products – the three amounting to roughly $12.5 billion – and saving forex reserves as well as reducing the negative trade balance.[60] It would also lead to renewed interest in R&D in the chemical industry, which has sharply declined in the past two decades.[61] A fifth of Israel's export relies on the chemical and petrochemicals industry.[62] In 2016, Israel exported $2.72 billion worth of plastics and rubbers (Bazan, Israel's largest oil refinery, also produces petrochemicals), the third largest industry in the export basket.[63] Natural gas can be used to maintain current levels of exports and build a new export sector based on gas as raw material.

It is important to note that in the ministry's projection, the absolute demand for methanol in the twenty years between 2020–2040 will remain unchanged in absolute terms, but in relative terms the volume of gas required will increase

TABLE 3.8 Impact of natural gas on different sectors, 2016

Level of technology	Potential for natural gas penetration	Product	Product details	Export value ($)	Import value ($)
Low	High	Animal hides	Equine, bovine and sheep hides, trunks and cases, leather sheets, leather articles, etc.	25.4 million	189 million
		Chemical products	Packaged and unpackaged medicaments, pesticides, industrial fatty acids, oil and alcohols, mixed minerals or chemical fertilisers	12.9 million	5.74 billion
		Footwear and headwear	Leather footwear, other footwear, fake hair, knitted hats	54.4 million	570 million
		Textiles	Non-woven textiles, non-retail synthetic filament yarn, light rubberised knitted fabric, raw cotton, house linen, knits wear, etc.	902 million	2.44 billion
		Mineral products	Refined petroleum, calcium phosphate, magnesium carbonate, salt, coal tar, petroleum jelly, and sand	722 million	4.12 billion
Medium-low	Medium-high	Paper goods	Brochures, toilet papers, uncoated paper, other printed material, paper labels, shaped paper, etc.	345 million	928 million
Medium	Medium	Plastics and rubbers	Raw plastic sheeting, other plastic products, plastic leads, propylene, polymers, plastic pipes, plastic house wares, plastic building materials, etc.	2.5 billion	2.72 billion
		Animal and vegetable by-products	Oil, wool, waxes, margarine	31.6 million	201 million
		Animal products	Cheese, poultry, fish, animals, butter, concentrated milk, etc.	38.9 million	1.37 billion
		Food stuff	Fruit juice, other edible preparations, baked goods, chocolates, pasta, wine, sauces, etc.	682 million	2.34 billion
		Stone and glasses	Cement articles, safety glass, float glass, building stones, milling stone, bathroom ceramics, etc.	414 million	899 million

		Products		
Medium high	Medium–low	Metals	Tool plates, other iron products, interchangeable tool parts, iron pipes, magnesium, scrap aluminium, scrap iron, scrap copper, copper and aluminium bars, cutting blades, etc.	2 billion	3.27 billion
		Miscellaneous	Prefabricated buildings, other furniture, stuffed animals, seed, light fixtures, video and card game, etc	.376 million	1.31 billion
		Wood products	Wood carpentry, wood ornaments, wood fibre board, particleboard, wood crates, plywood, wood frames, wood kitchen wares, etc.	8.61 million	596 million
High	Low	Arts and antiques	Sculpture, antiques, prints	86.1 million	41.2 million
		Instruments	Medical instruments, measuring instruments, x-ray equipment, orthopaedic appliances, eyewear, LCD, optical fibres, etc.	3.86 billion	3.86 billion
		Machines	Integrated circuits, telephones, other electrical, industrial printers, computers, audio alarm, electrical registers, batteries, etc.	12.8 billion	14.8 billion
		Precious metals	Diamond, precious stones, gold	16.3 billion	6.43 billion
		Transportation	Planes, helicopters, spacecraft, vehicle parts, aircraft parts, railway track fixtures, passenger, and cargo ships, etc.	422 million	7.81 billion
—		Vegetable products	Tropical fruits, citrus, sowing seed, vegetables, cut flowers, nuts, etc.	1.3 billion	1.75 billion
		Unspecified	—	23.3 million	631 million

Source: Author; Based on Yaniv Bar, Natural Gas Sector in Israel, January 2017; Alexander JG Simoes and CA Hidalgo, The Economic Complexity Observatory: An Analytical Tool for Understanding the Dynamics of Economic Development, Workshops at the Twenty-Fifth AAAI Conference on Artificial Intelligence, 2011, https://atlas.media.mit.edu/en/profile/country/isr/

Petrochemical industry based on natural gas

every year (Figure 3.7). As gas supply in the economy increases with the development of Leviathan and Karish–Tanin, it is expected to lead to the development of chemical/petrochemical industries based on the use of gas as feedstock. Low-cost feedstock in the market would present profitable opportunities for petrochemical firms interested in entering the local industry.

Global experience shows that the availability of low-cost feedstock is the key driving force in the development of petrochemical industry. Along with accesible low-cost energy, either in the form of electricity or fuel, an economically feasible petrochemical plant can be established.[64] In countries with surplus natural gas, such as the Persian Gulf states,[65] a large petrochemical industry has developed in recent years. Gas-rich countries, in general, strive for a vibrant petrochemical sector.[66]

Feedstock security is important not only for continuity but also for competitiveness of the industry since the cost of raw materials account for 40–60 percent of the total production cost, depending on the procurement source and price.[67] In Israel, natural gas can lead to the establishment of industries that manufacture traditional methane-based products, such as raw material for fertiliser industry and petrochemical products (ammonia and methanol), produce fuel substitutes (methanol and Dimethyl Ether or DME),[68] produce olefins (methanol to olefins (MTO) technology), and produce high quality liquid fuels (using gas-to-liquid (GTL) technology) such as super clean synthetic diesel.[69]

Ammonia is the basic building block for a wide variety of nitrogen-based fertilisers and industrial products. Fertiliser use accounts for over 80 percent of global ammonia demand.[70] Nitrogenous fertilisers are the most widely used fertilisers in the world, accounting for close to 60 percent of all fertilisers.[71] Uses of ammonia in industrial applications include, production of ammonium nitrates that are used to make among many others products, explosives, acrylic fibres, plastics, and pharmaceuticals. With the exception of China, where much of the ammonia is produced from coal gasification, most of the world's ammonia is produced from natural gas. The shares of naphtha and gas oil as feedstock is declining as natural gas becomes more readily available on a continuing basis.[72] According to IHS Markit,[73] during 2016–2021, 97 percent of the planned ammonia capacity increases will be based on natural gas and these increases will be in areas where cost of natural gas are lower, in particular the United States and Middle East.

Petrochemical industry plays a vital role in the economy of a country, with the creation of several backward and forward linkages, from the upstream to downstream sectors of petroleum production. Petrochemicals have backward linkages with industries in petroleum refining and natural gas processing, as well as forward linkages with industries that produce a variety of downstream petroleum distillate items. According to an ICRIER study, "the industry offer alternatives, which serve as substitutes for natural products and hence, has the capacity to meet the constantly growing demand that would otherwise strain the natural resources. In addition, downstream processing units contribute to employment generation and entrepreneurial development in SME (small and medium-sized enterprises) segment, serving a vital need of the economy."[74] Petrochemicals constitute a very important segment of world chemicals market with a share of nearly 40 percent[75] and, therefore, have high export value.

Ammonia market in Israel

Israel does not produce ammonia[76] and domestic consumption of around 120,000 tonnes a year[77] is based on import. The two biggest consumers are Haifa Chemicals Ltd. (HCL) and Israel Chemicals Ltd. (ICL) Fertilizers (division of ICL), both of which export most of their products. HCL consumes around 80,000 tonnes of ammonia a year (in factories both in the north and south) to produce nitrogenous fertilisers based on potash and phosphates procured from ICL's plants near the Dead Sea,[78] of which around 97 percent are exported, mainly to customers in China and India.[79] The company is the second-largest producer of potassium nitrate fertiliser after Chile's SQM.[80] ICL Fertilizers consumes around 40,000 tonnes of ammonia a year for its own production of fertilisers and special purpose chemicals.[81] Other consumers include industrial chemical companies and companies that manufacture cooling systems that consume less than 3 percent of the total imported amount.[82]

Haifa Chemicals established an import terminal at the Haifa port through which ammonia was imported annually using refrigerated ships with a capacity of 12,000 tonnes (about one month's supply). Liquid ammonia used to be offloaded to an equal capacity storage tank installed in 1989 at the Kishon terminal and from there the chemical was piped to HCL and ICL plants in the south. The tank was a key part of HCL's manufacturing operation, but was a bone of contention between the company and people of Haifa because of the risks it posed to people's health and the environment in the bay area.

In October 2013, the Israeli government issued a tender to establish an ammonia production factory in Mishor Rotem, some 22 km from Dimona in the Negev, in order to move the risky operation to an unpopulated area.[83] After extending the tender process twice and recognising that no company had sent in a bid, the environment ministry announced its failure in November 2016. In view of the government's failure, Haifa Mayor Yona Yahav commissioned a technical committee of scientists and engineers to submit a detailed study on the operations of the ammonia plant. The report submitted by the experts found that the ammonia operations posed a serious risk to the environment and endangered the lives of over 600,000 people if the tank suffered a leak, rupture, or collapse.[84] What is more, the committee also found that any mishap on the delivery ship carrying ammonia could be a greater threat to lives in the Haifa bay area. Upon the municipality petition filed following the publication of the report, the Haifa District Court ordered the closure of the ammonia storage tank in February 2017, which was upheld by the Supreme Court and accordingly emptied five months later in July 2017.

As an alternative arrangement and in the absence of Haifa municipality's permission to allow the delivery of imported ammonia to the plant by pipeline, the government has decided that the ammonia will be stored in so-called ISO tanks, which are containers designed to carry liquids in bulk on ships, off the coast of Haifa. The ships will each hold only several weeks' supply of ammonia, so that in the event of a leak or other problem, the environmental damage can be easily contained. The project will require anticipating the needs of customers and delivering the ammonia accordingly.

The failure of the government to attract bidders for its tender to build an ammonia plant revealed the economic issues preventing the establishment of an ammonia production plant in Israel. Cheap feedstock is the basis for the establishment of a petrochemical plant, which is not available at present in Israel. Since the government does not intervene in the price of gas agreed in the contract between the purchasing company and the natural gas suppliers (in the absence of a NEC), low-priced feedstock is just not available (as in Saudi Arabia or Iran).

Concern over the absorptive capacity of a small market like Israel and the absence of permission to export the produce kept companies away from the bid. These two reasons point to a critical feature of the nature of Israel's gas industry, i.e., since the total volume of gas (contingent and prospective) is small, it cannot be 'used away' in a segment of petrochemical industry for which the domestic market is limited and profitability of a private company would rest on export. In the absence of a NEC, a 'breakeven' ammonia plant that would cater solely to Israeli requirements appears improbable in the near future.

Global methanol market and Israel

Israel's energy ministry includes production of methanol in the natural gas utilisation mix. Methanol the simplest of alcohol (CH_3OH) manufactured worldwide mainly from natural gas (CH_4) but also from a variety of raw materials including coal, biomass, landfill gas, oil distillates, and even waste CO_2. However, production of methanol from natural gas is currently the most economical and is a well-developed technology. Because of its flexible origin both from conventional fossil sources and emerging renewable feedstock, methanol is often called a 'future proof' molecule – a fuel source that is inexhaustible.

As a versatile molecule, methanol is widely used in a diverse set of industries and applications. Therefore, it has a well-established production and distribution infrastructure, with more than 90 production plants globally.[85] Methanol can be substituted directly for gasoline or blended into gasoline to create high octane and less polluting transportation fuel. Through a thermal-chemical process, the molecule can also be converted into gasoline, ethanol, and substitutes of LPG and diesel (such as DME from methanol, which can act as a substitute for diesel fuel). Extensive world markets also exists for MTBE, a chemical compound manufactured from methanol and used as a fuel additive in motor gasoline to raise the oxygen content and increases its octane value.

Methanol is used to manufacture many consumer and industrial products and thus constitutes the key component of the petrochemical industry. The molecule can be used an alternative feedstock for production of light olefins, which are the building blocks of life's everyday supplies such as plastics, paints, detergents, ropes, car interiors, and synthetic textiles that would otherwise be made from crude oil. In many countries, methanol is almost exclusively used to produce a resin used in adhesives, finishes, particleboard, MDF, ropes, and moulded objects.

In recent years, demand for methanol to produce light olefins or MTO process has grown rapidly in China. With MTO capacity shuttered in the United States in early 2000s, about nearly 1 in 5 tonnes of global methanol production by 2021, will be used for the MTO process to satisfy the expanding Chinese demand.[86]

According to IHS Markit, global methanol demand reached 70mt in 2015 and is set to reach 95mt by 2021, being driven by the emerging energy applications for methanol, which now accounts for 45 percent of methanol consumption.[87] China is the global leader in methanol use, consuming around 49mt a year in 2017, more than half of global consumption and mostly derived from domestic production. The country's methanol supply soared through the increasing use of methanol in chemical industry and as fuel additive.[88] About two-thirds of China's methanol production is from coal (directly or through coking gas, a by-product of steel production) and the remainder from natural gas.[89]

As the major raw material for methanol is methane, the largest component of natural gas Methanol plants are traditionally located in the proximity of natural gas sources. In Saudi Arabia, these are situated in the Jubail industrial complex of the gas-rich al-Hasa province. Similarly, Iran's Zagros Petrochemical Company that produces methanol, is based in Asaluyeh located near the gigantic South Pars gas field, whereas the Fanavaran Petrochemical Company housed in Bandar Imam Khomeini special economic zone, is located in the Iran's gas- and oil-rich Khuzestan province. The Egyptian methanol plant built as a joint venture with Canadian company Methanax is located on the shores of the Mediterranean Sea in Damietta, and gets its feedstock from the northern offshore gas fields. Gas-rich countries typically create a petrochemical sector to diversify gas utilisation and meet domestic demand of secondary industries that use methanol.

The feasibility of developing MTO plants on the basis of natural gas reserves should be examined. Israel's Carmel Olefins of the Bazan Group uses oil derivates (naphtha and LPG) as feedstock,[90] which creates a strong rationale for adoption of technology that produce olefins from methanol. Production of methanol in Israel makes economic sense for three reasons: first, the easy availability of natural gas as feedstock; second, methanol can prove to be a substitute transportation fuel for gasoline produced from imported crude oil; third, local production of methanol creates potential for the expansion of the petrochemical industry. Since methanol can be transported easily at half the cost of gasoline (because methanol occupies double the volume of gasoline in transportation vessel), it can bring down the per unit cost of usable energy.

According to a Bank Leumi report and the projections of MoE, methanol production will be one of the long-term outcome of the natural gas discoveries. While the authors of Bank Leumi report believe that investment in a methanol plant will occur during 2020–2030, with methanol production commencing closer to 2030,[91] the ministry's forecast of methanol production starting 2020 (Figure 3.7) seems far-fetched, especially as there is no plant in Israel at the time of writing. Bank Leumi estimates that, "There will be one major producer with a medium sized plant, with capital costs of approximately $500 million. However, a smaller plant in the area of US$ 200 million could initially be constructed with the potential for increased capacity in the future."[92]

Natural gas as a transportation fuel

Israel's land transportation is entirely dependent on imported oil, despite the absorption of natural gas in other sectors of the economy. In 2016, the consumption of motor gasoline and diesel for transportation grew at the rate of 3.6 percent to 5.53mt as compared to 5.34mt in 2015, with consumption reaching approximately 2.94mt of gasoline and 2.60mt of diesel.[93] In view of the government's objective to reduce the share of oil in transportation to about 30 percent by 2020 and approximately 60 percent by 2025, the challenge is how to rapidly incorporate natural gas and its derivatives into the transportation sector.

The Prime Minister's Fuel Choice Initiative (FCI, discussed in Chapter 1) considers natural gas the best short-term replacement for oil in transportation and a bridge towards fully sustainable energy solutions[94] that involve electric mobility,[95] use of biofuels, and waste-to-energy conversion.

Under FCI, the energy ministry is involved in the entire technical, regulatory, and economic aspects of the incorporation of natural gas and natural-gas-based synthetic fuels in Israel's transportation sector. The ministry is wholly responsible for the processes relating to 'well to wheel' experimental projects, including an examination of their application to the Israeli market. In order to integrate natural gas and natural gas-based petroleum alternatives in land transportation,[96] the government's effort is gradually converging on three areas: a) CNG solutions for trucks, light duty vehicles, buses, and private vehicles; b) Methanol as a gasoline blend for private vehicles; and c) GTL technologies that can turn natural gas into drop-in fuels.[97]

Compressed natural gas

As a fuel, CNG is expedient both in terms of environmental sustainability and customer profitability. With regard to emissions, natural gas is the cleanest burning fuel in the market today, thanks to its reduced particulate emissions (95 percent as compared to diesel) and 35 percent less NOx (nitrogen oxide and nitrogen dioxide). Furthermore, due to lower carbon dioxide emissions (15–20 percent lower than gasoline), switching to CNG can help mitigate greenhouse gas emissions. However, if biomethane (landfill biogas) is used, carbon dioxide (CO_2) emissions in CNG-powered vehicles can go down from 10 percent up to 100 percent.[98] In terms of cost effectiveness, total cost of ownership (TCO) savings stand at up to 10 percent. Lower prices for natural gas in comparison to gasoline and diesel also equate to higher profitability, which translates into up to 40 percent in fuel expense reductions-- the most important aspect relating its adoption.[99]

CNG has been implemented globally in the mass transport sector, founded on the abundant availability of natural gas. As low-cost fuel CNG is projected to see a period of high market growth until 2024, led by demand augmentation from the Asia Pacific and riding on increasing investment in infrastructure for storage and distribution facilities in the region, according to Credence Research.[100] Governmental support in the form of subsidies, coupled with growing awareness of the deleterious impact of greenhouse gases and particulate emissions are the key factors pushing up the demand for CNG in automobiles across the globe. The trend is on a sharp growth curve in the Middle East, Asia Pacific, and Latin America.[101]

The extraction of natural gas from tight gas, coal-bed methane, and shale gas in North America have increased supply and further brought down the global CNG prices. A majority of the governments in key consuming economies are in the process of converting gasoline-based public transportation to CNG. However, the high cost of installing CNG storage tanks in vehicles, combined with a limited number of refuelling infrastructures present the key disadvantages and extant challenges for the users.[102]

CNG is a low energy density fuel: A gallon of CNG has only a quarter of the energy in a gallon of gasoline. CNG vehicles therefore require bulky fuel tanks, making CNG practicable mainly for large fleet vehicles such as buses, taxis, and delivery trucks. These vehicles park in the same place every night, where they can refuel without having to develop a costly refuelling infrastructure network. However, the use of CNG in passenger cars require a much more extensive spread infrastructure.[103] Natural gas is the fastest growing vehicular fuel: Natural gas vehicles worldwide increased from 7.40 million in 2007 to 25.0 million in 2017 with a CAGR of 12.95 percent.[104] The global CNG vehicles market is expected to grow at a CAGR of 4.9 percent during the period 2017–2021, as CNG gets momentum from growing use of CNG in luxury vehicles.[105]

The Tzemach Committee predicted that about a third of the total private vehicle and two-thirds of all public vehicles will convert to CNG[106] and that the consumption of natural gas in transportation would reach 40 bcm.[107] The Alternative Fuels Administration argued in a report in 2012 that assimilation of natural gas-powered vehicles could begin as early as 2014–2015 and more than 40 percent penetration could be achieved within a decade (Figure 3.8).[108] However, at the time of writing, natural gas-based fuels for transportation is at zero start,

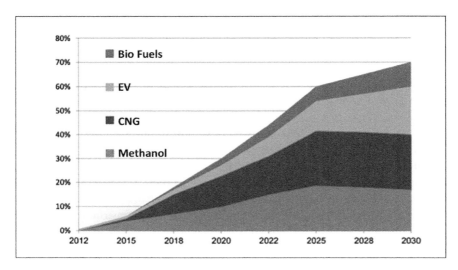

FIGURE 3.9 Expected penetration rate for transportation fuel alternatives in Israel

Source: Based on Alternative Fuels Initiative, Prime Minister's Office, State of Israel, 2012

except for a lone Stralis heavy truck supplied from CNH Industrial's commercial vehicles brand Iveco to Fridenson Group, one of Israel's logistics companies, on an experimental basis.[109]

According to MoE, the delay in implementation of the CNG project is primarily procedural and is related to the award of permits for installation of refuelling stations. Others suggest that delay is due to the absence of a policy on the taxes to be levied on gas-powered vehicles, causing potential natural gas vehicle (NGV) investors to hesitate about setting up the infrastructure.[110]

The government has allocated 100 million shekels for the construction of CNG fuelling stations,[111] mainly for heavy vehicles – urban trucks and bus fleets – categorised as major polluters. It is offering grants of NIS 1 million ($250,000) per station to qualifying companies, with the resolve to establish a network of 30 to 40 CNG stations within two years.[112] More specifically, the plan to fuel 11 garbage trucks in Haifa with natural gas has been budgeted at NIS 3 million.[113] Delek Israel Fuel Corporation Ltd., a subsidiary of the Delek Group, has proposed the installation of CNG gas pumps in 12 filling stations across Israel at a cost of 36 million shekels ($9.9 million), for which it has built a $50-million facility for compressing natural gas at Ashdod.[114]

Methanol as a transportation fuel: world

Both the United States and Australia are currently examining the practicality of methanol as a locomotive fuel, as it can be produced from low-cost natural gas. Chinese provincial governments are supporting methanol use by adopting standards ranging from M5 to M100 (5–100 percent methanol and gasoline pro-portion). In 2009, national fuel blending standards for M85 and M100 went into effect across China, and currently a national M15 standard is under review.[115]

Compared to gasoline and diesel fuel, methanol offers a substantial improve-ment over the toxic emissions released from the combustion of traditional fuels. Methanol cuts emissions of NOx and volatile organic compounds that imme-diately contaminate the air and are the key precursors of ground-level ozone or 'smog.'[116] Since methanol contains no sulphur, there is no sulphur dioxide emission. When used as a fuel in a combustion engine, methanol has shown to emit 15 to 20 percent less carbon than gasoline. It has been demonstrated that methanol-fuelled auto emissions meet and exceed California's stringent ultra low emission vehicle (ULEV) emission targets.[117] Methanol is also safer than gaso-line because it requires a much higher temperature for ignition and, therefore, reduces the risks of car fires and explosions in collision accidents. It also biode-grades quickly compared to petroleum fuels in case of a spill.

As a transportation engine fuel, methanol has chemical and physical prop-erties similar to ethanol, commonly used in US gasoline blends. More than 97 percent of US gasoline contains ethanol, typically E10 (10 percent ethanol, 90 percent gasoline), as a fuel oxygenator.[118] Ethanol is also available as E85 (or flex fuel), which can be used in flexible fuel vehicles (FFV), designed to oper-ate on any blend of gasoline and ethanol up to 85 percent. In the 1980s and 1990s, methanol was more popular than ethanol in US, riding on the oil crisis of 1970s and the drive to improve air quality. The whole-hearted adoption of methanol as the new fuel for cars by the state of California generated a popular interest in methanol.

Abundant availability of indigenous feedstock (i.e., coal and natural gas) and low production cost led to methanol's popularity as an alternative fuel, such that a national M85 standard (covering mixtures containing between 70 percent and 85 percent in gasoline) was put in place in the United States.[119] However, a vari-ety of factor prevented methanol from becoming a significant fuel. Political fac-tors, including pressure from oil companies and OPEC, combined with rapidly falling oil prices and the arrival of shale oil caused methanol to slide in popular-ity. The introduction of a 'renewable fuel standard' (RFS), requiring that certain percentage of transportation fuel in a geographical area be replaced by renewable fuels – and methanol produced from natural gas did not fall into the category of renewable fuel – led to the reduced interest in methanol. In the absence of strong advocacy, refiners switched wholesale to ethanol as the oxygenating agent of choice in the United States.[120]

Like ethanol, methanol is corrosive to vehicle parts, but requires relatively low-cost adaptation of the vehicular engine to accommodate higher blends. Methanol can be blended with gasoline and used at a lower level of 15 per-cent in existing vehicles or at a higher level of 85 percent in FFV. Aftermarket modifications of standard gasoline-only vehicles to run on alcohol fuels are also possible with low to moderate conversion prices.[121] Like ethanol, methanol has less energy per gallon than gasoline – methanol has only half the energy content per gallon of gasoline and ethanol is two-thirds the energy density of gasoline – which implies that fuel tanks using alcohol-based fuels deplete fast.[122] Therefore, the price per unit of methanol must remain significantly lower at least half or than gasoline to raise consumer acceptance.

Methanol as a transportation fuel: Israel

Israel's fundamentals – large gas finds and the strategic need to reduce oil dependence – make the use of methanol viable. Methanol has attractive features for use in transportation in Israel due to the following reasons:[123] First, as there is the availability of indigenous sources of gas, it can be produced at competitive prices relative to gasoline, advancing local fuel as compared to imported crude oil; second, due to the existence of a small market, it can be adapted easily without the enormous cost associated with fuel infrastructure (vessels, railroads, trucks, pipelines, etc.); third, being an isolated market in the region, the energetic efficiency of methanol-based fuel can be exploited at minimal incremental costs; fourth, the implausibility of ethanol production of a wide scale due to paucity of and water for crop growth; and fifth, it can reduce dependence on oil import and bring down the energy cost for the Israeli consumer.

In 2012–2015, the MoE-supported field trial of M15 (15 percent methanol and 85 percent gasoline) conducted by Dor Chemicals,[124] an Israeli company engaged in the manufacturing and trading of chemicals, revealed that "although there are very few and small modifications needed in the vehicles, M15 could not be used as a drop-in fuel in all existing gasoline-operated vehicles with no changes or adaptations of the vehicle."[125] In other words, existing gasoline vehicles will have to undergo modification that may not be popular. Therefore, officials prefer fuel with high methanol content in dedicated FFVs for the Israeli market, which also has strong economic advantage for the consumer.[126]

After Fiat Chrysler Automobiles N.V. (FCA) showed an interest in Dor's pilot project, a Memorandum of Understanding (MoU) was signed between FCA, Iveco (a brand of CNH Industrial, FCA's sister company), Magneti Marelli (a brand of FCA), and the Israel Fuel Choice Initiative (IFCI) for the development and trial of methanol blends based on natural gas. FCA also signed a MoU with Dor Chemicals to develop methanol for production, blending, infrastructure, regulations, and automotive technologies.[127] However, FCA suggested that instead of targeting FFVs directly, which posed a hazard in terms of technological risk management, M15 should be introduced as an immediate step.[128] In view of that, MoE supported another pilot project aimed at the adaption of FCA vehicles to run on methanol blends. Based on the detailed report of joint development and endurance tests performed in Israel, Israel's Ministry of Transport approved the regulatory standard for the use of M15 fuel in May 2016.[129] making Israel the first country in the world to issue a national standard for methanol flex-fuel vehicles.

At the Fuel Choices Summit in Israel in November 2016, FCA presented the Fiat 500 M15, a retail-ready version of the Fiat 500, capable of running on a blend of gasoline and methanol from 0 up to 15 percent and was compliant with Euro 6 New European Driving Cycle (NEDC) regulations. According to FCA, a Euro 6 compliant Fiat 500 M15, running on a blend of 85 percent gasoline and 15 percent methanol, would deliver a 2 percent CO_2 emission reduction when compared with the same Euro 6 version of the vehicle running on gasoline, without compromising vehicle performance.[130]

Before commercialisation of FVV can begin, FCA-Dor expects the government to have low excise duty for M15, disburse grants for the first gas stations adapting themselves to market the new fuel, facilitate purchase tax adjustments on vehicles approved for methanol fuel in accordance with the vehicle's emissions, and institute accelerated depreciation for investment of facilities producing methanol gasoline blends.[131] Dor Chemicals currently imports 100,000 tonnes per year of methanol for its petrochemical production to meet local demand. It has proposed replacing all methanol exports in the longer term by building a 500,000- tonne per year methanol plant in the Negev, utilising the local gas resources.[132]

While methanol substitution is supported by a number of economic considerations, non-economic drivers are no less important. Methanol substitution of crude oil is supported by the Chinese government's reported desire to reduce its dependence on imported oil. However, if low oil prices persist, methanol substitution will be more difficult to justify economically, as car manufacturers may seek ways to comply with emission regulations without engine conversions. To introduce methanol significantly into the Israeli market, both methanol vehicles and fuel infrastructure will have to be deployed simultaneously. It should be mentioned here that such a system is also amenable to renewable methanol produced from biomass for a more sustainable transportation alternative.

Gas-to-liquid (GTL) fuels

GTL is a process that converts natural gas to clean liquid fuels such as gasoline, diesel, and jet fuel that would otherwise be derived from crude oil. The most common technique used at GTL facilities is Fischer-Tropsch (synthesis) (F-T) developed in Germany in the 1920s. In general, GTL through the F-T route refers to technology for the conversion of natural gas to liquid; however, GTL is an umbrella term applicable to any hydrocarbon feedstock that can produce a set of synthetic hydrocarbon liquids. Although F-T synthesis has been in existence for nearly a century, it has barely penetrated the energy market, with currently only five GTL plants operating worldwide.[133] For decades, the relative parity in the cost of crude oil and natural gas curbed investment in GTL. However, with the growing discrepancy between higher the cost of petroleum products and the lower cost of natural gas assisted by the emergence of shale gas, has led investors to reconsider the potential of GTL.

As natural gas is relatively low in energy content per unit volume compared to gasoline or diesel, the transportation cost is significantly higher than it is for oil, which is one the key hurdles to its pervasive use. In view of the uncertainties surrounding pipeline construction, an increasingly difficult and costly undertaking, GTL technology offers the possibility of hauling gas to the market in an economic and efficient way.

Fuels produced by GTL have qualities that make substantial reductions in emissions possible. They contain almost none of the impurities – sulphur, aromatics, and nitrogen – that are found in crude oil. GTL diesel is sulphur free as is GTL kero, blend component for jet fuel production. GTL naphtha is sulphur free, and it is highly paraffinic, which renders it an ideal feedstock for olefins production. LPG can be either sold as product or reused as fuel inside a GTL plant. Natural gas being abundant, versatile, and affordable is thus suitable for addressing problems of remote gas utilisation, increase in crude oil price, depletion of fossil fuel, and environmental pollution.

Energy Information Administration (EIA) lists four major advantages of GTL technology: First, it provides energy security and diversity by affording the ability of a state to rely on self-produced fuel and hedge risk and dependencies associated with reliance on imported oil; second, the fuel can be used without requiring any modifications to existing infrastructure, vehicles, or driving habits; third, GTL can also lead to the production of various petroleum derivatives (kerosene, naphtha, lubricants, waxes, etc.) that hedge demand risks and give gas producers access to higher value markets; and fourth, GTL opens up the possibility of export to satisfy growing global demand for liquid products as new gas supplies come on-stream.

However, the critical downside of GTL technology is the high capital cost to the tune of $20,000 to $35,000 barrels per stream day, depending on the plant capacity and technology. It is believed that technological developments in syngas generation, FT reactor, and catalyst technology have resulted in a sizeable reduction in capital costs of GTL plants in recent years. GTL plants benefit significantly from economies of scale, which is driving most technology suppliers toward building larger plants. A large GTL plant would require a large feedstock source too, but for stranded, associated gas or smaller gas resources a small-scale GTL unit is the answer. Israel's gas resources are rather small as compared to Qatar, which has a large GTL plant (built by Shell), or Nigeria, where an equally large GTL plant is under construction (under the auspices of Chevron).[134]

GTL fuel in Israel

What appears feasible in Israel is a small-scale GTL plant, which can utilise gas from minor fields still awaiting development. In June 2014, MoE invited applications to submit standpoints, information, and expressions of interest regarding the possibility of building a GTL plant.[135] Only a few technology owners and engineering companies responded to this request for information (RFI), among them, Mayer Fitoussi, CEO of Aqua Soft, a Haifa-based company, presented proposal for a small GTL plant based on new catalyst technology.[136]

In what could be considered as the next step, the Israeli Government in October 2016 published a tender on aiding a pre-feasibility study for constructing and operating a GTL plant in Israel for specific technologies in specific locations. The winning tender will receive 50 percent of the cost of the pre-feasibility study from the ministry, an amount of up to NIS 200,000. Under the tender terms, the test will be for one or more sites on which the plant would be constructed.[137]

KTE,[138] a Haifa-based company providing technical and enterprises services for the industry and Givot Olam Oil Exploration, together are carrying out feasibility studies and working on designing a GTL project for the MoE. KTE is examining a GTL plant design and production of 900 billion barrel distillates blend, besides the manufacturing of LPG from associated gas procured at Givot's crude oil drilling in the Rosh Ha'ayin prospect in central Israel, based on the F-T reaction.[139] The oil potential in this 240-square-kilometre has been evaluated for hundreds of millions of barrels.[140]

KTE is also examining the prospect of production of 45,000 barrel per day of gasoline and diesel mentioned in the Pareto consulting services report,[141] "Integration of Alternative Fuels from Natural Gas in Israel Transportation System," commissioned by the energy ministry in 2012. The establishment of a GTL plant can also advance the Israeli government's much-discussed objective of eliminating oil from the transportation sector.

Creation of the sovereign wealth fund

Israel's natural gas discoveries are having a noticeable impact on the country's economic activity. There have been significant cost-cutting and productivity gains across several sectors together with increase in the competitiveness of the manufactured products. In addition, the revenues that the State of Israel is receiving from natural gas taxation and royalties are expected to be substantial creating enormous opportunities throughout the economy. However, the sudden injection of vast revenue derived from natural resource oil – natural gas, or mineral wealth – has a long history of wreaking havoc in both developed and developing economies, a phenomenon called the Dutch disease or 'resource curse,' which occurred in the Netherlands in the 1960s and 70s.

Following the discovery and rapid development of the supergiant Groningen gas field in 1959 and other gas fields in the North Sea in 1960s, the Netherlands led the world in the 1970s in natural gas exports volumes. The earnings from gas exports gave rise to a massive inflow of foreign currency into the Dutch economy that caused a sharp appreciation of the guilder, undermining price competitiveness of country's other exports. As a result of the decline in exports from these sectors, unemployment soared and fears of deindustrialisation gripped the Dutch economy.

Further, gas export earnings caused another internal difficulty to the Dutch economy. The gas industry "set the tone in nation-wide wage negotiations and dictate[d] wage settlements that other industries [could] ill afford."[142] A Bank Leumi report analyses thus:

> An additional problem resulting from the gas discovery occurred as the revenues from gas exports were used to increase local demand within Holland. This demand led to a rise in land prices, as well as in the prices of local services (restaurants, hospitality, and similar services). Consequently, labor wages in the local service sectors, which do not compete with import prices, increased. That in turn led to a wage increase also in other industries as employees began to switch over to the service industries. In other words, the use of revenue inflows from gas exports in the local market led to a rise in wages and to additional damage to the competitiveness of exports.[143]

Many resource-rich countries learnt their lesson from the Dutch experience and set up a SWF, to invest their earnings from natural resources or trade balance (basically any large inflow of money into the economy) in foreign currency abroad, with the purpose to shield the domestic economy from overheating and direct the returns for public expenditure. According to the *Investopedia*,

> SWF consists of pools of money derived from a country's reserves, set aside for investment purposes to benefit the country's economy and citizens. The funding for a SWF comes from central bank reserves that accumulate as a result of budget and trade surpluses, and from revenue generated from the exports of natural resources.[144]

In addition to Dutch disease concerns, one of the ideas behind the creation of a SWF is to effectively save today's wealth for the benefit of future generations, i.e., "to replace the temporary income from the sale of subsoil assets with permanent income from above-ground assets" in what is called a secure and appropriate intergenerational distribution of the proceeds. Many also raise the concern of stabilisation, implying the need to "insulate the budget from short-term fluctuations in commodity prices." The parking of funds, inherent in the understanding of a SWF, is to "hold revenues abroad until good investment opportunities arise."[145]

From Chile (copper mines) to Botswana (diamond and minerals) to Norway (oil) and Iran (oil and gas) as well as Singapore (balance of payment surplus), all have created SWFs to reduce their economic risks. According to the SWF Institute, as of January 2018, there are 77 country-based funds with oil and gas-related assets of $4266.76 billion, and land and mineral royalties among non-commodity based aggregation is $3314.70 billion.[146] The Government Pension Fund of Norway is the largest sovereign pension fund in the world, with assets worth $998.93 billion.[147] Saudi Arabia created the first SWF based on oil earnings and it has since created another SWF in 2008 to manage its vast oil revenues. Turkey's non-commodity Wealth Fund established in 2016 is of a more recent provenance.

The Israeli government in early 2011 commissioned the Milken Institute to examine how the country should structure a new sovereign fund in view of its newly-discovered natural gas resources. Subsequently, Prime Minister Benjamin Netanyahu, Finance Minister Yuval Steinitz and BoI Governor Stanley Fischer appointed an inter-ministerial steering committee to examine the manage-ment of state revenues from natural gas resources, in fulfilment of the provisions of the 2011 Taxation of Oil and Gas Revenues Law. The oil and gas taxation law required the government to bring forth a proposal to channelise fiscal revenues (the Sheshinski 'levy') from natural gas resources into a sovereign wealth fund that invests abroad in strategic projects. Holding the fund overseas will ensure the competitiveness in the economy (mitigate the impact of natural resource exports on the exchange rate), preserve employment, and strengthen the eco-nomic security of the state by shielding the deficit from fiscal leakage (provided the share kept aside for spending is kept at a low level). According to the commit-tee's recommendations submitted to the Cabinet on 19 February 2012:

> Approximately half of state revenues from oil and gas resources (incomes from the tax on excess profits) will be deposited in a fund that will invest abroad and will constitute a 'security cushion' for dealing with national events with extraordinary economic implications such as wars, natural disasters, economic crises, etc. Pursuant to a decision by Prime Minister Netanyahu, the fund's profits will be devoted to designated projects in the fields of education and security, which will be approved by the Cabinet. Should an extraordinary event take place, it will be possible to borrow from the fund.[148]

The Ministerial Committee on Legislation approved the management of fund's assets by BoI under a supervision and oversight mechanism – to be led by the Finance Ministry – that will ensure maximum public transparency. On that basis, the government authorised the creation of an SWF, called the Israeli Citi-zens Fund in July 2014.[149] As the name change suggests, the fund is aimed for the benefit of current and future generations, as it represents the earnings from the sale of a public asset.

To begin with, Israel's sovereign fund was envisaged on excess profit tax or levy from gas resources, but when Sheshinski II Committee in October 2014 suggested a progressive surtax on excess profit from the production of Israel's other mineral resources, it was also made a constituent part of the fund's poten-tial corpus. The Sheshinski II Committee suggested companies exploiting Israel's mineral resources will be charged a progressive tax rate on all windfall-profit of between 25 and 42 percent. A company reaching an annual rate of return on investment of 14–20 percent would pay a progressive tax rate starting at 25 per-cent; the rate would rise to 42 percent for a return above 20 percent. Companies would also pay the government royalties of 5 percent on their revenue, compared to the extant variable rate of 2–10 percent.[150] The recommendations of the committee, which went into effect in January 2017, mainly affects ICL, which holds the license to mine potash from the Dead Sea region, as well as phosphates and bromine in the Negev.

There are three types of revenue that accrue to the Israeli government from gas and other mineral resources. The first is royalties (12.5 percent royalty on gross natural gas sales and a 5 percent royalty on sales of other natural resources), the second comes from corporate tax, and the third includes income tax from surplus profits (that is, the profits that will be created after the return on investment in the reservoirs as well as the other mineral resources). While the royalties and corporate taxes are incorporated into the government budget, the source of the fund's revenue is the excess profits tax of up to 50 percent on the natural gas reservoirs, as recommended by the Sheshinski I Committee and up to 42 percent excess profits tax on other natural (mineral) resources, as recommended by the Sheshinski II Committee.

Israel's SWF will go into operation when the cumulative excess profits tax as recommended by the Sheshinski Committee (2011) reaches NIS 1 billion or $280 million, whose balance as of December 31 2016 was NIS 459 million (in 2015 it was also NIS 459 million) or $129 million. Mari-B reservoir, which depleted in 2012, contributed NIS 300 million in excess profits tax. Most of the fund's revenue will come from the Tamar reservoir but not before 2020, and in the middle of the next decade from the Leviathan reservoir.[151] In the case of ICL, the government decided that the company would start to pay natural resource tax on excess profit once they reach an annual return on investment of 11 percent, thus linking tax revenues to global potash prices.[152]

While according to OECD estimates, the size of Israel's SWF would be from $40 to $175 billion (that is, between 10 and 50 percent of Israel's GDP), by 2040, depending on the rate of new discoveries, according to a forecast presented to the Knesset by then-Governor of BoI Stanley Fischer in 2013, $72 billion will be accumulated in the fund by 2037. Revenue from excess profits tax on the production of potash, bromine, copper, and phosphates is expected to reach NIS 400 million or $112 million a year, according to the MoF estimate,[153] or NIS 280 million or $78 million a year according to the estimate presented by Prime Minister's Office.[154] A BoI 2015 assessment spoke of an accumulation of NIS 4 billion (around $1 billion), at the end 2019 based on the excess profits tax of gas and minerals.[155]

Since then, however, many issues have delayed the operation and accumulation of the projected funds in Israel's SWF. First, since the revenues are contingent upon the profits of the ventures, gas developers will start paying tax on profit only after they regain 150–230 percent of their recognised investment in the development of the fields. As part of the natural gas plan, government allowed the Tamar partnerships to make additional drillings for capacity expansion. Hence the estimated $2 billion worth of investment in Tamar second phase,[156] to increase the domestic supply and exports, would count as investment, which would delay the imposition of excess profits tax until 2020.

In view of the delays in the development of the Leviathan reservoir, revenues from taxes on surplus profits will not ensue before 2025. Moreover, global prices of oil (and gas) have plunged at least since 2014, which will have an impact on the revenues that will go into the fund. In 2017, as global potash prices dropped, ICL registered a lower profit than the previous year[157] indicating that the surtax profit would be lower and therefore less money will go into the sovereign fund.

Israel had two basic models to choose from while establishing its SWF. When SWF was established in 1990, the Bank of Norway assumed an independent charge of managing the oil fund to prevent political misuse of resource rents. On the other hand, Singapore established a non-governmental statutory authority – the Government Investment Corporation (GIC) – to manage the fund in addition to other asset management mandates from the public sector.[158] Israel has adopted the Norwegian model and under the mandate from MoF, a division within the BoI will manage the fund and its institutions (council and investment committee) will be established in 2018. Broadly, Israel's SWF will be invested overseas to expand investment options and thus secure better returns and evade a major inflow of foreign currencies that could strengthen the shekel and undermine export industries. However, income from the fund will be used nationally for national projects and emergencies. The decision to involve the BoI also stems from the costs associated with the functioning of a separate statutory body as well as the fact that a substantial sum is expected to accumulate not before the middle of the 2020s.

Looking forward

The growth in the use of natural gas in recent years in Israel is high in international comparison. Israel's rate of growth in natural gas consumption for 2017 was 7.4 percent, way higher than OECD average of 1.3 percent and 4.3 percent of the European Union (EU). Moreover, the natural gas consumption growth over ten-year period between 2006 and 2016 was a whopping 15.5 percent for Israel, whereas it recorded 1.6 percent for OECD, –1.3 percent for the EU, and 2.3 percent globally.[159] A trend typical of a developing sector, the high growth of Israel's natural gas consumption reflects the growing absorption of the fuel in the economy.

However, the high rate of natural gas penetration in Israeli economy is limited to primary energy consumption in electricity generation; a small amount in industry. It's use in non-energy transformation such as petrochemicals or transportation is virtually nil. While more than 80 percent of gas goes toward production of electricity, the average global is 29 percent.[160] Natural gas-based chemical industry is absent in Israel in the current scenario as compared with global average of 5.5 percent. Parallel to 3.4 percent of global natural gas consumption in transport, Israel still has to develop a commercially viable CNG-based transportation system. Though the share of natural gas in electricity generation was as high as 63 percent in 2017, there is ample scope for its further utilisation as substitute for coal.

Since 2013, Israel's priority has been to wean the industrial sector away from three oil products – diesel, Mazut, and LPG – and to substitute them with natural gas. Fostering the use of natural gas manufacturing is more than simply cost saving. As much as manufacturing is a wealth-producing sector – producing disposable income and employment in the economy – it is also crucial for the services using manufactured goods. Therefore, to expand the use of natural gas in the Israeli industrial/manufacturing sector, both supply and demand sides need to be addressed. On the supply side, a widespread distribution network is key to the expansion of natural gas use. Once gas fields besides Tamar come on stream, the uninterrupted availability of natural gas at a competitive price will accelerate absorption in the industrial sector. With the decline in cost of production due to the availability of a fuel supplied locally (as comported to imported oil products) would lead to a larger profit for exporters. That, in turn, can spur a virtuous cycle whereby factory owners and exporters would be willing to bear the cost of connection to the distribution network.[161]

A pervasive absorption of natural gas also plays a crucial role in the development of existing gas fields and energizing E&P.[162] One of the reasons why the gas licencing round of 2017 failed to attract major companies is the perception that Israel's market has limited scope for natural gas absorption. According to a latest 2017 appraisal report of MoE, towards the end of 2018, about 40 additional small consumers will connect to the distribution network so that in early 2019, there will be 97 consumers in total.[163] This is a very small number compared to the original target of 450–500 consumers through 2020.[164] However, measures by the government to provide support to companies for network deployment and subsidies to the manufactures to switch to natural gas will have a salutary impact on gas penetration in the economy and expanding the scope of utilisation. The second offshore bidding round launched in November 2018 will certainly test the impact of these measures.

While there is a trend towards progressive incorporation of natural gas in the manufacturing sector, NGA estimates its potential consumption through the distribution network will not be more than 720 mcm by 2030 and will increase to only 850 mcm in 2042 considering that for some units it may not be economical to make a fuel switchover.[165] A larger absorption will hence require expeditious development of petrochemicals and transportation sectors based on natural gas.

The full potential of gas in the domestic chemicals industry should be taken up for across the board sectorial utilisation. Israel currently imports products such as ammonia, methanol, and olefins from abroad – hence there is a place for use of natural gas to manufacture these locally. In 2016, Israel imported $5.74 billion worth of chemical products and $2.72 billion worth of plastic and rubbers products, many of which could use natural gas as base material or feedstock.[166] Israel also exported $12.9 million worth of chemical products and $2.5 billion worth of plastic and rubber products[167] – both areas could be enhanced using the indigenous resource either as feedstock or as source of electricity in their production.[168]

Further, a significant advancement for Israel may come through ammonia and methanol production, which may spur important developments in the organic chemical industry and transportation. The use of natural gas in transportation is an immense yet unrealised opportunity in the Israeli economy. Israel launched a national programme in 2011 to create a global hub for the development of oil independent technologies (Alternative Fuels Initiative) in Israel and allocated substantial sum of money for research and development in innovative technologies.

CNG in transportation is a well-developed technology and is being increasing adopted all over the world to bring down the cost of fuel, reduce emission levels, and extend the life of the vehicle (CNG does not contain lead, so spark plug life is prolonged because there is no fouling). It is possible to convert existing gasoline-powered vehicles to run on CNG; they can be dedicated (running only on natural gas) or bi-fuel (running on either gasoline or natural gas). However, an increasing number of vehicles worldwide are being manufactured to run on soley CNG.

Natural gas in an industrial plant's onsite electricity production is emerging as its most popular use. It is especially useful in desalination plants where cost of power may account for 30 percent to 60 percent of the operational costs.[169] Desalination plants in Hadera, Sorek, and Ashkelon are generating electricity using natural gas.[170] Israel's Water Authority plans for the years ahead envisages natural gas as the source of electricity.[171]

In addition, the use of natural gas as a source of energy in residential, commercial, and public facilities is common throughout the world. There is no reason why Israel cannot integrate it into potential areas of use, such as large shopping centres as well as residential gas connections (the use of household equipment that makes direct use of natural gas, such as central heating and laundry dryers). Electrification of the Israel Railways' line is a sectorial utilisation that will deepen the penetration of natural gas in the economy and contribute to the environmental goals of the state.

Natural gas has brought down electricity production costs and thereby electricity prices in the country. One of the prime reasons for the increase in public savings rate in the Israeli economy since 2014 is the savings from lower expenditure on import of energy products. The overall savings derive, among others, from the investments of tens of billions of dollars in the gas sector, creating economic growth and raising people's living standards. Gas royalties and taxes contribute to state revenues and create disposable income for investments in the social sectors for welfare of citizens – the argument emphasised by PM Netanyahu in his speech on the export of gas to Egypt.

Notes

1 Katharine Hayhoe is an atmospheric scientist and Professor of Political Science at Texas Tech University, where she is Director of the Climate Science Centre.
2 Israel's primary energy consumption from coal (electricity production as coal is not used in any other transformation) has continuously declined in the last five years

(2013–2017), from 7.4 mtoe to 5.2 mtoe (See Chapter 1: Figure 1.1 and Table 1.1). In the global scenario, compared to the strong growth in coal use in the 2000s, worldwide coal use remained flat in 2017. Coal is being increasingly replaced by natural gas, renewables, and nuclear power (in the case of China) for electric power generation, and demand for coal also weakens for industrial processes. See *BP Statistical Review of World Energy*, British Petroleum, London, UK, 2018; *International Energy Outlook 2017*, Energy Information Administration (EIA), United States Department of Energy, Washington, DC, United States, September 14, 2017, www.eia.gov/outlooks/ieo/exec_summ.php#2 (accessed on October 4, 2017).

3 Energy Minister Steinitz signed an order under the Electricity Law in coordination with the electricity authority in November 2017. See *Financial Reports for the Three Months Ended March 31, 2018*, Israel Electric Corporation Ltd., Haifa, Israel, p. 45, www.iec.co.il/EN/IR/Documents/The_Israel_Electric_Co-Financial_Reports_March_2018.pdf (accessed on August 2, 2018); *Israel Continues Policy of Reducing Emissions and Conversion to Natural Gas, Removes Barriers to Gas Flow From Leviathan Field*, Ministry of Environmental Protection, State of Israel, November 23, 2017, www.sviva.gov.il/English/ResourcesandServices/NewsAndEvents/NewsAndMessageDover/Pages/2017/11-Nov/Israel-Removes-Barriers-to-Gas-Flow-from-Leviathan-Fi.aspx.

4 The savings derive from fuel price differences only and do not take into account capital investments of the construction of power stations and conversion to natural gas. *Review of Developments in the Natural Gas Economy 2017* [Hebrew], Ministry of Energy and Natural Gas Authority, State of Israel, April 26, 2018, p. 11, www.gov.il/BlobFolder/guide/natural_gas_basics/he/ng_2017.pdf (accessed on August 2, 2018).

5 *CO$_2$ Emissions* (metric tonnes per capita), IEA Atlas of Energy, International Energy Agency, Paris, France, 2018.

6 *Greenhouse gas Emissions by Source, Nitrogen Oxides (Nox), All Sources*, Central Bureau of Statistics, Jerusalem, Israel, September 6, 2018.

7 See *Energy Economy Objectives for the Year 2030: Executive Summary*, Ministry of Energy, State of Israel, October 2018, pp. 1–18, www.gov.il/BlobFolder/news/plan_2030/en/energy_economy_objectives_2030.pdf (accessed on November 8, 2018); See also Dror Halavy, "Steinitz: Israel to Eliminate Coal Use Completely by 2030," *Hamodia*, October 25, 2018, https://hamodia.com/2018/10/25/steinitz-israel-eliminate-coal-use-completely-2030/ (accessed on November 8, 2018).

8 Erratic supply during 2011 and eventual cessation of gas flow in April 2012 reduced the supply flexibility to the economy. Electricity generation from natural gas fell more than half, from 21,995 million KWh (GWh) in 2010 to 10,566 million KWh (GWh) in 2012. Utilisation of gas in the industrial sector also remained sluggish during 2011–12 but picked up significantly as supply stabilised with production from Tamar in 2013, accompanied by some LNG imports. Industrial utilisation shot to 46,163 terajoule (TJ) in 2013 and then to 58,762 TJ in 2015 from 5,489 TJ in 2011. *Israel: IEA Gas Information 2018 & IEA Electricity Information 2018*, International Energy Agency (IEA) statistics, IEA, Paris, France.

9 *The Adiri Committee Report*, Ministry of Energy, State of Israel, July 2018, p. 4, www.gov.il/BlobFolder/rfp/ng_160718/he/Israel_Natural_Gas_report_draft.pdf (accessed on August 2, 2018).

10 "Assessment and Recommendations," *OECD Economy Surveys: Israel*, Organisation for Economic Co-operation and Development (OECD), Paris, France, March 2018, p. 21, https://read.oecd-ilibrary.org/economics/oecd-economic-surveys-israel-2018/assessment-and-recommendations_eco_surveys-isr-2018-3-en#page2 (accessed on August 2, 2018).

11 Yaniv Bar, *The Natural Gas Sector in Israel: An Economic Survey*, Bank Leumi, Tel Aviv, Israel, August 2018, p. 2, https://english.leumi.co.il/static-files/10/LeumiEnglish/Israel_Capital_Markets/Natural_Gas_in_Israel_August_2018_global.pdf?reffer=deposit_check_hp_banner (accessed on August 5, 2018).

12 The first phase of development (Phase IA) of the project is expected to cost around $3.75 billion. *East Med E&P: Our Assets*, Delek Group, Netanya, Israel, 2017, www. delek-group.com (accessed on October 7, 2017).

13 Phase 2 would include the possibility of integrating drilling to deeper prospective oil targets located at a depth of more than 7,000 metres below sea level, which could contain approximately 560 million barrels of oil with a geological probability of about 15 percent. *East Med E&P: Our Assets*, Delek Group; *Leviathan: A Regional Energy Anchor*, Delek Drilling, Herzeliya Pituah, Israel, undated, www.delekdrilling.co.il/ (accessed on October 7, 2017).

14 However, it is notable that within the plan there is a clause that permits a lower magnitude of development of the reservoir (only in the initial stage – 12 bcm) in the event an export agreement will not be signed in the end with Egypt or with Turkey.

15 FPSO is a floating vessel used by offshore industry for the processing and storage of oil and gas. It is designed to receive oil and gas produced from nearby platforms, process it and store it until oil or gas can be offloaded or transported.

16 "Israeli Court Dismisses Petition Against Karish-Tanin Development," *Offshoreenergytoday.com*, May 3, 2018, www.offshoreenergytoday.com/israeli-court-dismisses-petition-against-karish-tanin-development/ (accessed on August 5, 2018).

17 "Delek to Sell 9.25 Percent Stake in Tamar and Dalit Fields Offshore Israel," *Offshoretechnology.com*, July 7, 2017, www.offshore-technology.com/news/newsdelek-to-sell-925-stake-in-tamar-and-dalit-fields-offshore-israel-5864571 (accessed on October 7, 2017).

18 *Tamar Petroleum: Investors Presentation*, Tamar Petroleum, Herzeliya Pituach February 2018, https://ir.tamarpetroleum.co.il/wp-content/uploads/2018/02/Tamar-P-Investors-Presentation-Feb-2018-Eng.pdf (accessed on August 7, 2018).

19 The Leviathan developers have entered into finance agreements to recoup external financing: Out of the total cost, $1.5 billion would accrue to Noble Energy (incorporating the approximately 600 million it spent in 2016), $1.75 billion to the Delek Group, and $600 million to Ratio Oil Exploration. Delek Group has secured financing commitment from the HSBC Bank Plc. and J.P. Morgan Ltd. for its share in the first phase of the Leviathan project. Noble will fund Phase 1A of Leviathan through Tamar operating cash flows as well as the Eastern Mediterranean portfolio, and the company would secure access to a financing facility for additional funding flexibility. This includes the sale of 7.5 percent of the Tamar field, as required by the gas framework agreement, which will reduce Noble Energy's stake in Tamar to 25 percent from 32.5 percent. In addition, Noble is expected to sell off part of its share of Leviathan. It has already sold 35 percent of its stakes in the Cypriot Aphrodite field to BG, as well as its entire holdings in the smaller Tanin and Karish fields. Ratio Oil has signed an agreement for a $400 million loan from HSBC and BNP Paribas. In addition, Ratio issued a series of bonds to raise $160 million, to serve as its own equity for the project. It now has $250 million, including money raised recently from the sale of options. "Leviathan FID Reached," *The Oil and Gas Year*, February 23, 2017, www.theoilandgasyear. com/news/leviathan-fid-reached/ (accessed on October 10, 2017); Yacoov Benmeleh, "Delek Taps JPMorgan, HSBC for $1.75 Billion Leviathan Funds," *Bloomberg*, November 27, 2016, www.bloomberg.com/news/articles/2016-11-27/delek-taps-jpmorgan-hsbc-for-1-75-billion-to-finance-leviathan (accessed on October 10, 2017); *Signing of an Agreement for the Financing of the Delek Group Partnerships' Share in the Costs of Development of the Leviathan Project*, Press Release, Delek Group, February 21, 2017, https://ir.delek-group.com/news-releases/news-release-details/signing-agreement-financing-delek-group-partnerships-share-costs (accessed on October 10, 2017); *Noble Energy Sanctions Leviathan Project Offshore Israel*, Noble Energy, Press Release, February 23, 2017, http://investors.nblenergy.com/releasedetail.cfm?releaseid=1014140 (accessed on October 10, 2017); Eran Azran, "The Biggest-ever Infrastructure Project in Israel Gets Under Way," *Haaretz*, February 27, 2017, www.haaretz.com/

israel-news/1.774036 (accessed on October 10, 2017); "Israel's Ratio Secures $400 mln to Fund Leviathan Natgas Project," *Reuters*, March 21, 2017, www.reuters.com/article/ratio-oil-expl-funding-leviathan/israels-ratio-secures-400-mln-to-fund-leviathan-natgas-project-idUSL5N1GY38C (accessed on October 10, 2017).

20 See *Encouraging Small and Medium-sized Reservoirs and Declaring an Emergency in the Natural Gas Industry* [Hebrew], Government Decision No. 2592, April 2, 2017, pp. 1–18, www.gov.il/BlobFolder/pmopolicy/2017_dec2592/he/sitecollectiondocuments_mazkir_dec2592.pdf (accessed on October 17, 2017); *The Minister of Energy Submits the Plan for Promoting Marginal Fields for Government Approval*, Press Release, Ministry of Energy, State of Israel, March 13, 2017, www.gov.il/en/departments/news/promoting_marginal_fields (accessed on October 17, 2017).

21 *Review of Developments in the Natural Gas Economy 2017*, April 26, 2018, p. 1.

22 *Encouraging Small and Medium-sized Reservoirs*, April 2, 2017, p. 5.

23 Tamar is the only producing reservoir now and its current transmission system is a single pipeline to the shore that cannot provide all of the existing demand in the market.

24 *Review of Developments in the Natural Gas Economy 2017*, April 26, 2018, p. 6.

25 Ibid., p. 7.

26 *Revised Reserves Evaluation Report and Discounted Cash Flows for the Tamar Lease,* Regulatory Filing, Delek Drilling, July 2, 2017, https://ir.delek-group.com/news-releases/news-release-details/revised-reserves-evaluation-report-and-discounted-cash-flows (accessed on October 20, 2017).

27 In December 2015, the Ministry had directed the IEC to reduce its use of coal at the coal-fired power plants in Hadera and Ashkelon by 15 percent. Since then, 2015 has become baseline for reduction in coal consumption (electricity generation). As for the goal of 2018, Energy Minister Steinitz decided in early January, in conjunction with Environmental Protection Minister Zeev Elkin, that the IEC would reduce the use of coal to produce electricity by 30 percent, compared to 2015 – the base year. The declared goal in 2017 was a 20 percent reduction compared to the base year. The 30 percent drop will be a further reduction in coal use relative to 2017. As part of this decision, one of four coal-fired units in the Orot Rabin power plant in Hadera will be shuttered. The decision will lead to a significant reduction in air pollution from coal-fired power plants and is expected to increase market demand for natural gas. *Ministers Elkin and Steinitz: Electric Company Must Reduce Use of Coal by 30% Compared to 2015*, Ministry of Environmental Protection, State of Israel, January 3, 2018, www.sviva.gov.il/English/ResourcesandServices/NewsAndEvents/NewsAndMessageDover/Pages/2018/01-Jan/Ministers-Elkin-and-Steinitz-Electric-Company-Must-Reduce-Use-of-Coal-by-30-Compared-to-2015.aspx (accessed on August 8, 2018); Hedy Cohen, "The Cut in Coal Use Will Reduce Pollution But Increase Electricity Prices in 2016," *Globes*, December 29, 2015, www.globes.co.il/en/article-iec-to-reduce-coal-use-from-friday-1001091820 (accessed on October 20, 2017).

28 *Electricity Generation by Type of Energy and Producer,* Central Bureau of Statistics, State of Israel, 2018; *Review of Developments in the Natural Gas Economy 2017*, April 26, 2018, p. 9.

29 The supply of natural gas for the production of electricity includes the supply of gas to the IEC, private electricity producers, and industrial plants that generate electricity.

30 *Electricity Generation and Electricity Supply*, Central Bureau of Statistics, State of Israel, August 26, 2018.

31 Yaniv Bar, *The Natural Gas Sector in Israel: An Economic Survey*, Bank Leumi, Tel Aviv, Israel, January 2017, pp. 9–10, https://english.leumi.co.il/static-files/10/Leumi English/Leumi_Review/NaturalGasinIsraelacc.pdf (accessed on October 21, 2017).

32 Gallo Lior, *A Long-Term Forecast of Electricity Demand in Israel* [Hebrew], Bank of Israel, December 31, 2017, pp. 3, 7, www.boi.org.il/he/Research/DocLib/dp201713h.pdf (accessed on October 21, 2017).

33 Gallo Lior in an email conversation, June 11, 2018. Lior is an Economist at the Macroeconomic and Policy Division of the Bank of Israel.

34 Chen Herzog, Norden Shalabna, and Guy Maor, *Israel Natural Gas Demand Forecast 2017–2040*, BDO Consulting Group, Tel Aviv-Yafo, Israel, July 2, 2017, pp. 17–18, www.delek-group.com/wp-content/uploads/2017/09/BDO-Gas-Market-Forecast-2-07-2017-for-Delek-Group-with-final-letter-1.pdf (accessed on October 23, 2017).

35 MOE's low growth in electricity demand scenario is 2.07 percent. *The natural gas sector in Israel* [Hebrew], Ministry of Energy, State of Israel, http://archive.energy.gov.il/Subjects/NG/Pages/GxmsMniNGEconomy.aspx (accessed on October 23, 2017).

36 *The Electricity Sector in Israel* [Hebrew], Ministry of Energy, State of Israel, undated, http://archive.energy.gov.il/Subjects/Electricity/Pages/GxmsMniElectricityProduction.aspx (accessed on October 26, 2017).

37 Minister Elkin, *Decision to Shut Down Coal-Fired Units Is Bold and Historic*, Ministry of Environmental Protection, State of Israel, August 24, 2016, www.sviva.gov.il/English/ResourcesandServices/NewsAndEvents/NewsAndMessageDover/Pages/2016/08-August/Minister-Elkin-Decision-to-Shut-Down-Coal-Fired-Units-is-Bold-and-Historic.aspx (accessed on October 26, 2017).

38 *The Government Approved the Minister of Energy, Dr. Yuval Steinitz's Proposal: Shutting Down the Coal Power Station in Hadera in 4 Years*, Press Release, Ministry of Energy, State of Israel, July 29, 2018, www.gov.il/en/Departments/news/electricity_290718 (accessed on August 9, 2018).

39 *The Natural Gas Authority of the Ministry of Energy Has Granted Approval for the Flow of Natural Gas to Two Solar Thermal Power Stations Currently Being Constructed in Ashalim* [Hebrew] Ministry of Energy, State of Israel, December 26, 2016, www.gov.il/he/Departments/news/solar_power_ashalim (accessed on October 27, 2017).

40 *Review of Developments in the Natural Gas Economy 2017*, April 26, 2018, p. 9.

41 Self-generation is "production of electricity for own use with a captive power plant installed usually on one's own premises." It may be owned by the consumer, or by a third-party under a power-supply contract. "Self-generation," *Business Dictionary*, WebFinance Inc., Austin, Texas, United States, 2018, www.businessdictionary.com/definition/self-generation.html. Antonio2207, ust

42 The cogeneration power plant typically has a high level of energy utilisation due to usage of the technology, which supplies electricity and steam in a single production process. By capturing the residual heat, which is typically rejected to the environment, cogeneration facilities accomplish the goal of energy efficiency and energy savings, reduced dependency on imported fuel, peak power demand levelling, as well as contribute to lowering pollution.

43 *The Electricity Sector Regulations (Cogeneration), 2004* [Hebrew], Planning Administration, State of Israel, December 3, 2004, www.gov.il/he/Departments/legalInfo/infrastructure_8 (accessed on October 27, 2017); www.nevo.co.il/law_html/Law01/999_373.htm (accessed on October 27, 2017).; Jeremy Ben-Shalom, *National Report for CSD-14/15 Thematic Areas*, Ministry of Environmental Protection, October 29, 2006, pp. 23–24, www.sviva.gov.il/InfoServices/ReservoirInfo/DocLib2/Publications/P0401-P0500/P0401.pdf (accessed on October 27, 2017).

44 See *Israel: 2018 Article IV Consultation*, IMF Country Report No. 18/111, May 2018, p. 41, www.mof.gov.il/ChiefEcon/InternationalConnections/DocLib3/Article_IV_2018.pdf (accessed on August 9, 2018).; Shoshanna Solomon, "Knesset Approves 'Historic' Reform of Electricity Sector," *The Times of Israel*, July 19, 2018, www.timesofisrael.com/knesset-votes-in-historic-reform-of-electricity-sector/ (accessed on August 9, 2018); Barnea, Jaffa, Lande & Co., "Reform in the Electricity Sector and in the Israel Electric Corporation," *Lexology*, June 13, 2018, www.lexology.com/library/detail.aspx?g=fb6381f1-27e9-44de-b3e0-0c5b83dcc0e7 (accessed on August 9, 2018); *The Reform in the Israeli Electricity Sector*, Meitar Law Firm, Ramat Gan, Israel, June 2018, p. 3, http://meitar.com/files/Publications/2018/electricity_reform-_english_version.pdf (accessed on August 9, 2018).

45 *Infrastructure for Energy Independence*, Israel Natural Gas Lines (IGNL), Tel Aviv, Israel, 2013, www.ingl.co.il/?page_id=105&lang=en (accessed on October 30, 2017).

46 The Jerusalem region distribution license is the last of the six regions for which natural gas distribution licenses have been signed. Due to the difficulty in deploying the pipeline network, due to Jerusalem's high population density, the ministry has awarded the company a subsidy of NIS 60 million out of the estimated NIS 320–350 million in total cost. Hedy Cohen, Jerusalem natural gas distribution license signed, *Globes*, February 23, 2016, www.globes.co.il/en/article-jerusalem-gas-distribution-license-signed-1001105702 (accessed on October 30, 2017).; For information on network, see *The Distribution Network*, Ministry of Energy, State of Israel; Also see, Gina Cohen, "Natural Gas Distribution Tender"; "Natural Gas Distribution Network (Israel)," *Hebrew-English Energy Dictionary*, October 22, 2009, www.hebrewenergy.com/natural-gas-distribution-tender-natural-gas-distribution-network-israel/ (accessed on October 30, 2017).

47 In November 2009, Supergas and Shapir Engineering (owners of SuperNG Natural Gas Distribution Company) won a tender to distribute natural gas in the Central Region – the area between Gedera and Hadera, including Tel Aviv and Gush Dan, for a period of 25 years.

48 Sonia Gorodeisky and Michal Raz-Chaimovich, "Ben Gurion Airport Signs Gas Production Electricity Deal," *Globes*, November 15, 2018, https://en.globes.co.il/en/article-ben-gurion-airport-signs-gas-production-electricity-deal-1001260838 (accessed on November 15, 2018).

49 Delek Israel Fuel Corporation Ltd., a subsidiary of Delek Group, signed a NIS 50 million contract with food company Strauss Group Ltd. in January 2014 to supply four mcm of CNG a year to Strauss company's dairy at the Bar Lev Industrial Zone in the Galilee (Northern District) and the confectionary plant in Nazareth. Amiram Barakat, "Delek Will Supply Compressed Natural Gas to Strauss Dairy and Confectionary Plant in the Galilee," *Globes*, January 9, 2014, https://en.globes.co.il/en/article-1000908240 (accessed on November 2, 2017).

50 Ora Cohen, "Israeli Natural Gas Program Fails to Meet Quota," *Haaretz*, May 31, 2018, www.haaretz.com/whdcMobileSite/israel-news/business/israeli-natural-gas-program-fails-to-meet-quota-1.6135063 (accessed on November 2, 2017).

51 *Review of Developments in the Natural Gas Economy 2017*, April 26, 2018, pp. 1, 10.

52 *INGL Finished The Construction Of Eshel HaNasi PRMS For The Distribution Network*, Israel Natural Gas Lines, 2013, www.ingl.co.il/hello-world/?lang=en (accessed on November 3, 2017).

53 Hedy Cohen, "Bureaucracy Blocks the Gas," *Globes*, January 27, 2015, www.globes.co.il/en/article-the-bureaucratic-gas-blockage-1001004598 (accessed on November 3, 2017).

54 Some of the major reforms simplifying procedures were: (a) Validation from inspecting bodies and not from the Commissioner of Safety at the Gas Authority; (b) Shortening statutory planning procedures for deployment of the distribution network; and (c) Establishment of an Infrastructure Coordination Committee in order to facilitate coordination among the various companies. The authority of the committee is to rule on the disputes of the holder of a distribution license and public infrastructure companies (railways, public authorities), local authorities, or water corporations. In respect of a dispute relating to the scope of the payment or the date of payment, the Committee may order that the final decision be given that the execution of the work will not be delayed. The decision of the Committee is a judgement or an interim order of a Magistrate's Court. See *Review of Developments in the Natural Gas Economy 2016* [Hebrew], Ministry of Energy and Natural Gas Authority, State of Israel, pp. 1–2, http://archive.energy.gov.il/ (accessed on November 6, 2017).

55 *Review of Developments in the Natural Gas Economy 2017*, April 26, 2018, p. 10.

56 *Call No. 75/2018 -Acceleration of the Deployment of the Distribution Network* [Hebrew], *Ministry of Energy*, State of Israel, May 28, 2018, www.gov.il/he/Departments/publications/Call_for_bids/tender75_18 (accessed on August 12, 2018).

57 *Review of Developments in the Natural Gas Economy 2017*, April 26, 2018, p. 2.

58 *The Transmission Network*, Israel Natural Gas Lines, 2017, www.ingl.co.il/?page_id=1521&lang=en;%20www.ingl.co.il/?p=2534&lang=en (accessed on November 8, 2017).

59 Derived from Yaniv Bar, *Natural Gas Sector in Israel*, January 2017, pp. 11–12.

60 As of 2016 Israel had a negative trade balance of $16.8 billion in net imports, compared to their trade balance in 1995 when Israel still had a negative trade balance of $7.3 billion in net imports. *The Observatory of Economic Complexity*, MIT Media Lab, 2016.

61 Herzog, Shalabna, and Maor, *Israel Natural Gas Demand Forecast 2017–2040*, BDO Consulting Group, July 2, 2017, p. 79.

62 In 2016, chemical products, mineral products, and plastics and rubbers constituted $16.12 billion out of the total export of $55.85billion. *The Observatory of Economic Complexity*, 2016.

63 *The Economic Complexity Observatory*, 2011.

64 See Jasem M. Al-Besharah, "The Petrochemical Industry and Natural Gas: A Strategic Alliance," in P.N. Prasad et al. (eds.), *Science and Technology of Polymers and Advanced Materials* (New York: Plenum Press, 1998), p. 781.

65 Saudi Arabia and Iran, both leading petrochemical producing countries in the Middle East, established the basis for a large and competitive global petrochemical industrial sector by first establishing the plan for the continuous and low-priced supply of feedstock. See "Jubail Industrial City: Top Choice of Investors," *Arab News*, November 24, 2014, www.arabnews.com/saudi-arabia/news/664951 (accessed on November 10, 2017); "Iran Decreases Feedstock Gas Price for Petrochemical Plants," *Azer News*, January 16, 2016, www.azernews.az/region/91723.html (accessed on November 10, 2017).

66 For instance, Algeria, Egypt, and Iraq have a thriving petrochemical industry in which national companies play a leading role. The main value added petrochemical products of Algeria's Sonatrach are methanol and fertiliser. Similarly, Egypt's national petrochemical company, the EPC (Egyptian Petrochemical Company) manufactures polyvinyl chloride resin, propylene, and polypropylene. Further, Iraq's State Company for Petrochemical Industries (SCPI) is involved in the manufacture of polyethylene and sodium hypochlorite products. *Algeria Petrochemicals Report*, BMI Research, April 1, 2018; *Egyptian Petrochemical Company*, Alexandria, Egypt, undated; *State Company For Petrochemical* Industries, Basra, Iraq, undated.

67 Saon Ray, Amrita Goldar, and Swati Saluja, *Feedstock for the Petrochemical Industry*, Indian Council for Research on International Economic Relations (ICRIER), Working Paper 271, February 2014, p. 5, www.econstor.eu/bitstream/10419/176289/1/icrier-wp-271.pdf (accessed on November 11, 2017).

68 When dehydrated, methanol can be turned into Dimethyl Ether (DME), which can be used as a diesel substitute in heavy-duty trucks and ships.

69 See Yacov Sheinin and Chen Herzog, *Natural Gas Forecast Demand*, Economic Models Ltd., Ramat Gan, Israel January 26, 2014, p. 89, https://vdocuments.us/chen-herzog-natural-gas-delek.html (accessed on November 16, 2017).

70 *2016 GCC Fertilizer Industry Indicators*, Gulf Petrochemical and Chemicals Association (GPCA), Dubai, United Arab Emirates, p. 7, http://gpcafertilizers.com/wp-content/uploads/2017/10/2016-GCC-Fertilizer-Indicators.pdf (accessed on November 16, 2017).

71 "Ammonia," *Chemical Economics Handbook*, IHS Markit, London, UK, July 2017, https://ihsmarkit.com/products/ammonia-chemical-economics-handbook.html (accessed on November 16, 2017).

72 *Annual Energy Outlook 2011: With Projections to 2035*, EIA, US Department of Energy, Washington, DC, April 2011, p. 70, www.eia.gov/outlooks/aeo/pdf/0383(2011).pdf (accessed on November 18, 2017).

73 "Ammonia," *Chemical Economics Handbook*, July 2017.

74 Ray, Goldar, and Saluja, *Feedstock for the Petrochemical Industry*, February 2014, p. 5.

75 Ibid.
76 The ammonia manufacturing plant in the ICL Fertilizers (Deshanim) was closed several years ago because it became unprofitable to operate on naphtha feedstock.
77 *Next Stage Begins in Process to Remove Ammonia Tank From Haifa Bay*, Ministry of Environmental Protection, State of Israel, June 23, 2015, www.sviva.gov.il/English/ResourcesandServices/NewsAndEvents/NewsAndMessageDover/Pages/2015/06-June/Next-Stage-Begins-in-Process-to-Remove-Ammonia-Tank-from-Haifa-Bay.aspx (accessed on November 19, 2017).
78 Sheinin and Herzog, *Natural Gas Forecast Demand*, January 26, 2014, p. 93.
79 Ehud Keinan, "An Executive Summary of the Professors' Report," *The Israel Chemist and Engineer (ICE)*, Issue 3 (June 2017), p. 43, https://ice.digitaler.co.il/ice3/files/assets/common/downloads/publication.pdf (accessed on November 22, 2017).
80 Yoram Gabison, "Haifa's Ammonia Tank Ruling Will Be Felt Far Beyond Israel's Borders," *Haaretz*, March 8, 2017, www.haaretz.com/israel-news/business/ammonia-tank-ruling-will-be-felt-beyond-israels-borders-1.5446022 (accessed on November 22, 2017).
81 Sheinin and Herzog, *Natural Gas Forecast Demand*, January 26, 2014, p. 94.
82 Keinan, "An Executive Summary of the Professors' Report," June 2017, p. 43.
83 In 2013, the government took a decision (Govt. Decision No. 766) to shut down the ammonia storage tank in Haifa Bay by 2017 and set up a new production plant in the Negev instead, a long-standing demand of the residents and environmentalists in the region that would better serve the local market and make the country less reliant on the import of the hazardous chemical into the country. The project would be the first petrochemical plant that could be powered by domestic gas and would also see the ammonia storage tank in Haifa removed amid long-held fears that it poses a safety risk to tens of thousands of local residents and is a potential target for terrorists. The winning firm will be able to lease the plot for 49 years, and the state is willing to offer a construction grant of up to US $60 million for setting it up. In addition, the plant contactor would be granted a compensation of US $120 million as a guarantee against forced closure of the factory. In addition, the company will be able to produce related products such as urea, methanol, and melamine. *Government Hasn't Received Proposals to Build Ammonia Plant*, Ministry of Environmental Protection, State of Israel, November 14, 2016, www.sviva.gov.il/English/ResourcesandServices/NewsAndEvents/NewsAndMessageDover/Pages/2016/11-November/Government-Hasnt-Received-Proposals-to-Build-Ammonia-Plant.aspx (accessed on November 22, 2017); *Final Proposals Being Submitted in Haifa Bay Ammonia Tank Tender*, MOEP, State of Israel, June 23, 2016, www.sviva.gov.il/English/ResourcesandServices/NewsAndEvents/NewsAndMessageDover/Pages/2016/06-June/Final-Proposals-Being-Submitted-in-Haifa-Bay-Ammonia-Tank-Tender.aspx (accessed on November 22, 2017); Sharon Udasin, "ILA, Environment Ministry Publish Tender for New Ammonia Plant in Rotem," *Jerusalem Post*, January 28, 2014, www.jpost.com/Enviro-Tech/ILA-Environment-Ministry-publish-tender-for-new-ammonia-plant-in-Rotem-339650 (accessed on November 22, 2017).
84 Chana Roberts, "Haifa Mayor: Ammonia Tanks Endanger 600,000 Lives," *Arutz Sheva*, January 2, 2017, www.israelnationalnews.com/News/News.aspx/224240 (accessed on November 23, 2017).
85 *The Methanol Industry*, Methanol Institute, Alexandria, Virginia, United States, 2018, www.methanol.org/the-methanol-industry/ (accessed on August 13, 2018).
86 "IHS Markit: Methanol Demand Growth Driven by Methanol-to-olefins, China Demand," *Hydrocarbon Processing*, June 13, 2017, www.hydrocarbonprocessing.com/news/2017/06/ihs-markit-methanol-demand-growth-driven-by-methanol-to-olefins-china-demand (accessed on November 26, 2017); Marc Alvarado, "The Changing Face of the Global Methanol Industry," *IHS Chemical Bulletin* (Methanol Institute), Issue 3 (2016), pp. 1–2, www.methanol.org/wp-content/uploads/2016/07/IHS-ChemicalBulletin-Issue3-Alvarado-Jun16.pdf (accessed on November 26, 2017).

87 "Global Methanol Demand Growth Driven by Methanol to Olefins as Chinese Thirst for Chemical Supply Grows, IHS Markit Says," *IHS Markit*, June 12, 2017, http://news.ihsmarkit.com/press-release/country-industry-forecasting-media/global-methanol-demand-growth-driven-methanol-olefi (accessed on November 26, 2017); *The Methanol Industry*, Methanol Institute; *About Methanol*, Methanex Corporation, Vancouver, Canada, 2015, www.methanex.com/about-methanol/how-methanol-used (accessed on November 26, 2017).

88 "China Methanol Apparent Consumption Grows 5% on yr in Jan-Nov," *Sxcoal*, December 12, 2017, www.sxcoal.com/news/4566401/info/en (accessed on August 13, 2018).

89 Candace Dunn, *China's Use of Methanol in Liquid Fuels Has Grown Rapidly Since 2000*, February 23, 2017, EIA, US Department of Energy, Washington DC, www.eia.gov/todayinenergy/detail.php?id=30072 (accessed on November 27, 2017).

90 Einat Yarhi and Sigal Issaschar, *Carmel Olefins Ltd.*, Midroog (A subsidiary of Moody's), Tel Aviv, Israel, December 2008, p. 11, www.bazan.co.il/investors/Content/Images/CreditRatingCaol_27Jan09_En.pdf (accessed on November 27, 2017).

91 Gil Michael Bufman, Eyal Raz, and Noach Hager, *The Potential of Natural Gas in the Israeli Economy*, The Finance & Economics Division, Bank Leumi, Israel, April 2014, p. 11, www.chamber.org.il/media/150344/the-potential-of-natural-gas-in-the-israeli-economy-april-2014.pdf (accessed on November 30, 2017).

92 Ibid.

93 Israel: Oil for 2015 & 2016, *IEA Oil Information 2018*, IEA statistics.

94 Anat Bonshtien, *Israel Fuel Choices Initiative*, Prime Minister's Office (PMO), undated, www.weizmann.ac.il/SAERI/sites/AERI/files/fuelchoicesppt_anatbonstein.pdf (accessed on November 30, 2017).

95 The MoE through a press release in August 2018 stated that it is planning to provide a subsidy of NIS 25 million to establish recharging stations for electric vehicles nationwide, intending to drive the emerging electric vehicle market forward in order to resolve its 'chicken and egg' problem. A sample survey conducted by the MoE found the Israeli public willing to buy an electric vehicle subject to the availability of recharging stations. The ministry will support the establishment of recharging stations in three kinds of spaces – public, semi-public, and workplaces. *Another Important Step Taken in the Israeli Electric Vehicle Market: The Ministry of Energy Is Investing NIS 25 Million to Establish Recharging Stations for Electric Vehicles Nationwide!* Press Release, Ministry of Energy, State of Israel, August 20, 2018, www.gov.il/en/Departments/news/electric_car_200818 (accessed on August 16, 2018).

96 For objectives and jurisdiction of fuel alternatives, see Shlomo Wald, *Research and Development 2012–2014*, The Chief Scientist Office, Ministry of Energy, State of Israel, September 2014, p. 10, http://archive.energy.gov.il/gxmsmnipublications/rd2012_2013.pdf (accessed on December 1, 2017).

97 Bonshtien, *Israel Fuel Choices Initiative*; Eyal Rosner, *Strategic Plan*, Fuel Choices Initiative, PMO, undated, www.gaz-mobilite.fr/docs/upload/doc_20150210110215.pdf (accessed on December 1, 2017).

98 It should be noted that methane in the CNG is a very strong greenhouse gas and its global warming potential is 21 times higher than that of carbon dioxide. Any leakage, both in the direct use of CNG operated vehicle and in the production and delivery of the fuel, represent greenhouse gas emissions into the atmosphere. The ability of CNG to reduce greenhouse gas emissions over the entire fuel lifecycle (production, manufacture, distribution, use, and emission) depends on the source of the natural gas (well or biomass) and the fuel it is replacing (diesel or gasoline). CNG produced from landfill biogas was found by the California Air Resources Board (CARB) to have the lowest greenhouse gas emissions of any fuel analysed, with a value of 11.26 gCO_2e/MJ (more than 88 percent lower than conventional gasoline), providing a great incentive to harness biogas. In general, care is taken to completely seal the CNG fuel system so as to eliminate evaporative emissions. "Can Natural Gas Help Lower

Pollution Levels?" *Economic Times*, 2016, https://economictimes.indiatimes.com/can-natural-gas-help-lower-pollution-levels/changetheair_show/54777201.cms (accessed on December 1, 2017); *Environmental Impacts of Natural Gas*, Union of Concerned Scientists (UCS), Cambridge, MA, United States, undated, www.ucsusa.org/clean-energy/coal-and-other-fossil-fuels/environmental-impacts-of-natural-gas#references (accessed on December 1, 2017); Avinash Kumar Agarwal, Prakhar Bothra, and Pravesh Chandra Shukla, *Particulate Characterization of CNG Fuelled Public Transport Vehicles at Traffic Junctions*, Aerosol and Air Quality Research (Taiwan Association for Aerosol Research), Volume 15 (2015), p. 2168, www.aaqr.org/files/article/526/39_AAQR-15-02-TN-0084_2168-2174.pdf (accessed on December 1, 2017); J. T. Houghton et al. (eds.), *Climate Change 1995: The Science of Climate Change. Contribution of Working Group I to the Second Assessment Report of the Intergovernmental Panel on Climate Change*, Volume 2 (Cambridge: Cambridge University Press, 1996), p. 22.

  99 *Israel's First Ever Natural Gas Powered Vehicle Is an Iveco Stralis*, Press Release, Fiat Chrysler Automobiles, FCA Group, June 15, 2015, www.fcagroup.com/en-US/media_center/fca_press_release/2015/june/Pages/Israel%E2%80%99s_first_ever_natural_gas_pow-ered_vehicle_is_an_Iveco_Stralis.aspx (accessed on December 2, 2017).

100 *Compressed Natural Gas (CNG) Market-Growth, Future Prospects And Competitive Analysis, 2016–2024*, Credence Research, Credence Research Limited, London and San Jose, January 2017, www.credenceresearch.com/press/global-compressed-natural-gas-cng-market (accessed on December 2, 2017).

101 *Compressed Natural Gas Market Analysis By Source, Applications and Segment Forecasts to 2020*, Grand View Research, San Francisco, CA, United States and Pune, MH, India, December 2014, www.grandviewresearch.com/industry-analysis/compressed-natural-gas-cng-market (accessed on December 4, 2017).

102 See Fang-Yu Liang, Marta Ryvak, Sara Sayeed, and Nick Zhao, "The Role of Natural Gas as a Primary Fuel in the Near Future, Including Comparisons of Acquisition, Transmission and Waste Handling Costs of as With Competitive Alternatives," *Chemistry Central Journal* (Springer Open), Volume 6, Supplement 1 (2016), www.ncbi.nlm.nih.gov/pmc/articles/PMC3332260/ (accessed on December 4, 2017).

103 Alan Krupnick, Zhongmin Wang, and Yushuang Wang, "Sector Effects of the Shale Gas Revolution in the United States," *Resources for the Future*, Discussion Paper 13–20, July 2013, p. 21, www.rff.org/files/sharepoint/WorkImages/Download/RFF-DP-13-21.pdf (accessed on December 4, 2017); *Natural Gas as a Transportation Fuel: Prospects and Challenges*, Environmental and Energy Study Institute (EESI), Washington, DC, March 16, 2011, www.eesi.org/briefings/view/natural-gas-as-a-transportation-fuel-prospects-and-challenges (accessed on December 4, 2017).

104 "Current Natural Gas Vehicle Statistics: Natural Gas Vehicles Worldwide," *NGV Global*, April 26, 2018, www.iangv.org/current-ngv-stats/ (accessed on August 16, 2018).

105 "Global Compressed Natural Gas (CNG) Vehicles Market to Grow at a CAGR of 4.9%, 2017–2021 With Ford, Volkswagen, GM, Honda & Nissan Dominating," *PR Newswire*, May 30, 2017, www.prnewswire.com/news-releases/research-and-markets-global-compressed-natural-gas-cng-vehicles-market-to-grow-at-a-cagr-of-49-2017-2021-with-ford-volkswagen-gm-honda-nissan-dominating-300465021.html (accessed on December 5, 2017).

106 *Full Report of the Tzemach Committee* [Hebrew], p. 53, http://archive.energy.gov.il/Subjects/NG/Documents/NGReportSep12.pdf (accessed on December 5, 2017).

107 Ibid., pp. 54–55.

108 Eyal Rosner, *The Israel Alternative Fuels Initiative Reducing World Dependence on Oil in Transportation*, PMO, State of Israel, undated, p. 13, www.pmo.gov.il/SiteCollection Documents/oil/FuelsPresentation.pdf (accessed on December 5, 2017).

109 This order falls under the 2015 Memorandum of Understanding (MoU) signed between Fiat Chrysler Automobiles (FCA), CNH Industrial, and Israel's Fuel Choices Initiative (FCI), which foresees a partnership between the companies and FCI in research, development, and implementation of transportation based on natural gas and natural

gas-based fuels. *An Iveco Stralis Is the First Ever Natural Gas Powered Vehicle in Israel*, Press Release, IVECO (Industrial Vehicles Corporation), CNH Industrial Group, Turin, Italy, undated, www.iveco.com/africa-mideast-en/events/pages/israels-first-ever-nat ural-gas-powered-vehicle-is-an-iveco-stralis.aspx (accessed on December 5, 2017).

110 Delek Energy, subsidiary of Delek Group, has an ongoing project from the ministry, the scope of which includes the construction and operation of a public Compressed Natural Gas (CNG) fuelling station. See Wald, *Research and Development 2012–2014*, September 2014, p. 35; Hedy Cohen, "US Instructing Israel on Gas-Powered Vehicles," *Globes*, September 9, 2015, www.globes.co.il/en/article-us-instructing-israel-on-gas-powered-public-transport-1001068073 (accessed on December 8, 2017).

111 Bracha Halaf, *Research and Development 2016–2018*, The Chief Scientist Office, Ministry of Energy, p. 13, www.gov.il/BlobFolder/guide/rd_chief_science/he/R_D_2018_ acc.pdf (accessed on August 16, 2018).

112 "Israel Steps Up CNG Implementation Program," *NGV Global News*, January 22, 2016, www.ngvglobal.com/blog/israel-steps-up-cng-implementation-program-0122 (accessed on December 11, 2017).

113 "Launching a Clean Car Revolution in Israel," *Israel Environment Bulletin* (Ministry of Environmental Protection, State of Israel), Volume 44 (March 2018) p. 8, www.sviva. gov.il/english/resourcesandservices/publications/bulletin/documents/bulletin-vol44-march2018.pdf (accessed on August 17, 2018).

114 Ora Cohen, "Delek Israel Planning to Install Compressed Natural Gas Pumps in 12 Filling Stations," *TheMarker*, July 11, 2018, www.haaretz.com/israel-news/busi ness/.premium-israel-s-together-to-sell-cosmetics-based-on-cannabis-dead-sea-minera-1.6265734 (accessed on August 17, 2018).

115 Peter Gross, *China's Use of Fuel Methanol and Implications on Future Energy Trends*, Washington Methanol Policy Forum, June 13, 2017, p. 3, www.methanol.org/wp-content/ uploads/2017/06/Peter-Gross-Global-Methanol-Fuel-Blending-Initiatives-Panel. pdf (accessed on December 11, 2017); *China: The Leader in Methanol Transportation*, Methanol Facts, Methanol Institute, July 2011, http://greenmethanol.dk/wp-content/ uploads/2013/12/Methanol-Institute-Methanol-in-China.pdf (accessed on December 11, 2017).

116 Hai Guo, "Volatile Organic Compounds (VOCs) Emitted from Petroleum and their Influence on Photochemical Smog Formation in the Atmosphere," *Journal of Petroleum & Environmental Biotechnology*, Volume 3, Issue 1 (2012), p. 1, www.omicsonline.org/vol atile-organic-compounds-vocs-emitted-from-petroleum-and-their-influence-on-pho tochemical-smog-formation-in-the-atmosphere-2157-7463.1000e104.php?aid=3828 (accessed on December 11, 2017).

117 *Methanol Fuel in the Environment*, Methanol Fuels, Methanol Institute, undated, http:// methanolfuels.org/about-methanol/environment/ (accessed on December 12, 2017).

118 Ethanol (CH3CH2OH), ethyl alcohol, or grain alcohol is produced from starch- and sugar-based feedstock, such as corn grain (as it primarily is in the United States), sugarcane (as it primarily is in Brazil), or from cellulosic feedstock (such as wood chips or crop residues). More than 97 percent of US gasoline contains ethanol, typically E10 (10 percent ethanol, 90 percent gasoline), to oxygenate the fuel and reduce air pollution. See *Ethanol Fuel Basics*, Alternative Fuel Data Centre, US Department of Energy, Washington, DC, United States, undated, www.afdc.energy.gov/fuels/ethanol_fuel_ basics.html (accessed on December 12, 2017).

119 Richard J. Pearson and James W.G. Turner, "The Role of Alternative and Renewable Liquid Fuels in Environmentally Sustainable Transport," in Richard Folkson (ed.), *Alternative Fuels and Advanced Vehicle Technologies for Improved Environmental Performance: Towards Zero Carbon Transportation* (Cambridge: Elsevier Woodhead Publishing, 2014), p. 28.

120 The RFS originated with the Energy Policy Act of 2005 (EP Act 05) that changed US energy policy by providing tax incentives and loan guarantees for energy production of various types, including renewable energy, nuclear energy, and biofuels.

While biofuels were included in the tax reductions and generating methanol from biomass thermo-chemically is a well-developed technology, there is little advocacy for that as a pathway towards replacing petroleum fuel with renewables. Instead, the federal government has promoted crop-based ethanol as the transition fuel towards advanced biofuel (i.e., cellulosic, biodiesel or sugarcane ethanol). Gail Mosey and Claire Kreycik, *State Clean Energy Practices: Renewable Fuel Standards*, National Renewable Energy Laboratory, U.S. Department of Energy, July 2008, pp. 2–3, www.nrel.gov/docs/fy08osti/43513.pdf (accessed on December 12, 2017); Leslie Bromberg and Wai K. Cheng, *Methanol as an Alternative Transportation Fuel in the US: Options for Sustainable and/or Energy-secure Transportation*, Sloan Automotive Laboratory, Massachusetts Institute of Technology (Cambridge MA), November 28, 2010, pp. 8–9, https://afdc.energy.gov/files/pdfs/mit_methanol_white_paper.pdf (accessed on December 12, 2017); *Overview for Renewable Fuel Standard*, United States Environmental Protection Agency, Washington, DC, June 7, 2017, www.epa.gov/renewable-fuel-standard-program/overview-renewable-fuel-standard#structure (accessed on December 12, 2017).

121 *Avenues for Collaboration: Recommendations for US-China Transportation Fuel Cooperation*, United States Energy Security Council, Potomac, Maryland, United States, 2015, p. 12, www.iags.org/USChinaFC.pdf (accessed on December 14, 2017).

122 George A. Olah, Alain Goeppert, and G.K. Surya Prakash, *Beyond Oil and Gas: The Methanol Economy* (Weinheim: Wiley-VCH Verlag GmbH & Co. KGaA, 2009), pp. 159, 219.

123 See Sheinin and Herzog, *Natural Gas Forecast Demand*, January 26, 2014, pp. 99–100.

124 *Dor Chemicals, Fiat Chrysler Automobiles (FCA) and IFCI Present Jointly the New Choice of Fuel, the M15: A Methanol Powered Vehicle FIAT 500 M15 Is Launched at the Fuel Choices 2016 Summit*, Press Release, Dor Chemicals, November 3, 2016, www.methanol.org/wp-content/uploads/2016/11/Dor-Press-Release.pdf (accessed on December 14, 2017).

125 *IEA Advanced Motor Fuel Annual Report: Israel*, International Energy Agency (IEA) Energy Technology Network, IEA, Paris, France, 2015, p. 7, http://iea-amf.org/app/webroot/files/file/Country%20Reports/Israel.pdf (accessed on December 14, 2017).

126 Ibid.

127 *Fiat Chrysler Automobiles Presents the First Methanol-powered Euro 6 Vehicle*, Fiat Chrysler Automobiles NV, London, United Kingdom, November 2, 2016, www.fcagroup.com/en-US/sustainability/fca_news/Pages/FCA_Methanol.aspx (accessed on December 17, 2017).

128 *IEA Advanced Motor Fuel Annual Report: Israel*, 2015, p. 7.

129 Virgilio Cerutti, *The Methanol Project*, Fuel Choices Summit, Fuel Choice Initiative, Jerusalem, Israel, November 3, 2016, p. 8, www.fuelchoicessummit.com/Portals/37/Virgillio%20Cerutti.pdf (accessed on December 17, 2017).

130 "FCA Presents Fiat 500 M15 (methanol); to Be Sold in Israel," *Green Car Congress*, November 3, 2016, www.greencarcongress.com/2016/11/20161103-fcam15.html (accessed on December 17, 2017).

131 *Dor Chemicals, Fiat Chrysler Automobiles and IFCI*, Dor Chemicals, Press Release, November 3, 2016.

132 "Israel's Dor to Double Methanol Imports to Meet Transport Demand Surge," *Platts*, November 13, 2013, www.platts.com/latest-news/petrochemicals/jerusalem/israels-dor-to-double-methanol-imports-to-meet-27628729 (accessed on December 17, 2017).

133 With capacities ranging from 2,700 barrels per day (bbl/d) to 140,000 bbl/d, Shell operates two in Malaysia and one in Qatar, Sasol operates one in South Africa, and the fifth is a joint venture between Sasol and Chevron in Qatar. *Gas-to-Liquids Plants Face Challenges in the U.S. Market*, EIA, February 19, 2014, www.eia.gov/todayinenergy/detail.php?id=15071 (accessed on December 18, 2017).

134 *Gas-To-Liquid (GTL) Technology Assessment in Support of Annual Energy Outlook 2013*, Biofu-
     els and Emerging Technologies Team, Energy Information Administration, Washington,
     DC, United States, January 7, 2013, p. 9, www.eia.gov/outlooks/documentation/work
     shops/pdf/AEO2013_GTL_Assessment.pdf (accessed on December 21, 2017).
135 *An Invitation to Submit Standpoints, Information, and Express Interest Regarding the Possibil-
     ity of Building and Operating a GTL (Natural Gas to Liquid Fuels) Facility in Israel*, Ministry
     of Energy, State of Israel, June 2014, http://archive.energy.gov.il/english/publicinfo/
     tenders/documents/tender24_14.pdf (accessed on December 21, 2017).
136 Mayer Fitoussi, *GTL vs LNG: Economics, Challenges and Value Proposition*, http://
     archive.energy.gov.il/Subjects/NG/Documents/%D7%94%D7%AA%D7%99%D7%9
     9%D7%97%D7%A1%D7%95%D7%AA/GTL_gas_to_liquid.pdf (accessed on Decem-
     ber 21, 2017).
137 *Public Tender No. 55/2016 on Providing Assistance in Prefeasibility Study for Constructing
     and Operating a GTL (Gas to Liquid) Plant in Israel*, Ministry of Energy, State of Israel,
     2016, http://archive.energy.gov.il/informationforpublic/tenders/documents/2016/
     tender55_16english.pdf (accessed on December 22, 2017).
138 *GTL*, KTE Co. Technologies and Enterprises, Haifa, Israel, 2014, http://kte.co.il/
     energy/gtl/ (accessed on December 22, 2017).
139 Ibid.
140 Sonia Gorodiesky, "Givot Olam Oil Exploration License Deadline Extended," *Globes*,
     April 11, 2018, www.globes.co.il/en/article-givot-olam-oil-exploration-license-dead
     line-extended-1001231439 (accessed on August 17, 2018).; Sharon Udasin, "SPNI
     Files High Court Petition Against Meged Oil Drilling in Central Israel," *Jerusalem
     Post*, March 10, 2015, www.jpost.com/Israel-News/SPNI-files-High-Court-petition-
     against-Meged-oil-drilling-in-central-Israel-393503 (accessed on December 22, 2017).
141 "CNG Fuel Implementation Guidance Provided to Israel," *NGV Global News*, Sep-
     tember 17, 2015, www.ngvglobal.com/blog/israel-steps-up-cng-implementation-
     program-0122 (accessed on December 25, 2017).
142 Thorvaldur Gylfason, *The Dutch Disease: Lessons From Norway* (written for the Trini-
     dad Tobago Chamber of Commerce and Industry), December 1, 2006, p. 2, https://
     notendur.hi.is/gylfason/Trinidad2006.pdf (accessed on December 25, 2017).
143 Gil Michael Bufman, *Establishing a Sovereign Wealth Fund for Israel as Part of a Mecha-
     nism for Dealing With the Forces Supporting Appreciation of the Shekel, Finance & Economics
     Division*, Department of Economics, Bank Leumi, Israel, December 10, 2013, p. 2,
     https://english.leumi.co.il/static-files/10/LeumiEnglish/December102013Israeland-
     DutchDisease.pdf?reffer=9293 (accessed on December 25, 2017).
144 "Sovereign Wealth Fund – SWF," *Investopedia*, New York City, United States, www.
     investopedia.com/terms/s/sovereign_wealth_fund.asp (accessed on December 26, 2017).
145 Samuel E. Wills, Lemma W. Senbet, and Witness Simbanegavi, "Sovereign Wealth
     Funds and Natural Resource Management in Africa," *Journal of African Economies*, Vol-
     ume 25, AERC Supplement 2 (2016), p. ii6. (accessed on December 26, 2017).
146 *Sovereign Wealth Fund Ranking*, Sovereign Wealth Fund Institute, Seattle, Washington,
     United States, 2018, www.swfinstitute.org/sovereign-wealth-fund-rankings/ (accessed
     on August 17, 2018).
147 Ibid.
148 *Management of State Revenues From Natural Gas Resources*, Ministry of Foreign Affairs,
     State of Israel, February 19, 2012, http://mfa.gov.il/MFA/PressRoom/2012/Pages/
     Management_state_revenues_natural_gas_resources_19-Feb-2012.aspx (accessed on
     December 26, 2017).
149 *Israel Citizens' Fund Law 2014* [Hebrew], Ministry of Finance, State of Israel, http://
     fs.knesset.gov.il/19/law/19_lsr_303823.PDF (accessed on December 26, 2017); Angela
     Cummine, *Citizens' Wealth: Why (and How) Sovereign Funds Should be Managed by the
     People for the People* (New Haven and London: Yale university Press, 2016), p. 205.

150 "Sheshinski Committee Sets Out Mineral Exploration Rights," *The Economist Intelligence Unit*, October 23, 2014, http://country.eiu.com/article.aspx?articleid=1832414767 (accessed on December 27, 2017).

151 Meir Arlosoroff, "Why Hasn't Israel's Windfall-profit Tax Blown in Yet?" *Haaretz*, August 30, 2017, www.haaretz.com/israel-news/business/why-hasnt-israels-windfall-profit-tax-blown-in-yet-1.5446722 (accessed on December 27, 2017); Amiram Barakat, "Sovereign Wealth Fund to Begin Operating in 2017," *Globes*, November 11, 2015, www.globes.co.il/en/article-sovereign-wealth-fund-to-begin-operating-in-2017-1001080258 (accessed on December 27, 2017).

152 "Israel's SWF: New Kid on the Block 2020 or Stillborn?" *Arab Sovereign Wealth Fund Monitor* (The Netherlands), Volume 2, Issue 3 (March 19, 2017), p. 9, https://verocy.com/wp-content/uploads/Documents/Newsletters/ASWFM/PDFs/ASWM_3-2017.pdf (accessed on December 29, 2017).

153 Sharon Udasin, "Socioeconomic Cabinet approves Sheshinski 2 Committee Recommendations," *Jerusalem Post*, November 10, 2014, www.jpost.com/Business/Socioeconomic-cabinet-approves-Sheshinski-2-Committee-recommendations-381352 (accessed on December 29, 2017).

154 Barakat, "Sovereign Wealth Fund to Begin Operating in 2017," November 11, 2015.

155 Amiram Barakat, "Sovereign Wealth Fund Won't Operate Before 2020," *Globes*, February 15, 2017, https://en.globes.co.il/en/article-sovereign-wealth-fund-wont-operate-before-2020-1001177034 (accessed on December 29, 2017).

156 *East Med E&P: Our Assets*, Delek Group, 2017.

157 "Israel Chemicals Q2 Revenue, Profit Drop," *Reuters*, August 3, 2017, www.reuters.com/article/icl-results/israel-chemicals-q2-revenue-profit-drop-idusl5n1kp1vh (accessed on December 31, 2017).

158 Abdullah Al-Hassan, Michael Papaioannou, Martin Skancke, and Cheng Chih Sung, *Sovereign Wealth Funds: Aspects of Governance Structures and Investment Management*, International Monetary Fund, WP/13/231, November 2013, p. 10, www.imf.org/en/Publications/WP/Issues/2016/12/31/Sovereign-Wealth-Funds-Aspects-of-Governance-Structures-and-Investment-Management-41046 (accessed on December 31, 2017).

159 *BP Statistical Review of World Energy*, June 2018.

160 IEA Statistics, 2018.

161 The fees for connecting is NIS 600,000 shekels for using the infrastructure to transmit the gas is $1–2/mmbtu and the additional operational fines/fees is $0.5–1.5/mmbtu, depending on the swing/consuming profile of the consuming industry. Cohen and Korner, *Israeli Oil & Gas Sector, Economic and Geopolitical Aspects*, April 2016, p. 27, www.neaman.org.il/Files/6-459.pdf (accessed on December 31, 2017).

162 Israel plans a second offshore bid round in late 2018 or early 2019, which will involve about 25 southern blocks, a highly prospective area that has experienced less exploration than elsewhere offshore. "Israel Seeking Interest for Second Offshore Bid Round," *Oil and Gas Journal*, June 13, 2018, www.ogj.com/articles/2018/06/israel-seeking-interest-for-second-offshore-bid-round.html (accessed on August 18, 2018).

163 *Review of Developments in the Natural Gas Market During 2016*, 2016, p. 9.

164 Yaniv Bar, *The Natural Gas Sector in Israel: An Economic Survey*, January 2017, p. 15.

165 Yaniv Bar, *The Natural Gas Sector in Israel: An Economic Survey*, August 2018, p. 8.

166 *The Observatory of Economic Complexity* (OEC), The MIT Media Lab.

167 ibid.

168 Some of the prominent companies in these areas of manufacturing are Oil Refineries Ltd. (Carmel Olefins, and Gadiv Petrochemicals Industries are part of ORL), Israel Chemicals Ltd. (ICL), Keter Plastic, and Haifa Chemicals.

169 Ali Al-Karaghouli and Lawrence Kazmerski, "Renewable Energy Opportunities in Water Desalination," in Michael Schorr (ed.), Desalination, Trends and Technologies (Rijeka, Croatia: InTech, 2011), p. 150.

170 *Fact Sheet: Seawater Desalination in Israel*, Research Office, Legislative Council Secretariat, Hong Kong, July 4, 2017, www.legco.gov.hk/research-publications/english/1617fsc19-seawater-desalination-in-israel-201704-e.pdf (accessed on January 2, 2018).

171 See Benjamin Walsh, *Israel's New Desalination Plants Offset More Than Just Drought*, Future Directions International, Nedlands, Australia, May 2, 2018, www.futuredirec tions.org.au/publication/israels-new-desalination-plants-offset-just-drought/ (accessed on August 18, 2018).

4

STRATEGIC IMPLICATIONS FOR THE MEDITERRANEAN REGION

The changing political-economic scenario and Israeli gas exports

Natural gas is the future. It is here.

−*Bill Richardson*[1]

The question everyone is asking is, can Israel leverage its natural gas reserves to improve political relations in the region? Gas discoveries have been a turning point in Israel's energy status, creating greater energy independence for the state in an isolating region and from far flung foreign suppliers. Besides an assurance of supply for at least 30 years, Israel has acquired the potential to export natural gas, a radical change from being an importer only a few years ago. For Israeli policymakers, the nation's gas resource can become an effective instrument of foreign policy that can foster cooperation between the Jewish state and its regional adversaries. But in a fractious environment of the Middle East, can economics outflank politics? Will realpolitik underpinned by gas requirement and security lead Israel's regional enemies to ignore issues that have bedevilled their relations for decades?

Prime Minister Benjamin Netanyahu believes gas export from Leviathan can bring Israel closer to her Arab neighbours and help integrate firmly with the region. It "will promote cooperation with countries in the region [and] the ability to export gas [would make Israel] more immune to international pressure. We don't want to be vulnerable to boycotts."[2] The idea of 'economic peace,' repeatedly expressed by Israeli officials, relies on the premise that by fulfilling the demand for energy among its hostile neighbours, a transformed regional relationship based on mutual interest and underpinned by long-term gas contract is possible. According to Ron Adams, "Gas is a diplomatic–strategic resource tied to Israel's foreign policy objectives."[3] It offers "an opportunity to rethink regional relations and how Israel as a gas producer and exporter sketches a modus vivendi with its proximate neighbours."[4]

However, many doubt the proposition that Israel's gas resources will have a positive impact on relations with the Arab world in any fundamental way as long as the Palestinian issue festers without a resolution. Two related questions are pertinent here: Are Israel's neighbours, not in the best of relations with the Jewish state, interested in its gas resources and normalising relations? If not, then, given its geopolitical location, where does Israel look to export gas? With domestic regulations in place, Israel is planning to export gas to the region as well as trans-regionally, in two possible ways. First, direct export through pipelines to Jordan, Egypt, and Turkey, as well as through a lengthy pipeline across the Mediterranean, that passes through Cyprus and touches Europe in Greece. Second, Israel is vying to use Egypt's two liquefaction plants on the Mediterranean coast to sell LNG to far off consumers in Europe and Asia.

Israel's gas developers have signed at least four gas export deals with Jordanian and Egyptian companies. Pipeline export to Turkey, an eminently doable project both technically and economically, has been thwarted in recent years by Israel's deteriorating political relations with Ankara and continued Turkey–Cyprus conflict. These factors have led Israel to consider an alternative route to sell gas to Europe through a long-distance maritime pipeline. While hectic diplomacy between Israel, Cyrus, Greece, and Italy has swirled around the idea of a trans-Mediterranean pipeline, difficulties with regard the amount of gas that would flow through the pipeline and funding of the project in the face global decline in gas prices, persist. At present, Egypt is the most important pillar of Israel's gas export strategy. The North African country is not only geographically close, which facilitates easy transmission of gas, but is also linked to Israel through a pipeline.

For Israel, the Jordanian market has always been the first destination for its gas exports, spurred by considerations of security and stability, and share as they do a long and sometimes contentious border. It is not surprising that Israel has signed its first gas deal with Jordan. Israel has also picked up the threads from its earlier gas trade with Egypt and signed an export deal, involving use of pipeline already in place between the two countries. Moreover, Egypt's two liquefaction terminals located on the country's northern coast are of great interest to Israel, where gas from Tamar and Leviathan could be liquefied for export to Europe.

Turkey, a voracious gas consumer, much as it has space for additional gas from Israel among its various imports from Russia, Central Asia, and Iran, could also become the trans-shipment hub for onward transport of Israeli gas to Europe. A possible route could be through the the southern gas corridor (SGC) that aims to bring gas resources from the Caspian, Central Asian, Middle Eastern, and East Mediterranean gas into European markets.[5] "Another advantage of a pipeline from Israeli gas field to Turkey is its long-term use as carriage for reverse flow of gas from Central Asia and Russia when Israel runs short of indigenous supply," says Cenk Pala, an official from TurkStream pipeline project.[6]

Besides Israel, there have been several other gas discoveries in the Eastern Mediterranean since 2000 (Figure 4.1). These offshore discoveries have the potential to significantly alter energy supply dynamics in the region, historically deficient in indigenous sources of energy as compared to its Arabian counterpart. With the exception of Syria, energy deficiency and supply insecurity are not only real for Israel, Lebanon, and Cyprus, but also for Jordan and, for some time, Egypt. The issue of export of Israeli gas has brought into reckoning the possibility of linking gas resources and infrastructure of Israel, Cyprus, and Egypt through bilateral and multilateral trade agreements. The idea of a gas regime in the Eastern Mediterranean brings into focus issues of the location and configuration of export infrastructure as well as difficulties posed by regional political and territorial disputes to the utilisation of the resources.

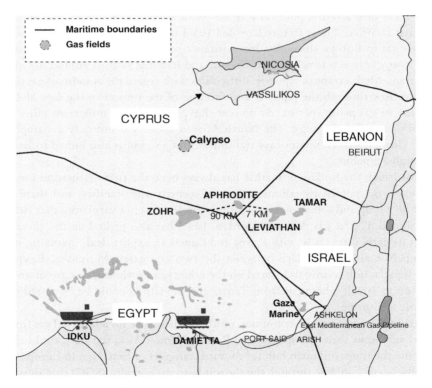

FIGURE 4.1 Geographical location of major gas fields in the Eastern Mediterranean

Source: Author's figure; referenced from Middle East Economic Survey, 2016

Disclaimer: Map not to scale

Israeli gas exports to Jordan

A successful example of gas trade in the Mediterranean region involving Israel is between Israeli gas producers and Jordanian companies: Two agreements of gas export from Israel to Jordan were signed in 2015 and 2016. Jordan and Israel have had diplomatic relations, often turbulent, since 1994, but that did not stand in the way of forging of bilateral energy trade. In the conflict-ridden reality of the Middle East, energy trade may not bring about peace but can support ties that already exist.

What appear to have clinched the Jordanian–Israeli deals are Jordan's need for energy and its easy availability from Israel. "Dependence here is the key," says Eyal Winter, from the Hebrew University of Jerusalem, who specialises in political economy and the Middle East.[7] Jordan, partially reliant on gas import from Egypt to satisfy domestic demand, started experiencing gas shortages starting in 2011. As Egypt faced disruptions in gas production and a declining surplus due to the disturbances caused by the Arab Spring, it faltered on export commitments to Jordan and Israel. The Hashemite Kingdom had to switch to using heavy fuels, widening trade deficit due to a higher than ever energy import bill.[8]

Jordan's energy crisis has been exacerbated by the influx of Syrian refugees, adding to the severity of energy demand, not the least the cost to the national exchequer that in October 2017 was reportedly $10 billion.[9] To alleviate the crisis, King Abdullah II authorised import of gas from Israel, despite significant opposition in the Jordanian parliament – 70 percent of the population is Palestinian, and they are hostile to Israel.

Israeli-Jordanian strategic relations

It is not surprising that Israel's first gas deal should be with Jordan. Israel and Transjordan (after 1949, the Hashemite Kingdom of Jordan) have shared a history of close ties dating back to the early 20th century and early years of the creation of the State of Israel.[10] Although Jordan's King Abdullah I bin Al-Hussein (great-grandfather of the present king) fought alongside other Arab countries in the first Arab–Israeli War in 1948, he negotiated with Israel to convert the Armistice Agreement of 1949 into a peace treaty, whereby he could legitimise the annexation of the West Bank to Jordan. Abdullah I was assassinated for negotiating with the enemy Jewish state, which had just defeated the Arabs and established itself by force.

In 1967, King Abdullah's grandson and immediate successor, King Hussein, ignored Israeli implorations and forewarnings not to join the coalition arrayed against Israel to fight alongside Egypt and Syria in the June War of 1967. By the end of the war, Hussein had suffered the consequences of losing control of the West Bank to Israel, a crucial piece of territory for the Jordanian economy. After the war, however, a pragmatist Hussein conferred with Israel through secret backchannels on matters of mutual interest in context of the changed circumstances. Yet, the imperative of staying within the Arab consensus on anti-Israeli stances, primarily because a large portion of Jordan's population was Palestinian, introduced a measure of complexity and, sometimes, hostility in the Israeli-Jordanian relationship.[11]

In 1970, as Jordanian government prepared to expel the PLO from their country in what came to be known as Black September, Israel quietly mobilised the IDF along the border and dispatched fighter jets to prevent Syrian leader Hafiz al-Assad from intervening on behalf of the Palestinians.[12] In return, in September 1973, King Hussein warned Prime Minister Golda Meir of war on the Egyptian–Israeli and Syrian–Israeli fronts[13] and stayed out of the Yom Kippur War that began on 6 October 1973, thus restricting the fighting to two fronts.[14]

While a formal state of war existed for more than four decades from 1948 until the peace treaty between the two countries in 1994, Israel and Jordan maintained a "functional relationship," predicated first and foremost on the opposition to the establishment of a separate Palestinian state.[15] Palestinian nationalism, on one hand "threatened the very existence of the Jewish state and Israel's control over West Bank and Gaza and Jordanian state on the other. After all the majority of Jordanian populations consists of Palestinian refugees from 1948 and 1967."[16]

Other mutual interest included peace and quiet along their 500-km long border from infiltration by Palestinian guerillas and influx of Palestinian refugees into Jordan. Finally, certain issues such as water sharing and security of navigation in the Gulf of Aqaba kept the two states tied to each other notwithstanding the formal state of war.[17] However, despite cooperation on these issues, Jordan strongly opposed Israeli policies in the West Bank and demanded a full Israeli withdrawal. King Hussein was opposed to the Jordanian option promoted by Israeli Prime Minister Shimon Peres that "proposed the creation of three political entities: Israeli, Jordanian and a Palestinian entity that would be administered by Israel and Jordan jointly."[18]

Jordan's geographic location ensured that the Hashemite Kingdom acted as a buffer between Israel and enemy Arab states, especially Iraq, which was more hostile to Israel than others. Jordan was no less a balancer in the hostility emanating from Egypt and Syria in the 1950s and 1960s. In short, "Jordan relations with Israel were generally characterized by tacit strategic cooperation against Palestinian nationalism and the hegemonic impulses emanating from Cairo, Damascus and Baghdad."[19] When Israel and the Jordan signed a peace treaty in 1994 in the wake of Oslo Accords, it underscored the "understanding that had been a feature of Israeli–Jordanian relations for years."[20] The two countries have since then expanded on economic and security cooperation. Jordan is the only country after Egypt to sign a peace treaty with Israel.

The relationship with Hashemite Kingdom of Jordan is of great strategic significance in Israeli foreign policy. Israel longest border, extending from Yarmouk River in the north to Eilat in the south, continues to be a stable frontier, largely peaceful for 25 years since the peace treaty. If it weren't for the Jordanian efforts at keeping the border quiet, Israel would have had to deploy a large number of its forces all along their common border. Security issues of the first few decades after 1948 that spurred the 'special relationship' have acquired renewed salience today. Jordan is seen as a buffer to radical Islamism emanating from Iraq and Syria. While neither country has troops or military presence in the other, Israel and Jordan are coordinating security measures to prevent radical groups in Syria from entering the Jordanian territory.[21]

The two neighbours "maintain tacit and effective security cooperation, and Jordan can reasonably assume that it can count on an Israel safety net in the event of a major crisis emanating from the Islamic State or from Syria."[22] Even as the civil war in Syria draws to a close, and power equations change in the region, indicating the likely Iranian presence on Israel's border, Jordan remains a reliable partner, keeping constancy in its ties with Israel. "Relations with Jordan is the kind of ideal relationship that Israel would like to establish with all its neighbours," observes Haviv Gur of the *Times of Israel*.[23] The Western capitals firmly support the closeness of the two Middle Eastern countries, ensuring Jordan gets continued US military aid, because a stable Jordan ensures a secure Israel.[24] Israel has a stake in the preservation of the status quo in Amman, most importantly, the continued stability of the Hashemite monarchy with which it has a functioning peace treaty.

Since the beginning of the Arab Spring uprisings, the Hashemite regime headed by King Abdullah II is imperilled by its own challenges. It continues to struggle over political reform and economic development. It faces internal challenges from a growing and restive population among which the political and economic goals of the Arab Spring uprisings resonate, including "rising public anger resulting from economic austerity, insufficient political reform, and perceived government tolerance of corruption,"[25] as they do throughout the Arab world.

The Hashemite regime witnessed a series of protests that began in July 2011 from traditional quarters, including the Kingdom's leftist and pan-Arab nationalist political parties, in addition to the Muslim Brotherhood's Action Front, as well as the country's local Boycott, Divestment and Sanctions (BDS) groups.[26] But the protests have also drawn their strength ominously from the Jordanians in the 'East Bank' that have historically been the backbone of the Hashemite monarchy.[27] Though the unrest never reached the magnitude of the uprisings in countries such as Yemen, Egypt, and Libya, the risk of domestic instability is greater today, as Jordan faces a host of economic and social problems due to the refugee problem created by the eight-year civil war in Syria.

The internal protests may have subsided in 2013, but the stream of refugees from Syria has presented a new set of problem to the Jordanian state. Accommodating 1.4 million Syrian refugees has put a major burden on Jordan's weak economy and weight on energy import, thus depleting the exchequer of crucial foreign exchange and significantly contributing to the country's $3.2 billion deficit 2015.[28] Worse has been the increasingly radicalisation of the Jordanian population due to the civil war next door. Some refugees, influenced by the ideology of the so-called Islamic State or Salafi Islam, have had a 'domino effect' on the Jordanian population, evident in a series of reports on terrorist-related incidents, arrests, trials, and internments of Islamist militants, both locals and Syrian nationals, in the Jordanian press throughout 2015–2016.[29]

While toward the end of 2015, Amman tried to establish a 'safe zone' on the Syrian side of the frontier, providing humanitarian and security assistance, an expanded Russian and Iranian campaign caused migration to continue toward the Jordanian border. Israel and Jordan are quietly cooperating in policing the Syrian–Jordanian border.[30]

The Hashemite regime also faces resistance from the conservative nationalists who have flagged the fear of Jordan emerging as 'the alternative nation' (*al-Watan al-Badeel*) for its open policy toward international refugees. Such talks have featured time and again in international discussions on the future resettlement of Syrian refugees or the resolution of the Palestinian question.[31] Though Jordan's uncertain position on Palestinian statehood continues, King Abdullah II, under domestic pressure to reconsider the peace agreement with Israel in the wake of the Arab Spring, has been more vocal in insisting that Israel restart negotiations with the Palestinians and sign a peace agreement.

As much as it would like to shore up the regime, Israel has limited ability to do so in the face of hostility on the Arab street. Be as it may, Israel relations with Jordan have not lost any of the complexity of what has been called, "a remarkable cooperation within the context of an enduring rivalry,"[32] within the larger context of the Arab-Israeli conflict.

Israel–Jordan gas deals

Israel–Jordanian relations, characterised pithily as an "adversarial partnership," is reflected in their gas trading deals. None of the political problems have vanished but Israel and Jordan have still executed GSPAs, underpinned by Jordan's energy and strategic vulnerabilities. A series of deft diplomatic maneuvers on the part of US – particularly the Department of State's Bureau of Energy Resources[33] – nudged its most important allies in the region to stabilise their relationship by giving it a solid economic foundation.

Noble energy, the operator of the Leviathan field, executed a GSPA in September 2016 to supply natural gas from the Leviathan field to Jordan's NEPCO, Israel's first gas customer from that Mediterranean reservoir. The deal will enable Jordan to import 300 million cubic feet of gas per day (8.5 mcm per day or 3.1 bcm per year), which represents 40 percent of the Kingdom's power generation needs.[34] Under the agreement, Leviathan partners will supply a gross quantity of 45 bcm of natural gas over a 15-year period at a cost of $10 billion, under the industry-standard take-or-pay (ToP) contract. NEPCO also has an option to purchase an incremental 0.5 bcm/year for a total of up to 3.6 bcm/year, which the Leviathan partners are not obliged to supply. Leviathan developers expect to accomplish the first delivery in early 2020.[35]

As required by the Expropriations Law Number 12 (1987),[36] Jordan's Ministry of Energy and Mineral Resources published an announcement in newspapers in January 2018, notifying the public of its intention to request Council of Ministers to authorise expropriation of land for the construction of a pipeline that will transmit gas received at the border from Israel (Article 4 of the Expropriations Law).[37] *Jordan Times*[38] in March 2018 reported that the government has completed land acquisition for the pipeline in the northern provinces of Irbid and Mafraq.

The 65-km pipeline, which would be complete by December 2019, will run from Jordan's border with Israel in the north to Mafraq province through Irbid. It will connect to an existing pipeline in Mafraq that will then distribute gas to the Kingdom's power plants for electricity production. The Israeli–Jordanian pipeline could also open up the possibility of a 'northern connection' (at Al Rihab in Mafraq) with the Arab gas pipeline passing through Jordan. The Israeli section of the pipeline will transmit gas from Israel's Eastern Mediterranean shore to the border with Jordan is also under construction (Figure 4.2).[39]

Another Israeli–Jordanian gas contract is between the Tamar partnership and Jordanian state-owned fertiliser plants, Arab Potash Company (APC) and its affiliate and Jordan Bromine for use at their facilities near the Dead Sea. In February 2014, the two Jordanian companies signed a $500 million contract with Tamar developers to obtain 1.8 bcm of gas from Tamar for 15 years.[40] In January 2017, Israel began exporting natural gas to the two Jordanian plants through a newly-built pipeline, which partly uses the Israeli national pipeline network.

Gas from the Ashkelon receiving station flows through the national pipeline network to the Sodom area by the Dead Sea, from where it connects to an underground 15.5-kilometre pipeline running along Highway 90 (Dead Sea Road or Arava Road), to a receiving station on the Israeli-Jordanian border.[41] In view of the political sensitivities in Jordan about doing business with Israel, according to *Haaretz*,[42] the supply is channelled through the American NBL Eastern Mediterranean Marketing and not directly by the Tamar partners themselves. The functioning of the pipeline has been deliberately kept low profile.

Israeli–Jordanian gas agreements have weathered significant political opposition from across the Jordanian society in recent years. Thousands of Jordanians taking part in the demonstrations against the deals have accused the Hashemite Kingdom of making an "ethical compromise" in importing gas from Israel, the proceeds from which would go into financing the occupation of the Palestinian territories.[43] The Jordanian government was put on the defensive, particularly over the NEPCO deal, because the company's gas import for nation-wide power supply would render the country dependent on the Jewish state for a critical requirement. The opposition raised the question of the compromise of Jordanian sovereignty and asked as to why other options, such as import of gas from Saudi Arabia and Algeria, were not pursued by the government.

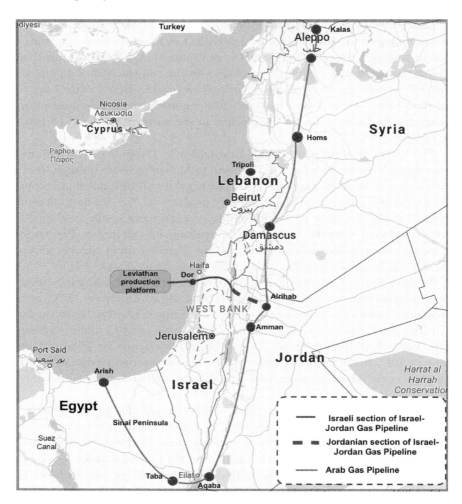

FIGURE 4.2 Pipelines to Jordan

Source: Author

Disclaimer: Map not to scale

The Jordanian energy ministry defended NEPCO's contract with Israeli developers, portraying it as a transaction concluded by private stakeholders of the electric company in which it did not have a controlling share. The government also drew attention to the economic and strategic benefits of the transaction: Jordan would save around $600 million a year (on power-generation costs) and the deal would enhance the country's energy security by diversifying sources of supply. In effect, the Jordanian government presented the deal as an exercise of prudence in public expenditure and national security.[44]

NEPCO validated the government's line, stating that the deal was a part of the strategy to diversify energy resources in light of disruption in gas supply from Egypt and in the absence of better options: Gas import from both Algeria and Saudi Arabia would prove to be very costly because of the difficulties in transportation. The company also suggested the deal with Israel would become a stepping stone to enhanced regional cooperation in the Mediterranean by means of infrastructural development. A statement issued by NEPCO[45] at the time said the agreement, "enhances opportunities for regional cooperation and will make Jordan part of the EU and the Union for the Mediterranean project to utilize the gas fields discovered in the East Mediterranean." Furthermore, NEPCO stated, the deal will allow Jordan to utilise the gas fields discovered in Palestine, Cyprus, and Egypt.

In the end, Jordan is not a democracy and government can disregard public opinion without the fear of periodic accountability, as "democratisation is weak in the absence of political parties and group opposition politics is not serious enough to effect policies." "The only real opposition are the Islamists of the Muslim Brotherhood who have been increasingly co-opted by the regime," said an official who did not want to be named.[46] The Jordanian monarch stuck to the agreement and went on to allocate 1.5 million dinars (around $2.1 million) in the 2018 national budget[47] for the gas pipeline, even after the parliamentarians tried to stop it with a negative vote.[48]

In view of the Kingdom's overwhelming energy imports (97 percent of its supplies), the deal would assure of continuous energy supply at reasonable price[49] – the two critical components of energy security for any country. Jordan would be able to obtain natural gas from a stable source with pricing linked to Brent oil and a firm floor price. Together with the existing LNG import from Qatar at Aqaba, the Kingdom would be able to fortify itself against any future supply disruption.[50]

From the Israeli standpoint, export agreement with NEPCO[51] is a crucial step towards raising finances for the development of the Leviathan field. Moreover, the State of Israel would get a share in the profits accruing to the developers, and thus augmenting the public revenue. Leviathan's development is vital for Israel's own gas supply, currently sourced wholly from the Tamar field.

A report by the German Marshall Fund of US about the Jordanian gas supply option observes that in transactional terms, Jordan is an obvious market for Israeli gas, given the short distances between the two nations; the Israeli pipeline network can be easily linked with that of Jordan. NEPCO is known to be a reliable customer that pays its bills on time. Besides, "In the future, gas supplies from Israel could be supplemented by gas from the Gaza Marine field if political circumstances permit this resource to be developed."[52]

Despite the commercial logic of gas trade with Israel, the groundswell of Jordanian anger over business with Israel, begs the question whether more than two decades of peace between the two countries – long portrayed by Western countries as a perfect model for Arab-Israeli coexistence – has brought the people of the two countries any closer? While "the country's authoritarian monarchy has mostly been able to absorb the rancor of a broadly anti-Israel public (Jordan is home to a major anti-normalisation movement), [but] it is sensitive to the population's strongly held convictions."[53] However, by signing a long-term agreement on a strategic resource such as gas, amidst ongoing unrest in the Palestinian territories as well as in Jordan itself, the Hashemite regime of Jordan affirmed its willingness to continue cooperating with Israel.[54] Although export contract with NEPCO offered Leviathan developers with an export outlet, "the amount that would be exported to Jordan is not enough to anchor the development of the second phase of the field: What is needed is a mega customer for that field to develop to full capacity."[55]

Israel's gas exports to Egypt

Another option for profitable use of Israeli gas is export to Egypt. Although endowed with vast deposits of natural gas, the North African country currently suffers from gas shortages. In 2003, after the discovery of sizeable reserves and the establishment of pipelines and LNG facilities, Egypt began exporting gas to Jordan, Israel, and Syria and harboured ambitious plans for export to Lebanon and Turkey. This phase of increased gas export also coincided with an increased thirst for gas locally.[56] The Egyptian energy market also expanded to consume a significant amount of gas domestically. Between 2000 and 2012, overall energy consumption in Egypt rose by 5.6 percent, but demand for gas grew by 8.7 percent. By 2012, gas was providing more than 50 percent of the total energy needs of the country compared to 35 percent in 2000.[57]

With the use of gas spread across power generation, industry, residential, and commercial purposes, energy industry own use (upstream operations and LNG facilities), and non-energy use (gas used as feedstock in petrochemicals),[58] it was inevitable that in the long run demand would outstrip supply. A soaring demand for energy, coupled with the lack of investment in the country's upstream sector following the political upheaval of 2011, and an untenable regulatory environment of subsidies led to severe natural gas supply shortages. Egypt lost its exporter status in 2015 and started importing LNG from Algeria and Russia.[59]

Israel needs Egypt as a market to export gas and gateway to markets in Europe. On one hand, Israel is focussing on the sale of gas to the Egyptian market and, on the other, it is keen on using Egypt's liquefaction facilities as export terminals.[60] In their March 2018 deal with an Egyptian entity for export of gas, Israeli field developers have bought majority shares in the EMG pipeline to transport gas from the Israeli fields to Egyptian shores, once the engineering for reverse flow is completed. Noble Energy and Delek Group are looking at finalising long-term deals to supply gas directly from Israel's largest fields to two liquefaction plants in Egypt:[61] If the Idku complex of the Egyptian Liquefied Natural Gas Company

(ELNG), comprising two liquefaction terminals, and the Spanish Egyptian Gas Company (SEGAS) LNG complex in Damietta that has one terminal,[62] are connected to Tamar and Leviathan through underwater pipelines (Figure 4.3),[63] it can pave the way for the flow of Israel's gas to European markets.

Israel–Egypt strategic relations

Israel and Egypt share a history of gas trade predicated on the peace treaty of March 1979 that established the Jewish state's first diplomatic relations with an Arab state. It was Egypt under the military regime of President Anwar Al-Sadat, which forged the peace treaty with Israel in the aftermath of the 1973 Arab–Israeli War and continues to steadfastly safeguard it against domestic and regional oppositions. Peace between the two countries continues to serve their national strategic interests. Israeli and Egyptian militaries have cooperated on a number of security related matters, including intelligence sharing. In fact, both countries have greatly benefitted from reduced security expenditures, resulting from diminution of inter-state tension and security preparedness against each other.

Unlike Jordan, Egypt has been less consistent in its relations with Israel over the period of four decades. Despite signing a peace agreement that ended military hostilities, political events in the Middle East prevent Egypt and Israel from establishing a warm relationship associated with mutual recognition. This has to some degree delayed the progress in energy cooperation. Egypt has resisted vigorous Israel's overtures for new bilateral activities, arguing that the atmosphere between the two countries must be improved first with the resolution of the Palestinian-Israeli conflict. The Egyptian–Israeli relationship continued to be bedevilled by regional and bilateral issues throughout the 1980s and 1990s. Much like ties with Jordan, two factors were salient: First, Israel's array of actions toward the Arab world in the broad regional landscape and, second, continuing differences between Israel and Egypt over the issue of self-determination of the Palestinians.

On the regional front, the Israeli bombing of Osiraq nuclear reactor in June 1982, invasion of Lebanon, annexation of Golan Heights, and the resistance of the Arab state towards accepting Israel without the resolution of outstanding Arab–Israeli issues, cast a long shadow over Egyptian–Israeli relations. As for the Palestinian issue, failure of the Palestinian autonomy talks (an integral part of the Camp David Accords), Israel's violent reaction to the first Intifada, expansion of settlements in the West Bank, and the annexation of East Jerusalem issues prevented Egypt from deepening ties with Israel in the 1980s. As Jacob Abadi writes, "issues relating to its [Egypt's] role as leader of the Arab world have weighed more heavily on its Israel policy than actual hostility towards the Jewish state."[64]

In view of Israel's actions and policies towards the other Arab states, many Egyptians had serious doubts about Israel's aims and stated desire for a

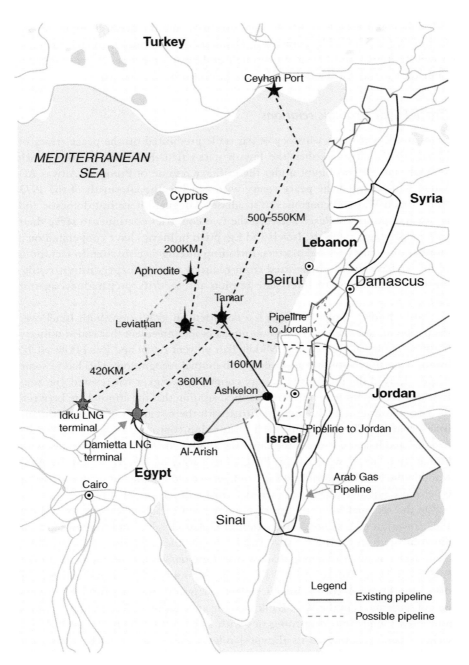

FIGURE 4.3 Possible routes for export of gas from Israel's fields to Egypt

Source: Author's figure; referenced from Delek Drilling, 2017

Disclaimer: Map not to scale

comprehensive peace in the Middle Eastern region. Israel's military exploits reinforced the belief among Egypt's populace that their national interests were intertwined with those of their Arab brethren. The trail of destruction left behind in Sinai and the refusal to vacate Taba[65] introduced more resentment in bilateral relations. However, Israel and Egypt continued to uphold the peace treaty without much cooperation "in all fields – economic, social, cultural,"[66] as Menachem Begin had yearned for.

Hosni Mubarak, who assumed power in 1981 upon Sadat's assassination, kept Israel at arm's-length, given the masses' sensitivity towards the sufferings of the Palestinians "The Palestinian issue remained unresolved, and therefore significant sections of the rival Egyptian society remained hostile and did not wish to move to the next phase of completely transforming the nature of Egyptian-Israeli relations."[67] The Egyptian-Israeli peace agreement my have eased the level of conflict and reduced the likelihood of inter-state war, but "relations did not move beyond the governmental diplomatic channels . . . in other words, peace is between governments, not respective societies."[68] Consequently what exists between Israel and Egypt now is 'cold peace.'

In contrast, Mubarak moved rapidly to enhance diplomatic relations with Arab countries and declared that his country's return to Arab fold was only natural. As a result of feverish behind the scenes diplomacy, Egypt's membership in the Organisation of Islamic Countries (OIC) was restored in 1984, five years after it had been rescinded and, in late 1987, the League of Arab States allowed Arab countries to restore relations with Egypt, although in reality they had never been entirely terminated.[69] Mubarak became actively involved in the Madrid Conference, encouraging the Palestinians to adopt a pragmatic approach and facilitating bilateral talks between Israel and the Arab parties.[70] At Madrid, Egypt was the only Arab country that had diplomatic relations with Israel, although formal Egyptian representation was only in the multilateral track of the negotiations.

As with Jordan, Egyptian–Israeli relations improved when Israel and the Palestinians represented by PLO, signed the Oslo Accord on 13 September 1993. Mubarak continued to act as a mediator in the Arab–Israeli negotiations, moderating disputes and preventing the escalations of the conflict between Israel and the Palestinians so that the peace process launched with the agreement in Oslo, remained on track. It is for this primary reason (besides Mubarak's anti-Muslim stance and his domestic political tussle with Hamas' predecessor, the Muslim Brotherhood) that the president of Egypt supported Al-Fatah against its political and military rival Hamas.[71] Mubarak condemned Hamas' suicide bombings in Israel but, at the same time, he also linked the attacks to Israel's refusal to halt the building of settlements in the West Bank and delay in the redeployment of its forces from the Occupied Territories. In March 1996, the Egyptian president hosted a 'terrorism summit' of 27 heads of state and government in the wake of suicide bomb attacks in Israel; however, during the summit he criticized, "what he described as Netanyahu's 'lack of action' in implementing the Israeli/PLO peace accord" [and] "intensified his attacks on Netanyahu in 1997, particular in regard to the expansion of Jewish settlements in the West Bank."[72]

Even so, Egypt partnered with Israel (supported by the United States) in imposing a blockade on Gaza when Hamas seized power in 2007 and declared its rule over the territory. There was a distinct concurrence of interests: While Israel was concerned that a regular traffic at the Rafah border crossing would enable Hamas acquire weapons, Mubarak's failed mediation attempt to end the conflict between Hamas and Fatah and return the Gaza strip to the control of the PA, drove the Egyptian regime to close its border as a sign of support for the PA.[73]

Egyptian officials also feared that Hamas' victory in Gaza would embolden its own Islamists and threaten the fragile peace with Israel. The Gaza land blockade on the Egyptian side, which prevented Hamas from moving weapons and other materials through the crossing, also affected "Gazan trade, civilian traffic, and humanitarian access."[74] Egypt also took forceful actions against the co-called "tunnel economy" installing "underground steel barrier meant to block off the smuggling tunnels that provide both a vital lifeline to Gaza's blockaded economy and a pipeline to resupply the arsenals of Hamas."[75] For the next four years from the Hamas' ascension to power in the Strip, the Gaza issue kept Mubarak on the horns of a dilemma: Whereas, the regime was averse to dealing with Hamas, it did not want to be seen as backing Israel's blockade, given the support for the Palestinian cause on the Egyptian street.[76]

However, even at the height of the domestic turmoil following the fall of Mubarak, when activists raised the banner of Palestine in demonstrations, the Supreme Council of the Armed Forces (SCAF) acting as the provisional government, announced on February 2011 that, "Egypt would honour all the obligation and agreements commitments it had signed."[77] When former Muslim Brotherhood leader Mohammad Morsi assumed the presidency of Egypt in June 2012, Hamas expected an end to Mubarak's policy of cooperation with Israel on the Gaza blockade. However, even as Morsi eased travel for Palestinians across the Rafah crossing, he also put constraints on the tunnel traffic, as the Egyptian military and intelligence officials viewed Hamas a foremost strategic threat to their country.[78] While nominally allowing some traffic through 'holes' in the large steel barriers to mollify Hamas, the Muslim Brotherhood regime in Egypt could escape the allegation that they were doing enemy Israel's bidding.[79]

Morsi declared his intention of preserving the Israel–Egypt Peace Treaty of 1979, and maintaining ties with the Jewish state. In his first address to the nation, Morsi observed he would respect all international treaties that Egypt had previously signed, in a clear reference to the peace treaty with Israel.[80] He kept lines of communication to Israel and the United States open so as to keep receiving US aid for the Egyptian military. When tensions between Israel and Palestinians escalated in 2012 – as Hamas militants fired a barrage of rockets at southern

Israeli towns in retaliation for the killing of Hamas' top military leader and Israel responded by airstrikes on the Gaza Strip for eight days – Morsi brokered a truce between Israel and Hamas in November. Like his predecessors, as Milton-Edwards says, "Morsi and his government had to balance Egyptian national interest with responsiveness to Egyptian popular sentiment on the Palestinian issue."[81] All in all, the Muslim Brotherhood leader was not inclined to alienate Israel and blindly back his fellow Islamists in Gaza.

Since the military takeover of July 2013, that ousted Morsi from presidency and replaced him with General Abdel Fattah el-Sisi, Egypt's security and intelligence cooperation with Israel has increased. Combating the threat posed by ISIS-Sinai Province and other militants operating in the Sinai has become the centrepiece of Egyptian–Israeli cooperation in recent years. Some observers believe that this cooperation has led to an improvement in relations, at least at the official level, though the realisation of peace between the people of the two countries remains a far cry. "Cooperation on the Sinai has largely driven the improvement in relations," says David Schenker, former Levant Country Director, Office of the Secretary of Defense. United States.[82]

ISIS-Sinai Province has used the peninsula to launch rockets towards the southern cities of Israel, at least on two occasions in 2017, and it, "continues to conduct daily attacks against the Egyptian Armed Forces (EAF) and security services, causing hundreds of casualties, while other extremist organizations have carried out attacks on the mainland," according to a testimony of General Joseph Votel, the Commander of US Central Command before the House Armed Services Committee.[83] The *New York Times* reportage by David Kirkpatrick in February 2018, has revealed Egypt's near-total dependency on Israel for security in Sinai, as it was unable to stop the killing of its soldiers and police officers at the hands of the terrorists. President Sisi frequently consented to Israel's airstrikes inside Egypt that "helped the Egyptian military regain the command in its nearly five-year battle against the militants. For Israel, the strikes have bolstered the security of its borders and the stability of its neighbour."[84] Kirkpatrick believes, "the remarkable cooperation marks a new stage in the evolution of their singularly fraught relationship."[85]

Will security cooperation enhance the possibility of engagements in other bilateral areas. There are some definite signs. In February 2018, Egyptian and Israeli gas companies signed a gas trade deal worth billions of dollars, adding an economic dimension to the relationship dominated by security. If this deal is made to follow through and Israel indeed begins exporting gas to Egypt, it could herald further normalization of relations between the two countries, long constrained by the Egyptian people's silent rejection of Israel and tacit support given to it by their government. "There is a clear understanding in Cairo," says Eran Lerman, "that the two countries face the same enemies and the same challenges, namely the terrorist threat in the Sinai Peninsula – and that Israel can be a major contributor to Egypt's long-term security and stability. This a a sold base to build multi-faceted ties."[86]

Feasibility of gas trade

In August 2017, President Sisi authorised a legislation (Law 196/2017) that partially deregulates the energy sector, opening up the import of natural gas to the private sector in return for gas-transit fees on the Egyptian pipeline network, and sanctions the establishment of a gas regulatory authority.[87] In the backdrop of these developments, the Tamar and Leviathan developers on 19 February 2018, announced a $15 billion contract to export 64 bcm of natural gas to Egypt over a period of ten years. The deal is based on a MoU from October 2014 between the Noble-Delek partnership and Dolphinus Holdings, a natural gas trading company. As stipulated in the contract terms, supplies from both Tamar and Leviathan fields will continue until the amounts agreed are delivered or until December 2030, whichever is earlier.[88] Gas deliveries in small quantities will begin in early 2019 on a trial basis. However, by spring 2019, the daily supply is projected to steady at 19.8 mcm.[89] The deal, as former Israeli Ambassador to Egypt Zvi Mazel says, "enables Israel to make the most of short distances and lower transportation costs."[90]

An export contract in one of the key markets in the region enables the Noble Energy and Delek Group to raise a part of the capital required for the development of the second phase of the Leviathan field. Besides, from Israel's point of view, as opening up a large export market such as Egypt, would generate interest on the part of big oil companies in the new license round of Israel's offshore areas, including areas close to the Leviathan field.[91] With the conclusion of the contract with Dolphinus, the Israeli gas reservoirs are tied up with no less than four transactions for export : export of gas to Egypt joins the export from Tamar to the Jordanian companies located near the Dead Sea and the gas trade agreement between Leviathan developers and NEPCO.

It is reasonable to assume that the governments of both Israel and Egypt played a crucial role in securing the gas contract between the companies on each side. PM Netanyahu called the deal "historic" and stated it will, "bring in millions to the state treasury, and this money will then be spent on education, health services, and welfare for the good of Israeli citizens."[92] While Ministry of Petroleum issued a statement saying it had no comment to make on negotiations involving private companies, President Sisi, in an impromptu address broadcast on television, stressed Egypt had, "scored a goal" by moving closer to becoming a regional hub for gas trade. "[It] has a lot of advantages for us [Egyptians]. And I want people to be reassured,"[93] Sisi tried to address the nation's wariness about ties with a country people still consider an enemy.

The news of the deal with Israel unsurprisingly sparked off a wave of public questioning in Egypt.[94] Opposition factions denounced the creation of dependency on Israel, asking why there was a need to import gas when the country was moving towards self-sufficiency, as asserted by Petroleum Minister Tariq al-Mulla at the inauguration of the gigantic Zohr gas field, a few weeks earlier to the agreement. The lack of public transparency on the deal, including the route of the natural gas import as well as the price at which it would be imported, irked the Egyptian public and brought back recollections of the gas deal with Israel a decade ago. Oil Minister Mulla also downplayed the singularity of the deal with Israel, stating that Egypt "welcomes any quantities of natural gas from any country for processing in the country's liquefaction plants" that will transform the nation "into a hub for gas and petroleum trading and transport."[95] Given that the Egyptians continue to hold a negative view of Israel, it was an attempt to distance from something that was bound to be unpopular. The voices of opposition soon died down: Egypt is not a democracy and lack of governmental accountability ensured the deal remained intact, unencumbered by people's resistance to it.

For Israel, the deal reflects its huge appetite for cooperation with Egypt. It is a step towards adding an economic layer to a relationship dominated by security, since the two countries signed a peace treaty four decades ago. An interdependent transaction implies further stabilisation of Israel's position in the region. Nadav Perry of Delek Drilling rightly opines that "every agreement is a step forward; it alone will not contribute to safety and security for Israel, but it will have a positive impact on the momentum towards resolution of conflicts."[96]

Likewise, Cairo's nod to the gas deal exposed a series of pressing concerns:[97] First, Egypt wanted to reach a settlement on the $1.76 billion in compensation that the state-owned Egyptian gas companies were required to pay to IEC as part of an international arbitration award. In an arbitration procedure of the International Chamber of Commerce (ICC) in December 2015, the court pronounced that EGAS and EGPC stood in violation of the 2005 deal to supply natural gas to Israel, when they terminated the contract in 2012.[98] Indeed, parallel to the negotiations between Noble-Delek and their Egyptian partner, East Gas, and the stakeholders of EMG Company, on acquisition of stakes in its Al-Arish–Ashkelon pipeline, *Bloomberg* reported in August 2018[99] of an agreement between the Egyptian government and IEC that reduced the arbitration fine to around $470 million and spread the payments over multiple years.

On 27 September 2018, Delek's disclosure filed with Israel Securities Authority and Tel Aviv Stock Exchange stated that Emed, a special-purpose company established by Delek, Noble Energy, and Sphinx (a wholly owned subsidiary of East Gas Company) for the pipeline transaction, had purchased a 39 percent stake in EMG. The East Gas acquired an additional 9 percent share, clearing the way for the export of gas from Israeli fields to Egypt through the Al-Arish–Ashkelon pipeline.[100] The pipeline agreement also conferred Delek and Noble Energy the right to use the Arab pipeline section between Al-Arish (Egypt) and Aqaba (Jordan), giving Israel's field developers another route for export of gas to Jordan.

Second, gas from Israel would cover a crucial shortfall in supply to Egypt's two liquefaction terminals. Despite Zohr's phenomenal development, the need to substitute costly fuel oil usage at power plants and replace exorbitant LNG imports, together with inevitable decline in production from other fields, necessitated gas import to run the facilities at Damietta and Idku, lying idle or operating below capacity since 2014 at great cost to the government.

Third, gas from Israel is required to cover a possible shortfall in Egyptian gas supply in coming years. While officials in Cairo declared supply self-sufficiency in September 2018 and talked of terminating CNG imports,[101] according to a CI Capital – one of the largest investment banks in Egypt – report,[102] the situation, if true at all, is unlikely to last for more than two years. Domestic demand has soared exponentially with the arrival of major new fields – Zohr, Atoll in Damietta concession, and the West Nile Delta project (Taurus and Delta fields) – into the production zone during 2015–2016, and the trend will continue as the Egyptian economy grows.[103] Neither will Egypt regain its status as a major gas exporter in the near future. The estimated production levels required for this purpose might only be available from subsequent development phases of these fields.[104]

Even though, the daily production rate of 187 bcm per day (68 bcm per year) in September 2018 exceeded the country's total gas consumption of 169.9 mcm per day (62 bcm per year),[105] demand is steadily increasing to outpace domestic supply. State-owned EGAS estimates that the average domestic gas consumption will increase to about 255 mcm per day (93 bcm per year) by 2020–2021, driven by the industrial development plan, growth in power production using natural gas, delivery of gas to homes, and the conversions of cars to CNG to replace petroleum products.[106] Moreover, Egypt started to export small quantities of gas to Jordan in July 2018 in fulfilment of the 2004 agreement, entailing a supply of 7 mcm per day or more than 2.5 bcm per year for 15 years. After a five-year hiatus of 2013–2017, during which Egyptian government diverted supply to the domestic arena, the petroleum ministry intends to restore a full-bodied supply in early 2019.[107] In effect, Egypt's self-sufficiency is borderline and probably short-lived.

In fact, the Egyptian government's protracted negotiations with the operator of Damietta facility Union Fenosa Gas (UFG) on an arbitration award to the latter, reveals how domestic energy demand has outstripped supply. EGAS stopped supplying gas to Damietta LNG plant as the country faced internal energy shortages in the wake of the turbulence unleashed by the Arab Spring uprisings. UFG took the case to the International Centre for Settlement of International Disputes (ICSID), a World Bank arbitration body, in 2014, which awarded a $2 billion in compensation from Egypt.[108] LNG exports halted entirely in 2015 but have since restarted with Idku's producing around one cargo per month after its partial reopening in 2016, amidst concerns about the continued availability of gas. In the medium term, provision of feedstock gas to the two LNG plants on a continuous basis appears an uphill task.[109]

A McKinsey analysis of gas production from the existing and new fields in the coming years predicts that in 2030, total production from the Egyptian fields will fall below 50 bcm a year.[110] The prognosis of fall in production capacity and surge in demand explains why Egypt, despite having discovered large reserves, is eager to import gas, not only from Israel but also from Cyprus and Lebanon (if and when gas reservoirs are discovered). An import deal of 6.4 bcm per year from Israel immediately fulfils the critical mass of gas required to restore operations in the LNG plants that have a combined capacity of 16.59 bcm.[111] The tentative plan of the Egyptian–Israeli gas deal is to allocate a portion for national consumption, while the remaining supply is to be pumped into liquefaction for export.[112]

Fourth, the deal portends strengthening of Egypt's economic ties with Europe. Cairo's strategy is to import gas from Eastern Mediterranean countries, including Israel and Cyprus, and use the liquefaction infrastructure to create a centre of gas production at Europe's doorstep. If this strategy were to materialise, it would serve a two-pronged political-economic thrust. Egypt would be able the wrest the aspiration of becoming a 'gas hub' from Turkey, which at present controls the overland passage of gas to Europe. It is pertinent to add here that in the aftermath Sisi's ouster of President Morsi in a coup, Turkish President Erdoğan has emerged as Egypt's bitter critic and rival. In economic terms, Egypt would benefit from tolls and transit fees from transport of gas bound for Europe.

A steady stream of gas supply to Europe from the Egyptian shores would not only lessen its excessive dependence on Russia, but also serve as an alternative to the decline in North Sea production[113] and the shutdown of Groningen gas fields by 2030.[114]

> For Egypt, EU, in addition to being a long-term viable gas customer, is a source of finance and technology for its upstream and downstream oil and gas as well as for the renewable sector.[115]

Israel has not only struck the cheapest delivery option to supply gas to Egypt, but has also consolidated an important future outlet options for its gas through the Arab gas pipeline. The ability to use a portion of the Arab Gas Pipeline to Aqaba will allow Israel to supply additional quantities of gas to Egypt or Jordan in the future. As of now, the EMG pipeline will require technical intervention to equip it for the reverse flow of gas, although the Sinai portion of the pipeline, which connects Al-Arish to Port Said, is replete with security challenges of bombings and sabotage as in 2011. With the removal of the obstacle to the transport of gas from the Israeli fields to Egyptian shore, Dolphinus will begin to import gas from Israel's biggest fields in mid-2019.[116]

At the same time, in recognition of a potential shortfall in supply, the Egyptian government is negotiating on a fast-track basis to bring piped gas from Cyprus' Aphrodite[117] to Damietta anf Idku liquefaction facilities. Indeed, to justify the investment for development of the 'Zohr-like' gas-bearing structure in the Calypso-1 well, discovered in the Cypriot waters in February 2018,[118] field developers would need to secure export markets, a dilemma similar to that facing the Israeli companies. An Egyptian–Cypriot deal suits both parties, much like the Egyptian–Israeli deal. Both deals are predicated on two intersecting interests: The Egyptian need to put Idku and Damietta terminals into full operation and reclaim the export market share, and the imperatives of Israel and Cyprus to secure export markets for their gas to finance the development of their gas sectors.

With Leviathan aiming to achieve the first production by the end of 2019, the development of its second phase still requires a critical mass of buyers through gas sales deals with Turkey and Europe, and further deals with Egypt. Can Israel leverage Egyptian gas requirements and close security cooperation to sign more deals? As far as the routes for export of Israel's gas are concerned, Egypt is a natural partner because of the proximity between the two nations. The construction of undersea pipelines connecting Tamar and Leviathan fields directly to Egyptian liquefaction terminals on the Mediterranean coast, is technically the simplest option. Gas from these two fields could also be pooled with Cypriot gas from Aphrodite and directed through a pipeline to Idku for liquefaction and export. Gas aggregation is emerging as a strong option, given that Noble-Delek consortium is the common developer of Tamar, Leviathan, and Aphrodite; and Shell, which has shares in Aphrodite, is the operator of the Idku plant in which it holds a 35 percent stake.[119] "While these routes are ideal, the only disadvantage is politics," observes Nasr Agiza, "as Israel ties with Egypt still lack dynamism, despite emerging engagements in several areas."[120]

If more gas from Israel and from Cyprus start flowing into Egyptian liquefaction terminals, it would not only potentially make Cairo a major player in the energy market but would also ensure hefty revenue earnings. The Egyptian-Israeli gas deal alone allows Cairo to earn an estimated $2 billion on an annual basis in exchange for liquefaction.[121] Moreover, royalties will be paid for the use of the national grid and taxes will be collected.[122] In addition to the expected profit, Egypt as a regional gas hub will also advance its petrochemical industry, diversifying its natural gas industry and creating jobs, both important aspects of President Sisi's economic reforms.[123]

Potential routes for Israeli gas: Turkey and Europe

The Obama Administration-brokered rapprochement between Israel and Turkey in 2016, after a six-year rupture following the Mavi Marmara incident in 2010,[124] led to the initiation of the 'energy dialogue' between the two estranged allies. There have been hectic mediation efforts by US to assist the two parties reach an agreement that would allow Israel to Turkey and onward to Europe.[125] In fact, Turkey's resilient economic relationship with Israel is a favourable pointer of the success of a project of this nature, despite fears about internal political opposition in Ankara to cooperation with Tel Aviv. Trade between Israel and Turkey in 2014 increased by 11.5 percent compared to 2013, as bilateral trade reached an all-time high at $5.44 billion, despite the political crisis and increasingly hostile anti-Israel rhetoric in Turkey.[126]

According to Eser Ozdil, Turkey is an excellent market for Israeli gas for three important reasons:

> It is a growth market where 99 percent of energy need is imported; it is a big market with large demand in power generation and industrial applications; and that most of Turkey's long-term energy contracts will expire in 2020 creating need for further contracts to secure energy supply.[127]

Further, as Nimrod Goren observes, "Turkey and Israel have a history of cooperation, so Turkey is a natural partner for Israel gas export plans."[128]

Through 2017, Turkey was seen as another major pillar of Israel's gas export strategy among policymakers. Discussions on the pipeline connection between Israeli gas fields and Turkey's Ceyhan port were reportedly at an advanced stage in that year. On the sidelines of 22nd World Petroleum Congress in Istanbul in July 2017, Israel's energy minister Yuval Steinitz stated that Turkey and Israel would soon conclude an inter-governmental umbrella agreement, enabling the construction of the pipeline by the year's end.[129] However, the direction of talks between Israel and Turkey changed with US recognition of Jerusalem as Israel's capital in December 2017. In response, Erdoğan escalated his public denunciations of Netanyahu and his policies towards Palestinians in the Occupied Territories. While Erdoğan may have had the resonance of anti-Israeli rhetoric with the domestic audience in mind ahead of the domestic elections of June 2018, the pace of negotiations on gas trade fell by the wayside. A Turkish–Israeli pipeline deal is in serious trouble, especially as Turkish president's criticism of Israel becomes more vocal and intense.

Turkey, nonetheless, has an undeniable interest in gas from Israel that can be attributed to a variety of reasons. As a high-growth economy, Turkey's energy needs are immense and a diversification of supply sources is required to safeguard energy security. Ankara could not only import gas from Israel for its own use, but can also serve as a supply route to Europe. That would add another justification to its ambition of becoming a transit hub for oil and gas extracted from the Central Asian and Eastern Mediterranean reserves.[130] For Israel, Turkey's stable economy and energy demands are assets for gas trade. "Since natural gas price in Turkey is higher than European averages, Turkey is in a position to offer the price advantage for Israeli gas," says Mert Bilgin, a professor of International Relations at Medipol University, Istanbul.[131]

Likewise, gas from Israel will be the cheapest option for Turkey, considering that an assumed price could be $199 per thousand cubic metres, which will be very competitive compared to $425 for Russian gas and $335 for Azerbaijani gas.[132] Israel's perusal of other gas export routes to European markets – such as, through Egypt's LNG terminals or a pipeline via Cyprus – is likely to be perceived in Turkey as attempts to weaken its coveted status of being the 'Rotterdam for gas'.[133] Given the complementarity of aims and interests, an Israeli–Turkish gas trade regime would be advantageous for both nations. However, political stains between Israel and Turkey, which are of recent origin, as those between Cyprus and Turkey that have been existent for decades, highlight the long-term risks and the influence of the region's tortured geopolitics on economic cooperation.

Pipeline to Turkey

Israeli-Turkish negotiations revolved around the construction of a 500-km underwater pipeline from the Leviathan field to Ceyhan port on Turkey's Mediterranean coast. With an annual capacity of 30 bcm, of which 7–10 bcm would be utilised in Turkey, an add-on pipeline from the Turkish port could transfer the remaining volume to Europe.[134] The ideal route for an Israeli–Turkish pipeline is along the Levantine coastline of Lebanon and Syria because of the shallow seabed, but political and security risks preclude this option. (Figure 4.4).

The longstanding Israeli–Lebanese enmity over the Palestinian issue and Israel's continued occupation of the Sheeba farms – a narrow strip of disputed land at the intersection of the Lebanese–Syrian border and the Golan Heights – which Lebanon claims as its own, stand in the way of the resolution of their conflict. In the offshore arena, Israel and Lebanon do not have a mutually agreed demarcation of their economic waters in the Eastern Mediterranean. The two countries

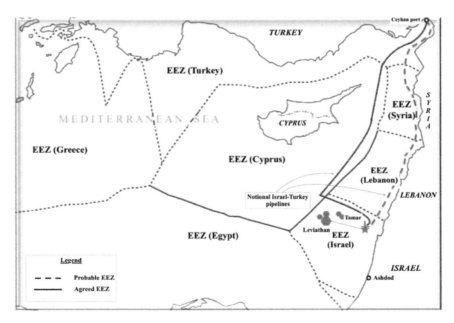

FIGURE 4.4 Prospective Israel–Turkey pipelines

Source: Author

Disclaimer: Map not to scale

are at daggers drawn over 700 square miles of disputed maritime territory, which both claim to own. Israel's occupation of Golan Heights and lack of diplomatic relations with Damascus, beats any idea of a pipeline from Israel navigating the Mediterranean shores of Syria.

An alternative route for the Israeli–Turkish pipeline could bypass Lebanon and Syria, but must go across the Cypriot EEZ to reach Ceyhan port (Figure 4.4). Any development, however, on this track will depend on the resolution of the Cyprus issue. The Republic of Cyprus (Greek Cypriot part) has refused to allow a pipeline to Turkey unless Ankara agrees to end the island's 40-year-old division and respects its EEZ. Turkey invaded the northern third of the island in response to an impending coup backed by the military rulers of Greece. Neither Turkey nor the Turkish Republic of Northern Cyprus (TRNC) – which declared independence from the Republic of Cyprus in November 1983 and is only recognised by Turkey – accept the Greek Cypriot's maritime border agreements with Egypt, Israel, and Lebanon.[135]

Turkey has for years opposed the Greek Cypriot efforts to exploit natural gas reserves, claiming that its drilling activities infringe upon the inalienable rights of the Turkish Cypriot, who are the co-owners of the island and its natural resources. In insisting that a permanent peace deal between the Republic of Cyprus and TRNC must be precede any international agreements on the island's hydrocarbon reserves, Ankara calls Nicosia's gas licensing to IOCs illegal. The Republic of Cyprus, rejects Turkey's claims, asserting that its actions are fully in accordance with international law and the potential wealth from oil and gas deposits in the islands' EEZ will be shared once a peace agreement reunifying the island is reached.

Nicosia asserts that instead of trying to reunify the island, Ankara is constantly trying to create a crisis to undermine Cyprus' energy projects in the Mediterranean. To counter the Republic of Cyprus' (Greek Cypriot administration) delineation of licensing blocks in the island's EEZ, TNRC has projected its own licensing blocks, as apparent in Figure 4.5. The overlapping areas between the Greek and Turkish Cypriot licensing blocks add another layer to the longstanding political conflict between Turkey and the Republic of Cyprus. To make matter worse, the state-run TPAO (Turkish Petroleum) is lining up to carry out exploration in the TRNC's licensing blocks, whilst there have been no exploratory surveys.

The dispute between Turkey and the Republic of Cyprus intensified in 2018, riding on several developments in the Eastern Mediterranean region. Early in the year, Turkish naval forces on manoeuvres off Cyprus, blocked an Eni-chartered drillship from reaching Block 3 of the Greek Cypriot licensing area, which overlaps with Block F of TRNC.[136] In November 2018, Ankara issued a strong rebuke of the attempt by the Republic of Cyprus to seek bidders for its Block 7, a part of which overlaps with the boundaries of the continental shelf claimed by Turkey. Meanwhile, reports suggest, Ankara prevented a Greek frigate in October from harassing Turkish Barbaros seismographic research/survey vessel stationed in the Eastern Mediterranean.[137] It is not surprising that Turkey's perceives an emerging

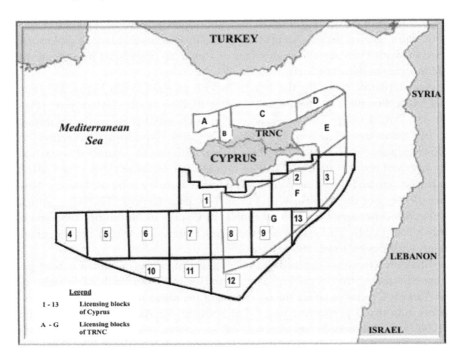

FIGURE 4.5 Overlapping Greek and Turkish Cypriot licensing blocks

Source: Author's figure; referenced from the Ministry of Foreign Affairs, Republic of Turkey, www. mfa.gov.tr/default.en.mfa

Disclaimer: Map not to scale

anti-Turkish bloc comprising of Greece, Israel, and Cyprus and that fuels its belligerent response to Cyprus' gas-related activities.

Turkey is still not a part of any gas trade deal, actual or potential, in the region, given its deteriorating political relations with Israel, Cyprus, and Egypt, as well as with Greece over maritime border demarcation in the Aegean Sea. Hence, Ankara not only feels 'left out' but also threatened by the hectic parleys on the gas trade among the Eastern Mediterranean countries, which can effectively undermine its primacy of being an operational and effective land route for transfer of oil and gas to Europe.

Turkey's Cyprus dilemma also reflects the response of a late comer to the region's 'gas game,' having launched its first drilling ship in November 2018, several years following its rivals' leap into the exploration business. When Eni and Total made an announcement in February 2018 about a potentially large gas discovery at the Calypso drilling site in Block 6 (a part of which falls lies in what Aankra considers its EEZ), suggesting an extension of Zohr-like play further northwest,[138] it sparked off tensions with Turkey.[139] The estimated size of Calypso find appears to be the immediate trigger. When the Aphrodite gas field in Block 12 (overlapping with TRC's G Block) was discovered in 2011 (Figure 4.6), Turkey adopted a less militaristic approach to the offshore drilling activities of the Greek Cypriots, not least because it was a small field and its prospective assets were then unknown. The Calypso discovery, according to a 2018 estimate, could be as high as around 570 bcm.[140] The Republic of Cyprus' existent and potential gas discoveries represent a challenge to Turkey. Ankara fears, along with Israel and Egypt, Cyprus might carve out a network of gas trade relations in the Eastern Mediterranean, excluding it from consumption and transit benefits.

Many analysts believe that instead of using gas as a carrot and stick in negotiations to resolve the intractable Cyprus dispute, Greek Cypriots should jointly develop and explore the EEZ of the island with the Turkish Cypriots.[141] The Republic of Cyprus maintains that Turkey needs to agree to the reunification of the island before any resource sharing can take place between the two parts. Turkey and Turkish Cypriots have refused to negotiate unless the Greek Cypriots discontinue drilling for oil and gas. In this vicious cycle marked by the hardened positions of the disputing parties, the possibility of the construction of the Turkish–Israeli gas pipeline through Cyprus' territorial waters appears far-fetched.

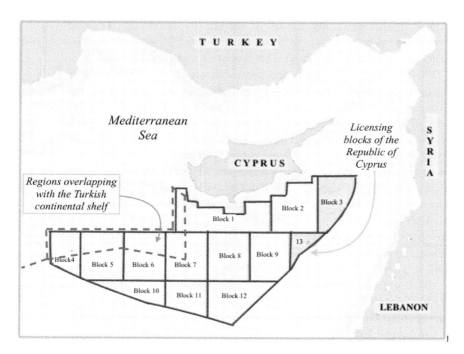

FIGURE 4.6 Areas of Cyprus' EEZ claimed by Turkey as part of its continental shelf

Source: Author

Disclaimer: Map not to scale

The Greek Cypriots have struck a conciliatory note since the discovery of the natural gas deposits, believing that tensions would impede the development of the resource.[142] "Sharing of resources is given once the political and security issues with Turkey are sorted out,"[143] says Demetrios Theophylactou, the High Commissioner to India. UN-led negotiations aimed at reunifying the ethnically divided island took place on and off from April 2015 – raising hope of unification with prospects linked to gas developments. In July 2017, however, the much-touted Turkish–Cypriot peace talks collapsed amidst accusations and counter-accusations of intransigence, further damaging the prospects of Israeli–Turkish energy relations. Any future development on the resolution of the Cyprus issue will go on to increase Israel's odds in favour of laying an underwater pipeline to Turkey.[144]

East Mediterranean gas pipeline

The idea of the EastMed pipeline that would link Israel's Leviathan field with the Cypriot Aphrodite field to export gas to the European mainland through Greece, is an outcome of the improvement in Israel's once frosty relations with Greece and Cyprus over the last decade. That occurred when relations between Israel and Turkey began to deteriorate in late 2008, which led the Israeli leadership to look for alternative alliances in the Eastern Mediterranean. The traditionally pro-Arab Greeks were won over through consistent diplomatic interactions and positioning of a common ground on economic and security issues.[145]

The EastMed project envisages the construction of a 1900-km long (1,300-km offshore pipeline and a 600-km onshore) pipeline that will connect Israel's offshore gas fields to the European pipeline network (Figure 4.7). To begin with, gas will be transmitted from the Israeli fields to Cyprus, where a pooling with gas from Cyprus' deposits will follow. From Cyprus, a pipeline of about 700-km under the sea will transport a large quantity of gas to Crete, before it can latch on to the transmission network in Greece. The connection shall subsequently extend through the Grecian mainland to Italy. Egypt and Lebanon (if it discovers gas and political contingencies permit) might link up with the pipeline at a later stage.[146] The project, equally owned by IGI Poseidon, a joint venture between Greece's state-owned natural gas firm Depa and Italian energy group Edison, is estimated to cost $7.3 billion. With a capacity of 10 bcm per year and sunk at a depth of 3 km in the Mediterranean Sea, the EastMed pipeline would be the world's longest and deepest offshore pipeline.[147] Designated as one of the 173 'projects of common interest' by the European Commission in the field of energy infrastructure, the project could see the light of day by 2025.[148]

On 3 April 2017, the energy ministers of Cyprus, Greece, Israel, and Italy met in Tel Aviv to sign a preliminary agreement on the EastMed pipeline project. Significantly, the EU Commissioner for Climate Action and Energy was also present at the event, indicating Europe's interest in the project. The EastMed pipeline is being increasingly envisaged by the stakeholder countries as a means

FIGURE 4.7   EastMed pipeline

Source: Author

Disclaimer: Map not to scale

to foster cooperation in their otherwise turbulent neigbourhood. Economically, it is perceived as the surest way for regional gas to have access to a larger European market.

To its European promoters, the appeal of the EastMed pipeline rests in the fact that it offers an opportunity to reduce their dependence on Russian gas through a diversification of imports, particularly since political relations get riskier with Brussels–Moscow differences on Ukraine, Syria, and a host of other international issues. Europe's gas need-related vulnerability present an opening for Israel to tether their energy policies to gas supply chains emanating from its fields.[149] That would allow Israel to forge a relationship with Europe, which looks beyond the prism of Palestinian–Israeli conflict, to a long-term strategic partnership.

However, many in the energy industry remain unconvinced about the pipeline's commercial viability. Some analysts question the cost competitiveness of the gas reaching European borders, given the project's enormous cost at a time of low gas prices. Others have raised doubt over the long-term viability of the project in the backdrop of changes in European energy consumption that is increasingly moving away from fossil fuels to renewable energy. It is uncertain if the demand or gas in Europe will remain high enough over the long term to support the cost-effectiveness. Some observers also draw attention to the expansion of the global LNG market as an alternative and possibly cheaper source of supply for Europe, including the flow of shale gas LNG from the United States. LNG is considered the simplest, fastest, and most economical way to utilise gas for export.

In addition, the EastMed gas pipeline to Europe may be commercially unrealistic unless it receives a substantial subsidy from the EU and stakeholders can prove that there is enough available gas to keep the pipeline operational for at least 25 years. Many analysts question whether enough gas will be available for export after domestic market prioritisations. They believe volumes larger than that available with Israel and Cyprus is required to make the construction of a pipeline of such magnitude viable even though it might be technically feasible. Egypt, the largest gasholder in the Eastern Mediterranean, can energise the project but it is not enthusiastic about the EastMed pipeline, having at its disposal two LNG terminals that have been underutilised since 2014.

Further, Cyprus' gas export to Egypt could damage the prospects of the EastMed pipeline. In September 2018, Egypt and Cyprus signed an agreement to build a direct pipeline that will allow natural gas from the Aphrodite field to flow onto Egyptian shores and then to the LNG facility in Idku. Cyriot gas will be eventually sold to mainland Europe as LNG. Israel alone cannot create the economies of scale needed to make the EastMed exports competitive.[150] The pipeline with an annual capacity 20 bcm per year requires 500 bcm of gas in 25 years at full capacity operations. Theoretically, there might be enough gas, if all the prospecting in Israel and Cyrpus yields positive results. As of 2018, Israel's total proven reserves of around 455 bcm and Cyprus' 125 bcm do not evoke investors' confidence in the EastMed.[151]

Even if the reserves do turn up in a few years, it would require complex manoeuvrings to link the Leviathan field to Aphrodite and Zohr for the EastMed pipeline, given Egypt's reluctance to prioritise a trans-Mediterranean pipeline over its liquefaction facilities.[152] The discovery of Zohr field in 2015 and its fast-tracked startup within two years opened up the possibility of the emergence a gas regime in the Eastern Mediterranean that would facilitate gas trade. However, in the fast-changing political and economic milieu of the region, drift in the events, nonetheless, stands out: If Eastern Mediterranean energy resources are to be developed and traded, Egypt will play a central role.

The fast-emerging Egyptian option

The net effect of tensions in Israel's maritime neighbourhood is to make the Egyptian export option increasingly appealing. The 'northern routes' to European markets for Israel's gas via Greece and Turkey do not hit the mark on the economic, technical, and political aspects. Egyptian liquefaction facilities saves Israel (and Cyprus) the burden of building their own terminals. While Egypt appears as a natural gateway for Israeli gas, its ability to become a conduit for re-export depends on a number of factors. First, the volume of gas that can be exported from Egyptian liquefaction plants in the long run remains unclear. While the capacity of the plants are known, it is unknown how much gas from Egyptian fields or from import by private sector companies would be used, say in a 15-year period, for domestic consumption and liquefaction. One of the features of President Sisi's economic reforms initiated in 2016 is to boost the use of natural gas in power generation given the escalation in demand for electricity from the household and industrial sectors.[153] Considering this factor, the exact proportion of gas available from internal and foreign sources to meet domestic requirements as well as export cannot be ascertained at a given point. Egypt needs to sustain its macroeconomic reforms, including reduction in fuel subsidy, to create a favourable environment for international investments in its upstream and downstream sectors. If a third LNG terminal does come up as a result, it could easily accommodate the additional gas from neighbouring countries, including Israel.[154] Lastly, the ubiquitous political factors can have a direct bearing on Egypt's receive gas from Israel for re-export.

EuroAsia interconnector

Israel's electricity is entirely generated domestically – a product of its strategy of energy self-sufficiency – and there are no grid connections with neighbouring countries. That is set to change with Israel's participation in the EuroAsia Interconnector, a leading Project of Common Interest of the European Union. It involves the creation of an 'electricity highway' by connecting the national grids of Israel, Cyprus, and Greece that allows for bi-directional transmission of electricity (Figure 4.7). Through subsea cables and onshore converter stations at

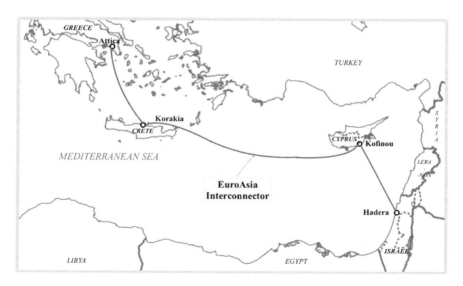

FIGURE 4.8 The projected Israel–Cyprus–Greece electricity interconnector

Source: Author

Disclaimer: Map not to scale

each connection point, the EuroAsia Inter-connector[155] with a total capacity to transmit 2,000 MW, will transmit electricity across 1518 km length from east to west. The interconnector will start near Hadera in Israel and take the route to Cyprus where it will connect at the Kofinou station. From there it will head west and take a subsea route to Korakia point in Crete, Greece, and from there continue to Attica on mainland Greece.

The idea of an interconnected electricity emerged amid improved relations between the three counties, coupled with the discovery of gas deposits in Israel and Cyprus that could be used to generate electricity. It will end electricity isolation of the two countries and also keep EU countries securely supplied with electricity produced by the gas reserves in Cyprus and Israel. Especially beneficial for Israel will be the fact that IEC could sell excess electricity to Cyprus or any other buyer further west.

Risks of conflict

In the above, we have seen how regional conflicts hinder Israel's attempt to move gas to profitable markets. Discussed below are two conflicts in which Israel is a direct party, and these have the potential to further complicate matters to its detriment. The conflicts with Lebanon, a regional country with which Israel has no diplomatic relations, and Palestinians, whose territory Israel continues to occupy, however, offer distinctive insights into the question whether economic engagement can pave the way for settlement of political differences.[156]

Israel and Lebanon

Formally at war for years, and without diplomatic relations, Israel and Lebanon have never agreed on delimitation of their maritime boundaries. Israel is not a party to United Nations Convention on the Law of the Sea (UNCLOS) of 1982, but tacitly accepts the notion of EEZ. In October 2010, Lebanon deposited its maritime boundary scheme to the United Nations to register its EEZ delimitation following on an agreement with Cyprus in 2007, which included geographical coordinates of its southern boundary with Israel.[157] However, the coordinates submitted by Lebanon was determined by the Lebanese parliament in May 2009, and was at variance with the coordinates specified in the 2007 agreement.[158]

Likewise, Israel officially adopted its own EEZ after negotiating a maritime delimitation agreement with Cyprus, and submitted the geographical coordinates, including the northern limits of its territorial sea, to the United Nations in July 2011.[159] Since, Lebanon and Israel have not agreed to the delimitation of their southern and northern territorial seas respectively, the difference between the maritime boundary coordinates submitted by the two countries to the United Nations, creates a triangular sliver of disputed sea area believed to be rich in oil and gas resources (Figure 4.9).[160]

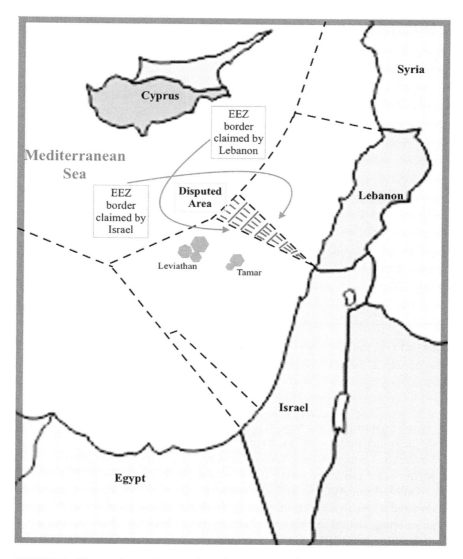

FIGURE 4.9 Disputed maritime territory between Israel and Lebanon

Source: Author

Disclaimer: Map not to scale

Both Lebanon and Israel have been unofficially exploring the Mediterranean waters for several years now, with a tacit understanding of keeping out of each other's way. In March 2017, however, Lebanon broke the status quo by publishing a tender for auction of oil and gas exploration blocks in the Eastern Mediterranean. A look at the licensing area reveals that Block 9 protrudes into the disputed triangular area (Figure 4.10). On the heels of the Lebanese licensing announcement,

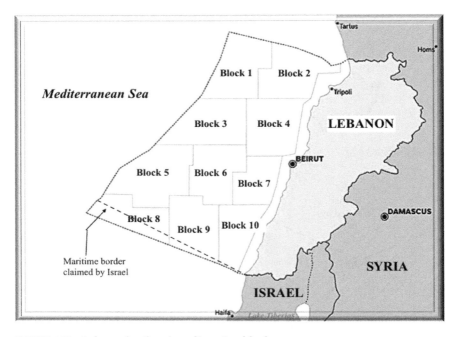

FIGURE 4.10 Lebanon's oil and gas licensing blocks

Source: Author; referenced from Lebanese Petroleum Administration, 2018

Disclaimer: Map not to scale

the Israeli government announced that the Knesset would deliberate upon a bill to define its maritime economic border with Lebanon.

Under the United Nations Vienna Convention on the Law of Treaties, states as parties must ratify the treaty to be bound by them.[161] The 2007 Cyprus–Lebanon Maritime Agreement does not bind Lebanon as the Lebanese parliament has refused its ratification. Hence, an agreement between Cyprus and Lebanon requires renegotiation for international acceptance. Equally, under international law, maritime boundary schemes submitted by Lebanon and Israel to UN are only unilateral proposals that have no legal standing. The arrangement must be made legal by an interim agreement between the two countries. Lebanon, like many other Arab countries in the region, does not recognise Israel and herein rests the core of the dispute.

As the Mediterranean is a semi-enclosed sea, Article 123, Part IX of UNCLOS, says, "states of this area have a general obligation to cooperate when facing a disagreement." To reduce the burden on the disputing parties, Article 74, paragraph 3, stresses that, "pending a final agreement, the States concerned shall make every effort to enter into provisional arrangements of a practical nature." In order to avoid implicit recognition of Israel, Lebanon does not want to determine the triple point delimitation between its own territorial waters, Cyprus and Israel. Evidently, once the three parties have agreed upon this triple point, the conflict, at least in its legal aspect would be resolved.[162] However, Lebanon's continued non-recognition towards Israel and the consequent absence of negotiations between the two parties, prevents the use of procedures from international law involving conciliation, arbitration, or submitting the case to the International Tribunal for the Law of the Sea (ITLOS). Even the International Court of Justice is unlikely to be successful, as Israel does not recognise its jurisdiction.[163]

In October 2017, Lebanon concluded its first offshore licensing round for E&P rights in five blocks (1, 4, 8, 9, and 10) which was re-launched after a three-year disruption caused by political instability. Not a very popular tendering due to regional turmoil and low gas prices, a consortium composed of France's Total SA, Eni International BV and JSC Novatek bid for just two blocks (4 and 9).[164] While available data suggests there are oil and gas deposits in Lebanon's waters, but so far, no exploratory drilling has taken place to estimate the size of the reserves. Initial seismic exploration in 2012 by UK-based Spectrum, estimated that at least 25 tcf (708 bcm) of gas could be found.[165] Block 9 is one of the most promising blocks and includes the area disputed by Israel (Figure 4.10). When the Lebanese Petroleum Authority (LPA) surveyed companies in 2013 to assess their interest in Lebanon's offshore, Block 9 received the highest number of votes.[166] The disputed triangular area of sea extends along the edge of three (blocks 8, 9 and 10) of the five blocks put up for tender (Figure 4.10). It seems that the dispute did not discourage the companies in bidding for the blocks in the contested zone.[167] Block 9, which has about 150 square kilometres in size zone, is close to the Karish field in Israeli waters, indicating a high probability of natural gas discovery.

Since the beginning of the Lebanese–Israeli maritime dispute, the United States has mediated between the two parties. Special envoys were sent to the region several times to encourage negotiations but they were met with repeated failures. On the heels of the award of E&P license by the Lebanese government, US Assistant Secretary of State for Near Eastern Affairs David Satterfield shuttled between the two countries in February 2018, to mediate on the maritime boundary dispute, which took on increased importance because of anticipated discovery of oil and gas deposits. Satterfield failed, too, because following his meetings with Lebanese officials, parliamentary Speaker Nabih Berri announced the rejection of a dispute resolution proposal endorsed by the United States.

The US proposal was the revival of the Hof's scheme that had been rejected by Lebanon: In 2012, Frederic Hof, then a diplomat with the US State Department and an expert on the borders in the Middle East, the proposed a line that would give Lebanon about two-thirds of a disputed maritime area in the Mediterranean and Israel one-third. Lebanese officials assert that the zone in its entirety belongs to Beirut.[168]

While Israel insists the entire area lies solidly within its economic waters. Reports emanating from Israel quoted energy minister Steinitz as communicating to Satterfield that both sides preferred a diplomatic solution, indicating perhaps a thaw.[169] Yet, if oil and gas deposits are indeed found in the three blocks protruding into the disputed maritime area, the current low level discord could rapidly degenerate into open hostility between the two neighbours. it is important to note that Israel and Lebanon have exchanged threats and condemnations over the Lebanese oil and gas licensing. Lebanon's foreign minister Gebran Bassil even called the approval of oil and gas exploration licenses an act of "economic resistance" against Israel.[170] It goes on to show how tenuous the situation is and that underlines the urgent need for an agreement. Without a peaceful and calm sea, the cost of developing the resources would mount significantly. The trend is evident in Israel's case, where expenses relating to defence of offshore energy infrastructure has soared over the last decade; in addition, the IOCs have shown little interest in investment in Israel's offshore exploration.

Lebanon, a country that depends heavily on energy imports, hopes to find oil or gas, or both, for the requirements of the domestic market and export. Imported fuels account for 95 percent of Lebanon's energy consumption, with the total aggregate expense adding up to $5.11 billion, or 11.4 percent of GDP in 2013. The focus of the country ought to be to reduce its dependence on energy imports and improve the efficiency of its energy utilisation. As far as export is concerned, high capital cost of new infrastructure development and relatively low global prices of oil and gas would diminish the commercial competitiveness of the prospective Lebanese reserves, unless the economies of scale take effect: Either Lebanon discovers huge quantities of hydrocarbon reserves or is able to pool its resources with other regional players for export.

Demand for natural gas is expected to increase, especially in Asia, and the markets will be able to absorb additional supplies, while competition will be tougher for suppliers as new producers join the club. Lebanon would have an obvious advantage as compared to Israel in terms of supplying to the regional countries. There are discussions on reversing the flow of Arab gas pipeline or supply to Jordan. Export of gas to Turkey, which is a closer and an easily accessible destination, is a strong possibility.

Above all, regional turmoil and slower rates of gas sales may discourage IOCs to invest hundreds of millions in the future licensing rounds in Lebanese economic waters. In addition, continued conflict with Israel may inhibit Lebanon's participation in regional gas infrastructural projects in which Israel is increasingly becoming an essential member. Israel is stridently pursuing several pipeline export options to Egypt, Cyprus, Turkey, and Europe. If these prospects materialise by the time gas from Lebanese fields come on-stream, Lebanon will find it difficult to manoeuvre multilateral frameworks supporting them. Given the scenario of hostility, the parties will find it extremely difficult to break the political stalemate so as to resolve their differences. Indeed, Antoine Dagher believes,

> the 'only way' for Israel to sell gas to Europe is to sign peace agreements with Lebanon and Syria towards which there should be genuine efforts. Israel

cannot sell in European markets without cooperating with all the gas-possessing countries of the region, given the limited size of their supply. The resolution of Israel's geopolitical problems would give the necessary push to Israel's desire to sell gas: Peace is required to sell gas and not the other way around.[171]

Equation with the Palestinians

Israel and the Palestinians discovered gas almost simultaneously in 1999. Around the time of the discovery of the Gaza Marine field, Israel too discovered its Yam Tethys' Mari–B field, located at the maritime border with the Gaza Strip. Gaza Marine gas field (Figure 4.11) has long been seen as a golden opportunity that could help the Palestinians solve their electricity crisis. However, despite persistent efforts by the investors, several disputes have prevented its development. In the initial years, Israel put restrictions on the development of the field, as it sought commercially favourable terms for purchase of gas in return for the transfer of revenues to the Palestinian Authority.

With the outbreak of the second Intifada in September 2000, there was a complete breakdown of mutual trust between Israel and the Palestinians, that had been built over the implementation of the Oslo Accord. The Likud-led government that came to power in Israel in 2001, vetoed any purchase of Palestinian gas, believing that anti-Israeli fighters could benefit from the sale of gas from the offshore Gaza field. The IEC then moved on to sign a gas import deal with EMG. Still, interest in the Gaza Marine remained, and Israel now sought to purchase the gas at a price below the market rate. In conjunction, Israel refused to grant security clearance to Gaza Marine's operator BG Group to conclude export contracts.[172] Once Hamas took control of the Gaza Strip following Fatah's ouster in June 2007,

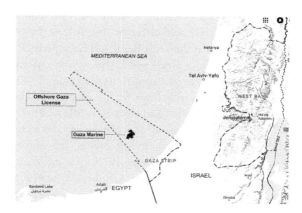

FIGURE 4.11   The Gaza Marine gas field

Source: Author

Disclaimer: Map not to scale

Israel's 'security concerns' argument received a new lease of life.[173] Israel procrastinated on signing a gas purchase contract with BG and as the blockade of the Strip took shape, it effectively stalled the Palestinian gas development project. The refusal of Israel and much of the international community to engage with Hamas forced Gaza Marine field developers to not put forth any further efforts. Kattan argues, until 2009, Israel viewed the gas the Gaza Strip an essential component of its energy security since the Yam Tethys reservoirs were nearing depletion. Moreover, as Lior Herman believes, "Gaza Marine was too small to be an export source and too big for sole Palestinian consumption, so the natural consumer was Israel."[174]

When Israel discovered large quantities of gas in Tamar and Leviathan in 2009, it no longer coveted the gas from the Gaza fields. The opposition to the development of Palestinian gas was then linked to conditions of the blockade.[175] PM Netanyahu reportedly agreed to discuss the development of the Gaza Marine gas field with PA in 2012,[176] and assured the Quartet[177] of his intention to allow the Palestinians to develop their gas field as part of a broader strategy to stabilise the Gaza Strip. However, nothing moved forward on the development of the Gaza Marine. On the contrary, the blockade of the Gaza Strip perpetuated a near total dependence of the Palestinians on Israel for their energy requirements. It is well known that "almost all petroleum products and most of the electricity [used by the Palestinians] are imported from Israel and the possibility of diversifying the energy imports from other countries is currently limited."[178] As a result, the West Bank and Gaza Strip are almost completely integrated within Israel's electricity grid; around 88 percent of total consumption is supplied by IEC, with the West Bank importing all the electricity from Israel. Considering that Palestinians have not been able to access and develop their natural resources since almost twenty years, a situation of complete dependency on Israel endures and continues to be a thorny subject between the two sides.[179]

Although small in size, Gaza Marine is more than sufficient to make the Palestinian energy sector entirely self-sufficient for at least 15 years at current Palestinian consumption levels in the West Bank and Gaza Strip. Palestinians will not have to import electricity from Israel and Egypt, saving crucial revenues, and will aslo be able to solve Gaza's chronic electricity shortages.[180] The PA's control over fuel purchases and transfers into Gaza for production of electricity[181] and "Israel's control over the supply of fuel and electricity allows it to restrict, reduce or halt the supply"[182] as 'weapon' against Hamas have created a chronic humanitarian crisis in the beleaguered strip, amongst others, the enforced closure of medical services and cessation of sewage disposal. "Linking Gaza Marine's development to security is fallacious," says Omar Kittaneh, "because the funds generated would have been monitored by the World Bank and other international agencies. As long as Israel is dealt as a country above international law, there can be no solution to Gaza's crisis."[183]

While there is no doubt that the development of the Gaza Marine will allow energy independence to the Palestinians and generate revenues for their fiscal sustainability, as long a Hamas controls the Gaza Strip, Israel will continue to reinforce the decade-long blockade and thwart the development of the gas fields. To maintain the security of its sovereign territory, Israel will not stop short of total control of the Strip to reign Hamas. "The siege on Gaza might not be only a punishment on Hamas, but a way to solidify its control over Gaza as well. It is easier to control a closed territory than an open one, where people can move in and out," say two World Bank studies authored by a group of Palestinian and Israeli economists.[184] "Israel often fights against Hamas, but also negotiates with Hamas through Egypt, and thus accepts its control over Gaza"[185] that gives rise to confusion, much as it raises hope of Gaza's offshore gas development.

To establish independent power generation capacity has been an important goal of PA and Israel is not averse to it. In April 2016, Israel notionally approved the construction of the first Palestinian power station of 450 MW capacity in the West Bank city of Jenin.[186] Whereas, in the long run, the Jenin power plant is expected to run on gas from the Gaza Marine fields, in early 2014, the Palestine Power Generation Company (established in 2010) signed an MoU with Leviathan leaseholders to buy 4.75 bcm of gas over 20 years, which they later terminated citing delay in the development of the Leviathan.[187] There are two ways in which Gaza Marine gas field can supply to the Palestinian territories: through an electricity swap with Israel (selling gas to Israel in exchange for electricity), proposes initially by the British Gas Group and/or through Israel's underwater pipeline infrastructure that can bring the extracted gas onshore. Both options face the challenge of the lack of trust between the parties, as also several political and economic obstacles, not the least opposition by the Palestinian wing of the boycott, disinvestment and sanctions (BDS) movement.

The Boycott National Committee (BNC) argues that any Palestinian cooperation with Israel on the gas issue will further entrench the occupation. "Whatever might be the nature of Palestinian-Israeli relations in future," says Uzi Landau, "in the existing circumstances, the Marine-Ashkelon-Gaza/West Bank route, offers the best possible way to move Palestinian gas from Israel's Ashkelon natural gas terminal) to supply to the Palestinian territories. Gas can become a strategic tool for stability in the Gaza Strip, providing energy for critical activities such as desalination and sewage treatment."[188]

Royal Dutch Shell took over the ownership of Gaza Marine gas field following its acquisition in 2016 of the BG Group. Given the internal Palestinian political disputes and conflict with Israel and recurrent delays in the development of the field, Shell had been struggling to find a buyer for its 55 percent stake in the field. However, in April 2018, it reached an agreement with the PIF to divest its share. Under a new structure agreed with the PA, the PIF and its investment partner, CCC Oil and Gas Ltd., would hold 27.5 percent of development rights each, and a future foreign operator would hold rest of the 45 percent.[189] The two partners effort to identify an international operator for the field brings into spotlight the political dimensions of Gaza Marine's development.[190] Can Palestinians develop the field in the context of the blockade of the Gaza Strip and the intensification of the BDS movement? Some argue that if Gazans were to cooperate with Israel in the economic arena, it would pave the way for the resolution of outstanding political issues. Equally, others argue that Israel has used the relative prosperity of the West Bank to perpetuate the occupation. The not so infrequent violent eruptions in both the West Bank and Gaza support the argument that political solution to the Palestinian–Israeli conflict must precede the economic development of the Palestinian territories. The conflict with the Palestinians poses a pervasive threat to Israel's own gas assets by creating a perpetual sense of insecurity along its borders.

Looking ahead

Israel is pursuing a multilateral arrangement to export its gas based on the notion of 'associational power sharing,' implying compliance to rules of the trade will go on to generate a beneficial outcome for all the actors involved. Natural gas discoveries present an opportunity for Israel to forge strong relationships that did not exist before, involving not just with the Arab neighbours but also Cyprus, Greece, Turkey, Europe.

Israel does not have pipeline connections to big consumers, such as, Turkey or Europe, nor the liquefaction facilities to export gas as LNG. Therefore, Egypt has emerged as the most important pillar of Israel's gas export strategy. Egypt is geographically close to facilitate easy movement of gas from Israeli shores or fields either to its domestic market or for re-export through its liquefaction terminals. However, the Egyptian option is not without its imponderables. The first question to ask is, what are the options for Israel if the forecasted shortfall of gas in the Egyptian market turns out to be exaggerated with the disovery of more gas in Egypt? There are indeed reports citing the discovery of massive reservoirs (about three times the size of Zohr) in the Noor gas field in North Sinai and the likelihood of finding new deposits in the western desert.[191] Egypt, in that case, may not be amenable to concluding any further gas deals with Israel, either for domestic consumption or for the liquefaction facilities.

Moreover, "given that the commercial basis of the current deal (between Noble-Delek and Dolphinus) is unknown, it is unclear from which Egypt would profit more: exporting its own gas or re-exporting Israeli gas."[192]

Investigative reports reveal that gas produced locally costs less than half of the cost of importing gas from Israel; its further export to Europe then becomes even less cost effective.[193] Any future gas deals with Israeli field developers is bound to raise heckles in Egypt, for commercial considerations of price and transport, as well as political consideration of people's repugnance to deeper engagement with Israel. That said, the Egyptian authoritarian regime is not constrained by democratic pressures of accountability or transparency, and it remains beholden to Israel for security in the Sinai. In fact, to compensate UFG for the losses resulting from cessation of gas for export in 2014, the Egyptian government might permit Damietta's operator to import gas from Israel's fields.[194] In Israel's dealings with Egypt, political and economic factors are invariably intertwined.

For Israel, the most profitable export route is transport gas via a pipeline to Turkey – an energy import-dependent market that strategises diversification of sources of supply and serves as a transit oveland route for oil and gas supply to Europe – but the option is riddled with geopolitical difficulties. The export from Israeli gas fields to Turkey is far more complicated than export to Egypt because of two political problems: first, the Israeli–Turkish relations remain uneasy; and second, a pipeline cannot be built without the political Cyprus the Cyrpus issue. Despite the normalisation agreement signed in June 2016 after six years of deteriorating relations, Turkish–Israeli bilateral relations slid downhill with greater intensity through 2017–2018 on the heels of the violent events at the Al-Aqsa mosque and in the Gaza Strip. Erdoğan's reelection in June 2018 and expansion of his powers intensifies the difficulties of Israel–Turkey engagement. As far as the Cyprus issue is concerned, it is still an open question whether negotiations will ever succeed, because the underlying issues are complex and acrimonious. The parties to the Cyprus conflict have used "natural gas as a political bargaining chip, and presumably an agreement for laying the pipeline will require a broad resolution of all the drilling and exploration rights around Cyprus,"[195] which could infinitely delay the process of moving forward with the project.

All may not be lost for Israel, however, because in the quicksand of Middle Eastern politics, things rarely turn out as expected. The Egyptian–Israeli gas deal, publicized by President's Sisi's as an evidence of his desire to make Egypt a gas hub, clashes with Turkey's similar long-standing aspiration. That clash might push the Turks to sign a deal making sure that the majority of gas from the Leviathan's second phase goes to Turkey. "Erdoğan has had a volatile relationship with Israel over the years, but he wants to supplant Egypt as the leader of the Sunni Muslim world. Furthermore, Turkey – unlike Egypt – could really use Israeli gas imports."[196] The Turkish economy's demand for imported natural gas is projected to grow significantly in the coming years, from 51.7 bcm in 2017 to 75 bcm in 2025 and 81 bcm in 2030.[197] With this rapid growth projection, the government faces the onerous tasks of ensuring Turkey's energy security, meeting demand in the medium and long term and ensuring that no episodes of shortages occur in the next decade. In 2017, Russian supplied half of this quantity, i.e., 51.8 percent, followed by Iran at 9.2 percent and Azerbaijan at 6.5 percent.[198] The rest of the supplies came from Algeria, Nigeria, Qatar, and spot LNG purchases.[199]

While the existing combination of suppliers to Turkey is expected to remain through 2025, shortages might occur during the 2020s, as BOTAŞ's (Turkey's state-owned Petroleum Pipeline Corporation) long-term contracts with its suppliers of gas begin to expire: Azerbaijan in 2021, Iran in 2026, and Russia in 2025 creating a shortfall of 36 bcm per year.[200] Natural gas exporters such as Iraq (in the form of LNG), Turkmenistan (in case the trans-Caspian pipeline is built), and perhaps Israel might also be able to compete for a share in the Turkish market. It is estimated that Israel is capable of supplying Turkey with between 5 and 10 bcm of gas per year.[201]

The Jordanians and Palestinians are in a different category. Even as Jordan is small buyer and not a major market, it is the most important country for Israel in the entire region. Jordan shares the longest border with Israel and its stability is important for Israel's long-term interests. Since the beginning of the Arab uprisings in 2011, Jordanians have had to navigate the difficulties of hosting a vast influx of Syrian refugees on their soil and providing for their welfare. In the same year, Jordan lost 2 percent of the GNP because of the collapse of gas supply system from Egypt and faced an energy crisis. In the backdrop of economic instability, King Abdullah was able to overcome political opposition to conclude gas imports deals with Israel, citing the need for additional supply – other than FLNG import from Qatar and recommenced import from Egypt – to safeguard the country's energy security. However, political opposition to economic engagement with Israel has been strong in Jordan, particularly since the beginning of weekly Gaza protests in March 2018 against the blockade of the strip. The Hashemite regime, through in close cooperation with Israel on security matters, is more responsive to the people's will because of the presence of a large number of Palestinians in Jordan: It implies that, additional deals with Jordanian entities may not be easy in the near term.

The development of Palestinian Gas off the coast of Gaza is contingent upon the resolution of the Palestinian-Israeli conflict. Gaza Marine, though sufficient for the consumption of the Palestinian population of the West Bank and Gaza Strip for several years, is a small deposit that just not justify the construction of infrastructure related to transmission of the gas. The most natural course would be a gas and electricity swap between the Palestinians and Israel. An alternative could be the utilisation of Israel's pipelines to transmit gas to the Palestinian power plants. A combination of the two supply methods can also be evaluated.

The EastMed pipeline will be economically viable only if it is trilaterally envisaged, transporting gas not only from Israel and Cyprus, but also from Egypt, which will be conceivably the largest contributor. The Egyptian gas situation is in flux, facing local demand pressures and the need to keep up with the operation of the liquefaction facilities. Its recent gas self-sufficiency does not sit well with the idea of the construction of a grandiose pipeline that would burden its economy with an export allocation load, when an alternative in the form of LNG export is already available.

An immediate task for Israel is to resolve the outstanding maritime conflict with Lebanon, which would go a long way in improving the investment climate in its economic waters. Lebanon has already issued the E&P concessions for blocks 8 and 9 that stick out into an area of water claimed by the two antagonists. Albeit the operators of the blocks have no plans to drill in the disputed part, contesting claims over the maritime territory, is potentially a flare-up point between the two countries, if oil and gas are discovered in these blocks. The US officials have reportedly put forward new ideas to resolve the dispute during the backchannel mediation[202] and that raises the possibility of a resolution.

From the above, it appears that, despite the existence of demand in the region and trans-regional markets, Israel's export plans are contingent upon a number of factors that impinge on one another. An appreciation of the peculiarities of Israel's situation was one of the several reasons why the debate on the export of gas was so furious in the country. The critics of export vociferously argued for gas to be kept for local use – even buried and not subject to a hurried extraction strategy – believing that it is tactically more beneficial to hold rather than export. Its incremental internal use will assure energy security over several generations ensures intergenerational energy security from an indigenous source, especially as Israel's relations with its neighbours continue to be inconsistent, even after peace deals and gas contracts.

Notes

1　William Blaine Richardson III is an American politician, author, and diplomat who served as the 30th Governor of New Mexico from 2003 to 2011.
2　Keith Johnson, "For Israel and Its Neighbors, Energy Finds Power Big Dreams," *Foreign Policy*, December 11, 2015, https://foreignpolicy.com/2015/12/11/for-israel-and-its-neighbors-energy-finds-power-big-dreams-zohr-leviathan/ (accessed on January 5, 2018).
3　Author's interview with Ambassador Ron Adams, Special Envoy on Energy, Ministry of Foreign Affairs, State of Israel, Jerusalem, January 11, 2016.
4　Author's interview with Professor Oren Barak, Professor of Political Science and International Relations, Hebrew University of Jerusalem, January 12, 2016, Jerusalem, Israel.
5　The three conduits of the SGC, the Azerbaijan-Turkey Trans-Anatolian Gas Pipeline (TANAP), South Caucasus Pipeline (SCP), and Trans Adriatic Pipeline (TAP), when operational would bolster the security and diversity of the EU's energy supply. At present, the primary supply source for the SGC is the Shah Deniz gas field (Phase 2), located in the Azerbaijani sector of the Caspian Sea; the proposed trans-Caspian gas pipeline would bring gas from Turkmenistan. The SCP through Azerbaijan and Georgia is functional and TANAP through Turkey will become operational in 2020. TANAP will link up with the planned TAP, starting at the Greece-Turkey border at Kipoi/Ipsala via Albania and the Adriatic Sea to Italy and further to Western Europe. See Leman Zeynalova, "Israeli Gas Supply to Europe Part of SGC Concept," *Trend News Agency*, July 14, 2017, https://en.trend.az/business/energy/2777256.html (accessed on January 5, 2018); Sara Israfilbayova, "Expert: Southern Gas Corridor Efficient Route for Israeli Gas Export," *Azernews*, August 30, 2017, www.azernews.az/oil_and_gas/118329.html (accessed on January 5, 2018); "Southern Gas Corridor," *Trans Adriatic Pipeline*, www.tap-ag.com/the-pipeline/the-big-picture/southern-gas-corridor (accessed on January 5, 2018).
6　Author's interview with Mr Cenk Pala, Government Relations Coordinator, Turk-Stream, Ankara, June 7, 2017.
7　Keren Setton, "Can Israel Leverage Its Newly Found Gas Reserves?" *Xinhua*, January 12, 2018, www.xinhuanet.com/english/2018-01/12/c_136889167.htm (accessed on August 19, 2018).
8　Moign Khawaja, "Jordan King Demands Peace in Syria as Country Suffers From Record Trade Deficit," Arabian Gazette, June 20, 2012, https://arabiangazette.com/jordan-king-calls-syria-peace-amid-growing-trade-deficit/ (accessed on January 6, 2018).
9　"Jordan Says Hosting Syrian Refugees Has Cost $10 Billion," *Arab News*, October 10, 2017, www.arabnews.com/node/1175541/middle-east (accessed on January 6, 2018).
10　Avi Shlaim, *Collusion Across the Jordan: King Abdullah, the Zionist Movement, and the Partition of Palestine* (New York: Columbia University Press, 1988); Zeev Maoz, *Defending the Holy Land: A Critical Analysis of Israel's Security and Foreign Policy* (Ann Arbor: University of Michigan Press, 2009), pp. 395–398.
11　"Israel-Jordan Peace Treaty," in Spencer C. Tucker (ed.), *The Encyclopaedia of the Arab-Israeli Conflict: A Political, Social, and Military History* (Santa Barbara: ABC-CLIO, Inc.), p. 514.
12　Norrin M. Ripsman, "Top Down Peacemaking: Why Peace Begins With States Not Societies," in T. V. Paul (ed.), *International Relations Theory and Regional Transformation* (Cambridge: Cambridge University Press, 2012), p. 267.

13 King Hussein's warning went unheeded, as senior military officers from the Israeli military intelligence believed that the warning from King Hussein was "not unequivocal." See Mitch Ginsburg, "Account of King Hussein's 1973 War Warning Still Deemed Too Harmful to Release," *The Times of Israel*, September 12, 2017, www.timesofisrael.com/account-of-king-husseins-1973-war-warning-still-deemed-too-harmful-to-release (accessed on January 6, 2018).

14 See Hemda Ben-Yehuda and Shmuel Sandler, *Arab-Israeli Conflict Transformed, The: Fifty Years of Interstate and Ethnic Crises* (Albany: State university of New York Press, 2002) p. 110.

15 Yehuda Lukacs, *Israel, Jordan, and the Peace Process* (New York: Syracuse University Press, 1997), pp. 181–182.

16 Ripsman, "Top Down Peacemaking," 2012, p. 268.

17 Lukcas, 1997, *Israel, Jordan, and the Peace Process*, p. 181; Ben Soetendorp, *The Dynamics of Israeli-Palestinian Relations: Theory, History, and Cases* (New York: Palgrave Macmillan, 2007), p. 45.

18 Soetendorp, *The Dynamics of Israeli-Palestinian Relations: Theory, History, and Cases*, 2007, p. 44.

19 Efraim Inbar, *Israel's National Security: Issues and Challenges Since the Yom Kippur War* (London: Routledge, 2008), p. 75.

20 Cathy Hartley and Paul Cossali, *A Survey of Arab-Israeli Relations*, 2nd edition (London and New York: Europa Publications, Taylor and Francis, 2004), p. 190.

21 Jonah Naghi, "The Value of Security Cooperation With Jordan," *Matzav*, February 22, 2017, www.matzavblog.com/2017/02/value-security-cooperation-jordan/ (accessed on January 9, 2018).

22 Itamar Rabinovich, *Israel and the Changing Middle East*, Middle East Memo, Number 34, January 2015, Brookings Institution, p. 6, www.brookings.edu/wp-content/uploads/2016/06/Israel-Rabinovich-01292015-1.pdf (accessed on January 9, 2018).

23 Author's interview with Haviv Rettig Gur, senior analyst at *The Times of Israel*, Jerusalem, January 4, 2016.

24 Teresa Welsh, "Israel and Jordan: The Middle East's Odd Couple," *US News*, November 14, 2014, www.usnews.com/news/articles/2014/11/14/israel-and-jordan-the-middle-easts-odd-couple (accessed on January 9, 2018).

25 *Political Instability in Jordan*, Contingency Planning Memorandum No. 19, Council on Foreign Relations, May 15, 2013, www.cfr.org/report/political-instability-jordan (accessed on January 9, 2018).

26 Natanel Abramov, "Israel's Plan to Supply the Arab World with Energy is Under Threat in Jordan," *Newsweek*, October 11, 2016, www.newsweek.com/israel-jordan-energy-supply-arab-world-ties-zionist-508955 (accessed on January 11, 2018).

27 Nur Koprulu, "Interplay of Palestinian and Jordanian Identities," in Kenneth Christie and Mohammad Masad (eds.), *State Formation and Identity in the Middle East and North Africa* (New York: Palgrave Macmillan, 2013), p. 81; Sean L Yom, "The New Landscape of Jordanian Politics: Social Opposition, Fiscal Crisis, and the Arab Spring," *British Journal of Middle Eastern Studies*, Volume 42, Issue 3 (2014), pp. 296, 298–299.

28 Kirk H. Sowell, "Jordan is Sliding Toward Insolvency," *Carnegie Endowment for International Peace*, March 17, 2016, http://carnegieendowment.org/sada/63061 (accessed on January 11, 2018).

29 David Schenker, "The Growing Islamic State Threat in Jordan," January 10, 2017, The Washington Institute for Near East Policy, www.washingtoninstitute.org/policy-analysis/view/the-growing-islamic-state-threat-in-jordan (accessed on January 11, 2018).

30 See Robert Satloff and David Schenker, *Growing Stress on Jordan*, March 10, 2016, Council on Foreign Relations, Center for Preventive Action, www.cfr.org/report/growing-stress-jordan (accessed on January 12, 2018).

31 See Sarah A. Tobin, "Jordan's Arab Spring: The Middle Class and Anti-Revolution," *Middle East Policy*, Volume XIX, Issue 1 (Spring 2012), www.mepc.org/jordans-arab-spring-middle-class-and-anti-revolution (accessed on January 12, 2018).

32 Ripsman, "Top Down Peacemaking," 2012, p. 268.

33 Brenda Shaffer, "Israel-Jordan Gas Trade Portends Brighter Future in Middle East," *The Hill*, March 7, 2017, http://thehill.com/blogs/pundits-blog/energy-environment/322703-israel-jordan-gas-trade-portends-bright-future-in (accessed on January 12, 2018).

34 "NEPCO and Israeli-American Noble Energy Gas Company Sign Agreement," *Al-Ghad* [Arabic], September 26, 2016, http://english.alghad.com/articles/1150842-NEPCo-and-Israeli-American-Noble-Energy-Gas-Company-Sign-Agreement (accessed on January 15, 2018).

35 Ashok Swain and Anders Jägerskog, *Emerging Security Threats in the Middle East: The Impact of Climate Change and Globalisation* (Lanham: Rowman and Littlefield, 2016), p. 107; *Signing of an Agreement for Export of Natural Gas From the Leviathan Project to the National Electric Power Company of Jordan*, Delek Group, September 26, 2016; "Noble Energy Will Supply Leviathan Gas (Israel) to NEEPCO (Jordan)," *Enerdata*, September 27, 2016, www.enerdata.net/publications/daily-energy-news/noble-energy-will-supply-leviathan-gas-israel-neepco-jordan.html (accessed on January 15, 2018).

36 *Acquisition Law No. 12 of 1987 and Its Amendments* [Arabic], www.fuqahalaw.com; *Acquisition Law and Its Amendments No. 6 of 1980* [Arabic], *Qistas*, www.qistas.com/legislations/jor/view/81254 (accessed on January 18, 2018).

37 "Landowners Waiting for Next Step in Jordan-Israel Gas Pipeline," *Al-Monitor*, March 29, 2018, www.al-monitor.com/pulse/originals/2018/03/jordan-israel-gas-deal-import-pipeline-expropriation-lands.html (accessed on August 19, 2018).

38 Raed Omari, "Lands for Israel Gas Pipeline Acquired," *The Jordan Times*, March 8, 2018, www.jordantimes.com/news/local/lands-israel-gas-pipeline-acquired%E2%80%99 (accessed on August 19, 2018).

39 "The Government Decides to Acquire and Lease Land for Citizens in Irbid and Mafraq to Extend the Gas Line With Israel," *Saraya News* [Arabic], February 20, 2018, www.sarayanews.com/article/474065 (accessed on August 19, 2018); Mohammad Tayseer and Yaacov Benmeleh, "Jordan Pipeline for Israeli Gas Set for Completion by End of 2019," *World Oil*, July 4, 2018, www.worldoil.com/news/2018/7/4/jordan-pipeline-for-israeli-gas-set-for-completion-by-end-of-2019 (accessed on August 19, 2018); Oded Eran, Elai Rettig, and Ofir Winter, *The Gas Deal With Egypt: Israel Deepens its Anchor in the Eastern Mediterranean*, INSS Insight No. 1033, March 12, 2018, www.inss.org.il/publication/gas-deal-egypt-israel-deepens-anchor-eastern-mediterranean/ (accessed on August 19, 2018).

40 "Jordan Agrees Gas Purchase Deal With Israel," *The Economist Intelligence Unit*, September 29, 2017, http://country.eiu.com/article.aspx?articleid=1894657373 (accessed on January 18, 2018).

41 See Hedy Cohen, "Israel-Jordan Gas Pipeline to Begin Operating in 2017," *Globes*, March 10, 2016, www.globes.co.il/en/article-israel-jordan-gas-pipeline-to-begin-operating-in-2017-1001109296 (accessed on January 21, 2018); "Israel Approves Pipeline Construction for Exporting Natural Gas to Jordan," *Port2Port*, September 24, 2105, www.port2port.com/article/Industry-Trade/Infrastructure/Israel-approves-pipeline-construction-for-exporting-natural-gas-to-Jordan/ (accessed on January 21, 2018).

42 Eran Ezran, "Israel Quietly Begins Exporting Natural Gas to Jordan Amid Political Sensitivities," *Haaretz*, March 2, 2017, www.haaretz.com/israel-news/business/israel-quietly-begins-exporting-gas-to-jordan-1.5443894 (accessed on January 22, 2018).

43 Beverley Milton-Edwards, "Protests in Jordan Over Gas Deal With Israel Expose Wider Rifts," Brookings, October 26, 2016, www.brookings.edu/blog/markaz/2016/10/26/protests-in-jordan-over-gas-deal-with-israel-expose-wider-rifts/ (accessed on January 22, 2018); Oded Eran, "How Would the New Gas Deal Affect Israel-Jordan Relations?" *Israel Defense*, December 4, 2016, www.israeldefense.co.il/en/node/27785 (accessed on January 22, 2018).

44 Zena Tahhan, "Jordanians Reject 'Stolen Gas' in Israel-Jordan Deal," *Al Jazeera*, October 6, 2016, www.aljazeera.com/news/2016/10/jordanians-reject-stolen-gas-israel-

jordan-deal-161002131442112.html (accessed on January 22, 2018); Donna Abu-Nasr, "Unwanted: The $10 Billion Gas Deal With Israel That Jordan Needs," *Bloomberg*, October 27, 2016, www.bloomberg.com/news/articles/2016-10-26/unwanted-the-10-billion-gas-deal-with-israel-that-jordan-needs (accessed on January 22, 2018).

45 "Jordan Allocates Initial $2 Million for Joint Pipeline Project With Israel," *Middle East Monitor*, January 2, 2018, www.middleeastmonitor.com/20180102-jordan-allocates-initial-2-million-for-joint-pipeline-project-with-israel/ (accessed on January 27, 2018).

46 Author's interview with a Jordanian official in New Delhi, April 17, 2018.

47 According to Amman-based Al-Ghad newspaper on Sunday, the cost of the joint Jordanian-Israeli project is expected to rise to 3 million dinars ($4.2 million) in 2019, and to 6 million dinars ($8.5 million) by 2020. www.middleeastmonitor.com/20180102-jordan-allocates-initial-2-million-for-joint-pipeline-project-with-israel/ (accessed on August 21, 2018).

48 Zaid Al-Dabisiyyeh, "Jordan's Gas Deal With Israel Hangs in the Balance," *The New Arab*, December 11, 2014, www.alaraby.co.uk/english/news/2014/12/12/jordans-gas-deal-with-israel-hangs-in-the-balance (accessed on January 27, 2018).

49 Gas from the region would be cheaper than LNG because there are no liquefaction and regasification costs. Andrea Gamba, *New Energy Sources for Jordan: Macroeconomic Impact and Policy Considerations*, IMF Working Paper 15/115, IMF, May 2015, p. 8.

50 See Sharon Udasin, "Israel to Supply Gas to Jordan in $10 Billion Deal," *Jerusalem Post*, September 26, 2016, www.jpost.com/business-and-innovation/environment/israels-leviathan-reservoir-to-supply-gas-to-jordan-468742 (accessed on January 27, 2018).

51 Rory Jones, "Investors in Israeli Natural Gas Agree to Supply Deal With Jordan," *The Wall Street Journal*, September 26, 2016, www.wsj.com/articles/investors-in-israeli-natural-gas-agree-supply-deal-with-jordan-1474903108 (accessed on January 28, 2018).

52 Simon Henderson, *Jordan's Energy Supply Options the Prospect of Gas Imports From Israel*, Foreign and Security Policy Paper Series, The German Marshall Fund of the United States, October 2015, pp. 2, 8.

53 Evan Gottesman, "Netanyahu's Dangerous Jordanian Fantasy," *Matzav*, October 27, 2017, www.matzavblog.com/2017/10/netanyahus-dangerous-jordanian-fantasy/ (accessed on January 28, 2018).

54 Neri Zilber, "Israel's Secret Arab Allies," *The New York Times*, July 14, 2017, www.nytimes.com/2017/07/14/opinion/israels-secret-arab-allies.html (accessed on January 31, 2018); Amos Harel, "Israel and Jordan Grow Closer as Iranian Foothold in Southern Syria Grows Stronger," *Haaretz*, June 21, 2017; "Israel Gives Jordan Helicopters for Border Security," *Reuters*, July 23, 2015, www.reuters.com/article/mideast-crisis-israel-jordan-idUSL8N0ZO15120150723 (accessed on January 31, 2018).

55 Author's interview with Ambassador Alon Leil, former Director General, Ministry of Foreign Affairs, Israeli Chargé d'Affaires in Ankara, and Israeli Ambassador to South Africa, Jerusalem, Israel, January 11, 2016.

56 Adel Abdel Ghafar, "Egypt's New Gas Discovery: Opportunities and Challenges," *The Brookings Institution* (Washington, DC), September 10, 2015, www.brookings.edu/opinions/egypts-new-gas-discovery-opportunities-and-challenges/ (accessed on January 31, 2018); M. Cherif Bassiouni, *Chronicles of the Egyptian Revolution and its Aftermath: 2011–2016* (New York: Sheridan Books and Cambridge University Press, 2017), p. 517.

57 Nikos Tsafos, *Egypt: A Market for Natural Gas From Cyprus and Israel?* Foreign and Security Policy Paper Series 2015, The German Marshall Fund of the United States, Washington, DC, October 2015, p. 2.

58 Ibid.

59 Ghafar, "Egypt's New Gas Discovery: Opportunities and Challenges," September 10, 2015.

60 Antonia Dimou, "Israel and Cyprus: In Search of Solutions to Natural Gas Challenges in the Eastern Mediterranean," *Foreign Policy News*, October 10, 2016, http://foreignpolicynews.org/2016/10/10/israel-cyprus-search-solutions-natural-gas-challenges-eastern-mediterranean/ (accessed on February 3, 2018).

61 The Leviathan developers announced at the end of June 2014 that they had signed a non-binding Letter of Intent (LoI) with UK's BG Group for the sale of 7 bcm of gas per year to be transported from the field by undersea pipeline to the Idku LNG plant, east of Alexandria. BG was the majority shareholder in ELNG, the operator of Idku, at that time. The plant was barely operating, as most of the gas that BG produced in Egypt was diverted to the local market to make up for a chronic supply shortfall. The imports from Leviathan were sufficient to enable the two trains of ELNG to operate near their full capacity of about 9.6 bcm per year. Leviathan was then slated for production in 2017. Likewise, in May 2014, Noble Energy-Delek partners signed a LoI with UFG to export 70 bcm of natural gas from Tamar field to SEGAS liquefaction facility for 15 years. However, the agreement with UFG was scrapped in March 2018, according to public filings by Delek Drilling, one of Tamar's partners, on the Tel Aviv Stock Exchange. "Will Israeli Natural Gas Flow in Egypt's Pipelines?" *Energy Egypt*, July 15, 2016, https://energyegypt.net/2016/07/15/will-israeli-natural-gas-flow-in-egypts-pipelines/ (accessed on February 3, 2018); "BG to Discuss Exporting Israeli Gas via Idku LNG," *The Economist Intelligence Unit*, July 2, 2014, http://country.eiu.com/article.aspx?articleid=1861978970 (accessed on February 3, 2018); *BP Statistical Review of World Energy*, 2014; Mohamed Samir, "Will Israeli Natural Gas Flow in Egypt's Pipelines?" July 14, 2016, https://dailynewsegypt.com/2016/07/14/will-israeli-natural-gas-flow-in-egypts-pipelines/ (accessed on February 3, 2018); *Delek Group Announces Consolidated Full Year & Fourth Quarter 2017 Results*, March 28, 2018, www.bloomberg.com/press-releases/2018-03-28/delek-group-announces-consolidated-full-year-fourth-quarter-2017-results (accessed on August 22, 2018).

62 Situated approximately 50 km east of Alexandria, the ELNG's two LNG trains have the capacity of 3.6 mt each per year. ELNG is a joint venture comprising of the two state-owned companies, EGPC and EGAS, as well as the Shell Group plc, PETRONAS, and Engie (Gaz de Suez). UFG operates the SEGAS LNG complex, located 60 km west of Port Said, in conjunction with EGAS (10 percent) and EGPC (10 percent). Union Fenosa of Spain and Eni own the UFG (80 percent) in a 50/50 partnership. The output capacity of the plant is 5 mt of LNG per year. Both the LNG terminals became operational in 2005. See "Our Shareholders," *Egyptian LNG*, www.egyptianlng.com/Pages/About/OurShareholders.aspx (accessed on February 4, 2018); "Egyptian LNG," PETRONAS, www.petronas.com.my/our-business/gas-power/lng/Pages/egyptian_lng.aspx (accessed on February 4, 2018); "SEGAS Liquefied Natural Gas Complex, Damietta," *Hydrocarbons Technology*, www.hydrocarbons-technology.com/projects/seagas/ (accessed on February 4, 2018).

63 Antonia Dimou, "East Mediterranean Gas Cooperation and Security Challenges," *National Security and the Future* (Zagreb, Croatia), Volume 17, Issue 1–2 (2016), p. 102.

64 Jacob Abadi, "Egypt's Policy Towards Israel: The Impact of Foreign and Domestic Constraints," *Israel Affairs*, Volume 12, Issue 1 (2006), 159–176.

65 See "Egypt-Israel: The Taba Boundary Dispute," Central Intelligence Agency (CIA), May 21, 1986, www.cia.gov/library/readingroom/docs/CIA-RDP86T01017R000100960001-4.pdf (accessed on February 7, 2018).

66 David K. Shipler, "Israeli Completes Pullout, Leaving Sinai to Egypt," *The New York Times*, April 26, 1982, www.nytimes.com/1982/04/26/world/israeli-completes-pullout-leaving-sinai-to-egypt.html?pagewanted=all (accessed on February 7, 2018).

67 Daniel Bar-Tal, *Intractable Conflicts: Socio-Psychological Foundations and Dynamics* (Cambridge: Cambridge University Press, 2013), p. 368.

68 Benjamin Miller, "Explaining the Warm Peace in Europe Versus the Shifts Between Hot War and Cold Peace in the Middle East," in Carmela Lutmar and Benjamin Miller (eds.) *Peacemaking and Conflict Management: A Comparative Approach* (London: Routledge, 2016), p. 10.

69 See Jacqueline S. Ismael, Tareq Y. Ismael, and Glenn Perry, *Government and Politics of the Contemporary Middle East: Continuity and Change* (London: Routledge), p. 474.

70 See Mordechai Gazit, "The Middle East Peace Process," in Ami Ayalon (ed.), *Middle East Contemporary Survey*, Volume XV, 1991 (Boulder, Colorado: Westview Press, 1993), pp. 122–123.

71 Paul J. Zwier, *Principled Negotiation and Mediation in the International Arena: Talking With Evil* (Cambridge: Cambridge University Press, 2013), p. 104.

72 Tom Lansford, "Arab Republic of Egypt," *Political Handbook of the World 2012* (Thousand Oaks, CA: CQ Press, 2012), p. 422.

73 See William Mark Habeeb, *The Middle East in Turmoil: Conflict, Revolution, and Change* (Santa Barbara, CA: Greenwood, 2012), pp. 11–12.

74 Khaled Elgindy, "Egypt, Israel, Palestine," *Brookings*, August 25, 2012, www.brookings. edu/articles/egypt-israel-palestine/ (accessed on February 13, 2018).

75 Abigail Hauslohner, In the Siege of Gaza, Egypt Walks a Delicate Line, *Time*, January 11, 2010, http://content.time.com/time/world/article/0,8599,1953015,00.html (accessed on February 13, 2018).

76 Habeeb, *The Middle East in Turmoil: Conflict, Revolution, and Change,* 2012, p. 12.

77 Artur Pohl, "Egypt-Israel Relations After 2010," in Radoslaw Fiedler and Przemyslaw Osiewicz (eds.), *Transformation Processes in Egypt After 2011: The Causes, Their Course and International Response* (Berlin: Logos Verlag Berlin GmbH, 2015), p. 148.

78 "The tunnels were considered a transit point for extremists of all kinds that posed a threat to the country. As a result, the Egyptian Military would occasionally, while the Muslim Brotherhood was in charge, close tunnels and erect steel barriers. . . . The Muslim Brotherhood did not want to alienate the military so they kept quiet about the issue and followed the lead of the military commanders, as needed." Richard Davis, *Hamas, Popular Support and War in the Middle East: Insurgency in the Holy Land* (London: Routledge, 2016), 145.

79 Ibid., Davis, *Hamas, Popular Support and War in the Middle East: Insurgency in the Holy Land*, 2016, p. 145.

80 Dala Hatuqa, "Morsi's Election as Seen From Palestine," *Al-Jazeera*, July 7, 2012, www. aljazeera.com/indepth/features/2012/07/20127311434932728.html (accessed on February 16, 2018).

81 Beverley Milton-Edwards, *The Muslim Brotherhood: The Arab Spring and Its Future Face* (London: Routledge, 2016), p. 73.

82 Bennett Seftel, "Persistent ISIS Sinai Threat Drives Israel-Egypt Cooperation," *The Cipher Brief*, March 14, 2018, www.thecipherbrief.com/persistent-isis-sinai-threat-drives-israel-egypt-cooperation (accessed on August 22, 2018).

83 Statement of General Joseph L. Votel Commander U.S. Central Command Before The House Armed Services Committee on the Posture of US Central Command Terrorism And Iran: Defense Challenges in the Middle East, February 27, 2018, p. 25, http:// docs.house.gov/meetings/AS/AS00/20180227/106870/HHRG-115-AS00-Wstate-VotelJ-20180227.pdf (accessed on August 22, 2018).

84 David D. Kirkpatrick, "Secret Alliance: Israel Carries Out Airstrikes in Egypt, With Cairo's O.K.," *The New York Times*, February 8, 2018, www.nytimes.com/2018/02/03/ world/middleeast/israel-airstrikes-sinai-egypt.html (accessed on February 17, 2018).

85 Ibid.

86 Author's interview with Eran Lerman, former Deputy for Foreign Policy and International Affairs at Israel's National Security Council.

87 Ahmed Saeed and Asmahan Soliman, "An Egyptian-Israeli Agreement: New Maritime Borders and Israeli Gas Imports for a Reduced Gas Fine," *Madamasr*, August 30, 2017, www.madamasr.com/en/2017/08/30/feature/politics/an-egyptian-israeli-agreement-new-maritime-borders-and-israeli-gas-imports-for-a-reduced-gas-fine/ (accessed on February 20, 2018).

88 *Signing of Agreements for Export of Natural Gas to Egypt*, Delek Drilling, February 20, 2018, https://ir.delek-group.com/news-releases/news-release-details/signing-agreements-export-natural-gas-egypt (accessed on February 20, 2018); *$15 Billion Agreements Signed for the Sale of Israeli Natural Gas to Egypt*, February 19, 2010, www.delekdrilling.

co.il/sites/default/files/wysiwyg_uploads/Dolphinus.pdf (accessed on February 20, 2018).

89 Asmahan Soliman, "Noble and Delek in Talks to Acquire East Mediterranean Gas Pipeline," *Madamasr*, February 28, 2018, www.madamasr.com/en/2018/02/28/feature/ politics/companions-to-the-israeli-gas-deal-noble-and-delek-in-talks-to-acquire-east- mediterranean-gas-pipeline/ (accessed on August 22, 2018).

90 Zvi Mazel, "Will the Eastern Mediterranean Become a World Hub for the Natural-gas Trade?" *Jewish News Syndicate*, February 27, 2018, www.jns.org/opinion/will-the-east ern-mediterranean-become-a-world-hub-for-natural-gas-trade/ (accessed on August 23, 2018).

91 *Why Developing Israel's Leviathan Gas Field Is a Mammoth Task*, Wharton School, Uni- versity of Pennsylvania, August 25, 2017, http://knowledge.wharton.upenn.edu/ article/developing-israels-leviathan-gas-field-proven-mammoth-task/ (accessed on Sep- tember 17, 2018).

92 "The $15 billion deal will bring in approximately 50 percent of the revenues for the government of Israel. Soon after the activation of one of the pipelines, Israel would start receiving around $1–1.5 billion, annually. The state will be in a position to impose a royalty of about 12.5 percent on the revenue and income tax will receive about 23 per- cent on the total profits. The excess revenue tax will range anywhere between 22 to 24 percent. A part of the excess revenue tax will go to the sovereign wealth fund of Israel," according to the *Eurasia Times*, report. "$15 Billion Israel-Egypt Deal Signed; The Biggest for Israel's Natural Gas Industry," *Eurasia Times*, February 21, 2018, https:// eurasiantimes.com/israel-egypt-deal-natural-gas/ (accessed on February 21, 2018).

93 "Sisi on Egypt-Israel Gas Deal: 'We Scored a Big Goal'," Middle East Monitor, Febru- ary 20, 2018, www.middleeastmonitor.com/20180222-sisi-on-egypt-israel-gas-deal- we-scored-a-big-goal/ (accessed on February 21, 2018); "President Sisi Says Dream of Turning Egypt into Regional Energy Hub Is Becoming Reality," Al Ahram Online, February 21, 2018, http://english.ahram.org.eg/NewsContent/3/12/291412/Busi ness/Economy/President-Sisi-says-dream-of-turning-Egypt-into-re.aspx (accessed on February 21, 2018).

94 Shahira Amin, "Egypt Faces Public Backlash After Signing $15 Billion Gas Deal With Israel," *Al-Monitor*, February 23, 2018, www.al-monitor.com/pulse/originals/2018/02/ egypt-gas-deal-israel-public-anger-sisi.html (accessed on August 23, 2018).

95 Al-Masry al-Youm, "Egypt Welcomes Natural Gas From All Countries: PM," *Egypt Independent*, February 24, 2018, www.egyptindependent.com/egypt-welcomes-natural- gas-countries-pm/ (accessed on August 23, 2018).

96 Author's interview with Nadav Perry, Head of Foreign Relations, Delek Drilling, Her- ziliya, January 5, 2016.

97 See Eran, Rettig, and Winter, *The Gas Deal With Egypt*, March 12, 2018, www.inss. org.il/publication/gas-deal-egypt-israel-deepens-anchor-eastern-mediterranean/ (accessed on August 24, 2018).

98 In the wake of the uprising in 2011, Egypt experienced a decline in gas production and diverted much of its gas for domestic use, especially to fulfil the increased demand from the electric power plants. Besides, the pipeline serving natural gas to Israel was hit by a series of explosions, prompting EGAS and EAPC to halt gas supplies and terminate the contract with EMG and IEC.

99 Mirette Magdy and Yaacov Benmeleh, "Delek, Noble and Egypt Said to Put Final Touches on Gas Deal," *Bloomberg*, August 8, 2018, www.bloomberg.com/news/arti cles/2018-08-08/delek-noble-and-egypt-are-said-to-put-final-touches-on-gas-deal (accessed on August 24, 2018).

100 EMED (whose shares are constituted of Noble Energy 25 percent; Delek Drilling 25 percent; and Sphinx 50 percent) purchased a 37 percent stake in EMG from busi- nessmen Yossi Maiman and Sam Zell and a 2 percent stake from Mediterranean Gas Pipeline Ltd., a private company controlled by the Evsen Group, a company headed by Ali Evsen, a Turkish businessman. The additional 9 percent stake of East Gas also

came from Evsen. Maiman and Zell, who had successfully filed arbitration cases against Egypt over the previous aborted gas deal, agreed to the buyout and dropped the cases. With the newly obtained EMG shares, in addition to the 10 percent stakes owned by EGPC in EMG, the Egyptian government had the majority stakes to drop/reduce the award in arbitration cases against state gas companies' non-compliance to the contract obligation in 2012. In fact, the resolution of the arbitration was the condition for providing Israel with an outlet for its gas. The buyout of Maiman and Zell's share cleared a major obstacle to the use of EMG's pipeline. The Egyptian–Israeli tradeoff in the transaction makes sense only when knows about the true nature of the East Gas Company. Why would a private company, namely East Gas, bail out government-owned EGAS and EAPC? Investigation by *Mada Masr* reveals that East Gas is no ordinary private firm: It is majority-owned by the Egyptian General Intelligence Service (GIS), and the share may be as high as 80 percent. Given the nature of the East Gas Company, it is important to note that the profits from gas trade will go into the coffers of the intelligence agency and not the state budget. *Engagement in Agreements for the Purchase of EMG Shares and the Purchase of Rights in the EMG Pipeline*, September 27, 2018, http://ir.delek-group.com/static-files/9146ef07-86d7-475e-aeb8-caac3b92669f (accessed on November 2, 2018); Hossam Bahgat, "Who's Buying Israeli Gas? A Company Owned by the General Intelligence Service," *Mada Masr*, October 23, 2018, https://madamasr.com/en/2018/10/23/feature/politics/whos-buying-israeli-gas-a-company-owned-by-the-general-intelligence-service/ (accessed on November 2, 2018).

101 Mohammed Hammad, "Egypt Is Self-sufficient of Gas and Stopped Importing It, Saving $ 2.5 Billion Annually and 6.6 Billion Cubic Feet of Production," *Al-Ahram* [Arabic], September 30, 2018, www.ahram.org.eg/NewsQ/673126.aspx (accessed on November 2, 2018).

102 Mohammad Samir, "Egypt's Energy Future Between Reality and Fantasies," *Daily News Egypt*, June 6, 2017, www.dailynewsegypt.com/2017/06/06/egypts-energy-future-reality-fantasies/ (accessed on February 24, 2018).

103 The installed capacity of Zohr, discovered in 2015, increased to 34 mcm from 31 mcm per day since its start date in May 2018. Eni is targeting a production level of 56.6 mcm per day by the end 2018 and a peak capacity at Zohr at 76.5 mcm per day or about 29 bcm per year in 2019. The BP-manage Atoll field, discovered in March 2015, began producing from its first phase in February 2018, delivering 9.9 mcm per day in April 2018. Taurus and Libra, of the West Nile Delta development started delivering to Egypt's national grid in March 2017. These two fields are currently producing more than 19.8 mcm per day gas sales. When fully onstream in 2019, combined production from Taurus and Libra is expected to reach up to almost 42.5 mcm a day, equivalent to about 30 percent of Egypt's current gas production. Zohr, Atoll, Taurus, and Libra added 45.3 mcm of gas per day to raise Egypt's daily production to 155.7 mcm a day in April 2018. "Italy's ENI Ramps-up Production Capacity at Egypt's Zohr Gas Field," *New Europe*, May 10, 2018, www.neweurope.eu/article/italys-eni-ramps-production-capacity-egypts-zohr-gas-field/ (accessed on August 25, 2018); *Eni Strengthens Record Production From Nooros Field Offshore Egypt*, *Eni.com*, Press Release, March 15, 2018, www.eni.com/en_IT/media/2018/03/eni-strengthens-record-production-from-nooros-field-offshore-egypt (accessed on August 25, 2018); "Production From Atoll Gas Field Reaches 350M cfd," *Egypt Today*, April 15, 2018, www.egypttoday.com/Article/3/47920/Production-from-Atoll-gas-field-reaches-350M-cfd (accessed on August 25, 2018); "Atoll Field Enters Production, Adds 300 mcfd to Output," *Egypt Today*, December 6, 2017, www.egypttoday.com/Article/3/35657/Atoll-field-enters-production-adds-300-mcfd-to-output (accessed on February 24, 2018); "Gas Deal With Israel Is Solution Regarding Arbitration With EMG: PM," *Egypt Today*, February 23, 2018, www.egypttoday.com/Article/3/43635/Gas-deal-with-Israel-is-solution-regarding-arbitration-with-EMG (accessed on February 24, 2018); "West Nile Delta – Taurus / Libra, Egypt," *British Petroleum*, March 24, 2017, www.bp.com/en/global/corporate/

investors/upstream-major-projects/major-projects-2017/west-nile-delta-egypt.html (accessed on February 24, 2018); "BP Starts Gas Production From Taurus, Libra Fields in Egypt," *Offshoreenergytoday.com*, May 10, 2017, www.offshoreenergytoday.com/bp-starts-gas-production-from-taurus-libra-fields-in-egypt/ (accessed on February 24, 2018).

104 Waad Ahmed, "Export Dreams: Will Zohr Gas Production Allow Egypt to Light Europe and Its Own Cities?" *Mada Masr*, February 6, 2018, www.madamasr.com/en/2018/02/06/feature/economy/export-dreams-will-zohr-gas-production-allow-egypt-to-light-europe-and-its-own-cities/ (accessed on February 27, 2018).

105 Ghada Raafat, "Egypt Stops Gas Imports, on Its Way to Become Self-Sufficient," *Ahram Online*, October 4, 2018, http://english.ahram.org.eg/NewsContent/3/12/312755/Business/Economy/Egypt-stops-gas-imports,-on-its-way-to-become-self.aspx (accessed on November 2, 2018).

106 "Egypt's Gas Consumption Will Rise to 9bn scf/day by 2020/21," *Daily New Egypt*, September 23, 2018, https://dailynewsegypt.com/2018/09/23/egypts-gas-consumption-will-rise-to-9bn-scf-day-by-2020-21/ (accessed on September 23, 2018).; Yvonne Andiva, "Egypt to Construct US \$2.3bn Gas-fired Combined Cycle Plant," *Construction Review Online*, November 6, 2018, https://constructionreviewonline.com/2018/11/egypt-to-construct-us-2-3bn-gas-fired-combined-cycle-plant/ (accessed on November 12, 2018).

107 "Egypt to Increase Natural Gas Exports to Jordan to 150m scfd by December," *Hellenic Shipping Worldwide*, November 10, 2018, www.hellenicshippingnews.com/egypt-to-increase-natural-gas-exports-to-jordan-to-150m-scfd-by-december/ (accessed on November 12, 2018).

108 Egypt's dry natural gas production declined by 31 percent from 2012 to 2016, due to Arab Spring instability, high energy subsides, and lack of investment. These factors led Egypt to divert its natural gas supply away from exports to the domestic market and to rely on LNG imports to address the shortfall in consumption. See *Egypt*, Energy Information Administration, May 24, 2018, www.eia.gov/beta/international/analysis.php?iso=EGY&scr=email (accessed on August 25, 2018); Myles McCormick and David Sheppard, "Egypt to Pay Spanish-Italian JV \$2bn in Natural Gas Dispute," *Financial Times*, September 3, 2018, www.ft.com/content/0d0dfd96-af6c-11e8-8d14-6f049d06439c (accessed on November 12, 2018).

109 The liquefaction terminals at Idku represent the only currently operating facilities in Egypt for the export of LNG. There too the number of LNG cargo ships leaving Idku has been at extremely low levels for the past three years. *Shell Oil Company's Idku LNG Ramps Up Exports*, AllSource Analysis, June 20, 2017, https://allsourceanalysis.com/wp-content/uploads/2017/06/AR-20170620-EG-A-Shell-Oil-Companys-Idku-LNG-Ramps-Up-Exports.pdf (accessed on August 26, 2018).

110 Dan Zaken, "Egypt Has Good Reasons to Buy Israeli Gas," *Globes*, November 5, 2018, https://en.globes.co.il/en/article-egypt-has-good-reasons-to-buy-israeli-gas-1001259029 (accessed on November 12, 2018).

111 "Egypt Poised to Become Net Natural Gas Exporter Again," *Compressor Tech2*, May 25, https://compressortech2.com/egypt-poised-to-become-net-natural-gas-exporter-again/ (accessed on August 26, 2018).

112 Asmahan Soliman, "Companions to the Israeli Gas Deal: Noble and Delek in Talks to Acquire East Mediterranean Gas Pipeline," *Mada Masr*, February 28, 2018, www.madamasr.com/en/2018/02/28/feature/politics/companions-to-the-israeli-gas-deal-noble-and-delek-in-talks-to-acquire-east-mediterranean-gas-pipeline/ (accessed on August 26, 2018).

113 Kevin Keane, "North Sea Oil and Gas Exploration 'at Lowest Level Since 1970s'," *BBC*, March 20, 2018, www.bbc.com/news/uk-scotland-north-east-orkney-shetland-43461811 (accessed on August 26, 2018).

114 "Netherlands to Shut Europe's Biggest Gas Field to Limit Quake Risk," *Deutsche Welle*, March 29, 2018, www.dw.com/en/netherlands-to-shut-europes-biggest-gas-field-to-limit-quake-risk/a-43190065 (accessed on August 27, 2018).

115 Cyril Widdershoven, "Egypt Could Become Europe's Next Big Energy Hub," *Oilprice. com*, April 26, 2018, https://oilprice.com/Energy/Natural-Gas/Egypt-Could-Become-Europes-Next-Big-Energy-Hub.html (accessed on August 27, 2018).

116 "Egyptian Company to Start Gas Imports From Israel Next Year, Sources Say," *Reuters*, August 5, 2018, www.reuters.com/article/us-egypt-energy-israel/egyptian-company-to-start-gas-imports-from-israel-next-year-sources-say-idUSKBN1KQ05N (accessed on August 27, 2018).; Tsvetana Paraskova, "Egypt to Start Importing Israeli Gas for Re-export in Early 2019," *Oilprice*, August 7, 2018, https://oilprice.com/Latest-Energy-News/World-News/Egypt-To-Start-Importing-Israeli-Gas-For-Re-export-In-Early-2019.html (accessed on August 27, 2018).

117 Avie Andreou, "Gas Pipeline Deal Reached With Egypt – CyBC," *Cyprus Mail*, https://cyprus-mail.com/2018/08/06/gas-pipeline-deal-reached-with-egypt-cybc/ (accessed on August 30, 2018).

118 "Egypt Holds Keys to East Mediterranean Gas," *The Economist Intelligence Unit*, February 23rd 2018, http://country.eiu.com/article.aspx?articleid=1396458923&Country=Israel&topic=Economy (accessed on March 2, 2018).

119 Stelios Orphanides, "Lakkotrypis Confirms Shell's Interest to Buy Cypriot Gas," *Cyprus Business Mail*, March 13, 2108, http://cyprusbusinessmail.com/?p=60873 (accessed on August 30, 2018); Yaacov Benmeleh, "Shell Mulls 15-Year Deal for Israeli, Cypriot Gas, Partner Says," *Bloomberg Quint*, March 23, 2018, www.bloombergquint.com/business/2018/03/21/shell-mulls-15-year-deal-for-israeli-cypriot-gas-partner-says (accessed on August 30, 2018).

120 Author's interview with Nasr Agiza at Cambridge (UK) on August 17, 2016. Agiza is a consultant at the TIBA (Petroleum Services and Consultation), Cairo, Egypt.

121 Jamal Jawahar, "Winners and Losers From the Egypt-Israel Gas Deal," *Asharq Al-Awsat*, February 24, 2018, https://aawsat.com/english/home/article/1185581/exclusive-winners-and-losers-egypt-israel-gas-deal (accessed on March 5, 2018).

122 The Gas Regulatory Authority of Egypt has set a tariff of $0.38 per million British thermal units (mmBtu) for firms seeking to use its national gas network across the country that would allow companies to tap into the national gas grid and use it for private imports. See "Egypt Sets Tariff of $0.38 for Use of National Gas Grid," *Egypt Independent*, August 3, 2018, www.egyptindependent.com/egypt-sets-tariff-of-0-38-for-use-of-national-gas-grid/ (accessed on August 31, 2018).

123 Abdellatif El-Menawy, "How Egypt Will Gain From Private Gas Deal With Israel," *Arab News*, February 27, 2018, www.arabnews.com/node/1255476 (accessed on March 5, 2018).

124 Relations between the two regional powers crumbled after Israeli marines stormed an aid ship in May 2010 to enforce a naval blockade of the Hamas-run Gaza Strip, killing 10 Turkish activists on board.

125 See Emre Tunçalp, "Turkey's Natural Gas Strategy: Balancing Geopolitical Goals & Market Realities," *Turkish Policy Quarterly* (Istanbul), Volume 14, Issue 3 (Fall 2015), p. 72.

126 *Turkey's Import and Exports With Israel*, Turkstat, Turkey, 2015, www.turkstat.gov.tr/; Central Bureau of Statistics, Israel, 2015, www.cbs.gov.il/www/fr_trade/d4t21.htm (accessed on March 5, 2018).

127 Author's interview with Mr. Eser Ozdil, Secretary General, Petform, Ankara, June 7, 2017.

128 Author's interview with Dr. Nimrod Goren, Founder and Head of Mitvim – The Israeli Institute for Regional Foreign Policies and a Teaching Fellow in Middle Eastern Studies at the Hebrew University of Jerusalem, Jerusalem, Israel, January 18, 2016.

129 Nuran Erkul Kaya, "2020 Critical for Turkey's Gas Market," *Energy Observer*, November 19, 2017, www.energyobserver.com/en/post/5833 (accessed on March 5, 2018).

130 Gurel Ayla, Tzimitras Harry, and Faustmann Hubert, *East Mediterranean Hydrocarbons, Geopolitical Perspectives, Markets and Regional Cooperation* (PRIO Cyprus Centre Friedrich Ebert Stiftung Brookings Institution, March 2014), p. 106, http://library.fes.de/pdf-files/bueros/zypern/11607.pdf (accessed on March 8, 2018).

131 Author's interview with Professor Mert Bilgin, Medipol University, Istanbul, June 9, 2017.

132 Akhmed Gumbatov, "Prospects of Delivering Israeli Gas to the Turkish Market," *Turkish Policy Quarterly*, January 26, 2016, http://turkishpolicy.com/blog/10/prospects-of-delivering-israeli-gas-to-the-turkish-market (accessed on March 8, 2018).

133 Ebru Oğurlu, *Turkey Amidst The Shifting Geopolitics in the Eastern Mediterranean*, Rethink Institute (Washington D. C.), Paper 9, May 2013, Summary.

134 Matthew Bryza, "Eastern Mediterranean Natural Gas: Potential for Historic Breakthroughs Among Israel, Turkey, and Cyprus," in Sami Andoura and David Koranyi (Eds.), *Energy In The Eastern Mediterranean: Promise Or Peril?* Egmont Paper 65, Egmont Institute and the Atlantic Council (Ghent, Belgium: Academia Press, May 2014), pp. 24, 41, 46, www.egmontinstitute.be/content/uploads/2014/05/ep65.pdf?type=pdf (accessed on March 9, 2018); Harald Hecking et al., *Options for Gas Supply Diversification for the EU and Germany in the Next Two Decades*, ewi Energy Research & Scenarios (ewi ER&S), Cologne and The European Centre for Energy and Resource Security (EUCERS), London, October 2016, p. 22, www.ewi.research-scenarios.de/cms/wp-content/uploads/2016/10/Options-for-Gas-Supply-Diversification.pdf (accessed on March 9, 2018).

135 Ertan Karpazli, "Gas Fueling New Hope in Eastern Mediterranean," *TRT World* (Istanbul), May 24, 2016, http://www2.trtworld.com/in-depth/gas-fueling-new-hope-in-eastern-mediterranean-112203 (accessed on March 12, 2018).

136 Easwaran Kanason, "Geopolitical Eruptions in the Eastern Mediterranean," *OilVoice*, March 30, 2018, https://oilvoice.com/Opinion/14953/Geopolitical-Eruptions-in-the-Eastern-Mediterranean (accessed on September 1, 2018); "Başbakandan Kıbrıs'ta doğalgaz aramaya gelen ABD'li Exxon'a: Karşılığını görecek [Turkish]," *Diken*, March 7, 2018, www.diken.com.tr/kalindan-kibrista-dogalgaz-aramaya-gelen-abdli-exxona-haklarimizi-koruyacagiz/ (accessed on March 12, 2018).

137 "Turkish Jets Prevent British Warplanes," *Yeni Safak* [Turkish], October 29, 2018, www.yenisafak.com/gundem/turk-jetlerinden-ingiliz-savas-ucaklarina-onleme-3405223 (accessed on November 6, 2018).

138 "Eni Announces a Gas Discovery Offshore Cyprus," *Eni.com*, February 8, 2018, www.eni.com/en_IT/media/2018/02/eni-announces-a-gas-discovery-offshore-cyprus (accessed on March 16, 2018).

139 Turkey's Foreign Ministry immediately responded to the new discovery with a statement that accused the Greek Cypriot government of "acting as though it were the sole owner of the island." *No: 43, 11 February 2018, Press Release Regarding the Greek Cypriot Administration's Hydrocarbon-related Activities in the Eastern Mediterranean*, Ministry of Foreign Affairs, Ankara, Turkey, www.mfa.gov.tr/no_-43_-gkrynin-dogu-akdenizdeki-hidrokarbon-faaliyetleri-hk.en.mfa (accessed on March 16, 2018).

140 Jonathan Gorvett, "Mediterranean Gas Hunt Threatened by Cyprus Stand-off," *Asia Times*, October 29, 2018, www.atimes.com/article/mediterranean-gas-hunt-threatened-by-cyprus-stand-off/ (accessed on October 29, 2018).

141 Chase Winter, "Gas, Pipeline Dreams and Gunboat Diplomacy in the Mediterranean," *Deutsche Welle*, April 2, 2018, www.dw.com/en/gas-pipeline-dreams-and-gunboat-diplomacy-in-mediterranean/a-43228234 (accessed on September 1, 2018).

142 "Cyprus President Says Gas Can Help Reunification,"*Euractiv*, April 11, 2014, www.euractiv.fr/section/all/news/cyprus-president-says-gas-can-help-reunification/ (accessed on March 18, 2018).

143 Author's interview with Mr. Demetrios Theophylactou, High Commissioner of Cyprus to India, October 20, 2017.

144 *Supplying The EU Natural Gas Market, Final Report*, November 2010, https://ec.europa.eu (accessed on March 18, 2018).

145 The icebreaker was the Moscow meeting in 2010 followed by the bilateral visits of Prime Ministers George Papandreou and Benjamin Netanyahu to Jerusalem and Athens, respectively. Papandreou's multidimensional foreign policy, in which he saw

security and economic benefits from a rapprochement with Israel, paved the way for cooperation on several issues, not least the military. See Jean-Loup Samaan, The East Mediterranean Triangle at Crossroads, Strategic Studies Institute and U.S. Army War College, Carlisle, PA, March 2016; George N. Tzogopoulos, "The Future of Greece-Israel Relations," BESA Center Perspectives, Paper No. 788, April 8, 2018, https://besacenter.org/perspectives-papers/greece-israel-relations/ (accessed on September 1, 2018).

146 Gerald Butt, "Can Greece Jump on the Gas-transit Train?" *Petroleum Economist*, September 4, 2018, www.petroleum-economist.com/articles/midstream-downstream/pipe lines/2018/can-greece-jump-on-the-gas-transit-train (accessed on November 6, 2018).

147 "A Direct Link to New Sources for Europe," *IGI Poseidon*, www.igi-poseidon.com/en/eastmed; *The East Med Pipeline Project: A Project of Common Interest for the Diversification of Gas Supplies to Europe*, Edison EDF Group, March 8, 2017, www.eurogas.org/uploads/media/EDISON_MargheriEastMed_EP_8.03.2017.pdf (accessed on March 21, 2018).

148 "Projects of Common Interest," https://ec.europa.eu/energy/en/topics/infrastructure/projects-common-interest (accessed on March 21, 2018).

149 David Wurmser, "The Geopolitics of Israel's Offshore Gas Reserves," *Jerusalem Centre for Public Affairs*, April 4, 2013, http://jcpa.org/article/the-geopolitics-of-israels-offshore-gas-reserves/ (accessed on March 23, 2018).

150 There has been no significant discovery in Israeli EEZ; many wells have turned out dry or semi-dry. Israel's failed bid to attract major oil companies to drill in its 24 blocks has left it with a limited reserve of gas. Isramco Negev and Modiin Energy announced in August 2017 that they are returning the licenses to develop the 252 bcm Daniel East and West fields because of the geological risks, difficulties expected in commercialising the gas, and the lack of interest by new investors, "Israeli Exploration Group to Return Daniel Natgas Field Licenses," *Reuters*, August 20, 2017, www.reuters.com/article/israel-natgas-isramco-negev-2-idUSL8N1L608C (accessed on March 23, 2018).

151 There has been no significant discovery in Israeli EEZ; many wells have turned out dry or semi-dry. Israel's failed bid to attract major oil companies to drill in its 24 blocks has left it with a limited reserve of gas. Isramco Negev and Modiin Energy announced in August 2017 that they are returning the licenses to develop the 252 bcm Daniel East and West fields because of the geological risks, difficulties expected in commercialising the gas, and the lack of interest by new investors, "Israeli Exploration Group to Return Daniel Natgas Field Licenses," *Reuters*, August 20, 2017.

152 See Simone Taglipietra, "Is the East Med Gas Pipeline Just Another EU Pipe Dream?" *Bruegel*, May 10, 2017, http://bruegel.org/2017/05/is-the-eastmed-gas-pipeline-just-another-eu-pipe-dream/ (accessed on March 28, 2018).

153 "Egypt Year in Review 2016," *Oxford Business Group*, December 26, 2016, https://oxfordbusinessgroup.com/news/egypt-year-review-2016 (accessed on March 29, 2018).

154 Noble had initially planned to link the gas from Tamar, Leviathan, and Cyprus' Aphrodite fields to a land-based or floating LNG facility for export to the global market. The Noble-Delek consortium struck a deal with Woodside Petroleum, an Australian oil and gas company with expertise in LNG to pursue the project. However, the Israeli authorities did not warm up to the idea of a LNG export, considering the export of gas to regional markets through pipeline as a more feasible option. As the consortium pursued export agreements in neighbouring countries in 2014, Woodside backed out of the project and the idea of an LNG export facilities was abandoned. See "New Great Game Over Natural Gas," *Stratfor*, February 22, 2018, https://worldview.stratfor.com/article/eastern-mediterraneans-new-great-game-over-natural-gas (accessed on March 29, 2018); John Reed, "Woodside Backs Out of $2.7bn Israel Gas Project," *Financial Times*, May 21, 2014, www.ft.com/content/2ce420d0-e0b5-11e3-a934-00144feabdc0 (accessed on March 29, 2018).

155 *EuroAsia Interconnector Concludes Strategic Alliance Agreement With Elia Grid,* EuroAsia Interconnector, Press Release, December 11, 2017, www.euroasia-interconnector.com/news-euroasia_interconnector_concludes_strategic_alliance_agreement_with_elia_

grid1078period2017-12/ (accessed on March 31, 2018); "End to Cyprus' Electricity Isolation One Step Closer," *Cyprus Mail Online*, October 2017, https://cyprus-mail. com/2017/10/16/end-cyprus-electricity-isolation-one-step-closer/ (accessed on March 31, 2018).

156 See Nizan Feldman, "Economic Peace: Theory Versus Reality," *Strategic Assessment*, Volume 12, Issue 3 (November 2009), pp. 19–29.

157 UN Maritime Space: Maritime Zones and Maritime Delimitation, February 16, 2011, www.un.org/depts/los/LEGISLATIONANDTREATIES/ (accessed on March 31, 2018).

158 Félicité Barrier and Ali Ahmad, *The Geopolitics of Oil and Gas Development in Lebanon*, Issam Fares Institute for Public Policy and International Affairs, American University of Beirut, Policy Brief 1, 2018, p. 1.

159 See *List of Geographical Coordinates for the Delimitation of the Northern Limit of the Territorial Sea and Exclusive Economic Zone of the State of Israel* (transmitted by a communication dated 12 July 2011 from the Permanent Mission of Israel to the United Nations addressed to the Secretariat of the United Nations), www.un.org/depts/los/LEGIS LATIONANDTREATIES/PDFFILES/isr_eez_northernlimit2011.pdf (accessed on April 3, 2018).

160 The so-called Point 1 on the map, which was set as a shared dividing point the 2007 Lebanon-Cyprus agreement, which the Cypriot government ratified immediately, is crucial. Lebanon 2010 maritime boundary submission uses a different coordinate, Point 23, 17 km southwest of Point 1 and includes an area that overlaps with territory claimed by Israel. See Martin Withlisch, "Israel-Lebanon Offshore Oil and Gas Dispute – Rules of International Maritime Law," *American Society of International Law*, Volume 15, Issue 21 (December 5, 2011), www.asil.org/insights/volume/15/issue/31/ israel-lebanon-offshore-oil-gas-dispute-%E2%80%93-rules-international-maritime (accessed on April 3, 2018).; Andrew Shibley, "Blessings and Curses: Israel and Lebanon's Maritime Boundary Dispute in the Eastern Mediterranean Sea," *The Global Business Law Review*, Volume 5, Issue 1 (2016), pp. 74–75; Andreas Stergiou, "Turkey – Cyprus – Israel Relations and the Cyprus Conflict," *Journal of Balkan and Near Eastern Studies*, Volume 18, Issue 4 (July 2016), pp. 375–392.

161 "Consent to Be Bound by a Treaty Expressed by Ratification, Acceptance or Approval," Article 14, 1(a), *United Nations Vienna Convention on the Law of Treaties*, May 23, 1969, www.jus.uio.no/lm/un.law.of.treaties.convention.1969/14.html (accessed on April 6, 2018).

162 Barrier and Ahmad, *The Geopolitics of Oil and Gas Development in Lebanon*, 2018, p. 2; Withlisch, "Israel-Lebanon Offshore Oil and Gas Dispute – Rules of International Maritime Law," December 5, 2011.

163 Barrier and Ahmad, *The Geopolitics of Oil and Gas Development in Lebanon*, 2018, p. 2.

164 "Lebanon Offers Five Blocks in First Oil & Gas Licensing Round," *OffshoreEnergy-Today.com*, January 26, 2017, https://www.offshoreenergytoday.com/lebanon-offers-five-blocks-in-first-oil-gas-licensing-round/ (accessed on April 6, 2018); *First Offshore Licensing Round Results*, Lebanese Petroleum Administration, 2018, https://www.lpa. gov.lb/first%20licensing%20round%20results.php (accessed on April 6, 2018).

165 Haytham Tabesh, "Lebanon's Politicians Set Aside Differences on Oil and Gas Policy," *Al-Arabiya*, July 22, 2016, http://english.alarabiya.net/en/business/energy/2016/07/22/ Lebanon-s-politicians-set-aside-differences-on-oil-and-gas-policy-.html (accessed on April 6, 2018).

166 "Lebanon's Oil & Gas Licensing Round Attracts Bids From Total-Eni-Novatek," Italian trade Agency, October 19, 2017, www.ice.gov.it/it/news/notizie-dal-mondo/100401 (accessed on April 7, 2018).

167 Total does not believe this is a major issue. It said in a press release in February 2018 that the consortium was "fully aware" of the Israeli-Lebanese border dispute in the south part of the block. It added that this covers only a "very limited area," at less than 8 percent of the block's surface. "Given that the main prospects are located more than 25 km from the disputed area, the consortium confirms that the exploration well on block

9 will have no interference at all with any fields or prospects located south of the border area," Total said. *Total Strengthens Its Position in the Mediterranean Region by Entering Two Exploration Blocks Offshore Lebanon*, Press Release, February 9, 2018, www.total.com/ en/media/news/press-releases/total-strengthens-position-in-mediterranean-region-by-entering-two-exploration-blocks-offshore-lebanon (accessed on April 7, 2018).

168 "Lebanon has a strong case for sticking by its maritime boundary claim. Lebanon's endpoint, 123 km out to sea, follows a cartographic rule of being equidistant between three locations on shore – the Akrotiri Peninsula in Cyprus, the promontory of Haifa in Israel and Ras Naqoura on the Lebanon-Israel border. Further, Lebanon's line appears to have been tacitly accepted by Israel before it was delivered by Beirut to the United Nations in 2010. The northern edges of Israel's own gas exploration blocks follow the same path. Buoys placed by the Israeli Navy off Ras Naqoura correspond to the Lebanese line. This is why Lebanese officials said they would not accept a compromise. Lebanon is sticking by its refusal." Israel argues for the entire zone, says Nicholas Branford, a correspondent for the *Christian Science Monitor*, writing on Lebanon and other areas of the Middle East, since 2002. Nicholas Branford, "US Mediates Border Dispute Between Lebanon and Israel Amid Rising Tensions," *The Arab Weekly*, February 25, 2018, https://thearabweekly.com/us-mediates-border-dispute-between-lebanon-and-israel-amid-rising-tensions (accessed on April 10, 2018).

169 "US Envoy Continues Shuttle Diplomacy Over Israel-Lebanon Gas Dispute," *The New Arab*, February 21, 2018, www.alaraby.co.uk/english/news/2018/2/21/us-envoy-con tinues-shuttle-diplomacy-over-israel-lebanon-gas-dispute (accessed on April 10, 2018).

170 "Bassil Says Oil and Gas Deal Is 'Economic Resistance'," *The Daily Star*, December 16, 2017, www.dailystar.com.lb/News/Lebanon-News/2017/Dec-16/430463-bassill-labels-oil-and-gas-exploration-economic-resistance.ashx (accessed on April 13, 2018).

171 Author's interview with Mr Antoine Dagher, Editor in Chief, *East Med Energy* (Ante-lias, Lebanon), Cambridge, August 17, 2016.

172 Victor Kattan, "The Gas Fields off Gaza: A Gift or a Curse?" *Al-Shabaka*, April 24, 2012, https://al-shabaka.org/briefs/gas-fields-gaza-gift-or-curse/ (accessed on April 13, 2018).

173 Tareq Baconi, "How Israel Uses Gas to Enforce Palestinian Dependency and Pro-mote Normalization," *Al-Shabaka*, March 12, 2017, https://al-shabaka.org/briefs/ israel-uses-gas-enforce-palestinian-dependency-promote-normalization/ (accessed on April 15, 2018).

174 Author's interview with Lior Herman, Lecturer of International Relations with exper-tise in Political Economy at Hebrew University, Jerusalem, Israel, January 25, 2016.

175 Kattan, "The Gas Fields off Gaza: A Gift or a Curse?" April 24, 2012.

176 "Gift or Curse? Israel Okays Development of Gaza Offshore Gas Field," *Middle East Online*, September 23, 2012, www.middle-east-online.com/english/?id=54515 (accessed on April 15, 2018).

177 "PM Netanyahu and Quartet Rep Blair Announce Economic Steps to Assist Pales-tinian Authority," February 4, 2011, *Israel Ministry of Foreign Affairs*,www.mfa.gov.il/ mfa/pressroom/2011/pages/pm_netanyahu_quartet_rep_blair_economic_steps_pa_4–feb-2011.aspx (accessed on April 18, 2018).

178 *Note Prepared by the EuroMed and Middle East Unit for Information Only Purposes for the DPAL [Delegation for Relations With Palestine] Meeting of 26–5–2015*, www.europarl. europa.eu/meetdocs/2014_2019/documents/dpal/dv/background_note_hala/back ground_note_halaen.pdf (accessed on April 18, 2018).

179 The purchase of fuel is in line with the Protocol on Economic Relations or the Paris Protocol, enshrined between Israel and the PLO as part of the Oslo Accords. Baconi, "How Israel Uses Gas to Enforce Palestinian Dependency and Promote Normaliza-tion," March 12, 2017; Tareq Baconi, *A Flammable Peace: Why Gas Deals Won't End Conflict In The Middle East*, European Council for Foreign Relations, Policy Brief, December 2017, www.ecfr.eu/publications/summary/a_flammable_peace_why_gas_ deals_wont_end_conflict_in_the_middle_east (accessed on April 18, 2018).

180 Gaza requires 450–500 MW of power a day but is receiving barely a third of that. About 30 MW produced by its own ageing power plant, Egypt sends 30 MW and Israel supplies 120 MW. The local power plant, Gaza Power Generation Company located in the Gaza Strip, which began operating in 2002, was built with a capacity to produce 140 MW. However, that capacity was never fully realised as the transmission network in Gaza city, its main site of operation, had limited carrying capacity. Never fully repaired after the damage incurred by Israeli bombing in the wake of Hamas' abduction of Israeli soldier Gilad Shalit, it is capable of producing 60 to 80 MW, about half of its potential capacity. The power plant could produce slightly more but is hampered by lack of enough funds to purchase fuel. Unpaid consumer bills are one of the reasons for paucity of funds. More importantly, the PA, which pays for power supplied to the strip through the Israeli and Egyptian grids, normally transfers fuel to Gaza and exempts it from most taxes, is no longer absorbing the cost because of its own financial constraints, and this has had a snowball effect on the capacity of the power plant to produce consistently. Above all, Israel's restrictions and prohibitions on the entry of equipment and parts, both for repair and maintenance of the power plant and transmission network due to their 'dual use' status, has further reduced power production. See Maayan Niezna, *Who's Responsible for Gaza's Infrastructure Crisis?* Gisha – Legal Centre for Freedom of Movement (Tel Aviv), January 2017, pp. 2–6; Elior Levy and Yoav Zitun, "Situation in Gaza Approaches Critical Point," *Ynetnews.com*, February 5, 2018, www.ynetnews.com/articles/0,7340,L-5090907,00.html (accessed on April 21, 2018); Nidal al-Mughrabi, "Energy Crisis Leaves Gaza With Barely Four Hours of Power a Day," *Reuters*, January 12, 2017, www.reuters.com/article/us-palestinians-gaza-energy/energy-crisis-leaves-gaza-with-barely-four-hours-of-power-a-day-iduskbn14w1yg (accessed on April 21, 2018); *Palestine Electric Company Annual Report 2015*, www.pec.ps

181 The PA controls most of the public and external funds, and since it opposes Hamas' rule in Gaza, several difficulties often crop up, including hindrances to energy supply and trade flows to and from the strip.

182 Niezna, January 2017, p. 6.

183 Author's interview with Dr Omar Kittaneh, Minister, Palestinian Energy and Natural Resources Authority, State of Palestine, January 21, 2016.

184 *Improving the Gazan Economy and Utilizing the Economic Potential of the Jordan Valley*, The Aix Group, January 2017, p. 54, http://aix-group.org/wp-content/uploads/2017/02/Aix-Group-Two-further-studies-10.pdf (accessed on April 23, 2018).

185 Ibid., p. 29.

186 *Note Prepared by the EuroMed and Middle East Unit for Information Only Purposes for the DPAL [Delegation for Relations With Palestine] Meeting of 26–5–2015.*

187 Sharon Udasin, "Palestinian Power Company Nixing Leviathan Gas Import Deal," *Jerusalem Post* March 11, 2015, www.jpost.com/Business/Palestinian-Power-Generation-Company-nixing-Leviathan-gas-import-deal-393570 (accessed on April 24, 2018).

188 Author's interview with Uzi Landau, former Minister of Energy and Water (2009–2013), Ra'anana, Israel, January 15, 2016.

189 Eoin O'Cinneide, "Palestine Seeks New Gaza Marine Operator," *Upstream*, April 4, 2018, www.upstreamonline.com/live/1465563/palestine-seeks-new-gaza-marine-operator?utm_medium=email&utm_source=free_article_access&utm_content=224422912 (accessed on April 26, 2018).

190 The Greek oil and gas company, Energean, has expressed its willingness to buy and operate the 45 percent stake in the Gaza Marine, it has been reported. Any change in ownership of the Gaza Marine depends on both the Israeli and Palestinian authorities giving their green signal. "Energean to Buy 45% Stake in Gaza Marine Field," *Energy East-Med News*, July 8, 2018, http://energynews.co.il/?p=33510 (accessed on September 1, 2018).

191 Eni alone plans to invest more than $10bn in Egypt by 2022. It and other firms have struck onshore gas in the western desert, where the government is keen to explore further, reports the *Economist*. In the meanwhile, SDX Energy Inc. has discovered more

gas in the South Disouq Concession in the Nile Delta. It announced in July 2018 that it had encountered gas at its SD-3X well. In early 2017, it had discovered gas at the SD-1X well. Andreas Exarheas, "SDX Hits Gas Onshore Egypt," *Rigzone*, July 23, 2018, www.rigzone.com/news/sdx_hits_gas_onshore_egypt-23-jul-2018-156371-article/ (accessed on September 2, 2018); "SDX to Exit South Ramadan, Switch Focus to South Disouq in Egypt," *Energy Egypt*, July 30, 2017, https://energyegypt. net/sdx-to-exit-south-ramadan-switch-focus-to-south-disouq-in-egypt/ (accessed on September 2, 2018); "Egypt Is Optimistic About New Gas Discoveries in the Mediterranean," *The Economist*, July 5, 2018, www.economist.com/middle-east-and-africa/2018/07/05/egypt-is-optimistic-about-new-gas-discoveries-in-the-mediterra nean (accessed on September 2, 2018).

192 Dania Akkad, "The Egypt-Israel Gas Deal: What's the Chance It Will Go Up in Smoke?" *Middle East Eye*, July 17, 2018, www.middleeasteye.net/news/business-egypt-israel-gas-deal-LNG-pipeline-delek-drilling-dolphinus-tamar-leviathan-field-mediterranean-energy-2125842654 (accessed on September 4, 2018).

193 Bahgat, "Who's Buying Israeli Gas?" October 23, 2018.

194 Mohamed Adel, "Damietta LNG Plant Exports Gas Again After Six-year Suspension," *Daily News Egypt*, September 4, 2018, www.dailynewsegypt.com/2018/09/04/dami etta-lng-plant-exports-gas-again-after-six-year-suspension/ (accessed on September 4, 2018).

195 Oded Eran and Elai Rettig, *New Obstacles Facing Israeli Natural Gas Exports*, INSS Insight No. 1073, July 10, 2018, www.inss.org.il/publication/new-obstacles-facing-israeli-natural-gas-exports/ (accessed on September 4, 2018).

196 "Why Developing Israel's Leviathan Gas Field Is a Mammoth Task," August 25, 2017, *The K@W Network* (University of Pennsylvania), http://knowledge.wharton.upenn. edu/article/developing-israels-leviathan-gas-field-proven-mammoth-task/ (accessed on April 23, 2018).

197 *BP Statistical Review of World Energy*, 2018; Eran and Rettig, *New* Obstacles, 2018, Gul-mira Rzayeva, *Natural Gas in the Turkish Domestic Energy Market: Policies and Challenges*, Oxford Institute for Energy Studies (OIES), February 2014, p. 1, www.oxfordenergy. org/wpcms/wp-content/uploads/2014/02/NG-82.pdf (accessed on April 24, 2018).

198 "Turkey Hits Record Gas Consumption and Imports in 2017," *Anadolu Agency*, Febru-ary 21, 2018, www.aa.com.tr/en/energy/turkey/turkey-hits-record-gas-consumption-and-imports-in-2017/18943 (accessed on April 26, 2018).

199 *Turkish Natural Gas Market Report2016*, Energy Market Regulatory, Republic of Turkey, Ankara 2017, http://yourmaninturkey.com.tr/business-news-detail/epdk-publishes-its-turkish-natural-gas-market-report-2016/ (accessed on April 26, 2018); *Turkey-Qatar Economic and Trade Relations*, Ministry of Foreign Affairs, Republic of Turkey, www.mfa.gov.tr/turkey_s-commercial-and-economic-relations-with-qatar. en.mfa (accessed on September 3, 2018).

200 Gulmira Rzayeva, *Turkey's Gas Demand Decline: Reasons and Consequences*, Energy Insight 11, OIES April, 2017, p. 1, www.oxfordenergy.org/wpcms/wp-content/uploads/2017/04/Turkeys-gas-demand-decline-reasons-and-consequences-OIES-En ergy-Insight.pdf (accessed on April 29, 2018).

201 "Turkey, Israel Working on Commercial Details of Possible Gas Pipeline: Israeli Official," *Hurriyet Daily News*, May 2 2017, www.hurriyetdailynews.com/turkey-israel-working-on-commercial-details-of-possible-gas-pipeline-israeli-official-112654 (accessed on April 29, 2018).

202 "Lebanese President: Israel Rejects Settling Disputed Maritime Border," *E&P*, June 27, 2018, www.epmag.com/lebanese-president-israel-rejects-settling-disputed-maritime-border-1707106 (accessed on September 3, 2018).

CONCLUSIONS

Learning from the past, looking into the future

Natural gas production from the Leviathan field at the end of 2019 will have a substantial impact on Israel's supply and consumption, much as it will transform the availability of energy in the Eastern Mediterranean region. In the domestic arena, it will resolve the precarious condition of dependence on a single reservoir and strengthen the nation's energy security. Leviathan's gas supply will wholly meet the current peak-hour demand and is likely to increase the market uptake, leading to the growth of the industrial sector based on natural gas. The development of infrastructure associated with higher demand for natural gas will also get a boost, strengthening the economy. A cross-sectoral impact will be the de-escalation in the electricity price with the participation of independent power producers and adoption of distributed generation. The growth in supply and demand, will send a positive signal to the investors that it is worthwhile to invest in Israel's upstream sector.

Leviathan will bring redundancy to Israel's gas supply. The simultaneous development of the Tanin and Karish fields – expected to come on stream in 2022 – combined with the beginning of exports from the Tamar field in 2019, will give a significant fillip to Israel's growth story and improve external relations. Energy scarce countries, such as, Jordan, which has signed import agreements with Israel, and Turkey, which wants to diversify sources of energy supply, would have an affordable and reliable source of energy within their reach.

While the maritime gas fields have transformed Israel – from an energy deficient to an energy surplus country – the country, while building an entire natural gas industry from scratch within a short period of time, was confronted with a host of challenges. The specific challenges of gas development in Israel related to devising a set of regulatory procedures and establishment of essential infrastructures. Those required at start the fostering of synergy – between the government, gas companies, and the people – so that each party could benefit from the development of the resource. As a result of positive decisions and right policies, Israel's gas industry has seen a phenomenal rise in less than a decade and that has had a significant impact on quality and quantity of energy consumption.

Israel over successive administrations has continued the development of petroleum industry exclusively private sector investments. The governments have refrained from directly investing in the oil and gas sector and instead have managed the industry through laws, rules, and regulations. These have ensured developers make fair profit, so that they invest and reinvest in the development of the industry. A new taxation regime has also ensured that people through the government get equitable share of the profits from the development of the oil and gas resource.

Should the state invest directly in oil and gas development through a national energy company (NEC)? This has been a recurrent question in the industry. The need for a NEC in Israel is acutely faced when the development of a reservoir is deemed unprofitable by the private developers. For instance, Isramco Negev and Modiin Energy returned the licenses to develop the Daniel gas fields in August 2017, citing lack of interest on the past of investors. Daniel is estimated to hold some 250 bcm, making it almost as big as Tamar. If Daniel does not develop, it is a loss to society and setback to the national objective of energy self-sufficiency. A NEC would be in a position to resolve such a crisis. In this context, it would be worthwhile to watch the second phase of the development of the Leviathan. If contracts of sufficient volume do not come by, the private sector will have difficulty financing the development of the reservoir. As the BoI report suggests[1] the government could consider investing in the form of assistance to the developers in return for a share in the profits from the sale of the gas.

NECs are also crucial for the creation of value in the economy. From upstream production, national oil and gas companies often create downstream assets in a forward linkage. Refining and production of refined value-added products for domestic consumption as well as export add to the expansion of the national industrial base. In Israel, the absence of technology seems to be the reason thwarting the advantages of 'vertical integration.'[2] Israeli oil and gas companies, lacking technology, repeatedly met with failures in E&P, obliging the government to invite international private investment into the petroleum sector. However, with the discovery of vast reserves, and the potential for more discoveries, there is room for the establishment of a public sector energy company.

The biggest beneficiary of the natural gas 'revolution' in Israel has been the electricity sector that has undergone the greatest change in fuel consumption mix. Once the Yam Tethys field came on stream in 2004, it together with the import of piped gas from Egypt, helped expand the production of electricity from natural gas. As the natural gas import agreement with Egypt collapsed in 2011 and Yam Tethys depleted in 2012, Israel faced a severe shortage of electricity, creating a crisis in supply. Conditions improved with the beginning of gas production from the Tamar field in 2013 that once again enabled the economy to revert to electricity generation from natural gas. With about two-thirds of electricity supply in Israel based on natural gas in 2017, it is a welcome improvement from the more polluting and expensive coal and oil. The shift to a natural gas-based electricity sector has allowed Israel to increase the share of domestic energy production and has helped the economy to overcome the vulnerabilities associated with the purchase of expensive liquid fuels and potential disruptions in supply.

Israel's gas bonanza has also benefitted its manufacturing sector a great deal gas bonanza is the manufacturing sector. Large industrial plants were the first to adopt natural gas. Because of their massive operation, the cost of using natural gas relative to cost of alternative fuels is low. Small consumers in the manufacturing sector have been less enthusiastic about incorporating natural gas in their production process, due to the high cost of connecting to natural gas network. Lack of a widespread gas distribution network has also played a role in the sluggish response of such consumers, discussed in Chapter 3. However, as gas prices become competitive for the industry with the onset of new fields operated by diverse players, and with the expansion of distribution infrastructure, the cost of converting to natural gas for small industrial units will become more efficient. This trend is already apparent in GSPAs concluded between the industrial units and Leviathan and Karish – Tanian developers. A reduction in the cost of production will have a salutary impact on the export competitiveness of Israeli products.

The conversion of the industrial sector to natural gas-based energy use is also beneficial to the environment. At the interface of economy and society lies the looming problem of pollution and climate change. Natural gas burns cleaner than coal, diesel or gasoline, producing 50–60 percent less carbon dioxide than coal and 20–30 percent less than oil and negligible emissions of greenhouse gases – and lowers the discharge of greenhouse gases.[3] Therefore, the Israeli government has an interest in creating a preference for natural gas over diesel and oil for industrial use. At present, excise tax on coal (used exclusively in electricity generation and diesel related to transportation) is heavy; If the fuel excise duty is raised up, it would act as a break on the preference of the manufacturing sector for oil over natural gas, even as the era of depressed oil prices is bringing down the cost of production. It will also drive the manufacturers to make environmentally informed choices about the type of fuel they choose for their businesses. A similar tax on natural gas in the manufacturing would ensure a prudent use of the internal resource.

Natural gas is not only a source of energy for the manufacturing sector, but also a raw material for the production of methanol – the basic molecule that can set into motion the establishment of a host of subsidiary industries. The emergence of a petrochemical industry in Israel will depend on the availability of natural gas at a price that can justify the domestic production of petrochemicals relative to import. Similarly, the use of natural gas in transportation has suffered a blow with the global drop in oil prices. Not seen as cost-efficient in the private vehicle segment in Israel, if natural gas does become a transportation fuel in the future, tax on CNG should reflect the externalities – such as pollution, crowding of roads, parking, and use of infrastructure – intrinsic to the use of such vehicles.

The increase in the availability of natural gas along with the reform of the electricity sector will encourage private companies to enter the power production market. Already, IPPs operating in industrial zones and factory complexes are using cogeneration power plants to provide, onsite electricity and energy.[4] Small power producers (SPPs) can use the expanding gas supply to generate electricity for direct retail sales to kibbutzim, shopping malls, recreation centres, hospitals, factories, and universities. Excess electricity can be sold to the national electricity grid nearest to the energy-producing site. However, these consumers are not likely to completely back off the national electricity grid since they will continue to depend on it for cover case of a breakdown. The SPPs, utilising natural gas and renewable sources foretell the emergence of smart grid that detect and respond to local changes in usage, through hi-tech digital technology, thus enhancing the efficiency of power consumption.

The transition to the use of natural gas has led to cumulative earning of about $2.83 billion for the Israeli economy in the 10-year period between 2004 and 2013.[5] Israel has had a current account surplus since 2003, the year in which natural gas came online. In 2013 and 2014, it expanded to 2.9 percent and 3.8 percent of GDP, respectively, as an upshot of production from the Tamar reservoir. Further, in 2015, the surplus expanded further to 5.2 percent of GDP due to improved terms of trade, ensuing from the decline in energy prices (oil prices declined by more than 50 percent in 2015). As oil prices firmed up comparatively in 2016 and stabilised, Israel's surplus remained high at 3.8 percent.[6] In 2016, the BoI purchased $4.9 billion in foreign currency, of which $1.5 billion was to, offset the impact of the appreciation of the shekel on the current account.[7] The negative effect of the appreciation of the domestic currency on inflation and export are among the considerations for BoI's monetary accommodation.[8]

Dealing with currency appreciation requires both short-term and long-term measures. The BoI has employed two short-term instruments: These are the direct interventions in the foreign currency market through the purchase of US dollars in inter-bank trade, and the reduction of the short-term interest rate. As far as the long-term approach is concerned, Israel has set up a SWF to stabilise its currency when tax on excess profits or levy begin to accrue to the government. The BoI announced in early November 2018 that it will halt the foreign exchange acquisition programme once the Leviathan starts production. That is because Israel's SWF is expected to begin operations in 2020.

Israel may have formulated an export policy for its gas resource, but securing export contracts and building export infrastructure to far-off consumers is proving to be a tricky proposition. The difficulties associated with export were one of the several reasons why the debate on the export of gas was so furious in Israel. The critics of gas export vociferously argued that the country should build up a strategic reserve in the first instance and then export if geopolitical and security expediencies of the state so demand. It is pertinent to remember here that the gas contract with the NEPCO is still subject to political risks, as it is being attacked on the Jordanian street; the with Dolphinus of Egypt is highly unpopular as well. An additional reason for keeping the gas within the country comes from the geologists,[9] who believe it is unlikely that Israel will find more gas that could be commercially extractable. Moreover, Israel's upstream gas sector has had no exploratory drilling between 2013 and 2018. They are critical of the government's push for export and instead favour a policy that builds strategic reserves for the next 40 years and incentivises local use of the proven reserve.

Turkey–Israel ties have hurtled downhill following US recognition of Jerusalem as the capital of Israel, and their worsening diplomatic relations is affecting the prospect of a pipeline from Leviathan to Ankara's Ceyhan port. The lack of a maritime agreement between Cyprus and Turkey adds to the complications and, of late, Turkey's belligerent attitude towards the Republic of Cyprus' offshore drilling offers little scope for optimism on the Israeli-Turkish pipeline. The breakdown of relations between Israel and the PA has stalled discussions on the development of the Gaza Marine field, as it has for export of gas from Israeli fields to a planned power station in Jenin in the north of the West Bank.

Israeli gas field developers' successful gas export deal with a private Egyptian company is too small and hardly the anchor agreement required to finance the second phase of the Leviathan's development. Egypt's gas production recovery during 2016–2018 had made the country sufficient transitorily in terms of its gas requirement; Egypt will continue to import some gas in gas, but it might still have to import in view of its galloping demand. Moreover, close security cooperation between Israel and Egypt has created a quid pro quo situation: Greater economic cooperation in return for Israeli security. Hence, gas deals between Israeli field developers and private Egyptian players or with the international companies operating its LNG facilities are possible in the future. The United States remains a strong backer of greater Israeli–Egyptian and Israeli-Jordanian economic cooperation, believing it would catalyse, the normalisation of Arab-Israeli relations.

It is instructive that the US Assistant Secretary of State for Energy Resources, Francis R. Fannon, travelled to Israel, Egypt, and Cyprus on a three-nation visit in November 2018 to discuss regional cooperation and energy security. His visit took place in the wake of the agreement between Noble-Delek and East Gas that will facilitate the delivery of natural gas from the Leviathan and Tamar gas fields to Egypt. However, regional energy cooperation with Israel is unlikely to gather momentum in a swift manner. Energy contracts, particularly gas deals, are notoriously difficult to get off the ground, given the difficulties involved in transportation and storage. The sensitivity of the Egyptians to a tighter embrace of Israel is an ubiquitous intervening factor in transactions between Israel and Egypt.

Israel's proclivity for the EastMed pipeline is mired in a host of political and economic issues discussed in Chapter 4. Neither Israel's Leviathan nor Cyprus' Aphrodite have secured 'anchor' export contracts to make EastMed look profitable.

The leaders of both countries, along with those of Greece and Italy, have been making upbeat statements about the project, that emerges more from geopolitical posturing against Turkey, than from the confidence in its commercial feasibility.

In view of the difficulties stemming from the exercise of the export option, the question whether the most suitable utilisation of Israel's gas is in the domestic market crops up. Two factors are worth taking into consideration here: first, Israel's proven gas reserve is small and, second, the share of gas is still surpassed by oil in the primary energy mix, which indicates the vast scope for absorption of gas in the economy. Using one's own gas reserve will boost the country's energy security, provide savings on import, allow for the delivery of environmental benefits to the people, as well as meet international emission obligations. Israel has already started converting coal-fired powered stations to gas, all private power producers use gas as a fuel, and new power plants will solely run on natural gas. In contrast, the geopolitical and geoeconomic challenges to export are too many. While these challenges are unlikely to be resolved soon and export pipelines may not materialise quickly, the changes in domestic regulations suggested by the Adiri Committee have the potential to attract investments in the upstream sector and propel the development of the gas industry in Israel.

Israel's success in discovering gas reserves in the Eastern Mediterranean region has induced its neighbours to begin or accelerate exploration for oil and gas. Cyprus has successfully explored its EEZ and discovered two gas fields, and Lebanon held its first offshore licensing round in 2017. The Israeli – Lebanon conflict over the demarcation of the maritime boundary potentially rich in resources is an ongoing problem that has triggered fiery rhetoric from both sides about their readiness to defend their resources using every means, including military action. A resolution of the dispute here would go a long way in alleviating the insecurity of oil and gas companies and towards making the area more secure for investment. In particular, the gas resource presents Israel with the prospect of engaging in bilateral and multilateral discussions with regional countries on issues of common interest that can only have positive outcomes. Israel's improved relations with Cyprus and Greece are cases in point and worth are replicating in the larger Arab world.

Notes

1 "Economy and Economic Policy," *Bank of Israel Annual Report – 2015*, March 28, 2016, p. 24, www.boi.org.il/en/NewsAndPublications/RegularPublications/Pages/Doch BankIsrael2015.aspx (accessed on September 9, 2018).

2 Silvana Tordo with Brandon S. Tracy, and Noora Arfaa, *National Oil Companies and Value Creation*, World Bank Working Paper No. 218, The World Bank Washington, DC, 2011, p. xiv, https://siteresources.worldbank.org/INTOGMC/Resources/9780821388310.pdf (accessed on September 11, 2018).

3 However, its production generates large amounts of condensate – a low-density mixture of hydrocarbon liquids present in the raw natural gas, which is toxic with prolonged or repeated exposure. Concerns and fears about condensate contamination have driven the

people of the Hof Hacarmel regional council in north-western Israel to protest against the building of Leviathan's production platform a few kilometres away from the shore.

4 See *The Future of Israel's Electricity Market*, Budget Department, Ministry of Finance, State of Israel, pp. 14–15, https://energy.org.il/wp-content/uploads/2017/01/%D7%9 E%D7%A6%D7%92%D7%AA-%D7%90%D7%95%D7%93%D7%99-%D7%90%D7% 93%D7%99%D7%A8%D7%99.pdf (accessed on September 11, 2018).

5 "Natural Gas Rents," *The World Bank* data, 2013, https://data.worldbank.org/indica tor/NY.GDP.NGAS.RT.ZS?locations=IL; "GDP (current US$)," *The World Bank* data, https://data.worldbank.org/indicator/NY.GDP.MKTP.CD?locations=IL (accessed on September 16, 2018).

6 Based on *Central Bureau of Statistics*, June 2018, www.cbs.gov.il/reader/?MIval=cw_usr_ view_SHTML&ID=829 (accessed on September 20, 2018); *World Bank National Accounts Data, and OECD National Accounts Data Files*, https://data.worldbank.org/indicator/ NY.GDP.MKTP.CD?locations=IL (accessed on September 20, 2018); "The Economy and Economic Policy," Bank of Israel Annual Report – 2015, p. 21.

7 "The Economy and Economic Policy," *Bank of Israel Annual Report – 2016*, March 29, 2017, p. 11, www.boi.org.il/en/NewsAndPublications/RegularPublications/Pages/ DochBankIsrael2016.aspx (accessed on September 23, 2018).

8 "The Economy and Economic Policy," *Bank of Israel Annual Report – 2017*, March 28, 2018, p. 10, www.boi.org.il/en/NewsAndPublications/RegularPublications/Pages/ DochBankIsrael2017.aspx (accessed on September 26, 2018).

9 David Israel, "Geologist: Israel Plans Excessive Natural Gas Exports, Draining Finite Resources," *The Jewish Press*, October 24, 2018, www.jewishpress.com/news/politics/geol ogist-israel-plans-excessive-natural-gas-exports-draining-finite-resources/2018/10/24/ (accessed on October 24, 2018).

GLOSSARY

A current account surplus is a positive current account balance, indicating that a country is exporting a greater value of goods and services than it is importing. When this happens, it implies that the country is a net lender to the rest of the world, i.e., it has surplus foreign exchange it can use to invest in other countries. Thus, a country with a current account surplus, will have a deficit on the financial/capital account, suggesting the country is increasing its ownership of foreign assets.

An Independent Power Producer (IPP) is an entity, which is not owned by the national electricity company or public utility, but which owns facilities to generate electric power and sometimes heat via cogeneration, for sale to the utility and end users.

An ISO tank is a tank container, which is built to the ISO standard (International Organisation for Standardisation). ISO tanks are designed to carry liquids, gases, and powders, both hazardous and non-hazardous, as bulk cargoes. The tank is made of stainless steel and is surrounded by several protective layers that offer enhanced safety and security for shipping chemicals by taking chemicals off roadways and reducing the incidence of accidents. ISO containers are also intermodal, that is, they can be used across different modes of transport without the need to unload and reload the cargo.

Cogeneration power plant or Combined Heat and Power (CHP) plant is one in which heat generated during electricity production (and allowed to escape and go waste) is used to provide cooling or heating for industrial facilities. CHP plants are frequently located inside industrial complexes close to end users to help reduce transmission and distribution losses, and can help achieve energy savings by 40 percent.

Combined-Cycle power generation is the typical process, which uses both gas turbine and steam turbine to generate the electricity, and which produces

50 percent more electricity from the same fuel than the normal process. First, the gas turbine burns the fuel. Then, a heat recovery system captures heat produced in the process to create steam. That steam is routed to the nearby steam turbine, which produces additional power.

Compound Annual Growth Rate (CAGR) is a measure of growth over multiple time periods. It can be thought of as the growth rate in the initial value of a quantity, if the assumption is that the value of the quantity has compounded over the time periods. Growth over a period of time is subject to several factors, each having different impacts in different years. Therefore, to understand an average growth of a quantity over a period of time, taking into account all the factors, one needs to use the CAGR.

Condensate is a very light hydrocarbon (such as gas oil and naphtha and gas liquids like ethane, butane, and propane) that remains liquid at room temperature and pressure. In underground formations, condensate can exist separately from the crude oil and gas or dissolve in crude oil and gas. Recovered mainly from gas reservoirs, condensates are very similar to light stabilised crude oil and are used as feedstock for oil refining and other petrochemical industries.

Diversification of energy means using different energy resources in the energy mix, buying energy from varied suppliers as shield against intimidation, coercion, and manipulation, and using several transportation routes such as tankers and pipelines to reduce dependence on a single resource or provider. A country that diversifies its energy mix insulates itself from energy disruptions, such as, supply or price shocks and strengthens its energy security. Renewable energy is increasingly becoming the leitmotif of global energy security because any country can produce it.

Electricity generation is power generated from fossil fuels, nuclear power plants, hydropower plants (excluding pumped storage), geothermal systems, solar panels, biofuels, wind, etc. It includes electricity produced in electricity-only plants and in cogeneration (combined heat and power) plants. It is the secondary production of the transformation of primary energy sources.

Emissions are releases of pollutants into the atmosphere from motor vehicles or factories.

Energy transformation is the process of transforming primary energy into secondary energy or further levels of energy. For example, crude oil is transformed into gasoline, diesel, and aviation fuel through the refining process for use in transportation. Similarly, coal and natural gas are used to produce heat and electricity in industrial processes and power plants. Further, primary energy derived from solar, water, and wind are utilised to generate heat and electricity.

Excess profit tax is the tax imposed by certain businesses on profit over and above what is estimated to be a normal return on capital investment and is assessed in addition to corporate income tax and royalty.

Exploration and production is the upstream sector in the oil and gas industry; the companies involved focus on finding, producing, and selling different types of oil and gas.

Floating production, storage, and offloading (FPSO) vessel is a ship-shaped offshore production facility that gathers hydrocarbon (oil and gas) from subsea production wells through a series of in-field pipelines, processes it, and stores it until oil or gas can be transported to the shore by pipeline or offloaded into shuttle tankers.

Fossil fuels, of which coal, oil, and natural gas are primary, are produced from the fossilisation of plants and animals over millions of years. Fossil fuels have fuelled the fast pace of global economic development over the past century and are currently the world's primary energy source. However, fossil fuels are finite resources and their burning produces harmful gases that can also irreparably damage the environment in a way that can cause change in Earth's climate.

Gas field is an area consisting of one or more reservoirs, all of which are related to the same geological structure or rock layer. A single field may support commercial production from several separate reservoirs at varying depths.

Gas reservoir is a naturally occurring storage area for natural gas (and/or oil) in a formation of rock. The oil and gas collect in the small, interconnected pore spaces of rock and are sealed below ground surface by an impervious layer of rock. These reservoirs do not occur as 'puddles' or 'lakes' of gas (and/or oil) beneath the surface so it might seem as if there are no vast open cavities that contain oil.

Government take is the total amount of revenue a government receives from production processes, including taxes, royalties, and government participation.

Ground level ozone or 'smog' is air pollution that reduces visibility and can trigger a variety of respiratory problem in humans as well as damage to plants and ecosystems. Ozone is a gaseous molecule that contains three oxygen atoms (O3). In the stratospheric level of the atmosphere, it shields the earth against harmful ultraviolet radiation from the sun. Close to the troposphere or ground level, it is the main component of smog. Ground level ozone is created when oxides of nitrogen (NOx) and volatile organic compounds (VOC or quick evaporating hydrocarbons) emitted from motor vehicle exhaust, power plants using fossil fuels, industrial boilers, refineries, chemical plants, and other sources chemically react in the presence of sunlight. Also called photochemical ozone, the 'haze' can be transported over distances by wind, so areas with low pollution can also experience high ozone level.

High-octane fuels are those which can stand high compression before igniting. When the air fuel/gasoline mixture ignites by the heat of compression rather than because of the spark from the spark plug, it causes a knocking sound and can be damaging for the engine. The higher the fuel's octane number, the more resistant it will be to knock. High-octane fuels are compatible with high compression or powerful, fuel-efficient engines while potentially reducing emissions by burning the fuel more completely. An octane rating, or octane number, is therefore a standard measure of the performance of an engine or fuel. Ethanol is partly used to increase the octane rating of the gasoline

Hydrocarbons are chemical compounds that contain hydrogen and carbon bonded into molecules in a variety of ways. Hydrocarbon-based fuels such as gasoline, diesel, and CNG power motor vehicles. Pollution from unburned or partially burned fuel is emitted from the engine in the form exhausts are responsible for grave harm to the environment. They combine with nitrogen oxides in the presence of sunlight to form ozone that could cause serious health troubles. These chemicals are also the basis for everyday products such as fabricated wood, paints, fibres, and plastic. Hydrocarbons have both positive and negative value to living beings.

Licensing round is the award of licenses of specified and demarcated piece of geographical areas at land or sea to an oil and gas company or a joint venture to allow them to search for commercially feasible deposits of petroleum and to maximise economic recovery if such resources are found. The procedure for the award of the licenses vary greatly from one country to another, but the most common is the bid system where the highest bidder obtains the petroleum exploration rights for a limited period of time.

Natural gas is a colourless, odourless, and highly flammable hydrocarbon consisting primarily of methane, created from the decomposition and pressurisation of algae, plankton, and other organisms deposited millions of years ago in environments such as swamps, lakes, river deltas, and seabeds. It is gaseous in its natural state and can also be liquefied for easy transportation. Unlike oil or coal, natural gas burns extremely cleanly and produces very low levels of harmful waste and byproducts.

Nitrogen Oxides (NO_x) are a group of highly reactive gases that contain nitrogen and oxygen in varying amounts. The common pollutant nitrogen dioxide (NO_2) is produced from the burning of fossil fuels. In areas of high motor vehicular traffic (cars, trucks, and buses), the amount of nitrogen oxides emitted into the atmosphere can be significant. Nitrogen oxides are also produced by power plants and industrial sources that burn fuels. NO_2 combines with particles in the air as a reddish-brown layer, making the air hazy and harmful to breathe. NO_2 and other NO_x interact with water, oxygen, and other chemicals in the atmosphere to form acid rain, harmful to humans and sensitive ecosystems such as lakes and forests.

Nitrogenous fertilisers are one of the most common categories of fertilisers produced from the nitrogen element. Since the deficiency of nitrogen in the soil is the foremost issue in crop cultivation, such fertilisers are essential to increasing the production of crops. Crops respond to nitrogen better than to other nutrients.

Olefins, also known as alkenes, are one of the most common types of petrochemical that constitute the basis for polymers used to make plastic, resins, fibres, lubricants, and gels.

Petroleum literally means 'rock oil' and in common parlance is the name given to crude oil. In industry, it is a general term for crude oil and natural gas.

Petroleum products / Petrochemicals are those obtained from crude oil and natural gas during processing in the refineries. These include transportation fuels (automotive gasoline and aviation gasoline), fuel oils for heating and electricity generation, asphalt and road oil for laying metalled roads, Naptha, LPG, lubricants waxes, and feedstocks for making the chemicals, plastics, fibres, and synthetic materials that constitute nearly everything we use in daily life. The petrochemical industry, thus, has direct interface with the petroleum industry.

Potassium nitrate fertilisers are sources of two major essential plant nutrients, potassium and nitrogen. It is commonly used as a fertiliser to increase the yield of high-value crops. Applications of such fertilisers to soil require careful calibration.

Primary energy is an energy form found in nature that has not been subjected to any anthropogenic conversion process. Secondary energy source is obtained from primary energy sources through a transformation process. For example, gasoline, the secondary product better suited for motor transport, is obtained from crude oil, the primary product from. Primary energy can be non-renewable or renewable.

Primary energy consumption refers to the direct use at the source, or supply to users without transformation, of crude energy, that is, energy that has not been subjected to any conversion or transformation process.

Primary energy supply is defined as energy at the disposal of the economy in the period under review in terms of local production plus energy imports, exports, minus international bunkers, and stock changes. Data on export of energy and marine bunkers are deducted and stock changes are added or subtracted to arrive at the amount of energy at the disposal of the economy.

Renewable energy originates from sources that are continually replenished or replenished on a human timescale, such as solar power, wind, rain, tides, waves, geothermal heat, and production of energy through biological processes (biogas).

Shale gas (and/or oil) is a natural gas found in several different types of rocks, including shale, sandstone, and coal seams. Shales are fine-grained sedimentary rocks and are often very rich sources of oil and natural gas. As they have low permeability, i.e., interconnectivity between pores within a rock, it becomes difficult to extract oil or gas from a reservoir. Greater permeability can be artificially created by applying hydraulic fracturing or ('fracking') to the reservoir.

Stream day is a method of defining a refinery's production capacity during continuous operation for a single day when running at full capacity and ignoring any slowdowns or outages. In contrast, a refiner's capacity is also recorded as calendar day, which is total production or actual hour operation in a year divided by the days in that year. Similarly, barrels per stream day

(BSD or BPSD), is the quantity of oil processed by a refining unit during a 24-hour period of continuous operation.

Upstream and downstream sectors are two major areas of the petroleum industry. The upstream sector concerns E&P, that is, search for oil and gas underground on land and offshore in seas. It involves drilling exploratory wells on the basis of seismic data and maps of petroleum plays and, if the hydrocarbon is discovered in situ, then its recovery to the surface and transfer to the processing site. Downstream industry includes operations such as processing, storage, and sale of the discovered oil and gas. Oil refineries and petrochemical units are parts of the downstream sector, as are petroleum product distribution through retail outlets. Natural gas distribution companies are also part of the downstream operations.

BIBLIOGRAPHY

Primary sources: reports, articles, and presentations

$15 Billion Agreements Signed for the Sale of Israeli Natural Gas to Egypt, February 19, 2010, 3pp., www.delekdrilling.co.il/sites/default/files/wysiwyg_uploads/Dolphinus.pdf

About the Company, Eilat Ashkelon Pipeline Co. Ltd. (EAPC), 2018, http://eapc.com/about-us/company-profile/

About National Coal Supply Corporation, The National Coal Supply Corporation Limited, undated, http://ncsc.co.il/?page_id=101&lang=en

Additional Prospect: Dalit, Delek Group, 2017, www.delek-group.com/our-operations/east-med/

"Addressing Oil Shale Extraction in Israel," *Environment Bulletin*, Volume 41 (January 2015), pp. 27–30, Israel Ministry of Environmental Protection (MoEP), State of Israel.

Adoption of the Main Recommendations of the Committee to Examine the Government's Policy Regarding the Natural Gas Market in Israel, Government Resolution 442, Ministry of Energy, State of Israel, June 23, 2013, https://www.gov.il/he/Departments/policies/2013_des442

Adoption of Tzemach Committee Conclusions Could Harm the Public and Could Cause Irreparable Damage to the Economy and the Environment, Ministry of Environmental Protection, State of Israel, April 4, 2013, www.sviva.gov.il/English/ResourcesandServices/NewsAndEvents/NewsAndMessageDover/Pages/2012/08_August_2012/TzemachCommitteeConclusionsHarmful.aspx

Adopting the Main Recommendations of the Professional Team for the Periodic Review of the Recommendations of the Committee to Examine the Government's Policy on the Natural Gas Sector in Israel and the Amendment of the Government Decision, Government Decision 442, Prime Minister's Office, January 6, 2019, https://www.gov.il/he/Departments/policies/dec4442_2019 (accessed on February 11, 2019).

Alona Sheafer-Caro, *The Position of the Ministry of Environmental Protection – Recommendations of the Committee to Examine Government Policy in the Natural Gas Industry* [Hebrew], September 12, 2012, 6pp., http://archive.energy.gov.il/Subjects/NG/Documents/NGSviva.pdf

Alternative Fuels Administration, Prime Minister's Office, State of Israel, www.pmo.gov.il/English/PrimeMinistersOffice/DivisionsAndAuthorities/OilFree/Pages/IsraelOilFreeInitiative.aspx

Amendment of the Outline for Increasing the Quantity of Natural Gas Produced From the Tamar Natural Gas Field and the Rapid Development of the Leviathan, Shark and Tannin Natural Gas Fields and Other Natural Gas Fields, Government Decision 1465, Prime Minister's Office, May 22, 2016, www.gov.il/he/Departments/policies/2016_dec1465

Annual Energy Outlook 2011: With Projections to 2035, April 2011, EIA, 246pp., www.eia.gov/outlooks/aeo/pdf/0383(2011).pdf

Annual Report on Competition Policy Developments in Israel, Directorate for Financial and Enterprise Affairs, Organisation for Economic Co-operation and Development, June 11, 2013, 17pp., www.oecd.org/officialdocuments/publicdisplaydocumentpdf/?cote=DAF/COMP/AR(2013)15&docLanguage=En

Annual Report on Competition Policy Developments in Israel – 2015, Organisation for Economic Co-operation and Development (OECD), June 15–17, 2016, 13pp., www.oecd.org/officialdocuments/publicdisplaydocumentpdf/?cote=DAF/COMP/AR(2016)5&docLanguage=En

Another Important Step Taken in the Israeli Electric Vehicle Market: The Ministry of Energy Is Investing NIS 25 Million to Establish Recharging Stations for Electric Vehicles Nationwide! Press Release, Ministry of Energy, State of Israel, August 20, 2018, www.gov.il/en/Departments/news/electric_car_200818

Aphrodite Gas Field, Delek Drilling, undated, www.delekdrilling.co.il/en/project/aphrodite-gas-field

Approval of the Development Plan for the Leviathan Field of 21 bcm Per Year by the Petroleum Commissioner, Delek Group, June 7, 2016, https://ir.delek-group.com/news-releases/news-release-details/approval-development-plan-leviathan-field-21-bcm-year-petroleum

Are We Entering the Golden Age of Gas? Special Report, World Energy Outlook, IEA, 2011, 121pp., www.iea.org/publications/freepublications/publication/WEO2011_GoldenAgeofGasReport.pdf

Article 52, Restrictive Trade Practices Law, 5748–1988, The Antitrust Authority, State of Israel, www.antitrust.gov.il/eng/Antitrustlaw.aspx

Ashalim, BrightSource, 2015, www.brightsourceenergy.com/ashalim-solar-project#.WP9ScCN962w

Ashalim Power Station, Israel, GE Renewable Energy, 2016, www.ge.com/content/dam/gepower-renewables/global/en_US/downloads/brochures/solar-csp-ashalim-gea32278.pdf

Assessment of Undiscovered Oil and Gas Resources of the Levant Basin Province, Eastern Mediterranean, United States Geological Survey (USGS), Virginia, United States, March 12, 2010, https://pubs.usgs.gov/fs/2010/3014/ (accessed on August 14, 2016).

"At a Glance: News in Brief About the Environment in Israel," *Israel Environment Bulletin*, Volume 39 (July 2013), MoEP, pp. 6–7, www.sviva.gov.il/English/ResourcesandServices/Publications/Bulletin/Documents/Bulletin-Vol39-July2013.pdf

At the Weekly Cabinet Meeting, Prime Minister's Office, June 28, 2015, www.pmo.gov.il/english/mediacenter/secretaryannouncements/pages/govmes280615.aspx

At the Weekly Cabinet Meeting, PMO, State of Israel, July 31, 2005, www.pmo.gov.il/english/mediacenter/secretaryannouncements/pages/govmes310705.aspx

At the Weekly Cabinet Meeting, PMO, State of Israel, August 16, 2015, www.pmo.gov.il/english/mediacenter/secretaryannouncements/pages/govmes160815.aspx

Avenues for Collaboration: Recommendations for US-China Transportation Fuel Cooperation, United States Energy Security Council, Potomac, Maryland, United States, 2015, 42pp., www.iags.org/USChinaFC.pdf

Bank of Israel Annual Report – 2015, March 28, 2016, www.boi.org.il/en/NewsAnd Publications/RegularPublications/Pages/DochBankIsrael2015.aspx

Bank of Israel Annual Report – 2016, March 28, 2017, www.boi.org.il/en/NewsAnd Publications/RegularPublications/Pages/DochBankIsrael2016.aspx

Bank of Israel Annual Report – 2017, March 28, 2018, www.boi.org.il/en/NewsAnd Publications/RegularPublications/Pages/DochBankIsrael2017.aspx

Bank of Israel to Offset Effect of Natural Gas, Israeli Missions Around the World, undated, http://embassies.gov.il/MFA/InnovativeIsrael/economy/Pages/Bank-of-Israel-to-offset-effect-of-natural-gas.aspx

Bar, Yaniv, *The Natural Gas Sector in Israel: An Economic Survey*, Bank Leumi, January 2017, 19pp., https://english.leumi.co.il/static-files/10/LeumiEnglish/Leumi_Review/Natural GasinIsraelacc.pdf

Barbe, Andre and David Riker, *Obstacles to International Trade in Natural Gas*, Office of Industries, US International Trade Commission, Washington, DC, No. ID-15-043, December 2015, 39pp., www.usitc.gov/publications/332/obstacles_natural_gas_final_pdf_accessible.pdf

Bonshtien, Anat, *Israel Fuel Choices Initiative*, Prime Minister's Office, undated, www.weizmann.ac.il/SAERI/sites/AERI/files/fuelchoicesppt_anatbonstein.pdf

Cabinet Approves Increase in Quantity of Gas for the Israeli Economy, PMO, State of Israel, June 23, 2013, www.pmo.gov.il/English/MediaCenter/Spokesman/Pages/spokegas 230613.aspx

Cabinet Approves National NIS 250 Million Plan to Advance Smart Transportation, January 22, 2017, Prime Minister's Office, State of Israel, www.pmo.gov.il/English/MediaCenter/Spokesman/Pages/spokeTransportation220117.aspx

Calculation of Reserves, Tethys Oil, undated, www.tethysoil.com/en/operations/oil-and-natural-gas/calculation-of-reserves

Call No. 75/2018 – Acceleration of the Deployment of the Distribution Network, Ministry of Energy, State of Israel, May 28, 2018, www.gov.il/he/Departments/publications/Call_for_bids/tender75_18

Chairman Cabel, *In Israel It Is Easy to Make Everything a Security Issue*, The Knesset, Press Release, December 14, 2015, www.knesset.gov.il/spokesman/eng/PR_eng.asp?PRID=11815

A Comparison of Fiscal Regimes: Offshore Natural Gas in Israel, Special Report, IHS CERA, 2010, www.mof.gov.il/Committees/PreviouslyCommittees/PhysicsPolicy Committee/ServedOpinion_NovelEnergy_Appendix_d.pdf

Conclusions of the Committee for the Examination of the Fiscal Policy on Oil and Gas Resources in Israel, State of Israel [Sheshinski Committee] [Hebrew], Ministry of Finance, State of Israel, January 2011, https://mof.gov.il/BudgetSite/reform/Documents/shashinskiFullReport_n.pdf

Conclusions of the Professional Committee for the Periodic Review of the Recommendations of the Committee for Examination of Government Policy on the Natural Gas Sector in Israel, Which Were Adopted in Government Decision 442 of 23 June 2013 [Adiri Committee] [Hebrew] Ministry of Energy, State of Israel, December 2018 (accessed on February 5, 2019).

Conclusions of the Professional Team for the Periodic Examination of the Recommendations of the Committee on Examining the Government's Policy in the Natural Gas Market Adopted in Government Decision 442 Dated June 23 2013 [Adiri Committee], Executive Summary, Ministry of Energy, State of Israel, December 2018, http://www.energy-sea.gov.il/English-Site/PublishingImages/Pages/Forms/EditForm/Adiri%20Committee%20Final%20Recommendations%2018.12.2018%20Executive%20Summary%20-%20Translation.pdf (accessed on February 11, 2019).

Consent to be Bound by a Treaty Expressed by Ratification, Acceptance or Approval, Article 14, 1(a), United Nations Vienna Convention on the Law of Treaties, May 23, 1969, www.jus.uio.no/lm/un.law.of.treaties.convention.1969/14.html

Consumption and Demand, Israel Natural Gas Lines, Ministry of Energy, State of Israel, 2013, www.ingl.co.il/facts-and-information/national-transmission-network/?lang=en

Council Decisions, Council for Natural Gas Affairs, Ministry of Energy, State of Israel, undated, http://archive.energy.gov.il/Subjects/NG/Pages/GxmsMniNGPublications Aggregator.aspx

Country Comparison: Natural Gas – Proved Reserves, The World Factbook, Central Investigation Agency, undated, www.cia.gov/library/publications/the-world-factbook/rankorder/2253rank.html

Country Focus: Israel, Ernst and Young Global Limited, undated, www.ey.com/gl/en/industries/power-utilities/recai-israel

Daniel Johnston, *Israel Hydrocarbon Fiscal Analysis and Commentary*, Daniel Johnston & Co., Inc., November 15, 2010, 6pp. [opinion to the Sheshinski Committee], 42pp., www.eisourcebook.org/cms/Israel,%20Hydrocarbon%20Fiscal%20Analysis%20and%20Commentary.pdf

The Deep Water LNG Terminal, Israel Natural Gas Lines, Ministry of Energy, State of Israel, 2013, www.ingl.co.il/the-deep-water-lng-terminal/?lang=en

Delek Group Announces Consolidated Full Year & Fourth Quarter 2017 Results, March 28, 2018, www.bloomberg.com/press-releases/2018-03-28/delek-group-announces-consolidated-full-year-fourth-quarter-2017-results

"Description of Actions Resulting From Implementation of the Proposed Plan," *National Outline Plan NOP 37/H – Marine Environment Impact Survey*, June 2013, pp. 30–110, https://www3.opic.gov/Environment/EIA/nobleenergy/ESIA/TranslatedTAMA 37HEIAOffshoresections/Offshore_EIA_Chapters_3_4_5.pdf

A Direct Link to New Sources for Europe, IGI Poseidon, www.igi-poseidon.com/en/eastmed

The Distribution Network [Hebrew], Ministry of Energy, State of Israel, undated, http://archive.energy.gov.il/Subjects/NG/Pages/GxmsMniNGDistributionNetwork.aspx (accessed on June 4, 2017).

Dor Chemicals, Fiat Chrysler Automobiles (FCA) and IFCI Present Jointly the New Choice of Fuel, the M15. A Methanol Powered Vehicle FIAT 500 M15 Is Launched at the Fuel Choices 2016 Summit, Press Release, Dor Chemicals (Haifa, Israel), November 3, 2016, 3pp., www.methanol.org/wp-content/uploads/2016/11/Dor-Press-Release.pdf

Draft Recommendations: Committee for Increasing Competition in the Economy [Hebrew], Ministry of Finance, State of Israel, October 11, 2011, 325pp., http://mof.gov.il/Committees/CompetitivenessCommittee/TyuyatRec_Report.pdf

Dunn, Candace, *China's Use of Methanol in Liquid Fuels Has Grown Rapidly Since 2000*, February 23, 2017, EIA, US Department of Energy, Washington, DC, www.eia.gov/todayinenergy/detail.php?id=30072

East Med E&P: Our Assets, Delek Group, 2017, www.delek-group.com/our-operations/east-med/

East Med E&P: Our Business Environment, Delek Group, 2017, www.delek-group.com/our-operations/east-med-our-business-environment/

Economic & Commercial Report for October 2010, Embassy of India, Tel Aviv, 23pp., http://pharmexcil.org/uploadfile/ufiles/293698897_Israel_Annual_Eco_and_Com_Rep_2010.pdf

"The Economy and Economic Policy," *Bank of Israel Annual Report – 2015*, April 2016, pp. 1–32, www.boi.org.il/en/NewsAndPublications/RegularPublications/Pages/DochBankIsrael2015.aspx

Egypt-Israel Peace Treaty, March 26, 1979, Israel ministry of Foreign Affairs, www.mfa. gov.il/mfa/foreignpolicy/peace/guide/pages/israel-egypt%20peace%20treaty.aspx

Egypt-Israel: The Taba Boundary Dispute, CIA, May 21, 1986, 31pp., www.cia.gov/library/ readingroom/docs/CIA-RDP86T01017R000100960001-4.pdf

Egyptian LNG, PETRONAS, www.petronas.com.my/our-business/gas-power/lng/Pages/ egyptian_lng.aspx

The Electricity Sector in Israel [Hebrew], Ministry of Energy, State of Israel, undated, http:// archive.energy.gov.il/Subjects/Electricity/Pages/GxmsMniElectricityProduction. aspx (accessed on August 20, 2017).

The Electricity Sector Regulations (Cogeneration), 2004 [Hebrew], Planning Administration, State of Israel, December 3, 2004, www.gov.il/he/Departments/legalInfo/infra structure_8; www.nevo.co.il/law_html/Law01/999_373.htm

Encouraging Small and Medium-Sized Reservoirs and Declaring an Emergency in the Natural Gas Industry [Hebrew], Government Decision No. 2592, April 2, 2017, 18pp., www. gov.il/BlobFolder/pmopolicy/2017_dec2592/he/sitecollectiondocuments_mazkir_ dec2592.pdf

Energy Economy Objectives for the Year 2030: Executive Summary, Ministry of Energy, State of Israel, 18pp., www.gov.il/en/Departments/news/plan_2030;www.gov.il/Blob-Folder/news/plan_2030/en/energy_economy_objectives_2030.pdf

Engagement in Agreements for the Purchase of EMG Shares and the Purchase of Rights in the EMG Pipeline, September 27, 2018, http://ir.delek-group.com/static-files/9146ef07-86d7-475e-aeb8-caac3b92669f

Ethanol Fuel Basics, Alternative Fuel Data Centre, US Department of Energy, Washington DC, undated, United States, www.afdc.energy.gov/fuels/ethanol_fuel_basics.html

EuroAsia Interconnector Concludes Strategic Alliance Agreement with Elia Grid, EuroAsia Interconnector, Press Release, December 11, 2017, www.euroasia-interconnector.com/ news-euroasia_interconnector_concludes_strategic_alliance_agreement_with_elia_ grid1078period2017-12/

Examination of the Fiscal Policy With Respect to Oil and Gas Resources in Israel, State of Israel [Sheshinski Committee], Ministry of Finance, State of Israel, January 2011, www. financeisrael.mof.gov.il/financeisrael/Docs/En/publications/02_Full_Report_ Nonincluding_Appendixes.pdf

Executive Summary of the Recommendations of the Inter-Ministerial Committee to Examine the Government's Policy Regarding Natural Gas in Israel, Natural Resources Administration, Ministry of Energy, September 2012, 20pp., www.gov.il/BlobFolder/ reports/tzemach_report/en/pa3161ed-B-REV%20main%20recommendations%20 Tzemach%20report.pdf

Fact Sheet: Seawater Desalination in Israel, Research Office, Legislative Council Secretariat, Hong Kong, FSC19/16–17, July 4, 2017, 7pp., www.legco.gov.hk/research-publications/english/1617fsc19-seawater-desalination-in-israel-201704-e.pdf

Final Proposals Being Submitted in Haifa Bay Ammonia Tank Tender, MOEP, State of Israel, June 23, 2016, www.sviva.gov.il/English/ResourcesandServices/NewsAndEvents/ NewsAndMessageDover/Pages/2016/06-June/Final-Proposals-Being-Submitted-in-Haifa-Bay-Ammonia-Tank-Tender.aspx

Financial Reports for Six and Three Months, June 6, 2017, IEC, www.iec.co.il/en/ir/pages/ financialstatements.aspx

Financial Reports for Three Months, March 31, 2012, IEC, www.iec.co.il/en/ir/pages/ financialstatements.aspx

Financial Reports for the Year Ended December 31, 2011, The Israel Electric Corporation Limited (IEC), www.iec.co.il/en/ir/pages/financialstatements.aspx

Financial Reports for the Year Ended December 31, 2012, IEC, www.iec.co.il/en/ir/pages/financialstatements.aspx

Financial Reports for the Year Ended December 31, 2017, IEC, www.iec.co.il/en/ir/pages/financialstatements.aspx

First Offshore Licensing Round Results, Lebanese Petroleum Administration, 2018, https://www.lpa.gov.lb/first%20licensing%20round%20results.php

Fitoussi, Mayer, *GTL vs. LNG: Economics, Challenges and Value Proposition*, 28pp., http://archive.energy.gov.il/Subjects/NG/Documents/%D7%94%D7%AA%D7%99%D7%99%D7%97%D7%A1%D7%95%D7%AA/GTL_gas_to_liquid.pdf

Friedmann, Yoav, *The Natural Gas Production Industry – Government Policy Seven Years After the "Tamar" Discovery* [Hebrew], Bank of Israel, Periodical Papers 2016.01, March 2016, 25pp., www.boi.org.il/he/NewsAndPublications/PressReleases/Documents/%D7%9E%D7%97%D7%A8-%20%D7%9E%D7%93%D7%99%D7%A0%D7%99%D7%95%D7%AA%20%D7%94%D7%9E%D7%9E%D7%A9%D7%9C%D7%94%20%D7%91%D7%A2%D7%A0%D7%A3%20%D7%94%D7%A4%D7%A7%D7%AA%20%D7%94%D7%92%D7%96%20%D7%94%D7%98%D7%91%D7%A2%D7%99.pdf

Fuel Choices and Smart Mobility Initiative, Prime Minister's Office (PMO), State of Israel, www.fuelchoicesinitiative.com/our-mission/

Fuel Choices Initiative, Israel Energy Week, Ministry of Economy and Industry (MoEI), Foreign Trade Administration, State of Israel, http://itrade.gov.il/india/events/israel-energy-week-december-3-9-2014-tel-aviv-israel/

Full Report of the Tzemach Committee [Hebrew], Ministry of Energy, State of Israel, 128pp., http://archive.energy.gov.il/Subjects/NG/Documents/NGReportSep12.pdf

The Future of Israel's Electricity Market, Budget Department, Ministry of Finance, State of Israel, pp. 14–15, https://energy.org.il/wp-content/uploads/2017/01/%D7%9E%D7%A6%D7%92%D7%AA-%D7%90%D7%95%D7%93%D7%99-%D7%90%D7%93%D7%99%D7%A8%D7%99.pdf

Gas in Electricity and Industry, Delek Drilling, www.delekdrilling.co.il/en/natural-gas/gas-electricity-and-industry

Gas-To-Liquids Plants Face Challenges in the U.S. Market, EIA, February 19, 2014, www.eia.gov/todayinenergy/detail.php?id=15071

Gas-To-Liquid (GTL) Technology Assessment in support of Annual Energy Outlook 2013, Biofuels and Emerging Technologies Team, Energy Information Administration (EIA), United States Department of Energy, Washington, DC, United States, January 7, 2013, 29pp., www.eia.gov/outlooks/documentation/workshops/pdf/AEO2013_GTL_Assessment.pdf

The General Director of Restrictive Trade Practices Considers Declaring Delek to Have a Monopoly in the Supply of Natural Gas and to Determine that Delek, Avner, Noble and Ratio Were Sides to a Restrictive Arrangement in Relation to the 'Leviathan' Joint Venture, The Antitrust Authority, Government of Israel, Press Release, September 6, 2011, www.antitrust.gov.il/eng/subject/182/item/32860.aspx

The General Director of Restrictive Trade Practices Declares the Partners in the Natural Gas Reservoir 'Tamar' to Have a Monopoly on Israel's Natural Gas Supply, The Antitrust Authority, Government of Israel, Press Release, November 13, 2012, www.antitrust.gov.il/eng/subject/182/item/32858.aspx

Giorno, Claude, *Boosting Competition in Israeli Markets*, Economics Department Working Papers No. 1287, Organization for Economic Co-operation and Development (OECD), April 4, 2016, pp. 30–40.

The Government Approved the Minister of Energy, Dr. Yuval Steinitz's Proposal: Shutting Down the Coal Power Station in Hadera in 4 Years, Press Release, Ministry of Energy, State of Israel, July 29, 2018, www.gov.il/en/Departments/news/electricity_290718

Government Hasn't Received Proposals to Build Ammonia Plant, MOEP, State of Israel, November 14, 2016, www.sviva.gov.il/English/ResourcesandServices/NewsAnd Events/NewsAndMessageDover/Pages/2016/11-November/Government-Hasnt-Received-Proposals-to-Build-Ammonia-Plant.aspx

Government OKs Decision to Shut Coal-Fired Power Plants in Hadera by 2022, MoEP, State of Israel, August 9, 2018, www.sviva.gov.il/English/ResourcesandServices/News AndEvents/NewsAndMessageDover/Pages/2018/08-Aug/Government-OKs-Decision-to-Shut-Coal-Fired-Power-Plants-in-Hadera-by-2022.aspx

GTL, KTE Co. Technologies and Enterprises, Haifa, Israel, 2014, http://kte.co.il/energy/gtl/

Gylfason, Thorvaldur, *The Dutch Disease: Lessons From Norway* (written for the Trinidad Tobago Chamber of Commerce and Industry), December 1, 2006, 4pp., https://notendur.hi.is/gylfason/Trinidad2006.pdf

Halaf, Bracha, *Research and Development 2016–2018*, The Chief Scientist Office, Ministry of Energy, 64pp., www.gov.il/BlobFolder/guide/rd_chief_science/he/R_D_2018_acc.pdf

Hatrurim License, Israel Opportunity Energy Resources, www.oilandgas.co.il/englishsite/assetsmap/hatrurim-license.aspx

Hemmings, Philip, *Assessing Challenges to the Energy Sector in Israel*, OECD Economics Department Working Paper No. 914, December 6, 2011, 32pp., www.oecd.org/official documents/publicdisplaydocumentpdf/?cote=ECO/WKP(2011)83&docLanguage=En

High Court of Justice 4374/15, 7588/15, 8747/15, 262/16, *The Movement for Quality Government v. The Prime Minister*, Summary of Judgment [English translation], 9pp., http://versa.cardozo.yu.edu/sites/default/files/upload/opinions/Movement%20 for%20Quality%20Government%20v.%20Prime%20Minister_0.pdf

Historic Inauguration of Ketura Sun – Israel's First Solar Field, Arava Power Company, June 5, 2011, www.aravapower.com/Ketura%20Sun

Honi Kabalo, *The Israeli Net Metering Scheme – Lessons Learned*, Public Utilities Authority Electricity, State of Israel, September 29, 2014, 4pp., https://pua.gov.il/English/Documents/The%20Israeli%20Net%20Metering%20Scheme%20%20lessons%20learned.pdf

IEA Advanced Motor Fuel Annual Report: Israel, International Energy Agency (IEA) Energy Technology Network, IEA, Paris, France, 2015, 10pp., http://iea-amf.org/app/webroot/files/file/Country%20Reports/Israel.pdf

Infrastructure for Energy Independence, Israel Natural Gas Lines, Tel Aviv, Israel, 2013, www.ingl.co.il/?page_id=105&lang=en

INGL Finished the Construction of Eshel HaNasi PRMS for the Distribution Network, Israel Natural Gas Lines, 2013, www.ingl.co.il/hello-world/?lang=en

International Energy Outlook 2017, EIA, United States Department of Energy, Washington, DC, September 14, 2017, www.eia.gov/outlooks/ieo/exec_summ.php#2

In the Supreme Court Sitting as the High Court of Justice, HCJ 4491/13 [Hebrew], October 21, 2013, 96pp., http://elyon1.court.gov.il/files/13/910/044/s12/13044910.s12.pdf

An Invitation to Submit Standpoints, Information, and Express Interest Regarding the Possibility of Building and Operating a GTL (Natural Gas to Liquid Fuels) Facility in Israel, Ministry of energy, State of Israel, June 2014, http://archive.energy.gov.il/english/publicinfo/tenders/documents/tender24_14.pdf

Ishai Lease, Israel Opportunity Energy Resources LP, Ramat Gan, Israel, www.oilandgas.co.il/englishsite/assetsmap/pelagic-licenses.aspx

"Israel–Energy," *Export.gov*, June 9, 2017, www.export.gov/apex/article2?id=Israel-Energy

Israel, Fossil Fuel Support Country Note, Organization for Economic Cooperation and Development (OECD), September 2016.

Israel: 2018 Article IV Consultation, IMF Country Report No. 18/111, May 2018, 66pp., www.mof.gov.il/ChiefEcon/InternationalConnections/DocLib3/Article_IV_2018.pdf

Israel Citizens' Fund Law 2014 [Hebrew], Ministry of Finance, State of Israel, 11pp., http://fs.knesset.gov.il/19/law/19_lsr_303823.PDF

Israel Commits to Reducing GHG Emissions 26% by 2030, MoEP, October 7, 2015, www.sviva.gov.il/English/ResourcesandServices/NewsAndEvents/NewsAndMessageDover/Pages/2015/Oct-10/Israel-Commits-to-Reducing-GHG-Emissions-26-percent-by-2030.aspx

Israel Continues Policy of Reducing Emissions and Conversion to Natural Gas, Removes Barriers to Gas Flow From Leviathan Field, Ministry of Environmental Protection, State of Israel, November 23, 2017, www.sviva.gov.il/English/ResourcesandServices/NewsAndEvents/NewsAndMessageDover/Pages/2017/11-Nov/Israel-Removes-Barriers-to-Gas-Flow-from-Leviathan-Fi.aspx

The Israel Electric Corporation Ltd. Financial Reports for the Three Months Ended March 31, 2018, www.iec.co.il/EN/IR/Documents/The_Israel_Electric_Co-Financial_Reports_March_2018.pdf

Israel – Excess SH-60F Sea-Hawk Helicopter Equipment and Support, Defence Security Cooperation Agency, News Release, July 6, 2016, www.dsca.mil/major-arms-sales/israel-excess-sh-60f-sea-hawk-helicopter-equipment-and-support

Israeli Gas Opportunities, Ministry of Energy, State of Israel, 2016, http://archive.energy.gov.il/English/Subjects/Natural%20Gas/Pages/GxmsMniNGLobby.aspx

Israeli Government's Vision of the Natural Gas Market, Delek Group, Netanya, Israel, 2017, www.delek-group.com/our-operations/east-med-our-business-environment/

Israel National Plan for Implementation of the Paris Agreement, Israel Ministry of Environmental Protection, State of Israel, September 2016, 44pp., http://www.sviva.gov.il/InfoServices/ReservoirInfo/DocLib2/Publications/P0801-P0900/P0836eng.pdf; Honi Kabalo, *The Israeli Net Metering Scheme – Lessons Learned*, Public Utilities Authority-Electricity, State of Israel, September 29, 2014, https://pua.gov.il/English/Documents/The%20Israeli%20Net%20Metering%20Scheme%20%20lessons%20learned.pdf

Israel Natural Gas Lines, 2018, www.ingl.co.il/?page_id=105&lang=en

Israel Oil, International Energy Agency Statistics, www.iea.org/statistics/statisticssearch/report/?country=ISRAEL&product=oil&year=2015

Israel's Fuel Economy, Ministry of Energy, State of Israel, http://energy.gov.il/English/Subjects/Subject/Pages/GxmsMniIsraelsFuelEconomy.aspx

Israel's Renewable Energy Sector, National Sustainable Energy and Water Program, Ministry of Economy and Industry, undated, http://israelnewtech.gov.il/English/Energy/Pages/aboutus.aspx

Karish, Energean Oil and Gas, Tel Aviv and Haifa, Israel, undated, www.energean.com/operations/israel/israel/karish/

"Launching a Clean Car Revolution in Israel," *Israel Environment Bulletin* (MOEP), Volume 44 (March 2018), pp. 6–9, www.sviva.gov.il/english/resourcesandservices/publications/bulletin/documents/bulletin-vol44-march2018.pdf

"Launching a Clean Car Revolution in Israel," *Israel Environmental Bulletin*, MoEP, Volume 44 (March 2018), 4pp., www.sviva.gov.il/English/SearchResults/Pages/GeneralSearchResults.aspx

Law for Promotion of Competition and Reduction of Concentration, The Antitrust Authority, 2013, State of Israel, www.antitrust.gov.il/eng/Law%20of%20Concentration.aspx

Lebanon's Oil & Gas Licensing Round Attracts Bids From Total-Eni-Novatek, Italian Trade Agency, October 19, 2017, www.ice.gov.it/it/news/notizie-dal-mondo/100401

Letter of Appointment Establishing Inter-Ministerial Committee to Examine the Government's Policy Regarding Natural Gas in Israel, Ministry of Energy, State of Israel, October 4, 2011, www.gov.il/he/Departments/news/gas_com (accessed on October 8, 2017).

Leviathan Gas Field, Delek Drilling, undated, www.delekdrilling.co.il/en/project/leviathan-gas-field

Leviathan: The Levant Basin's Game Changing Discovery, East Med and Our Assets, Delek Group, www.delek-group.com/our-operations/east-med/

Leviathan: A Regional Energy Anchor, Delek Drilling, undated, www.delekdrilling.co.il/en/project/leviathan-gas-field#_ftnref1

Lior, Gallo, *A Long-Term Forecast of Electricity Demand in Israel* [Hebrew], Bank of Israel, December 31, 2017, 56pp., www.boi.org.il/en/Research/Pages/dp201713h.aspx; www.boi.org.il/he/Research/DocLib/dp201713h.pdf

List of Geographical Coordinates for the Delimitation of the Northern Limit of the Territorial Sea and Exclusive Economic Zone of the State of Israel (transmitted by a communication dated 12 July 2011 from the Permanent Mission of Israel to the United Nations addressed to the Secretariat of the United Nations), www.un.org/depts/los/LEGISLATION-ANDTREATIES/PDFFILES/isr_eez_northernlimit2011.pdf

LNG Supply Projects and Regasification Plants, Shell Global, www.shell.com/energy-and-innovation/natural-gas/liquefied-natural-gas-lng/lng-supply-projects-and-regasification-plants.html

Management of State Revenues From Natural Gas Resources, Ministry of Foreign Affairs (MFA), State of Israel, February 19, 2012, http://mfa.gov.il/MFA/PressRoom/2012/Pages/Management_state_revenues_natural_gas_resources_19-Feb-2012.aspx

Marine Buoy to Absorb Natural Gas From LNG Ships [Hebrew], Israel Natural Gas Lines, 2013, www.ingl.co.il/%D7%A0%D7%AA%D7%95%D7%A0%D7%99-%D7%94%D7%9E%D7%A2%D7%A8%D7%9B%D7%AA/%D7%A4%D7%A8%D7%95%D-7%99%D7%A7%D7%98%D7%99%D7%9D/%D7%94%D7%9E%D7%A6%D7%95%D7%A3-%D7%94%D7%99%D7%9E%D7%99-%D7%9C%D7%A7%D7%9C%D7%99%D7%98%D7%AA-%D7%92%D7%96-%D7%98%D7%91%D7%A2%D7%99-%D7%9E%D7%90%D7%A0%D7%99%D7%95%D7%AA-lng-%D7%9E%D7%92%D7%96%D7%96/

Market Overview: Renewables, Green Energy Association of Israel (GEA-IL), 2018, www.greenrg.org.il/he-il/english.htm

Memorandum of Agreement Between the Governments of Israel and the United States, September 1, 1975, Volume 1252, No. 20410, pp. 67–71, https://treaties.un.org/doc/Publication/UNTS/Volume%201252/volume-1252-I-20410-English.pdf

Memorandum of Agreement Between the Governments of the United States of America and Israel-Oil, Ministry of Foreign Affairs, State of Israel, March 26, 1979, www.mfa.gov.il/MFA/ForeignPolicy/Peace/Guide/Pages/US-Israel%20Memorandum%20of%20Agreement.aspx

Memorandum of Understanding on a Strategic Partnership on Energy Between the European Union and the Arab Republic of Egypt 2018–2022, April 23, 2018, European Commission, 10pp., https://ec.europa.eu/energy/sites/ener/files/documents/eu-egypt_mou.pdf

The Methanol Industry, Methanol Institute, Alexandria, Virginia, United States, 2018, www.methanol.org/the-methanol-industry/

Minister Elkin: "Decision to Shut Down Coal-Fired Units is Bold and Historic," Ministry of Environmental Protection, State of Israel, August 24, 2016, www.sviva.gov.il/English/ResourcesandServices/NewsAndEvents/NewsAndMessageDover/Pages/2016/08-August/Minister-Elkin-Decision-to-Shut-Down-Coal-Fired-Units-is-Bold-and-Historic.aspx

The Minister of Energy Submits the Plan for Promoting Marginal Fields for Government Approval, Press Release, Ministry of Energy, State of Israel, March 13, 2017, www.gov.il/en/departments/news/promoting_marginal_fields

"Minister of Environment at the Economic Affairs Committee: 'We Are Not a Gas Empire, We Should Keep Reserves of the bcm 600 for the Israeli Market'," *Press Release* [English], The Knesset, June 5, 2013, www.knesset.gov.il/spokesman/eng/PR_eng.asp?PRID=10766

The Minister of Finance Appoints A Committee to Examine the Policy on Oil and Gas Resources in Israel, Press Release [Hebrew], Ministry of Finance, State of Israel, April 13, 2010, https://mof.gov.il/Releases/Documents/2010-667.doc;https://mof.gov.il/pages/searchresults.aspx?k=%D7%A9%D7%A8%20%D7%94%D7%90%D7%95%D7%A6%D7%A8%20%D7%9E%D7%9E%D7%A0%D7%94%20%D7%95%D7%95%D7%A2%D7%93%D7%94%20%D7%9C%D7%91%D7%97%D7%99%D7%A0%D7%AA%20%D7%94%D7%9E%D7%93%D7%99%D7%A0%D7%99%D7%95%D7%AA%20%D7%91%D7%A0%D7%95%D7%A9%D7%90%20%D7%9E%D7%A9%D7%90%D7%91%D7%99%20%D7%A0%D7%A4%D7%98%20%D7%95%D7%92%D7%96%20%D7%91%D7%99%D7%A9%D7%A8%D7%90%D7%9C%20Path%3Ahttps%3A%2F%2Fmof%2Egov%2Eil

The Ministerial Committee on Legislation Approved the Oil Profits Tax Law, Which Regulates the New Taxation System for Gas and Oil Discoveries [Hebrew], Ministry of Finance, State of Israel, February 23, 2011, https://mof.gov.il/Releases/Pages/News_320.aspx

Ministers Elkin and Steinitz: "Electric Company Must Reduce Use of Coal by 30% Compared to 2015," January 3, 2018, Ministry of Environmental Protection, State of Israel, www.sviva.gov.il/English/ResourcesandServices/NewsAndEvents/NewsAndMessageDover/Pages/2018/01-Jan/Ministers-Elkin-and-Steinitz-Electric-Company-Must-Reduce-Use-of-Coal-by-30-Compared-to-2015.aspx

Ministry Director General: The Tzemach Committee Should Reconsider Its Gas Export Policy Recommendations, Ministry of Environmental Protection, State of Israel, October 25, 2012, www.sviva.gov.il/English/ResourcesandServices/NewsAndEvents/NewsAndMessageDover/Pages/2012/10_October_2012/TzemachCmteRecommendations.aspx

The Ministry of Energy's Plan to Rescue Israel From Energy Pollution, Ministry of Energy, Government of Israel, October 22, 2018, www.gov.il/en/Departments/news/plan_2030

Ministry Is Ordering Israel Electric Corporation to Reduce Coal Use, MoEP, December 13, 2015, www.sviva.gov.il/English/ResourcesandServices/NewsAndEvents/NewsAndMessageDover/Pages/2015/12-Dec/Ministry-is-Ordering-Israel-Electric-Corp-to-Reduce-Coal-Use.aspx

The Ministry of National Infrastructures, Energy and Water Resources Has Taken Another Step Towards Constructing and Operating a GTL (Gas to Liquids) Facility in Israel, June 1, 2014, www.gov.il/en/Departments/news/constructing_operating_gtl

Mosey, Gail and Claire Kreycik, *State Clean Energy Practices: Renewable Fuel Standards*, National Renewable Energy Laboratory, US Department of Energy, July 2008, 19pp., www.nrel.gov/docs/fy08osti/43513.pdf

National Plan for Implementation of the Greenhouse Gas Emissions Reduction Targets and for Energy Efficiency, Government Decision No. 1403, Ministry of Environmental Protection, State of Israel, April 10, 2016, 8pp., http://www.sviva.gov.il/English/env_topics/climatechange/NatlEmissionsReductionPlan/Documents/Govt-Decision-1403-National-GHG-Reduction-Plan-April-2016.pdf.

National Security and Foreign Relations, Delek Drilling, undated, www.delekdrilling.co.il/en/natural-gas/national-security-and-foreign-relations (accessed on July 18, 2018).

Natural Gas, IEA Atlas of Energy, http://energyatlas.iea.org/#!/tellmap/-1165808390

The Natural Gas Authority, Ministry of Energy, State of Israel, July 4, 2018, www.gov.il/en/Departments/Guides/natural_gas_authority_cuncil?chapterIndex=1

The Natural Gas Authority of the Ministry of Energy Has Granted Approval for the Flow of Natural Gas to Two Solar Thermal Power Stations Currently Being Constructed in Ashalim [Hebrew] Ministry of Energy, State of Israel, December 26, 2016, www.gov.il/he/Departments/news/solar_power_ashalim

Natural Gas Distribution Network (Israel), October 22, 2009, www.hebrewenergy.com/natural-gas-distribution-tender-natural-gas-distribution-network-israel/

The Natural Gas Sector in Israel [Hebrew], Ministry of Energy, State of Israel, undated, http://archive.energy.gov.il/Subjects/NG/Pages/GxmsMniNGEconomy.aspx

Netanyahu, Sinaia and Shlomo Wald, *The Policy of Managing Natural Gas Resources in Israel Opinion on the Subject of Natural Gas Export Option From Israel* [Hebrew], March 19, 2012, 41pp., http://archive.energy.gov.il/Subjects/NG/Documents/%D7%94%D7%AA%D7%99%D7%99%D7%97%D7%A1%D7%95%D7%AA/NGExportMarch2012.pdf

Next Stage Begins in Process to Remove Ammonia Tank from Haifa Bay, Ministry of Environmental Protection, State of Israel, June 23, 2015, www.sviva.gov.il/English/ResourcesandServices/NewsAndEvents/NewsAndMessageDover/Pages/2015/06-June/Next-Stage-Begins-in-Process-to-Remove-Ammonia-Tank-from-Haifa-Bay.aspx

No: 43, 11 February 2018, Press Release Regarding the Greek Cypriot Administration's Hydrocarbon-Related Activities in the Eastern Mediterranean, Ministry of Foreign Affairs, Ankara, Turkey, www.mfa.gov.tr/no_-43_-gkrynin-dogu-akdenizdeki-hidrokarbon-faaliyetleri-hk.en.mfa

Noble Energy, *Eastern Mediterranean*, Energy Analysts Conference Presentation, December 6, 2012, 162pp., http://files.shareholder.com/downloads/ABEA-2D0WMQ/2473688728x0x620347/477d484f-655f-4c8e-8c6f-390ad9a75988/NBL_Analyst_Day_Presentation.pdf

Noble Energy Sanctions Leviathan Project Offshore Israel, Noble Energy, Press Release, February 23, 2017, http://investors.nblenergy.com/releasedetail.cfm?releaseid=1014140

Note Prepared by the EuroMed and Middle East Unit for Information Only Purposes for the DPAL [Delegation for Relations with Palestine] Meeting of 26–5–2015, 16pp., www.europarl.europa.eu/meetdocs/2014_2019/documents/dpal/dv/background_note_hala/background_note_halaen.pdf

"Notes to the Consolidated Financial Statements," *IEC Financial Reports*, December 31, 2017.

OECD Economy Surveys: Israel 2018, Organisation for Economic Co-operation and Development (OECD), Paris, France, March 2018, https://read.oecd-ilibrary.org/economics/oecd-economic-surveys-israel-2018/assessment-and-recommendations_eco_surveys-isr-2018-3-en#page2

Offshore Levant Basin Petroleum System and HC Resource Assessment, Petroleum Unit, Natural Resources Administration, Ministry of Energy, State of Israel, 33pp., www.energy-sea.gov.il/English-Site/Pages/News%20And%20Media/Highlights%20of%20%20Basin%20Analysis%20of%20the%20Levantine%20Basin%20Offshore%20%E2%80%93%20Extracted%20from%20%20BeiCip%20FranLab%20Final%20Report%20%282015%29.pdf

Oil Development in Israel, Intelligence Memorandum (Secret), Central Intelligence Agency (CIA), June 1970, Date of Release, October 31, 2011, 22pp., www.cia.gov/library/readingroom/docs/CIA-RDP85T00875R001600030086-4.pdf

Oil & Gas in Israel – Exploration History, Ministry of Energy, State of Israel, undated, www.energy-sea.gov.il/English-Site/Pages/Oil%20And%20Gas%20in%20Israel/History-of-Oil-Gas-Exploration-and-Production-in-Israel.aspx

Oil Profits Tax Law, 5771–2011 [Hebrew], April 10, 2011, https://mof.gov.il/Committees/NatureResourcesCommittee/MoreFiles_TaxesLaw.pdf

Our Shareholders, Egyptian LNG, www.egyptianlng.com/Pages/About/OurShareholders.aspx

Overview for Renewable Fuel Standard, United States Environmental Protection Agency (EPA), Washington, DC, June 7, 2017, www.epa.gov/renewable-fuel-standard-program/overview-renewable-fuel-standard#structure

Ownership in Petroleum Rights, Oil and Gas Section, Ministry of Energy, State of Israel, January 8, 2018, 4pp., www.gov.il/BlobFolder/guide/oil_gas_license/he/OwnershipPetroleumRights_1.pdf

Palestine Electric Company Annual Report 2015, www.pec.ps

Petroleum Law, 5712–1952, State of Israel, http://www.energy-sea.gov.il/English-Site/SiteAssets/PETROLEUM%20%20LAW,%201952.pdf (accessed on August 19, 2017)

Pindyck, Robert S. and Analysis Group, Inc., *A Framework for the Taxation of Natural Resources in Israel,* Ministry of Finance, State of Israel, September 22, 2014, 39pp., https://mof.gov.il/Committees/NatureResourcesCommittee/Maskanot_Appendix3.pdf

PM Netanyahu and Quartet Rep Blair Announce Economic Steps to Assist Palestinian Authority, MFA, State of Israel, February 4, 2011, www.mfa.gov.il/mfa/pressroom/2011/pages/pm_netanyahu_quartet_rep_blair_economic_steps_pa_4-feb-2011.aspx

PM Netanyahu's Remarks on the Decision to Increase to 60% the Amount of Natural Gas Designated for the Israeli Market, PMO, June 16, 2013, www.pmo.gov.il/english/mediacenter/events/pages/eventgas190613.aspx

Policy on the Integration of Renewable Energy Sources into the Israeli Electricity Sector, Ministry of Energy, State of Israel, February 14, 2010, 31pp., http://archive.energy.gov.il/English/PublicationsLibraryE/REPolicy.pdf

Proaktor, Gil et al., *Israel National Plan For Implementation of the Paris Agreement, September 2016,* MoEP, 44pp., www.sviva.gov.il/InfoServices/ReservoirInfo/DocLib2/Publications/P0801-P0900/P0836eng.pdf

Projects of Common Interest, European Commission, https://ec.europa.eu/energy/en/topics/infrastructure/projects-common-interest

Public Tender No. 55/2016 on Providing Assistance in Prefeasibility Study for Constructing and Operating a GTL (Gas to Liquid) Plant in Israel, Ministry of Energy, State of Israel, 2016, http://archive.energy.gov.il/informationforpublic/tenders/documents/2016/tender55_16english.pdf

Reducing Israeli Dependence on Petroleum-Based Fuels in Transportation, Government Resolution No. 5327, Prime Minister's Office, 4pp., www.pmo.gov.il/English/PrimeMinistersOffice/DivisionsAndAuthorities/OilFree/Documents/GovernmentResolution5327.pdf

Renewable Energy, Israel Ministry of Environmental Protection, State of Israel, February 2, 2017, www.sviva.gov.il/English/env_topics/climatechange/renewable-energy/Pages/RE-default.aspx

Renewable Energy: Catalyst for a Clean Energy Transition, OECD, 2016, www.oecd.org/environment/renewable-energy-catalyst-clean-energy-transition.htm

Renewable Energy Planning and Policy: An Overview: Lawmakers Pass First Solar Energy Legislation, MoEP, February 19, 2017, www.sviva.gov.il/English/env_topics/climatechange/renewable-energy/Pages/Renewable-Energy-Planning-And-Policy.aspx

Report of the Professional Team's Conclusions for Periodic Review of the Recommendations of the Government Policy Review Committee on the Issue of the Natural Gas Sector in Israel that Were Adopted in Government Decision 442 of 23 June 2013: Draft for Public Reference [Adiri Committee Interim Report] [Hebrew], Ministry of Energy, State of Israel, July

2018, www.gov.il/BlobFolder/rfp/ng_160718/he/Israel_Natural_Gas_report_draft. pdf

Reverse Flow Project, EAPC, 2018, http://eapc.com/reverse-flow-project/

Review of Developments in the Natural Gas Economy 2016 [Hebrew], Ministry of Energy and Natural Gas Authority, State of Israel, 13pp., http://archive.energy.gov.il/Subjects/ NG/Pages/GxmsMniNGEconomy.aspx; http://archive.energy.gov.il/Subjects/NG/ Documents/Publication/NGPublication2016.pdf

Review of Developments in the Natural Gas Economy 2017 [Hebrew], Ministry of Energy and Natural Gas Authority, State of Israel, April 26, 2018, 11pp., www.gov.il/BlobFolder/ guide/natural_gas_basics/he/ng_2017.pdf

Revised Reserves Evaluation Report and Discounted Cash Flows for the Tamar Lease, Regulatory Filing, Delek Drilling, July 2, 2017, https://ir.delek-group.com/news-releases/ news-release-details/revised-reserves-evaluation-report-and-discounted-cash-flows

Ron-Tal, Yiftach and Eli Glikman, *Israel Electric Corporation Ltd.*, 2012, 2pp., www.iec. co.il/Community/Documents/Hevrat%20Hashmal_eng_2012.pdf

Rosner, Eyal, *The Israel Alternative Fuels Initiative Reducing World Dependence on Oil in Transportation*, Prime Minister's Office, State of Israel, undated, 26pp., www.pmo. gov.il/SiteCollectionDocuments/oil/FuelsPresentation.pdf

Rosner, Eyal, *Israel's Fuel Choices Initiative*, Fuel Choices Initiative, Prime Minister's Office, State of Israel, http://inrep.org.il/wp-content/uploads/2017/07/FuelChoices-Initiative-update-%D7%90%D7%99%D7%99%D7%9C-%D7%A8%D7%95%D7%96% D7%A0%D7%A81.pdf

Rosner, Eyal, *Strategic Plan*, Fuel Choices Initiative, Prime Minister's Office, 2pp., undated, www.gaz-mobilite.fr/docs/upload/doc_20150210110215.pdf

Royee, Ratio Oil, 2017, www.ratioil.com/en/assets/royee/

2nd Bid Round, Ministry of Energy, State of Israel, November 2018, http://www.energy-sea.gov.il/English-Site/Pages/Offshore%20Bid%20Rounds/2nd-Bid-Round.aspx (accessed on February 11, 2019).

Security Cabinet Unanimously Approves Moving Quickly to Develop and Expand Israel's Gas Fields, Prime Minister's Office, Government of Israel, June 25, 2015, www.pmo.gov. il/English/MediaCenter/Spokesman/Pages/spokeGaz250615.aspx

Signing of an Agreement for Export of Natural Gas from the Leviathan Project to the National Electric Power Company of Jordan, Delek Group, September 26, 2016, https://ir.delek-group. com/news-releases/news-release-details/signing-agreement-export-natural-gas-leviathan-project-national

Signing of Agreements for Export of Natural Gas to Egypt, Delek Drilling, February 20, 2018, https://ir.delek-group.com/news-releases/news-release-details/signing-agreements-export-natural-gas-egypt

Signing of an Agreement for the Financing of the Delek Group Partnerships' Share in the Costs of Development of the Leviathan Project, Press Release, February 21, 2017, https:// ir.delek-group.com/news-releases/news-release-details/signing-agreement-financing-delek-group-partnerships-share-costs

Solution Found for Framework for Developing Israel's Natural Gas Fields – The Stability Provision Will Be Revised, May 19, 2016, Ministry of Energy, www.gov.il/en/departments/ news/framework_developing_natural_gas_fields

Southern Gas Corridor, Trans Adriatic Pipeline, www.tap-ag.com/the-pipeline/the-big-picture/southern-gas-corridor

Speech of Professor David Gilo, Israel Antitrust Authority General, Annual Conference of the Israeli Institute of Energy, The Antitrust Authority, State of Israel, May 26, 2015, www. antitrust.gov.il/eng/subject/182/item/33641.aspx

State Company For Petrochemical Industries, Basra, Iraq, undated, http://pchemiq.com/xabout.htm

Statement of General Joseph L. Votel Commander U.S. Central Command Before The House Armed Services Committee on the Posture of US Central Command Terrorism and Iran: Defence Challenges in the Middle East, February 27, 2018, 45pp., http://docs.house.gov/meetings/AS/AS00/20180227/106870/HHRG-115-AS00-Wstate-VotelJ-20180227.pdf

Summary of Attack on IDF Ship, Ministry of Foreign Affairs, State of Israel July 15, 2006, www.mfa.gov.il/mfa/foreignpolicy/terrorism/hizbullah/pages/summary%20of%20attack%20on%20idf%20missile%20ship%2015-jul-2006.aspx

Summary of Main Conclusions of the Committee for the Examination of Fiscal Policy on Oil and Gas Resources in Israel Headed by Prof. Eytan Sheshinski, Ministry of Finance, State of Israel, January 3, 2011, https://mof.gov.il/pages/searchresults.aspx?k=%D7%97%D7%95%D7%A7%20%D7%9E%D7%99%D7%A1%D7%95%D7%99%20%D7%A0%D7%A4%D7%98%20%20Path%3Ahttps%3A%2F%2Fmof%2Egov%2Eil#k=%D7%97%D7%95%D7%A7%20%D7%9E%D7%99%D7%A1%D7%95%D7%99%20%D7%A0%D7%A4%D7%98%20%20Path%3Ahttps%3A%2F%2Fmof.gov.il;https://mof.gov.il/Releases/Documents/2011-19.doc

Tamar Gas Field, Delek Drilling, undated, www.delekdrilling.co.il/en/project/tamar-gas-field

Tamar Petroleum: Investors Presentation, Tamar Petroleum, Herzeliya Pituach, Israel, February 2018, https://ir.tamarpetroleum.co.il/wp-content/uploads/2018/02/Tamar-P-Investors-Presentation-Feb-2018-Eng.pdf

Tanin, Energean Oil and Gas, Tel Aviv and Haifa, Israel, undated, www.energean.com/operations/israel/tanin/

Thermo Solar Power, Negev Energy, undated, http://www.negevenergy.co.il/en/

Total Strengthens Its Position in the Mediterranean Region by Entering Two Exploration Blocks Offshore Lebanon, Press Release, February 9, 2018, www.total.com/en/media/news/press-releases/total-strengthens-position-in-mediterranean-region-by-entering-two-exploration-blocks-offshore-lebanon

Transmission and Distribution System [Hebrew], Ministry of Energy, www.gov.il/he/Departments/Guides/distribution_area

The Transmission Network, Israel Natural Gas Lines, 2017, www.ingl.co.il/?page_id=1521&lang=en;%20www.ingl.co.il/?p=2534&lang=en

Turkey-Qatar Economic and Trade Relations, Ministry of Foreign Affairs, Republic of Turkey, www.mfa.gov.tr/turkey_s-commercial-and-economic-relations-with-qatar.en.mfa

Turkey's Energy Profile and Strategy, Ministry of Foreign Affairs, Republic of Turkey, www.mfa.gov.tr/turkeys-energy-strategy.en.mfa

Turkey's Import and Exports With Israel, Turkstat, Turkey, 2015, www.turkstat.gov.tr/

Turkish Natural Gas Market Report 2016, Energy Market Regulatory, Republic of Turkey, Ankara 2017, http://yourmaninturkey.com.tr/business-news-detail/epdk-publishes-its-turkish-natural-gas-market-report-2016/

United Nations Framework Convention on Climate Change, Israel Ministry of Environmental Protection, September 24, 2017, www.sviva.gov.il/English/env_topics/InternationalCooperation/IntlConventions/Pages/UNFCCC.aspx

UN Maritime Space: Maritime Zones and Maritime Delimitation, February 16, 2011, www.un.org/depts/los/LEGISLATIONANDTREATIES/

Update on the Natural Gas Issue, The Antitrust Authority, State of Israel, December 24, 2014, www.antitrust.gov.il/eng/item/33459/search/785c3118847a4ee381ae044651cb82b3.aspx

Wald, Shlomo, *Research and Development 2012–2014*, The Chief Scientist Office, Ministry of Energy, State of Israel, September 2014, 44pp., http://archive.energy.gov.il/gxmsmnipublications/rd2012_2013.pdf

Wald, Shlomo and Ilan Yaar, *The Need for Nuclear Power Stations in Israel*, IAEA Panel, February 11, 2014, www.iaea.org/inis/collection/NCLCollectionStore/_Public/45/114/45114735.pdf

West Nile Delta – Taurus/Libra, Egypt, British Petroleum, March 24, 2017, www.bp.com/en/global/corporate/investors/upstream-major-projects/major-projects-2017/west-nile-delta-egypt.html

What We Do, British Petroleum, 2018, www.bp.com/en_tt/trinidad-and-tobago/about-bp-in-trinidad-and-tobago/BPinTT.html

The Winners of the Eric and Sheila Samson Prime Minister's Prize for Innovation in Alternative Fuels for Transportation, Fuel Choices and Smart Mobility Initiatives, Prime Ministers' Office, State of Israel, 2017, www.fuelchoicessummit.com/Award.aspx

Yam Tethys: The Transition to Natural Gas, Delek Drilling, undated, www.delekdrilling.co.il/en/project/yam-tethys

Primary sources: website for statistics

BP Statistical Review of World Energy
Central Bureau of Statistics, State of Israel
Energy Information Administration statistics
International Energy Agency statistics
The Observatory of Economic Complexity, The MIT Media Lab
Turkstat, Republic of Turkey
The World Bank data

Primary sources: interviews

1. Mr. Haviv Rettig Gur, Jerusalem, Israel, January 4, 2016.
2. Dr. Eyal Propper, Jerusalem, January 4, 2016.
3. Mr. Nadav Perry, Herziliya, Israel, January 5, 2016.
4. Ambassador Ron Adams, Jerusalem, Israel, January 11, 2016.
5. Ambassador Alon Leil, Jerusalem, Israel, January 11, 2016.
6. Prof. Oren Barak, Jerusalem, Israel, January 12, 2016.
7. Ambassador Oded Eran, Tel Aviv, January 13, 2016.
8. Dr. Uzi Landau, Ra'anana, Israel, January 15, 2016.
9. Dr. Nimrod Goren, Jerusalem, Israel, January 18, 2016.
10. Dr. Omar Kittaneh, Minister, Ramallah, The West Bank, January 21, 2016.
11. Prof. Alfred Tovias, Jerusalem, Israel, January 21, 2016.
12. Dr. Eran Lerman (Telephonic interview), Jerusalem, January 24, 2016.
13. Mr. Amnon Portugali (Telephonic interview), Jerusalem, January 24, 2016.
14. Dr. Lior Herman, Jerusalem, Israel, January 25, 2016.
15. Mr. Noam Segal (Telephonic interview), Jerusalem, Israel, January 26, 2016.
16. Mr. Nasr Agiza, Cambridge, UK, August 17, 2016.
17. Mr Antoine Dagher, Cambridge, UK, August 17, 2016.
18. Mr. Eser Ozdil, Ankara, Turkey, June 7, 2017.
19. Mr Cenk Pala, Ankara, Turkey, June 7, 2017.
20. Dr. Necdet Pamir, Ankara, Turkey, June 7, 2017.
21. Prof. Mert Bilgin, Medipol University, Istanbul, Turkey, June 9, 2017.
22. Ambassador Demetrios Theophylactou, New Delhi, October 20, 2017.
23. Undisclosed Jordan official posted in New Delhi, India.

Wikileaks

Consul General Jake Walles, *Update on Commercial Development of Offshore Gaza Natural Gas Field*, Confidential, Wikileaks, February 27, 2007, https://wikileaks.org/plusd/cables/07JERUSALEM401_a.html

ECPO Counsellor John Desrocher, Egypt and Israel Signed Gas Deal, June 30, 2005, Confidential, Wikileaks, https://wikileaks.org/plusd/cables/05CAIRO4972_a.html

Secondary sources: books and book chapters

Abir, Mordechai, *Oil, Power and Politics: Conflict of Arabia, the Red Sea and the Gulf* (London: Frank Cass and Co. Ltd., 1974. Republished by Taylor & Francis e-Library, 2005).

Al-Besharah, Jasem M., "The Petrochemical Industry And Natural Gas: A Strategic Alliance," in P.N. Prasad et al. (eds.), *Science and Technology of Polymers and Advanced Materials* (New York: Plenum Press, 1998), pp. 781–795.

Al-Karaghouli, Ali and Lawrence Kazmerski, "Renewable Energy Opportunities in Water Desalination," in Michael Schorr (ed.), *Desalination, Trends and Technologies* (INTECH Open Access Publisher, 2011), pp. 149–184.

Bahgat, Gawdat, *Alternative Energy in the Middle East* (Basingstoke, Hampshire: Palgrave Macmillan, 2013).

Bard, Mitchell and Moshe Schwartz, *1001 Facts Everyone Should Know About Israel* (Oxford: Rowman and Littlefield Publishers, 2005).

Bar-Tal, Daniel, *Intractable Conflicts: Socio-Psychological Foundations and Dynamics* (Cambridge: Cambridge University Press, 2013).

Bassiouni, M. Cherif, *Chronicles of the Egyptian Revolution and Its Aftermath: 2011–2016* (New York: Sheridan Books and Cambridge University Press, 2017).

Ben-Yehuda, Hemda and Shmuel Sandler, *Arab-Israeli Conflict Transformed, The: Fifty Years of Interstate and Ethnic Crises* (Albany: State University of New York Press, 2002).

Bryza, Matthew, "Eastern Mediterranean Natural Gas: Potential for Historic Breakthroughs Among Israel, Turkey, and Cyprus," in Sami Andoura and David Koranyi (eds.), *Energy in the Eastern Mediterranean: Promise or Peril?* Egmont Paper 65, Egmont Institute and the Atlantic Council (Ghent, Belgium: Academia Press, May 2014), pp. 39–48, 98pp.

Buzan, Barry, *People, States and Fear: An Agenda for International Security Studies in the Post-Cold War Era*, 2nd edition (Colchester: ECPR Press, 2009).

Buzan, Barry, Ole Wæver, and Jaap de Wilde, *Security: A New Framework for Analysis* (Boulder: Lynne Rienner Publishers, 1998).

Cohn, Margit, *Energy Law in Israel* (Alphen an den Rijn, The Netherlands: Kluwer Law International BV, 2010).

Colantoni, Lorenzo et al., "Introduction," in Silvia Colombo, Mohamed El Harrak and Nicolò Sartori (eds.), *The Future of Natural Gas Markets and Geopolitics Editors* (The Netherlands: Lenthe Publishers/European Energy Review, 2016), pp. 19–24.

Cordesman, Anthony H., *Energy Developments in the Middle East* (Westport: Praeger Publishers, 2004).

Crandall, Maureen S., *Energy, Economics, and Politics in the Caspian Region: Dreams and Realities* (Westport: Praeger Security International, 2006).

Cummine, Angela, *Citizens' Wealth: Why (and How) Sovereign Funds Should Be Managed by the People for the People* (New Haven and London: Yale University Press, 2016).

Dahan, Momi, "Policy Analysis in the Treasury: How Does the Israeli Ministry of Finance Arrive at a Policy Decision," in Gila Menahem and Amos Zehavi (eds.), *Policy Analysis in Israel* (Bristol: Policy Press, 2016), pp. 123–140.

Davis, Richard, *Hamas, Popular Support and War in the Middle East: Insurgency in the Holy Land* (London: Routledge, 2016).

Dietl, Gulshan, *India and the Global Game of Gas Pipelines* (New Delhi: Routledge, 2017).

Europa Publication, *The Middle East and North Africa 2004* (London and New York: Taylor and Francis Group, 2004).

Franza, Luca, Dick de Jong and Coby van der Linde, "The Future of Gas: The Transition Fuel?" in Silvia Colombo, Mohamed El Harrak and Nicolò Sartori (eds.), *The Future of Natural Gas Markets and Geopolitics* (Diepenheim, The Netherlands: Lenthe Publishers/European Energy Review, Istituto Affari Internazionali, and OCP Policy Centre, 2016), pp. 25–40.

Gardosh, Michael et al., "Hydrocarbon Exploration in the Southern Dead Sea," in Zvi Ben-Avraham, Tina M. Neimi and Joel R. Gat (eds.), *The Dead Sea: The Lake and Its Setting* (New York and Oxford: Oxford University Press, 1997), pp. 57–72.

Habeeb, William Mark, *The Middle East in Turmoil: Conflict, Revolution, and Change* (Santa Barbara, CA: Greenwood, 2012).

Hartley, Cathy and Paul Cossali, *A Survey of Arab-Israeli Relations*, 2nd edition (London and New York: Europa Publications, Taylor and Francis, 2004).

Houghton, J. T. et al. (eds.), *Climate Change 1995: The Science of Climate Change. Contribution of Working Group I to the Second Assessment Report of the Intergovernmental Panel on Climate Change*, Volume 2 (Cambridge: Cambridge University Press, 1996).

Inbar, Efraim, *Israel's National Security: Issues and Challenges Since the Yom Kippur War* (London: Routledge, 2008).

Ismael, Jacqueline S., Tareq Y. Ismael, and Glenn Perry, *Government and Politics of the Contemporary Middle East: Continuity and Change* (London: Routledge, 2011).

Koprulu, Nur, "Interplay of Palestinian and Jordanian Identities," in Kenneth Christie and Mohammad Masad (eds.), *State Formation and Identity in the Middle East and North Africa* (New York: Palgrave Macmillan, 2013), pp. 59–85.

Lansford, Tom, "Arab Republic of Egypt," in Thomas C. Muller and Judith F. Isacoff (eds.), *Political Handbook of the World 2012* (Thousand Oaks, CA: CQ Press, 2012), pp. 418–429.

Lukacs, Yehuda, *Israel, Jordan, and the Peace Process* (New York: Syracuse University Press, 1997).

Mansfield, Edward D. and Brian M. Pollins, "Interdependence and Conflict: An Introduction," in Edward D. Mansfield and Brian M. Pollins (eds.), *Economic Interdependence and International Conflict: New Perspectives on an Enduring Debate* (Ann Arbor: University of Michigan Press, 2003), pp. 1–30.

Maoz, Zeev, *Defending the Holy Land: A Critical Analysis of Israel's Security and Foreign Policy* (University of Michigan Press, 2009).

Miller, Benjamin, "Explaining the Warm Peace in Europe Versus the Shifts Between Hot War and Cold Peace in the Middle East," in Carmela Lutmar and Benjamin Miller (eds.), *Peacemaking and Conflict Management: A Comparative Approach* (London: Routledge, 2016), pp. 7–44.

Milton-Edwards, Beverley, *The Muslim Brotherhood: The Arab Spring and Its Future Face* (London: Routledge, 2016).

Nakhle, Carole, *Petroleum Taxation: Sharing the Oil Wealth: A Study of Petroleum Taxation Yesterday, Today and Tomorrow* (London and New York: Routledge, 2008).

Olah, George A., Alain Goeppert, and G.K. Surya Prakash, *Beyond Oil and Gas: The Methanol Economy* (Weinheim: Wiley-VCH Verlag GmbH & Co. KGaA, 2009).

Pearson, Richard J. and James W.G. Turner, "The Role of Alternative and Renewable Liquid Fuels in Environmentally Sustainable Transport," in Richard Folkson (ed.),

Alternative Fuels and Advanced Vehicle Technologies for Improved Environmental Performance: Towards Zero Carbon Transportation (Cambridge: Elsevier Woodhead Publishing, 2014), pp. 17–50.

Pierpaoli Jr, Paul G., "Israel-Jordan Peace Treaty," in Spencer C. Tucker (ed.), *The Encyclopaedia of the Arab-Israeli Conflict: A Political, Social, and Military History* (Santa Barbara: ABC-CLIO, Inc.), pp. 514–515.

Pohl, Artur, "Egypt-Israel Relations After 2010," in Radoslaw Fiedler and Przemyslaw Osiewicz (eds.), *Transformation Processes in Egypt After 2011: The Causes, Their Course and International Response* (Berlin: Logos Verlag Berlin GmbH, 2015), pp. 143–154.

Press-Barnathan, Galia, *The Political of Transitions to Peace: A Comparative Perspective* (Pittsburgh and Pasadena: University of Pittsburgh Press, 2009).

Ripsman, Norrin M., "Top Down Peacemaking: Why Peace Begins With States Not Societies," in T.V. Paul (ed.), *International Relations Theory and Regional Transformation* (Cambridge: Cambridge University Press, 2012), pp. 255–281.

Samuel-Azran, Tal, *Al Jazeera and US War Coverage* (New York: Peter Lang, 2010).

Shaham, Shiri, Simon Weintraub, Noam Meir and Josh Hersch, "Israel," in Christopher B. Strong (ed.), *The Oil and Gas Law Review*, 2nd edition (London: Law Business Research Ltd., 2014), pp. 179–188, www.arnon.co.il/files/e3b84790d602b8d3179de6a92b-2be89a/The%20Oil%20and%20Gas%20Review.pdf

Shlaim, Avi, *Collusion Across the Jordan: King Abdullah, the Zionist Movement, and the Partition of Palestine* (New York: Columbia University Press, 1988).

Soetendorp, Ben, *The Dynamics of Israeli-Palestinian Relations: Theory, History, and Cases* (New York: Palgrave Macmillan, 2007).

Swain, Ashok and Anders Jägerskog, *Emerging Security Threats in the Middle East: The Impact of Climate Change and Globalisation* (Lanham: Rowman and Littlefield, 2016).

Tawadros, Edward, *Geology of North Africa* (Boca Raton: BRC Press, 2011).

Zwier, Paul J., *Principled Negotiation and Mediation in the International Arena: Talking With Evil* (Cambridge: Cambridge University Press, 2013).

Secondary sources: reports, research papers, and policy papers

About Methanol, Methanex Corporation, Vancouver, Canada, 2015, www.methanex.com/about-methanol/how-methanol-used

Agarwal, Avinash Kumar, Prakhar Bothra and Pravesh Chandra Shukla, *Particulate Characterization of CNG Fuelled Public Transport Vehicles at Traffic Junctions*, Aerosol and Air Quality Research (Taiwan Association for Aerosol Research), Volume 15 (2015), pp. 2168–2174, www.aaqr.org/files/article/526/39_AAQR-15-02-TN-0084_2168-2174.pdf

Al-Hassan, Abdullah, Michael Papaioannou, Martin Skancke, and Cheng Chih Sung, *Sovereign Wealth Funds: Aspects of Governance Structures and Investment Management*, International Monetary Fund, Working Paper /13/231, November 2013, 34pp., www.imf.org/en/Publications/WP/Issues/2016/12/31/Sovereign-Wealth-Funds-Aspects-of-Governance-Structures-and-Investment-Management-41046

"Ammonia," *Chemical Economics Handbook*, IHS Markit, London, UK, July 2017, https://ihsmarkit.com/products/ammonia-chemical-economics-handbook.html

Arbell, Dan, *The US-Turkey-Israel Triangle*, Centre for Middle East Policy at Brookings, Washington, DC, Analysis Paper No. 34, October 2014, 54pp., www.brookings.edu/wp-content/uploads/2016/07/USTurkeyIsrael-Triangle.pdf

Ayla, Gurel, Tzimitras Harry, and Faustmann Hubert, *East Mediterranean Hydrocarbons, Geopolitical Perspectives, Markets and Regional Cooperation,* Peace Research Institute Oslo (PRIO, Cyprus Centre), Friedrich Ebert Stiftung (Cyprus Centre) Brookings Institution (Washington, DC), PCC Report 3/2014, 126pp.

Baconi, Tareq, *A Flammable Peace: Why Gas Deals Won't End Conflict in the Middle East,* European Council for Foreign Relations, Policy Brief, December 2017, www.ecfr.eu/publications/summary/a_flammable_peace_why_gas_deals_wont_end_conflict_in_the_middle_east

Baconi, Tareq, *How Israel Uses Gas to Enforce Palestinian Dependency and Promote Normalization,* Al-shabaka Policy Brief, New York, March 12, 2017, https://al-shabaka.org/briefs/israel-uses-gas-enforce-palestinian-dependency-promote-normalization/

Bar, Yaniv, *The Natural Gas Sector in Israel An Economic Survey,* Bank Leumi, January 2017, 19pp., https://english.leumi.co.il/static-files/10/LeumiEnglish/Leumi_Review/Natural GasinIsraelacc.pdf

Bar, Yaniv, *The Natural Gas Sector in Israel: An Economic Survey,* Bank Leumi, August 2018, 16pp., https://english.leumi.co.il/static-files/10/LeumiEnglish/Israel_Capital_Markets/Natural_Gas_in_Israel_August_2018_global.pdf?reffer=deposit_check_hp_banner

Barrier, Félicité and Ali Ahmad, *The Geopolitics of Oil and Gas Development in Lebanon,* Issam Fares Institute for Public Policy and International Affairs, American University of Beirut, Policy Brief 1, 2018, 4pp.

Ben-Shalom, Jeremy, *National Report for CSD-14/15 Thematic Areas,*

Bromberg, Leslie and Wai K. Cheng, *Methanol as an Alternative Transportation Fuel in the US: Options for Sustainable and/or Energy-Secure Transportation,* Sloan Automotive Laboratory, Massachusetts Institute of Technology (Cambridge, MA), November 28, 2010, 78pp., https://afdc.energy.gov/files/pdfs/mit_methanol_white_paper.pdf

Bufman, Gil Michael, *Establishing a Sovereign Wealth Fund for Israel as Part of a Mechanism for Dealing with the Forces Supporting Appreciation of the Shekel,* Finance & Economics Division, Department of Economics, Bank Leumi, Tel Aviv, Israel, December 10, 2013, 7pp., https://english.leumi.co.il/static-files/10/LeumiEnglish/December102013Israel andDutchDisease.pdf?reffer=9293

Bufman, Gil Michael, Eyal Raz, and Noach Hager, *The Potential of Natural Gas in the Israeli Economy,* The Finance & Economics Division, Bank Leumi, Israel, April 2014, 16pp., www.chamber.org.il/media/150344/the-potential-of-natural-gas-in-the-israeli-economy-april-2014.pdf

Cerutti, Virgilio, *The Methanol Project,* Fuel Choices Summit, Fuel Choice Initiative, Jerusalem, Israel, November 3, 2016, 15pp., www.fuelchoicessummit.com/Portals/37/Virgillio%20Cerutti.pdf

China: The Leader in Methanol Transportation, Methanol Facts, Methanol Institute, July 2011, 2pp., http://greenmethanol.dk/wp-content/uploads/2013/12/Methanol-Institute-Methanol-in-China.pdf

Cohen, Gina, "Natural Gas Distribution Tender"; "Natural Gas Distribution Network (Israel)," *Hebrew-English Energy Dictionary,* October 22, 2009, www.hebrewenergy.com/natural-gas-distribution-tender-natural-gas-distribution-network-israel/

Cohen, Gina and Miki Korner, *Israeli Oil & Gas Sector, Economic and Geopolitical Aspects: Distinguish between the Impossible, the Potential and the Doable,* Samuel Neaman Institute, Haifa, Israel, April 2016, 34pp., www.neaman.org.il/Files/6-459.pdf

Compressed Natural Gas Market Analysis by Source, Applications and Segment Forecasts to 2020, Grand View Research, San Francisco, CA, United States and Pune, MH, India, December 2014, www.grandviewresearch.com/industry-analysis/compressed-natural-gas-cng-market

Compressed Natural Gas (CNG) Market-Growth, Future Prospects And Competitive Analysis, 2016–2024, Credence Research, London and San Jose, January 2017, www.credence research.com/press/global-compressed-natural-gas-cng-market

Country Focus: Israel, Ernst and Young Global Limited, www.ey.com/gl/en/industries/power-utilities/recai-israel

Efron, Shira, *The Future of Israeli-Turkish Relations*, RAND Corporation, Santa Monica, California, 2018, 69pp., www.rand.org/content/dam/rand/pubs/research_reports/RR2400/RR2445/RAND_RR2445.pdf

Egyptian Petrochemical Company, Alexandria, Egypt, undated, www.egy-petrochem.com/

Egypt Year in Review 2016, Oxford Business Group, December 26, 2016, https://oxford businessgroup.com/news/egypt-year-review-2016

Elgindy, Khaled, *Egypt, Israel, Palestine*, Centre for Middle East Policy, Brookings, August 25, 2012, www.brookings.edu/articles/egypt-israel-palestine/

Eni Announces a Gas Discovery Offshore Cyprus, Eni.com, February 8, 2018, www.eni.com/en_IT/media/2018/02/eni-announces-a-gas-discovery-offshore-cyprus

Environmental Impacts of Natural Gas, Union of Concerned Scientists (UCS), Cambridge, MA, United States, undated, www.ucsusa.org/clean-energy/coal-and-other-fossil-fuels/environmental-impacts-of-natural-gas#references

Eran, Oded and Elai Rettig, *New Obstacles Facing Israeli Natural Gas Exports*, Institute for National Security Studies (INSS) Insight No. 1073, July 10, 2018, www.inss.org.il/publication/new-obstacles-facing-israeli-natural-gas-exports/

Eran, Oded, Elai Rettig, and Ofir Winter, *The Gas Deal With Egypt: Israel Deepens Its Anchor in the Eastern Mediterranean*, INSS Insight No. 1033, March 12, 2018, www.inss.org.il/publication/gas-deal-egypt-israel-deepens-anchor-eastern-mediterranean/

FCA Presents Fiat 500 M15 (Methanol); To be Sold in Israel, Green Car Congress Newsletter, November 3, 2016, www.greencarcongress.com/2016/11/20161103-fcam15.html

Fiat Chrysler Automobiles Presents the First Methanol-Powered Euro 6 Vehicle, Fiat Chrysler Automobiles NV, London, United Kingdom, November 2, 2016, www.fcagroup.com/en-US/sustainability/fca_news/Pages/FCA_Methanol.aspx

Friedman, Yoav, *The Government's Policy in the Field of Natural Gas Production, Seven Years After the Discovery of 'Tamar'* [Hebrew], Research Department, BOI, Periodical Papers 2016.1, March 2016, 25pp.

Gamba, Andrea, New *Energy Sources for Jordan: Macroeconomic Impact and Policy Considerations*, IMF Working Paper 15/115, May 2015, 21pp.

Ghafar, Adel Abdel, *Egypt's New gas Discovery: Opportunities and Challenges*, The Brookings Institution (Washington, DC), September 10, 2015, www.brookings.edu/opinions/egypts-new-gas-discovery-opportunities-and-challenges/

Gross, Peter, *China's Use of Fuel Methanol and Implications on Future Energy Trends*, Washington Methanol Policy Forum, June 13, 2017, 17pp., www.methanol.org/wp-content/uploads/2017/06/Peter-Gross-Global-Methanol-Fuel-Blending-Initiatives-Panel.pdf

Grossman, Gershon and Naama Shapira, *Natural Gas for Transportation in Israel: Summary and Recommendations of the Discussion* [Hebrew], The Samuel Neaman Institute of Energy, The Samuel Neaman Institute of National Policy Research, July 2017, www.neaman.org.il/EN/Energy-Forum-40-Natural-gas-for-transportation-in-Israel

Gylfason, Thorvaldur, *The Dutch Disease: Lessons From Norway*, Trinidad Tobago Chamber of Commerce and Industry, December 1, 2006, 4pp.

Hadera Deepwater LNG Terminal: Israel's First LNG Import Terminal, Excelerate Energy, undated, http://excelerateenergy.com/project/hadera-deepwater-lng-terminal/

Hecking, Harald et al., *Options for Gas Supply Diversification for the EU and Germany in the Next Two Decades*, ewi Energy Research & Scenarios (ewi ER&S), Cologne and The

European Centre for Energy and Resource Security (EUCERS), London, October 2016, 167pp.

Hemmings, Philip, *Assessing Challenges to the Energy Sector in Israel*, OECD Economics Department Working Paper No. 914, December 6, 2011, 7pp.

Henderson, Simon, *Jordan's Energy Supply Options: The Prospect of Gas Imports From Israel*, Foreign and Security Policy Paper Series, The German Marshall Fund of the United States, October 2015, 17pp.

Herzog, Chen, Norden Shalabna, and Guy Maor, *Israel Natural Gas Demand Forecast 2017–2040*, BDO Consulting Group, Tel Aviv-Yafo, Israel, July 2, 2017, 96pp., www.delek-group.com/wp-content/uploads/2017/09/BDO-Gas-Market-Forecast-2-07-2017-for-Delek-Group-with-final-letter-1.pdf

Hever, Shir, *Flammable Politics: Political-Economic Implications of Israel's Natural Gas Find*, The Economy of the Occupation: A Socioeconomic Bulletin, No. 27–28, Alternative Information Centre, Jerusalem, December 2011, 60pp., www.shirhever.com/wp-content/uploads/2018/01/Bulletin-27-28-Natural-Gas-Discovery.pdf

Hochberg, Michael, *Israel's Natural Gas Potential: Securing the Future*, Middle East Institute (MEI) Policy Focus 2016–20, August 2016, 19pp., www.mei.edu/sites/default/files/publications/PF20_Hochberg_IsraelGas_web.pdf

I know What Reserves Are, But What Are Contingent and Prospective Resources, Gaffney, Cline and Associates, July 29, 2016, http://gaffney-cline-focus.com/i-know-what-reserves-are

Inbari, Pinhas, *Stabilizing Israel-Hamas Relations in Gaza: Can It Be Achieved?* Jerusalem Issue Brief, Jerusalem Centre for Public Affairs, August 6, 2018, http://jcpa.org/stabilizing-israel-hamas-relations-in-gaza-can-it-be-achieved/

Israel-Egypt Disengagement Agreement (1974), Economic Cooperation Foundation (ECF), January 1, 1974, https://ecf.org.il/issues/issue/179

Israeli-Egyptian Interim Agreement (Sinai II, 1975), ECF, September 4, 1975, https://ecf.org.il/issues/issue/180

The Israeli Renewable Energy and Energy Efficiency Industry: Executive Summary, Samuel Neaman Institute for National Policy Research, Israel Institute of Technology, October 2015, 6pp., www.neaman.org.il/Files/6-449.pdf

Israel: Monetary Policy Status Quo, BNP Paribas, January 30, 2018, http://economic-research.bnpparibas.com/html/en-US/Monetary-policy-status-1/30/2018,30610

Israel Science & Technology: Oil & Natural Gas, Jewish Virtual Library, 2018, www.jewishvirtuallibrary.org/oil-and-natural-gas-in-israel

Israel-Turkey Reconciliation: A Progress Report, Britain Israel Communications and Research Centre (BICOM) Briefing, 2017, 4pp., www.bicom.org.uk/wp-content/uploads/2017/04/Turkey-paper-2017-Final-pdf.pdf

Israel's First Ever Natural Gas Powered Vehicle Is an Iveco Stralis, Press Release, Fiat Chrysler Automobiles, FCA Group, June 15, 2015, www.fcagroup.com/en-US/media_center/fca_press_release/2015/june/Pages/Israel%E2%80%99s_first_ever_natural_gas_powered_vehicle_is_an_Iveco_Stralis.aspx

Israel's Upstream Natural Gas Sector Against the Backdrop of the New Gas Framework, Meitar Law Firm, June 7, 2016, 5pp., http://meitar.com/files/Publications/2016/1-israels_upstream_natural_gas_sector_against_the_backdrop_of_the_new_gas_framework.pdf

Kattan, Victor, *The Gas Fields off Gaza: A Gift or a Curse?* Al-shabaka Policy Brief, April 24, 2012, https://al-shabaka.org/briefs/gas-fields-gaza-gift-or-curse/#fnref-390-2

Krupnick, Alan, Zhongmin Wang, and Yushuang Wang, *Sector Effects of the Shale Gas Revolution in the United States*, Resources for the Future Discussion Paper 13–20, July 2013, 58pp., www.rff.org/files/sharepoint/WorkImages/Download/RFF-DP-13-21.pdf

LNG Supply Projects and Regasification Plants, Shell Global, www.shell.com/energy-and-innovation/natural-gas/liquefied-natural-gas-lng/lng-supply-projects-and-regasification-plants.html

Methanol Fuel in the Environment, Methanol Fuels, Methanol Institute, undated, http://methanolfuels.org/about-methanol/environment/

The Methanol Industry, Methanol Institute, 2015, www.methanol.org/the-methanol-industry/

Milton-Edwards, Beverley, *Protests in Jordan Over Gas Deal with Israel Expose Wider Rifts*, Brookings Doha Centre, October 26, 2016, www.brookings.edu/blog/markaz/2016/10/26/protests-in-jordan-over-gas-deal-with-israel-expose-wider-rifts/

Ministry of Environmental Protection, State of Israel, October 29, 2006, 45pp., www.sviva.gov.il/InfoServices/ReservoirInfo/DocLib2/Publications/P0401-P0500/P0401.pdf

Nakhle, Carole, *Licensing and Upstream Petroleum Fiscal Regimes: Assessing Lebanon's Choices* (Ras Beirut: The Lebanese Centre for Policy Studies, 2015), 40pp., www.lcps-lebanon.org/publications/1436792630-edt_lcps_carol_n_policy_paper_2015_high_res.pdf

Natural Gas as a Transportation Fuel: Prospects and Challenges, Environmental and Energy Study Institute (EESI), Washington, DC, March 16, 2011, www.eesi.org/briefings/view/natural-gas-as-a-transportation-fuel-prospects-and-challenges

Niezna, Maayan, *Who's Responsible for Gaza's Infrastructure Crisis?* Gisha – Legal Centre for Freedom of Movement (Tel Aviv), January 2017, 34pp.

Noble Energy Will Supply Leviathan Gas (Israel) to NEEPCO (Jordan), Enerdata Intelligence and Consulting, September 27, 2016, www.enerdata.net/publications/daily-energy-news/noble-energy-will-supply-leviathan-gas-israel-neepco-jordan.html

Oei, Pao-Yu and Roman Mendelevitch, *Perspectives and Colombian Coal Exports on the International Steam Coal Market Until 2030*, Rosa Luxemburg Stiftung, November 2016, 47pp., www.rosalux.de/en/publication/id/9251/perspectives-on-colombian-coal/

Oğurlu, Ebru, *Turkey Amidst the Shifting Geopolitics in the Eastern Mediterranean*, Paper 9, Rethink Institute, Washington, DC, May 2013, 25pp.

Palestine Electric Company Annual Report 2015, Palestine Electric Company, March 19, 2016, 55pp., http://www.pec.ps/Control/Files/Annual%20Report%202015%20English.pdf

Political Instability in Jordan, Contingency Planning Memorandum No. 19, Council on Foreign Relations, May 15, 2013, www.cfr.org/report/political-instability-jordan

The Potential of Natural Gas in the Israeli Economy, Finance & Economics Division, Bank Leumi, State of Israel, April 2014, 16pp., www.chamber.org.il/media/150344/the-potential-of-natural-gas-in-the-israeli-economy-april-2014.pdf

Press Release, Central Bureau of Statistics, State of Israel, Jerusalem, January 6, 2019, https://www.cbs.gov.il/he/mediarelease/DocLib/2019/001/03_19_001b.pdf

2016 GCC Fertilizer Industry Indicators, Gulf Petrochemical and Chemicals Association (GPCA), Dubai, United Arab Emirates, 30pp., http://gpcafertilizers.com/wp-content/uploads/2017/10/2016-GCC-Fertilizer-Indicators.pdf

Rabinovich, Itamar, *Israel and the Changing Middle East*, Middle East Memo, No. 34, January 2015, Cntre for Middle East Policy, Brookings Institution, 12pp.

Ray, Saon, Amrita Goldar, and Swati Saluja, *Feedstock for the Petrochemical Industry*, Indian Council for Research on International Economic Relations (ICRIER), Working Paper 271, February 2014, 31pp., www.econstor.eu/bitstream/10419/176289/1/icrier-wp-271.pdf

The Reform in the Israeli Electricity Sector, Meitar Law Firm, Ramat Gan, Israel, June 2018, 5pp., http://meitar.com/files/Publications/2018/electricity_reform-_english_version.pdf

Reich, Arie, *Israel's Foreign Investment Protection Regime in View of Developments in Its Energy Sector*, European University Institute Department of Law, EUI Working Paper

LAW, February 2017, 39pp., https://poseidon01.ssrn.com/delivery.php?ID=67406609
20200810721210050050810171010380460070200590341270660891101261020
99072029028056033058006042055014025020105118119091096053082054001060l
22115073004110103078006061053066087028066090075031125012071024065024l
21087029025082127077070018122098077024104&EXT=pdf

Rzayeva, Gulmira, *Natural Gas in the Turkish Domestic Energy Market: Policies and Challenges*, Oxford Institute for Energy Studies (OIES), OIES Paper: NG 82, February 2014, 79pp.

Rzayeva, Gulmira, *Turkey's Gas Demand Decline: Reasons and Consequences*, Energy Insight 11, OIES, April 2017, 16pp.

Samaan, Jean-Loup, *The East Mediterranean Triangle at Crossroads*, Strategic Studies Institute and U.S. Army War College, Carlisle, PA, March 2016, 63pp.

Satloff, Robert and David Schenker, *Growing Stress on Jordan*, Council on Foreign Relations, Centre for Preventive Action, March 10, 2016, www.cfr.org/report/growing-stress-jordan

Schenker, David, *The Growing Islamic State Threat in Jordan*, The Washington Institute for Near East Policy, January 10, 2017, www.washingtoninstitute.org/policy-analysis/view/the-growing-islamic-state-threat-in-jordan

Segal, Noam, *Israel: The 'Energy Island's' Transition to Energy Independence*, Heinrich Boll Stiftung (Israel), July 7, 2016, https://il.boell.org/en/2016/07/07/israel-energy-islands-transition-energy-independence

Shaham, Shiri and Simon Weintraub, *Update on Israeli Natural Gas Industry*, Yigal Arnon & Co., Tel Aviv and Jerusalem, January 11, 2017; www.engineerlive.com/content/update-israeli-natural-gas-industry

Sharp, Jeremy M., *1979 Memorandum of Agreement Between the United States and Israel on Oil*, Congressional Research Service, May 8, 2014, 9pp.

Sheinin, Yacov and Chen Herzog, *Natural Gas Forecast Demand*, Economic Models Ltd., Ramat Gan, Israel, January 26, 2014, 122pp., https://vdocuments.us/chen-herzog-natural-gas-delek.html

Shell Oil Company's Idku LNG Ramps Up Exports, AllSource Analysis, June 20, 2017, https://allsourceanalysis.com/wp-content/uploads/2017/06/AR-20170620-EG-A-Shell-Oil-Companys-Idku-LNG-Ramps-Up-Exports.pdf

Sinai II Accords, Egyptian-Israeli Disengagement Agreement, Centre for Israel Education (Atlanta, Georgia), September 4, 1975, https://israeled.org/resources/documents/sinai-ii-accords-egyptian-israeli-disengagement-agreement/

Southern Gas Corridor, Trans Adriatic Pipeline, 2018, www.tap-ag.com/the-pipeline/the-big-picture/southern-gas-corridor

Sovereign Wealth Fund Ranking, Sovereign Wealth Fund Institute, 2018, Seattle, Washington, DC, United States, www.swfinstitute.org/sovereign-wealth-fund-rankings/

Sowell, Kirk H., *Jordan Is Sliding Toward Insolvency*, Carnegie Endowment for International Peace, March 17, 2016, http://carnegieendowment.org/sada/63061

Supplying the EU Natural Gas Market, Final Report, Mott MacDonald, November 2010, 70pp., https://ec.europa.eu/energy/sites/ener/files/documents/2010_11_supplying_eu_gas_market.pdf

Swirski, Shlomo with Guy Pade, Yaron Dishon, and Adi Sofer, *No Paradigm Change in Sight: The Economic Policies of the Second Netanyahu Government (2009–2012)*, Friedrich Ebert Stiftung and the Adva Center (Tel Aviv, Israel), November 2013, 30pp., http://adva.org/wp-content/uploads/2015/01/miracle21.pdf

Taglipietra, Simone, *Is the East Med Gas Pipeline Just Another EU Pipe Dream?* Bruegel (Brussels) Blog, May 10, 2017, http://bruegel.org/2017/05/is-the-eastmed-gas-pipeline-just-another-eu-pipe-dream/

Tordo, Silvana with Brandon S. Tracy and Noora Arfaa, *National Oil Companies and Value Creation*, World Bank Working Paper No. 218, The World Bank, Washington, DC, 2011, 148pp.

Tsafos, Nikos, *Egypt: A Market for Natural Gas From Cyprus and Israel?* Foreign and Security Policy Paper Series, The German Marshall Fund of the United States, Washington, DC, October 2015, 19pp.

Tzogopoulos, George N., *The Future of Greece-Israel Relations*, BESA Center Perspectives, Paper No. 788, April 8, 2018, https://besacenter.org/perspectives-papers/greece-israel-relations/

Ülgen, Sinan and Mitat Çelikpala, *TurkStream: Impact on Turkey's Economy and Energy Security*, Centre for Economics and Foreign Policy Studies (EDAM), November 11, 2017, 66pp., http://edam.org.tr/wp-content/uploads/2017/11/turkstream_report_eng.pdf

Walsh, Benjamin, *Israel's New Desalination Plants Offset More than Just Drought*, Future Directions International, Nedlands, Australia, May 2, 2018, www.futuredirections.org.au/publication/israels-new-desalination-plants-offset-just-drought/

West Nile Delta – Taurus/Libra, Egypt, British Petroleum, March 24, 2017, www.bp.com/en/global/corporate/investors/upstream-major-projects/major-projects-2017/west-nile-delta-egypt.html

What Is the Foremost Consideration for Subsea Tiebacks? Audubon Companies, November 5, 2015, www.auduboncompanies.com/what-is-the-foremost-consideration-for-subsea-tiebacks/

Why Developing Israel's Leviathan Gas Field Is a Mammoth Task, Wharton School, University of Pennsylvania, August 25, 2017, http://knowledge.wharton.upenn.edu/article/developing-israels-leviathan-gas-field-proven-mammoth-task/

Will the Bank of Israel Succeed Once Again to Stop the Shekel From Strengthening? The Economic Sector, Bank Leumi, Israel, April 2013, 7pp., https://english.leumi.co.il/static-files/10/LeumiEnglish/June2013shekelstrengthening.pdf

Workman, Daniel, *Israel's Top 10 Imports*, World's Top Exports, March 11, 2018, www.worldstopexports.com/israels-top-10-imports/

Wurmser, David, *The Geopolitics of Israel's Offshore Gas Reserves*, Jerusalem Centre for Public Affairs Special Report, April 7, 2013, http://jcpa.org/article/the-geopolitics-of-israels-offshore-gas-reserves/

Yaalon, Moshe, *Does the Prospective Purchase of British Gas From Gaza Threaten Israel's National Security?* Jerusalem Issue Briefs, Jerusalem Centre for Public Affairs, Volume 7, No. 17, October 19, 2007, http://jcpa.org/article/does-the-prospective-purchase-of-british-gas-from-gaza-threaten-israel%E2%80%99s-national-security/

Yarhi, Einat and Sigal Issaschar, *Carmel Olefins Ltd.*, Midroog (A subsidiary of Moody's), Tel Aviv, Israel, December 2008, 14pp., www.bazan.co.il/investors/Content/Images/CreditRatingCaol_27Jan09_En.pdf

Secondary sources: newspapers, journals, and magazines

+972 Magazine (Israel/Palestine)
21st Century (Yerevan, Armenia)
Ahram Online (Cairo, Egypt)
Al-Ahram Weekly (Cairo, Egypt)
Al-Arabiya (Dubai, UAE)
Al-Ghad (Amman, Jordan)
Al Jazeera (Doha, Qatar)
Al-Masdar (Beirut, Lebanon)

Al-Monitor (Houston, TX, USA)
American Society of International Law (Washington, DC, USA)
Anadolu Agency (Ankara, Turkey)
Arab News (Jeddah, Saudi Arabia)
Arabian Gazette (Dubai, UAE)
Arutz Sheva (Beit El, The West Bank)
Asharq Al-Awsat (London, UK)
Azer News (Baku, Azerbaijan)
BBC News (London, UK)
Bloomberg (New York, USA)
Bloomberg Quint (Mumbai, India)
Calcalist-Tech (Rishon LeZion, Israel)
Christian Science Monitor (Boston, USA)
The Cipher Brief (Washington, DC, USA)
The Citizen (New Delhi, India)
Clean Energy Wire (Berlin, Germany)
Cyprus Business Mail (Nicosia, Cyprus)
Cyprus Mail Online (Nicosia, Cyprus)
Daily New Egypt (Dokki, Giza, Egypt)
The Daily Star (Beirut, Lebanon)
Defense News (Tysons, VA, USA)
Defense Update (Kadima, Israel)
Deutsche Welle (Bonn, Berlin, Germany)
Digital Journal (Toronto, ON, Canada)
Diken (Istanbul, Turkey)
DMEA – Downstream Middle East & Africa (London, UK)
Duke Energy (Charlotte, NC, USA)
The Economic Times (New Delhi, India)
The Economist (London, UK)
The Economist Intelligence Unit (London, New York and Hong Kong)
Egypt Independent (Cairo, Egypt)
Egypt Today (Cairo, Egypt)
Energy East-Med News (Jerusalem, Israel)
Energy Egypt (Cairo, Egypt)
Energy Matters (Victoria, Australia)
Energy Observer (Belgrade, Serbia)
Energy Quarterly (Cambridge, UK)
Energy Security (Potomac, MD, USA)
energy-pedia news (London Colney, UK)
E&P Magazine (Houston, TX, USA)
Euractiv (Brussels, Belgium)
Eurasia Times (Brussels, Belgium)
EuroAsia Interconnector (Nicosia, Cyprus)
Executive (Beirut, Lebanon)
Financial Times (London, UK)
Forbes (Jersey City, NJ, USA)
Foreign Policy (Washington, DC, USA)
Fortune (New York, USA)
Front News International (Kiev, Ukraine)

Gas Strategies (London, UK)

The Global Business Law Review (Cleveland State University, Cleveland, OH, USA)

GlobalSecurity.org (Alexandria, VA, USA)

Globes (Tel Aviv, Israel)

Green Car Congress (San Francisco, CA, USA)

Haaretz (Jerusalem, Israel)

Hamodia (New York, USA)

Hellenic Shipping News (Piraeus, Greece)

Hurriyet Daily News (İstanbul, Turkey)

Hydrocarbon Processing (Houston, TX, USA)

Hydrocarbons Technology (New York, USA)

I-CONnect: Blog of the International Journal of Constitutional Law (Oxford University Press, Oxford, UK)

IHS Markit (Englewood, CO, USA)

The Independent (London, UK)

Insight Turkey (Ankara, Turkey)

International Crisis Group (Brussels, Belgium)

Investopedia (New York, USA)

Israel Defense (Kfar Saba, Israel)

Israel Hayom (Jerusalem, Israel)

Israel21c (Tel Aviv, Israel)

Jane's Defence Weekly (Coulsdon, Surrey, UK)

The Jerusalem Post (Jerusalem, Israel)

Jewish Business News

The Jewish Chronicle (London, UK)

Jewish News Syndicate (New York, USA)

Jewish Telegraphic Agency (New York, USA)

JewishPress.com (New York, USA)

JOC.com (New York, USA)

The Jordan Times (Amman, Jordan)

Journal of Balkan and Near Eastern Studies (London, UK)

Journal of Energy Security (Institute for Analysis of Global Security, Potomac, MD, USA)

Knowledge@Wharton (University of Pennsylvania, USA)

LNG World Shipping (Enfield, UK)

Madamasr (Cairo, Egypt)

The Marker (Tel Aviv, Israel)

Matzav Blog (Israel Policy Forum, New York, USA)

Matzav Blog (New York, USA)

Mediterranean Affairs (Reggio Calabria, Italy)

Middle East Eye (London, UK)

Middle East Monitor (London, UK)

Middle East Online (London, UK)

Middle East Policy (New Jersey, USA)

Middle East Quarterly (Philadelphia, UK)

Middle East Strategic Perspective (Beirut, Lebanon)

Mondaq (London, New York, Sydney)

Nasdaq (New York, USA)

Natural Gas Europe (Vancouver, Canada)

Natural Gas World (Vancouver, Canada)

Naval Technology (New York, London, and Victoria)
The New Arab (London, UK)
New Europe (Brussels, Belgium)
Newsweek (New York, USA)
The New York Times (New York, USA)
NGV Global (Auckland, New Zealand)
NoCamels – Israeli Innovation News (Herzliya, Israel)
Offshore Engineer (Houston, TX, USA)
Offshore Technology (New York, London, and Victoria)
OffshoreEnergyToday.com (Rotterdam, Netherlands)
Oil and Gas Journal (Tulsa, OK, USA)
The Oil and Gas Year News (Dubai, UAE)
Oilfield Technology (Surrey, UK)
Oilprice.com (London, UK)
OilVoice (Milton Keynes, UK)
Petroleum Economist (London, UK)
Platts (New York, London and Singapore)
Port2Port (Tel Aviv, Israel)
PR Newswire (New York, USA)
Proceedings (United States Naval Academy, Annapolis, MD, USA)
Renewable Energy Magazine (Madrid, Spain)
Renewable Energy World (Plymouth, MN, USA)
Renewables Now (Sophia, Bulgaria)
Reuters (London, UK)
Rigzone (Houston, London, Dubai and Singapore)
RT.com (Moscow, Russia)
Saraya News (Amman, Jordan)
Search and Discovery (Boulder, Tulsa, USA)
Slate (New York and Washington, DC, USA)
Society of Petroleum Engineers (Richardson, TX, USA)
Strategic Assessment (Tel Aviv-Yafo, Israel)
Stratfor (Austin, TX, USA)
Sustainability (Basel, Switzerland)
Sxcoal (Taiyuan, Shanxi, China)
Syrian Times (Damascus, Syria)
Tablet Magazine (New York, USA)
Tethys Oil (Stockholm, Sweden)
Time Magazine (New York, USA)
The Times of Israel (Jerusalem, Israel)
Tishreen (Damascus, Syria)
Trend News Agency (Baku, Azerbaijan)
TRT World (Turkish Radio and Television Corporation, Istanbul, Turkey)
Turkish Policy Quarterly (Istanbul, Turkey)
United Press International (Washington, DC, USA)
US News (Washington, DC and New York, USA)
The Wall Street Journal (New York, USA)
Wind Power Monthly (London, UK)
World Bulletin News (Istanbul, Turkey)
World Oil (Houston, TX, USA)
Xinhua (Beijing, China)
Yeni Safak (Istanbul, Turkey)

Ynet News.com (Tel Aviv, Israel)
Zion Oil (Dallas, TX, USA)

Secondary sources: newspapers, journals, and magazine articles

"$15 Billion Israel-Egypt Deal Signed; The Biggest for Israel's Natural Gas Industry," *Eurasia Times*, February 21, 2018, https://eurasiantimes.com/israel-egypt-deal-natural-gas/

"Israeli project secures funding," *Wind Power Monthly*, July 18, 2018, https://www.windpowermonthly.com/article/1487419/israeli-project-secures-funding

Abadi, Jacob, "Egypt's Policy Towards Israel: The Impact of Foreign and Domestic Constraints," *Israel Affairs*, Volume 12, Issue 1 (2006), pp. 159–176.

Abilov, Shamkhal, "The Azerbaijan-Israel Relations: A Non-Diplomatic, But Strategic Partnership," *The Journal of Central Asian and Caucasian Studies* (OAKA) (USAK, Ankara International Strategic Research Organization), Volume 4, Issue 8 (2009), pp. 147–167.

Abramov, Natanel, "Israel's Plan to Supply the Arab World With Energy Is Under Threat in Jordan," *Newsweek*, October 11, 2016, www.newsweek.com/israel-jordan-energy-supply-arab-world-ties-zionist-508955

Abu-Nasr, Donna, "Unwanted: The $10 Billion Gas Deal With Israel that Jordan Needs," *Bloomberg*, October 27, 2016, www.bloomberg.com/news/articles/2016-10-26/unwanted-the-10-billion-gas-deal-with-israel-that-jordan-needs

Adato, Edna, Hezi Sternlicht, Ze'ev Klein, and Dan Lavie, "High Court Upholds Government's Gas Export Policy," *Israel Hayom*, October 22, 2013, www.israelhayom.com/site/newsletter_article.php?id=12749

Adel, Mohamed, "Damietta LNG Plant Exports Gas Again After Six-Year Suspension," *Daily News Egypt*, September 4, 2018, www.dailynewsegypt.com/2018/09/04/damietta-lng-plant-exports-gas-again-after-six-year-suspension/

"AGR, Partners Make Big Israeli Gas Find," *Platts*, January 3, 2013, www.platts.com/latest-news/natural-gas/jerusalem/agr-partners-make-big-israeli-gas-find-6978742

Ahmed, Waad, "Export Dreams: Will Zohr Gas Production Allow Egypt to Light Europe and Its Own Cities?" *Madamasr*, February 6, 2018, www.madamasr.com/en/2018/02/06/feature/economy/export-dreams-will-zohr-gas-production-allow-egypt-to-light-europe-and-its-own-cities/

Akkad, Dania, "The Egypt-Israel Gas Deal: What's the Chance It Will Go Up in Smoke?" *Middle East Eye*, July 17, 2018, www.middleeasteye.net/news/business-egypt-israel-gas-deal-LNG-pipeline-delek-drilling-dolphinus-tamar-leviathan-field-mediterranean-energy-2125842654

Akkad, Dania, "Why Hasn't Gaza Marine Produced Gas," *Mid East Eye*, April 26, 2015, www.middleeasteye.net/news/why-hasnt-gaza-marine-produced-gas-257418634

Al-Dabisiyyeh, Zaid, "Jordan's Gas Deal With Israel Hangs in the Balance," *The New Arab*, December 11, 2014, www.alaraby.co.uk/english/news/2014/12/12/jordans-gas-deal-with-israel-hangs-in-the-balance

"Allowing U.S. Oil Drilling in Golan Breaches UN Resolutions," *Syrian Times*, February 25, 2013, http://syriatimes.sy/index.php/golan/3229-allowing-u-s-oil-drilling-in-golan-breaches-un-resolutions

"Alma Oilfields Returned to Egypt," *Jewish Telegraphic Agency*, November 26, 1979, www.jta.org/1979/11/26/archive/alma-oilfields-re-turned-to-egypt

al-Mughrabi, Nidal, "Energy Crisis Leaves Gaza With Barely Four Hours of Power a Day," *Reuters*, January 12, 2017, www.reuters.com/article/us-palestinians-gaza-energy/energy-crisis-leaves-gaza-with-barely-four-hours-of-power-a-day-iduskbn14w1yg

Alster, Paul and David Andrew Weinberg, "The Daunting Challenge of Defending Israel's Multi-Billion Dollar Gas Fields," *Forbes*, January 1, 2014, www.forbes.com/sites/realspin/2014/01/08/the-daunting-challenge-of-defending-israels-multi-billion-dollar-gas-fields/#ce039c03b929

Alvarado, Marc, "The Changing Face of the Global Methanol Industry," *IHS Chemical Bulletin* (Methanol Institute), Issue 3 (2016), p. 2, www.methanol.org/wp-content/uploads/2016/07/IHS-ChemicalBulletin-Issue3-Alvarado-Jun16.pdf

al-Youm, Al-Masry, "Egypt Welcomes Natural Gas From All Countries: PM," *Egypt Independent*, February 24, 2018, www.egyptindependent.com/egypt-welcomes-natural-gas-countries-pm/

Amin, Shahira, "Egypt Faces Public Backlash After Signing $15 Billion Gas Deal With Israel," *Al-Monitor*, February 23, 2018, www.al-monitor.com/pulse/originals/2018/02/egypt-gas-deal-israel-public-anger-sisi.html

"Analysis: Israel's Plans to Tap Into Wind Power Take Shape," *Wind Power Monthly*, January 30, 2015, www.windpowermonthly.com/article/1331651/analysis-israels-plans-tap-wind-power-shape

Andiva, Yvonne, "Egypt to Construct US $2.3bn Gas-Fired Combined Cycle Plant," *Construction Review Online*, November 6, 2018, https://constructionreviewonline.com/2018/11/egypt-to-construct-us-2-3bn-gas-fired-combined-cycle-plant/

Andreou, Avie, "Gas Pipeline Deal Reached With Egypt – CyBC," *Cyprus Mail*, https://cyprus-mail.com/2018/08/06/gas-pipeline-deal-reached-with-egypt-cybc/

Antreasyan, Anais, "Gas Finds in the Eastern Mediterranean: Gaza, Israel and Other Conflicts," *Journal of Palestine Studies*, Volume XLII, Issue 3 (Spring 2013), pp. 29–47.

Arlosoroff, Meirav, "Why Hasn't Israel's Windfall-Profit Tax Blown in Yet?" *Haaretz*, August 30, 2017, www.haaretz.com/israel-news/business/why-hasnt-israels-windfall-profit-tax-blown-in-yet-1.5446722

"Ashalim's Solar Tower Is World's Tallest," *Renewable Energy Magazine*, December 27, 2017, www.renewableenergymagazine.com/solar_thermal_electric/ashalima-s-solar-tower-is-worlda-s-20171227

"At Least 10 Firms Bid for Israel-Turkey Gas Pipeline: Report," *Hurriyet Daily News*, March 25, 2014, www.hurriyetdailynews.com/at-least-10-firms-bid-for-israel-turkey-gas-pipeline-report-64066

"Atoll Field Enters Production, Adds 300 MCFD to Output," *Egypt Today*, December 6, 2017, www.egypttoday.com/Article/3/35657/Atoll-field-enters-production-adds-300-mcfd-to-output

Aviel, David, "Economic Implications of the Peace Treaty Between Egypt and Israel," *Case Western Reserve Journal of International Law*, Volume 12, Issue 1 (Winter 1980), pp. 57–75.

Azran, Eran, "The Biggest-ever Infrastructure Project in Israel Gets Under Way," *Haaretz*, February 27, 2017, www.haaretz.com/israel-news/1.774036

Azran, Eran, "Geologist Reports Major Oil Find in Israel; Firm Stays Mum," *Haaretz*, October 8, 2015, www.haaretz.com/israel-news/business/.premium-geologist-reports-golan-oil-find-firm-stays-mum-1.5406510

Azran, Eran, "Israel Quietly Begins Exporting Natural Gas to Jordan Amid Political Sensitivities," *Haaretz*, March 2, 2017, www.haaretz.com/israel-news/business/israel-quietly-begins-exporting-gas-to-jordan-1.5443894

Azran, Eran, "Israel's Capital Market: A Swamp of Concentration," *Haaretz*, August 1, 2011, www.haaretz.com/israel-news/business/1.5038269

Azulay, Moran, "Netanyahu Fighting to Build Majority for Natural Gas Plan," *Reuters*, June 29, 2015, www.reuters.com/article/israel-gas-idUSL8N0ZG0J820150630

Baatout, Faisal, "Qatar Ready to Boost Ties With Israel," *Middle East Online*, May 15, 2003, www.middle-east-online.com/english/?id=5562

Bahgat, Gawdat, "Energy and the Arab-Israeli Conflict," *Middle Eastern Studies*, Volume 44, Issue 6 (November 2008), pp. 937–944.

Bahgat, Gawdat, "Israel's Energy Security: The Caspian Sea and the Middle East," *Israel Affairs*, Volume 16, Issue 3 (2010), pp. 406–415.

Bakal, Shai, "Israel: Competition Regulation In Israel: The Law, Recent Trends and Insights," *Mondaq*, May 2, 2017, www.mondaq.com/x/590348/Trade+Regulation+Practices/Competition+Regulation

Ball, Jeffrey, "Germany's High-Priced Energy Revolution," *Fortune*, March 14, 2017, http://fortune.com/2017/03/14/germany-renewable-clean-energy-solar/

Barakat, Amiram, "Delek Will Supply Compressed Natural Gas to Strauss Dairy and Confectionary Plant in the Galilee," *Globes*, January 9, 2014, https://en.globes.co.il/en/article-1000908240

Barakat, Amiram, "Sheshinski: Bring Gas Ashore Early, Pay Less Tax," *Globes*, January 31, 2011, www.globes.co.il/en/article-1000613046

Barakat, Amiram, "Sovereign Wealth Fund to Begin Operating in 2017," *Globes*, November 11, 2015, www.globes.co.il/en/article-sovereign-wealth-fund-to-begin-operating-in-2017-1001080258

Barakat, Amiram, "Sovereign Wealth Fund Won't Operate Before 2020," *Globes*, February 15, 2017, https://en.globes.co.il/en/article-sovereign-wealth-fund-wont-operate-before-2020-1001177034

Barbara Opall-Rome, "Israel Navy Readies for Third-Generation USV," *Defense News*, July 27, 2016, www.defensenews.com/naval/2016/07/27/israel-navy-readies-for-third-generation-usv/

Bar-Eli, Avi, "Antitrust Chief Warns He May Break Up Natural Gas Monopoly," *Haaretz*, December 23, 2014, www.haaretz.com/israel-news/business/.premium-1.633228

Bar-Eli, Avi, "Steinitz Blasts 'Pressure Campaign' Against Gas Royalties Committee," *Haaretz*, August 26, 2010, www.haaretz.com/1.5105440

Bar-Eli, Avi, Moti Bassok and Zvi Zrahiya, "Cabinet Approves Sheshinski Committee Recommendations," *Haaretz*, January 24, 2011, www.haaretz.com/israel-news/business/cabinet-approves-sheshinski-committee-recommendations-1.338809

Barkat, Amiram, "Gas Developers, Owe Sheshinski Debt of Gratitude," *Globes*, May 20, 2015, www.globes.co.il/en/article-gas-developers-owe-sheshinski-a-debt-of-gratitude-1001038366

Barnea, Jaffa, Lande & Co., "Reform in the Electricity Sector and in the Israel Electric Corporation," *Lexology*, June 13, 2018, www.lexology.com/library/detail.aspx?g=fb6381f1-27e9-44de-b3e0-0c5b83dcc0e7

Baroudi, Admiral Nazih, "The Commanders Respond: Lebanese Navy," *Proceedings*, Volume 138/3/1,309 (March 2012), www.usni.org/magazines/proceedings/2012-03/commanders-respond-lebanese-navy

Baroudi, Admiral Nazih, "The Commanders Respond: Lebanese Navy," *Proceedings*, Volume 139/3/1,321 (March 2013), www.usni.org/magazines/proceedings/2013-03/commanders-respond-lebanese-navy

"Başbakandan Kıbrıs'ta doğalgaz aramaya gelen ABD'li Exxon'a: Karşılığını görecek [Turkish]," *Diken*, March 7, 2018, www.diken.com.tr/kalindan-kibrista-dogalgaz-aramaya-gelen-abdli-exxona-haklarimizi-koruyacagiz/

"Bassil Says Oil and Gas Deal Is 'Economic Resistance'," *The Daily Star*, December 16, 2017, www.dailystar.com.lb/News/Lebanon-News/2017/Dec-16/430463-bassill-labels-oil-and-gas-exploration-economic-resistance.ashx

Bassok, Moti, "Chairman of Israel's Gas Panel Receives Death Threats," *Haaretz*, January 24, 2011, www.haaretz.com/1.5112015

"Belectric Cuts Ribbon on 30-MW Solar Park in Israel," *Renewables Now*, January 31, 2018, https://renewablesnow.com/news/belectric-cuts-ribbon-on-30-mw-solar-park-in-israel-600026/

Bengio, Ofra, "Surprising Ties Between Israel and the Kurds," *Middle East Quarterly*, Volume 21, Issue 3 (Summer 2014), pp. 1–12.

Benmeleh, Yacoov, "Delek Taps JPMorgan, HSBC for $1.75 Billion Leviathan Funds," *Bloomberg*, November 27, 2016, www.bloomberg.com/news/articles/2016-11-27/delek-taps-jpmorgan-hsbc-for-1-75-billion-to-finance-leviathan

Benmeleh, Yaacov, "Shell Mulls 15-Year Deal for Israeli, Cypriot Gas, Partner Says," *Bloomberg Quint*, March 23, 2018, www.bloombergquint.com/business/2018/03/21/shell-mulls-15-year-deal-for-israeli-cypriot-gas-partner-says

Benovadia, Dov, "Israel Navy Completes Gas Platforms Defensive Drill," *Hamodia*, June 6, 2018, https://hamodia.com/2018/06/06/israel-navy-completes-gas-platforms-defensive-drill/

Ben-Zion, Ilan, "Government Secretly Approves Golan Heights Drilling," *The Times of Israel*, May 13, 2012, www.timesofisrael.com/government-secretly-approves-golan-heights-drilling/

Berger, Ariella, "Natural Gas at the Supreme Court: Far-Reaching Consequences," *Jerusalem Post*, August 7, 2013, www.jpost.com/Opinion/Op-Ed-Contributors/When-the-wider-public-sphere-becomes-the-correct-forum-322380

"BG to Discuss Exporting Israeli Gas Via Idku LNG," *The Economist Intelligence Unit*, July 2, 2014, http://country.eiu.com/article.aspx?articleid=1861978970; BP *Statistical Review of World Energy*, British Petroleum, London, UK, 2014.

"Black Gold Under the Golan," *The Economist*, November 7, 2015, www.economist.com/news/middle-east-and-africa/21677597-geologists-israel-think-they-have-found-oilin-very-tricky-territory-black-gold

Bob, Yonah Jeremy, "Netanyahu to High Court: Gas Deal Helps Chance of Peace With Many Countries," *Jerusalem Post*, February 14, 2016, www.jpost.com/Israel-News/Politics-And-Diplomacy/Netanyahu-confronts-High-Court-to-defend-natural-gas-policy-in-unprecedented-personal-appearance-444846

Boehm, Omro, "Did Israel Just Stop Trying to Be a Democracy?" *The New York Times*, July 26, 2018, www.nytimes.com/2018/07/26/opinion/israel-law-jewish-democracy-apartheid-palestinian.html

"BP Starts Gas Production From Taurus, Libra Fields in Egypt," *Offshoreenergytoday.com*, May 10, 2017, Offshoreenergytoday.com, www.offshoreenergytoday.com/bp-starts-gas-production-from-taurus-libra-fields-in-egypt/

Branford, Nicholas, "US Mediates Border Dispute Between Lebanon and Israel Amid Rising Tensions," *The Arab Weekly*, February 25, 2018, https://thearabweekly.com/us-mediates-border-dispute-between-lebanon-and-israel-amid-rising-tensions

Butt, Gerald, "Can Greece Jump on the Gas-Transit Train?" *Petroleum Economist*, September 4, 2018, www.petroleum-economist.com/articles/midstream-downstream/pipelines/2018/can-greece-jump-on-the-gas-transit-train

Butt, Gerald, "Troubled Waters Ahead in Israel-Lebanon Border Dispute," *Petroleum Economist*, March 8, 2018, www.petroleum-economist.com/articles/politics-economics/middle-east/2018/troubled-waters-ahead-in-israel-lebanon-border-dispute

Calculation of Reserves, Tethys Oil, Stockholm, Sweden, undated, www.tethysoil.com/en/operations/oil-and-natural-gas/calculation-of-reserves

"Can Natural Gas Help Lower Pollution Levels?" *Economic Times*, 2016, https://economictimes.indiatimes.com/can-natural-gas-help-lower-pollution-levels/change theair_show/54777201.cms

Childs, Nick, "Russia Seeks Mid-East Role," *BBC News*, April 27, 2005, http://news.bbc.co.uk/2/hi/middle_east/4490447.stm

"China Methanol Apparent Consumption Grows 5% on yr in Jan-Nov," *Sxcoal*, December 12, 2017, www.sxcoal.com/news/4566401/info/en

"CNG Fuel Implementation Guidance Provided to Israel," *NGV Global News*, September 17, 2015, www.ngvglobal.com/blog/israel-steps-up-cng-implementation-program-0122

"CNG Fuel Implementation Guidance Provided to Israel," *NGV Global*, September 17, 2015, www.ngvglobal.com/blog/israel-steps-up-cng-implementation-program-0122

"Coal in Germany," *Clean Energy Wire*, December 5, 2017, www.cleanenergywire.org/factsheets/coal-germany

Cohen, Gina, "Israel: More Gas Customers, Please," *Petroleum Economist*, September 12, 2017, www.petroleum-economist.com/articles/midstream-downstream/lng/2017/israel-more-gas-customers-please

Cohen, Hedy, "Bureaucracy Blocks the Gas," *Globes*, January 27, 2015, www.globes.co.il/en/article-the-bureaucratic-gas-blockage-1001004598

Cohen, Hedy, "The Cut in Coal Use Will Reduce Pollution But Increase Electricity Prices in 2016," *Globes*, December 29, 2015, www.globes.co.il/en/article-iec-to-reduce-coal-use-from-friday-1001091820

Cohen, Hedy, "Israel Electric Corp to Reduce Coal Use Friday," *Globes*, December 29, 2015, www.globes.co.il/en/article-iec-to-reduce-coal-use-from-friday-1001091820

Cohen, Hedy, "Israel-Jordan Gas Pipeline to Begin Operating in 2017," *Globes*, March 10, 2016, www.globes.co.il/en/article-israel-jordan-gas-pipeline-to-begin-operating-in-2017-1001109296

Cohen, Hedy, "Jerusalem Natural Gas Distribution License Signed," *Globes*, February 23, 2016, www.globes.co.il/en/article-jerusalem-gas-distribution-license-signed-1001105702

Cohen, Hedy, "US Instructing Israel on Gas-powered Vehicles," *Globes*, September 9, 2015, www.globes.co.il/en/article-us-instructing-israel-on-gas-powered-public-transport-1001068073

Cohen, Ora, "Delek Israel Planning to Install Compressed Natural Gas Pumps in 12 Filling Stations," *TheMarker*, July 11, 2018, www.haaretz.com/israel-news/business/.premium-israel-s-together-to-sell-cosmetics-based-on-cannabis-dead-sea-minera-1.6265734

Cohen, Ora, "Israeli Natural Gas Program Fails to Meet Quota," *Haaretz*, May 31, 2018, www.haaretz.com/whdcMobileSite/israel-news/business/israeli-natural-gas-program-fails-to-meet-quota-1.6135063

Cohen, Ora, "Israel's 5% Claim on Gas in Cypriot Field Causes Dispute With Nicosia," *Haaretz*, May 11, 2018, www.haaretz.com/israel-news/business/israel-s-5-claim-on-gas-in-cypriot-field-causes-dispute-with-nicosia-1.6075918

Collins, Ryan and Kevin Varley, "A U.S. Shale Gas Cargo Is Heading to Israel for the First Time," *Bloomberg*, May 11, 2018, www.bloomberg.com/news/articles/2018-05-10/a-u-s-shale-gas-cargo-is-heading-to-israel-for-the-first-time

"Company Overview of Palestine Investment Fund PLC," *Bloomberg*, 2018, www.bloomberg.com/research/stocks/private/snapshot.asp?privcapId=62147909

"Controversial Natural Gas Deal Passes Knesset," *The Times of Israel*, September 7, 2015, www.timesofisrael.com/controversial-natural-gas-deal-passes-knesset/

Crisis Group, "Can Gas Save Cyprus? The Long-Term Cost of Frozen Conflicts," *International Crisis Group*, March 22, 2013, http://blog.crisisgroup.org/europe-central-asia/2013/03/22/can-gas-save-cyprus-the-long-term-cost-of-frozen-conflicts/

"Current Natural Gas Vehicle Statistics: Natural Gas Vehicles Worldwide," *NGV Global*, April 26, 2018, www.iangv.org/current-ngv-stats/

"Cyprus President Says Gas Can Help Reunification," *Euractiv*, April 11, 2014, www.euractiv.fr/section/all/news/cyprus-president-says-gas-can-help-reunification/

Damiras, Vassilios, "Greece, Cyprus and Israel in an Era of Geostrategic Friendship and Geoeconomic Cooperation," *Mediterranean Affairs*, January 9, 2015, http://mediterraneanaffairs.com/greece-cyprus-and-israel-in-an-era-of-geostrategic-friendship-and-geoeconomic-cooperation/

David Israel, "Geologist: Israel Plans Excessive Natural Gas Exports, Draining Finite Resources," *The Jewish Press*, October 24, 2018, www.jewishpress.com/news/politics/geologist-israel-plans-excessive-natural-gas-exports-draining-finite-resources/2018/10/24/

"Deepwater Risks-1: Challenges, Risks Can Be Managed in Deepwater Oil and Gas Projects," *Oil and Gas Journal*, November 27, 2006, www.ogj.com/articles/print/volume-104/issue-44/exploration-development/deepwater-risks-1-challenges-risks-can-be-managed-in-deepwater-oil-and-gas-projects.html

"Definition of Libor," *Financial Times*, undated, http://lexicon.ft.com/Term?term=LIBOR

"Delek, Noble to Invest in EMG Pipeline to Egypt," *DMEA – Downstream Middle East & Africa*, Week 27, Issue 363, July 12, 2018, https://newsbase.com/topstories/delek-noble-invest-emg-pipeline-egypt

"Delek to Sell 9.25 Percent Stake in Tamar and Dalit Fields Offshore Israel," *Offshore Technology*, July 7, 2017, www.offshore-technology.com/news/newsdelek-to-sell-925-stake-in-tamar-and-dalit-fields-offshore-israel-5864571

Dimou, Antonia, "East Mediterranean Gas Cooperation and Security Challenges," *National Security and the Future* (Zagreb, Croatia), Volume 17, Issue 1–2 (2016), pp. 99–112.

Dimou, Antonia, "Israel and Cyprus: In Search of Solutions to Natural Gas Challenges in the Eastern Mediterranean," *Foreign Policy News*, October 10, 2016, http://foreignpolicynews.org/2016/10/10/israel-cyprus-search-solutions-natural-gas-challenges-eastern-mediterranean/

Dubin, Rhys, "Netanyahu Finally Supports a Two-State Solution – In Iraq," *Foreign Policy*, September 13, 2017, http://foreignpolicy.com/2017/09/13/netanyahu-finally-supports-a-two-state-solution-in-iraq/

"Eastern Mediterranean Gas Discoveries Redefine LNG Playing Field," *LNG World Shipping*, March 28, 2018, www.lngworldshipping.com/news/view,eastern-mediterranean-gas-discoveries-redefine-lng-playing-field_51240.htm

"East Med Natural Gas Reserves Could Meet Turkey's Energy Needs for 572 Years," *Yeni Safak*, July 24, 2018, www.yenisafak.com/en/news/east-med-natural-gas-reserves-could-meet-turkeys-energy-needs-for-572-years-3437159

"Edison Stops Gas Exploration in Israel," *Trend News Agency*, August 7, 2018, https://en.trend.az/world/europe/2937789.html

Editors, "Germany Is Burning Too Much Coal," *Bloomberg*, November 14, 2017, www.bloomberg.com/view/articles/2017-11-14/germany-is-burning-too-much-coal

"EGAS to Launch Bid Round for Gas Exploration in 9 Areas in Q2 2018," *Energy Egypt*, April 3, 2018, https://energyegypt.net/2018/04/03/egas-to-launch-bid-round-for-gas-exploration-in-9-onshore-offshore-areas/

"Egypt, Cyprus to Sign Deal to Connect Aphrodite Gas Field With Egypt," *The Economic Times*, April 30, 2018, https://energy.economictimes.indiatimes.com/news/oil-and-gas/egypt-cyprus-to-sign-deal-to-connect-aphrodite-gas-field-with-egypt/63966328

"Egypt Holds Keys to East Mediterranean Gas," *The Economist Intelligence Unit*, February 23, 2018, http://country.eiu.com/article.aspx?articleid=1396458923&Country=Israel&topic=Economy

"Egyptian Company to Start Gas Imports From Israel Next Year, Sources Say," *Reuters*, August 5, 2018, www.reuters.com/article/us-egypt-energy-israel/egyptian-company-to-start-gas-imports-from-israel-next-year-sources-say-idUSKBN1KQ05N

"Egypt Is Optimistic About New Gas Discoveries in the Mediterranean," *The Economist*, July 5, 2018, www.economist.com/middle-east-and-africa/2018/07/05/egypt-is-optimistic-about-new-gas-discoveries-in-the-mediterranean

"Egypt Petroleum Ministry Keen to Resolve Gas Export Disputes: Official," *Arab News*, February 20, 2018, www.arabnews.com/node/1250651/business-economy

"Egypt Scraps Gas Supply Deal," *BBC News*, April 23, 2012, www.bbc.com/news/world-middle-east-17808954

"Egypt Sets Tariff of $0.38 for Use of National Gas Grid," *Egypt Independent*, August 3, 2018, www.egyptindependent.com/egypt-sets-tariff-of-0-38-for-use-of-national-gas-grid/

"Egypt Signals that $15 Billion Gas Deal Will Hinge on Israeli Debt Concessions," *Haaretz*, February 26, 2018, www.haaretz.com/israel-news/egypt-signals-that-giant-gas-deal-will-hinge-on-israeli-concessions-1.5848582

"Egypt to Develop Sinai Oil Fields 'Over-Exploited' by Israel," *World Bulletin News* (İstanbul), November 25, 2013, www.worldbulletin.net/news/123659/egypt-to-develop-sinai-oil-fields-over-exploited-by-israel

"Egypt to Increase Natural Gas Exports to Jordan to 150m SCFD by December," *Hellenic Shipping Worldwide*, November 10, 2018, www.hellenicshippingnews.com/egypt-to-increase-natural-gas-exports-to-jordan-to-150m-scfd-by-december/

"Eilat Class Multi-Mission Naval Corvettes," *Naval Technology*, undated, www.naval-technology.com/projects/saar5/

El-Menawy, Abdellatif, "How Egypt Will Gain From Private Gas Deal With Israel," *Arab News*, February 27, 2018, www.arabnews.com/node/1255476

"The End of Lignite Coal for Power in Germany," *Deutsche Welle*, October 27, 2015, www.dw.com/en/the-end-of-lignite-coal-for-power-in-germany/a-18806081

"End to Cyprus' Electricity Isolation One Step Closer," *Cyprus Mail Online*, October 2017, https://cyprus-mail.com/2017/10/16/end-cyprus-electricity-isolation-one-step-closer/

"Energean to Buy 45% Stake in Gaza Marine Field," *Energy East-Med News*, July 8, 2018, http://energynews.co.il/?p=33510

"Energy Firm Says Old Dead Sea Well Could Hold $322 MLN of Oil," *energy-pedia News*, May 1, 2016, www.energy-pedia.com/news/israel/new-167342

"Energy Minister Uzi Landau Has Decided to Renew Exploration Licenses on the Golan, Despite Syrian Objections," *Globes*, May 13, 2013, www.globes.co.il/en/article-1000748091

Engber, Daniel, "Where Does Israel Get Oil," *Slate*, July 14, 2006, www.slate.com/articles/news_and_politics/explainer/2006/07/where_does_israel_get_oil.html

Eppelbaum, Lev, Youri Katz and Zvi Ben-Avraham, "Israel – Petroleum Geology and Prospective Provinces," *Search and Discovery*, No. 10533 (2013), www.searchanddiscovery.com/pdfz/documents/2013/10533eppelbaum/ndx_eppelbaum.pdf.html

Eran, Oded, "How Would the New Gas Deal Affect Israel-Jordan Relations?" *Israel Defense*, December 4, 2016, www.israeldefense.co.il/en/node/27785

"Erdoğan Says Israel Is the World's 'Most Fascist, Racist' State," *TRT World*, July 24, 2018, www.trtworld.com/turkey/erdogan-says-israel-is-the-world-s-most-fascist-racist-state-19119

Eshel, Tamir, "Israel Shipyards Introduces the SAAR 72 Mini-Corvette Design," *Defense Update*, May 16, 2013, http://defense-update.com/20130516_saar-72.html

"EuroAsia Interconnector Front-End Engineering Design (FEED) Study," *EuroAsia Interconnector*, February 10, 2017, www.euroasia-interconnector.com/news-euroasia_interconnec tor_frontend_engineering_design_feed_study_and_support_services_tender_no_2 5101820161065period2017-01/

Exarheas, Andreas, "SDX Hits Gas Onshore Egypt," *Rigzone*, July 23, 2018, www.rigzone. com/news/sdx_hits_gas_onshore_egypt-23-jul-2018-156371-article/;

"Excess Profits Tax," *Investopedia*, www.investopedia.com/terms/e/excess-profits-tax. asp (accessed on January 18, 2018).

"Exploration History," *Zion Oil*, 2006, www.sec.gov/Archives/edgar/data/1131312/ 000113131206000077/exploration.htm

Fallon, Paul, "Israel Uses Syrian Chaos to Drill for Oil in the Golan Heights," *The Citizen*, July 27, 2015, www.thecitizen.in/index.php/en/newsdetail/index/1/4524/ israel-uses-syrian-chaos-to-drill-for-oil-in-the-golan-heights

"FCA Presents Fiat 500 M15 (Methanol); to Be Sold in Israel," *Green Car Congress*, November 3, 2016, www.greencarcongress.com/2016/11/20161103-fcam15.html

Feldman, Nizan, "Economic Peace: Theory Versus Reality," *Strategic Assessment*, Volume 12, Issue 3 (November 2009), pp. 19–29.

Fink, Daniel, "Turning Off the Egyptian Gas Spigot: Implications for Israel," *Journal of Energy Security*, May 31, 2011, http://ensec.org/index.php?option=com_content&vie w=article&id=313:turning-off-the-egyptian-gas-spigot-implications-for-israel&cati d=116:content0411&Itemid=375

Flectcher, Martin, "Israel's Big Gusher," *Slate*, February 26, 2014, www.slate.com/articles/ news_and_politics/moment/2014/02/israel_s_natural_gas_deposits_tel_aviv_s_off-shore_gas_fields_will_make_it.html

Gabison, Yoram, "Haifa's Ammonia Tank Ruling Will Be Felt Far Beyond Israel's Borders," *Haaretz*, March 8, 2017, www.haaretz.com/israel-news/business/ammonia-tank-ruling-will-be-felt-beyond-israels-borders-1.5446022

Gabizon, Yoram Gabizon, "Largest Wind Energy Project in Israel Commences – Will Bring in NIS 105 Million Per Year," *The Marker* [Hebrew], June 10, 2018, https:// www.themarker.com/markets/1.6159248

"Gas Deal With Israel Is Solution Regarding Arbitration With EMG: PM," *Egypt Today*, February 23, 2018, www.egypttoday.com/Article/3/43635/Gas-deal-with-Israel-is-solution-regarding-arbitration-with-EMG

"The Gaza Marine Field: Left Behind," *Natural Gas Europe*, May 11, 2015, www.natural-gaseurope.com/the-gaza-marine-field-left-behind-23564

"Gaza Marine Gas Field," *Offshore Technology*, 2018, www.offshore-technology.com/ projects/gaza-marine-gas-field/

"Germany Subsidizes Sale of Four Warships to Israel," *Reuters*, May 11, 2015, http:// in.reuters.com/article/germany-israel-warships/germany-subsidizes-sale-of-four-warships-to-israel-idINL5N0Y21IL20150511

"Gift or Curse? Israel Okays Development of Gaza Offshore Gas Field," *Middle East Online*, September 23, 2012, www.middle-east-online.com/english/?id=54515

Ginsburg, Mitch, "Account of King Hussein's 1973 War Warning Still Deemed Too Harmful to Release," *The Times of Israel*, September 12, 2017, www.timesofisrael.com/ account-of-king-husseins-1973-war-warning-still-deemed-too-harmful-to-release

"Global Compressed Natural Gas (CNG) Vehicles Market to Grow at a CAGR of 4.9%, 2017–2021 With Ford, Volkswagen, GM, Honda & Nissan Dominating," *PR Newswire*, May 30, 2017, www.prnewswire.com/news-releases/research-and-markets-global-compressed-natural-gas-cng-vehicles-market-to-grow-at-a-cagr-of-49-2017-2021-with-ford-volkswagen-gm-honda-nissan-dominating-300465021.html

"Global Methanol Demand Growth Driven by Methanol to Olefins as Chinese Thirst for Chemical Supply Grows, IHS Markit Says," *IHS Markit*, June 12, 2017, http://news.ihsmarkit.com/press-release/country-industry-forecasting-media/global-methanol-demand-growth-driven-methanol-olefi

Gorodiesky, Sonia, "Egypt: We've an Understanding on $1.8b IEC Compensation," *Globes*, February 23, 2018, www.globes.co.il/en/article-egypt-weve-an-understanding-on-18b-iec-compensation-1001225107

Gorodiesky, Sonia, "Givot Olam Oil Exploration License Deadline Extended," *Globes*, April 11, 2018, www.globes.co.il/en/article-givot-olam-oil-exploration-license-deadline-extended-1001231439

Gorodeisky, Sonia, "Knesset C'tee Approves 'Green Tax' to Boost Gas Use," *Globes*, March 15, 2018, www.globes.co.il/en/article-knesset-ctee-approves-green-taxation-to-boost-natgas-usage-1001227926

Gorodeisky, Sonia and Michal Raz-Chaimovich, "Ben Gurion Airport Signs Gas Production Electricity Deal," *Globes*, November 15, 2018, https://en.globes.co.il/en/article-ben-gurion-airport-signs-gas-production-electricity-deal-1001260838

Gorvett, Jonathan, "Mediterranean Gas Hunt Threatened by Cyprus Stand-off," *Asia Times*, October 29, 2018, www.atimes.com/article/mediterranean-gas-hunt-threatened-by-cyprus-stand-off/

Gottesman, Evan, "Netanyahu's Dangerous Jordanian Fantasy," *Matzav Blog* (Israel Policy Forum), October 27, 2017, www.matzavblog.com/2017/10/netanyahus-dangerous-jordanian-fantasy/

"The Government Decides to Acquire and Lease Land for Citizens in Irbid and Mafraq to Extend the Gas Line With Israel," *Saraya News* [Arabic], February 20, 2018, www.sarayanews.com/article/474065

Graham, Karen, "Israel Will Soon Have World's Tallest Solar Power Tower," *Digital Journal*, January 8, 2017, www.digitaljournal.com/tech-and-science/technology/israel-will-soon-have-world-s-tallest-solar-power-tower/article/483220

Grossman, Michelle Malka, "Oil Drilling to Go on in Golan Heights," *Jerusalem Post*, February 1, 2016, www.jpost.com/business-and-innovation/environment/drilling-to-go-on-in-the-golan-443533

Gumbatov, Akhmed, "Prospects of Delivering Israeli Gas to the Turkish Market," *Turkish Policy Quarterly*, January 26, 2016, http://turkishpolicy.com/blog/10/prospects-of-delivering-israeli-gas-to-the-turkish-market

Guo, Hai, "Volatile Organic Compounds (VOCs) Emitted From Petroleum and their Influence on Photochemical Smog Formation in the Atmosphere," *Journal of Petroleum & Environmental Biotechnology*, Volume 3, Issue 1 (2012), pp. 1–2, www.omicsonline.org/volatile-organic-compounds-vocs-emitted-from-petroleum-and-their-influence-on-photochemical-smog-formation-in-the-atmosphere-2157-7463.1000e104.php?aid=3828

Gutman, Lior, "Israel Announces $28.5 Million Grants Program for CNG Fueling Infrastructure," *Calcalist-Tech*, March 29, 2018, www.calcalistech.com/ctech/articles/0,7340,L-3735247,00.html

Hadar, Leon, "The Collapse of Israel's 'Periphery Doctrine'," *Foreign Policy*, June 26, 2010, http://foreignpolicy.com/2010/06/26/the-collapse-of-israels-periphery-doctrine/

Halavy, Dror, "Steinitz: Israel to Eliminate Coal Use Completely by 2030," *Hamodia*, October 25, 2018, https://hamodia.com/2018/10/25/steinitz-israel-eliminate-coal-use-completely-2030/

Harel, Amos, "Fearing Hezbollah Attacks, Israeli Military Insists Gas Rigs Be Close to Shore," *Haaretz*, July 31, 2018, www.haaretz.com/israel-news/.premium-fearing-hezbollah-attacks-israeli-military-insists-gas-rigs-be-close-to-shore-1.6334588

Harel, Amos, "Israel and Jordan Grow Closer as Iranian Foothold in Southern Syria Grows Stronger," *Haaretz*, June 21, 2017, https://www.haaretz.com/israel-news/.premium-israel-and-jordan-grow-closer-amid-iranian-foothold-in-syria-1.5486599

Harkov, Lahav, "Gas Deal Still Stuck Despite Knesset Approval," *Jerusalem Post*, September 7, 2015, https://www.jpost.com/Israel-News/Politics-And-Diplomacy/Gas-deal-still-stuck-despite-Knesset-approval-415489 (accessed on September 8, 2017).

Harris, Leon, "Your Taxes: What the Sheshinski Committee Report Means?" *Jerusalem Post*, November 16, 2010, www.jpost.com/Business/Commentary/Your-Taxes-What-the-Sheshinski-Committees-report-means

Hatuqa, Dala, "Morsi's Election as Seen from Palestine," *Al Jazeera*, July 7, 2012, www.aljazeera.com/indepth/features/2012/07/20127311434932728.html

Hauslohner, Abigail, "In the Siege of Gaza, Egypt Walks a Delicate Line," *Time*, January 11, 2010, http://content.time.com/time/world/article/0,8599,1953015,00.html

Herzog, Shirin, "Israel's Anti-Concentration Law: An Opportunity for New Players," *The Times of Israel*, November 30, 2017, http://blogs.timesofisrael.com/israels-anti-concentration-law-an-opportunity-for-new-players/

"Hizbullah Hits Israel's INS Hanit With Anti-Ship Missile," *Jane's Defence Weekly*, July 18, 2006, www.janes.com/defence/news/jdw/jdw060718_1_n.shtml

Hoch, Dov, "Israel Discusses Import of Gas from Egypt, Qatar," *JOC.com*, August 25, 1994, www.joc.com/israel-discusses-import-gas-egypt-qatar_19940825.html

Hossam Bahgat, "Who's Buying Israeli Gas? A Company Owned by the General Intelligence Service," *Mada Masr*, October 23, 2018, https://madamasr.com/en/2018/10/23/feature/politics/whos-buying-israeli-gas-a-company-owned-by-the-general-intelligence-service/

"IHS Cambridge Energy Research Associates Inc.," *Bloomberg*, 2018, www.bloomberg.com/profiles/companies/376925Z:US-ihs-cambridge-energy-research-associates-inc

"IHS Markit: Methanol Demand Growth Driven by Methanol-to-Olefins, China Demand," *Hydrocarbon Processing*, June 13, 2017, www.hydrocarbonprocessing.com/news/2017/06/ihs-markit-methanol-demand-growth-driven-by-methanol-to-olefins-china-demand

"Iran Decreases Feedstock Gas Price for Petrochemical Plants," *Azer News*, January 16, 2016, www.azernews.az/region/91723.html

"'Iron Dome of Seas': Israel's Navy Version of Missile Defence System Declared Operational," *RT.com*, November 28, 2017, www.rt.com/news/411189-israel-iron-dome-warship/

"Israel Approves Noble's Leviathan Development Plan," *OffshoreEnergyToday.com*, June 2, 2016, www.offshoreenergytoday.com/israel-approves-nobles-leviathan-development-plan/

"Israel Approves Pipeline Construction for Exporting Natural Gas to Jordan," *Port2Port*, September 24, 2105, www.port2port.com/article/Industry-Trade/Infrastructure/Israel-approves-pipeline-construction-for-exporting-natural-gas-to-Jordan/

"Israel Chemicals Q2 Revenue, Profit Drop," *Reuters*, August 3, 2017, www.reuters.com/article/icl-results/israel-chemicals-q2-revenue-profit-drop-idusl5n1kp1vh

"Israel Council Approves First License to Drill for Oil in Golan Heights," *Platts*, February 21, 2013, www.platts.com/latest-news/oil/jerusalem/israel-council-approves-first-license-to-drill-8167166

"Israel Electric Coal Consumption to Drop Further in 2017," *Platts*, March 15, 2017, www.platts.com/latest-news/coal/telaviv/israel-electric-coal-consumption-to-drop-further-26685600

"Israel Eyes Second Import Terminal," *Hellenic Shipping News*, August 11, 2016, www.hellenicshippingnews.com/israel-eyes-second-import-terminal/

"Israel Gives Jordan Helicopters for Border Security," *Reuters*, July 23, 2015, www.reuters.com/article/mideast-crisis-israel-jordan-idUSL8N0ZO15120150723

"Israeli Co Enlight to Buy PV, Wind in Central Europe," *Renewables Now*, January 22, 2018, https://renewablesnow.com/news/israeli-co-enlight-to-buy-pv-wind-in-central-europe-598988/

"Israeli Court Dismisses Petition Against Karish-Tanin Development," *Offshoreenergytoday.com*, May 3, 2018, www.offshoreenergytoday.com/israeli-court-dismisses-petition-against-karish-tanin-development/

"Israeli Exploration Group to Return Daniel Natgas Field Licenses," *Reuters*, August 20, 2017, www.reuters.com/article/israel-natgas-isramco-negev-2-idUSL8N1L608C

"Israeli Government Approves 40 Pct Limit on Natural Gas Exports," *Reuters*, June 23, 2013, www.reuters.com/article/israel-natgas-idUSL5N0EZ0BQ20130623

"Israeli Navy to Get 2 German Frigates to Shield Natural Gas Fields," *United Press International*, December 17, 2013, www.upi.com/Business_News/Security-Industry/2013/12/17/Israeli-navy-to-get-2-German-frigates-to-shield-natural-gas-fields/UPI-40851387306062/

"Israel Plans to Close Coal Power Plants Until 2025," *Front News International*, September 27, 2017, https://frontnews.eu/news/en/14344

"Israel Seeking Interest for Second Offshore Bid Round," *Oil and Gas Journal*, June 13, 2018, www.ogj.com/articles/2018/06/israel-seeking-interest-for-second-offshore-bid-round.html

"Israel Steps Up CNG Implementation Program," *NGV Global*, January 22, 2016, www.ngvglobal.com/blog/israel-steps-up-cng-implementation-program-0122

"Israel Targets Coal-for-Power Use at Less Than 10% of Fuel Mix by 2025," *Platts*, April 5, 2017, www.platts.com/latest-news/electric-power/telaviv/israel-targets-coal-for-power-use-at-less-than-26704398

"Israel to Build World's Tallest Solar Tower in Symbol of Renewable Energy Ambition," *Independent*, January 5, 2017, www.independent.co.uk/news/world/middle-east/israel-solar-tower-power-energy-renewable-tech-ambitions-a7510901.html

"Israel to Import Natural Gas for Less than Its Own Field's Rates," *JewishPress.com*, April 6, 2016, www.jewishpress.com/news/breaking-news/israel-to-import-natural-gas-for-less-than-its-own-fields-rates/2016/04/06/

"Israel: Production Capacities," *The Wind Power*, December 27, 2016, www.thewindpower.net/country_en_60_israel.php

"Israel's Dor to Double Methanol Imports to Meet Transport Demand Surge," *Platts*, November 13, 2013, www.platts.com/latest-news/petrochemicals/jerusalem/israels-dor-to-double-methanol-imports-to-meet-27628729

"Israel's Energy Minister: No Coal, Gasoline by 2030," *Globes*, December 4, 2017, www.globes.co.il/en/article-israels-energy-minister-no-coal-gasoline-by-2030-1001214304

"Israel's Ketura Solar Farm Connected to Grid," *Energy Matters*, July 30, 2015, www.energymatters.com.au/renewable-news/ketura-solar-farm-em4960/

"Israel's Ratio Secures $400 MLN to Fund Leviathan Natgas Project," *Reuters*, March 21, 2017, www.reuters.com/article/ratio-oil-expl-funding-leviathan/israels-ratio-secures-400-mln-to-fund-leviathan-natgas-project-idUSL5N1GY38C

"Israel's SWF: New Kid on the Block 2020 or Stillborn?" *Arab Sovereign Wealth Fund Monitor* (The Netherlands), Volume 2, Issue 3 (March 19, 2017), pp. 9–12, https://verocy.

com/wp-content/uploads/Documents/Newsletters/ASWFM/PDFs/ASWM_
3-2017.pdf

Israfilbayova, Sara, "Expert: Southern Gas Corridor Efficient Route for Israeli Gas
Export," *Azernews*, August 30, 2017, www.azernews.az/oil_and_gas/118329.html

"Italy's ENI Ramps-up Production Capacity at Egypt's Zohr Gas Field," *New Europe*,
May 10, 2018, www.neweurope.eu/article/italys-eni-ramps-production-capacity-
egypts-zohr-gas-field/

Jawahar, Jamal, "Winners and Losers from the Egypt-Israel Gas Deal," *Asharq Al-Awsat*,
February 24, 2018, https://aawsat.com/english/home/article/1185581/exclusive-winners-
and-losers-egypt-israel-gas-deal

Johnson, Keith, "For Israel and Its Neighbors, Energy Finds Power Big Dreams," *Foreign
Policy*, December 11, 2015, https://foreignpolicy.com/2015/12/11/for-israel-and-its-
neighbors-energy-finds-power-big-dreams-zohr-leviathan/

Johnson, Keith, "Israel's Reconciliation With Turkey Could Lead to New Energy
Deals," *Foreign Policy*, June 27, 2016, https://foreignpolicy.com/2016/06/27/israels-
reconciliation-with-turkey-could-lead-to-new-energy-deals/

Jones, Rory, "Investors in Israeli Natural Gas Agree to Supply Deal With Jordan," *The
Wall Street Journal*, September 26, 2016, www.wsj.com/articles/investors-in-israeli-
natural-gas-agree-supply-deal-with-jordan-1474903108

"Jordan Agrees Gas Purchase Deal With Israel," *The Economist Intelligence Unit*, September 29, 2017, http://country.eiu.com/article.aspx?articleid=1894657373

"Jordan Allocates Initial $2 Million for Joint Pipeline Project With Israel," *Middle East
Monitor*, January 2, 2018, www.middleeastmonitor.com/20180102-jordan-allocates-
initial-2-million-for-joint-pipeline-project-with-israel/

"Jordan Says Hosting Syrian Refugees Has Cost $10 Billion," *Arab News*, October 10,
2017, www.arabnews.com/node/1175541/middle-east

"Jordan to Resume Gas Imports From Egypt in January," *Hellenic Shipping News
Worldwide*, July 24, 2018, www.hellenicshippingnews.com/jordan-to-resume-gas-
imports-from-egypt-in-january/

"Jordan Unions Protest Against Israel Gas Deal," *Middle East Monitor*, July 25, 2018, www.
middleeastmonitor.com/20180725-jordan-unions-protest-against-israel-gas-deal/

"Jubail Industrial City: Top Choice of Investors," *Arab News*, November 24, 2014, www.
arabnews.com/saudi-arabia/news/664951

Julian, Hana Levi, "Israel, Cyprus Move to International Arbitration on Aphrodite Gas Reservoir," *JewishPress.com*, May 1, 2018, www.jewishpress.com/news/business-economy/
israel-cyprus-move-to-international-arbitration-on-gas-reservoir/2018/05/01/

Kalman, Matthew, "Israel Minister Seeks End to Coal, Diesel and Gasoline by 2030,"
Bloomberg, April 17, 2018, www.bna.com/israel-minister-seeks-n57982091179/

Kanason, Easwaran, "Geopolitical Eruptions in the Eastern Mediterranean," *OilVoice*,
March 30, 2018, https://oilvoice.com/Opinion/14953/Geopolitical-Eruptions-in-the-
Eastern-Mediterranean

Karpazli, Ertan, "Gas Fueling New Hope in Eastern Mediterranean," *TRT World*
(Istanbul), May 24, 2016, http://www2.trtworld.com/in-depth/gas-fueling-new-hope-
in-eastern-mediterranean-112203

Kaya, Nuran Erkul, "2020 Critical for Turkey's Gas Market," *Energy Observer*, November
19, 2017, www.energyobserver.com/en/post/5833

Keane, Kevin, "North Sea Oil and Gas Exploration 'at Lowest Level Since 1970s',"
BBC News, March 20, 2018, www.bbc.com/news/uk-scotland-north-east-orkney-
shetland-43461811

Keinan, Ehud, "An Executive Summary of the Professors' Report," *The Israel Chemist and Engineer (ICE)*, Issue 3 (June 2017), pp. 42–47, https://ice.digitaler.co.il/ice3/files/assets/common/downloads/publication.pdf

Khawaja, Moign, "Jordan King Demands Peace in Syria as Country Suffers From Record Trade Deficit," *Arabian Gazette*, June 20, 2012, https://arabiangazette.com/jordan-king-calls-syria-peace-amid-growing-trade-deficit/

Kirkpatrick, David D., "Secret Alliance: Israel Carries Out Airstrikes in Egypt, With Cairo's O.K.," *The New York Times*, February 8, 2018, www.nytimes.com/2018/02/03/world/middleeast/israel-airstrikes-sinai-egypt.html

"Landowners Waiting for Next Step in Jordan-Israel Gas Pipeline," *Al-Monitor*, March 29, 2018, www.al-monitor.com/pulse/originals/2018/03/jordan-israel-gas-deal-import-pipeline-expropriation-lands.html

Lavi, Zvi, "Landau: Energy Firm May Favor Egypt Gas," *Ynetnews.com*, December 13, 2010, www.ynetnews.com/articles/0,7340,L-3997847,00.html

Lazaroff, Tovah and Michael Wilner, "U.N. and Egypt Pressure all Sides to Halt Gaza Violence," *Jerusalem Post*, July 29, 2018, www.jpost.com/Arab-Israeli-Conflict/UN-and-Egypt-pressuring-all-sides-to-halt-Gaza-violence-563653

"Lebanese Army Chief Urges Military to Remain Alert to 'Defy Israeli Enemy'," *Al-Masdar*, July 31, 2018, www.almasdarnews.com/article/lebanese-army-chief-urges-military-to-remain-alert-to-defy-israeli-enemy/

"Lebanon Offers Five Blocks in First Oil & Gas Licensing Round," *OffshoreEnergy Today.com*, January 26, 2017, https://www.offshoreenergytoday.com/lebanon-offers-five-blocks-in-first-oil-gas-licensing-round/

"Lebanese President: Israel Rejects Settling Disputed Maritime Border," *E&P Magazine*, June 27, 2018, www.epmag.com/lebanese-president-israel-rejects-settling-disputed-maritime-border-1707106

"Lebanon's Oil & Gas Licensing Round Attracts Bids From Total-Eni-Novatek," *Middle East Strategic Perspective*, October 13, 2017, www.mesp.me/2017/10/13/lebanons-oil-gas-licensing-round-attracts-bids-total-eni-novatek/

"Leviathan FID Reached," *The Oil and Gas Year News*, Dubai, UAE, February 23, 2017, www.theoilandgasyear.com/news/leviathan-fid-reached/

"Leviathan Gas Field Group Submits $6.5 B Development Plan," *Ynetnews.com*, October 1, 2014, www.ynetnews.com/articles/0,7340,L-4576570,00.html

"Leviathan Partners Submit FPSO Field Development Plan," *Gas Strategies*, October 1, 2016, www.gasstrategies.com/information-services/gas-matters-today/leviathan-partners-submit-fpso-field-development-plan

Levitt, William J., "Israel Told to Keep Sinai Oil," *The New York Times*, November 6, 1978, www.nytimes.com/1978/11/06/archives/israel-told-to-keep-sinai-oil.html

Levy, Elior and Yoav Zitun, "Situation in Gaza Approaches Critical Point," *Ynetnews.com*, February 5, 2018, www.ynetnews.com/articles/0,7340,L-5090907,00.html

Liang, Fang-Yu, Marta Ryvak, Sara Sayeed and Nick Zhao, "The Role of Natural Gas as a Primary Fuel in the Near Future, Including Comparisons of Acquisition, Transmission and Waste Handling Costs of as With Competitive Alternatives," *Chemistry Central Journal*, Volume 6, Supplement 1 (2016), www.ncbi.nlm.nih.gov/pmc/articles/PMC3332260/

"Libor," *Fedprimerate.com*, 2018, www.fedprimerate.com/libor/index.html

Lidman, Melanie, "10 Things to Know About Israel's Natural Gas," *The Times of Israel*, November 29, 2015, www.timesofisrael.com/top-10-things-to-know-about-israels-natural-gas/

Lidman, Melanie, "Israelis to Dedicate Largest Solar Field in East Africa," *The Times of Israel*, February 4, 2015, www.timesofisrael.com/israelis-to-dedicate-largest-solar-field-in-east-africa/

Lidman, Melanie, "With $1b Africa Deal, Israel's Solar Power Exports Eclipse Local Usage," *The Times of Israel*, June 5, 2017, www.timesofisrael.com/with-1b-africa-deal-israels-solar-power-exports-eclipse-local-usage/

Lief, Louise, "Egypt Puts Stamp on Sinai," *Christian Science Monitor*, April 22, 1982, www.csmonitor.com/1982/0422/042255.html

"Long-Range Surface-to-Air Missile (LRSAM)/Barak 8," *GlobalSecurity.org*, undated, www.globalsecurity.org/military/world/india/lr-sam.htm

Magdy, Mirette and Yaacov Benmeleh, "Delek, Noble and Egypt Said to Put Final Touches on Gas Deal," *Bloomberg*, August 8, 2018, www.bloomberg.com/news/articles/2018-08-08/delek-noble-and-egypt-are-said-to-put-final-touches-on-gas-deal

Maoz, Epstein Rosenblum, "Israel Launches First International Bid Round for Offshore Oil and Gas Exploration Blocks," *Mondaq*, April 28, 2017, www.mondaq.com/x/589814/Oil+Gas+Electricity/Israel+Launches+First+International+Bid+Round+For+Offshore+Oil+And+Gas+Exploration+Blocks

Marta Silva, "Securitization as a Nation-building Instrument," *Politikon: The IAPSS Academic Journal*, Volume 29 (March 2016), pp. 201–214.

Maverik, Jack Bogart, "What Is the Difference Between Proven and Probable Reserves in the Oil and Gas Sector?" *Investopedia*, September 14, 2018, www.investopedia.com/ask/answers/060115/what-difference-between-proven-and-probable-reserves-oil-and-gas-sector.asp

Mazel, Zvi, "Will the Eastern Mediterranean Become a World Hub for the Natural-gas Trade?" *Jewish News Syndicate*, February 27, 2018, www.jns.org/opinion/will-the-eastern-mediterranean-become-a-world-hub-for-natural-gas-trade/

McCormick, Myles and David Sheppard, "Egypt to Pay Spanish-Italian JV $2bn in Natural Gas Dispute," *Financial Times*, September 3, 2018, www.ft.com/content/0d0dfd96-af6c-11e8-8d14-6f049d06439c

Melman, Yossi, "How Israel Lost to the Iranians," *Haaretz*, November 1, 2017, www.haaretz.com/print-edition/features/how-israel-lost-to-the-iranians-1.209838

Minasian, Sergey, "The Israeli-Kurdish Relations," *21st Century*, No. 1 (2007), pp. 15–32.

The Ministerial Committee on Legislation Approved the Oil Profits Tax Law, Which Regulates the New Taxation System for Gas and Oil Discoveries, Press Release [Hebrew], Ministry of Finance, State of Israel, February 23, 2011, https://mof.gov.il/Releases/Pages/News_320.aspx

Musarra, Sara Parker, "Israel Attempts to Balance Regulations, Infrastructure With LNG Growth," *Offshore Engineer*, October 22, 2013, www.oedigital.com/geoscience/item/4277-israel-attempts-to-balance-regulations-infrastructure-with-lng-growth

Naghi, Jonah, "The Value of Security Cooperation with Jordan," *Matzav Blog*, February 22, 2017, www.matzavblog.com/2017/02/value-security-cooperation-jordan/

Nasr, Nirvana, "Egypt, Jordan Agree on Amending Gas Import Deals," *Ahram Online*, August 9, 2018, http://english.ahram.org.eg/NewsContent/3/12/309338/Business/Economy/Egypt,-Jordan-agree-on-amending-gas-import-deals-.aspx

"Natural Gas Vehicle Statistics," *NGV Global*, July 6, 2018, www.iangv.org/current-ngv-stats/

"NEPCO and Israeli-American Noble Energy Gas Company Sign Agreement," *Al-Ghad* [Arabic], September 26, 2016, http://english.alghad.com/articles/1150842-NEPCo-and-Israeli-American-Noble-Energy-Gas-Company-Sign-Agreement

"Netherlands to Shut Europe's Biggest Gas Field to Limit Quake Risk," *Deutsche Welle*, March 29, 2018, www.dw.com/en/netherlands-to-shut-europes-biggest-gas-field-to-limit-quake-risk/a-43190065

"New Great Game Over Natural Gas," *Stratfor*, February 22, 2018, https://worldview. stratfor.com/article/eastern-mediterraneans-new-great-game-over-natural-gas

"Noble Brings Noa North Gas Field on Stream," *OffshoreEnergyToday.com*, June 25, 2012, www.offshoreenergytoday.com/noble-brings-noa-north-gas-field-on-stream-israel/

Norlen, Anders, "Turkey's Floating LNG Imports Deliver Cheaper Gas and Energy Security," *Mckinsey Energy Insights*, April 2017, www.mckinseyenergyinsights.com/ insights/turkey-s-floating-lng-imports-deliver-cheaper-gas-and-energy-security/

Norris, Andrew, "Block 9: Flashpoint for the Next Lebanon War?" *Tablet Magazine*, undated, www.tabletmag.com/jewish-news-and-politics/263356/block-9-flashpoint-for-the-next-lebanon-war

Noy, Kfir and Moshe Givoni, "Is 'Smart Mobility' Sustainable? Examining the Views and Beliefs of Transport's Technological Entrepreneurs," *Sustainability*, Volume 10, Issue 2 (February 2018), pp. 1–19, www.mdpi.com/2071-1050/10/2/422/htm

O'Cinneide, Eoin, "Palestine Seeks New Gaza Marine Operator," *Upstream*, April 4, 2018, www.upstreamonline.com/live/1465563/palestine-seeks-new-gaza-marine-operator? utm_medium=email&utm_source=free_article_access&utm_content=224422912

Oil Profits Tax Law, 5771–2011 [Hebrew], April 10, 2011, https://mof.gov.il/Commit-tees/NatureResourcesCommittee/MoreFiles_TaxesLaw.pdf

Omari, Raed, "Lands for Israel Gas Pipeline Acquired," *The Jordan Times*, March 8, 2018, www.jordantimes.com/news/local/lands-israel-gas-pipeline-acquired%E2%80%99

Orphanides, Stelios, "Lakkotrypis Confirms Shell's Interest to Buy Cypriot Gas," *Cyprus Business Mail*, March 13, 2108, http://cyprusbusinessmail.com/?p=60873

"Owners of Israeli Field Seek to Stop Cyprus Deal With Egypt," *Cyprus Mail Online*, March 14, 2018, https://cyprus-mail.com/2018/03/14/owners-israeli-field-seek-stop-cyprus-deal-egypt/

Pamir, Necdet, "Cyprus and Its Natural Resources Are a Vital Part of Our 'Blue Home-land'," *Insight Turkey*, February 23, 2018, https://sigmaturkey.com/2018/02/23/cyprus-natural-resources-vital-part-blue-homeland/

Paraskova, Tsvetana, "Egypt to Start Importing Israeli Gas for Re-export in Early 2019," *Oilprice.com*, August 7, 2018, https://oilprice.com/Latest-Energy-News/World-News/ Egypt-To-Start-Importing-Israeli-Gas-For-Re-export-In-Early-2019.html

"Partners in Israel's Tamar Raise Gas Reserves Estimate by 13 Pct," *Reuters*, July 2, 2017, www.reuters.com/article/israel-natgas-idUSL8N1JT09K

Patel, Prachi and Anat Bonshtien, "Israel Makes an Ambitious Move on Alternative Fuels," *Energy Quarterly*, Volume 39, Issue 3 (March 2014), pp. 214–215.

Peskin, Doron, "Report: Qatar Offering Israel Gas," *Ynetnews.com*, May 5, 2011, www. ynetnews.com/articles/0,7340,L-4064547,00.html

Petroleum Resources Classification System and Definitions, Society of Petroleum Engineers, Texas, United States, 2003–2018, www.spe.org/industry/petroleum-resources-classification-system-definitions.php

"President Sisi Says Dream of Turning Egypt into Regional Energy Hub Is Becoming Real-ity," *Al Ahram Online*, February 21, 2018, http://english.ahram.org.eg/NewsContent/ 3/12/291412/Business/Economy/President-Sisi-says-dream-of-turning-Egypt-into-re.aspx (accessed on February 21, 2018)

Press, Viva Sarah, "Enlight, Migdal to Invest $147 Million in Renewable Energy," *Israel21c*, January 3, 2016, www.israel21c.org/enlight-migdal-to-invest-147-million-in-renewable-energy/

Price, Yisrael, "Natural-Gas Facilities Too Close for Safety, Say Northern Residents," *Hamodia*, August 20, 2017, https://hamodia.com/2017/08/20/natural-gas-facilities-close-safety-say-northern-residents/

"Production From Atoll Gas Field Reaches 350M cfd," *Egypt Today*, April 15, 2018, www.egypttoday.com/Article/3/47920/Production-from-Atoll-gas-field-reaches-350M-cfd

Raafat, Ghada, "Egypt Stops Gas Imports, on Its Way to Become Self-Sufficient," *Ahram Online*, October 4, 2018, http://english.ahram.org.eg/NewsContent/3/12/312755/Business/Economy/Egypt-stops-gas-imports,-on-its-way-to-become-self.aspx

Rabinovitch, Ari, "Israel's New Motor Fuels Strategy Leans on Gas," *Reuters*, December 17, 2013, www.reuters.com/article/us-israel-cars-fuels/israels-new-motor-fuels-strategy-leans-on-gas-idUSBRE9BN0BC20131224

Rashty, Sandy, "Roll Out Israel's Oil Barrels," *The Jewish Chronicle*, August 4, 2013, www.thejc.com/business/features/roll-out-israel-s-oil-barrels-1.47310

Raz, Hila, "Rejected Petitions Against Sheshinski Law; 'There Is No Retroactive Taxation'," *The Marker* [Hebrew], August 15, 2012, www.themarker.com/law/1.1801962

Redler, Ori, "Crime and Punishment: The Social Protests Chase Away Investors," *Mida* [Hebrew], December 9, 2015, https://mida.org.il/2015/12/09/%D7%94%D7%97%D7%98%D7%90-%D7%95%D7%A2%D7%95%D7%A0%D7%A9%D7%95-%D7%94%D7%9E%D7%97%D7%90%D7%95%D7%AA-%D7%94%D7%97%D7%91%D7%A8%D7%AA%D7%99%D7%95%D7%AA-%D7%9E%D7%91%D7%A8%D7%99%D7%97%D7%95%D7%AA-%D7%90/

Reed, John, "Israel: Oil Secrets to Spill," *Financial Times*, January 27, 2016, www.ft.com/content/6260b762-c067-11e5-846f-79b0e3d20eaf?mhq5j=e5

Reed, John, "Woodside Backs Out of $2.7bn Israel Gas Project," *Financial Times*, May 21, 2014, www.ft.com/content/2ce420d0-e0b5-11e3-a934-00144feabdc0

"Regulator Orders Delek, Noble Energy to Sell Gas Fields," *Globes*, March 27, 2014, www.globes.co.il/en/articleregulator-orders-delek-noble-energy-to-sell-gas-fields-1000927892

Rinat, Zafrir, "Building New Natural Gas Rig Off Israel's Shores Poses High Ecological Risks, Expert Warns," *Haaretz*, July 30, 2018, www.haaretz.com/israel-news/.premium-expert-warns-of-ecological-risk-posed-by-offshore-natural-gas-rig-1.6334688

Rinat, Zafrir, "Energy Plan Sees Need for Nuclear Power Plants in Israel," *Haaretz*, January 26, 2016, www.haaretz.com/israel-news/.premium-1.699485

Roberts, Chana, "Haifa Mayor: Ammonia Tanks Endanger 600,000 Lives," *Arutz Sheva*, January 2, 2017, www.israelnationalnews.com/News/News.aspx/224240

Rosen, Edward R., "The Effect of Relinquished Sinai Resources on Israel's Energy Situation and Policies," *Middle East Review*, Volume 14, Number 3–4 (1982), pp. 5–12.

Rosenbaum, Amir, "Hatrurim Land License Drilling Finds Oil Near Dead Sea; Israeli Oil Reserve Worth $319 Million," *Jewish Business News*, May 1, 2016, http://jewishbusinessnews.com/2016/05/01/hatrurim-land-license-drilling-finds-oil-near-dead-sea-israeli-oil-reserve-worth-319-million/

Saeed, Ahmed and Asmahan Soliman, "An Egyptian-Israeli Agreement: New Maritime Borders and Israeli Gas Imports for a Reduced Gas Fine," *Madamasr*, August 30, 2017, www.madamasr.com/en/2017/08/30/feature/politics/an-egyptian-israeli-agreement-new-maritime-borders-and-israeli-gas-imports-for-a-reduced-gas-fine/

Samir, Mohamed, "Will Israeli Natural Gas Flow in Egypt's Pipelines?" *Daily New Egypt*, July 14, 2016, https://dailynewsegypt.com/2016/07/14/will-israeli-natural-gas-flow-in-egypts-pipelines/

Schindler, Max, "Energy Minister: Natural Gas Can Transform Israel's Geopolitical Status," *Jerusalem Post*, November 27, 2017, www.jpost.com/business-and-innovation/energy-minister-natural-gas-can-transform-israels-geopolitical-status-515293

Schindler, Max, "Pipeline Failure for Tamar Gas Field to Cause Hiccup in Electricity Rates," *Jerusalem Post*, September 24, 2017, www.jpost.com/Business-and-Innovation/Environment/Israelis-electric-bills-to-increase-following-gas-pipeline-failure-505827

"SDX to Exit South Ramadan, Switch Focus to South Disouq in Egypt," *Energy Egypt*, July 30, 2017, https://energyegypt.net/sdx-to-exit-south-ramadan-switch-focus-to-south-disouq-in-egypt/

Seftel, Bennett, "Persistent ISIS Sinai Threat Drives Israel-Egypt Cooperation," *The Cipher Brief*, March 14, 2018, www.thecipherbrief.com/persistent-isis-sinai-threat-drives-israel-egypt-cooperation

"SEGAS Liquefied Natural Gas Complex, Damietta," *Hydrocarbons Technology*, www.hydrocarbons-technology.com/projects/seagas/

"Self-Generation," *Business Dictionary*, WebFinance Inc., Austin Texas, 2018, www.businessdictionary.com/definition/self-generation.html

Setton, Keren, "Can Israel Leverage Its Newly Found Gas Reserves?" *Xinhua*, January 12, 2018, www.xinhuanet.com/english/2018-01/12/c_136889167.htm

Setton, Keren, "Rocky Israel-Turkey Ties Hit New Low, But Full-blown Crisis Could Be Prevented," *Xinhua*, May 17, 2018, www.xinhuanet.com/english/2018-05/17/c_137186839.htm

Shaffer, Brenda, "Israel-Jordan Gas Trade Portends Brighter Future in Middle East," *The Hill*, March 7, 2017, http://thehill.com/blogs/pundits-blog/energy-environment/322703-israel-jordan-gas-trade-portends-bright-future-in

Shaham, Shiri and Simon Weintraub, "Israeli Natural Gas Industry – Where Do We Go Now?" *Oilfield Technology*, June 24, 2016, www.energyglobal.com/upstream/drilling-and-production/24062016/israeli-natural-gas-industry-where-do-we-go-now-part-1/

Sheizaf, Noam, "Bill Clinton Tried to Dismantle Israeli Natural Gas Revenue Committee," *+972 Magazine*, April 16, 2013, https://972mag.com/bill-clinton-tried-to-dismantle-israeli-natural-gas-revenue-committee/69394/

"Shell's Idku LNG Ramps Up Exports," *Energy Egypt*, July 15, 2017, https://energyegypt.net/2017/07/15/allsource-analysis-shells-idku-lng-ramps-up-exports/

Sheppard, David, John Reed, and Anjli Raval, "Israel Turns to Kurds for Three-Quarters of Its Oil Supplies," *Financial Times*, August 23, 2015, www.ft.com/content/150f00cc-472c-11e5-af2f-4d6e0e5eda22

"Sheshinski Committee Sets Out Mineral Exploration Rights," *The Economist Intelligence Unit*, October 23, 2014, http://country.eiu.com/article.aspx?articleid=1832414767

"Sheshinski Eases Proposed Tax for Gas Exploration Firms," *Jerusalem Post*, April 1, 2011, www.jpost.com/National-News/Sheshinski-eases-proposed-tax-for-gas-exploration-firms

Shibley, Andrew, "Blessings and Curses: Israel and Lebanon's Maritime Boundary Dispute in the Eastern Mediterranean Sea," *The Global Business Law Review*, Volume 5, Issue 1 (2016), pp. 50–80.

Shipler, David K., "Israeli Completes Pullout, Leaving Sinai to Egypt," *The New York Times*, April 26, 1982, www.nytimes.com/1982/04/26/world/israeli-completes-pullout-leaving-sinai-to-egypt.html?pagewanted=all

"A Shortcut for Russian Oil to Asia," *Energy Security*, Institute for the Analysis of Global Security, March 31, 2004, www.iags.org/n0331044.htm

"Sisi on Egypt-Israel Gas Deal: 'We Scored a Big Goal'," *Middle East Monitor*, February 20, 2018, www.middleeastmonitor.com/20180222-sisi-on-egypt-israel-gas-deal-we-scored-a-big-goal/

"Sisi: Egypt Govt Not a Party on Gas Deal With Israel," *Al-Arabiya*, February 21, 2018, http://english.alarabiya.net/en/News/middle-east/2018/02/21/Sisi-on-gas-deal-with-Israel-Egyptian-government-is-not-a-party.html

Soliman, Asmahan, "Companions to the Israeli Gas Deal: Noble and Delek in Talks to Acquire East Mediterranean Gas Pipeline," *Madamasr*, February 28, 2018, www.madamasr.com/en/2018/02/28/feature/politics/companions-to-the-israeli-gas-deal-noble-and-delek-in-talks-to-acquire-east-mediterranean-gas-pipeline/

Soliman, Asmahan, "Noble and Delek in Talks to Acquire East Mediterranean Gas Pipeline," *Madamasr*, February 28, 2018, www.madamasr.com/en/2018/02/28/feature/politics/companions-to-the-israeli-gas-deal-noble-and-delek-in-talks-to-acquire-east-mediterranean-gas-pipeline/

Solomon, Shoshanna, "Israel Aims to Eliminate Use of Coal, Gasoline and Diesel by 2030," *The Times of Israel*, February 27, 2018, www.timesofisrael.com/israel-aims-to-eliminate-use-of-coal-gasoline-and-diesel-by-2030/

Solomon, Shoshanna, "Knesset Approves 'Historic' Reform of Electricity Sector," *The Times of Israel*, July 19, 2018, www.timesofisrael.com/knesset-votes-in-historic-reform-of-electricity-sector/

"Sovereign Wealth Fund – SWF," *Investopedia*, www.investopedia.com/terms/s/sovereign_wealth_fund.asp

Steinblatt, Ron, "National Capital Markets Recommends Ratio: Improving Prospects for Exports," *Globes*, May 6, 2013, www.globes.co.il/news/article.aspx?did=1000841866

Stergiou, Andreas, "Turkey-Cyprus-Israel Relations and the Cyprus Conflict," *Journal of Balkan and Near Eastern Studies*, Volume 18, Issue 4 (July 2016), pp. 375–392.

Sukkarieh, Mona, "Aphrodite's Blues: Cyprus and Israel Diverge Over Shared Gas Reservoir," *Executive*, June 6, 2018, www.executive-magazine.com/economics-policy/aphrodites-blues

"Sulphur Dioxide Scrubbers," *Duke Energy*, undated, www.duke-energy.com/our-company/environment/air-quality/sulfur-dioxide-scrubbers

Surkes, Sue, "State Comptroller Probing Why Gas Platform Being Built Close to Israeli Coast," *The Times of Israel*, August 10, 2018, www.timesofisrael.com/state-comptroller-probing-why-gas-platform-being-built-close-to-israeli-coast/

"Syria to UN: Israel's Licensing US Company to Drill for Oil in Occupied Syrian Golan Violates SC Resolution," *Tishreen* (Damascus) [Arabic], March 2, 2013, http://archive.tishreen.news.sy/tishreen/public/read/28145 (accessed on May 5, 2018).

Tabesh, Haytham, "Lebanon's Politicians Set Aside Differences on Oil and Gas Policy," *Al-Arabiya*, July 22, 2016, http://english.alarabiya.net/en/business/energy/2016/07/22/Lebanon-s-politicians-set-aside-differences-on-oil-and-gas-policy-.html

Tahhan, Zena, "Jordanians Reject 'Stolen Gas' in Israel-Jordan Deal," *Al Jazeera*, October 6, 2016, www.aljazeera.com/news/2016/10/jordanians-reject-stolen-gas-israel-jordan-deal-161002131442112.html

Tayseer, Mohammad and Yaacov Benmeleh, "Jordan Pipeline for Israeli Gas Set for Completion by End of 2019," *World Oil*, July 4, 2018, www.worldoil.com/news/2018/7/4/jordan-pipeline-for-israeli-gas-set-for-completion-by-end-of-2019

Tiryakioglu, Muhsin Baris, "Egypt's Sisi Denies Govt. Involved in Israeli Gas Deal," *Anadolu Agency*, February 22, 2018, https://aa.com.tr/en/energy/international-relations/egypts-sisi-denies-govt-involved-in-israeli-gas-deal/18958

Tobin, Sarah A., "Jordan's Arab Spring: The Middle Class and Anti-Revolution," *Middle East Policy* (Wiley-Blackwell), Volume XIX, Issue 1 (Spring 2012), www.mepc.org/jordans-arab-spring-middle-class-and-anti-revolution

Trilnick, Itai, "Israel's Gas Reserves Insufficient for Exports," *Haaretz*, July 18, 2012, www.haaretz.com/israel-news/business/israel-s-gas-reserves-insufficient-for-exports-1.451838

Tully, Andy, "Major Shale Find Could Guarantee Israel's Oil Supply for Years," *Nasdaq*, October 9, 2015, www.nasdaq.com/article/major-shale-find-could-guarantee-israels-oil-supply-for-years-cm528693

Tunçalp, Emre, "Turkey's Natural Gas Strategy: Balancing Geopolitical Goals & Market Realities," *Turkish Policy Quarterly*, Volume 14, Issue 3 (Fall 2015), p. 72.

"Turkey and the Law of the Sea: Some Facts," *Cyprus Mail Online*, February 11, 2018, https://cyprus-mail.com/2018/02/11/turkey-law-sea-facts/

"Turkey Hits Record Gas Consumption and Imports in 2017," *Anadolu Agency*, February 21, 2018, www.aa.com.tr/en/energy/turkey/turkey-hits-record-gas-consumption-and-imports-in-2017/18943

"Turkey, Israel Working on Commercial Details of Possible Gas Pipeline: Israeli Official," *Hurriyet Daily News*, May 2, 2017, www.hurriyetdailynews.com/turkey-israel-working-on-commercial-details-of-possible-gas-pipeline-israeli-official-112654

"Turkish Jets Prevent British Warplanes," *Yeni Safak* [Turkish], October 29, 2018, www.yenisafak.com/gundem/turk-jetlerinden-ingiliz-savas-ucaklarina-onleme-3405223

Tzanetakou, Nefeli, "September Meeting in Israel for the EastMed Pipeline," *Independent Balkan News Agency*, July 6, 2018, www.balkaneu.com/september-meeting-in-israel-for-the-eastmed-pipeline/

Udasin, Sharon, "Hadera Coal Chimneys to Be Shut Down, Replaced by Gas Within Six Years," *Jerusalem Post*, August 25, 2016, www.jpost.com/Israel-News/Hadera-coal-chimneys-to-be-shut-down-replaced-by-gas-within-six-years-465968

Udasin, Sharon, "ILA, Environment Ministry Publish Tender for New Ammonia Plant in Rotem," *Jerusalem Post*, January 28, 2014, www.jpost.com/Enviro-Tech/ILA-Environment-Ministry-publish-tender-for-new-ammonia-plant-in-Rotem-339650

Udasin, Sharon, "Israel Branching Out," *Jerusalem Post*, April 1, 2017, www.jpost.com/International/Branching-Out-485711

Udasin, Sharon, "Israel to Supply Gas to Jordan in $10 Billion Deal," *Jerusalem Post*, September 26, 2016, www.jpost.com/business-and-innovation/environment/israels-leviathan-reservoir-to-supply-gas-to-jordan-468742

Udasin, Sharon, "Palestinian Power Company Nixing Leviathan Gas Import Deal," *Jerusalem Post*, March 11, 2015, www.jpost.com/Business/Palestinian-Power-Generation-Company-nixing-Leviathan-gas-import-deal-393570

Udasin, Sharon, "Report: Majority of Israeli Oil Imported From Kurdistan," *The Jerusalem Post*, August 24, 2015, www.jpost.com/Business-and-Innovation/Israel-importing-77-percent-of-its-oil-from-Iraqi-Kurdistan-report-says-413056

Udasin, Sharon, "Socioeconomic Cabinet Approves Sheshinski 2 Committee Recommendations," *Jerusalem Post*, November 10, 2014, www.jpost.com/Business/Socioeconomic-cabinet-approves-Sheshinski-2-Committee-recommendations-381352

Udasin, Sharon, "SPNI Files High Court Petition Against Meged Oil Drilling in Central Israel," *Jerusalem Post*, March 10, 2015, www.jpost.com/Israel-News/SPNI-files-High-Court-petition-against-Meged-oil-drilling-in-central-Israel-393503

"The Underbelly of Eastern Mediterranean Gas," *Journal of Energy Security*, August 13, 2013, www.ensec.org/index.php?option=com_content&view=article&id=445:the-under-belly-of-eastern-mediterranean-gas&catid=137:is

"US Envoy Continues Shuttle Diplomacy Over Israel-Lebanon Gas Dispute," *The New Arab*, February 21, 2018, www.alaraby.co.uk/english/news/2018/2/21/us-envoy-continues-shuttle-diplomacy-over-israel-lebanon-gas-dispute

"US: Israel to Get 8 Seahawk Helicopters, Related Equipment," *Israel Hayom*, July 11, 2016, www.israelhayom.com/2017/07/20/us-israel-to-get-8-seahawk-helicopters-related-equipment/

Vogelman, Justice Uzi, Nadiv Mordechay, Yaniv Roznai, and Tehilla Schwartz, "Developments in Israeli Constitutional Law: The Year 2016 in Review," *I-CONnect: Blog of the International Journal of Constitutional Law*, October 4, 2017, www.iconnectblog.com/2017/10/developments-in-israeli-constitutional-law-the-year-2016-in-review/

Wahba, Abdel Latif, "Egypt Resolving Dispute Holding Up $15 Billion Israel Gas Deal," *Bloomberg*, February 22, 2018, www.bloomberg.com/news/articles/2018-02-19/noble-delek-sign-15-billion-deal-to-export-israel-gas-to-egypt

Wahish, Niveen Wahish, "The Deal and Beyond," *Al-Ahram Weekly*, March 8–15, 2017, http://weekly.ahram.org.eg/News/23873.aspx

Waldoks, Ehud Zion, "All Coal-Fired Power Stations to Get Filters," *Jerusalem Post*, December 27, 2010, www.jpost.com/enviro-tech/all-coal-fired-power-stations-to-get-filters

Welsh, Teresa, "Israel and Jordan: The Middle East's Odd Couple," *US News*, November 14, 2014, www.usnews.com/news/articles/2014/11/14/israel-and-jordan-the-middle-easts-odd-couple

"What Is Libor," *Investopedia*, 2018, www.investopedia.com/terms/l/libor.asp

"Why Developing Israel's Leviathan Gas Field Is a Mammoth Task, Knowledge," *Knowledge@Wharton* (University of Pennsylvania), August 25, 2017, http://knowledge.wharton.upenn.edu/article/developing-israels-leviathan-gas-field-proven-mammoth-task/

Widdershoven, Cyril, "Egypt Could Become Europe's Next Big Energy Hub," *Oilprice.com*, April 26, 2018, https://oilprice.com/Energy/Natural-Gas/Egypt-Could-Become-Europes-Next-Big-Energy-Hub.html

"Will Israeli Natural Gas Flow in Egypt's Pipelines?" *Energy Egypt*, July 15, 2016, https://energyegypt.net/2016/07/15/will-israeli-natural-gas-flow-in-egypts-pipelines/

Wills, Samuel E., Lemma W. Senbet, and Witness Simbanegavi, "Sovereign Wealth Funds and Natural Resource Management in Africa," *Journal of African Economies*, Volume 25, AERC Supplement 2 (2016), pp. ii3–ii19.

Winter, Chase, "Gas, Pipeline Dreams and Gunboat Diplomacy in the Mediterranean," *Deutsche Welle*, April 2, 2018, www.dw.com/en/gas-pipeline-dreams-and-gunboat-diplomacy-in-mediterranean/a-43228234

Withlisch, Martin, "Israel-Lebanon Offshore Oil and Gas Dispute – Rules of International Maritime Law," *American Society of International Law*, Volume 15, Issue 21 (December 5, 2011), www.asil.org/insights/volume/15/issue/31/israel-lebanon-offshore-oil-gas-dispute-%E2%80%93-rules-international-maritime

Yom, Sean L., "The New Landscape of Jordanian Politics: Social Opposition, Fiscal Crisis, and the Arab Spring," *British Journal of Middle Eastern Studies*, Volume 42, Issue 3 (2014), pp. 284–300.

Zaken, Dan, "Egypt Has Good Reasons to Buy Israeli Gas," *Globes*, November 5, 2018, https://en.globes.co.il/en/article-egypt-has-good-reasons-to-buy-israeli-gas-1001259029

Zalel, Ya'acov, "Day of High Drama Sees Egypt Freeze Gas Negotiations With Israel," *Natural Gas Europe*, October 2, 2012, www.naturalgaseurope.com/egypt-freezes-gas-negotiations-israel-after-ordered-to-pay-1.76-billion-compensation-26965

Zalel, Ya'acov, "Israel Electric Company Signed an Agreement to Import LNG," *Natural Gas World*, April 6, 2016, www.naturalgasworld.com/report-israel-to-import-lng-cheaper-than-local-natural-gas-28946

Zalel, Ya'acov, "Tamar Gas Supply to Israel Halted," *Natural Gas World*, September 22, 2017, www.naturalgasworld.com/gas-supply-from-tamar-to-israel-completely-stopped-55492

Zetelny, Itay, Ernst and Young, "Renewable Energy Recap: Israel," *Renewable Energy World*, January 2, 2012, www.renewableenergyworld.com/articles/2012/01/renewable-energy-recap-israel.html

Zeynalova, Leman, "Israeli Gas Supply to Europe Part of SGC Concept," *Trend News Agency*, July 14, 2017, https://en.trend.az/business/energy/2777256.html

Zilber, Neri, "Israel's Secret Arab Allies," *The New York Times*, July 14, 2017, www.nytimes.com/2017/07/14/opinion/israels-secret-arab-allies.html

Zion Oil and Gas, Zion Oil & Gas, Inc., 2001–2006, www.sec.gov/Archives/edgar/data/1131312/000113131206000077/exploration.htm

INDEX